ORGANIZATION AND MANAGEMENT
A SYSTEMS AND CONTINGENCY APPROACH

McGRAW-HILL SERIES IN MANAGEMENT
Keith Davis and Fred Luthans, Consulting Editors

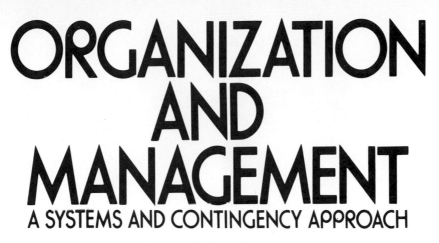

ORGANIZATION AND MANAGEMENT
A SYSTEMS AND CONTINGENCY APPROACH

Third Edition

FREMONT E. KAST
JAMES E. ROSENZWEIG

Graduate School of Business Administration
University of Washington

McGRAW-HILL BOOK COMPANY

New York • St. Louis • San Francisco • Auckland
Bogotá • Düsseldorf • Johannesburg • London • Madrid • Mexico
Montreal • New Delhi • Panama • Paris • São Paulo
Singapore • Sydney • Tokyo • Toronto

To
Boots
and
Phyllis

ORGANIZATION AND MANAGEMENT
A Systems and Contingency Approach

1 2 3 4 5 6 7 8 9 0   FGRFGR   7 8 3 2 1 0 9 8

This book was set in Times Roman by Rocappi, Inc. The editors were William J. Kane,
Barbara Brooks, and M. Susan Norton; the designer was A Good Thing, Inc.;
the production supervisor was Dominick Petrellese. New drawings were done by
J & R Services, Inc.
Fairfield Graphics was printer and binder.

Library of Congress Cataloging in Publication Data

Kast, Fremont Ellsworth, date
    Organization and management.

    (McGraw-Hill series in management)
    Bibliography: p.
    Includes indexes.
    1. Organization. 2. Management. I. Rosenzweig,
James Erwin, date   joint author. II. Title.
HD31.K33 1979   658.4   78-8976
ISBN 0-07-033346-7

Contents

PART FIVE
THE PSYCHOSOCIAL SYSTEM

PART SIX
THE MANAGERIAL SYSTEM

PART SEVEN
COMPARATIVE ANALYSIS AND
CONTINGENCY VIEWS

PART EIGHT
ORGANIZATIONAL CHANGE AND THE FUTURE

Preface

This book is about organizations and their management. We are all aware of the dramatic changes that have taken place in our society over the past century. The transformation from a predominantly agrarian society with emphasis on the family, informal groups, and small communities to a complex industrial society characterized by the emergence of large, formal organizations has affected our lives in many ways. We are amazed at accelerating and apparently unbounded scientific and technological achievements, but a second thought causes us to recognize a major factor underlying these achievements—our ability to develop and manage a vast array of *social organizations* for accomplishing our purposes. Designing and managing complex organizations is a social technology that is comparable to the physical manifestations of technology evident in our communication systems or space programs. *Effective management* of human endeavor is truly one of our greatest accomplishments, and it is a continuing challenge.

You are affected by organizations and management in many of your daily activities—sometimes for the good and sometimes for the bad. Indeed, some aspects of your life may seem disorganized and mismanaged. Organizations designed to serve you—schools, government agencies, businesses, and so on—may appear to hinder progress toward your individual goals. Your new car is recalled by the manufacturer because of a defective brakeline, transit employees are on strike to protest management's use of part-time drivers, and the first class you attend (after hitchhiking to school) is cancelled because of lack of staff. These are examples of unintended consequences of organization and management which, although they are evident and noteworthy, often obscure the predominantly functional aspects of organizational endeavors.

Families, clubs, schools, hospitals, restaurants, retail stores, distributors, manufacturers, financial institutions, cities, states, and federal agencies provide goods and services that we, as individuals, cannot provide for ourselves. We are members of an organizational society—people cooperating in groups to accomplish a variety of purposes. Overall, the system works reasonably well.

Organizations come in various types, sizes, and forms and are designed to accomplish specific goals. Our purpose in this book is to help you understand organizations better—what makes them work well and what makes them not work so well. Understanding the factors and forces involved should help prepare you to be a more effective organizational member. In addition, increased knowledge plus skill gained through experience should enhance your potential as a manager and leader.

Systems and contingency concepts have become key considerations in the study of organization and management. A systems philosophy is a way of thinking about complex human endeavors. It facilitates recognition of the context within which organizations operate and emphasizes *understanding* the interrelationships among the various activities that are required to accomplish goals. A contingency view is a way of thinking about managing organizational endeavor. It facilitates situational diagnosis that leads to managerial *action* that is appropriate in specific circumstances.

In this edition we have continued to develop the open-system model as an overall framework for understanding organizations and their management. We have illustrated contingency views throughout our discussion of the various organizational subsystems. We have expanded our treatment of comparative analysis by incuding more material on organization and management in other countries. We have added a chapter on the city to complement earlier coverage of the hospital and the university.

This book is not meant to be the last word. Rather, we hope that it is an integrated view of organization theory and management practice at one particular time. The field is evolving and dynamic; it is difficult to keep the concepts and research findings up to date with actual practices.

We wish to thank our students and colleagues in the Department of Management and Organization, University of Washington, who have questioned many of our ideas—lending both support and criticism. In academia, an active, intellectually stimulating environment is essential for research and writing. Our colleagues help provide this. It is quite likely that many ideas that we think are original were first suggested by our professional colleagues. Numerous organizations and managers have provided us with illustrative material. It has been particularly helpful to share ideas with managers and colleagues in other countries.

We appreciate the resources made available by the Graduate School of Business Administration. Excellent typing, clerical, and artistic support was provided by Beth Verdin and Sheryl Rosenzweig.

Fremont E. Kast
James E. Rosenzweig

ORGANIZATION AND MANAGEMENT
A SYSTEMS AND CONTINGENCY APPROACH

Whenever I have studied human affairs, I have carefully labored not to mock, lament, nor condemn, but only to understand.
Spinoza

Where there is much desire to learn, there of necessity will be much arguing, many opinions; for opinion in good men is but knowledge in the making.
Milton

A good theory is one that holds together long enough to get you to a better theory.
D. O. Hebb

The dissenting opinions of one generation become the prevailing interpretation of the next.
Burton Hendrick

Sooner or later, we shall learn what everything is made of and how everything works—everything, that is, except men and their societies. . . . Attempts to develop the scientific laws of human nature are likely to have limited success and application. But we can try to find out where we are, how we got there, what we know and do not know, and we can try to discern tendencies and probable results.
Robert Hutchins

In one way or another, we are forced to deal with complexities, with "wholes" or "systems," in all fields of knowledge. This implies a basic re-orientation in scientific thinking.
Ludwig von Bertalanffy

Conceptual
Foundations

1

Part 1 is designed to set the stage for the entire book. It establishes a framework within which the other seven parts can be integrated.

In Chapter 1, the pervasiveness and importance of organization and management is stressed. The eclectic nature of organization theory is emphasized, indicating the role played by various disciplines. Organization theory is described as the foundation for management practice. Key concepts that recur throughout the book are introduced. And, finally, the plan of the book is set forth by parts and chapters.

Chapter 2 traces management values over many centuries. The impact of contemporary cultural or societal values on management thought is emphasized. The evolution of Western culture and value systems has had an important influence on managerial attitudes. Of particular concern are the developments since the industrial revolution and the accelerating changes in the twentieth century. Contemporary society, with its pluralistic values, provides an exceedingly complex and dynamic setting for organizations and managers.

The Setting of Organization and Management

One

We are social animals with a propensity for organizing and managing our affairs. We do so in an increasingly complex and dynamic environment. Many disciplines are contributing to an eclectic body of knowledge—organization theory—which, coupled with experience, is the foundation for management practice. In this chapter the setting of organization and management will be introduced via the following topics:

Our Organizational Society
Relevant Research and Knowledge
Increasing Complexity of Organizations
Major Themes and Concepts
Systems Approach—Understanding
Contingency View—Acting
Performance
Outline of Book

Our Organizational Society

Groups and organizations are a pervasive part of our existence. Typically, we are born into a family with the aid of a medical organization, the hospital. We spend a great deal of time in educational institutions. Informal groups develop spontaneously when several people have common interests and agree (often implicitly) to pursue common goals—a picnic or a fishing trip. Work organizations account for a large part of our time, with formal or informal relationships often carrying over into the leisure-time activities such as bowling or softball teams. It is easy to see that all of us, except for hermits, are involved in a variety of groups and organizations. We tend to develop cooperative and interdependent relationships.

Humans are activists. We have created and destroyed civilizations. We have developed vast technological complexes. We have utilized natural resources in ingenious ways and in the process have wreaked havoc with the ecosystem. We have even broken the umbilical cord holding us to mother earth; we have been to the moon and returned. Future generations may see us go to the planets and beyond. We are all amazed at (and probably fail to comprehend fully) the enormity of modern scientific and technological achievements. But a second thought causes us to recognize a major factor underlying these achievements—our ability to develop *social organizations* for accomplishing our purposes. The development of these organizations and *effective management* of them is truly one of our greatest achievements.

It is worth reminding ourselves that management does not really exist. It is a word, an idea. Like science, like government, like engineering, management is an abstraction. But managers exist. And managers are not abstractions; . . . they are human beings. Particular and special kinds of human beings. Individuals with a special function: to lead and move and bring out the latent capabilities—and dreams—of other human beings. . . . This I believe, and this my whole life's experience has taught me: the managerial life is the broadest, the most demanding, by all odds the most comprehensive and the most subtle of all human activities. And the most crucial. [1]

This book is about organizations and their management. It is an attempt to facilitate understanding of the managerial role in a complex and dynamic organizational society. The tendency to organize or cooperate in interdependent relationships is inherent in human nature. Although conflict within families and clans is evident, the group provides a means of protection and hence survival. Organized activity today ranges on a continuum from informal, ad hoc groups to formal, highly structured organizations. Military activities and religious affairs were among the first to become formally organized. Elaborate systems were developed and by and large have persisted, with modifications, to the present. Business, government, and education are other spheres of activity that have developed formal organizations geared to task accomplishment. We engage in many voluntary organizations in our leisure time—some recreational, some philanthropic, and some of a crusading nature.

Many different definitions of organization have been set forth, but they have certain fundamental or essential elements. Organization behavior is directed toward objectives that are more or less understood by members of the group. The organization uses knowledge and techniques in the accomplishment of its tasks. *Organization* implies structuring and integrating activities, that is, people working or cooperating together in interdependent relationships. The notion of interrelat-

---

1 David E. Lilienthal, *Management: A Humanist Art,* Columbia University Press, New York, 1967, p. 18.

edness suggests a social system. Therefore we can say that organizations are: (1) *goal-oriented,* people with a purpose; (2) *psychosocial systems,* people interacting in groups; (3) *technological systems,* people using knowledge and techniques; and (4) *an integration of structured activities,* people working together in patterned relationships.

The Importance of Management

Management involves the coordination of human and material resources toward objective accomplishment. We often speak of individuals managing their affairs, but the usual connotation suggests group effort. Four basic elements can be identified: (1) *toward objectives,* (2) *through people,* (3) *via techniques,* and (4) *in an organization.* Typical definitions suggest that management is a process of planning, organizing, and controlling activities. Some increase the number of sub-processes to include assembling resources and motivating; others reduce the scheme to include only planning and implementation. Still others cover the entire process with the concept of decision making, suggesting that decisions are the key output of managers.

Management is the primary force within organizations that coordinates the activities of the subsystems and relates them to the environment. The study of management is relatively new in our society, stemming primarily from the growth in size and complexity of business and other large-scale organizations since the industrial revolution.

The emergence of management as an essential, a distinct and a leading institution is a pivotal event in social history. Rarely, if ever, has a new basic institution, a new leading group, emerged as fast as has management since the turn of this century. Rarely in human history has a new institution proven indispensable so quickly; and even less often has a new institution arrived with so little opposition, so little disturbance, so little controversy . . . . Management, which is the organ of society specifically charged with making resources productive, that is, with the responsibility for organized economic advance, therefore reflects the basic spirit of the modern age. It is in fact indispensable—and this explains why, once begotten, it grew so fast and with so little opposition. [2]

Managers convert diverse resources of people, machines, material, money, time, and space into a useful enterprise. Essentially, management is the process whereby these unrelated resources are integrated into a total *system for objective accomplishment.* Managers get things done by working with people and physical resources in order to accomplish the objectives of the system. They coordinate and integrate the activities and work of others.

A recurring question is the distinction between the terms *management*

---

2 Peter F. Drucker, *The Practice of Management,* Harper & Row, Publishers, Incorporated, New York, 1954, pp. 3–4.

and **administration.** "Administration" often has had the connotation of governmental or other nonprofit organizations, whereas "management" has been relegated to business enterprises. However, there is considerable overlap in usage. YMCAs have boards of managers, for example. The military has program managers with overall responsibility for mission accomplishment. On the other hand, many colleges of business administration have management departments. We will use the terms interchangeably and tend toward the use of the term management regardless of whether the specific example involves business organizations, hospitals, philanthropic institutions, or government bureaus. On this basis, management is a most pervasive activity. According to Hertz, "the single ubiquitous mind-driven activity of mankind is management."[3] We are all involved in management—of ourselves, of our economic and social activities, and of society as a whole.

order to remain in a dynamic equilibrium with their environment. Information flow is essential for the decision-making process. It involves knowledge of the past, estimates of the future, and timely feedback concerning current activity. Management's task is implementing this information-decision system to coordinate effort and maintain a dynamic equilibrium.

 With organization and management as pervasive as they are, we might naturally assume a well-defined body of knowledge that provides a framework for research, teaching, and practice. There is a body of knowledge, but it is not particularly well defined, and currently it appears to be evolving rapidly. A number of conditions have hampered the development of a well-defined body of knowledge—particularly the increasing complexity within organizations and the dynamic nature of their environment. Theories developed to fit organizations in the early 1900s are not likely to be appropriate for many organizations in the 1980s.

Relevant Research and Knowledge

 Scientific disciplines have emerged as separate and distinct bodies of knowledge as our search for enlightenment has continued. However, the entire social science field, behavioral science in particular, has been relatively slow in developing.[4] Anthropology, sociology, and psychology are products of the last 100 years. Economics and political science emerged somewhat earlier as specific disciplines. Organization theory and/or management practice did not receive concerted attention until the twentieth century.

---

 3 David B. Hertz, "The Unity of Science and Management," *Management Science,* April 1965, p. B-89.
 4 Kenneth E. Boulding, *The Impact of the Social Sciences,* Rutgers University Press, New Brunswick, N.J., 1966.

Within this historical context, a well-developed body of knowledge may be too much to ask of this fledgling discipline. Yet significant strides have been made, and a body of knowledge has been developing which in turn has been useful in managing organizations of diverse characteristics and objectives.

We think it is helpful to distinguish organization theory and management in order to provide a useful framework for research, teaching, and practice. We suggest that organization theory is the body of knowledge, including hypotheses and propositions, stemming from research in a definable field of study which can be termed **organization science.** [5] The study of organizations is an applied science because the resulting knowledge is relevant to problem solving or decision making in ongoing enterprises or institutions.

Because of the pervasiveness of organizations, the related theory and scientific study are extremely broad-based. It is an eclectic theory, a total system comprised of many subsystems of relevant disciplines such as parts of sociology, psychology, anthropology, economics, political science, philosophy, and mathematics (see Figure 1.1). Not all these above-mentioned disciplines are applicable to the same degree; only a small subpart of a particular subject-matter area may be relevant. During the twentieth century, however, society's organizations have received increasing attention, and the study of organizations has evolved as an important, visible, and definable field.

As indicated in Figure 1.1 contributions to organization theory come from many sources. Deductive and inductive research in a variety of disciplines provides a theoretical base of propositions that are useful for understanding organizations and for managing them. Experience gained in management practice is also an important input to organization theory. In short, Figure 1.1 illustrates how the art of management is based on a body of knowledge generated by practical experience *and* scientific research concerning organizations.

Organization theory itself stems from an applied science that draws upon the basic disciplines and their relatively more abstract theories only as they are relevant to organizations found in society. Management technology stems from organization theory and is even more applied in the sense that it focuses on the practice of management in ongoing organizations. With this view of the relationship between organization theory and management in mind, let us turn to a more specific discussion of the requirements of an organization science.

Foundations of Organization Theory

The pervasiveness of organizations and management argues for considerable latitude with regard to the organizations studied and the scientific methods used. Moreover, the value systems of researchers, teachers, and practitioners are quite diverse, and hence the determination of relevance and scientific method may

---

5 "Organizationology" might be appropriate if the term were less cumbersome.

Figure 1.1 The Foundations of Organization Theory and Management Practice.

Managerial role
Business
Government
Education
Church
Military

Technology and structure

Environmental systems

Economic, political, social

Systems concepts

History

Political science

Economics

Social science

Management Art/Practice

Managerial decision making
Judgmental
Computational

Managerial subsystems
Strategic
Coordinative
Operating

Organization Theory/Knowledge

Value systems; goals
Individual
Group

Principles of organization
Principles of management
Contingency views

Philosophy

Statistics

Comparative analysis

Mathematics

Quantitative methods

Organization Science/Research

Managerial process
Planning
Assembling resources
Organizing
Motivating
Controlling

Motivation
Status, roles
Group dynamics
Influence, power, authority
Leadership

Sociology

Psychology

Anthropology

Behavorial science

vary considerably. On the other hand, the concerted effort toward the development of organization theory during the mid-twentieth century has resulted in useful dialogue, cross-fertilization, and mutual understanding among participants. While no well-defined consensus has yet appeared, there are consistent threads of inquiry and agreement with regard to the general scope of organization theory. Although not exhaustive, Figure 1.1 indicates many of the key concepts and areas of interest.

Early management concepts came from practitioners. Texts were often the distillation of experience in ongoing enterprises. Such contributions are important and valuable additions to the body of knowledge comprising organization theory. We need continued observation and conceptualization from astute practicing managers. Meanwhile, scientist-scholars have become more and more involved in research related to organizations but carried on in the context of basic disciplines. Other scholars have been engaged in integrating findings from basic disciplines and translating the results into meaningful concepts or propositions.

Integration of the body of knowledge comes from two directions. Those primarily engaged in studying organizations and management have looked toward the basic disciplines for new insight. Simultaneously, those engaged in the work of basic disciplines have become increasingly aware of the pervasiveness of organizations in society and have begun to concentrate attention on relevant problems. Industrial psychology and industrial sociology are two subfields that give evidence of this trend.

Two Kinds of Knowledge

There have been many references to the exact versus the inexact sciences. However, as new findings continue to come in on all fronts in our search for knowledge, we find that exactness is a relative concept. Some disciplines are relatively more exact than others, and all knowledge developed to date remains open to further refinement. Increasingly, propositions are stated in terms of probabilities, which vary between 0 and 1, depending on the discipline and the particular proposition in question. In short, the concept of knowledge in the absolute sense can be ruled out for science in general and organization science in particular.

What are the characteristics of knowledge in a more moderate sense? "The properties of knowledge in this moderate sense are that it consists of propositions which are (1) testable by reference to evidence, (2) subject to rational criticism, and either (3) corrigible or rectifiable or (4) falsifiable."[6] This framework is much more amenable to the study of organizations. These properties connote the probabilistic nature of propositions in organization theory. They imply an evolving body of knowledge that is adjusted as new evidence is developed or as new

6 Mortimer J. Adler, *The Conditions of Philosophy,* Dell Publishing Co., Inc., New York, 1965, pp. 21–31.

concepts emerge from astute criticism. Refinements are made continually in the theory, and there is always the chance that some propositions may be eliminated altogether if they prove to be false on the basis of new findings. Taken together, these properties indicate that a body of knowledge can be described as responsible, reliable, well-founded, reasonable opinion.

An Emerging Discipline

The study of organizations and their management is an intellectually respectable discipline. Organization theory sets forth propositions that are testable. It is also conducted as a public enterprise with many contributors. Everyone has theories concerning individual and organizational behavior—at least implicit if not explicit. Research and the resulting literature have increased at an accelerating rate and will continue to do so. Research is conducted by scholars from many disciplines; indeed, the same organization is often studied from several points of view. The results are compared at separate points in time, for organizations in various cultures, and for different types of institutions within a given culture. All this activity has made the study of organizations one of the most visible and public enterprises in society.

Organization science has questions of its own that set it apart as a relatively autonomous discipline. That is, it is concerned with questions that other disciplines are not. Obviously many questions cross discipline boundaries with perhaps some variation in emphasis. Some of the topics of particular interest to organization students are:

1 Goals and value systems
2 The use of technology and knowledge in organizations
3 The structuring of organizations
4 Formal and informal relationships
5 Differentiation and integration of activities
6 Motivation of organizational participants
7 Group dynamics in organizations
8 Status and role systems in organizations
9 Organizational politics
10 Power, authority, and influence in organizations
11 Managerial processes in organizations
12 Organization strategy and tactics
13 Information-decision systems in organizations
14 Stability and innovation in organizations
15 Organizational boundaries and domains

16 Interface between organizations

17 Planned change and improvement

There is a danger at times that a scientific discipline may begin to exist for its own sake and emphasize esoteric concepts. It is true that there is a gradation from applied to pure research. However, there is no absolutely "pure" research. In the long run everything is applied; hence, a discipline must keep in touch with the real world. In an evolving body of knowledge such as organization theory, there are many tentative conclusions and propositions. However, the real world cannot wait for the ultimate body of knowledge (there is none!). Practicing managers in business firms, hospitals, and government agencies continue to operate on a day-to-day basis. Therefore, they must use whatever theory is available. Practitioners must be included in the search for new knowledge because they control access to an essential ingredient—organizational data. Mutual understanding among managers, teachers, and researchers will facilitate the development of a relevant body of knowledge.

Increasing Complexity of Organizations

Organizations have become increasingly complex over time. The trend begins with the evolution of organisms, of which human beings are the most complex example.

There is a characteristic trend in this development—the units are bound to become more and more complicated. They lose the simple features they had at the beginning of life's history. Most changes are steps toward higher differentiation, toward change of nucleic acids which produce more proteins with more specialized tasks. Hence from the moment when units exist that can form replicas of themselves, a development toward more and more complicated units is bound to start. Better adaptation to external conditions leads almost always to more complicated units. [7]

Haskins describes this phenomenon by saying: "Paleontological research has yielded dramatic evidence that in the evolutionary development of living matter there has been an unmistakable broad trend from the simple to the complex. Both the variety of life on earth and the intricacy of its organization reflect and emphasize this trend." [8] The essential element in this trend is that of specialization. It allows organisms a means of dividing up the work in performing each subpart more effectively and efficiently. However, specialization requires integration of activities in pursuit of identified goals. It is a process of analysis and synthesis;

---

7 Victor F. Weisskopf, *Knowledge and Wonder*, Doubleday & Company, Inc., Garden City, N.Y., 1966, p. 251.

8 Caryl P. Haskins, *Of Societies and Men*, The Viking Press, Inc., New York, 1960, p. 15.

that is, breaking up the task into parts according to specialized activities and integrating those activities toward objective accomplishment. The tendency to integrate is a "companion feature" of specialization.

These same trends are evident in organizations. More specialization requires increasingly sophisticated methods of coordination and integration. Tendencies toward both cooperation and conflict are evident among organizational participants. The question of individualism versus conformism is relevant and important. In short, many forces are at work in organizations—some divisive, some cohesive, all somewhat confounding. These factors have led to increasing complexity within organizations and hence have made the job of management more and more difficult.

Size
Of
Organizations

For small face-to-face groups in a rather stable environment, the job of management is relatively straightforward. Once a particular approach is found effective, it can be applied indefinitely with likely success. As groups grow in size, face-to-face relationships become impossible; the number of interrelationships among organizational participants increases dramatically; and managers cannot hope to maintain personal contact throughout the organization.

Trends toward increased organizational size are not likely to taper off. The population continues to grow. Thus sheer numbers of people will provide a complex environment for society and its subunits. The trend from a sparse, rural population to urban concentrations has been in effect for many centuries. Crises of many kinds—housing, crime, transit, air pollution—are evident in large metropolitan areas. What if the earth were one giant megalopolis? However unlikely such a future condition may be, the possibility indicates the accelerating nature of environmental developments that pose organizational and managerial problems.

Science
and
Technology

Scientific knowledge and technological developments are also accelerating. Again, we might gain perspective by referring to developments throughout the evolution of humanity. If our time on earth is taken as 240,000 years and if we imagine that those years take place in one hour, we spent fifty-five minutes of that time in Paleolithic (Old Stone Age) culture.

Five minutes ago, he embarked upon the neolithic culture, the cultivation of plants, the domestication of animals, the making of pottery, weaving, and the use of the bow and arrow; 3½ minutes ago he began the working of copper; 2½ minutes ago he began to mold bronze; 2 minutes ago he learned to smelt iron; ¼ of a minute ago he learned printing; 5 seconds ago the Industrial Revolution began; $3\frac{1}{3}$ seconds ago he learned to apply electricity; and the time he has had the automobile is less than the interval between the ticks of a watch, i.e., less than one second.[9]

With the industrial revolution representing only five seconds of an imaginary hourglass, the accelerating nature of technology is apparent. And a concerted effort toward organization theory and principles of management is a post-industrial revolution phenomenon. Think of the developments since the automobile was introduced—"less than one second ago." Television, jet airplane travel, birth control pills, and space exploration are examples of science and technology proceeding at an accelerating pace. One recalls the phrase, "If it works, it is obsolete."

Developments in science and technology have magnified trends toward specialization. Scientists, researchers, technicians, and other "knowledge workers" are becoming increasingly prevalent in organizations. Integration of their efforts toward organizational accomplishment can be difficult. There may be differences in value systems between scientists and managers. The former may be concerned with the effectiveness of a product or process (i.e., striving for perfection), while the manager may be more interested in efficiency (i.e., cost as related to effectiveness).

Other Considerations

Science and technology are only a part of the picture. The general increase in the education, knowledge, and diversity of human participants provides a more sophisticated atmosphere in organizations. People are becoming less tractable and more prone to "think for themselves." This trend is also accelerating and provides another confounding variable for management.

An increasing governmental role is another consideration. Organizations must keep tuned to governmental propensities for regulatory action in many areas of interest. The most obvious are economic and defense matters, but the spectrum of influence widens over time. Trends in all the areas of governmental concern— federal, state, and local—provide meaningful background for managerial decision making in organizations.

Coupled with developments in the sciences (natural, social, and behavioral) is progress in the philosophy of management. In a sense all of us are philosophers because we hold views concerning what *is* or happens in the world as well as what we *ought* to do or seek. Some development can proceed prescriptively via common sense, experience, and reflection. It is more likely, however, that a combination of the experiential approach and inputs from scientific research will round out an individual's philosophy of management.

[9] Wilson D. Wallis, as cited in Charles R. Walker, *Modern Technology and Civilization*, McGraw-Hill Book Company, New York, 1962, p. 10.

The hallmark of management is change—swift, incessant, fundamental change. The only thing that is constant is change. The dynamic interplay of forces in the environment of organizations is evident. Similarly, within organizations the situation is becoming much more complex from the point of view of management. Thus it becomes increasingly important to understand the trends and developments taking place. The pace of change is likely to increase; therefore, managers must better understand the behavior of individuals and organizations in order to be able to predict and ultimately coordinate effort toward objectives. The aim of this book is to contribute to this understanding.

Major Themes and Concepts

One approach to solving complex problems is to assume away much of the complexity and then solve a much simpler problem. Theoretically, the interim step provides insight into how the more complex problem might be solved. Many introductory texts treat problem solving in this way. However, unless students pursue the subject in later courses, they are left with an oversimplified view of the real world, one which may be more dysfunctional than functional. "A little knowledge is a dangerous thing." We hope to avoid that in this book.

Our general purpose will be to understand the increasingly complex nature of organizations in a dynamic environment and the attendant difficult problem-solving task of managers. We may use abstractions and models from time to time but in all cases hope to link them adequately to the real world. Our primary purpose is to recognize and understand the dynamic complexity rather than to simplify the real world in order to develop straightforward cookbook approaches.

We are concerned in this book with a wide variety of organizations or institutions and are interested in those propositions that have broad applicability—in business, governmental, medical, educational, religious, military, philanthropic, voluntary, and other types of organizations. Also of interest is diversity, not only in type of institution but in size as well. For the most part, organization theory and management principles have been developed within the context of large organizations. Consideration will be given to the applicability of findings to small- and medium-sized organizations as well.

Although we have not emphasized it to the same degree as institutional comparisons, we will be interested in management and organization theory as it applies across cultures. What findings hold in Japan or Yugoslavia as well as in the United States or Great Britain? Unless otherwise stated, the material presented will refer primarily to developments in the United States; however, our discussions with managers and academicians in numerous countries suggest that there are many common threads in research endeavors, organization theory, and management practice.

We are interested in both descriptive findings and normative considerations. There is a great need for empirical research concerning organizations and management. At times there seems to be a tendency in the behavioral sciences toward conducting experimental research in unrealistic settings as a way of emulating the physical sciences. It might be more useful to emulate the zoologists and biologists, whose observation of what *is and happens* in the real world has occupied a considerable amount of time and attention. There is a need to understand clearly how individuals and organizations behave in a variety of circumstances. Once we have a more complete understanding of what *is*, we can begin to consider normative propositions of what managers *ought to do or seek*. Such an approach facilitates the development of conceptual schemes that will provide useful frames of reference for managers in organizations.

Major changes in all fields of science occur with the development of new conceptual schemes, or **paradigms.** These paradigms do not just represent a step-by-step advancement in "normal" science (the science generally accepted and practiced) but rather a revolutionary change in the way the scientific field is perceived by the practitioners. New paradigms frequently are rejected by the scientific community. (At first they may seem crude and limited—offering very little more than older paradigms.) They frequently lack the apparent sophistication of the older paradigms, which they ultimately replace. They do not display the clarity and certainty of older paradigms that have been refined through years of research and writing. But a new paradigm does provide for a new start and opens up new directions that were not possible under the old. "We must recognize how very limited in both scope and precision a paradigm can be at the time of its first appearance. Paradigms gain their status because they are more successful than their competitors in solving a few problems that the group of practitioners has come to realize as acute. To be more successful is not, however, to be either completely successful with a single problem or notably successful with any large number." [10]

Systems theory provides a new paradigm for the study of social organizations and their management. In some ways it may not be much better than older paradigms that have been accepted and used for a long time (such as the management process approach). As in other fields of scientific endeavor, the new paradigm must be applied, clarified, elaborated, and made more precise. But it does provide a fundamentally different view of the reality of social organizations and can serve as the basis for progress.

The systems approach facilitates analysis and synthesis in a complex and dynamic environment. It considers interrelationships among subsystems as well as interactions between the system and its suprasystem and also provides a means of

---

10 Thomas S. Kuhn, *The Structure of Scientific Revolutions*, University of Chicago Press, Chicago, 1962, p. 23.

understanding synergistic aspects.[11] This conceptual scheme allows us to consider organizations—individuals, small-group dynamics, and large-group phenomena—all within the constraints of an external environmental system.

Systems Approach— Understanding

The systems view of organizations and their management serves as the basic conceptual framework for this book. A *system* is an organized, unitary whole composed of two or more interdependent parts, components, or subsystems and delineated by identifiable boundaries from its environmental suprasystem.

Systems of various types are all around us. For example, we have mountain systems, river systems, and the solar system as part of our physical surroundings. The body itself is a complex organism including the skeletal system, the circulatory system and the nervous system. We come into daily contact with such phenomena as transportation systems, communication systems (telephone, telegraph), and economic systems. We obviously can't consider all these systems—their study would involve most of the subject matter of a major university and even more. We will concentrate our attention on a narrower subset of systems—social organizations.

We need a general definition and a conceptual model of organizations that will be appropriate for all types: small and large, informal and formal, simple and complex, and those engaged in a wide variety of activities and functions. In this context, we define an organization as:

1 A subsystem of its broader environment, consisting of
2 Goal-oriented people with a purpose
3 A technical subsystem—people using knowledge, techniques, equipment, and facilities
4 A structural subsystem—people working together on integrated activities
5 A psychosocial subsystem—people in social relationships
6 A managerial subsystem—which coordinates the subsystems and plans and controls the overall endeavor

As illustrated by Figure 1.2 a basic premise is that the organization, as a *subsystem of the society*, must accomplish its goals within constraints that are an integral part of the environmental suprasystem. The organization performs a function for society; if it is to be successful in receiving inputs, it must conform to social constraints and requirements. Conversely, the organization influences its environmental suprasystem.

---

11 Synergy: the whole is greater than (or at least different from) the sum of its parts.

The internal organization can be viewed as composed of several major subsystems. Organizational **goals and values** represent one of the more important subsystems. While the organization takes many of its values from its broader sociocultural environment, it also influences societal values.

The **technical subsystem** refers to the knowledge required for the performance of tasks. By organizational technology we mean the techniques, equipment, processes, and facilities used in the transformation of inputs into outputs. The technical subsystem is determined by the purposes of the organization and

Figure 1.2   The Organization System

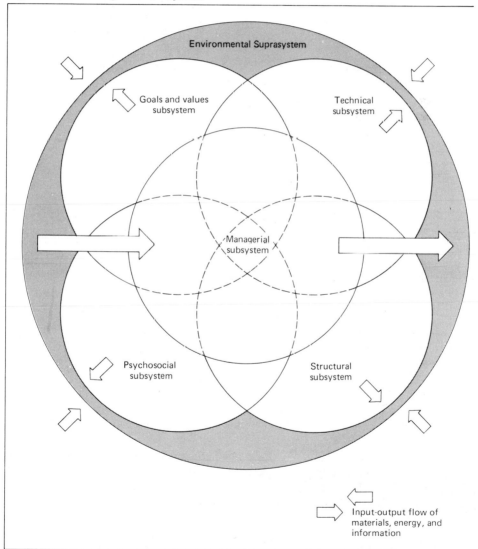

will vary according to the task requirements. The technology frequently proscribes the type of organization structure and affects the psychosocial system.

Every organization has a **psychosocial subsystem**, which consists of individual behavior and motivation, status and role relationships, group dynamics, and influence networks. This subsystem is, of course, affected by external environmental forces as well as by the technology, tasks, and structure of the internal organization.

Intermeshed with the technical and the psychosocial subsystems is the organization **structure**. Structure is concerned with the ways in which the tasks of the organization are divided (differentiation) and with the coordination of these activities (integration). In a formal sense, structure can be set forth by organization charts, job descriptions, and rules and procedures. It is concerned with patterns of authority, communication, and work flow.

The **managerial subsystem** plays a central role in goal setting, planning, designing organizations, and controlling activities, as well as in relating the organization to its environment. Managerial functions and practices are vital to the integration of activities in all the other subsystems.

Contingency View— Acting

Throughout the book we will stress the relationship of organization theory and management practice in specific situations. The contingency view depends on a body of knowledge and research tasks that focus on interrelationships among key variables and subsystems in organizations, It also emphasizes the role of the manager as a diagnostician, pragmatist, and artist. In terms of the systems model set forth above, we can say that:

The contingency view of organizations and their management suggests that an organization is a system composed of subsystems and delineated by identifiable boundaries from its environmental suprasystem. The contingency view seeks to understand the interrelationships within and among subsystems as well as between the organization and its environment and to define patterns of relationships or configurations of variables. It emphasizes the multivariate nature of organizations and attempts to understand how organizations operate under varying conditions and in specific circumstances. Contingency views are ultimately directed toward suggesting organizational designs and managerial actions most appropriate for specific situations. [12]

The essence of this view is that there is *no one best way* and that there is a middle ground between "universal principles" and "it all depends." This approach recognizes the complexity involved in managing modern organizations but uses the existing body of knowledge to relate environment and design, to match structure

[12] Fremont E. Kast and James E. Rosenzweig, *Contingency Views of Organization and Management,* Science Research Associates, Inc., Palo Alto, Calif., 1973, p. ix.

and technology, to integrate strategy and tactics, or to determine the appropriate degree of subordinate participation in decision making, given a specific situation. Success in the art of management depends on a reasonable success rate for actions taken in a probabilistic environment.

Performance

Why study organization and management? We have indicated that they are a pervasive part of our existence. We are affected by a wide variety of organizations and their management. It seems obvious that we would be better off with increased understanding of anything that affects us. Beyond this, however, there is an implicit notion that increased knowledge will somehow lead to better organization and management. But what do we mean by better? An overall concept is:

Performance = f(ability, motivation)

Ability is comprised of human and technical capabilities that provide an indication of the range of possible performance. Just how much of that latent capability is realized depends on the degree to which individuals and/or groups are motivated to perform. For organizations, performance results from the aggregation of individual and group efforts to achieve relevant goals.

Measuring and evaluating results is important in determining performance. Output per work-hour, share of the market, and net profits are relatively straightforward indicators of performance. However, most organizations have multiple goals, some of which are not easily measured. Examples might be customer satisfaction, increased managerial skill, or long-run viability. It is important to recognize multiple goals and evaluate organizational performance on a variety of relevant dimensions. [13] It is particularly important to identify substantive functions that spell success or failure in order to give priority attention to them.

Throughout this book we will refer to three dimensions of organizational performance—effectiveness, efficiency, and participant satisfaction. **Effectiveness** is concerned with the accomplishment of explicit or implicit goals. What is the degree of accomplishment of objectives in key results areas? **Efficiency** refers to the ratio of output to input, or benefit to cost. It is possible to be effective but inefficient—thus squandering human and material resources. Similarly, it is possible to be efficient and ineffective. Organizations sometimes emphasize *doing things right* at the expense of *doing the right things*. For us, a basic ingredient of organizational performance is **participant satisfaction.** In most organizations people have to be satisfied enough to continue their membership. If not, they quit and go elsewhere. An important relationship is that good task performance typically leads to satisfaction so that we can work on participant satisfaction by being both effective and efficient.

13 Richard M. Steers, "When Is An Organization Effective?" *Organization Dynamics*, Autumn, 1976, pp. 50–63.

Another consideration is improvement in capability. Long-run viability depends on both short-run achievements and the potential to sustain and improve performance in the future. Balanced development of individual and group capability is important for the well-being of the organization as a whole.

Our study of organization and management will be concerned with better understanding of organizational phenomena so that appropriate managerial actions can be taken. The systems approach is a way of thinking about organizational variables and relationships. A contingency view provides a framework for doing the right things at the right times, depending on the situation. Hopefully, better understanding and improved practice can result in improved organizational performance as measured by a variety of relevant dimensions.

Outline
of
Book

Part 1 presents conceptual foundations for studying organization and management. In this chapter we have emphasized the pervasiveness of organization and management, shown the relationship of management practice to organization theory, indicated the newness and evolving nature of organization science, and stressed its increasingly complex and dynamic environment. Chapter 2 is concerned with the evolution of value systems over time and with their impact on management thinking. This is a key step in the development of later materials because value systems and ideologies underlie organization design and managerial behavior.

Part 2 traces the evolution of organization theory and management practice with particular reference to the twentieth century. The traditional concepts involved in scientific management, bureaucracy, and administrative management are set forth. The behavioral and management science contributions are then discussed, and their impact on the evolving theory is evaluated. In Chapter 5 systems concepts and contingency views are elaborated as a framework for modern theory, stressing their usefulness in the study of complex organizations. This provides the primary framework for the remainder of the book.

Part 3 covers the environmental suprasystem of organizations—both general and specific. The concept of boundaries delineating organizations is important because it helps focus analysis on reasonably well-defined systems. The subject of organizational goal setting (in an environmental context) is also covered in Part 3.

Part 4 looks at the technical and structural subsystems. The impact of rapidly changing technology on modern organizations is discussed, and the relationship of the technical system to the other subsystems is evaluated. The ways in which organization design establishes a formal structuring of relationships in order to accomplish its purposes are then discussed.

Part 5 is concerned with the psychosocial systems within the organization. Attention is given to individual behavior in organizations and to the various influences affecting motivation. Status and role systems are presented as inevitable phenomena in social groups. The discussion then turns to group dynamics and its role in organization improvement. The concept of an influence system is set forth and related to power and authority. Finally, the impact of leadership styles on the psychosocial system is discussed.

Part 6 considers the managerial system within complex organizations with emphasis on decision making as the most pervasive activity. Information-decision systems are discussed in terms of their role in the planning and control functions. As a background for considering decision-making processes and specific management tasks, the concept of open and closed systems is explored in detail. Typical management science techniques are discussed in terms of their usefulness in relatively closed systems and computational decision making. Behavioral aspects of decision making (value and ethical considerations, for example) are considered as they relate to open-system models of organizations. The functions of planning and control are viewed as means for coordinating organizational activities.

In Part 7 we reemphasize systems concepts, highlight contingency views of organization theory and management practice, and set forth a model for comparative analysis across institutions and cultures. The framework provides the means to analyze a variety of society's basic organizations—hospitals, universities, schools, public agencies, and businesses.

Part 8 includes a consideration of organization change and renewal, emphasizing the delicate and necessary balance between stability/continuity and adaptation/innovation. Organization and management in the future are previewed in Chapter 24. With the eclectic nature of organization theory in mind, we set forth some notions about trends and developments in organizations and the role of management in the future.

Questions and Problems

1 Define organization. Why are organizations so pervasive?
2 Define management. Do you agree that management is the "single ubiquitous mind-driven activity of humanity?" Why or why not?
3 Illustrate the continuum of organizations ranging from small, informal groups to large, complex institutions (such as General Motors, a university, a large hospital, or a city). What common characteristics can you cite?
4 Compare and contrast organization science, organization theory, and management practice.

5 Is management an art or a science? Why?

6 Discuss *(a)* the eclectic nature of organization theory and *(b)* the relative new-ness of some of the relevant underlying disciplines.

7 Screen current periodicals in the behavioral and social sciences (such as *American Sociological Review, American Economic Review, Journal of Applied Psychology, Journal of Anthropology,* and *Behavioral Science*) and list the various articles that relate to organization theory and management practice.

8 Discuss the tentativeness of knowledge about organizations.

9 What basic trends have led to increasing complexity within organizations as well as in their external environment? What impact does this increasing complexity have on organization theory and management practice?

10 Consider a particular organizational type, such as a business corporation, university, hospital, or city, and discuss the forces that have led to greater internal and environmental complexity for that institution.

11 For the same organizational type (question 10), list and discuss criteria for measuring and evaluating performance.

Perspectives on Management Values

Two

The modern manager operates in a dynamic system with rapidly changing technologies and in an increasingly complex environment. The development of organization theory and management practice is strongly influenced by these forces. Concepts and actions are affected by value systems determined not only from within the organization but by the sociocultural norms of the broader society as well. It is necessary to understand the evolution of values in order to comprehend some of the underlying forces that have affected the development of management thought. This chapter considers the influences of sociocultural values on managerial concepts and practices, beginning with a brief discussion of the historical evolution of the capitalistic ethic and the transformation to modern industrialism. Closely related to values is the question of professionalism of management. The following topics provide the framework for the chapter.

Evolution of Sociocultural Values
Historical Evolution of Capitalistic Ethic
Transformation of Capitalistic Ethic
Current Business Ideologies
Professionalization of Management
Social Control over Business Activity
Influence of Changing Values on Management Concepts

Evolution of Sociocultural Values

The organization can be thought of as a subsystem of the broader sociocultural environment in which it operates. "It seemed appropriate to define an organization as a social system which is organized for the attainment of a particular type of goal; the attainment of that goal is at the same time the performance of

25

a type of function on behalf of a more inclusive system, the society."[1] The values of the organization are therefore strongly influenced by norms and ideologies of the broader society. In this sense the values of the organization legitimate its existence and activities in the broader social system. Our fundamental thesis is that values are a primary basis for guiding decision making and other actions and therefore set the basic framework for the development of organization theory and management practice.

Values and ideologies are closely related. "We conceive of values as normative propositions, held by individual human beings of what human beings *ought* to desire, e.g., the desirable. They are supported by internalized sanctions and functions as (a) imperatives in judging how one's social world ought to be structured and operated, and (b) standards for evaluating and rationalizing the propriety of individual and social choices."[2] This approach emphasizes that values are normative standards by which human beings are influenced in their choice of actions. The primary function of values in terms of managerial behavior is that they serve as determinants and guidelines for decision making and action.

Ideologies are "the aggregate of the ideas, beliefs, and modes of thinking characteristic of a group, such as a nation, class, caste, profession or occupation, religious sect, political party, etc. These ideologies are conditioned and determined by the geographical and climatic situation, habitual activities, and cultural environment of their respective groups. They are not necessarily mutually exclusive and may overlap."[3] These definitions suggest that values are individually held and that ideologies emphasize group ideas, beliefs, and modes of thinking; however, we will use them interchangeably to represent both individuals and group beliefs.

Ideologies and values set the social roles that individuals fulfill in their society. According to the concept of "role theory," the individual attempts to operate within the expectations of the broader social group and also internalizes the values and norms which the group explicitly or implicitly prescribes. Thus the role prescribed for the manager is reinforced by personal motivation to fulfill it effectively. The managerial role in contemporary society has evolved substantially from that prescribed earlier under traditional capitalism.

We should not look at the issue of values as a one-way street. While the broad sociocultural system does influence the values of the manager, business organizations also have affected social norms. Ours has been characterized as a "business society" in which the ideology of the large corporate enterprise sets the dominant theme for the total system. The beliefs of business executives have

---

1 Talcott Parsons, "Suggestions for a Sociological Approach to the Theory of Organizations—II," *Administrative Science Quarterly,* September 1956, p. 238.

2 Philip E. Jacob and James J. Flink, with the collaboration of Hedvah L. Shuchman, "Values and Their Function in Decision-Making," Supplement no.9 to *The American Behavioral Scientist,* May 1962, p. 22.

3 H.P. Fairchild (ed.), *Dictionary of Sociology,* Philosophical Library, Inc., New York, 1944, p. 149.

always exerted a strong influence in the United States. The modern business organization is the primary mechanism for the transformation of accelerating technology into products and services. It is a dominant force in receiving inputs from the environment, in transforming them, and in distributing outputs. In performing this role, it influences society.

Other organizations have substantial impact on societal values. The greatly expanded activities of government—federal, state, and local—have had a profound effect, These are often difficult to measure, but they are nevertheless very important. For example, what was the impact on our value system of the creation of the National Aeronautics and Space Administration, successful landings on the moon, and other space explorations? Certainly the Vietnam war and the resulting social upheavals affected our values. Government-sponsored social security, unemployment compensation, and health care programs have tended to modify our traditional views concerning individualism and self-sufficiency.

Educational institutions also have an important impact on our values. Elementary and secondary schools are the primary institutional means within our society for the transmittal of ideologies and values to young people. The growing proportion of people attending colleges and universities has increased the impact of these institutions on individual and collective value systems. Religious organizations, unions, correctional institutions, the military, and all other types of organizations operate under certain values, which in turn affect the broader society.

There is a dynamic interplay between the organization and society. Every organization is a subunit of the broader sociocultural system. Organizations utilize resources provided by the environment and are granted a degree of autonomy to accomplish their purposes, but they are constrained by the requirement of meeting the needs of the broader society. They must operate under the general ideologies and values established by that society. But at the same time they are not passive; they modify social values.

In the following sections we will consider the evolution of values that have specifically affected business organizations. However, we should recognize that many of these changes have affected other types of organizations as well.

Historical Evolution of Capitalistic Ethic

The capitalistic ideology has not been the norm or standard ethic throughout Western history. In fact, for much of recorded history this ideology was unacceptable. Yet exchange and commercial activities are as old as recorded history. The books of the Old Testament, for example, are filled with examples of commercial activities and with laws and regulations for their governance. Archaeologists have discovered many artifacts that indicate commercial activities that were often subject to rather elaborate and sophisticated rules and codes of ethics. For example, the Code of Hammurabi, approximately 2000 BC, was set forth by the Babylonian ruler and provided guidelines for merchants and peddlers.[4]

Commerce in ancient Greece flourished in spite of the ideal of self-sufficiency with emphasis on an economic base of agriculture and animal husbandry, which provided ideological constraints against commercial activities. The Greek philosophers generally looked down on commercial activities as necessary but distasteful. The Roman view regarding commercial activities was patterned after the Grecian ideology and thus was tolerant of commerce and trade but relegated these activities to a low calling. Although the Roman aristocracy entered into agreements with business in return for the provision of money for more noble conquests, there was a general and persistent mistrust of the merchant. Thus both Grecian and Roman ideology shared a disdain for business practitioners but were pragmatic enough to recognize that these activities were necessary in order to accomplish the broader purposes of the empires.

The Medieval Period

The medieval age has been characterized as a period of stagnation and lack of economic and social development. It was dominated by the two primary social organizations of the time, the feudal system and the Catholic Church. The feudal system, with its closed structure and specific definition of roles for the lord and for the peasant-serf, dominated the economic life of Western Europe. The church provided the ideology and set forth the value system for the whole society. The primary concern was the salvation of the soul. The religious concept suggested that people were only on earth for a brief period of time, in which they must prepare for eternity and salvation. The church was the dominant institution that prevailed over the feudal community and national boundaries. Its influence was great in all areas of human activity.

In the early phases of the Middle Ages, in particular, the dominant church ideology held business and commercial activities in disdain and set forth strict rules and limitations. Usury was a sin, and trade itself was of dubious purity. Church doctrine reflected a hostility toward the business practitioner and commercial activity. However, there was an important transition in church views of business activities during the latter part of the medieval period, coincident with growing commercialism. The Italian city-states had a resurgence of trade within the Mediterranean area. There was growing commerce between local communities and an increase in the number of craftspeople under the guild system. The modification of the church views regarding commercial activities is seen in the pronouncements of St. Thomas Aquinas in the middle of the thirteenth century.

---

4 Edward C. Bursk, Donald T. Clark, and Ralph W. Hidy, "The Oldest Business Code: Nearly 4000 Years Ago," *The World of Business,* vol.1, Simon and Schuster, Inc., New York, 1962, pp. 9-10.

Although he continued to hold that trade was degrading and a necessary evil, he saw that the growing commercialism of the time did have a social role. He set forth the concept of a just price and accepted profit margins acquired in the process of trade as a wage for the labor of the trader. His view that there was a just price that might be determined by the market was a major concession to the merchants' activities.

In spite of these relaxations in church regulations concerning business activities, the dominant view during the medieval period was that trade and commerce were tolerated as necessary evils. Many business practices were not within the realm of the accepted ethic. Tawney describes the medieval period and its view of business activities as follows:

At every turn, therefore, there are limits, restrictions, warnings against allowing economic interests to interfere with serious affairs. It is right for man to seek such wealth as is necessary for a livelihood in his station. To seek more is not enterprise, but avarice, and avarice is a deadly sin. Trade is legitimate; the different resources of different countries show that it was intended by Providence. But it is a dangerous business. A man must be sure that he carries it on for the public benefit, and that the profits which he takes are no more than the wages of his labor. Private property is a necessary institution, at least in a fallen world; men work more and dispute less when goods are private than when they are common. But it is to be tolerated as a concession to human frailty, not applauded as desirable in itself. [5]

This negative view of business that predominated during medieval times still persists in many present-day cultures and among certain groups in the United States. It remains a part of modern ideology about business.

Rise of Capitalistic Ethic

It should be emphasized that the capitalistic creed did not appear suddenly in full bloom in Western society. Rather, it developed as an evolutionary process that had its roots in the changing views of the church regarding commercial activities during the latter part of the Middle Ages. By the beginning of the sixteenth century, many of the constraints of the medieval period were being broken down. The urbanization of the population and the development of communities and nations stimulated the growth of commerce and trade. The growing overseas trade of such nations as England, France, Holland, Portugal, and Spain further stimulated commercial activities.

A number of historians consider the changes in religious values and attitudes as an important basis for the development of the capitalistic ethic. Several consider Judaism as the primary force in the development of the capitalistic system. Sombart, for example, suggests that the Jewish religion did not invoke the

5 R. H. Tawney, *Religion and the Rise of Capitalism*, Mentor Books, New American Library of World Literature, New York, 1954, p. 35.

same restrictions against commerce and the accumulation of wealth that were evident in the Christian faith. The Jews in Europe were restrained from owning land and from participating in many other activities and therefore turned to trade and commerce as alternatives. The basic Judaic values of self-control, hard work, sobriety, thrift, and abidance by religious laws and teachings were conducive to economic development and were compatible with the growing capitalism.[6]

Other writers, most notably Max Weber, emphasized that the changes in the religious ethic resulting from the Reformation and the Protestant movement provided an ethical and hence economic climate that was highly favorable to the progress of capitalism. Weber suggested that the growing Protestantism in England, Scotland, the Netherlands, and later in New England was the primary reason why these countries were the first to undergo industrial development.[7] Others have indicated that the new spirit of individualism encouraged by humanism and Protestantism was a dominant force in the evolving capitalism. Eells and Walton summarize the role of the Reformation leaders in the development of this new ethic as follows:

Luther's emphasis on individual enterprise, on biblical interpretation, and on the importance of work was reinforced and expanded by Calvin, who placed frugality, thrift, and industry—virtues dear to those earlier businessmen—high in his schema of values. Furthermore, by focusing on the notion that worldly success and prosperity might be construed as signs of God's approval for the elect, Calvin provided a religious incentive that harmonized effectively with the spread of the profit motive in Western society.[8]

Thus the tenets of Calvinism provided the basic framework for the encouragement of capitalism and set the stage for the development of the Protestant ethic. In the new world, puritanism continued the stress on the virtues of hard work, sobriety, and an accumulation of worldly goods as a sign of being in God's grace. Weber saw in the pronouncements of Benjamin Franklin the essence of the Protestant ethic. He said that all Franklin's moral attitudes were colored by strong utilitarianism. "Honesty is useful, because it assures credit; so are punctuality, industry, frugality, and that is the reason they are virtues."[9] Weber cited Franklin's view that the accumulation of wealth was a sign of God's grace. "If we thus ask, *why* should 'money be made out of men,' Benjamin Franklin himself, although he was a colourless deist, answers in his autobiography with a quotation from the Bible, which his strict Calvinistic father drummed into him again and again in his youth: 'Seest thou a man diligent in his business? He shall stand before kings.' (Prov. xxii. 29)."[10]

6 Werner Sombart, *The Quintessence of Capitalism*, trans. and ed. by M. Epstein, T. Fisher Unwin, London, 1915, pp. 265–266.

7 Max Weber, *The Protestant Ethic and the Spirit of Capitalism*, trans. by Talcott Parsons, Charles Scribner's Sons, New York, 1958.

8 Richard Eells and Clarence Walton, *Conceptual Foundations of Business*, Richard D. Irwin, Inc, Homewood, Ill., 1961, pp. 29–30.

9 Weber, op. cit., p. 52.

10 Ibid., p. 53.

Adam Smith
and the
Triumph of
Laissez-Faire

At the time of the American Rovolution, the capitalist ethic was well entrenched in the Netherlands, England, and in the American Colonies. Although the philosophy of mercantilism had dominated the economic scene during the sixteenth and seventeenth centuries, by the mid-1700s it was breaking down. Under the mercantilistic concept, the individual was subordinate to the state, and economic and business activities were dedicated to the support of the power of the state. The acquisition of wealth was the important economic mission of the nation, and all economic activities were dedicated to this goal.

In 1776, with the publication of Adam Smith's *An Inquiry into the Nature and Causes of the Wealth of Nations,* the capitalistic ethic received its grand theory. His view set the theoretical background for the growing capitalistic ethic that has dominated economic thought in Western Europe and America since that time. Smith argued for economic freedoms on the premise that by maximizing self-interest, each individual would benefit the total society. The "invisible hand" of the market and competition would ensure maximization of social benefits. The beauty of the Smithonian theory was that it allowed each individual to maximize personal profit and wealth and yet automatically make the best possible allocation of resources for the broad social benefit. The control mechanism was the competition of the marketplace, which was automatic and needed neither state nor any other external control to ensure its effective operation.

Smith emphasized that any governmental interference with commercial activities would tend to upset the natural balance, and he championed the laissez faire concept of letting business alone to work out the allocation of resources within the constraints of the marketplace. This ideology fit admirably the technological and industrial developments of the time and provided a perfect justification for the growth of the industrialist. "Smith's theory of capitalism, reinforced and somewhat modified by Bentham and Ricardo, formed the philosophy of the Industrial Revolution and is still widely held in the Western world. It produces a wonderful world of full employment, lowest possible prices and costs, maximum efficiency, and progress and freedom. This dream is clearly seen in many of the pronouncements made by American business leaders today." [11]

Embracing
Science
and
Technology

The Protestant ethic and the emerging spirit of capitalism were favorable to the growing emphasis on scientific investigation and technological applications in Western societies. There are many common values in the Protestant ethic,

[11] Joseph W. McGuire, *Business and Society,* McGraw-Hill Book Company, New York, 1963, pp. 59–60.

capitalism, and science and technology: emphasis on rationality, empiricism, a utilitarian mentality, the view of humanity's need to utilize the resources of nature for personal betterment here on earth and for the glory of God, and the importance placed on knowledge and literacy. These movements converged during the seventeenth and eighteenth centuries to provide the basis for industrial societies. Merton suggests that "Puritanism and the scientific temper are in most salient agreement, for the combination of *rationalism and empiricism* which is so pronounced in the Puritan ethic forms the essence of the spirit of modern science." [12]

The Protestant ethic provided the ideology for both capitalism and the advancement of science. Capitalism encouraged the utilization of scientific knowledge for technical applications. The emergence of a market system organized around the principle of private property provided the institutional means for the accumulation of resources necessary to translate the growing scientific knowledge into an industrial technology.

These three forces were associated with another, perhaps even more fundamental, trend. Each of them—the Protestant ethic, the emergence of capitalism, and the development of science and technology—required a fundamental change in the education of people. They depended on a better educated citizenry, at least among the elites, and this led to an expansion of general and specialized education, particularly in the scientific and technical fields.

Social Darwinism and the Survival of the Fittest

In 1858 Charles Darwin published his classic *Origin of the Species,* in which he set forth the theory of evolution of biological organisms from lower to higher forms of life. He emphasized that in the evolutionary process the organism adapted itself successfully to its environment and that it was in a continual process of struggle. This concept of **survival of the fittest** was extended from the biological organism to the broader social order by Herbert Spencer in the latter part of the nineteenth century. Social Darwinism suggested that the most capable and resourceful people would rise to the top of the social hierarchy and that this was the natural order of things. Under Social Darwinism it was only natural that there would be poor and rich classes, and any attempt to upset this hierarchical order was considered unnatural and against the best interest of society. Social Darwinism clearly reinforced the Protestant ethic and Adam Smith's concept of laissez faire. It provided the basic ideology for the business practitioner in the late nineteenth century and helped justify the accumulation of resources and their use for self-interest.

Thus, these ideological strands converged during the latter part of the nineteenth century to provide the high point of the classical capitalistic ethic. But

---

12 Robert K. Merton, "Puritanism, Pietism and Science," in *Social Theory and Social Structure,* rev. ed., The Free Press of Glencoe, New York, 1957, p. 579.

even at that time there were dissenters from this ideology. Perhaps the most famous dissenter was Karl Marx, who wrote *The Communist Manifesto* with Frederick Engels in 1848 and *Das Kapital* in 1867. Marx and Engels saw the evolving
capitalistic system as a primary threat to the social structure and recommended
revolutionary remedies. The industrialists and capitalists were breaking down the
established social order. They said, "The *bourgeoisie*, wherever it got the upper
hand, put an end to all feudal, patriarchal, idyllic relations, pitilessly tore asunder
the motley feudal ties that bound man to his 'natural superiors,' and left remaining no other bond between man and man than naked self-interest and callous cash
payments." [13] Marx called for a proletarian revolution to break the capitalistic
order and to establish communism. However, there were many other dissenters in
the nineteenth century who advocated not revolution but rather revolutionary
reforms in the capitalistic ideology.

Transformation of Capitalistic Ethic

Prior to the Civil War, agriculture and small business enterprises dominated the American scene. Although there had been rapid developments in fledgling industries, trade, and transportation facilities in the early part of the nineteenth century, it was not until after the Civil War that large-scale industrial
developments took place. The industrial revolution, with its emphasis on the technology of production, utilization of machinery, and the factory system, required
the collective organization of people and resources. This was the era of the industrial capitalist who accumulated and utilized vast resources in shaping the new
world. The development of the corporate form of business provided the means for
accumulation of the capital necessary for the operations of the industrial empire.
Carnegie, Gould, Morgan, Vanderbilt, Cook, Hill, and others became the popular
heroes of the day and were the champions of Industrial Darwinism.

The evolving Protestant ethic, the competitive model of Adam Smith,
and Social Darwinism provided the ideological support for industrial capitalism.
This period, from the end of the Civil War until 1890, can be considered as the
apex in the evolution of the traditional capitalistic ethic. In American society the
basic ideological heritages and values merged with the expanding technology and
opportunities of the industrial revolution to achieve the high point of a militant
and frequently unremitting capitalistic ethic. Even though the growing concentration of power and monopolization of industry created a real situation totally
different from that envisioned in Adam Smith's pure, competitive model, the ideology of individualism and laissez faire continued to dominate business thinking.

Many of the captains of industry at this time engaged in highly unethical
practices as measured by today's standards. However, these actions should be

---

13 Cited in Tawney, op. cit., p. 223.

considered in terms of the prevailing norms of that period. Industrialists were the heroes of the day and had substantial popular support for their activities. However, toward the end of the nineteenth century many dissenters pointed to the antisocial consequences of the prevailing Industrial Darwinism.

Emerging Government Regulations

During much of the early part of the nineteenth century, governmental actions were highly favorable to the development of industry and commerce. Tariff laws that protected the emerging manufacturing interest were passed. The Supreme Court held that the private corporate form was legal, and this decision set the stage for the later development of huge corporate enterprises. The government provided vast sums of money and land for the development of the railroad transportation system. During the period from the formation of the United States to the 1880s, governmental actions, particularly those of the federal government, were quite favorable to the business system.

The antisocial actions of many industrialists in the late 1800s created substantial public dissatisfaction with the business system. The development of huge corporations and trusts—and the evident monopolistic powers that they maintained—led various forces within the society to demand some form of regulation or control. They suggested that the unfettered application of the laissez faire concept (built on Adam Smith's pure competitive model) might not be effective in a system of oligopoly and monopoly. Thus the period between 1880 and World War I saw the beginning of regulation and control of American business in a variety of ways. The Grange movement—a combination of farmers, local communities, and state legislatures—represented a popular uprising against the monopolistic powers of the big railroads. This movement resulted in the passage of many state acts to regulate the railroads and finally led to the enactment of the Interstate Commerce Act in 1887. Although in early phases this act was ineffectively enforced, it did set the stage for the broader regulation of business activities by the federal government.

The Sherman Antitrust Act was passed in 1890. Although this act was very general and its interpretation was left to the courts, it did set the groundwork for the view that the government should regulate business in the public interest. Actually, the Sherman Antitrust Act did not represent a major philosophical deviation from the laissez faire ethic of Adam Smith. The primary purpose of this act was to restrict monopolistic practices and to roll back the business system to that of the competitive model. This, however, was impossible in view of the changing industrial structure, and the government continued to pass laws to regulate business practices directly. The Pure Food and Drug Act was passed in 1906, and the Clayton Act and the Federal Trade Commission Act were enacted in 1914. Thus, during this period the basic framework for governmental regulation of certain aspects of business activities was established.

Rise of Labor Movements

Although there are incidents of organized labor activities in America dating back to the seventeenth century, labor unions did not become effective as a countervailing power to the industrialists until the latter part of the nineteenth century. During the early phases of the industrial revolution many legal restraints were placed on collective actions of work groups. Essentially, the courts held that unions were conspiracies in restraint of trade. Although there are numerous examples of small-scale unions during this period, the impact of organized labor was localized and not substantial. However, after the Civil War, with the growth of larger industrial organizations, the labor movement received added impetus.

The Knights of Labor was organized in 1869 and remained a secret society until 1879, when it began open activities. It was opened to all workers, and a coalition with agrarian groups was formed to advocate major social reform. The American Federation of Labor (AFL), established in 1886, set the pattern for the American labor movement. Under the pragmatic leadership of Samuel Gompers, it adopted a policy of operating within the capitalistic framework but with a view to gaining a greater share of the benefits of the economic system for labor. Although it did accept the capitalistic ideology, the AFL became a strong countervailing power against the large corporations and, in effect, did have a part in modifying and transforming this ideology.

Radical unions such as the Socialist Labor Party and the Industrial Workers of the World (IWW) developed between 1895 and 1920. The IWW, or "Wobblies," gathered workers into militant industrial unions with the purpose of overthrowing the capitalistic system. Although this movement passed from the American scene after World War I, it represented a violent reaction to the dominant Industrial Darwinism of the period.

The Great Depression and the Keynesian Revolution

The decade of the 1920s was the high point for American business and the industrial system, with predictions of endless prosperity. But the 1930s brought a low point for the esteem of the businessperson and the greatest challenge to the capitalistic ideology. The Great Depression, beginning with the stock market crash of 1929 and continuing with a massive economic collapse, threatened the very framework of our economic and social system. Widespread unemployment and the collapse of the market challenged the roots of the classical capitalistic ideology, and business was the scapegoat.

In classical economic theory, depressions, while accepted as inevitable, were considered to be short-term periods of adjustment that represented only minor dislocation in utilization of resources. Under this model, full employment and utilization of resources would be established at a new equilibrium. This, however, did not happen during the Great Depression. It extended with minor modifications from 1929 until the World War II stimulus to industrial activity caused the turn. The Depression, furthermore, cast grave doubts on some of the basic tenets of the Protestant ethic—individualism and the value of hard work and thrift. Individuals were not totally responsible for their own fate. Many forces operating in a complex industrial society could not be coped with by the individual—people were affected by events far beyond their control.

Although the Depression itself was evidence of the breakdown of the economic system and the classical capitalistic ethic, it took economist John Maynard Keynes in *The General Theory of Employment, Interest, and Money* in 1936 to provide the theoretical explanation. Keynes challenged a basic tenet of the Protestant ethic by saying that savings withheld from consumption could lead to dislocation and underutilization of economic resources. Even more important, the Keynesian thesis questioned the foundation of the classical economic doctrine of laissez faire, whereby the market mechanism and price system would automatically adjust to an equilibrium point for full utilization of resources and employment. The classical doctrine was a beautiful model of an automatically adjusting closed system. No interference or external force was necessary in order to ensure optimal allocation and full utilization of economic resources—and this to the broad social benefit. A wonderful ideology, unique in its simplicity! Keynes explained the Depression by suggesting that equilibrium could be reached in spite of a large number of involuntarily unemployed people and other nonutilized resources. He emphasized consumption rather than savings as the way to achieve full utilization of resources. Without a self-adjusting system operating at full employment of both people and other resources, it was necessary under this thesis to have an external force provide the balancing mechanism—this force was the government.

Although Keynes's theory was received with substantial hostility from the business community and still remains suspect in many circles, there is little doubt that the inescapable reality of the Great Depression and the persuasiveness of his views had a significant influence on the transformation of the capitalistic ethic.

Expansion of Governmental Activities

World War II required the massive interjection of the government into all phases of economic activity in our society in order to accumulate and manage the resources necessary for the war effort. Although most of these controls were relaxed after the war, the vestiges of this intervention remained. In 1946, a predominantly Republican Congress passed the Fair Employment Act of 1946, which established the policy that the federal government had prime responsibility for the maintenance of full employment and full utilization of economic resources. What a major transformation from the hostility toward Keynesian theory just ten years earlier! Although the United States did demobilize immediately after the end of the war, this period was short-lived, and by 1948 we were again in a state of continued preparedness. The cold war and the hot Korean and Vietnam wars caused our society to remain in a partial state of mobilization with a huge allocation of economic resources for "defense" efforts. During the past twenty-five years nearly 10 percent of our gross national product has been allocated to defense, an expenditure of hundreds of billions of dollars. Furthermore, the government has made other massive expenditures in areas such as atomic energy and space programs.

Over the past three decades governmental expenditures in the nondefense sector have expanded significantly. Social welfare, health care, support for education, natural resource development, highways, mass transit, equal employment opportunities, and environmental improvement are examples. These activities have expanded at all levels of government—federal, state, and local. In the federal government many new agencies have been established, such as the Environmental Protection Agency, the Consumer Product Safety Commission, and the Equal Employment Opportunity Commission. Older agencies, such as the Federal Trade Commission, the Securities and Exchange Commission, and the Food and Drug Administration have taken an increasingly active role in regulating business activities.

What has been the impact on the capitalistic ideology of this increasing governmental role in economic and social affairs? Most governmental interventions do not operate within the market mechanism assumed in the competitive model. With the expansion of these activities, the business community has had to share economic and social power with government. Increasingly, executives have been working with governmental agencies, and this process has affected managerial values.

Technological and Social Change

In the past three decades, we have seen profound technological and social change. The necessity for dealing with technological change within the complex organization has influenced the prevailing business ideology. The introduction of scientists, professionals, and other highly trained specialists into the organization has affected managerial concepts and approaches. Major social changes outside the business system have also had an impact on the ideology. The growing social awareness and activism of various groups—women, minorities, consumer advocates, and environmental protectionists—have caused managers to reconsider their own values.

**Projection
Into a
World
Consciousness**

One of the most fundamental changes since World War II has been the expansion of our sphere of consciousness from national to worldwide issues. Earlier we were predominantly isolationists and concerned almost exclusively with our internal economic and social development. However, we now have moved into a position of world leadership and a growing awareness that we are greatly influenced by many events beyond our national boundaries. We are also becoming more aware that we have responsibilities to other people and cultures. [14]

The growth of United States corporations and their expansion into other countries has had an impact on our ideologies. We cannot merely transfer a little island of the United States into a foreign country and expect it to operate according to our norms. Our corporations must adapt to the different cultural values of societies in which they are located. We are also beginning to see more of the process in reverse. Many more foreign multinational firms are locating within our boundaries, and we need to adapt to different managerial approaches.

Increased interaction with other countries and cultures has required us to reexamine and modify our traditional business ideologies. A dramatic illustration of the adaptiveness of capitalistic values is seen in the increasing commercial transactions with communist countries. This has required ideological compromises on both sides.

**Changing Views
on Growth
and Economic
Development**

Traditional capitalistic ideology emphasized continuing economic growth. Advancing science and technology and more effective organization for resource exploitation and utilization were the key instruments of growth. The fundamental ideology was that economic growth would lead to the betterment of the individual and the total society.

This ideology of continual growth was severely challenged in late 1973 when the Organization of Petroleum Exporting Countries (OPEC) oil cartel increased the price of crude oil from $2.75 per barrel to $10 per barrel. This severely limited growth in the United States and in the worldwide economy. By the end of 1976, it was estimated that the increase had cost the United States economy almost 3 million jobs and more than $60 billion in real gross national product (GNP). [15] Worldwide, it is estimated that the oil-consuming nations lost the stag-

---

14 Dean Rusk, "The Interdependence of All Peoples," *California Management Review*, Summer 1977, pp. 79-83.
15 "How OPEC's High Prices Strangle World Growth," *Business Week*, Dec. 20, 1976, pp. 44-50.

gering sum of $600 billion in economic output. Governments throughout the world reacted to the inflationary impact of the oil price increase by curtailing economic growth.

Although our economy is on the road to recovery from this major setback, the situation has raised many questions concerning the basic ideology of continued growth. This action dramatically provided the painful lesson that world resources are limited and that there is growing competition for them from other industrialized and developing countries. We are recognizing that business organizations may not have the luxury of operating in a continually expanding economy and that there are finite resources and limits to growth. [16]

More Voice for Others

Many other forces—beyond laissez faire and government—are trying to affect business organizations. Environmentalists, consumer protection groups, women activists, minorities, citizens' lobbying groups, and many others are trying to influence the decision making of managers directly. The call for social responsiveness in business is being heard from many sides. Responding to these voices requires further transformations in the traditional capitalistic ideology. These groups have utilized many forms of social pressure to obtain a hearing—publicity, consumer boycotts, minority stockholder proposals, influencing legislators, and direct legal action. With loud and often divergent messages, it is little wonder that managers are finding it difficult to establish a clear-cut value system that will guide their actions.

Figure 2.1 illustrates the long-term evolution and transformation of the capitalistic ethic. It gives us the historical development but doesn't provide a clear picture of the current ideology. The period since World War II has been one of major technological, economic, and social change, which has challenged the traditional ideology and raised major questions for the manager. What is the dominant business ideology today? What role should business play in society? What is the impact of the changing ideology on managerial concepts and practices? These questions will be discussed in the following sections.

Current Business Ideologies

It is impossible to define a single current dominant business ideology. Ours is a society of ethical pluralism, and the business manager as an element of this society is caught in the middle of conflicting values. Pluralism has been a dominant characteristic of the American social scene.

16 Donella H. Meadows, et al., *The Limits to Growth,* Universe Books, New York, 1972.

Figure 2.1   Evolution and Transformation of Capitalistic Ethic
The primary forces contributing to the rise and transformation of the capitalistic ethic are shown. The time periods are not to exact scale, and many of these forces influenced development for longer periods than could be indicated in this simplified model.

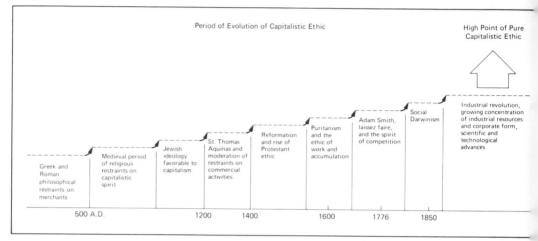

The great genius of the American pattern of society has always been its pluralism—its capacity to accommodate, in the peace of one society, the manifold private motives and energies which are generated by the social life. The society is one; the centers of initiative for its acts are many. Such a distributive pattern of power is inherently precarious, for it depends on the preservation of balance between the claims of the society and the claims of the centers of initiative which appear within it. [17]

Although there are many threads to this ethical pluralism, the major conflict appears to be between the Calvinistic or Protestant ethic and the Judeo-Christian ethic. Farmer suggests that the Calvinist ethic was the theme dominating American life from 1620 to 1930 but that the Judeo-Christian ethic, although much older and going back several thousand years, has come into prominence in the United States since 1930. [18] The Calvinistic ethic supports the view that laissez faire and the profit maximization ideology are the basis on which business operates; it places primary emphasis on production efficiency and the role of the business organization as a creator of goods and services. The Judeo-Christian ethic, on the other hand, suggests that the business enterprise has a broader social responsibility and should not be solely concerned with profit maximization. Farmer sees this as a major dilemma for American society. "The dilemma is that both groups are essentially correct. The Calvinist ethic is correct in economic terms, and this can be demonstrated historically. The Judeo-Christian ethic is

17 John F. A. Taylor, "Is the Corporation above the Law?" *Harvard Business Review,* March–April, 1965, p. 128.
18 Richard N. Farmer, "The Ethical Dilemma of American Capitalism," *California Management Review,* Summer 1964, pp. 47–58

Figure 2.1   (continued)

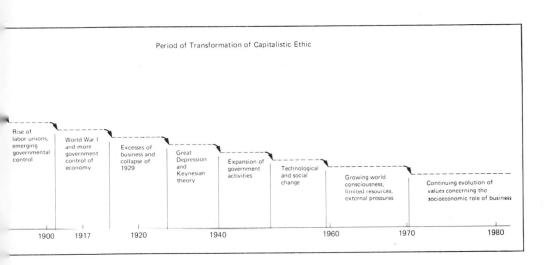

correct in personal terms, and it requires little imagination to project the ethic to the national scene. But there is little economic content in this ethic." [19]

One of the major contributions to this dilemma has been the traditional ideology, stemming from the laissez faire concept and reinforced by traditional economics, that the only objective of business enterprise is profit maximization. The dominant economic theory of the firm takes as its basic premise that the business manager operates as a profit maximizer and that the competitive market operates to ensure social welfare.

A more recent view is that business does not act as an individual profit maximizer but rather that the organization has a number of interest groups, such as customers, suppliers, stockholders, employees, unions, and various government agencies. Under this view, the business organization consists of a number of sometimes cooperating but frequently conflicting groups who make demands on its resources. The manager operating in this dynamic coalition must seek to satisfy the interests of these various groups in order to retain their cooperation and participation in organizational activities.

This view holds that profits are certainly one of the prime goals of the business enterprise and are vital to the long-range viability of the organization. However, it suggests that there are many additional goals of the various participants in the organization, which have to be satisfied. This obviously makes the role of the manager more ambiguous and strained than the profit maximization model. But is this not a realistic view? The objectives and motives of managers are

---

19 Ibid., p. 57.

social as well as economic in origin and are set by the broad culture. It is unrealistic to expect that managers can isolate themselves from this climate. They are intricately interwoven with the environment and should recognize that they will influence and be influenced by the broader social system.

Figure 2.2 outlines some of the major transitions from the traditional capitalistic ethic to the emerging contemporary views. It is primarily illustrative of the trends as we perceive them and does not suggest that we have totally discarded the old ethic and taken on the new. There is no one unified voice of business, just as there is no universally accepted prescription from society on how business should operate. In our contemporary society the environmental influences on business are many, and the responses to these pressures are varied.

Figure 2.2 Comparison of Traditional Capitalistic Ethic with Emerging Contemporary Ethic

Traditional Capitalistic Ethic	Emerging Contemporary Ethic
Protestant ethic of individualism, property rights, and self-determination	Growth of social ethic emphasizing community, group participation and responsibilities, and sociocultural influences on individual welfare
The individual maximizing self-interest leads to higher levels of social welfare	Need for cooperative social behavior
Increasing efficiency through division of labor and specialization	Recognition of limits of specialization in terms of human satisfaction
The business enterprise as an economic unit	The business organization as a *socioeconomic* institution
Profit maximization as a single objective	Profit as a major objective, but increasing recognition of social objectives. Satisfaction of multiple objectives
Total emphasis on effective and efficient economic performance	Emphasis on effectiveness, efficiency, and participant satisfaction
The business organization as a closed system	The business organization as an open system interacting with its environment
Responsive only to market and competitive environment	Responsive to many interest groups and social forces
Laissez faire view of governmental actions	Recognition of role of government in meeting social objectives
Humans seeking exploitation and control over nature	Living in harmony with and under the constraints of nature
Strong commitment to economic growth through exploitation of environmental resources	Recognition of the limits of growth and movement toward conservation of resources
Unrestrained utilization of science and technology. Laissez faire and deterministic view of technology	Recognition of limits of science and technology. Perceiving a need for controlling technological applications
Society's expectations of business limited to production of goods and services	Society expects business to deal with broader issues of the quality of life
Measuring business performance by profits	Measuring business by profits *and* other indicators of social performance

Many managers perceive similar shifts in ideologies. In a survey of 1844 readers of *Harvard Business Review*, Martin and Lodge asked the respondents to consider the two ideologies set forth in Figure 2.3. Ideology I fits closely with our description of traditional capitalistic ideology, and Ideology II matches our emerging contemporary ethic.

The value system of contemporary capitalism is pragmatic, and increasingly managers are recognizing that they operate not only in an economic but in

Figure 2.3 Ideological Preferences and Predictions

Ideology I

The first ideology, enunciated by philosopher John Locke 300 years ago, is the nucleus of the traditional "American way" extolling the values of individualism, private property, free competition in an open marketplace, and limited government. This is the way we stated Ideology I in the survey:

"The community is no more than the sum of the individuals in it. Self-respect and fulfillment result from an essentially lonely struggle in which initiative and hard work pay off. The fit survive and if you don't survive, you are probably unfit. Property rights are a sacred guarantor of individual rights, and the uses of property are best controlled by competition to satisfy consumer desires in an open market. The least government is the best. Reality is perceived and understood through the specialized activities of experts who dissect and analyze in objective study."

Ideology II

The second ideology defines the individual as an inseparable part of a community in which his rights and duties are determined by the needs of the common good. Government plays an important role as the planner and implementer of community needs. We expressed Ideology II this way in the survey:

"Individual fulfillment and self-respect are the result of one's place in an organic social process; we 'get our kicks' by being part of a group. A well-designed group makes full use of our individual capacities. Property rights are less important than the rights derived from membership in the community or a group—for example, rights to income, health, and education. The uses of property are best regulated according to the community's need, which often differs from individual consumer desires. Government must set the community's goals and coordinate their implementation. The perception of reality requires an awareness of whole systems and of the interrelationships between and among the wholes. This holistic process is the primary task of science."

Significant Findings

More than two thirds of the respondents prefer Ideology I. However, many readers sense its replacement by a new set of value definitions based on the communitarian principles of Ideology II. Some 62% of the readers regard Ideology I as the more dominant ideology in the United States today, whereas 73% anticipate that Ideology II will dominate in 1985.

Many readers think that the transformation from Ideology I to II could lead to social disaster, with burdensome government interference causing the disintegration of business and loss of personal freedom. A minority accept the change with cautious optimism, acknowledging that many perplexing problems—including resource shortages, explosive population growth, and environmental degradation—can be resolved only within the framework of Ideology II.

The U.S. and non-U.S. responses differed sharply. Two thirds of the Americans regard Ideology I as the more effective ideological framework for solving future problems, while the same proportion of foreign respondents believe Ideology II is more desirable.

William F. Martin and George Cabot Lodge, "Our Society in 1985—Business May Not Like It," *Harvard Business Review,* November–December 1975, pp. 143-150.

a total social environment. They should not be discouraged by the frequent ideological dilemmas that face them and by the various and often seemingly impossible demands made on them by different groups. We reject monolithic authority in
American society and have traditionally valued pluralistic expressions and conflicting views. "The coexistence of Puritanism, Hamiltonianism, Keynesism, and
the welfare state is one of the marvels of our still more or less capitalistic economy. The American melting pot, which works imperfectly with ethnic groups,
doesn't do much better with ideas or ideologies. But in the survival and clash of
opposing ideas may be found the explanation of much of the dynamism of American life—as well as of the abiding disorder and incompleteness of the American
experiment." [20]

Professionalization of Management

Concurrent with the rise of our industrial society and the large-scale,
complex organization has been the development of professionalism as a means for
delineation of role specialization. There is a close relationship between the issue of
managerial ideology and roles and the concept of professionalism.

The Concept of Professionalism

It is virtually impossible to get any authoritative agreement on the definition of a professional. The ministry, law, and medicine have been considered to
be the original professions. Increasingly other occupational groups are classifying
themselves as professions and are assuming some of the characteristics. However,
even the traditional professional groups fall short of an "ideal" professional model
in some respects. It is probably useful to describe professionalism in terms of a
continuum with the ideal type of profession at one end and unorganized occupational categories, or nonprofessions, at the other end, rather than as a unique set
of characteristics from which we can measure an occupational group on an all-or-
nothing basis. Professionalization is a process, then, that may affect any occupation to a greater or lesser degree.

Using this continuum, we may describe the essential elements in an ideal
profession as follows:

1 Professions have a systematic body of theory. Skill is achieved through a
lengthy process of training. The skills that characterize a profession flow from
and are supported by information which has been organized into an internally

consistent system, called a *body of knowledge*. Preparation for a profession must be an intellectual as well as a practical experience.

2 The professional has an authority based upon superior knowledge which is recognized by his clientele. This authority is highly specialized and is related only to the professional's sphere of competence.

3 There is a broad social sanction and approval of the exercise of this authority. The community sanctions the exercise of this authority within certain spheres by conferring upon professionals certain powers and privileges. Control over entry into the profession, licensing procedures, and the confidentiality of communications between the professional and the client are examples of these.

4 There is a code of ethics regulating relations of professional persons with clients and with colleagues such as the Hippocratic oath of the medical profession. Thus self-discipline is utilized as a basis of social control.

5 There is a culture sustained by organizations. A professional is a member of many formal and informal groups. The interactions of social roles required by these groups generate a social configuration unique to the profession, a professional culture.[21]

Is Management a Profession?

If we use this ideal model of professionalism, it is difficult to classify modern management as a profession. It has not developed these five elements to the extent of the traditional professional groups. Nevertheless, if we view the concept of professionalism on a continuum, it is apparent that the trend over the past several decades has been toward greater compliance with these elements of professionalism. There is a growing body of systematic knowledge concerning the management and administration of complex organizations; the authority role of the manager has been legitimated in our culture; this role has the sanction of the community; there is a growing number of professional management associations, particularly in the various specialized aspects of business; and finally, there is a nucleus of the development of self-control.

Technical Competence as a Basis of Professionalism

Parsons suggests that the distinction between professionals and managers based on the "self-interest" motives of business and the "altruistic" motives of the professionals has been overemphasized. He states that the central focus of the

---

21 Howard M. Vollmer and Donald Mills (eds.), *Professionalization,* Prentice-Hall, Inc., Englewood Cliffs, N.J., 1966, pp. 9–19.

professional role lies in the technical competence of the professional and the recognition of this by society. [22] Certainly, the management of complex organizations requires a high level of technical competence, and this role has been accepted by society. The fact that we do not classify management as an ideal type of profession does not diminish the importance of the managerial function. Indeed, it is our view that management of social organizations is one of the most vital and important functions in society.

Although management is not currently a profession as measured against the ideal model, the trend is in this direction. This is important when considering the question of the role of management because one of the primary attributes of professionalism is self-control rather than pure self-interest.

Social Control Over Business Activity

Figure 2.4 is a conceptual diagram showing several forms of social control over business and their changing relationships from the latter part of the nineteenth century until the present. Four primary forms of social control are (1) competition in the marketplace, where the control is exerted primarily through the market mechanisms, (2) governmental regulation, wherein control is exerted directly by federal, state, and local governments, (3) influence of other external groups, and (4) self-control, the growing professionalism of management.

The American business ideology has been transformed over the past century from one of total reliance on the classical capitalistic ideology and laissez faire to one that accepts the proper role of governmental regulations and control and also gives recognition to the importance of the social responsibilities of the corporate enterprise. It is obvious that it would be impossible to quantify these various forms of social control. It is important to place as much reliance as possible on the competitive mechanism because it provides the decentralized and automatic adjustment necessary for a viable economy and society. Nevertheless, it is not a perfect mechanism and must be balanced by judicious use of government regulation, responsiveness to other external groups, and by acceptance of self-control.

The growing professionalization of management has fostered a concept of social responsibility, which is becoming one of the accepted norms of business behavior. There certainly is not complete harmony between the four primary elements of social control. They are not always complementary; rather they are often in conflict when specific issues are considered. But this conflict is the very essence of our pluralistic American society, and it should be recognized that each of these types of social control has a legitimate role.

---

22 Talcott Parsons, "The Professions and Social Structure," *Essays in Sociological Theory,* rev. ed., The Free Press of Glencoe, New York, 1964, pp. 34–49.

Figure 2.4   Forms of Social Control over Business

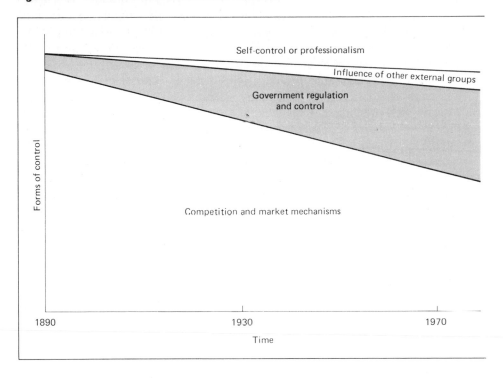

Influence of Changing Values on Management Concepts

There have been significant changes in the capitalistic ideology and in society's views of the legitimate role of the manager and the corporation. Heilbroner summarizes this change:

In the concept of a new capitalism, distinguished by its sense of professional responsibility, characterized by large-scale technological units, imbued with a concern for human values, and aware of the legitimacy of labor and government as centers of economic powers, we have an expression, however incomplete, of what capitalism means that is markedly different from what it meant to the late nineteenth—or early twentieth—century big businessman and considerably different from the lingering conservative depiction today. [23]

It is essential to recognize, particularly as a frame of reference for the next three chapters, that organization theory and management practice have been

---

23 Robert L. Heilbroner, "The View from the Top," in Earl F. Cheit (ed.) *The Business Establishment,* John Wiley & Sons, Inc., New York, 1964, p. 30.

strongly influenced by a changing society and the evolving ideology. Frederick Taylor's scientific management cannot be considered as an isolated force, but should be viewed in the light of the industrial and social situation within which it developed. The writings of Elton Mayo and the human relationists reflect a substantial evolution in management ideology.

The motivation and behavior of practicing managers are affected by value systems. A commonality of ideology is the basis for legitimating the organization as a social system. The managerial concepts that guide the actions of the participants are the primary unseen networks that hold the organization together and make it a functioning entity. They are prime determinants of management practices. Above all, it should be emphasized that modern business executives are not guided by a universal or monistic ethic. Rather, they are guided by contemporary ethical pluralism, which provides general guidelines for decision making but never specific answers.

Summary

Management concepts and practices are influenced by the ideologies of the broader society. Values are normative standards that influence human beings in their social roles and choice of actions. Values are subject to evolutionary change, and the modern manager is faced with a number of ethical norms that are often in conflict.

The capitalistic ideology has not been the norm or standard ethic throughout history. In ancient Greece and Rome, and throughout much of the medieval period, commercial activities were tolerated as necessary evils. The rise of the capitalistic ethic has been associated with changes in the religious ethic resulting from the Reformation and the Protestant movement.

Adam Smith provided the capitalistic ethic with its grand theory. He argued for economic freedoms on the premise that by maximizing their self-interests, each person would benefit the total society. The Protestant ethic and the emerging spirit of capitalism were favorable to the growing emphasis on scientific investigation and technological applications.

There were, however, dissenters from the capitalistic ideology. Marx and Engels saw the capitalistic system as a primary threat to the social structure and recommended revolutionary remedies. Other forces, such as emerging government regulation and labor unions, helped transform the classical capitalistic ethic.

The Great Depression of the 1930s brought a low point to the esteem for business and the greatest challenge to the capitalistic ideology. In 1936, Keynes provided the theoretical explanation for the breakdown. He called for governmental action to restore employment and to prevent depressions.

It is impossible to define a single, current business ideology. Ours is a society of ethical pluralism, and the manager is caught in the middle of conflicting values. There is increasing evidence of the business community's willingness to recognize the social consequence of the changes that it has created and to participate in finding some means for moderating any adverse effects. Furthermore, it has shown a greater tolerance for accepting the roles of other institutions, such as the government and unions, in dealing with social problems.

There is a close relationship between the role of management and the concept of professionalism. Although management is not a profession as measured against the "ideal" model, the trend is in that direction. Organization theory and management practice have been strongly influenced by a changing society and its evolving ideologies.

Questions and Problems

1 Why is our society characterized by "ethical pluralism"? Discuss the various components of our ethical system.

2 Discuss the various forces that led to the high point of the pure capitalistic ethic in the latter part of the nineteenth century. What contributed to the transformation of this ethic during the twentieth century? What will be the major changes in the future?

3 How were the values under the Protestant ethic and the norms of science and technology similar? Is this relationship still true today?

4 Discuss the basic distinctions between the Protestant and Judeo-Christian eth ics. What are the implications of these differences for managers?

5 How have the rise of labor unions and the growing governmental regulations affected the value systems of businesspeople?

6 Review current periodicals such as *Business Week, Fortune,* and *The Wall Street Journal* for current situations involving the question of the role of business in society.

7 What is your evaluation of the view that organizations seek to satisfy a number of objectives imposed by different groups rather than to maximize a single objective?

8 Discuss the concept that professionalism is a form of social control that modifies self-interest in favor of social interest.

9 Using Figure 2.4 as a point of reference, discuss the past and future trends in relative importance of these four forms of social control over business.

Here and elsewhere we shall not obtain the best insight into things until we actually see them growing from the beginning.
Aristotle

The learning process is simply a matter of progressing from cocksure ignorance to thoughtful uncertainty.
George Bernard Shaw

Scientific knowledge, like language, is intrinsically the common property of a group or else nothing at all. To understand it we shall need to know the special characteristics of the groups that create and use it.
Thomas S. Kuhn

Because we live in a time of great change, and because our philosophy of optimism makes us expectant of and receptive to change, we may easily overlook a deeply important aspect of historic development. This is its quality of inertia. It is a quality which is manifest not only in resistance to change—although that is one of its more important aspects—but in the viscosity which is imparted to history because people tend to repeat and continue their ways of life as long as it is possible for them to do so.
Robert L. Heilbroner

Open-system theory is . . . a framework, a meta-theory, a model in the broadest sense of that overused term. Open-system theory is an approach and a conceptual language for understanding and describing many kinds and levels of phenomena. It is used to describe and explain the behavior of living organisms and combinations of organisms, but it is applicable to any dynamic, recurring process, any patterned sequence of events.
Daniel Katz and Robert Kahn.

The rung of a ladder was never meant to rest upon, but only to hold a man's foot long enough to enable him to put the other somewhat higher.
Thomas Huxley

Evolution of Organization and Management Theory

2

The attempts to codify organization and management knowledge as a separate and identifiable field of study are relatively recent. It has been only during the twentieth century that attempts have been made to develop a general theory. The contributors to this development represent a heterogeneous group of practitioners as well as academic generalists and specialists. Much of the early management thought came from practicing executives and administrators who recorded their observations and experiences and set them forth as general guidelines for others. Scientific management, with its engineering approach and emphasis on observation and measurement, provided another source of knowledge. In academia, sociologists, influenced by Max Weber's bureaucratic model, have made contributions to the theory. Economists with their microeconomic theory set forth a limited and closed model of organization, but one which has had an influence. Finally, there has been a trend toward using scientific research in the study of organizations and management practices.

Many new developments have increased our understanding of organization theory and management practice. These developments can be broadly categorized as two types: (1) the behavioral sciences, which emphasize the psychosocial aspects of organization and management, and (2) the management sciences, which emphasize quantification, mathematical models, and applications of computer technology.

In this part, we will look at the evolution of organization and management concepts in three stages: (1) the traditional views, (2) the behavioral and management science revolutions, and (3) the development of modern systems and contingency concepts. In Chapter 3 we review traditional organization and management theories with a discussion of the primary contributors, the key ideas, and the limitations. In Chapter 4 we consider the behavioral and management science revolutions and their impact. In Chapter 5 we set forth systems and contingency concepts that are the basis for the development of current organization theory and management practice and that set the stage for the remainder of the book.

Traditional Organization and Management Concepts

Three

While we are primarily concerned with modern organization theory and management practice, there is value in looking at the traditional views and in tracing their development. Modern concepts are not completely distinct and unrelated; they evolved from earlier views. Moreover, many current management practices are influenced and guided, either consciously or subconsciously, by these traditional concepts. There are many ways to classify the components of traditional theory, and it is impossible to give credit to all the contributors. This chapter is not an exhaustive treatise, but it does provide the overall framework necessary for later consideration of current organization theory and management practice. The following topics are discussed:

Setting of Traditional Theory
Scientific Management
Administrative Management Theory
Bureaucratic Model
Microeconomics: Theory of the Firm
Public Administration
Major Assumptions of Traditional Theory
Critique of Traditional View

Setting of Traditional Theory

A systematic body of knowledge concerning organization and management is a product of the late nineteenth and of the twentieth centuries. However, there is a rich heritage of ideas from the past. Throughout recorded history, we have pondered the problems of human organizations and the administration of governments, churches, armies, empires, and other complex social groups.

The beginnings of a systematic body of knowledge are closely associated with the industrial revolution and the rise of large-scale economic enterprises, which required the development of new organizational forms and management practices. John Mee says:

There is evidence to support the proposition that management thought in the United States was initiated and influenced by the economic, social, political, and technological forces in the environment during the last portion of the nineteenth century. A relationship still exists between the cumulative forces in the environment of our organized society and the nature of management philosophy applied to business and industrial enterprises.

There seemed to be little interest in management thought or philosophy in the United States until the political and economic climate provided a fertile field for the seeds of management thought to germinate and develop. Management thought followed closely in the wake of the political and economic philosophies of our nation. [1]

Even after the start of large-scale commercial and industrial enterprises, the development of management thought was relatively slow. [2] We read of the capitalistic ideology of the dynamic industrialists of the latter part of the nineteenth century such as Carnegie, Rockefeller, and Cook but little about their management philosophies. During this period management style was very individualistic and depended more on the unique personality of the industrialist than on any well-defined body of knowledge. Jenks suggests this highly individualistic nature of management practices:

Problems of organization and the use of the labor force were solved *ad hoc,* empirically for each establishment. Knowledge about the solutions was transmitted by observation or word of mouth and had to be rediscovered by most new firms. This type of thinking probably predominated in American and British business concerns at the beginning of the twentieth century. Here management was an uncertain mixture of the traditional with the arbitrary or capricious—a personal autocracy of varying degrees of benevolence—an emanation of the personality of the owner-manager. [3]

It was not until the scientific management movement, the writings of Max Weber on bureaucracy, and the early administrative management theorists that there developed a systematic body of knowledge related to the management of complex business and other organizations.

---

1 John F. Mee, *Management Thought in a Dynamic Economy,* New York University Press, New York, 1963, pp. xvi–xvii.

2 There were some practitioners who did set forth their management philosophies during the early part of the nineteenth century. Most notable were the contributions of Andrew Ure and Charles Babbage. See Andrew Ure, *The Philosophy of Manufacturers,* Charles Knight, London, 1835; and Charles Babbage, *On the Economy of Machinery and Manufacturers,* Charles Knight, London, 1832.

3 Leland H. Jenks, "Early Phases of the Management Movement," *Administrative Science Quarterly,* December 1960, p.424.

Scientific Management

The scientific management movement was given its intital impetus under the driving force of Frederick W. Taylor (1856-1915) in the latter part of the nineteenth and early part of the twentieth centuries. Taylor was stimulated in his early thinking by a number of predecessors, particularly the American industrialist and engineer Henry R. Towne.

Taylor's views were strongly influenced by the Protestant ethic of the time. He emphasized the value of hard work, economic rationality, individualism, and the view that each person had a role to play in society. Taylor did not develop a broad, general theory of management. He was pragmatically oriented with an empirical, engineering, and mechanistic emphasis that focused primarily on increasing worker efficiency. In his earlier writings, he referred to his ideas as "task management." It was not until 1910 that the term "scientific management" was coined by Louis Brandeis in a statement before the Interstate Commerce Commission. The primary emphasis of scientific management was on planning, standardizing, and improving human effort at the operative level in order to maximize output with minimum input.

Taylor's ideas came from his actual work experiences at the Midvale Steel Company, Bethlehem Steel Company, and as a consultant to many industrial firms. Early in his career he became interested in improving work efficiency and methods and in ascertaining scientifically the "one best way" of doing each task. By this means increases in productivity could be achieved, and both employer and employee would benefit. "By maximizing the productive efficiency of each worker, scientific management would also maximize the earnings of workers and employers. Hence, all conflict between capital and labor would be resolved by the findings of science." [4]

Basic Approaches of Scientific Management

Taylor thought that work could be analyzed scientifically and that it was management's responsibility to provide the specific guidelines for worker performance. This led to the development of the one best method of doing the task, standardization of this method (usually through time and motion studies), selection of workers best suited to performing the specific tasks, and training them in the most efficient method for performing the work. It was an engineering approach and viewed the worker as an adjunct to the machine. The assumption was that workers would be motivated by greater economic rewards, which would come

4 Reinhard Bendix, *Work and Authority in Industry,* John Wiley & Sons, Inc., New York, 1956, pp. 274–275.

from the increasing productivity. "It is no single element, but rather this whole combination, that constitutes scientific management, which may be summarized as: Science, not rule of thumb. Harmony, not discord. Cooperation, not individualism. Maximum output, in place of restricted output. The development of each man to his greatest efficiency and prosperity." [5]

Role
of
Management

Under Taylor's philosophy the role of management changed significantly from that of the past. His emphasis was on making management a science rather than an individualistic approach based on rule of thumb. He set forth the new duties of management as follows: (1) Develop a science for each element of a person's work, which replaces the old rule-of-thumb method. (2) Scientifically select and then train, teach and develop the workers, whereas in the past they chose their own work and trained themselves as best they could. (3) Cooperate with the workers to ensure that all the work would be done in accordance with scientific principles. (4) Divide responsibility between management and workers. Management takes over all functions for which they are better fitted than the workers. [6]

Scientific management had a direct impact on the workers' relationships to their tasks. It removed the workers' discretion in the planning, organizing, and controlling of their own task performances. If the workers did exactly as they were told by the management specialist, they would profit through increased productivity and greater monetary rewards.

Scientific management required that management plan, organize, and control task performance. It demanded a new, more systematic approach to the processes of management. Taylor stated that although there was some resistance on the part of the workers to the scientific approach, the primary resistance came from management itself, which was required to give up the old rule-of-thumb methods in favor of scientific approaches. This strong role for management was emphasized by Taylor:

It is only through *enforced* standardization of methods, *enforced* adoption of the best implements and working conditions, and *enforced* cooperation that this faster work can be assured. And the duty of enforcing the adoption of standards and of enforcing this cooperation rests with the *management* alone. . . . The *management* must also recognize the broad fact that workmen will not submit to this more rigid standardization and will not work extra hard, unless they receive extra pay for doing it. [7]

5 Frederick Winslow Taylor, "The Principles of Scientific Mangement," *Scientific Management,* Harper & Row, Publishers, Incorporated, New York, 1947, p. 140.

6 Ibid., pp. 36–37.

7 Ibid., p. 83.

Followers of Scientific Management

Taylor had a major impact on management practices for the next several decades. Even today the basic principles he set forth are a key part of our management thought, particularly in factory and industrial operations. Taylor and his associates, Henry Gantt, Frank and Lillian Gilbreth, Harrington Emerson, Horace Hathaway, and Sanford Thompson, spread the gospel of scientific management through countless speeches, articles and books.[8] Scientific management became a "movement" with wide application and many spokespeople. This system had a major impact on industrial practice, not only in the United States but in Europe as well. It not only affected the task performance at the worker level, but also created many changes in industrial organization structures. Before scientific management, such departments as industrial engineering, personnel, maintenance, and quality control were nonexistent.

Opposition to Scientific Management

It is little wonder that Taylor and his followers had opposition and critics, because the new approach involved a complete overhauling of traditional managerial practices. Many managers resisted Taylor's approach because they opposed his substitution of the scientific method and techniques for their own judgment and discretion. "Taylor had questioned their good judgment and superior ability which had been the subject of public celebration for many years. Hence, many employers regarded his methods as an unwarranted interference with managerial prerogatives."[9]

Taylor anticipated that management would oppose his new approach. However, he may have been naïve in thinking that his views were compatible with the interests of workers. Resentment over many of the practices and techniques grew. Workers resisted time study procedures and standardization of every aspect of their performance. In their view, they were being treated like machines and were required to operate according to mechanistic rather than humanistic principles. They resisted Taylor's incentive systems, which required that they continuously perform at a high level. They objected to the distribution of the "savings" that had resulted from the adoption of scientific management, because an overwhelming proportion seemed to go to the company rather than to themselves. However, it was the leaders of organized labor who provided the greatest resist-

8 For a discussion of how the early proponents of scientific management disseminated their views and findings in the various engineering, mechanical, management, and industrial journals, see Jenks, op. cit., pp. 421–447.

9 Bendix, op. cit., p. 280.

ance. Although Taylor professed not to be an opponent of the union movement, a reading of his testimony before a special committee of the U.S. House of Representatives in 1912 suggests that he really did not believe unions were necessary and that he thought effective cooperation between employer and employees could exist without them. One senses that Taylor is suggesting that unions were only necessary when management did not do its job effectively, that is, by adopting the principles of scientific management. Union leaders saw Taylor's scientific management as a challenge to their role and to the growth of the union movement.

In spite of these criticisms, the principles of scientific management spread rapidly throughout American industry. Pragmatically they worked to increase the efficiency of industrial operations, and the resistance could be brushed aside in the drive for greater productivity. However, there was a growing philosophical confrontation with Taylor's ideas from many sources. It was stated that scientific management treated workers like cogs in a well-oiled machine and that the system destroyed humanistic practices in industry. This remains the primary criticism today. When we recognize the time setting in which Taylor and his followers were experimenting and writing about their management views, it is inconceivable that they could have the same views on "industrial humanism" that may exist today. Taylor was a product of his environment. He was strongly influenced by the Protestant ethic of his time and the rationalism of economic theory and engineering practices. Within this framework he made major contributions to management thought, contributions that are applied worldwide in industry today.

Scientific Management and Organization Theory

Taylor and his followers were not organizational theorists but were practitioners who operated at the shop level and who were concerned with efficient worker performance. However, Taylor did have a number of implicit concepts concerning management and organization that were important in the development of a general theory. He provided many of the ideas for the conceptual framework later adopted by administrative management theorists, including clear delineation of authority and responsibility, separation of planning from operations, the functional organization, the use of standards in control, the development of incentive systems for workers, the principle of management by exception, and task specialization. Many of the concepts from scientific management were similar to those in Max Weber's bureaucratic model. This was particularly true of Taylor's view that management itself should be governed by rational rules and procedures. He said, "I have tried to point out that the old-fashioned dictator does not exist under scientific management. The man at the head of the business under scientific management is governed by rules and laws which have been developed through hundreds of experiments just as much as the workman is, and the standards which have been developed are equitable." [10]

Administrative Management Theory

Scientific management was concerned with optimizing effort at the shop or operative level and thus was a micro approach. In contrast, there developed a body of knowledge during the first half of the twentieth century whose primary emphasis was on establishing broad administrative principles applicable to higher organizational levels. The emphasis was on the development of macro concepts. March and Simon refer to this body of knowledge as "administrative management theory." [11] Other writers call it the traditional or classical theory of management. It focuses on formal organization structure and the delineation of the basic processes of general management.

Henri Fayol: Early Management Theorist

Fayol, a leading French industrialist, was one of the earliest exponents of a general theory of management. He has been described as the father of management theory. His observations, based on experiences as a top manager, were first published in 1916 as *Administration Industrielle et Générale*. This work was not translated into English until 1929 and was not widely available in the United States until 1949. [12]

Despite the fact that Fayol's writings did not receive wide dissemination until years after the original publication, his concepts have had a profound impact. He defined administration in terms of five primary elements: planning, organization, command, coordination, and control. These five elements of administration have become the foundation for considering the basic processes or functions of management. Fayol and his followers advocated the idea that management was a universal function that could be defined in terms of the various processes that the manager performed. He emphasized that the managerial processes and the principles that he developed were applicable not only to business but to governmental, military, religious, and other organizations. Fayol developed

10 Frederick Winslow Taylor, "Testimony before the Special House Committee," *Scientific Management*, p. 189.

11 James G. March and Herbert A. Simon, *Organizations*, John Wiley & Sons, Inc., New York, 1958, p. 22.

12 This translation was Henri Fayol, *General and Industrial Management*, trans. by Constance Storrs, Sir Issac Pitman & Sons, Ltd., London, 1949.

a comprehensive list of principles to provide guidelines for the manager. In introducing these principles he said:

The soundness and good working order of the body corporate depend on a certain number of conditions termed indiscriminately principles, laws, rules. For preference I shall adopt the term principles whilst dissociating it from any suggestion of rigidity, for there is nothing rigid or absolute in management affairs, it is all a question of proportion. Seldom do we have to apply the same principle twice in identical conditions; allowance must be made for different changing circumstances. [13]

Fayol's fourteen principles were:

1 Division of work. The principle of specialization of labor in order to concentrate activities for more efficiency.
2 Authority and responsibility. Authority is the right to give orders and the power to exact obedience.
3 Discipline. Discipline is absolutely essential for the smooth running of business, and without discipline no enterprise could prosper.
4 Unity of command. An employee should receive orders from one superior only.
5 Unity of direction. One head and one plan for a group of activities having the same objectives.
6 Subordination of individual interests to general interests. The interest of one employee or a group should not prevail over that of the organization.
7 Remuneration of personnel. Compensation should be fair and, as far as possible, afford satisfaction to both personnel and the firm.
8 Centralization. Centralization is essential to the organization and is a natural consequence of organizing.
9 Scalar chain. The scalar chain is the chain of superiors ranging from the ultimate authority to the lowest rank.
10 Order. The organization should provide an orderly place for every individual. A place for everyone and everyone in their place.
11 Equity. Equity and a sense of justice pervade the organization.
12 Stability of tenure of personnel. Time is needed for the employees to adapt to their work and to perform it effectively.
13 Initiative. At all levels of the organizational ladder, zeal and energy are augmented by initiative.
14 Esprit de corps. This principle emphasized the need for teamwork and the maintenance of interpersonal relationships. [14]

13 Ibid., p. 19.
14 Ibid., pp. 19–42.

Although there have been modifications by later administrative management theorists, Fayol's fourteen principles provided the basic foundation for this school of thought. However, it should be emphasized that he recognized that these were neither absolute nor rigid. "Principles are flexible and capable of adaptation to every need; it is a matter of knowing how to make use of them, which is a difficult art requiring intelligence, experience, decision and proportion." [15] He suggested that there was no limit to the number of administrative principles and that new principles whose worth was determined by experience would evolve.

Other Administrative Management Theorists

During the 1920s and 1930s a number of other writers, primarily those actively engaged in management or consulting practices, set forth their views, following the pattern established by Fayol. Luther Gulick and Lyndall Urwick, in particular, carried on Fayol's work in the development of principles based on wide experience in industry and government. In 1937 they edited *Papers on the Science of Administration.* [16] In these papers and other writings they popularized such principles as (1) fitting people to the organization structure, (2) recognizing one top executive as the source of authority, (3) adhering to unity of command, (4) using special and general staffs, (5) departmentalizing by purpose, process, persons, and place, (6) delegating and utilizing the exception principle, (7) making responsibility commensurate with authority, and (8) considering appropriate spans of control.

Another major contributor to the development of management thought during this period was Mary Parker Follett. Although she was a contemporary of the other administrative management theorists and set forth certain general principles as guidelines for practice, her approach was significantly different. She brought to her writings and speeches a vast knowledge of governmental and business administration. She presented many lectures and wrote articles that, taken together, established a philosophy of management. [17] She was unique in emphasizing the psychological and sociological aspects of management. She viewed management as a social process and the organization as a social system. Her ideas in such areas as the acceptance of authority, the importance of lateral coordination, the integration of organizational participants, and the necessity for change in a dynamic administrative process differed substantially from those of other writers. In many ways her ideas can be viewed as a link between the classical administrative management theorists and the behavioral scientists (see Chapter 4).

15 Ibid., p. 19.

16 Luther Gulick and Lyndall Urwick (eds.), *Papers on the Science of Administration,* Institute of Public Administration, Columbia University, New York, 1937.

17 H. C. Metcalf and Lyndall Urwick (eds.), *Dynamic Administration: The Collected Papers of Mary Parker Follett,* Harper & Row, Publishers, Incorporated, New York, 1941.

In the United States the most important contribution to the development of administrative management theory came from two General Motors executives, James D. Mooney, and Alan C. Reiley. [18] The principles that Mooney and Reiley set forth had a major impact on management practice in the United States. They not only drew on their experiences as business executives but also utilized a historical evaluation of governmental agencies, the Roman Catholic Church, and military organizations as a basis for their views. Their ideas were developed around four major principles: (1) the coordinative principle, which provided for a unity of action in the pursuit of a common objective, (2) the scalar principle, which emphasized the hierarchical organizational form and authority, (3) the functional principle, which organized tasks into departmental units, and (4) the staff principle, which recognized the role of line management in the exercise of authority but provided a staff to give advice and information. Their ideas were related to the development of a pyramidal organizational structure with a clear delineation of authority, specialization of tasks, coordination of activities, and utilization of staff specialists. Application of their concepts led to the establishment of formal organizational charts, position descriptions, and organizational manuals.

The Management Process School

The basic ideas of the administrative management theorists are the antecedents of what has been termed the *management process school.*

This school analyzes the management process, establishes a conceptual framework for it, identifies its principles, and builds a theory of management from them. It regards management as a universal process, regardless of the type or level of enterprise, although recognizing that obviously the environment of managing differs widely between enterprises and levels. It looks upon management theory as a way of organizing experience so that practice can be improved through research, empirical testing of principles, and proper teaching of fundamentals. [19]

The basic approach of this school is to look at the processes of management—planning, organizing, assembling resources, motivating, and controlling—and to set forth certain fundamental principles. It is dedicated to the view that the knowledge concerning management practices can be set forth as a cohesive and coherent body of thought and that generalizations concerning good management practices can be transmitted.

18 James D. Mooney and Alan C. Reiley, *Onward Industry,* Harper & Row, Publishers, Incorporated, New York, 1931.
19 Harold Koontz and Cyril O'Donnell, *Principles of Management,* 4th ed., McGraw-Hill Book Company, New York, 1968, p. 36.

Contribution of Administrative Management Theorists

Although there have been serious questions raised regarding the appropriateness of the approach and principles of the administrative management theorists, many of the concepts from this school are currently applied in organizations. The pyramidal form, the scalar principle, the concept of unity of command, the exception principle, the delegation of authority, limited span of control, and departmentalization principles are currently being applied in the design of many organizations. Although the administrative management theorists have been criticized for their rigid approach with little recognition of human and sociological factors, their ideas still have applicability in the structuring of organizations and in providing general guidelines.

Many current management authors retain as their basic framework the classical approach and have integrated recent developments from the behavioral and management sciences into their views. They utilize the classical viewpoint as a first approximation in their development of organization and management concepts and then make substantial modifications based on recent empirical research and theory.

Even though, throughout this book, we make substantial modifications to the concepts of the administrative management theorists, we recognize that they provided an important link in the development of modern theory. One of their most fundamental contributions was the emphasis on management as a distinct field that should be observed, studied, and improved and that is therefore an important scientific and academic endeavor.

Bureaucratic Model

The third major pillar in the development of classical organization concepts was provided by Max Weber's bureaucratic model. Although Weber's views had a profound effect on sociologists and political scientists, it has only been in recent years that his concepts have been utilized by students of management.

He was one of the founders of modern sociology and was a significant contributor to economic, social, and administrative thought. Writing during the first part of the twentieth century, he was contemporary with the scientific management movement and the early phases of administrative management thought. However, he not only studied the administration of the single organization but was also interested in the broad economic and political structure of society. His ideas concerning the bureaucratic organization were only a part of a total social theory. In his various writings he traced the changes in religious views, discussed their impact on the growth of capitalism, and examined the effect of industrialization on organization structure. His discussions of the bureaucratic mechanism were a natural evolution from broader considerations of historical and social factors that led to the development of complex organizations.

The term *bureaucracy* as developed by Weber and his followers is not used in the popularized, emotionally charged sense of red tape and inefficiency. The bureaucratic model possesses certain structural characteristics and norms that are used in every complex organization. The concept of bureaucracy used herein connotes neither good nor bad in terms of performance but, rather, refers to certain characteristics of organizational design. Weber viewed bureaucracy as the most efficient form, that which could be used most effectively for complex organizations—business, government, military, for example—arising out of the needs of modern society.

The view of rational-legal authority was basic to Weber's concept of bureaucracy. It is the right to exercise authority based on position. "In the case of legal authority, obedience is owed to the legally established impersonal order. It extends to the persons exercising the authority of office under it only by virtue of the formal legality of their commands and only within the scope of the authority of the office."[20] Rational-legal authority is based on position within the organization, and when it evolves into an organized administrative staff, it takes the form of a "bureaucratic structure." Within this structure each member of the administrative staff occupies a position with a specific delineation of power, compensation is in the form of a fixed salary, the various positions are organized in a hierarchy of authority, fitness for office is determined by technical competence, and the organization is governed by rules and regulations. Weber suggests that the bureaucratic form is the most efficient instrument of large-scale administration that has ever been developed in the modern world. He says:

Experience tends universally to show that the purely bureaucratic type of administrative organization—that is, the monocratic variety of bureaucracy— is, from a purely technical point of view, capable of attaining the highest degree of efficiency and is in this sense formally the most rational known means of carrying out imperative control over human beings. It is superior to any other form in precision, in stability, in the stringency of its discipline, and in its reliability. It thus makes possible a particularly high degree of calculability of results for the heads of the organization and for those acting in relation to it. It is finally superior both in intensive efficiency and in the scope of its operations, and is formally capable of application to all kinds of administrative tasks.

The development of the modern form of the organization of corporate groups in all fields is nothing less than identical with the development and continual spread of bureaucratic administration. This is true of church and state, of armies, political parties, economic enterprises, organizations to promote all kinds of causes, private associations, clubs, and many others. Its development is, to take the most striking case, the most crucial phenomenon of the modern Western state. . . . The whole pattern of everyday life is cut to fit this

20 Max Weber, *The Theory of Social and Economic Organization,* trans. by A.M. Henderson and Talcott Parsons, The Free Press of Glencoe, New York, 1964, p. 328. This is a translation of Part One of Weber's *Wirtschaft und Gesellschaft* (Economics and Society), which was unfinished at his death in 1920.

framework. For bureaucratic administration is, other things being equal, always, from a formal, technical point of view, the most rational type. For the needs of mass administration today, it is completely indispensable. The choice is only that between bureaucracy and dilettantism in the field of administration. [21]

Thus Weber saw the bureaucratic form as emerging from the needs of the environment and as the most effective means for the administration of large, complex organizations in an industrial society.

Dimensions of Bureaucracy

The bureaucratic model has served as a point of departure for many writers, particularly sociologists and political scientists. Recently, a number of social scientists have suggested that bureaucracy is a condition that exists along a continuum rather than being in an absolute sense either present or absent. Hall, for example, suggests that the degree of bureaucratization can be determined by measuring the following six dimensions: (1) a division of labor based on functional specialization, (2) a well-defined hierarchy of authority, (3) a system of rules covering the rights and duties of positional incumbents, (4) a system of procedures for dealing with work situations, (5) impersonality of interpersonal relations, and (6) promotion and selection for employment based on technical competence. [22]

In the "ideal" type of bureaucracy all these dimensions would exist to a high degree, whereas in a less bureaucratic organization they would be present to a smaller degree.

Appraisal of large-scale, complex organizations suggests that these dimensions are always present in varying degrees. Bureaucracy is consistent with the general framework of the formal organization structure established by administrative management theorists such as Fayol, Mooney, and Reiley. Weber and his bureaucratic model have provided the theoretical framework and the point of departure for much of the current theory and empirical research on complex organizations.

Research and Modification of Bureaucratic Model

Students of bureaucracy have analyzed Weber's ideal model to determine both its functional and dysfunctional consequences. Merton, Selznick, Gouldner, and others have critically evaluated the bureaucratic form and have

---

21 Ibid., p. 337.

22 Richard H. Hall, "The Concept of Bureaucracy: An Empirical Assessment," *American Journal of Sociology*, July 1963, p. 33.

suggested that while it may describe an ideal type in terms of formal relationships, it does not take into account consequences dysfunctional to organizational effectiveness. Their studies indicate that the bureaucratic organization is influenced by behavioral factors that Weber did not consider. Merton says that one consequence of bureaucratic structuring on the behavior of organizational participants is disruption in goal achievement.[23] He suggests that the bureaucratic form affects its members' personalities and encourages rigid adherence to rules and regulations for their own sake, which may displace the primary goals of organization.

Gouldner's research empirically tested the appropriateness of the bureaucratic dimensions and suggested major modifications in Weber's concepts. He was concerned with the consequences of bureaucratic rules on the maintenance of organizational structure and effectiveness. He suggests that bureaucratic mechanisms develop certain forms of autocratic leadership and control that may have dysfunctional consequences for the organization.[24]

The modern view is to utilize the Weberian bureaucratic model as a point of departure but also to recognize the limitations and dysfunctional consequences of this highly structured approach. At the risk of oversimplification, the prevailing view suggests that (1) the bureaucratic form is most appropriate for routine organizational activities where productivity is the major objective and that (2) this form is not appropriate for the highly flexible organization that faces many nonroutine activities in which creativity and innovation are important. Many modern writers stress the view that in a dynamic society the innovative, creative organization is becoming the rule rather than the exception. Weber's model was highly mechanistic, and he had more in common with the administrative management theorists such as Fayol than with later writers who conducted empirical studies using the bureaucratic model.

Microeconomics: Theory of the Firm

The value system of classical economics and the "ideal competitive model" strongly influenced managerial thought and action and provided a rationale for the operation of the business firm within society. Economic theory is also related to organizational theory, particularly in regard to the assumptions about entrepreneurial behavior. It was a basic premise of classical economics that the role of the business manager in a competitive economy was primarily one of adaptation to market forces. The economic theory of the firm was an outgrowth of the broader, more inclusive macroeconomic theory and accepted its premises.

23 Robert K. Merton, "Bureaucratic Structure and Personality," in *Social Theory and Social Structure*, rev. ed., The Free Press of Glencoe, New York, 1957, pp. 195–206.
24 Alvin W. Gouldner, *Patterns of Industrial Bureaucracy*, The Free Press of Glencoe, New York, 1954.

A
Normative
Theory

Microeconomics is a normative theory in that it attempts to prescribe what the business person should do in order to maximize profits, given a set of simplifying assumptions. It does not describe how managers or firms actually operate.

The economist's view of the firm is not a theory of organization because it treats the firm as a single person. "The economic theory of the firm assumes a single decision maker who maximizes profit under environmental constraints." [25] While this approach certainly does not describe the complex business organization of today, economists suggest that viewing the firm in this way provides a simplifying assumption that does not basically limit the model's predictive utility.

In addition to the basic assumption of the firm acting as an individual entrepreneur with the goal of profit maximization, there are additional simplifying assumptions from the economic theory of the firm such as:

1 The firm has a goal (or goals) toward which it strives.
2 It moves toward its objectives in a "rational" manner.
3 The firm's function is to transform economic inputs into outputs.
4 The environment in which the firm operates is given.
5 The theory concentrates particularly on changes in the price and quantities of inputs and outputs. [26]

From the viewpoint of the management and organization theorists, it is difficult to accept these simplifying assumptions of the business organization. Furthermore, it is difficult for the astute observer to accept some of the premises relating to the economic environment. [27]

Modifications
in the Theory
of the Firm

To suggest that there have not been criticisms regarding the theory of the firm from economists themselves would do a disservice to the profession.

25 Julian Feldman and Herschel E. Kanter, "Organizational Decision Making," in James G. March (ed.), *Handbook of Organizations,* Rand McNally & Company, Chicago, 1965, p. 629.

26 Joseph W. McGuire, *Theories of Business Behavior,* © 1964, p. 47. Reprinted by permission of Prentice-Hall, Inc., Englewood Cliffs, N.J.

27 Cyert and March say, "In a modern market society, economic decisions on price, output, product lines, product mix, resource allocation, and other standard economic variables are made not by individual entrepreneurs but by a complex of private and public institutions. Many of these decisions are made within the large multifunctional, and complicated organizations called firms. These are simple facts. They may not be facts with which economic theory should concern itself, but the disparity between the process by which business decisions appear to be made by complex organizations in the real world and the way in which they are explained by economic theory has provided material for several decades of debate." Richard M. Cyert and James G. March, *A Behavioral Theory of the Firm,* © 1963, p. 4. Reprinted by permission of Prentice-Hall, Inc., Englewood Cliffs, N.J.

Many critics have suggested that these limiting assumptions not only present an unreal picture of actual business organizations but, even more pertinent, may restrict the predictive value of the theory. There appear to be at least two major difficulties with the traditional theory of the firm. First, the motivational and rationality assumptions of the theory are unrealistic. There is a question as to whether profit maximization is the single goal of the complex organization. Second, as Cyert and March say, "The 'firm' of the theory of the firm has few of the characteristics we have come to identify with actual business firms. It has no complex organization, no problems of control, no standard operating procedures, no budget, no controller, no aspiring 'middle management.' To some economists it has seemed implausible that a theory of an organization can ignore the fact that it is one." [28]

Many economists are recognizing that while the theory of the firm may be appropriate as a normative model for limited purposes, it has been severely abused by utilizing it as a descriptive model of actual organizational and managerial behavior. [29] The most important work in modifying this view was by Cyert and March, in which they developed a theory of the firm considering behavioral factors. "We believe that, in order to understand contemporary economic decision making, we need to supplement the study of market factors with an examination of the internal operations of the firm—to study the effects of organizational structure and conventional practice on the development of goals, the formation of expectations, and the execution of choices." [30] Their views represent a major modification to the traditional theory of the firm by integrating recent empirical research and findings from the behavioral sciences with economic theory.

Public Administration

There is a close relationship between traditional management theory as applied to business and the development of concepts of public administration. Max Weber, in establishing his bureaucratic model, drew on his observations of public agencies. In the early part of the twentieth century there was a continual cross-fertilization between the fields of business and public administration. Public administration was influenced by "scientific management" and the attempts to develop principles of administration. Writers in public administration emphasized the need for increased effectiveness and efficiency in government through improving managerial practices. One of the early leaders in advocating improved administrative practices in government was Woodrow Wilson. [31]

28 Ibid., p. 8.

29 For a discussion of this point, see Fritz Machlup, "Theories of the Firm: Marginalist, Behavioral, Managerial," *The American Economic Review,* March 1967, pp. 1–33.

30 Cyert and March, op. cit., p. 1.

31 Woodrow Wilson, "The Study of Administration," *Political Science Quarterly,* June 1887, pp. 197-222.

A dominant concept of early writers in public administration was the need for separation between policy making and administration. The policy-making function established the ends or objectives to be achieved and was assumed to be determined by legislative enactment or executive order. The implementation of decisions was the province of the administrative arm of the government. Emphasis was placed on the development of a nonpolitical civil service system for the administration of the policy decisions of the legislative branch. Consideration was also given to the development of efficient organizations through better financial and personnel management, more effective planning and control, and other administrative techniques. In these areas such writers as Gulick and Urwick had a major influence on public administration as well as business management.

In recent years a number of writers on public administration have challenged the traditional view of the separation of policy making and administration. "This simplified model of decision-making and administration based on a clear-cut separation of policy and administration has long dominated the literature in this area, but since World War II it has increasingly been regarded as an inadequate point of departure for the study of decision-making in public bureaucracies."[32] Many other traditional principles of public administration established in the earlier part of the twentieth century have been challenged. Increasingly, public administration has been concerned with such factors as informal organization, special-interest groups, authority and power, conflict, decision-making processes, and communications.

Writers with a primary interest in public administration have contributed to the development of organization theory. The bodies of knowledge or theories relevant to business and public organizations have merged.[33] Current emphasis is on the development of concepts concerning all types of formal organizations, rather than on highly specialized theories for individual types.

Major Assumptions of Traditional Theory

So far we have reviewed some of the most significant twentieth-century contributions to traditional theory—scientific management, the bureaucratic model, administrative management theory, the microeconomic theory of the firm, and public administration. Although these contributions come from a wide variety of sources based on different experiences and observations, there are certain common threads and similarities.

The basic premise of a rational economic man (complete knowledge and

---

32 Robert L. Peabody and Francis E. Rourke, "Public Bureaucracies," in March, op., cit., p. 805.

33 For a discussion of the similarities in the evolution of organization theory and political theory, see Herbert Kaufman, "Organization Theory and Political Theory," *The American Political Science Review,"* March 1964, pp. 5–14.

maximizing behavior) was integrated by the classical management writers into their views of the organization. Through specialization in a well-defined hierarchical relationship, work could be organized to accomplish the goals of the organization most efficiently. The organization was viewed as a mechanistic system that was planned and controlled by the legitimate authority of management.

The primary emphasis was on increasing efficiency through structuring and controlling the human participants. People were assumed to be motivated primarily by economic incentives. It was necessary to specialize tasks and to provide detailed instructions and controls. In order to ensure cooperation in meeting organizational goals, the participants had to be closely supervised. Management was the primary integrative force and the formal hierarchy was the mechanism for achieving coordination.

The classical management theory thus evolved into the development of concepts such as the pyramidal structure, unity of command, span of control, management by exception, specialization by function, line-staff dichotomy, and other generalized "principles of management" that were appropriate for all organizations.

Critique of Traditional View

One of the major criticisms of the classical theory is that it employed unrealistic closed-system assumptions about organizations.[34] It was a model that failed to consider many of the environmental influences on the organization as well as many important internal aspects. Simplifying assumptions were made in order to reduce uncertainty, a process that often led to an incomplete view of actual organizational situations.

assumption concerning human behavior. Many of the "principles" derived from the traditionalists have been questioned as being truisms or plain common sense and so general that they lack specific guidelines for application. It has been suggested that many of these concepts actually are internally contradictory.[35] The basic premise of authority related to the classical hierarchical structure has been questioned. Many current writers see a major conflict between the institution of hierarchy based on position within the organization and the growing importance of technical specialization with its authority of knowledge.

Another criticism of the classical concepts is that they were written by practitioners in management and were based only on personal experience and limited observation. The principles have not stood the test of rigorous empirical research using scientific methods.

---

34 James D. Thompson, *Organizations in Action,* McGraw-Hill Book Company, New York, 1967, p. 6.
35 Herbert A. Simon, *Administrative Behavior,* 3d ed., The Free Press, New York, 1976, pp. 20–36. These views are amplified in March and Simon, op. cit., pp. 12–33.

A primary focus of dissent concerns the view of people in the organization. Thus, March and Simon describe the classical theory as the "machine model." [36] Bennis suggests that the focus of the classical theory is on "organizations without people." [37]

However, it is unfair to criticize the classical theorists too severely for their restricted views. These theories were strongly influenced by the society of the time and the existing ideologies. When they were developed, during the latter part of the nineteenth and early twentieth centuries, there was a great need to create more rational organizational forms that would meet the requirements for greater productivity. During this period many of our mass-production industries were being developed, and the traditional theory was appropriate. It also fit well with the need for more effective utilization of existing industrial technology.

The traditional theory was compatible with existing views of people and the types of human resources available. Society was concerned with increasing productivity and industrial output to satisfy the more basic, materialistic needs of a rapidly growing population. Industrial growth at that time required the use of an uneducated and unskilled work force. Most of the available workers were recent immigrants from other countries or migrants from farms. The traditional concepts emphasizing detailed job specialization and a strong hierarchical system of authority and control were likely the most effective means for utilizing these human resources.

Technology interacts with contemporary social conditions in complex ways. Mass-production methods, for example, were first developed when the majority of the labor force had little education or technical training. It is doubtful that the level of technical knowledge at the turn of the century predetermined the nature of mass-production factories. What seems more likely is that the low level of available skills influenced the manner in which this knowledge was applied to the organization of work. Mass-production techniques simply made it possible to produce complex products with a largely unskilled work force. [38]

Obviously now, more than half a century after the development of this traditional theory, many things have changed, and these concepts may not be as appropriate. People are better educated and have a higher level of skills, they have more complex aspirations than just a paycheck, and they have the capacity for more effective participation in organizational activities. Our technologies have become more sophisticated and require different structural arrangements. The complexity of markets requires more adaptive organizations. The increasing number of highly trained specialists and professionals changed the human component of organizations. In short, the significant changes that have occurred during the

---

36 Ibid, p. 36.

37 Warren G. Bennis, "Leadership Theory and Administrative Behavior," *Administrative Science Quarterly*, December 1959, pp. 259–301.

38 Peter M. Blau, et al., "Technology and Organization in Manufacturing," *Administrative Science Quarterly*, March 1976, p. 39.

twentieth century have made traditional theory obsolete as the model for *all* organizations. However, the basic concepts may be appropriate for some types of organizations and situations. Current management thought has a heritage from many sources, and the traditional theory provides an important linkage. In the next two chapters we build on these traditional views toward a modern theory of organization and management.

Summary

A systematic body of knowledge concerning organization and management is relatively new. It is closely associated with the industrial revolution and the rise of large-scale enterprises, which required the development of new organizational forms and management practices. Traditional organization and management theory is based on contributions from a number of sources, including scientific management, administrative management theorists, the bureaucratic model, microeconomics, and public administration.

The primary emphasis of scientific management was on planning, standardizing, and improving the efficiency of human work. It viewed management as a science rather than an individualistic approach based on rule of thumb.

During the first half of the twentieth century there developed a body of knowledge termed "administrative management theory." The pyramidal form, scalar principle, unity of command, exception principle, authority delegation, span of control, and departmentalization concepts were set forth by this group.

Another thread in classical organization theory was provided by Max Weber and his bureaucratic model. He viewed bureaucracy as the most efficient form for complex organizations. His model included such dimensions as well-defined hierarchy of authority, division of labor based on functional specialization, a system of rules, impersonality of interpersonal relationships, a system of work procedures, and placement based on technical competence.

Traditional management theory operated under certain assumptions, such as that of the rational economic person. Management should plan, direct, and control the activities of the work group. Authority had its source at the top of a hierarchy and was delegated downward. Principles were established to guide managerial practices.

Classical theory has been criticized for employing unrealistic closed-system assumptions about the organization. It fails to consider many of the environmental and internal influences. It makes unrealistic assumptions about human behavior.

In spite of these criticisms, the classical concepts represent an important, although limited, part of organization theory. Many of them are still utilized in organizations and can serve as an initial or first approximation. They serve as the foundation for more modern views of organization theory and management practice.

Questions and Problems

1 Discuss the relationship between the Protestant ethic and scientific management.

2 Why would management resist scientific management principles? Why would workers and unions react adversely to this movement?

3 Why was the theory of bureaucracy established at a time in history that saw a tremendous increase in the number and size of organizations? How did this theory differ from the "old" order?

4 Select any large-scale organization and evaluate the degree to which it adheres to bureaucratic concepts.

5 Relate the development of a body of knowledge concerning organizations to the trend toward professionalism in management.

6 Investigate a business or other large organization to see whether any of the principles from the administrative management theorists are being applied.

7 Give your evaluation of the view of management and organizations contained in classical economic theory. Does this fit "real world" organizations? Why or why not?

8 Do you think business organizations and public agencies should have similar organization and management concepts?

9 Evaluate the major contributions and deficiencies of traditional organization theory.

10 Discuss the view that traditional organization theory emphasized "organizations without people."

11 What assumptions concerning human nature are represented by the traditional theory?

The Behavioral and Management Science Revolutions

Four

Many forces have affected the evolution of organization theory and management practice. New knowledge has come from conceptualization and empirical research in a number of related disciplines—psychology, economics, sociology, anthropology, political science, mathematics and statistics, and industrial engineering, for example. It is difficult to summarize these contributions. However, two broad categories emerge as fundamental: (1) the behavioral sciences, which emphasize the psychosocial system and the human aspects of administration, and (2) the management sciences, which emphasize quantification, mathematical models, and the application of computer technology. The contributions from these two areas have had a profound influence. They will be used as the basic framework for our discussion of the following specific topics:

Revolution in Two Directions
The Behavioral Sciences
The Management Sciences
Divergence and Convergence in Theory and Practice

Revolution in Two Directions

Many forces, both within organizations and in the external environment, have stimulated change in theory and practice. The growth in size and complexity of organizations has been unparalleled. Increased general educational levels provided people with more intellectual skills and required new inducements to secure effective cooperation. These and many other changes during the twentieth century have led to an evolution in organization theory and management practice. Traditional theory was based on the environmental and organizational characteristics of the industrial revolution. It has been modified by new intellectual inputs to meet the needs of a modern industrial society.

Much of the development in modern theory can be attributed to interdisciplinary contributions. Organizations and management have become focal points for research. This field is relatively new, and there is no single, well-defined community of scholars and practitioners. Researchers are active in diverse fields such as sociology, anthropology, economics, psychology, political science, and history as well as in closely related areas such as public administration, management science, industrial psychology, and industrial sociology. While these contributions have added greatly to our knowledge and understanding, the diversity of assumptions, models, and research findings has increased the problem of understanding and integration for the student.

The traditional school suggested a rather clear-cut concept of the process of management and provided definitive principles as guidelines to action. In so doing, it provided a relatively restricted model, which excluded many variables from consideration. Basically, the revolution resulted in the opening up of the traditional views to many mediating and confounding variables, which have become increasingly important in organization theory.

The two primary sources of new ideas have been the behavioral and management sciences. Management science can be considered as a basic extension of scientific management but with modification. It is concerned with the organization primarily as an **economic-technical system**. This approach has developed since the end of World War II with contributions from economics, engineering, mathematics, and statistics. The primary emphasis of this school is in the establishment of normative models of managerial and organizational behavior for maximizing efficiency. This view focuses on the manager as a decision maker and uses systematic analysis and quantitative techniques to optimize performance toward certain objectives. The growing sophistication and development of techniques in mathematics, statistics, economics, and engineering, together with advancing computer technology, have provided the primary tools for analyzing complex problems.

The second major segment of the revolution came from the behavioral sciences. In their study of organizations, the behavioral scientists emphasize the **psychosocial system** with primary consideration of the human components. They are concerned with studying organizations in the field and less interested in establishing normative models. Using an open-system approach, they have considered many variables that were excluded from the closed-system models. Whereas traditional management concepts were concerned with structure and task, the emphasis of the behavioral scientists is on human factors and the way people behave in actual organizations. The behavioral school is interested in empirical research to verify theories of organizational behavior. Typically, they have a "humanistic" view that differs substantially from the mechanistic orientation of the traditionalists and management scientists.

These two approaches, behavioral and management sciences, have made such important contributions to organization theory and management practice that they should be considered in detail.

The Behavioral Sciences

The behavioral sciences are relatively recent academic and intellectual disciplines. Much of the work in psychology, sociology, and anthropology is a product of this century, particularly the empirical research. They have provided new insights into human behavior over the whole spectrum of human activities. Obviously, in this section we cannot consider the whole body of knowledge developed in the behavioral sciences. Therefore, we will concentrate on those areas that are most pertinent to organization theory and management practices.

Definition of the Behavioral Sciences

Berelson and Steiner distinguish the behavioral sciences—psychology, sociology, and anthropology—from the social sciences as follows:

In our usage here, we do not equate the behavioral sciences with the social sciences. The latter term is usually understood to cover six disciplines: anthropology, economics, history, political science, psychology, and sociology. By the behavioral sciences we mean the disciplines of anthropology, psychology, and sociology—minus and plus: *Minus* such specialized sectors as physiological psychology, archeology, technical linguistics, and most of physical anthropology; *Plus* social geography, some psychiatry, and the behavioral parts of economics, political science, and law. In short, we are concerned here with the scientific research that deals directly with human behavior. [1]

To be classified as a behavioral science, a field of study must satisfy at least two basic criteria: (1) it must deal with human behavior and (2) it must use a "scientific" approach. "The scientific aim is to establish generalizations about human behavior that are supported by empirical evidence collected in an impersonal and objective way. . . . The ultimate end is to understand, explain, and predict human behavior in the same sense in which scientists understand, explain, and predict the behavior of physical forces or biological factors or closer to home, the behavior of goods and prices in the economic market." [2] Many research efforts and conceptualizations from the behavioral sciences have contributed to organization theory and management practice, beginning with the pioneer human relationists.

---

1 Bernard Berelson and Gary A. Steiner, *Human Behavior: An Inventory of Scientific Findings,* Harcourt, Brace & World, Inc., New York, 1964, pp. 10–11.

2 Bernard Berelson (ed.), *The Behavioral Sciences Today,* Basic Books, Inc., Publishers, New York, 1963, p. 3.

Pioneer
Human
Relationists

The human relations movement in industry began with the research of Elton Mayo and his associates in a series of studies carried out at the Hawthorne Plant of the Western Electric Company between 1927 and 1932.[3] The background of the Hawthorne experiments provides an interesting picture of the transition from scientific management to the early human relations movement. Employees had been considered as mechanistic elements in the productive system. Industrial engineers and psychologists made many investigations of the relationship of work environment to productivity. Studies on fatigue, rest periods, and physical surroundings were prevalent during the early part of the twentieth century.

The stimulus for the Hawthorne experiments resulted from earlier studies based on the scientific management tradition. At the Hawthorne Plant, the Western Electric Company, in collaboration with the National Research Council, initiated a study to determine the relationship between the intensity of illumination and the productivity of workers. Although good research methods were used, including control groups, the experiment failed to show any simple relationship between intensity of illumination and rate of output. In fact, when the engineers reversed the experiment and reduced the illumination in the experimental room, instead of output declining as predicted, it actually increased. This experiment suggested that variables other than physical conditions might be affecting output. Psychological and sociological factors might have an important bearing not only on worker motivation and attitude but on output as well. At this point Elton Mayo and his Harvard colleagues, F. J. Roethlisberger and T. N. Whitehead, were called in by the company to help establish more rigid controls for experimental purposes and to isolate these mediating variables.

The basic studies by Mayo and his group took place over a five-year period and covered three phases: (1) the relay assembly test room experiment, (2) the interviewing program, and (3) the bank wiring observation room. The relay assembly test room experiment involved the prolonged observation of six women making telephone assemblies. A series of studies was undertaken to determine the effects on output of working conditions, length of working day, frequency and length of rest periods, and other factors relating to the physical environment. As these studies continued, it was found that, regardless of variations in these conditions, production increased. Even more astounding, production continued to increase even after the women were returned to the original conditions with longer working days, without rest pauses, and with poor surroundings. Mayo and his

---

3 The research in the Hawthorne experiments has been described in detail in a number of books and reports. For example, Elton Mayo, *The Human Problems of an Industrial Civilization,* The Macmillan Company, New York, 1933; T. N. Whitehead, *The Industrial Worker,* Harvard University Press, Cambridge, Mass., 1938, vol. II; F. J. Roethlisberger and W. J. Dickson, *Management and the Worker,* Harvard University Press, Cambridge, Mass, 1939.

group hypothesized that the increased production was a result of changes in social relations, motivation, and supervision of workers.

This experiment provided a break from the tradition of scientific management and industrial psychology that held that illumination, work conditions, rest periods, fatigue, and other physical and physiological variables combined with strong monetary incentives were the primary factors influencing output and productivity. Social and psychological factors were now seen as important in determining worker satisfaction and productivity.

This led to the second stage of the Hawthorne studies, in which over 21,000 people were interviewed during a three-year period. It was initially started as directed interviewing but moved toward nondirective, in-depth interviewing. Although this phase of the program did not lead to a quantifiable result, it did indicate the importance of human and social factors in the total work situation.

The third and final phase of the research program consisted of a study to observe and record group behavior of workers. The bank wiring room study was an intensive observation of a small work group of fourteen male operators for a period of six months.[4] The informal work group established production norms that were often in conflict with those set forth by management. In spite of the fact that the workers were paid on a group piecework incentive plan, each worker restricted output, thereby reducing possible earnings. The work group determined the output of individual workers, indicating that production was more determined by social rather than aptitude and physiological factors. The work group established many other types of social norms in addition to output standards. These norms set forth various roles for individual workers and supervisory personnel.

The bank wiring room observations indicated the strength of the imformal social organization based on sentiments and feelings, status roles, and social interactions that were often far removed from the formal organizational policies and procedures.

Contributions of Human Relationists

The Hawthorne studies provided scientific verification for the changing view of many students of industrial organizations. Early human relationists brought to the forefront the concept of the organization as a social system encompassing individuals, informal groups, and intergroup relationships as well as formal structure. In effect, this view put the human element back into the organization—the aspect that the traditionalists had minimized.

The early human relationists had two primary orientations. The first was a basic concern for people in the organization. Scott calls this ideological approach *industrial humanism.* "Basic to the philosophy of industrial humanism is

---

4 The interpretations and conclusions are set forth in detail in Roethlisberger and Dickson, op. cit., chaps. 22 and 23.

the design of the work environment to provide for the restoration of man's dignity."[5] Mayo emphasized the necessity for reevaluating the traditional hypothesis of economic theory, which considered society to be made up of individuals who were trying to maximize self-interest. He called for modifications in the industrial system to give greater recognition to human values.[6]

The second major emphasis of the human relationists was the utilization of the scientific research methods in studying organizational behavior. The Hawthorne studies continue to be important examples of behavioral research in industry and set the foundation for later investigations.

Mayo, Roethlisberger, Whitehead, and other early human relationists developed many concepts about human behavior in organizations, such as:

1 The business organization is a social system as well as a technical-economic system. This social system defines individual roles and establishes norms that may be at variance with those of the formal organization.

2 The individual is not only motivated by economic incentives, but is motivated by diverse social and psychological factors. Behavior is affected by feelings, sentiments, and attitudes.

3 The informal work group became a dominant unit of consideration. The group has an important role in determining the attitudes and performance of individual workers.

4 Leadership patterns based on the formal structure and authority of position in the organization under the traditional view should be modified substantially in order to consider psychosocial factors. The human relationists emphasized "democratic" rather than "authoritarian" leadership patterns.

5 The human relations school generally associated worker satisfaction with productivity and emphasized that increasing satisfaction would lead to increased effectiveness.

6 It is important to develop effective communication channels between the various levels in the hierarchy that allow the exchange of information. Thus "participation" became an important approach of the human relations movement.

7 Management requires effective social skills as well as technical skills.

8 Participants can be motivated in the organization by fulfilling certain social-psychological needs.

In spite of the fact that the human relations school had a major impact on management thought, there has been substantial dissent. Few research pro-

---

5 William G. Scott, *Organization Theory,* Richard D. Irwin, Inc., Homewood, Ill., 1967, p. 43.

6 Elton Mayo, *The Social Problems of an Industrial Civilization,* Harvard Graduate School of Business Administration, Boston, 1945; and Elton Mayo, *The Human Problems of an Industrial Civilization*, The Macmillan Company, New York, 1933.

grams have been so thoroughly criticized or reinforced. They continue to be the subject of debate and discussion.[7]

As the traditional management writers overemphasized the technical and structural aspects, the human relationists overemphasized the psychosocial aspects. They have been criticized for viewing human relations in a closed system and for not considering economic, political, and other environmental forces. One of the major shortcomings of the early human relationists was inadequate consideration of the role of unions in industrial societies. The impression from many of Mayo's writings is that he thought unions were rather unnecessary if management was performing its functions effectively. This coincides with another criticism that Mayo was authoritarian and really was bent on the maintenance of the hierarchical structure but with the manager giving greater consideration to human factors in order to maintain the traditional system. In spite of these criticisms, there is little doubt that the early human relationists had an impact on management practices.[8]

Other
Behavioral
Transitionalists

Mayo, Roethlisberger, and other early human relationists were by no means the only behavioral scientists who contributed to the new developments. Actually, several intellectual currents prior to the Hawthorne studies supported the changing views. The writings of Freud and his followers concerning subconscious motivation, frustration of needs, and the effect of attitudes and sentiments on behavior had an impact on the human relationists. Pareto's work in general sociology provided the theoretical framework for the Hawthorne research. "A comparative analysis of Pareto's general sociology and the major works of the Hawthorne human relationists reveals striking similarities in the theoretical systems. . . . The concepts of the social system, logical and nonlogical behavior, equilibrium, the functions of language, and the circulation of the elite are the essential features of the theoretical scheme of Pareto and the human relationists."[9]

During the 1930s and 1940s others provided important behavioral insights for organization theory and management practice. Carl Rogers and his client-centered therapy and sociometric studies by Moreno were major landmarks. Rogers used a neo-Freudian, clinical approach to counseling therapy, clinical

---

7 For example, see Alex Carey, "The Hawthorne Studies: A Radical Criticism," *American Sociological Review,* June 1967, pp. 403–416; and "Hawthorne Revisited: The Legend and the Legacy," *Organizational Dynamics,* Winter 1975, pp. 66–80.

8 Many have suggested that the human relationists had more of an impact on managerial ideology than on actual practices. For example, Reinhard Bendix says, "My conclusion will be that Mayo's ideological synthesis has found only limited acceptance in managerial *practice,* but that its contribution to managerial *ideology* has been pervasive." *Work and Authority in Industry,* John Wiley & Sons, Inc., New York, 1956, p. 319.

9 Scott, op. cit., p. 38. Scott provides a detailed evaluation of the similarities in the theoretical systems of Pareto and the Hawthorne human relationists on pp. 40–41.

methods, and nondirective interviewing.[10] Moreno, in his studies of interpersonal relations, developed sociometric techniques that received wide attention.[11] Kurt Lewin and his followers contributed to group dynamics and emphasized field theory. Much of the current work in individual behavioral change through group dynamics (Alcoholics Anonymous, Weight Watchers, sensitivity training) and the action-research approach to organization development is based on his pioneering efforts. Concepts of organizational behavior have been strongly influenced by the theory of motivation advanced by Maslow.[12] His hierarchy directed the emphasis away from the satisfaction of basic economic and survival needs toward higher-level social, esteem, and self-actualization needs. These are but a few of the earlier behavioral scientists who contributed to the body of knowledge concerning human behavior, group dynamics, and interpersonal relations in organizations.

In addition, there were a number of management writers who had a definite behavioral orientation. As indicated previously, one of the earliest writers with a psychological-sociological orientation was Mary Parker Follett. Writing at the time of classical management theorists, her ideas represented a substantial departure. She viewed management as a social process and developed many ideas that have been supported by behavioral research.

One of the most profound and insightful treatises on organization and management was written by Chester Barnard, based on his many years of experience as president of the New Jersey Bell Telephone Company. Barnard can be called a transitionalist between traditional management theory and the evolving behavioral concepts. He stressed the psychosocial aspects of organization and management rather than economic and technical aspects. He developed a broad conceptual model based on practical experience and a wide intellectual contact with economics, sociology, psychology, philosophy, and many other fields. He was among the first to consider the organization as a social system. "It is the central hypothesis of this book that the most useful concept for the analysis of experience of cooperative systems is embodied in the definition of a formal organization as a *system of consciously coordinated activities or forces of two or more persons.*"[13]

Barnard set forth many concepts similar to the developing views of the behavioral scientists. The existence of the organization depends on the maintenance of an equilibrium between the contributions and the satisfactions of the organizational participants. Psychosocial rewards as well as material inducements should be provided. Informal organizations and their relationships to the formal structure should be considered. His "acceptance" theory of authority differed substantially from the legitimate positional authority of Max Weber and the management traditionalists. Authority depends basically on the willingness of the sub-

10 Carl P. Rogers, *Counseling and Psychotherapy,* Houghton Mifflin Company, Boston, 1942.

11 J. L. Moreno, *Who Shall Survive?* Beacon House, Inc., Beacon, N.Y., 1953.

12 A. H. Maslow, *Motivation and Personality,* Harper & Row, Publishers, Incorporated, New York, 1954.

13 Chester I. Barnard, *The Functions of the Executive,* Harvard University Press, Cambridge, Mass, 1938, p. 73.

ordinate to comply rather than on the position of the superior. He emphasized the role of communication in maintaining the organization as a cooperative system and stressed social and psychological factors in his discussion of the environment of the decision-making process.

Many other behavioral scientists and management writers with a behavioral orientation have made significant conceptual contributions and engaged in research in a wide variety of areas, such as leadership training, group dynamics, motivation and satisfaction, participative management, individual and group decision making, behavior modification, sensitivity training, job enlargement and enrichment, sociotechnical systems, organization change, management by objectives, and the quality of work life. It would be impossible to discuss each one; many of their findings and views will be interwoven into the discussion in the following chapters.

There has been a growing interest on the part of behavioral scientists in studying organizations. Professional schools of management or administration (such as business, public, education, and health care) have attracted behavioral scientists to their faculties and have encouraged interactions with other university departments. Many studies using behavioral research methods have been undertaken in areas such as leadership, motivation, intergroup relationships, communication, and control. Also, broad conceptual models for understanding complex organizations have been developed. Throughout this book we will integrate research findings and concepts from the behavioral sciences into the specific topical discussion. However, it is important to emphasize two trends—change agents and power equalization.

Behavioral Scientists as Change Agents

In our society there is a growing interest and concern for social as well as technological change. During the twentieth century we have moved away from the concept of non-intervention in social affairs that stemmed from the "natural law" and "invisible hand" ideology of the laissez faire doctrine of automatic adjustment. Today in a large number of our activities we are becoming concerned with the methods used in planning and controlling the forces of change. "Human interventions designed to shape and modify the institutionalized behaviors of men are now familiar features of our social landscape."[14] Increasingly, we are not only studying the social system but are actively engaged in shaping its course.

Behavioral scientists interested in the study of organization and management are not just neutral observers and describers but are taking an active interest in changing the system. "In short, behavioral scientists are not only *interpreting*

---

14 Warren G. Bennis, Kenneth D. Benne, Robert Chin, and Kenneth E. Corey (eds.), *The Planning of Change,* 3d ed., Holt, Rinehart, and Winston, Inc., New York, 1976, p. 15.

the world in different ways; some intend to *change* it." [15] This new role as a change agent presents many dilemmas in terms of professional versus organizational identification for the behavioral scientists. It also brings to the forefront basic questions of value systems. [16] There frequently develops an "understanding gap" between the perspective of the behavioral scientists and their psychosocial orientation and managers who must also consider economic-technical factors.

Power Equalization Emphasis of the Behavioral Scientists

The writings of many of the behavioral scientists emphasize the value of more democratic, less authoritarian, less hierarchically structured organizations than proposed in the traditional view. Shepard refers to a "coercion-compromise" system that relies heavily on internal systems of command, on authority and obedience, and on bureaucratic relations for governing the actions of participants. [17] He sees many adverse consequences of this approach. By comparison, most behavioral scientists advocate a "collaboration-consensus" or "power equalization" system. Leavitt describes this as follows·

Besides the belief that one changes people first, these power-equalization approaches also place major emphasis on other aspects of the human phenomena of organizations. They are, for example, centrally concerned with affect; with morale, sensitivity, psychological security. Secondly, they value evolutionary, internally generated change in individuals, groups, and organizations over externally planned or implemented change. Thirdly, they place much value on human growth and fulfillment as well as upon task accomplishment; and they often have stretched the degree of causal connection between the two. Finally, of course, the power-equalization approaches, in their early stages at least, shared a normative belief that power in organizations should be more equally distributed than in most existent "authoritarian" hierarchies. Operationally, this belief was made manifest in a variety of ways: in encouraging independent decision making, decentralization, more open communication, and participation. [18]

Many modern behavioral scientists advocate a democratic, participative approach. The concepts will be discussed in detail in Part 5: "The Psychosocial System." At this stage we will merely introduce them briefly. Likert suggests an "interaction-influence" system that uses the concept of supportive relationships between members in the organization as a central theme. He advocates the development of effective working groups linked to other such groups in a large organi-

15 Warren G. Bennis, "New Role for Behavioral Science," *Administrative Science Quarterly,* September 1963, p. 127.

16 B. F. Skinner, *Beyond Freedom and Dignity,* Alfred A. Knopf, Inc., New York 1971.

17 Herbert A. Shepard, "Changing Interpersonal and Intergroup Relations in Organizations," in James G. March (ed.), *Handbook of Organizations,* Rand McNally & Company, Chicago, 1965, p. 1130.

18 Harold J. Leavitt, "Applied Organizational Change in Industry: Structural, Technological and Humanistic Approaches," March, op. cit., p. 1154.

zational system.[19] McGregor also followed this theme by emphasizing the desirability of replacing the authoritarian Theory X by the more democratic-participative Theory Y.[20] Argyris reflects still more support for this view. He focuses on the need for the organization to provide an "authentic" relationship for its participants. In his view, the traditional organization restricts human growth and self-fulfillment.[21] Maslow has extended his theory of motivation to emphasize the importance of providing an organization environment in which the individual can achieve maximum "self-actualization."[22] Bennis is perhaps even more outspoken when he says "democracy is inevitable." In his view, the traditional concepts of Weber's bureaucracy and the administrative management theorists are inappropriate for modern organizations.[23] He advocates that behavioral scientists should be actively engaged in changing the traditional bureaucratic form toward more democratic social systems.

We have presented a few of the views of behavioral scientists, with varying academic specialties, who have a general humanistic orientation toward organization and management. They emphasize human values and, consequently, tend to depreciate economic and technical considerations, which may be overriding in some situations. Their views have profoundly influenced organization theory and management practices.

The Management Sciences

A second major revolution came about through the application of quantitative methods to decision making. This is a post-World War II development and has generally been termed *operations research* or *management science.* In

19 Rensis Likert, *New Patterns of Management,* McGraw-Hill Book Company, New York, 1961. See also: Rensis Likert, *The Human Organization,* McGraw-Hill Book Company, New York, 1967.

20 Douglas McGregor, *The Human Side of Enterprise,* McGraw-Hill Book Company, New York, 1960. In a later book, McGregor amplified this view as follows: "Management must seek to create conditions (an organizational environment) such that members of the organization at all levels can best achieve their own goals by directing their efforts toward the goals of the organization." *The Professional Manager,* ed. by Warren G. Bennis and Caroline McGregor, McGraw-Hill Book Company, New York, 1967, p. 13.

21 Chris Argyris, *Integrating the Individual and the Organization,* John Wiley & Sons, Inc., New York, 1964.

22 Abraham Maslow, *Toward a Psychology of Being,* D. Van Nostrand Company, Inc., Princeton, N.J., 1962.

23 Warren G. Bennis, *Changing Organizations,* McGraw-Hill Book Company, New York, 1966, p. 4.

many ways the approach is a descendant from the scientific management movement with the addition of more sophisticated (primarily mathematical) methods, computer technology, and an orientation toward broader problems. It adopts the **scientific method** as a framework for problem solving with emphasis on objective rather than subjective judgment. Like Taylor, the current management scientists are dedicated to the utilization of scientific approaches for the solution of management problems and emphasize a normative approach to provide the manager with optimal decisions. It prescribes how the manager should decide, given certain assumptions of economic-technical rationality and the objectives to be achieved.

In order to develop an approach that emphasizes optimal managerial decision making, certain assumptions about organizations and participant behavior have been made by the operations researchers or management scientists. These assumptions often differ from those made by behaviorial scientists. This difference may be basic to the background disciplines that have become interested in these two approaches. As indicated previously, the behavioral scientists were drawn primarily from the social sciences with a psychosocial orientation. In contrast, most of the contributors to management science come from mathematics, statistics, engineering, and economics and have an economic-technical orientation. It is normal, therefore, that these two approaches have different views and assumptions.

Definition and Nature of Management Science

It is difficult to define this area and even to select an appropriate label. It has been called management science, operations research, quantitative analysis, systems analysis, or decisions sciences, and is also related to industrial engineering and mathematical economics. We have selected a convenient title, management science, recognizing that there are differences of opinion. It is useful to look at the various fields in order to determine the broad boundaries and areas covered. Miller and Starr define operations research simply as *applied decision theory.* "Operations research uses any scientific, mathematical, or logical means to attempt to cope with the problems that confront the executive when he tries to achieve a thoroughgoing rationality in dealing with his decision problems." [24] They emphasize that operations research is directed toward solving actual problems facing the executive. It is not theoretically oriented; it is directed to problem solving and application. The Operations Research Society of America, Committee on Professional Standards, provides a similar definition: "Operations research is an experimental and applied science devoted to observing, understanding, and predicting the behavior of purposeful man-machine systems; and operations-research work-

---

[24] David W. Miller and Martin K. Starr, *Executive Decisions and Operations Research,* Prentice-Hall, Inc., Englewood Cliffs, N.J., 1960, p. 104.

ers are actively engaged in applying this knowledge to practical problems in business, government, and society." [25]

The term "management science" received its initial impetus with the establishment of The Institute of Management Sciences (TIMS) in 1953 with the objective, "to identify, extend, and unify scientific knowledge that contributes to the understanding and practice of management." Although numerous attempts have been made to distinguish between operations research and management science, it is difficult to make any clear-cut distinction. Several have suggested that the term management science is broader in that it encompasses within its sphere such fields as mathematical economics and behavioral sciences and also has a close relationship with engineering and the physical sciences. Others have suggested that operations research is operationally oriented, while management science is directed toward establishment of broad theory. Although this may be a sound theoretical separation, in practice it is difficult to see a distinction between people who call themselves management scientists or operations researchers. A look at recent issues of *Management Science* and *Operations Research,* the two major publications in this area, suggests that there is a good deal of similarity and that the authors of articles do not make a distinction between these terms. In fact, many authors use the designation MS/OR (management science/operations research) to designate the profession. [26] Simon summarizes his views on the relationship between scientific management, operations research, and management science as follows:

Except in matters of degree (e.g., the operations researchers tend to use rather high-powered mathematics) it is not clear that operations research embodies any philosophy different from that of scientific management. Charles Babbage and Frederick Taylor will have to be made, retroactively, charter members of the operations research societies. . . . No meaningful line can be drawn any more to demarcate operations research from scientific management or scientific management from management science. [27]

There is a close relationship between management science and industrial engineering. They are interested in many of the same problems and frequently use similar techniques. Industrial engineering often uses concepts and models developed by management science for direct applications. [28]

In recent years MS/OR also has been influenced by mathematical economists. Subjects such as marginal analysis, maximization, demand theory,

25 "Guidelines for the Practice of Operations Research," *Operations Research,* September 1971, p. 1138.

26 See, for example, William H. Gruber and John S. Niles, "Problems in the Utilization of Management Science/Operations Research: A State of the Art Survey," *Interfaces,* November 1971, pp. 12–19; and "ORSA/TIMS Collaboration," *Interfaces,* August 1973, pp. 32–42.

27 Herbert A. Simon, *The Shape of Automation: For Men and Management,* Harper & Row, Publishers Incorporated, New York, 1965, pp. 68–69.

28 Norman N. Barish, "Operations Research and Industrial Engineering: The Applied Science and its Engineering," *Operations Research,* May-June 1963, p. 391.

equilibrium analysis, input-output analysis, and utility theory have been included in the management sciences. Baumol suggests that a basic hallmark of the economic theorist's approach to the analysis of business problems is the concept of optimization. "The approach of optimality analysis is to take these alternatives into account and to ask which of these possible sets of decisions will come *closest* to meeting the businessman's objectives, i.e., which decisions will be best or *optimal.*" [29] He says that the operations researcher also attempts to use optimality as the normative criterion for managerial decision making but from a different viewpoint. The economist's focus is on theory development, while the operations researcher is concerned with practical application. However, there is substantial cross-fertilization between the fields.

Other disciplines have contributed to the development of the management sciences. Mathematics and statistics have provided many analytical tools; evolving computer technology has facilitated the utilization of sophisticated quantitative methods. Although MS/OR is a rather loose conglomeration of interests and approaches, there are key concepts that permeate the field:

1 Emphasis on scientific method
2 Systematic approach to problem solving
3 Mathematical model building
4 Quantification and utilization of mathematical and statistical procedures
5 Concern with economic-technical rather than psychosocial aspects
6 Utilization of electronic computers as tools
7 Emphasis on systems approach
8 Seeking rational decisions under varying degrees of uncertainty
9 Orientation to normative rather than descriptive models

Early Operations Research Approaches

As indicated, operations research (OR) and management science are descendants from the scientific management movement. However, there was a definite break between generations. Operations research as currently conceived is an outgrowth of World War II efforts in which scientists with a wide variety of skills were called on to assist in solving military problems. The first use of organized operations research groups occurred in England in 1940. One of the projects was a study of the application of the newly developed radar systems. The group studied radar-interceptor defense systems as an integrated man-machine system in order to develop optimal utilization of available resources. The effectiveness of the

29 William J. Baumol, *Economic Theory and Operations Analysis,* Prentice-Hall, Inc., Englewood Cliffs, N.J., 1961, p. 4.

British air defense during the Battle of Britain was increased dramatically as a result of these efforts. In Great Britain OR teams were established for each of the three military services and were used extensively. In the United States the military services also adopted the operations research approach to deal with such problems as deploying merchant marine convoys to minimize losses from enemy submarines, improving methods of search for submarines, and achieving greater accuracy in aerial bombing.

The success of these efforts set the foundation for the future development of operations research teams with applications to nonmilitary problems. However, it was not until the early 1950s that OR caught on in American industry. During this developmental period there were a wide variety of approaches, and it was not until the late 1950s that the field began to stabilize. Writing in 1957, Churchman, Ackoff, and Arnoff said: "Ten years ago it would have been difficult to get an operations researcher to describe a procedure for conducting OR. Today it is difficult to keep one from doing it. Each practitioner's version of OR's method (if recorded) would differ in some respect. But there would also be a great deal in common." [30] For example, there seems to be a consensus with regard to the following major phases of an OR project:

1 Formulating the problem.
2 Constructing a mathematical model to represent the system under study.
3 Deriving a solution from the model.
4 Testing the model and the solution derived from it.
5 Establishing controls over the situation.
6 Putting the solution to work: implementation. [31]

The early philosophy of operations research was directed toward total system optimality and toward interdisciplinary effort in order to ensure that all significant factors in the problem were given consideration. This theoretical approach was never achieved in practice. In looking at the results from OR projects, it is evident that many were not interdisciplinary team efforts, nor did they ensure total system optimality. It appears that the trend has moved more toward the development of techniques and toward problem solving at the subsystem level with a narrower interdisciplinary team than was envisioned by early operations researchers.

Of significance in the management science approach was the introduction of many scientists to actual military and business decision-making problems

---

30 C. West Churchman, Russell L. Ackoff, and E. Leonard Arnoff, *Introduction to Operations Research,* John Wiley & Sons, Inc., New York, 1957, pp. 12–13.
31 Ibid.

where they could apply their specialized knowledge and skills. Under scientific management it was the practicing manager and the industrial engineer who applied scientific methods to problem solving at the task level. In operations research many scientists with backgrounds in mathematics, physics, statistics, economics, and the other disciplines are contributing their knowledge to managerial problem solving.

Current Developments in Management Science

Information concerning management science techniques has been disseminated broadly. Until the 1950s, approaches such as linear programming, game theory, queuing theory, statistical decision theory, systems analysis, simulation, Monte Carlo techniques, and other similar analytical tools were relatively unknown. Today they have not only become commonplace in business and industry but also are a basic part of the curriculum in professional schools such as business and engineering. An indication of this development was the creation of the American Institute for Decision Sciences (AIDS) in 1968. This organization was created to promote the development and application of quantitative methodology to functional and behavioral problems of administration. Members of this organization come primarily from schools of business and management and share a common interest in the application of the methods of science and quantitative approaches to the solution of decision problems of organizations.

The rapid growth in the management sciences is reflected by the substantial increase in the number of practitioners in the field. One indication is the membership of the three related professional societies. In the early 1950s, both the Operations Research Society of America and the Institute of Management Sciences were formed with less than 100 members each. The American Institute for Decision Sciences was not even created until 1968. Today, these professional societies have over 20,000 members who have diverse academic backgrounds and are associated with many different organizations—business firms, universities, hospitals, and government agencies, for example. Research studies indicate that most of these MS/OR practitioners have academic training in mathematics and statistics, engineering, economics, and business administration. Many more people engaged in industrial operations research have training in the technical disciplines than in the social sciences or humanities.

There has also been a dramatic growth in MS/OR applications in governmental organizations, particularly in national defense and space activities. Many of the new approaches, such as systems analysis, cost-effectiveness analysis, network analysis, and planning-programming-budgeting systems, have a management science orientation. In military and space programs the term ***systems analy-***

sis is used to describe an integrative decision-making process using MS/OR approaches. [32]

Systems analysis can be thought of as an extension of the operations research utilized during World War II. During this early phase, operations research was concerned with tactical problems. In contrast, systems analysis also deals with longer-range strategic problems. It makes use of the quantitative approaches but also involves nonquantifiable inputs. Hitch suggests its broad, integrative nature by stating, "Systems analysis at the national level, therefore, involves a continuous cycle of defining military objectives, designing alternative systems to achieve those objectives, evaluating these alternatives in terms of their effectiveness and cost, questioning the objectives and the other assumptions underlying the analysis, opening new alternatives, and establishing new military objectives." [33]

MS/OR has made a major contribution toward the development and implementation of planning-programming-budgeting systems (PPBS) used extensively in federal as well as numerous state and local government agencies. Systems analysis, input-output analysis, and cost-effectiveness analysis are basic ingredients of PPBS.

On the industry level, management science typically has not been directed toward strategic problems but has been concerned primarily with tactical decisions. For the most part, management scientists have not been engaged in problem solving for those types of "ill-structured" problems that are the concern of top management and that generally have not been amenable to precise mathematical and statistical approaches. They have emphasized lower- to middle-level problems where quantification is possible.

The way is open, however, for management scientists to deal more effectively with ill-structured problems. Development in computer technology and programming over the past two decades has provided new resources. In the early development of the computer, the primary concern was the automation of many routine data processing activities. The next step was the utilization of the computer and management science approaches for programming lower-level, well-structured problems such as inventory control, production control, and allocation problems. With computer and programming developments there are greater opportunities to move to higher-level decision problems. Simulation approaches, for example, can be used for ill-structured problems. Recent developments in programming for "heuristic decision making" open new vistas for the management scientist. Greater emphasis on heuristic problem solving will move the manage-

32 E. S. Quade (ed.), *Analysis for Military Decisions,* The Rand Corporation, Santa Monica, Calif., 1964, p. 4.

33 Charles J. Hitch, ''A Planning-Programming-Budgeting System,'' in Fremont E. Kast and James E. Rosenzweig (eds.), *Science, Technology, and Management,* McGraw-Hill Book Company, New York, 1963, p. 64.

ment scientist away from concentration on statistical and mathematical techniques and will require the integration of knowledge from the behavioral sciences.

Role of the Management Scientist

In many ways the role of management scientists and their relationship to the operating manager are similar to those of the behavioral scientist. In the early stages management scientists were content with the development of an optimal decision which they presented to management for implementation. They were often most interested in the development of sophisticated, quantitative models and computer programming for these models and felt that their task was performed once their recommendations were presented. As a result of a communications gap, the manager often did not understand the basis of the recommendations, and therefore many OR reports became the last folder in a dusty file. Gruber and Niles summarize the problems involved in the utilization of MS/OR in practice:

1 Operations researchers do not emphasize enough human factors, since these factors are hard to model mathematically.
2 The task of explaining and convincing the customer should unconsciously shape the formulation and solution of the problem.
3 Management science must become involved in management as a total process.
4 Management quite often lacks the confidence to use the result that the operations research group has produced.
5 The inertia of management slows down implementation.
6 Operations research people should realize that management operates in a real-time, crisis environment. [34]

Management scientists have become increasingly concerned about the implementation of their recommendations and thus are having to deal with the organization as a social as well as an economic-technical system. They have begun to recognize the need for *both quality and acceptance* of solutions in organizational problem solving. Management scientists, like the behavioral scientists, have become agents of change in organizations. Often they develop new concepts and ideas that challenge traditional management approaches. Increasingly, they recognize that to carry out their role in applied problem solving, they cannot only be concerned with the development of esoteric, highly technical and refined mathematical models but also must be actively engaged in the communication and implementation of findings. [35] Furthermore, many management scientists are be-

34 Gruber and Niles, op. cit., p. 13.
35 Herbert Halbrecht, et al., "Through a Glass Darkly," *Interfaces*, August 1972, pp. 1–17.

coming more interested in strategic decision-making issues faced by top management.

Divergence and Convergence in Theory and Practice

The behavioral and management science revolutions have done much to modify traditional organization theory and management practice. Ideally, these two approaches would converge with the traditional one to provide a unified and clearly delineated modern theory. This has not happened. There are many reasons for this lack of integration—a basic difference in values and ideologies, varying academic disciplines, and a conflict between descriptive and normative theory. This latter dichotomy is an important difference. The normative approach has been used primarily in economics and the management sciences. "Economists and operations research analysts are interested in things as they should be: they observe organizations and their environments in order to develop analytical models which will enable the organization to make more rational decisions."[36] On the other hand, most psychologists, sociologists, and other behavioral scientists question the economic-technical assumptions of human behavior and are concerned with describing the way people and organizations actually behave.

As many more disciplines have become interested in organization and management, researchers have brought into consideration their own traditional preoccupation with certain selective subject matters. Instead of developing a more simplified, less complex organization theory, the tendency has been in quite the opposite direction—toward greater complexity and consideration of more variables. The development of a "general theory" is becoming even more difficult.

An indication of this diversity is seen in the evolution of one of the professional organizations in the field, the Academy of Management. This organization was established in the late 1930s with the primary objective of fostering the general advancement of research, learning, teaching, and practice in the field of management, and of encouraging the extension and unification of knowledge pertaining to management. In its earlier days it was organized as a general body to cover the entire field of management. Over the past decade it has been reorganized into the following major professional divisions:

Management History

Management Education and Development

Organizational Behavior

---

36 William R. Dill, "Desegregation or Integration? Comments about Contemporary Research on Organizations," in W. W. Cooper, H. J. Leavitt, and M. W. Shelly, II (eds.), *New Perspectives in Organization Research,* John Wiley & Sons, Inc., New York, 1964, p. 47.

Business Policy and Planning
Managerial Consultation
Production-Operations Management
Organization and Management Theory
Personnel-Human Resources
Social Issues in Management
International Management
Organization Development
Organizational Communication
Health Care Administration
Public Sector

This diversity of subject matter areas, all encompassed under the Academy of Management, is indicative of the expansion and heterogeneity of the field.

There is controversy over which approach—the traditional, behavioral science, or management science—is best. The arguments are often meaningless. "These three approaches are complementary rather than competitive; each occupies a different part of the broad field of organizational studies, with overlapping boundaries." [37] Much of the controversy stems from the "understanding gap" among the various fields. We have discussed the gap between behavioral scientists and managers and between management scientists and managers. In reality it is a three-way separation—behavioral scientist—management scientist—manager. Both behavioral and management scientists become impatient when managers do not seem to understand them or immediately recognize the value of their findings. Managers in turn are frequently suspicious of untried theories and recommendations that do not seem to fit the reality of their own organizations. These attitudes are a reflection of longstanding and deep-seated problems arising from the general backgrounds of the different cultures. [38] These differences are a mirror of the basic conflicts between the scientific and nonscientific cultures as discussed by C. P. Snow. [39] The cultural differences of behavioral scientists, management scientists, and members of management impose serious problems for communication and understanding. Value systems vary and are deep-seated; specialists are interested in different aspects of the organization and of society and emphasize the utility of different endeavors. It is essential that we recognize diverse contributions and do not refer to the efforts of other groups as inferior. All are valuable. All three have important contributions to make to understanding organizations and improving management practice.

37 Kenneth E. Boulding, "Evidences for an Administrative Science," *Administrative Science Quarterly,* June 1958, p. 4.
38 For a discussion of these different cultures, see James E. Rosenzweig, "Managers and Management Scientists (Two Cultures)," *Business Horizons,* Fall 1967, pp.79–86.
39 C. P. Snow, *The Two Cultures and the Scientific Revolution,* Cambridge University Press, New York, 1959.

Some Approaches toward Convergence

In spite of the fact that many contributions to management and organization theory by the behavioral and management sciences have been polarized and divergent rather than convergent, there have been attempts at integration. For example, March and Simon and their colleagues were among the first to take a broad interdisciplinary approach. Their overriding emphasis has been in looking at decision-making processes in organizations from an open-system viewpoint. Current work on computer simulation of human behavior represents a merging of various interests in decision-making processes. [40]

Students are faced with fragmented and diverse inputs concerning organizational theory and management practice. They are often required to take various courses that emphasize the traditional, or behavioral, or management science approaches. The integration of these separate approaches is left to the student. Yet there is a bright side; the diversity can provide a stimulating and exciting educational program.

The student should welcome these diverse contributions and should not seek a simplified, clear-cut body of knowledge. The subject matter is complex and dynamic, and the body of knowledge is continually evolving. Many disciplines can make contributions. Organizations are complex systems made up of psychological, sociological, technological, and economic elements, which in themselves require intensive investigation. The suggestion that we wrap it all up nicely in one bundle and tie it together with a ribbon of simplified theory is unrealistic. The student of organizations and the practicing manager should recognize and accept contributions from diverse fields. Attempts to freeze this field of study to a restricted view would reduce our flexibility and opportunity for continued investigation.

Future progress is tied closely with developments in the disciplines underlying organization and management theory. "The progress of management theory today is inextricably interwoven with techniques of observation and experiment, with sociology, psychology, and economics, and with the sharp tools of mathematics. In this respect, there is no more confusion than exists in other areas of scientific endeavor that has its observational techniques, its bodies of general theory, and its tools of analysis. Confusion, by another name, is progress to which we have not yet become accustomed." [41]

This is the excitement of the study of organization theory and management practice. It has become an important field of study for students in schools of

40 Edward A. Feigenbaum and Julian Feldman (eds.), *Computers and Thought,* McGraw-Hill Book Company, New York, 1963; John M. Dutton and William N. Starbuck, *Computer Simulation of Human Behavior,* John Wiley & Sons, Inc., New York, 1971; and James R. Emshoff, *Analysis of Behavioral Systems,* Macmillan Publishing Co., Inc., New York, 1971.

41 Herbert A. Simon, "Approaching the Theory of Management," in Harold Koontz (ed.), *Toward a United Theory of Management,* McGraw-Hill Book Company, New York, 1964, p.82.

Figure 4.1   Evolution of Organization and Management Theory

Traditional Theory		Modifications	
Scientific Management (Efficient task performance)			
Bureaucratic Model (Authority and structure)		Behavioral Sciences (Psychological, sociological, and cultural issues)	
Administrative Management theory (Universal management princples)		Management Sciences (Economic-technical rationality)	
1900	1920s	1940s	1960s

business administration, public administration, hospital administration, and other areas where professional managers are being trained, but it is also becoming an exciting laboratory for many other academic disciplines.

Figure 4.1 illustrates the past evolution of organization and management theory. After discussing the diverse contributions to the relevant body of knowledge and indicating that there has not been a convergence into one unified theory, we are seemingly left without a logical framework for the development of this book. We do, however, see one overriding approach that does provide a basis of integration—*systems and contingency concepts.* In every segment contributing to the development of organization theory and management practice, there has been a trend toward the use of these concepts. As discussed in the following chapter, they provide a framework for the remainder of this book.

Summary

Many forces have modified traditional organization and management theory. The two broad strands of change are the behavioral sciences, which emphasize the psychosocial system and the human aspects of administration, and the management sciences, which emphasize the economic-technical system and quantification, mathematical models, and the application of computer technology.

The behavioral sciences use an open-systems approach and consider many variables that were excluded from the traditional models. The behavioral approach has been developed primarily by psychologists, sociologists, and anthropologists who are interested in empirical investigation to verify their concepts. They have a humanistic orientation that differs from the traditional school and also from the management science approach.

Management science can be considered as a basic extension of scientific management, with modifications. It is concerned with the organization primarily as an economic-technical system. The increasing sophistication of quantitative techniques, together with advancing computer technology, has provided the basic tools for this approach.

The newer approaches have utilized knowledge from a wide variety of disciplines and have provided new informational inputs for organization theory and management practice. The behavioral scientists and the management scientists have frequently become change agents in organizations by advocating approaches and practices that differ from traditional ways of operating. Conflicts and a "communications gap" frequently develop between these scientists and managers.

A fully integrated body of knowledge called organization and management theory has not emerged. Each school of thought has emphasized the aspects of the organization that it considers most important. This diversity should not be considered undesirable. Rather, it is an indication of the active intellectual interest in the study of organizations and their management. Organizations are complex systems made up of psychological, sociological, technical, and economic elements that require intensive investigation. The view that is emerging as a basis for modern theory focuses on *systems and contingency concepts.*

Questions
And
Problems

1 Why have researchers become more interested in the study of organizations and their management?

2 What are the major distinctions between the management science and the behavioral science approaches?

3 Look at recent issues of *Management Science* and *Administrative Science Quarterly.* What are the major differences in emphasis between these two periodicals? How do you explain these differences?

4 How did the approach and findings of the pioneer human relationists differ from scientific management?

5 What is your evaluation of the eight concepts about organizational behavior listed on page 79?

6 Do you see any difficulty for behavioral and management scientists as change agents in organizations in maintaining scientific objectivity? Why or why not?

7 How are scientific management and management science related?

8 Discuss the various disciplines that are contributing to the development of management science. (An appraisal of authors and articles in recent issues of *Management Science, Operations Research,* and *Decision Sciences* will help in answering this question.)

9 Why has effort in operations research been primarily directed toward tactical rather than strategic decisions?

10 Discuss the gaps between behavioral scientists, management scientists, and managers.

11 Evaluate the probabilities of (1) divergence and (2) convergence in organization and management theory.

The Modern View: Systems and Contingency Concepts

Organization theory and management practice are evolving continually. Traditional theory has been modified and enriched by informational inputs from a variety of underlying disciplines. Scientific research and conceptual endeavors have, at times, resulted in divergent theories; however, in recent years an approach has emerged that offers an opportunity for convergence in organization and management theory. The systems approach provides a basis for integration by giving us a way to view the total organization in interaction with its environment and for conceptualization of relationships among internal components or subsystems. Systems concepts provide the basic frame of reference for the development of contingency views of organizations and their management. Systems and contingency approaches are discussed in this chapter via the following topics:

General Systems Theory
Systems Approach and Organization Theory
Organization as an Open System
An Integrated Systems View of Organizations
Managerial Systems
Contingency Views of Organizations
Contingency Views of Management
Systems and Contingency Concepts for Organization and
    Management

General Systems Theory

Over the past several decades the development of general systems theory has provided a basis for the integration of scientific knowledge across a broad spectrum. [1] We have defined a *system as an organized, unitary whole composed of two or more interdependent parts, components, or subsystems and delineated by identifiable boundaries from its environmental suprasystem.* The term *system* covers a broad spectrum of our physical, biological, and social world. In the universe there are galaxial systems, geophysical systems, and molecular systems. In biology we speak of the organism as a system of mutually dependent parts, each of which includes many subsystems. The human body is a complex organism including, among others, a skeletal system, a circulatory system, and a nervous system. We come into daily contact with such phenomena as transportation systems, communication systems, and economic systems.

General systems theory provides a basis for understanding and integrating knowledge from a wide variety of highly specialized fields. In the past, traditional knowledge has been along well-defined subject matter lines. Bertalanffy suggests that the various fields of modern science have had a continual evolution toward a parallelism of ideas. This parallelism provides an opportunity to formulate and develop principles that hold for systems in general. "In modern science, dynamic interaction is the basic problem in all fields, and its general principles will have to be formulated in General System Theory." [2] General systems theory provides the broad macro view from which we may look at all types of systems.

There is an important distinction between closed systems and open systems. Physical and mechanical systems can be considered as closed in relationship to their environment. On the other hand, biological and social systems are not closed but are in constant interaction with their environment. This view of biological and social phenomena as open systems has profound importance for the social sciences and organization theory. Traditional theory assumed the organization to be a closed system, whereas the modern approach considers it an open system in interaction with its environment. While the development of general systems theory has provided an overall conceptual view for dealing with all types of phenomena—physical, biological, and social—there have been many additional threads in intellectual development that have contributed to the development of the systems approach.

Pervasiveness of Systems Theory

The emergence of the systems approach in the study of organizations is a reflection of an even broader theoretical development. General systems theory

1 The name "general systems theory" and many of the basic concepts were set forth by the biologist Ludwig von Bertalanffy. For a general discussion of his views, see "The Theory of Open Systems in Physics and Biology." *Science,* Jan. 13, 1950. pp. 23–29; and *General System Theory,* George Braziller, Inc., New York, 1968.

2 Ludwig von Bertalanffy, *Problems of Life,* John Wiley & Sons, Inc., New York, 1952, p. 201. On page 176 he stresses this view: "If we survey the various fields of modern science, we notice a dramatic and amazing evolution. Similar conceptions and principles have arisen in quite different realms, although this parallelism of ideas is the result of independent developments, and the workers in the individual fields are hardly aware of the common trend. Thus, the principles of wholeness, of organization, and of the dynamic conception of reality become apparent in all fields of science."

provides a basis for understanding and integrating knowledge from a wide variety of specialized fields. In complex societies with rapid expansion of knowledge, the various scientific fields become highly differentiated and specialized. In many scientific fields, the concentration over the past several decades has been on analytical, fact-finding, and experimental approaches in highly specific areas. This has been useful in helping to develop knowledge and to understand the details of specific but limited subjects. At some stage, however, there should be a period of synthesis, reconciliation, and integration, so that the analytical and fact-finding elements are unified into broader, multidimensional theories. There is evidence that every field of human knowledge passes alternately through phases of analysis and fact finding to periods of synthesis and integration. Recently systems theory has provided this framework in many fields—physical, biological, and social.

The development and contagion of the modern systems perspective can be traced in part to the concern of several disciplines to treat their subject matter—whether the organism, the species, or the social group as a whole, an entity in its own right, with unique properties understandable only in terms of the whole, especially in the face of a more traditional reductionistic or mechanistic focus on the separate parts and a simplistic notion of how these parts fit together. [3]

The application of systems thinking has been particularly relevant to the social sciences. In sociology, Talcott Parsons led in the adoption of the general systems viewpoint. [4] Although Parsons acknowledges his debt to Pareto for the concept of systems in scientific theory, it is Parsons himself who has fully utilized the open-systems approach for the study of social structures. [5] He not only developed a broad social system framework but also related his ideas to the organization. Many of his concepts relating to the structure and processes of social systems will be used later in this book.

In the field of psychology, the systems approach has achieved prominence. The very word *gestalt* is German for configuration or pattern. [6] "The Gestaltists early adopted the concept of system, which is more than the sum of its

---

3 Walter Buckley (ed.), *Modern Systems Research for the Behavorial Scientist,* Aldine Publishing Co., Chicago, 1968, p. xxiii.

4 Talcott Parsons uses the systems approach in much of his writings. His *The Social System,* The Free Press of Glencoe, New York, 1951, presents a comprehensive treatise on his views.

5 For a view of Pareto's works, see Lawrence J. Henderson, *Pareto's General Sociology,* Harvard University Press, Cambridge, Mass. 1935.

6 "A *gestalt* is an organized entity or whole in which the parts, though distinguishable, are interdependent; they have certain characteristics produced by their inclusion in the whole, and the whole has some characteristics belonging to none of the parts. The gestalt thus constitutes a 'unit segregated from its surroundings,' behaving according to certain laws of energy distribution. It is found throughout human behaviour as well as in physiological and physical events and is thus a fundamental aspect of scientific data." Julius Gould and William L. Kolb (eds.), *A Dictionary of the Social Sciences,* The Free Press of Glencoe, New York, 1964, p. 287.

components, and which determines the activity of these components."[7] Kurt Lewin was among the first to apply the tenets of gestalt psychology to the field of individual personality. He found that purely psychological explanations of personality were inadequate and that sociocultural forces had to be taken into account. He viewed personality as a dynamic system, influenced by the individual's environment. Harry Stack Sullivan, in his *Interpersonal Theory of Psychiatry,* went even further in relating personality to the sociocultural system. He viewed the foundation of personality as an extension and elaboration of social relationships. A further extension of psychology to give greater consideration to broader interpersonal and social systems is seen in the rapidly expanding field of social psychology.

Modern economics has increasingly used the systems approach. Equilibrium concepts are fundamental in economic thought, and the very basis of this type of analysis is consideration of subsystems of a total system. Economics is moving away from static equilibrium models appropriate to closed systems toward dynamic equilibrium considerations appropriate to open systems.

The discipline of cybernetics is based on a systems approach. It is primarily concerned with communication and information flow in complex systems. Although cybernetics has been applied primarily to mechanistic engineering problems, its model of feedback, control, and regulation has a great deal of applicability for biological and social systems as well.

Even more recently, our society has become increasingly concerned over the pollution and deterioration of the natural environment. Traditionally, we viewed the environment and natural resources as available for our utilization and exploitation. We had a mechanistic, piecemeal, and suboptimal view of the ecosystem. Each act against nature was viewed separately. The accumulation of individual actions might lead to drastic environmental deterioration, but this was not understood. More recently, it is being recognized that our relationship to our environment must be viewed from a systems approach.

Another similar point of view permeating many of the social and physical sciences is the concept of holism—the view that all systems—physical, biological, and social—are composed of interrelated subsystems. The whole is not just the sum of the parts, but the system itself can be explained only as a totality. Holism is the opposite of elementarism, which views the total as the sum of its individual parts. The holistic view is basic to the systems approach. In traditional organization theory, as well as in many of the sciences, the subsystems have been studied separately, with the view to later putting the parts together into a whole. The systems approach emphasizes that this is not possible and that the starting point has to be with the total system.

---

7 Ian Whitaker, "The Nature and Value of Functionalism in Sociology," in *Functionalism in the Social Sciences,* Monograph 5, American Academy of Political and Social Science, February 1965, pp. 137–138.

The foregoing discussion has attempted to show how the systems approach and associate views have become the operating framework for many physical and social sciences.

Psychologists, sociologists, anthropologists, economists, and political scientists have been "discovering" and using the system model. In so doing, they find intimations of an exhilarating "unity" of science, because the system models used by biological and physical scientists seem to be exactly similar. Thus, the system model is regarded by some system theorists as universally applicable to physical and social events, and to human relationships in small or large units. [8]

Key Concepts from General Systems Theory

General concepts applicable to many different types of systems have been set forth by various writers. [9] They reflect a broad eclectic overview. The key concepts of general systems theory are set forth in Figure 5.1. Although all of these concepts have some relevance, several are particularly important in the study of organizations.

The concept of boundaries helps us understand the distinction between open and closed systems. The closed system has rigid, impenetrable boundaries, whereas the open system has permeable boundaries between itself and a broader supersystem. The boundaries set the "domain" of the organization's activities. In a physical, mechanical, or biological system the boundaries can be identified. In a social organization, the boundaries are not easily definable and are determined primarily by the functions and activities of the organization. It is characterized by rather vaguely formed, highly permeable boundaries.

Many systems grow through internal elaboration. In the closed system subject to the laws of physics, the system moves toward entropy and disorganization. In contrast, open systems appear to have the opposite tendency and move in the direction of greater differentiation and a higher level of organization. Bertalanffy points to the continual elaborations of biological organisms: "In organic development and evolution, a transition toward states of higher order and differentiation seems to occur. The tendency toward increasing complication has been

8 Robert Chin, "The Utility of System Models and Developmental Models for Practitioners," in Warren G. Bennis, et al., (eds.), *The Planning of Change,* 3d ed., Holt, Rinehart, and Winston, Inc., New York, 1976, pp. 91–92.

9 Russell L. Ackoff, "Towards a System of Systems Concepts," *Management Science,* July 1971, pp. 661–671; F. Kenneth Berrien, *General and Social Systems,* Rutgers University Press, New Brunswick, N.J., 1968; Kenneth E. Boulding, "General Systems Theory: The Skeleton of Science," *Management Science,* April 1956, pp. 197–208; Walter Buckley (ed.), *Modern Systems Research for the Behavioral Scientist,* Aldine Publishing Co., Chicago, 1968; A. D. Hall and R. E. Fagen, "Definition of System," *General Systems: Yearbook for the Society for the Advancement of General Systems Theory,* Vol. 1, 1956, pp. 18–28; James G. Miller, "Living Systems: Basic Concepts," *Behavioral Science,* July 1965, pp. 193–237; and Ludwig von Bertalanffy, *General System Theory,* George Braziller, Inc., New York, 1968.

Figure 5.1 Key Concepts of General Systems Theory

Subsystems or Components. A system by definition is composed of interrelated parts or elements. This is true for all systems—mechanical, biological, and social. Every system has at least two elements, and these elements are interconnected.

Holism, Synergism, Organicism, and Gestalt. The whole is not just the sum of the parts; the system itself can be explained only as a totality. Holism is the opposite of elementarism, which views the total as the sum of its individual parts.

Open Systems View. Systems can be considered in two ways: (1) closed or (2) open. Open systems exchange information, energy, or material with their environments. Biological and social systems are inherently open systems; mechanical systems may be open or closed. The concepts of open and closed systems are difficult to defend in the absolute. We prefer to think of open–closed as a dimension; i.e., systems are relatively open or relatively closed.

Input-Transformation-Output Model. The open system can be viewed as a transformation model. In a dynamic relationship with its environment, it receives various inputs, transforms these inputs in some way, and exports outputs.

System Boundaries. It follows that systems have boundaries that separate them from their environments. The concept of boundaries helps us understand the distinction between open and closed systems. The relatively closed system has rigid, impenetrable boundaries, whereas the open system has permeable boundaries between itself and a broader suprasystem. Boundaries are relatively easily defined in physical and biological systems but are very difficult to delineate in social systems such as organizations.

Negative Entropy. Closed physical systems are subject to the force of entropy which increases until eventually the entire system fails. The tendency toward maximum entropy is a movement to disorder, complete lack of resource transformation, and death. In a closed system, the change in entropy must always be positive; however, in open biological or social systems, entropy can be arrested and may even be transformed into negative entropy—a process of more complete organization and ability to transform resources—because the system imports resources from its environment.

Steady State, Dynamic Equilibrium, and Homeostasis. The concept of steady state is closely related to that of negative entropy. A closed system eventually must attain an equilibrium state with maximum entropy—death or disorganization. However, an open system may attain a state in which the system remains in dynamic equilibrium through the continuous inflow of materials, energy, and information.

Feedback. The concept of feedback is important in understanding how a system maintains a steady state. Information concerning the outputs or the process of the system is fed back as an input into the system, perhaps leading to changes in the transformation process and/or future outputs. Feedback can be both positive and negative, although the field of cybernetics is based on negative feedback. Negative feedback is informational input which indicates that the system is deviating from a prescribed course and should readjust to a new steady state.

Hierarchy. A basic concept in systems thinking is that of hierarchical relationships between systems. A system is composed of subsystems of a lower order and is also part of a suprasystem. Thus, there is a hierarchy of the components of the system.

Internal Elaboration. Closed systems move toward entropy and disorganization. In contrast, open systems appear to move in the direction of greater differentiation, elaboration, and a higher level of organization.

Multiple Goal Seeking. Biological and social systems appear to have multiple goals or purposes. Social organizations seek multiple goals, if for no other reason than that they are composed of individuals and subunits with different values and objectives.

Equifinality of Open Systems. In mechanistic systems there is a direct cause-and-effect relationship between the initial conditions and the final state. Biological and social systems operate differently. Equifinality suggests that certain results may be achieved with different initial conditions and in different ways. This view suggests that social organizations can accomplish their objectives with diverse inputs and with varying internal activities (conversion processes).

indicated as a primary characteristic of the living, as opposed to inanimate, nature." [10]

This same process appears to hold true for most social systems. There is a tendency for them to elaborate their activities and to reach higher levels of differentiation and organization. There is a tendency for complex organizations to achieve greater differentiation and specialization among internal subsystems. The increased number of specialized departments and activities in complex business organizations is readily apparent. The great proliferation of departments, courses, and subject matter in universities is another example of differentiation and elaboration.

Equifinality is an important characteristic of social systems. In physical systems there is a direct cause-and-effect relationship between the initial conditions and the final state. Biological and social systems operate differently. The concept of *equifinality* says that final results may be achieved with different initial conditions and in different ways. This view suggests that the social organization can accomplish its objectives with varying inputs and with varying internal activities. Thus, the social system is not restrained by the simple cause-and-effect relationship of closed systems.

The equifinality of social systems has major importance for the management of complex organizations. A closed-system cause-and-effect view adopted from the physical sciences would suggest that there is one best way to achieve a given objective. The concept of equifinality suggests that the manager can utilize a varying bundle of inputs into the organization, can transform them in a variety of ways, and can achieve satisfactory output. Extending this view further suggests that the management function is not necessarily one of seeking a rigid optimal solution but rather one of having available a variety of satisfactory alternatives.

Organizations display many of the characteristics set forth in Figure 5.1. However, it is important to recognize that there are significant differences among various types of systems. Social organizations are not natural like physical or biological systems, they are contrived. They have structure, but it is the structure of events rather than of physical components, and it cannot be separated from the processes of the system. The fact that social organizations are contrived by human beings suggests that they can be established for an infinite variety of objectives and do not follow the same life-cycle pattern of birth, maturity, and death as biological systems. Katz and Kahn say:

Social structures are essentially contrived. People invent the complex patterns of behavior that we call social structure, and people create social structure by enacting those patterns of behavior. Many properties of social systems derive from these essential facts. As human inventions, social systems are imperfect. They can come apart at the seams overnight, but they can also outlast by centuries the biological organisms that originally created them. The cement that holds them together is essentially psychological, rather

10 Ludwig von Bertalanffy, "The Theory of Open Systems in Physics and Biology," *Science,* Jan. 13, 1950, p. 26.

than biological. Social systems are anchored in the attitudes, perceptions, beliefs, motivations, habits, and expectations of human beings. [11]

Recognizing that the social organization is a contrived system cautions us against making an exact analogy between it and physical or biological systems.

The foregoing are a few of the characteristics of open systems. To the student who is initially exposed to some of these concepts, they may seem complicated. Much of our educational experience emphasizes closed-system approaches—mathematics and the physical sciences, for example. The open-system view, with the properties set forth in the previous sections, is pertinent for organization theory.

It is important for the student of organization and management to recognize that the developing body of knowledge and applications of the systems approach to complex organizations is but a part of the broad trend in many of the physical and social sciences and that this field is part of a pervasive stream of thought. Furthermore, understanding that organization theory can be put in the context of general systems theory allows for a growing community of interest and understanding with widely diverse disciplines. We will now look more closely at the direct relationship between the systems approach and organization theory.

Systems Approach and Organization Theory

Traditional organization theory used a highly structured, closed-system approach. Modern theory has moved toward the open-system approach. "The distinctive qualities of modern organization theory are its conceptual-analytical base, its reliance on empirical research data, and, above all, its synthesizing, integrating nature. These qualities are framed in a philosophy which accepts the premise that the only meaningful way to study organization is as a system." [12]

The historical roots of systems thinking related to organization and management go back many years. Mary Parker Follett, writing at the time of the classical management theorists, expressed many views indicative of a systems approach. She considered the psychological and sociological aspects of management, described management as a social process, and viewed the organization as a social system. [13]

---

11 Daniel Katz and Robert L. Kahn, *The Social Psychology of Organizations,* 2d ed., John Wiley & Sons, Inc., New York, 1978, p. 37.

12 William G. Scott and Terence R. Mitchell, *Organization Theory,* rev. ed., Richard D. Irwin, Inc., Homewood, Ill., 1972, p. 55.

13 H.C. Metcalf and Lyndall Urwick (eds.), *Dynamic Administration: The Collected Papers of Mary Parker Follett,* Harper and Row, Publishers, New York, 1941.

Chester Barnard was one of the first management writers to utilize the systems approach.[14] Herbert Simon and his associates viewed the organization as a complex system of decision-making processes. Simon has ranged widely in seeking new disciplinary knowledge to integrate into his organization theories. However, the one broad consistency in both his research and his writings has been the utilization of the systems approach. "The term 'systems' is being used more and more to refer to methods of scientific analysis that are particularly adapted to the unraveling of complexity."[15] He not only emphasizes this approach for the behavioral view of organizations but also stresses its importance in management science.

The systems approach has been advocated by a number of other writers in management science. Churchman and his associates were among the earliest to emphasize this view. "The comprehensiveness of O.R.'s aim is an example of a 'systems' approach, since 'system' implies an interconnected complex of functionally related components. Thus a business organization is a social or man-machine system."[16] Although the systems approach has been adopted and utilized in mangement science, the models typically used are closed in the sense that they consider only certain variables and exclude from consideration those not subject to quantification.

The sociologist George Homans uses systems concepts as a basis for his empirical research on social groups. He developed a model of social systems that can serve as an appropriate basis for small groups and also for larger organizations.[17] In his view, an organization is comprised of an external environmental system and an internal system of relationships that are mutually interdependent. There are three elements in a social system. *Activities* are the tasks that people perform. *Interactions* occur between people in the performance of these tasks, and *sentiments* develop between people. These elements are mutually interdependent.

Philip Selznick utilizes structural functional analysis and the systems approach in his studies of organizations. The institutional leader is concerned with the adaptation of the organization to its external systems. The organization is a dynamic system, constantly changing and adapting to internal and external pressures, and is in a continual process of evolution. "Cooperative systems are constituted of individuals interacting as wholes in relation to a formal system of coordination. The concrete structure is therefore a resultant of the reciprocal influences of the formal and informal aspects of organization. Furthermore, this structure is itself a totality, an adaptive 'organism' reacting to influences upon it from an

14 Chester I. Barnard, *The Functions of the Executive,* Harvard University Press, Cambridge, Mass., 1938.

15 Herbert A. Simon, "Approaching the Theory of Management," in Harold Koontz (ed.), *Toward a Unified Theory of Management,* McGraw-Hill Book Company, New York, 1964, pp. 82–83.

16 C. West Churchman, Russell I. Ackoff, and E. Leonard Arnoff, *Introduction to Operations Research,* John Wiley & Sons, Inc., New York, 1957, p. 7.

17 George C. Homans, *The Human Group,* Harcourt, Brace & World, Inc., New York, 1950.

external environment." [18] Selznick used this systems frame of reference for empirical research on governmental agencies and other complex organizations.

The systems approach has also been used in other countries. Miller points out that Alexander Bogdanov, the Russian philosopher, developed a theory of tektology or universal organization science in 1912 that foreshadowed general systems theory and used many of the same concepts as modern systems theorists. [19] In England the organizational researchers at the Tavistock Institute of Human Relations have viewed the organization as a sociotechnical system with a structuring and integration of human activities around various technologies toward the accomplishment of certain goals. [20] Burns and Stalker made substantial use of systems views in setting forth their concepts of mechanistic and organic managerial systems. [21] In France, Michel Crozier and his associates have used a comprehensive systems approach to investigate complex governmental relationships. [22]

The systems approach has also been adopted by social psychologists as a basis for studying organizations. Using open-systems theory as a general conceptual scheme, Katz and Kahn present a comprehensive theory of organization. [23] They suggest that the psychological approach has generally ignored or has not dealt effectively with the facts of structure and social organization, and they use systems concepts to develop an integrated model.

There are numerous examples of the utilization of the systems approach at operational levels. For example, the trend toward automation involves implementation of these ideas. Automation suggests a self-contained system with inputs, outputs, and a mechanism of control.

The systems approach has been utilized as a basis of organization for many of our advanced defense and space programs. Program management is geared to changing managerial requirements in research, development, procurement, and utilization. With the new complex space programs it became impossible to think of individual segments or parts of the program as separate entities, and it was necessary to move to a broader systems approach. [24] In many other types of

18 Philip Selznick, "Foundations of the Theory of Organization," *American Sociological Review*, February 1948, pp. 25–35.

19 Robert F. Miller, "The New Science of Administration in the USSR," *Administrative Science Quarterly*, September 1971, pp. 249–250; and George Gorelik, "Reemergence of Bogdanov's *Tektology* in Soviet Studies of Organization," *Academy of Management Review*, June 1975, pp. 345–357.

20 F. E. Emery and E. L. Trist, "Socio-technical Systems," in C. West Churchman and Michael Verhulst (eds.), *Management Sciences: Models and Techniques*, Pergamon Press, New York, 1960, vol. 2, pp. 83–97; A. K. Rice, *The Enterprise and its Environment*, Tavistock Publications, London, 1963; and P. G. Herbst, *Socio-Technical Design*, Tavistock Publications, London, 1974.

21 Tom Burns and G. M. Stalker, *The Management of Innovation,* Tavistock Publications, London, 1961.

22 Michel Crozier and Jean-Claude Thoening, "The Regulation of Complex Organized Systems," *Administrative Science Quarterly*, December 1976, pp. 547–570.

23 Katz and Kahn, op. cit.

24 For a discussion of the evolution of this approach in military and space programs, see Fremont E. Kast and James E. Rosenzweig, "Organization and Management of Space Programs," in Frederick I. Ordway, III (ed.), *Advances in Space Science and Technology*, Academic Press, Inc, New York, 1965, vol. 7, pp. 273–364.

governmental projects that require the integration of many agencies and activities—transportation problems, pollution control, and urban renewal, for example—the systems approach is being used.

The development of planning-programming-budgeting systems (PPBS) represents one of the most important and comprehensive examples of the application of the systems approach to the management of complex organizations. Essentially, PPBS is a systematic approach that attempts to establish goals, develop programs for their accomplishment, consider the costs and benefits of various alternative approaches, and utilize a budgetary process that reflects program activities over the long run. PPBS was first developed by the federal government and is currently being used by numerous state and local government agencies.

These examples of the trend toward adapting the systems approach to modern organization theory and management practice are by no means exhaustive; they merely illustrate current developments. However, they are sufficient to indicate that increasing attention is being given to the study of organizations as complex systems. "But on one thing all the varied schools of organizational analysis now seemed to be agreed: Organizations are systems—indeed, they are open systems." [25]

Reference to other scientific disciplines can help us understand what is occurring in the field of organization theory. Major changes in all fields of science occur with the development of new conceptual schemes or paradigms, which provide a different view and a "new start." [26] Systems theory provides a new paradigm for the study of organizations and their management, a basis for thinking of the organization as an open system in interaction with its environment. It also helps us understand the interrelationships between the major components of an organization—its goals, technology, structure, and psychosocial relationships. It provides an improved frame of reference for managerial practice.

Organization as an Open System

The organization can be considered in terms of a general open-system model, as in Figure 5.2. The open system is in continual interaction with its environment and achieves a "steady state" or dynamic equilibrium while still retaining the capacity for work or energy transformation. The survival of the system, in effect, would not be possible without continuous inflow, transformation, and outflow. In the biological or social system this is a continuous recycling process. The system must receive sufficient input of resources to maintain its opera-

25 Charles Perrow, "The Short and Glorious History of Organization Theory," *Organizational Dynamics,* Summer 1973, p. 11.

26 Thomas S. Kuhn, *The Structure of Scientific Revolutions,* 2d ed., University of Chicago Press, Chicago, 1970.

Figure 5.2   General Model of Organization as an Open System

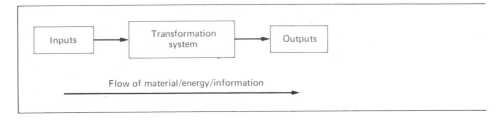

tions and also to export the transformed resources to the environment in sufficient quantity to continue the cycle. "Every surviving system must provide some output acceptable usually to a collateral or supra-system." [27]

For example, the business organization receives inputs from the society in the form of people, materials, money, and information; it transforms these into outputs of products, services, and rewards to the organizational members sufficiently large to maintain their participation. For the business enterprise, money and the market provide a mechanism for recycling of resources between the firm and its environment. The same kind of analysis can be made for all types of social organizations.

Although we will use the open system perspective throughout this book, we should recognize that the concept of open or closed is a matter of degree. In an absolute sense, all systems are open or closed, depending on the point of reference. Thus, all systems are "closed" in some degree from external forces. The system's boundaries always prevent *some* environmental factors from impacting on the system; it provides for selective inputs. We will discuss this issue of degrees of openness and closedness more completely in Chapter 6.

An Integrated Systems View of Organizations

We view the organization as an open, sociotechnical system composed of a number of subsystems, as illustrated in Figure 5.3. It receives inputs of energy, information, and materials from the environment, transforms these, and returns outputs to the environment. Under this view, an organization is not simply a technical or a social system. Rather, it is the structuring and integrating of human activities around various technologies. The technologies affect the types of inputs into the organization, the nature of the transformation processes, and the outputs from the system. However, the social system determines the effectiveness and efficiency of the utilization of the technology.

---

27 F. Kenneth Berrien, "A General Systems Approach to Organizations," in Marvin D. Dunnette (ed.), *Handbook of Industrial and Organizational Psychology,* Rand McNally College Publishing Company, Chicago, 1976, p. 45.

Figure 5.3   The Organizational System

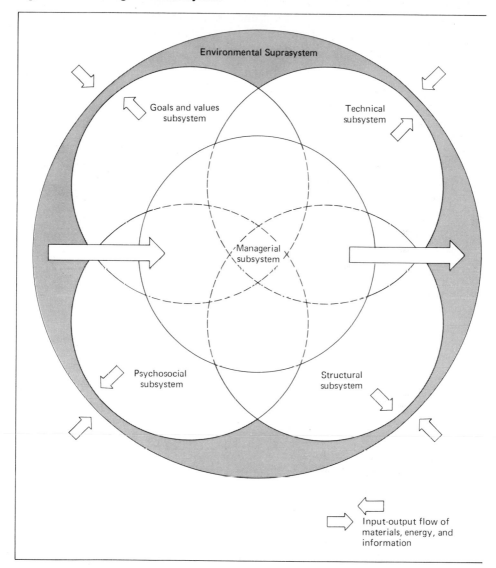

The internal organization can be viewed as composed of several major subsystems. The organizational ***goals and values*** are one of the more important of these subsystems. The organization takes many of its values from the broader sociocultural environment. A basic premise is that the organization as a subsystem of the society must accomplish certain goals that are determined by the broader system. The organization performs a function for society, and if it is to be success-ful in receiving inputs, it must conform to social requirements.

The **technical** subsystem refers to the knowledge required for the performance of tasks, including the techniques used in the transformation of inputs into outputs. It is determined by the task requirements of the organization and varies depending on the particular activities. The technology for manufacturing automobiles differs significantly from that used in an oil refinery or an electronics company. Similarly, the task requirements and technology in a hospital are different from those in a university. The technical subsystem is shaped by the specialization of knowledge and skills required, the types of machinery and equipment involved, and the layout of facilities. The technology affects the organization's structure as well as its psychosocial subsystem.

Every organization has a **psychosocial** subsystem that is composed of individuals and groups in interaction. It consists of individual behavior and motivation, status and role relationships, group dynamics, and influence systems. It is also affected by sentiments, values, attitudes, expectations, and aspirations of the people in the organization. Obviously, this psychosocial subsystem is affected by external environmental forces as well as by the tasks, technology, and structure of the internal organization. These forces set the "organizational climate" within which the human participants perform their roles and activities. We would therefore expect psychosocial systems to differ significantly among various organizations. Certainly the climate for the person on the assembly line is different from that of the scientist in the laboratory or the doctor in the hospital.

Structure involves the ways in which the tasks of the organization are divided (differentiation) and coordinated (integration). In the formal sense, structure is set forth by organization charts, by position and job descriptions, and by rules and procedures. It is also concerned with patterns of authority, communication, and work flow. The organization's structure provides for formalization of relationships between the technical and the psychosocial subsystems. However, it should be emphasized that this linkage is by no means complete and that many interactions and relationships occur between the technical and psychosocial subsytems that bypass the formal structure.

The **managerial** subsystem spans the entire organization by relating the organization to its environment, setting the goals, developing comprehensive, strategic, and operational plans, designing the structure, and establishing control processes.

Figure 5.3 provides one way of viewing the organization. The goals and values, as well as the technical, structural, psychosocial, and managerial subsystems, are shown as integral parts of the overall organization. This figure is an aid to understanding the evolution of organization theory. Traditional management theory emphasized the structural and managerial subsystems and was concerned with developing principles. The human relationists and behavioral scientists emphasized the psychosocial subsystem and focused their attention on motivation, group dynamics, and other related factors. The management science school emphasized the technical subsystem and methods for quantifying decision-making and control processes. Thus each approach to organization and management has tended to emphasize particular subsystems, with little recognition of the importance of the others. The modern approach views the organization as an open, sociotechnical system and considers *all* the primary subsystems *and* their interactions.

Managerial System

The managerial system spans the entire organization by directing the technology, organizing people and other resources, and relating the organization to its environment.

This last component, which determines the overall objectives and relates the subsystem standards to the overall, can be called the "management subsystem." It is the subsystem that thinks about the overall plan and implements its thinking. [28]

One approach to the study of management focuses attention on the fundamental administrative processes—planning, organizing, and controlling—that are essential if an organization is to meet its primary goals. These basic managerial processes are required for any type of organization—business, government, education—where human and physical resources are combined to achieve certain objectives. Furthermore, these processes are necessary regardless of the specialized area of management—production, distribution, finance, or facilitating activities.

Another way to help understand the managerial task is to look within organizations at various levels or subsystems. The model shown in Figure 5.4 is an extension of the work of Parsons, Petit, and Thompson. [29] There are basic differences in the orientation of the managerial system at these different levels. The operating subsystem is concerned primarily with economic-technical rationality and tries to create certainty by "closing the technical core" to many variables. Thompson says, "Under norms of rationality, organizations seek to seal off their core technologies from environmental influences. Since complete closure is impossible, they seek to buffer environmental influences by surrounding their technical cores with input and output components." [30] A relatively closed-system view is applicable to the "technical core" or operating subsystem of the organization.

By contrast, at the strategic level the organization faces the greatest degree of uncertainty in terms of inputs from its environment over which it has little or no control. Therefore, management at this level should have a relatively open-system view and concentrate on adaptive and/or innovative strategies. The

28 C. West Churchman, *The Systems Approach,* Dell Publishing Co., Inc, New York, 1968, p. 8.

29 Talcott Parsons, *Structure and Process in Modern Societies,* The Free Press, New York, 1960, pp. 60–96; Thomas A. Petit, "A Behavioral Theory of Management," *Academy of Management Journal,* December 1967, pp. 341–350; and James D. Thompson, *Organizations in Action,* McGraw-Hill Book Company, New York, 1967.

30 James D. Thompson, op. cit., p. 24.

Figure 5.4 The Organization as a Composite of Strategic, Coordinative, and Operating Subsystems/Levels

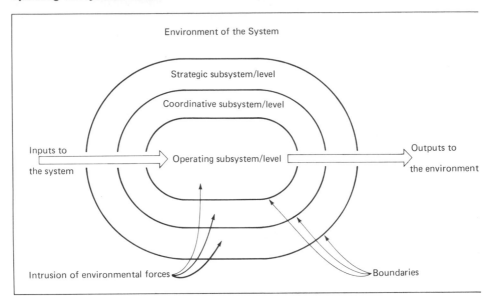

coordinative manager operates between the operating and the strategic levels and serves to mediate and coordinate the two. This level transforms the uncertainty of the environment into the economic-technical rationality necessary for input into the operating subsystem.

In many organizations these roles are separated theoretically. For example, in the university, the board of regents is thought of as fulfilling the strategic role, whereas the president, deans, and department heads are involved with coordinative aspects. The professors, under this concept, perform the operating functions. In a hospital, the board of trustees performs the strategic role, the hospital administrator's staff is involved with coordinative aspects, while the doctors, nurses, and other specialists perform the "operating" functions. Theoretically, in business the board of directors relates the organization to its environment, upper and middle management deal with coordinative aspects, and other employees perform the operating tasks. However, this distinction is not clear-cut in any of these organizations. For example, the president of a corporation usually has both strategic and coordinative roles.

Figure 5.5 illustrates in more detail the differences in managerial tasks at the various levels in organizations. The smaller the organization, the more likely that the various aspects of the managerial task will be carried out by one individual. Obviously, for a proprietorship, the owner-manager is involved in all the activities set forth in Figure 5.5. He or she must define the task in relation to the environment, plan activities over the short and long run, and then carry them out in order to achieve the objectives.

Figure 5.5   The Managerial Task: Strategic, Coordinative, and Operating Subsystems

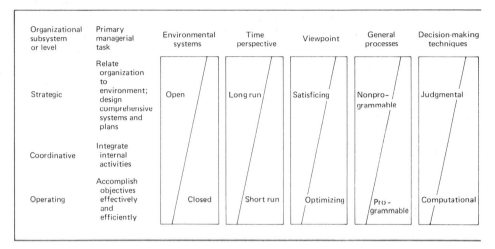

Organizational subsystem or level	Primary managerial task	Environmental systems	Time perspective	Viewpoint	General processes	Decision-making techniques
Strategic	Relate organization to environment; design comprehensive systems and plans	Open	Long run	Satisficing	Nonpro-grammable	Judgmental
Coordinative	Integrate internal activities					
Operating	Accomplish objectives effectively and efficiently	Closed	Short run	Optimizing	Pro-grammable	Computational

In larger, more complex organizations it is more likely that these subsystems are separable and identifiable. Top management is involved in relating the organization to its environment—identifying a niche that it must fill in order to survive and grow. Strategy formulation also involves designing comprehensive systems and plans. A systems philosophy is useful in conceptualizing the long-run nature of the organization and assembling the appropriate resources for achieving desired goals. The environmental system is relatively open; general processes are typically nonprogrammable; and the viewpoint is essentially one of satisficing—finding workable solutions to complex, ill-structured, novel problems. Decision making is largely judgmental and cogitative—reasoned evaluation of all relevant inputs to the problem-solving process.

In the operating subsystem the primary task is accomplishing stated objectives effectively and efficiently. It is here that the organization "does its thing"—producing bicycles or toothpaste, providing health care or fire protection. The environmental system is relatively closed and general processes can be programmed—for example, standard operating procedures or computer programs. Systems analysis provides a framework for a short-run, optimizing outlook and computational decision making through the use of quantitative techniques.

In the coordinative subsystem—ranging between the strategic and operating activities—the primary concern is integrating internal activities that have been specialized by function and/or level. Middle management is involved in translating comprehensive plans into operational plans and procedures. It is involved in interpreting the results of the operating system and in focusing existing resources in appropriate directions. Systems management facilitates coordination of several functions, projects, or programs within an overall organization. A pragmatic point of view is essential in integrating short- and long-run considerations.

Compromise is often necessary in decision making at this level in order to achieve a practical or utilitarian outcome via analysis and synthesis of problems.

The terms used in the various dimensions shown in Figure 5.5 are illustrative of general tendencies, i.e., most likely activities or approaches. It is not to say that judgment is not important in the operating system or that computational techniques are never used in developing comprehensive plans. However, the terms do provide a basic flavor of the managerial task in three relatively distinct organizational subsystems. Nor does this mean that the different managerial subsystems can operate independently. Quite the contrary—they are interdependent. For example, the strategic subsystem must perform effectively if the organization is to receive the necessary inputs for the operating subsystem. Also, the operating subsystem must produce outputs efficiently to ensure that the organization receives environmental support.

Role of Manager

The view of the organization as an open system suggests a substantially different role for management from the one it played in traditional theory. "A profound change in the way management is perceived has been produced by the advent of the so-called systems revolution." [31]

In the traditional theory, the emphasis was on economic-technical rationality. This closed-system view was appropriate for the operating level but not for the coordinative and strategic levels. The human relations emphasis did bring into focus the psychosocial subsystem but neglected the technical, structural, and environmental aspects. The management science approach adopted a closed-system view, focusing on the techniques of managerial decision making.

The view of an open sociotechnical system creates a more difficult role for management. It must deal with uncertainties and ambiguities and, above all, must be concerned with adapting the organization to new and changing requirements. Management is a process that spans and links the various subsystems of the organization.

The systems view suggests that management faces situations that are dynamic, inherently uncertain, and frequently ambiguous. Management is not in full control of all the factors of production, as suggested by traditional theory. It is strongly restrained by many environmental and internal (technological, structural, and psychosocial) forces. This does not mean, however, that management is passive, merely adapting to these constraints. Quite the contrary, management has a vital role in perceiving and determining environmental relationships and in designing the internal subsystems. One of the key functions of management is to develop congruence between the organization and its environment and to design internal subsystems that meet the objectives of effectiveness, efficiency, and par-

---

31 John A. Beckett, *Management Dynamics*, McGraw-Hill Book Company, New York, 1971, p. 13.

ticipant satisfaction. The systems approach provides a vital philosophical basis for *understanding* organizations. It is the conceptual foundation for the next step—contingency views that are *action oriented* and directed toward the implementation of systems concepts.

Contingency Views of Organizations

Systems concepts provide the broad framework for understanding organizations. One of the consequences of this approach is a rejection of simplistic statements concerning universal principles of organization design and management practice. Modern organization theory reflects a search for patterns of relationships, congruencies among subsystems, and a contingency view.

Systems concepts provide us with a macro paradigm for the study of organizations, but they involve a relatively high degree of generalization. Contingency views tend to be more concrete and to emphasize more specific characteristics and patterns of interrelationships among subsystems. This trend toward more explicit understanding of relationships among organizational variables is essential if the theory is to facilitate and improve management practice.

Using the systems perspective, we can describe the contingency view of organizations as follows:

The contingency view of organizations and their management suggests that an organization is a system composed of subsystems and delineated by identifiable boundaries from its environmental suprasystem. The contingency view seeks to understand the interrelationships within and among subsystems as well as between the organization and its environment and to define patterns of relationships or configurations of variables. It emphasizes the multivariate nature of organizations and attempts to understand how organizations operate under varying conditions and in specific circumstances. Contingency views are ultimately directed toward suggesting organizational designs and managerial actions most appropriate for specific situations.

Systems concepts are directed toward providing a broad model for understanding *all organizations.* Contingency views recognize that the environment and internal subsystems of each organization are somewhat unique and provide a basis for designing and managing *specific organizations.* Contingency views represent a middle ground between (1) the view that there are universal principles of organization and management and (2) the view that each organization is unique and that each situation must be analyzed separately.

An underlying assumption of the contingency view is that there should be a congruence between the organization and its environment and among the various subsystems.[32] The primary managerial role is to maximize this congru-

32 Donald V. Nightingale and Jean-Marie Toulouse, "Toward a Multilevel Congruence Theory of Organization," *Administrative Science Quarterly,* June 1977, pp. 264–280.

ence. The appropriate fit between the organization and its environment and the appropriate internal organizational design will lead to greater effectiveness, efficiency, and participant satisfaction.

The contingency view suggests that there are appropriate patterns of relationships for different types of organizations and that we can improve our understanding of how these relevant variables interact. For example, certain principles of organization and/or management might be appropriate for uniform operations in a relatively stable environment. A mass production operation such as a refrigerator assembly line might operate most efficiently under a rigid hierarchy with precise planning and control as well as routinization of activities. In contrast, other organizations, operating in an uncertain environment and with dynamic technologies, may operate more efficiently under a very different set of principles. An advertising agency, for example, might be characterized by a flexible structure, nonroutine activities, and adaptive planning and control. Contingency analysis thus may lead us to general conclusions about these patterns of relationships, such as:

The **stable-mechanistic** organization form is more appropriate when:

1 The environment is relatively stable and certain
2 The goals are well defined and enduring
3 The technology is relatively uniform and stable
4 There are routine activities and productivity is the major objective
5 Decision making is programmable and coordination and control processes tend to make a tightly structured, hierarchical system possible

The **adaptive-organic** organizational form is more appropriate when:

1 The environment is relatively uncertain and turbulent
2 The goals are diverse and changing
3 The technology is complex and dynamic
4 There are many nonroutine activities in which creativity and innovation are important
5 Heuristic decision-making processes are utilized and coordination and control occur through reciprocal adjustments. The system is less hierarchical and more flexible

These patterns of relations stemming from contingency analysis will be referred to and elaborated in subsequent sections of this book.

The movement from systems to contingency concepts describes the evolution of organization and management theory up to the present. These changes are depicted in Figure 5.6 and indicate the continuing evolution. And, as in biological evolution, there has not been a radical transformation that eliminated the

Figure 5.6 Evolution of Organization and Management Theory toward Systems Concepts and Contingency Views

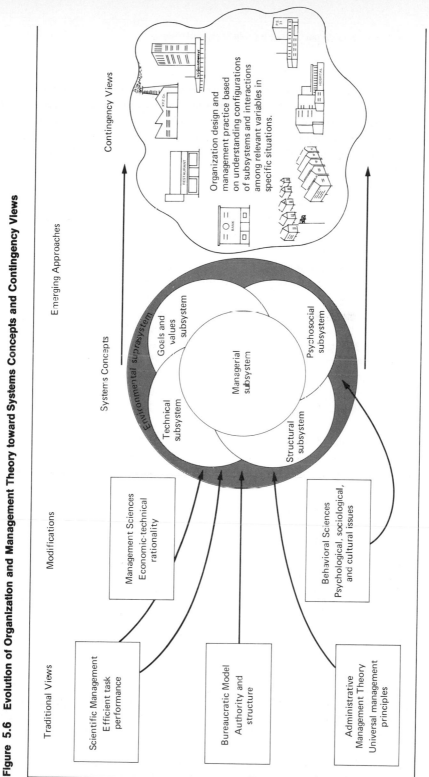

old and substituted the new. Rather, the resulting theories at each stage have been mutations of the old, retaining many of the more enduring concepts. We can attempt to take the best of existing theory, develop new insights about organizational relationships, and refine the body of knowledge accordingly. This process is basic to the development of theory that is applicable to a variety of organizations—the essence of the contingency view.

Contingency Views of Management

Noting the multivariate nature of organizations, it is no wonder that managers often say, "The theory may be appropriate in general, but our organization is different." The thrust of contingency views of management practice is to offset such claims by providing appropriate guidelines for action. Contingency views recognize both similarities and differences among organizations but still emphasize that the primary managerial role is to seek *congruence* between the organization and its environment and among its various subsystems. Systems and contingency concepts facilitate more thorough understanding of complex situations and increase the likelihood of appropriate managerial actions.

Although we think that some managers have utilized these concepts intuitively, most have not. Application of contingency concepts requires increased understanding and sophistication on the part of managers.

An applier of contingency views must recognize more and different kinds of goals and needs for his organization, consider more factors bearing on a decision, employ a wider variety of ways of making and carrying out decisions, and evaluate decisions not on a one-by-one basis, but in relation to each other. Therefore, practitioners must be made aware that they must learn new approaches to solving organizational problems if they choose to use contingency views. [33]

Research findings related to systems and contingency concepts provide an increasing body of knowledge that can be of significant operational use for practicing managers. For example, it can help managers develop an appropriate organizational design within certain environmental and technological contexts; it can provide guidelines for realistic planning and control processes in differing situations; it can help in determining appropriate leadership styles; and it can be instrumental in determining the most relevant means for organizational change and improvement. In effect, systems concepts and contingency views cannot provide general principles for managing all organizations, but they can provide important guidelines for organizational diagnosis and managerial actions in specific situations.

33 Dennis J. Moberg and James L. Koch, "A Critical Appraisal of Integrated Treatment of Contingency Findings," *Academy of Management Journal,* March 1975, p. 121.

Systems and Contingency Concepts for Organization and Management

This chapter sets the framework for the remainder of the book. The basic concepts will be discussed and illustrated in the following six parts:

Environment, Boundaries, and Goals
Technology and Structure
The Psychosocial System
The Managerial System
Comparative Analysis and Contingency Views
Organizational Change and the Future

This framework will be used as a basis for the development of modern organization theory and management practice. We will begin with a discussion of the environmental suprasystem and its impact on the organization. Next we will look at organizational goals. This will set the stage for the discussion of technology and an appraisal of its effects on the organization structure as well as on the psychosocial system. Structural relationships will then be considered in detail. The components of the psychosocial system are analyzed in depth. The managerial system is then reviewed, with emphasis on information flow, decision making, and the key functions of planning and controlling the activities of the organization. In effect, we will follow an orderly process of looking in more detail at each of the major subsystems of the organization as shown in Figure 5.3.

Throughout these discussions we will emphasize contingency views by looking at patterns of relationships among the subsystems and by suggesting appropriate organizational designs and managerial practices to fit various situations. We will make frequent references to *stable-mechanistic* and *adaptive-organic* organizational types. After we have considered the environment and various subsystems in detail, we will return to a more explicit consideration of patterns of relationships and configurations among the various subsystems (Chapter 19, "Comparative Analysis and Contingency Views"). We will set forth contingency propositions concerning organization design and management practice.

Summary

The systems approach provides an integrative framework for modern organization theory and management practice. General systems theory includes concepts for integrating knowledge in the physical, biological, and social sciences. Traditional management theory used closed-system thinking. Modern theory has moved toward considering the organization as an open system interacting with its environment.

There are several key characteristics of organizational systems. They are not natural, like physical or biological systems, but are *contrived.* There are *boundaries* that separate the organization from its environment. Open systems display *growth through internal elaboration.* They tend to move in the direction of greater differentiation and to a higher level of organization. Finally, open systems have the characteristic of *equifinality*—objectives may be achieved with varying inputs and in different ways.

The organization can be viewed as an open system in interaction with its environment and composed of five primary components—goals and values, and technical, structural, psychosocial, and managerial subsystems.

There are three subsystems or levels in the managerial system of complex organizations: operating, coordinative, and strategic. The *operating* subsystem is involved with actual task performance. The *strategic* level relates the activities of the organization to its environment. The *coordinative* subsystem serves to integrate activities vertically (strategic and operating) and horizontally (among different functions at the same level). The view of the organization as a sociotechnical system creates a different role for managers. They must integrate and balance the various subsystems and their activities in the environmental setting.

Systems concepts provide the broad framework for understanding organizations. Contingency views tend to be more concrete and to emphasize more specific characteristics and patterns of interrelationships among subsystems. A basic assumption of the contingency view is that there should be a congruence between the organization and its environment and among the various subsystems. Systems and contingency concepts facilitate more effective diagnosis of complex situations and increase the likelihood of appropriated managerial actions.

Questions and Problems

1 Define systems. Can you describe systems that fit the concepts of general systems theory set forth in Figure 5.1?

2 Compare and contrast mechanistic and biological or social systems.

3 Differentiate open and closed systems. Which model is more appropriate for business and for government organizations? Why?

4 Why might modern organization theory be considered a special element of general systems theory?

5 Relate a specific organization to the subsystems in Figure 5.3.

6 How can automation, electronic data processing, and network analysis (PERT, for example) be considered applications of the systems approach?

7 Why can an organization be considered a contrived system that operates under the concept of equifinality?

8 Relate the concept of "growth through internal elaboration" to a specific type of organization such as a business or university.

9 Discuss the major differences between the operating, coordinative, and strategic subsystems in the managerial system.

10 How does the systems approach affect management practices?

11 How would you use the systems approach to describe these types of organizations?

     a a business

     b a hospital

     c a university

     d a city

12 Describe in your own words what is meant by a contingency view of organization and management.

*Our main job today is learning how to make the
world safe for diversity.*
Norman Cousins

*Primitive randomness evolves into organized
complexity. This is true for the beginnings of life and, before
that, in the chemical evolution of the universe. It is equally
true of our social evolution.*
F. Kenneth Berrien

*Ecological survival does not mean the abandonment
of technology. Rather, it requires that technology be derived
from a scientific analysis that is appropriate to the natural
world on which technology intrudes.*
Barry Commoner

*An obvious characteristic of modern society is ever
increasing interdependency; little can be changed without
affecting a wide array of institutions, and many new
developments depend upon close, collaborative, and integrated
activities that criss-cross organizational boundaries and the
dividing line between the public and private sectors.*
Leonard R. Sayles and Margaret K. Chandler

*When a man does not know what harbor he is
making for, no wind is the right wind.*
Seneca

*Many define effectiveness in terms of a single
evaluation criterion (profit or productivity, for example). But
it is difficult to conceive of an organization that would survive
for long if it pursued profits to the exclusion of its employees'
needs and goals or those of society at large. Organizations
typically pursue multiple (and often conflicting) goals—and
these goals tend to differ from organization to organization
according to the nature of the enterprise and its environment.*
Richard M. Steers

Environment, Boundaries, and Goals

3

Every organization is a subsystem of an environment that provides resource inputs and utilizes the organization's outputs. Each society has certain fundamental characteristics, such as values, people, and resources, that greatly affect the nature of its organizations and their management. The social organization has a loosely defined boundary that separates it from its environmental suprasystem. However, organizations are open systems and this boundary is permeable to a variety of inputs and outputs. The environment in modern societies is becoming increasingly turbulent and organizations must continually adapt.

Organizational values and goals are determined through interactions with the environmental suprasystem. In this part we will begin to use the systems model developed in Chapter 5 to consider in depth the environmental suprasystem, the boundaries between organizations and their environment, and the goals and values subsystem.

Chapter 6, "Environmental Suprasystem," looks in detail at the nature of the environmental system and how it affects organizations. Both the general environment for all organizations and the specific task environment for each individual organization will be considered. As an illustration of these relationships, we will look at the interface between business organizations and society.

In Chapter 7 we turn to a consideration of organizational goals. Goals are considered from three perspectives—environmental constraints, system goals, and goals of individual participants. The role of management in setting goals and developing programs for their accomplishment is discussed. The problems of measuring the organization's performance in achieving its goals are also considered.

Environmental Suprasystem

Six

Organizations are subsystems of a broader suprasystem—the environment. They have identifiable but permeable boundaries that separate them from their environment. They receive inputs across these boundaries, transform them, and return outputs. As society becomes more and more complex and dynamic, organizations need to devote increasing attention to environmental forces. This chapter will look at the interrelationships between organizations and their external suprasystem and will consider more specifically the impact of societal forces on business organizations. The following topics are discussed:

Environment, Boundaries, and Organizations
The Societal (General) Environment
The Task (Specific) Environment
More Complex and Uncertain Environments
Organizations Influence Their Environments
Society's View of Business
Social Responsibilities of Business
The Issue of Personal Ethics

Environment, Boundaries, and Organizations

More explicit understanding of environmental impacts on organizations is important for the organization theorist, and it is significant for the practicing manager. Certain principles of organization and/or management may be appropriate for uniform operations in a relatively stable environment. A mass-production organization such as an automobile assembly line might operate most efficiently under a rather rigid hierarchy with precise planning and control and routinization of activities. This approach would also be appropriate for a routine service organization such as the post office. In contrast, other organizations, operating in an uncertain environment and with nonroutine technology, may perform most efficiently under a very different set of principles. A research and development laboratory or a university graduate program, for example, would have a very different environment and would be characterized by a flexible structure, nonroutine activities, and adaptive planning and control processes.

It is therefore essential in applying systems and contingency concepts to the study of organizations and their management to start with the environmental suprasystem rather than with any internal subsystem. "The first step should always be to go to the next higher level of system organization, to study the dependence of the system in question upon the supersystem of which it is a part, for the supersystem sets the limits of variance of behavior of the dependent system." [1]

Open-System View

The organization is an open system that exchanges information, energy, and materials with its environment. For example, the business organization receives inputs of money, people, and other resources; transforms these through its production processes; and exports products or services. The university receives inputs of students and financial and other resources, transforms them, and exports educated graduates and new knowledge. In this view organizations are dependent for their survival and efficiency on an exchange of goods and services with their environment.

This open-system view makes the study of organizations much more difficult than a closed-system perspective. It is simpler to study an organization as a closed system, to concentrate on internal operations, and to dismiss environmental influences. But this can lead to erroneous conclusions.

One point needs clarification. When speaking of organizations as open systems, we should qualify this by saying "relatively" open systems. In fact, most biological organisms and social organizations are "partially open" and "partially closed." Open and closed are a matter of degree. For example, human beings are certainly an open biological system and receive many inputs from their environment. However, we cannot receive all possible inputs and are therefore not totally open. For example, we can hear sounds only within a narrow range. We can see only a narrow spectrum of light rays. Thus we are severely limited with regard to the nature and type of inputs we receive from our environment. Conversely, we have only a limited range of behavioral outputs. The social organization is also "selectively" open to inputs. The organization cannot respond to all possible environmental influences; it must select the inputs it receives, the transformations it

---

1 Daniel Katz and Robert L. Kahn, *The Social Psychology of Organizations,* 2d ed., John Wiley & Sons, Inc., New York, 1978, p. 63.

performs, and the outputs it produces. In effect, it must establish a "domain" for its activities and boundaries that separate it from its external environment.[2]

Organizational Boundaries

The concept of boundaries helps one understand the distinction between open and closed systems. The relatively closed system has rigid, impenetrable boundaries, whereas the open system has permeable boundaries between itself and a broader suprasystem. Boundaries are relatively easily defined in physical and biological systems—they are visible. For example, we can define the physical boundaries of the human body very precisely. However, what happens when we depart from a purely physical description of the boundaries of the human being? How can we describe the sociological and psychological boundaries of human behavior? We must begin to define the boundary between the human being and society in terms of activities or processes rather than physical structures.

This point is even more important when considering social systems such as organizations. They do not have any precise physical boundaries. What are the boundaries of the U.S. Army, General Motors, the Teamsters, or the corner service station? Organizations have no clearly observable boundaries and are open to many inputs and outputs. Generally, those activities necessary for the organization's tranformation process define its boundary.

There are important differences among organizations concerning the degree of permeability. For example, the inner circle of a crime syndicate would generally have very closed, impenetrable boundaries, where people would be screened thoroughly; entering and leaving the system might be very difficult (often in a concrete block in the river). Institutions such as maximum security prisons and some mental hospitals also tend to have tight boundaries. The Communist Party in the United States and other revolutionary groups tend to be closed. In contrast, the boundaries of many other organizations are very permeable. It is not very difficult to become a member of the PTSA (in fact, it is difficult *not* to become a member). The Republican and Democratic parties have few constraints on membership.

The fact that organizations are social institutions composed of people contributes to openness and boundary permeability. People are continually moving back and forth between the environment and the work organization. Few of us spend a large part of our time in a single organization. We have a variety of activities and roles.

The organization is not the total world of the individual; it is not a society. People must fulfill other social roles; besides, society has shaped them in ways which affect their ability to perform organizational tasks. A man has a marital status, ethnic identification,

2 James D. Thompson, *Organizations in Action,* McGraw-Hill Book Company, New York, 1967, pp. 25–38.

religious affiliations, a distinctive personality, friends, to name only a few. . . . Daily, people come contaminated into the organization. [3]

In spite of the fact that boundaries of social organizations are somewhat open and permeable, they do provide a filtering function. Organizational boundaries screen the inputs and outputs. In this sense, the boundaries are barriers to the flow of energy, material, and information. This is a vital function of boundaries because it would be impossible for any organization to deal with *all possible* inputs. Frequently, the boundaries serve to homogenize the inputs so that the organization can deal with them more effectively. For example, elementary schools set forth certain age requirements for entry into the first grade, thus standardizing inputs. Universities generally require graduation from high school with a certain grade point average and course prerequisites. The business organization sets up requirements for employment, again homogenizing the human inputs. And it typically sets forth specifications to standardize raw material inputs.

Boundaries also filter the outputs of the organization. The organization cannot perform an infinite variety of transformation funtions but must restrict itself to certain activities. It therefore can return only certain specific outputs to its environment. The Red Cross requires trainees to pass certain tests before they are certified as lifeguards. A manufacturing company develops quality controls that standardize product outputs. However, it is difficult to be precise about the nature of all outputs. For example, there may be various indirect outputs that are not readily delineated in the input-transformation-output model. As a by-product of its production processes, the manufacturing plant may output waste products that pollute the environment. Even more subtly, a highly autocratic and coercive organization with little regard for human participants may output a great deal of human dissatisfaction.

Furthermore, as we indicated in Chapter 5, there may be internal boundaries or filtering processes that standardize inputs and outputs to the various operating subsystems. For example, in the university various courses (the operating subsystems) frequently have prerequisites that standardize the inputs. Thus, the strategic and coordinative subsystems "buffer" the operating subsystems of the organization from environmental influences. (See Figure 5.4.)

Organizational boundaries perform another vital function. They provide a degree of autonomy and independence for the organization from intrusion of environmental influences. For example, in our society the "private enterprise" system provides substantial autonomy for the business organization. This system allows the individual firm a great deal of discretion in conducting its internal operations as long as it meets broad social goals.

This view can also be transferred to the public sector. The individual organization, such as a school system, must have a certain amount of indepen-

---

3 From *Organizational Analysis: A Sociological View*, by Charles Perrow. Copyright 1970 by Wadsworth Publishing Company, Inc. Reprinted by permission of the publisher, Brooks/Cole Publishing Company, Monterey, California.

dence from environmental intrusions in order to carry out its transformation functions efficiently. The filtering and buffering functions of the organizational boundary are important in maintaining this autonomy.

Boundary-Spanning Components

Environmental forces have a direct impact on the way the organization structures its activities. When the environment is dynamic and heterogeneous, it is usually necessary to establish functional departments within the organization to deal with a specific set of environmental inputs or outputs. In business enterprises many specialized departments have a boundary-spanning function. Purchasing is engaged in receiving material inputs; personnel departments recruit and select employees; market research departments obtain information from the environment. On the output side, sales departments represent the major boundary-spanning component. Public relations departments are concerned with providing informational outputs to the environment that will enhance the reputation and prestige of the organization.

Generally speaking, the more heterogeneous and dynamic the environment, the more complex and differentiated the internal structuring of the organization. We see many examples of this. As environmentalists and other groups have become more vociferous and influential, companies have responded by establishing new environmental or ecology departments to deal with these specific groups. Most universities have established separate research offices to coordinate research grants from governmental agencies and private organizations. Hospitals establish special departments to coordinate their activities with Medicare and Medicaid, insurance companies, and other health care organizations.

These boundary-spanning positions are often stressful. They are caught in the middle between the demands made on them by their own organization and the requirements imposed by environmental forces.

In effect the BRP (boundary role person) is both the influencer and the recipient of influence from insiders and outsiders. This basic characteristic leads potentially to higher levels of role conflict and tension for the BRP than for other organization members; influences his approach to and manner of bargaining, and the outcomes he achieves; has implications for how the internal constituents of his organization perceive, evaluate, and trust him; affects his job satisfaction; and influences the strength of his organization bonds. [4]

For example, the sales department may have conflicts in responding to the needs of customers while recognizing the requirements for efficient production. The United States representative to the United Nations frequently has problems

---

[4] J. Stacy Adams, "The Structure and Dynamics of Behavior in Organizational Boundary Roles," in Marvin D. Dunnette (ed.), *Handbook of Industrial and Organizational Psychology*, Rand McNally College Publishing Company, Chicago, 1976, p. 1178.

of responding to contradictory demands. The union bargaining agent must represent the workers but also be responsive to the needs of the employer. At the same time that the boundary-spanning components must represent their organizations, in order to be effective they must be sensitive to the attitudes, needs, beliefs, goals, and aspirations of the environmental groups with which they are dealing.

The
Societal (General)
Environment

In the broadest sense, the environment is everything external to the organization's boundaries. However, it may be useful to think of the environment in two ways: (1) the societal *(general)* environment, which affects all organizations in a given society, and (2) the task *(specific)* environment, which affects the individual organization more directly.[5]

Many forces at the societal, general, or macro environmental level influence organizations. Frequently we take these conditions as given with little recognition of the ways they affect the internal operations of organizations.

In the United States we take for granted a whole set of cultural conditions which permit the efficient functioning of complex organizations—such as literacy, authority relations, and an emphasis upon achievement as a basis of judging people rather than characteristics ascribed at birth. But it is a mistake to take these conditions for granted, for they explain a good deal about our society and its organizations.[6]

A number of classification schemes have been suggested for environmental characteristics that affect all organizations.[7] (See Figure 6.1 for a composite framework.) These characteristics provide a homogenizing framework for businesses, unions, governmental agencies, and all other organizations. For example, although most of our large state universities do operate in different specific environments (the individual state), they have many similar characteristcs. Professors and students find that the Universities of Minnesota, Washington, and California have many more similarities than differences. City governments throughout the United States have similar structures and processes. Public school systems in New Jersey and Oregon have many similarities. These general environmental charac-

---

5 Richard H. Hall, *Organizations: Structure and Process,* Prentice-Hall, Inc., Englewood Cliffs, N.J., 1972, pp. 297-324; and Richard N. Osborn and James G. Hunt, "Environment and Organization Effectiveness," *Administrative Science Quarterly,* June 1974, pp. 231-246.

6 Perrow, op. cit., p. 94

7 See, for example, Hall, op. cit., pp. 298–306; Richard N. Farmer and Barry M. Richman, *Comparative Management and Economic Progress,* Cedarwood Publishing Company, Bloomington, Ind., 1970, pp. 25–31; Anant R. Negandhi (ed.), *Environmental Settings in Organizational Functioning,* Comparative Administration Research Institute, Kent State University, Kent, Ohio, 1970; and Billy J. Hodge and Herbert J. Johnson, *Management and Organizational Behavior,* John Wiley & Sons, Inc., 1970, pp. 65–83.

Figure 6.1   General Environmental Characteristics for Organizations

---

Cultural. Including the historical background, ideologies, values, and norms of the society. Views on authority relationships, leadership patterns, interpersonal relationships, rationalism, science, and technology define the nature of social institutions.

Technological. The level of scientific and technological advancement in society. Including the physical base (plant, equipment, facilities) and the knowledge base of technology. Degree to which the scientific and technological community is able to develop new knowledge and apply it.

Educational. The general literacy level of the population. The degree of sophistication and specialization in the educational system. The proportion of the people with a high level of professional and/or specialized training.

Political. The general political climate of society. The degree of concentration of political power. The nature of political organization (degrees of decentralization, diversity of functions, etc.). The political party system.

Legal. Constitutional considerations, nature of legal system, jurisdictions of various governmental units. Specific laws concerning formation, taxation, and control of organizations.

Natural Resource. The nature, quantity, and availability of natural resources, including climatic and other conditions.

Demographic. The nature of human resources available to the society; their number, distribution, age, and sex. Concentration or urbanization of population is a characteristic of industrialized societies.

Sociological. Class structure and mobility. Definition of social roles. Nature of the social organization and development of social institutions.

Economic. General economic framework, including the type of economic organization—private versus public ownership; the centralization or decentralization of economic planning; the banking system; and fiscal policies. The level of the investment in physical resources and consumption characteristics.

---

teristics have an important effect in determining the resources available for inputs, the specific mission, the most appropriate transformation processes, and acceptability of organizational outputs.

Climate for Creating Organizations

In the United States the environmental characteristics set forth in Figure 6.1 are generally favorable to the growth of diverse, complex social organizations. Stinchcombe suggests that the key societal conditions favorable to this process are *(a)* general literacy and specialized advanced schooling, *(b)* urbanization, *(c)* a money economy, *(d)* political change, *(e)* the density of social life, including especially an already rich organizational life. [8] This model suggests that a society with many complex, diverse organizations will find it easier to create new organizations and new organizational forms. Reflecting back over the past century, we can see this process working in our society. Development of the corporate form, conglom-

---

8 Arthur L. Stinchcombe, "Social Structure and Organizations," in James G. March (ed.), *Handbook of Organizations,* Rand McNally & Company, Chicago, 1965, p. 150.

erates, multinational businesses, multiversities, labor unions, complex hospital systems, and governmental organizations such as the Tennessee Valley Authority, the National Aeronautics and Space Administration, and the Environmental Protection Agency are examples. There is every evidence that this process is continuing, with more organizations being spawned and nurtured to meet social needs. At the same time, many organizations do not survive the changing conditions and go out of existence.

The Task (Specific) Environment

The individual organization, while operating in the general environmental setting set forth above, may not be directly influenced by nor can it respond to all of these forces. The **task environment** is defined as the more specific forces which are relevant to the decision-making and transformation processes of the individual organization.[9] The general environment is the same for all organizations in a given society. The task environment is different for each organization.

The distinction between the general environment and the task environment is not always clear-cut and is continually changing. Forces in the general environment are continually "breaking through" into the task environment of the specific organization. "Even beyond the task environment there are environmental factors and phenomena which may affect the organization (and be affected by it). Clearly, the environment is a continuum in which relevance is a matter of degree."[10] For example, universities have traditionally been able to maintain barriers to external forces (the ivory tower) and have restricted their task environment to a limited range of factors. Increasingly, forces from the general environment, such as international conflicts, political activities and minority and women's rights movements, have become relevant forces in their task environment. Business organizations have had to consider many broader social conditions, such as civil rights movements and environmental pollution, as being within their relevant task environment. The major components in the task environment for the typical business organization are shown in Figure 6.2.

Figure 6.3 shows the relationship between the general and task environments and the organizational system for an industrial firm. The figure also shows the strategic, coordinative, and operating subsystems of the organization. The strategic subsystem is a primary boundary-spanning component of the organization and buffers the inputs into the coordinative and operating subsystems. The operating subsystem or technical core must receive and transmit filtered (standardized and homogenized) inputs and outputs to perform the transformation

---

9 William R. Dill, "Environment as an Influence on Managerial Autonomy," *Administrative Science Quarterly*, March 1958, pp. 409–443.
10 Hans B. Thorelli, "Organization Theory: An Ecological View," *Academy of Management Proceedings*, Washington, D.C., 1967, p. 69.

**Figure 6.2   Relevant Components of the Task Environment for a Typical
Industrial Firm**

Customer Component
  Distributors of product or service
  Actual users of product or service

Suppliers Component
  New materials suppliers
  Equipment suppliers
  Product parts suppliers
  Labor supply

Competitor Component
  Competitors for suppliers
  Competitors for customers

Socio-political Component
  Government regulatory control over the industry
  Public political attitude towards industry and its particular product
  Relationship with trade unions with jurisdiction in the organization

Technological Component
  Meeting new technological requirements of own industry and related industries in production
  of product or service
  Improving and developing new products by implementing new technological advances in the
  industry

Robert B. Duncan, "Characteristics of Organizational Environments and Perceived Environmental Uncertainty," *Administrative Science Quarterly*, September 1972, p. 315.

functions effectively. Conceptually, there is a series of permeable boundaries,
moving from the general environment to the operating subsystem, that serve to
filter both inputs and outputs.

The "Perceived" Environment

The task environment has an impact on the goals and values, structure,
technology, human relationships, and managerial processes within organizations.
But the cause-effect relationship is not simple or clear-cut. The "objective" or
factual characteristics of the environment affect organizations, but the perceptions
and beliefs of internal members, particularly managers as decision makers, are
equally important. Information from the outside is passed through perceptive and
cognitive (thinking) processes that result in decisions affecting internal characteristics of the organization. Figure 6.4 illustrates this process.

Organizations engage in many activities that attempt to provide more
accurate information concerning their environments. They engage in long-range
forecasting of economic, technological, and social trends. They have market research staffs that attempt to ascertain changing consumer requirements and preferences. They hire legislative representatives and lobbyists to keep informed about
governmental actions. They keep close tabs on competitors. They engage in many

Figure 6.3   Relationship of General and Task Environments to the Organizational System

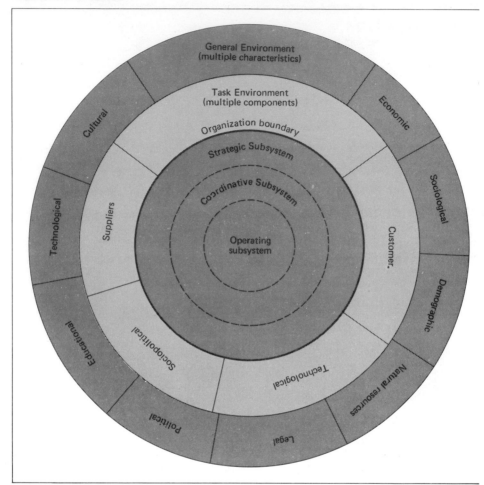

activities in order to acquire more information and reduce their uncertainties. But all of this "factual" information must still be filtered and interpreted by the human mind. Managers in two different organizations in the same industry may have differing views of that environment. These perceptual differences help explain the variations in organization design and managerial practices within the same industry or field.[11]

11 See for example, Robert B. Duncan, "Characteristics of Organizational Environments and Perceived Environmental Uncertainty," *Administrative Science Quarterly,* September 1972, pp. 313–327; H. Kirk Downey, Don H. Hellriegel, and John W. Slocum, Jr., "Environmental Uncertainty; the Construct and Its Application," *Administrative Science Quarterly,* December 1975, pp. 613–629; George P. Huber, Michael J. O'Connell, and Larry L. Cummings, "Perceived Environmental Uncertainty: Effects of Information and Structure," *Academy of Management Journal,* December 1975, pp. 725–740; and Jay Galbraith, *Designing Complex Organizations,* Addison-Wesley Publishing Company, Reading, Mass., 1973.

Figure 6.4 Managerial Perceptions of the Environment

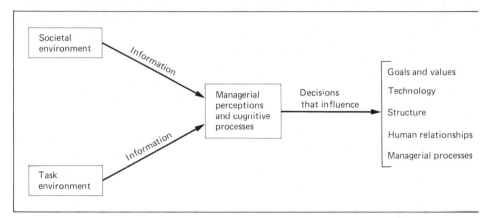

More Complex and Uncertain Environments

There is increasing evidence that the environment is becoming more dynamic and uncertain in our society. A close look at the general environmental characteristics shown in Figure 6.3 suggests that each involves an accelerating rate of change. Technological conditions are changing rapidly; major cultural and social changes are under way; and so on. "A main problem in the study of organizational change is that the environmental contexts in which organizations exist are themselves changing, at an increasing rate, and towards increasing complexity." [12] Emery and Trist suggest that the environments of organizations are moving from "placid, randomized" to "turbulent fields." Many writers, such as Alvin Toffler in *Future Shock,* suggest the increasing turbulence in modern societies.

The acceleration of change in our time is, itself, an elemental force. This accelerative thrust has personal and psychological, as well as sociological consequences. . . . *Future Shock* is a time phenomenon, a product of the greatly accelerated rate of change in society. It arises from the superimposition of a new culture on an old one. It is culture shock in one's own society. [13]

Organizations of the future will be even more subject to external forces and must be prepared to adapt. [14] This is evident from current experiences. Auto-

12 F. E. Emery and E. L. Trist, "The Causal Texture of Organizational Environments," *Human Relations,* February 1965, p. 21.

13 Alvin Toffler, *Future Shock,* Random House, Inc., New York, 1971, pp. 2 and 11.

14 Shirley Terreberry, "The Evolution of Organizational Environments," *Administrative Science Quarterly,* March 1968, pp. 590–613.

mobile companies are hearing more directly not only from customers concerning safety and performance, but also from "environmentalists" concerning air pollution. The hospital is being called on to expand its boundaries and to deal with the total health care needs of people in the community. On all fronts, organizations are facing a more heterogeneous and uncertain suprasystem.

This growing environmental turbulence creates many problems for organizations. We have suggested that organizations attempt to reduce or minimize environmental uncertainties in a number of ways, such as routinization of inputs and outputs and obtaining more accurate information. In a placid environment this process is not difficult. The organization need only respond to a limited number of inputs, which are relatively static over time. It can develop specific policies, rules, and regulations to deal with routine events. It can operate with a rigid structure, clearly defined hierarchy, and specific roles for all participants. In effect, it can become a highly structured bureaucracy and can operate effectively and efficiently *as long as the environment remains placid.* However, in a turbulent environment this form is not viable. The organization must develop a more adaptive-responsive system. Old principles of organization and management, geared to a placid environment, are no longer appropriate. Buckley suggests this difference:

Complex adaptive systems are open systems in intimate interchange with an environment characterized by a great deal of shifting variety ("booming, buzzing confusion") and its constraints (its structure of causal interrelations). The concept of equilibrium developed for closed physical systems is quite inappropriate and usually inapplicable to such a dynamic situation. Rather, a characteristic resultant is the elaboration of organization in the direction of the less probable and the less inherently stable. [15]

A word of caution. We should not get carried away in overemphasizing environmental turbulence. All organizations are not (nor will they be) operating in a dynamic setting. Some organizations, and some components and functions within organizations, are able to establish boundaries for their activities that allow them to operate within a more placid environment. We do not see a demise of the more routinized, structured organization in all fields. Systems concepts and contingency views consider the task environment as one of the key forces affecting the organization and its management. Task environments will be significantly different; therefore, the most appropriate structures and processes should vary among organizations.

Interorganizational Relationships

In modern societies, the environment itself is increasingly composed of other organizations. In developing societies the environment is characterized by informal social institutions. In an organizationally rich society, the environment of any one organization is composed of many other organizations.

15 Walter Buckley (ed.), *Modern Systems Research for the Behavioral Scientist,* Aldine Publishing Company, Chicago, 1968, p, 509.

The development of a comprehensive theory of interoganizational relations is still in its infancy. [16] In the past, management and organization theory has
concentrated on the individual organization and has been primarily concerned
with internal relationships. Classical economic theory provides an idealized model
of interrelationships between organizations—the free marketplace. In this view,
the marketplace and the pricing mechanism determine the relationships between
firms. However, in a complex society of many organizations, we need to develop
new means for interorganizational integration.

Organizational study has a long way to go before it will do justice to the crucial question
of the organization of organizations. The importance of this problem should not be underestimated. Modern society is composed more and more of larger and larger organizations. Society has long recognized that it cannot leave economic interaction to the free
play of market forces because this might not lead these organizations to pursue a course
that will bring the greatest happiness to the greatest number. The same holds for interaction among organizations that do not pursue economic goals, and for the non-economic
interactions of economic organizations. Modern society has found it necessary to build
more and more instruments to regulate this interaction to encourage increase not only in
the effectiveness and satisfaction within each one but also of the relations among them. [17]

There has been an increase in the development of new organizational
forms that integrate the activities of existing complex organizations. For example,
the construction of giant hydroelectric dams requires the combined efforts of several large construction companies, as did the construction of the Alaskan pipeline.
Space exploration requires the integration of numerous governmental agencies
and private contractors. The development of multistate port authorities, region-
wide waste disposal programs, area transportation systems, and regional health
services programs all require new interorganizational arrangements. Many of the
major social and environmental problems facing our society cannot be dealt with
by an individual organization. They require the combined efforts of many complex organizations, often both public and private. [18]

Over the past century we have learned a great deal about the design and
management of complex organizations. This knowledge will serve as the foundation for understanding and dealing with interorganizational relationships. Many
of the concepts we will discuss in later sections of this book are important for these
issues. In looking at interorganizational relationships we are expanding the
boundaries of the system under consideration to include many organizations
(rather than one).

16 William M. Evan, "The Organization-Set: Toward a Theory of Interorganizational Relations," in
James D. Thompson (ed.), *Approaches to Organizational Design,* University of Pittsburgh Press,
Pittsburgh, 1966, pp. 175-191.

17 Amitai Etzioni, *Modern Organizations,* Prentice-Hall, Inc., Englewood Cliffs, N.J., 1964, pp.
112–113.

18 Andrew H. Van de Ven, "On the Nature, Formation, and Maintenance of Relations Among Organizations," *Academy of Management Review,* October 1976, pp. 24–36.

One of the consequences of environmental turbulence and the increase in number and types of organizations is more interorganizational conflict. Increasingly, social conflict takes the form of one organization against another, corporation versus labor union, business versus organized consumer groups, and environmentalist groups versus public utilities.

We need new social mechanisms that provide the means for reduction and resolution of conflict between organizations. The current system of competition and legal means of conflict resolution appear to be inflexible and inadequate. We need to design new means for collaboration. Many of the concepts that organizations utilize to confront and deal with internal conflict may be appropriate for dealing with interorganizational conflict. Approaches such as team building, program management, participative management, legitimized bargaining, and integrated planning may provide the foundation for handling interorganizational conflicts.

Organizations Influence Their Environments

So far we have looked at environmental-organizational relationships as a one-way street; organizations react to external forces as if they were passive systems. A counterview suggests that the organization is *proactive* in selecting the environment within which it will operate and continually attempts to shape that environment to accomplish its goals. "To no small degree, an organization's environment is an arbitrary invention of the organization itself. The organization selects the environments it will inhabit, and it subjectively defines the environment it has selected." [19] Weick suggests that organizations are always proactive and uses the term "enacted environment" to indicate that people create the environment, to which the system then adapts. [20] This two-way influence process between environment and organization is evident in many situations. The business firm determines a market niche for its products or services. It may diversify into new product markets or expand into new geographic regions. The university makes many decisions that determine its environment. What types of educational programs does it offer? Does it have a law, medical, or business school? Does it emphasize teaching or research? The hospital also has discretion in its selection of environments. What geographic area should it cover? Should it treat short- or long-term patients? What kinds of facilities and equipment will it have in order to treat various types of illnesses? Will it engage in preventive health care as well as treatment? Every organization has some measure of discretion concerning its environment.

Furthermore, once established, the organization tries to manipulate its

19 William H. Starbuck, "Organizations and Their Environments," in Dunnette, op. cit, p. 1078.
20 Karl E. Weick, *The Social Psychology of Organizing,* Addison-Wesley Publishing Company, Reading, Mass., 1969, pp. 27–29 and 63–71.

environment in order to accomplish its purposes. The university influences public school systems to supply high-quality student input. It may negotiate with alumni, other potential donors, and legislatures to obtain financial support. The corporation engages in a major advertising campaign to stimulate demand for its products. It establishes long-term contracts to ensure a supply of raw materials. It may actively seek to influence governmental agencies and legislative bodies.

In the following section we will bring some of the foregoing discussion of the impact of environmental forces on organizations into sharper focus by considering more specifically the relationships between business and society.

Society's View of Business

The esteem in which society has held commercial activities has undergone significant fluctuations. In the medieval period commercial activities were viewed as a necessary evil. This view was gradually transformed, so that entrepreneurs were held in high regard, particularly during the second half of the nineteenth century. During the twentieth century there have been many fluctuations and variations. The regard for business reached a zenith during the 1920s but declined to a very low ebb during the Depression of the 1930s.

Public opinion surveys taken during the mid-1960s suggested a high degree of public acceptance. People regarded business favorably for its accomplishments in providing goods and services, for building up the economy, for providing jobs and good wages. However, there were indications of some misgivings. People were satisfied with the economic output and functioning of the business system, but there was a growing concern about the social consequences of business activities.

Recent public opinion surveys conducted by the Opinion Research Corporation and Louis Harris and Associates indicate more societal disenchantment with the performance of business. There is considerably lower public approval of the performance of corporations and business leaders than there was in the mid-1960s.

This skepticism is not directed exclusively at business organizations. There is evidence of a loss of public confidence in the performance of most institutions: business, government, education, courts, labor unions, religion, and the scientific community. Although we cannot begin to assess all the reasons for this growing suspicion of organizations and institutions in our society, the previous discussions suggest some of the possible roots of the problem. During periods of increasing environmental turbulence, it is very difficult for established organizations to respond and adapt. Organizations, by their very nature, routinize and standardize their operations and screen environmental inputs in order to operate effectively. In a sense, they are "conservative" and resistors of change. This also represents a source of strength because they provide stability.

Organizations have great difficulty in responding to all of the demands posed by society, many of which are not well articulated and are often in conflict with each other. This is occurring not only for private corporations, but for public agencies as well. For example, in our community there are many contradictory pressures on the municipally owned Seattle City Light. Customers demand more and improved electrical service. At the same time, ecology groups are strongly resisting the construction of new hydroelectric facilities that may have a deleterious effect on the natural environment. The apparently simple answer of moving to fuel-fired generation of power or nuclear power raises a number of other issues. These means of power generation also may create major environmental pollution. Electric utilities, both public and private, throughout the United States are facing confrontation with these divergent and conflicting forces within the community.

Frequently social demands outrun the ability of organizations to respond. In many cases we view social progress as too slow, not because improvements are not being made, but because aspirations outrun our ability to perform.

At any given moment the public must have in mind some criteria, however imprecise, of what constitutes a satisfactory performance by business. The public keeps raising its standards—as, in an achieving society, it should. Trouble develops because the public is not aware of how rapidly it raises its standards. Because it believes its standards are unchanging, it tends to perceive business performance as moving backward. [21]

Society appears to be changing the "rules of the game" for business organizations. No longer will effectiveness be measured exclusively in terms of economic performance. For example, there is a growing interest in the development of national social indicators and a program of social system accounting. [22] Development of such a system of social accounts will help in evaluating the performance of agencies and organizations in the accomplishment of goals. Increasingly, society is demanding that business organizations be responsive to and help alleviate many of the broader social problems, such as poverty, urban blight, and environmental deterioration. These questions raise some major issues concerning the social responsibilities of business and how managers should respond.

Social Responsibilities of Business

The modern business corporation has become a major source of power and influence on the American scene. Over the past 100 years the corporation has

21 Max Ways, "Business Needs to Do a Better Job of Explaining Itself," *Fortune,* September 1972, p. 86.
22 Raymond A. Bauer, *Social Indicators,* The M.I.T. Press, Cambridge, Mass., 1966; U.S. Department of Health, Education, and Welfare, *Toward a Social Report,* Government Printing Office, Washington, D.C., 1969; and Michael Springer, "Social Indicators, Reports, and Accounts: Toward the Management of Society," *The Annals of the American Academy of Political and Social Science,* March 1970, pp. 1–13.

become not only our most important economic institution but also a major force for social change. Although the business sector is often viewed as politically conservative, in many ways it is one of the more radical forces in society. The corporation has become the predominant device for the transformation of science and technology into economically useful goods and services. In performing this economic role the corporation has created significant social changes.

It would be misleading to suggest that business' view concerning its social role has undergone changes only in recent years. However, there appears to be an accelerated trend to consider social responsibilities in an ever-broadening context.

A report on social responsibilities of business by the Committee for Economic Development suggests the following expectations of society regarding the activities of business.

The fact is that the public wants business to contribute a good deal more to achieving the goals of a good society. Its expectations of business have broadened into what may be described as three concentric circles of responsibility.

The *inner circle* includes the clear-cut basic responsibilities for the efficient execution of the economic function—products, jobs, and economic growth.

The *intermediate circle* encompasses responsibility to exercise this economic function with a sensitive awareness of changing social values and priorities: for example, with respect to environmental conservation; hiring and relations with employees; and more rigorous expectations of customers for information, fair treatment, and protection from injury.

The *outer circle* outlines newly emerging and still amorphous responsibilities that business should assume to become more broadly involved in actively improving the social environment. Society is beginning to turn to corporations for help with major social problems such as poverty and urban blight. [23]

The public at large and many businesspeople, particularly in larger corporations, are prepared to accept the social responsibilities indicated in the first two circles. However, when it comes to business responsibilities for solving broader social problems, the issues become blurred. Even the largest corporation can deal with only a limited range of activities and cannot respond to all social needs. Which broad social problems does it assume responsibility for? It must be selective, but what are the criteria for decision making?

Although there are no easy solutions to this question of the extent of business responsibility, we can identify some broad guidelines. Where the corporation is clearly involved in the creation of social problems, such as air and water pollution, it should participate with other agencies in finding ways to ameliorate these harmful effects. On the other hand, some adverse consequences of economic activities are beyond the control of individual corporations. For example, product breakthroughs may make individual firms or entire industries obsolete. The social

23 *Social Responsibilities of Business Corporations,* A Statement by the Research and Policy Committee, Committee for Economic Development, New York, June 1971, p. 15.

consequences of the resulting unemployment may be devastating to an entire community. Yet, the company involved may be unable to cope with the situation.

Business is directly, but not exclusively, involved in social problems such as urban renewal, civil rights movements, energy conservation, and environmental improvement. These massive and complex domestic tasks require cooperative efforts on the part of business and government. Increasingly, business has been joining with other agencies—particularly federal, state, and local governmental units—in attempting to meet these problems. While we might not expect business managers to take the total responsibility on themselves to deal with these broader social problems, they should not close their eyes to the need for social change and should not resist programs that are directed toward social improvement. Active cooperation with governmental agencies in dealing with social issues is one of the emerging responsibilities of business.

There have been many recent pressures for businesses, particularly large corporations, to develop more precise means of measuring their "social accountability." A number of large corporations have initiated a *corporate social audit.* They "are looking into ways of measuring their performance in activities that affect the society around them or at least assess the true costs of such programs."[24] The social audit would be directed toward spelling out more precisely those areas in which the corporation contributes to social betterment that do not normally appear in traditional financial statements. What has the company done about pollution control? Consumer protection? Community development? It should be emphasized that the concept and practical application of the corporate social audit are still in their infancy. There are many difficulties and controversies involved. For example, what type of information should be included and how should it be reported? So far the primary emphasis has been on measuring the actual costs to the corporation of dealing with social issues. Little has been done to measure benefits. However, in spite of the difficulties in application, the concept of the corporate social audit is important. It is a first step in making the business organization more directly accountable for its performance in social endeavors.

In a recent Committee for Economic Development survey, nearly one half of the corporations responding thought that social audits would be mandatory in the future.[25] The Securities and Exchange Commission is considering this issue and in the future may establish requirements for social accountability reporting. Various professional accounting associations have established committees and study groups to consider standards for measuring business social performance.

[24] "The First Attempts at a Corporate 'Social Audit,'" *Business Week,* Sept. 23, 1972, p. 88. For a more comprehensive discussion, see Raymond A. Bauer and Dan H. Fenn, Jr., *The Corporate Social Audit,* The Russell Sage Foundation, New York, 1972; and John J. Corson and George A. Steiner, *Measuring Business's Social Performance: The Corporate Social Audit,* Committee for Economic Development, New York, 1974.

[25] Corson and Steiner, op. cit., pp. 36–37.

Environmental
Improvement

There is a growing concern today over the deterioration of the natural environment. Water and air pollution, accumulation of solid wastes, creation of radioactive materials, oil spills, and numerous cases of poisoning of humans, other animals, and plant life are clearly evident. There has been a gradual change in attitudes and views concerning the ecosystem. Traditionally, we have viewed nature as available for human exploitation; resources were to be used for our betterment. Science and technology accelerated this process. Resources—trees, animals, minerals, agricultural land, water, and air—were plentiful and considered expendable. Greater realization of the important balance between people and nature requires an overall systems view. [26]

The root cause of environmental depredation is not to be found in the "bad" behavior of any one group—businesses, government, or consumers. We are all polluters, and the higher the standard of living we develop, the more adverse consequences to the ecological system result. This obviously raises major question about economic, materialistic, and social progress, as well as other issues. Every industrialized society is facing problems of environmental deterioration, regardless of its political or economic-political system. The United States, Russia, Sweden, and Japan—all with different economic and political systems—are facing similar environmental problems. Radioactive fallout from atomic tests is just as much a pollutant from communist China as from the capitalistic United States. Thus, it is not just a matter of the particular political or economic system but, more fundamentally, our whole relationship with the environment. There is growing evidence that our traditional demands for greater industrialization, a higher standard of living, and more resource utilization have a disastrous effect on the environment.

Meeting environmental issues will require many reevaluations of our priorities and concepts. New ideologies, legal and structural arrangements, and management skills will be necessary to utilize organizational resources, both public and private, to deal with environmental problems and conservation of resources.

The
Issue of
Personal
Ethics

Closely associated with the general organizational issues of social responsibilities is the more specific question of the personal ethics of managers. Publicity from the Watergate investigations raised many questions concerning individual ethics in an organizational context. Throughout the hearings we heard a common theme: "I didn't think it was right, but I went along because it seemed

26 Harold M. Proshansky, William H. Ittelson, and Leanne G. Rivlin (eds.), *Environmental Psychology: Man and His Physical Setting,* Holt, Rinehart and Winston, Inc., New York, 1970, pp. 1–6.

to be for the good of the cause and I perceived that it was what my superior wanted." Subsequent disclosures of questionable business activities, such as illegal campaign contributions, lobbying practices, payoffs to foreign officials, and even intervention in the political affairs of other countries raised many questions concerning ethical behavior.

There is substantial evidence that corporate managers feel considerable pressure to compromise their personal ethics in meeting apparent company requirements. In a recent survey of 238 respondents from a wide variety of industries, Carroll found almost 65 percent agreed with the statement, "managers today feel under pressure to compromise personal standards to achieve company goals." [27] He suggested several interpretations from this survey:

The data suggest that managers experience pressure, real or perceived, to compromise their personal moral standards to satisfy organizational expectations. Furthermore, the data suggest that middle and lower level managers perceive this pressure more than top managers. . . .

The survey data suggest the real possibility that top management can be inadvertently insulated from organizational reality with respect to particular issues. . . .

Finally, the findings support earlier data by suggesting that young managers in business today would have done just what junior members of Nixon's reelection committee did— go along with their bosses to show their loyalty. [28]

Many managers have problems in accommodating their own ethical standards to organizational requirements. We should not be misled into thinking that this only happens in business. It is obvious from Watergate and other disclosures that it occurs in government. It happens in other organizations—hospitals, the military, universities, and unions, for example.

In another survey of 1200 subscribers to *Harvard Business Review,* Brenner and Molander found that there was little general agreement on whether or not the ethical standards in business have improved or deteriorated over the past 16 years. This survey also revealed that the majority of the respondents had experienced a conflict between what was expected of them as efficient managers and what was expected of them as ethical persons. In their conclusions, the authors suggested that in order to improve the ethical climate and reduce conflicts between personal ethics and organizational requirements, changes are necessary in two primary areas, managerial outlook and managerial actions:

Managerial Outlook

You will face ethical dilemmas, created by value conflicts, for which there may be no totally satisfactory resolution. But don't use this condition to rationalize unethical behavior on your part.

27 Archie B. Carroll, "Managerial Ethics: A Post-Watergate View," *Business Horizons,* April 1975, pp. 75-77. Surveys conducted by Pitney-Bowes, Inc., manufacturers of business equipment, and Uniroyal, Inc., producer of rubber and plastic products, revealed similar responses to this question. "The Pressure to Compromise Personal Ethics," *Business Week,* January 31, 1977, p. 107.

28 Ibid., pp. 79–80.

Don't expect ethical codes to help solve all problems. Codes can create a false sense of security and lead to the encouragement of violations.

If you wish to avoid external enforcement of someone else's ethical code, make self-enforcement work.

Don't deceive yourself into thinking you can hide unethical actions.

Managerial Actions

Fair dealing with customers and employees is the most direct way to restore confidence in business morality.

Corporate steps taken to improve ethical behavior clearly must come from the top and be part of the reward and punishment system.

If an ethical code is developed and implemented, have an accompanying information system to detect violations. Then treat violators equitably.

Test decisions against what you think is right rather than against what is expedient.

Don't force others into unethical conduct. [29]

These surveys suggest that ethical behavior must start from the top, and the reward systems within the organization must reflect these values. Even though managers may not directly condone unethical behavior, they may actually force others into such practices through pressures to accomplish unrealistic objectives. Increasingly it will be more difficult for top managers and administrators to escape all responsibility by saying, "I didn't know about or condone such practices, and besides, we have a definite policy against such acts." It is management's responsibility to establish the appropriate moral climate and to reinforce it through direct actions.

But what happens if the organization embarks on a course of action that the individual feels is unethical? Certainly, he or she can leave or perhaps be fired. Traditionally, the only proper course of action for an employee who could not in good conscience accept a superior's "order" has been to resign. But is there any other recourse? Increasingly, the act of "whistle blowing" is occurring in both public and private organizations. "Having decided at some point that the actions of the organization are immoral, illegal, or inefficient, he or she acts on that belief by informing legal authorities or others outside the organization." [30]

Some subordinates do not feel that it is appropriate just to resign and silently steal away. They consider it more ethical to remain with the organization and act as forces for change from within. Obviously, this is a rather drastic move and not likely to find favor with superiors. There is increasing evidence that in public organizations employees do have substantial protection when blowing the whistle, based on the First Amendment's provision that government cannot deny freedom of speech. In private organizations, employees do not have as much

---

29 Steven N. Brenner and Earl A. Molander, "Is the Ethics of Business Changing," *Harvard Business Review,* January–February 1977, p. 71.

30 Kenneth D. Walters, "Your Employees' Right to Blow the Whistle," *Harvard Business Review,* July-August 1975, p. 26.

protection. However, recent court decisions do indicate that these rights are being upheld and expanded.

One of the thorniest issues concerning ethical behavior is related to business practices in other countries. There have been many recent disclosures concerning questionable overseas payoffs.

The disclosure that U.S. corporations operating abroad pay—or are solicited to pay— bribes in order to obtain or engage in business, or to procure favorable tax and other administrative decisions from foreign governments, has opened a Pandora's box of complex and troublesome issues, which affect U.S. foreign relations, national security, and the investment and marketing policies of American international companies. [31]

Although there is substantial criticism of such practices from within the business community, many companies operating overseas suggest that some forms of payoff are a fact of life in many foreign countries and a necessary part of doing business. They suggest that the issue really is the extent and nature of such payoffs. To what extent can business firms hold to a code of ethics based on practices and standards existing within the United States? Must they have "situational ethics" based on the common practices within a given country? This is just one of many new and complex issues facing organizations and managers operating in diverse and complex environments.

Summary

Every organization is dependent on its broader suprasystem for inputs of resources and for acceptance of its outputs. It is therefore essential in applying systems and contingency concepts to the study of organizations and their management to start with the environmental suprasystem rather than with any internal subsystem.

The open-system view suggests that organizations are separated from their environment by a permeable boundary that filters inputs and outputs. Boundaries provide a degree of autonomy and independence for organizations from intrusion of external influences. Organizations utilize boundary-spanning components to deal with specific environmental forces. These boundary-spanning positions are often stressful and subject to conflicting pressures.

It is useful to think of the environment in two ways: (1) the societal (general) environment, which affects all organizations in a given society, and (2) the task (specific) environment, which affects the individual organization more directly. The environment is becoming more dynamic and uncertain, thus creating many problems for organizations.

---

[31] Peter Nehemkis, "Business Payoffs Abroad: Rhetoric and Reality." *California Management Review,* Winter 1975, p. 5.

Society's view of business has undergone significant modifications. In recent years the public image of business has become tarnished. This skepticism is not directed exclusively at business organizations; there is evidence of a loss of public confidence in the performance of most institutions—the "establishment" in general. One of the root causes of this disenchantment is the acceleration of societal change and the difficulties of timely organizational adjustments.

The question of the social responsibilities of business is a matter of growing concern. Traditionally, the role of business was limited to efficient production of goods and services. Increasingly, this role has expanded to include broader social consequences of business activities. One of the most important issues facing our society is the deterioration of the natural environment. Meeting environmental issues and conserving resources will require reevaluation of our concepts and priorities.

There are many difficult issues concerning personal ethics in an organizational context. Many employees feel pressure to compromise their personal ethics. Top managers are responsible for establishing a climate that enhances both individual and organizational social responsibility.

Questions and Problems

1 What is meant by organizational boundaries? Define the boundaries for a specific organization. How permeable are these boundaries?

2 What is meant by the term *boundary-spanning component?* Why are these roles stressful?

3 Select a specific organization and list those forces in the general and task environments that affect it.

4 Do you agree that our general environmental characteristics have been conducive to the development of new organizational forms? Speculate on the possible types of organizations that will emerge in the future.

5 Investigate a specific organization and describe it in terms of the model presented in Figure 6.3.

6 Why are there ambivalent feelings toward business? What are your own attitudes about business?

7 Do you see any evidence of businesspeople accepting greater social responsibilities? Document your answer with examples.

8 Based on your own experience or personal knowledge from friends or family, describe a situation in which there was a perceived conflict between personal ethics and organizational requirements. What were the factors contributing to this conflict and how was it resolved?

9 Why is it necessary to adopt a total system view when dealing with environmental issues? Briefly describe examples of where a subsystem approach has led to environmental depredation.

10 Who should deal with environmental issues? What is the role of the business community?

Organizational Goals

Seven

Formal organizations are contrived social systems designed to accomplish specific purposes. The basic values that underlie goal setting and decision making are a fundamental part of the organizational system. The organization performs some function for society in order to receive resource inputs. And it satisfies certain needs of internal participants in order to maintain their continuing involvement. The organization also has system goals that it strives to achieve. Therefore, goals should be considered from three perspectives—social goals imposed on the organization, system goals, and participant goals. The discussion in this chapter will be structured around the following topics:

The Issue of Values
What Are Goals?
Environmental Determinants of Organizational Goals
Organizational System Goals
Individual Participant Goals
The Role of Management in Goal Setting and Implementation
Measuring Organizational Performance

The Issue of Values

We have indicated that goals and values are one of the integral subsystems of every organization. Values are normative views held by individual human beings (consciously or subconsciously) of what is good and desirable. They provide standards by which people are influenced in their choice of actions. Social values reflect a system of shared beliefs about desired goals and norms for human conduct. In our society we place a high value on "winning" in competitive sports, but we also have social norms that prescribe how a "winner" or "loser" should behave. We get upset when one of our sports heroes (or our opponent) is an "arrogant winner" or a "poor loser."

Organizations appear to hold certain values, but defining them precisely and showing how they influence decision making is difficult. However, there are several broad generalizations. Organizations depend on a minimum level of shared values among internal participants and the external society for their very existence. Deeply ingrained cultural values provide a measure of cohesiveness. Values such as "individual human dignity," "individual property rights," "everyone should work for a living," and "acceptance of legitimate authority" provide a foundation without which organizations could not exist. Every human participant brings a certain set of values to the organization. Value inputs also come from a wide variety of external sources—customers, competitors, suppliers, and other elements of the organization's task environment. Therefore, in dealing with values issues we should consider at least five levels:

Individual values.

Those values held by individuals that affect their actions.

Group values.

Those values held by small informal and formal groups that effect the behavior of individuals and the actions of the organization.

Organizational values.

Those values held by the organization as a whole—a composite of individual, group, total organizational, and cultural inputs.

Values of constituents of the task environment.

Values held by those in direct contact with the organization—customers, suppliers, competitors, governmental agencies, and the like.

Cultural values.

Values held by the entire society.

Depending on specific issues, we might want to consider values from one, several, or all these perspectives. In discussing the goals and values subsystem, we are most concerned with those values that directly affect the internal operations and actions of the organization. But in an open system complete closure is not possible and interactions with the environment are inevitable. this is particularly true with value issues.

Because value issues affect so many levels—the culture, task environment, organization, group, and individual—we will not try to cover them directly in this chapter, but will deal them in the context of discussions of the environmental suprasystem and organizational subsystems. In Chapters 2 and 6 we have already dealt extensively with the evolution of management values as well as cultural values. In later chapters we will consider organizational, group, and individual values and how they affect decision making and behavior. We will try to consider value issues where they count rather than in the abstract. The remainder of this chapter will focus on organizational goals.

What
Are
Goals?

Simply stated, goals represent the desired future conditions that the organization strives to achieve. In this sense, goals include missions, purposes, objectives, targets, quotas, and deadlines. However, the concept of a goal has acquired a variety of meanings, depending on the perspective of the writer. It is sometimes used to legitimize and justify the role of the organization in society (the goal of General Motors is to make automobiles for people to use) or to provide a motive for the organization's activity (General Motors' goal is to make a profit). A goal may also be a specific accomplishment, such as manufacturing 15,000 automobiles during a given time period. In another sense, goals may be considered as the set of constraints that the organization must satisfy, i.e., profit for the stockholders, satisfaction of employees, meeting government demands for "safe" automobiles, pacifying the environmentalists, and meeting customer requirements. [1]

One of the major problems in the analysis of organizational goals is the distinction between official goals and actual operational goals. Official goals are often stated in broad, ambiguous terms to justify the activities of the organization. For example, the official goals of a mental institution may be to treat mental illness. However, the operational goals are those actually pursued. The mental hospital may provide little in the way of treatment and be geared to custodial care of patients.

The type of goals most relevant to understanding organizational behavior are not the official goals, but those that are embedded in major operating policies and the daily decisions of the personnel. . . . These goals will be shaped by the particular problems or tasks an organization must emphasize, since these tasks determine the characteristcs of those who will dominate the organization. [2]

The goals of an organization influence its interactions with the environmental suprasystem and other subsystems. The efforts to achieve goals affect the ability of the organization to receive resource inputs from the broader society and thus legitimize its existence. Goals focus the attention of participants on actions that are organizationally relevant. They provide the standards for measurement of success. They help determine the technologies required and also set the basis for

---

1 Herbert A. Simon, "On the Concept of Organizational Goal," *Administrative Science Quarterly,* June 1964, pp. 1–22.

2 Charles Perrow, "The Analysis of Goals in Complex Organizations," *American Sociological Review,* December 1961, p. 854.

specialization of effort, authority patterns, communication and decision networks, and other structural relationships. The nature of the goals affects the basic character of the organization. Perrow says:

They reflect more readily the uniqueness of organizations and the role of specific influences within the more general technological and structural categories. For goals are the product of a variety of influences, some of them enduring and some fairly transient. To enumerate some of these influences: the personality of top executives, the history of the organization, its community environment, the norms and values of the other organizations with which it deals (e.g., the "mentality of the steel industry"), the technology and structure of the organization, and ultimately the cultural setting. [3]

Management is directly involved with organizational goals. Chief executives generally establish broad institutional goals that help relate the organization to its environment. Management then translates these broad goals into operational objectives and provides means of control to measure the extent of accomplishment. It must continually deal with goal conflicts and find a means of satisfying the interests of many internal and external individuals and groups.

Do Organizations Have Goals?

We have defined organizations as goal-seeking systems. This personalization of the organization—attributing individual human qualities to a social system—is reflected in much of the thinking about organizational goals. Perhaps the origins of this view stem from classical economic theory of the firm, which considered the organization as a single entrepreneur—the goals of the firm and those of the entrepreneur are identical. Similarly, in public agencies the classical approach assumed that goals were determined by legislation and that the primary function of the agency was action planning and implementation. However, in reality there are many organization participants—stockholders, boards of directors, executives, and other employees—whose individual goals affect the activities of the organization. The goal structure of organizations is much more complex than that postulated by traditional economic and administrative theory. But we are left with a dilemma. If we do not accept the entrepreneurial goal as the organization goal, what is the organization goal? Cyert and March set forth this problem as follows:

1 People (i.e., individuals) have goals; collectivities of people do not.
2 To define a theory of organizational decision making, we seem to need something analogous—at the organization level—to individual goals at the individual level. [4]

3 From *Organizational Analysis: a Sociological View* by Charles Perrow. Copyright 1970 by Wadsworth Publishing Company, Inc. Reprinted by permission of the publisher, Brooks/ Cole Publishing Company, Monterey, California.
4 Richard M. Cyert and James G. March, *A Behavioral Theory of the Firm,* Prentice-Hall, Inc., Englewood Cliffs, N.J., 1963, p. 26.

They also suggest a solution to this problem by conceptualizing the organization as a coalition of many participants.

In a business organization the coalition members include managers, workers, stockholders, suppliers, customers, lawyers, tax collectors, regulatory agencies, etc. In the governmental organization the members include administrators, workers, appointive officials, elective officials, legislators, judges, clientele, interest group leaders, etc. In the voluntary charitable organization there are paid functionaries, volunteers, donors, donees, etc. [5]

These organizational members have different and frequently conflicting goals. The actual goals of the organization result from a continuous bargaining-learning process. Therefore, organizations do have multiple goals. These goals are frequently not officially stated and are often in conflict. There may be inconsistencies and ambiguities. The goal set of the organization is continually changing as a result of this learning-adapting process.

We need to look more closely at the forces influencing organizational goal setting. In order to do so, we will consider goals from three primary perspectives: (1) the environmental level—the constraints imposed on the organization by society; (2) the organizational level— the goals of the organization as a system; and (3) the individual level—the goals of organizational participants. Typically there are goal conflicts among these three levels. However, there must also be a minimum degree of goal compatibility if the organization is to survive.

Environmental Determinants of Organizational Goals

The societal and task environments both have an important impact on organizational goals. Thompson and McEwen suggest that the impact of the environment on organizational goal setting is influenced by the nature of the interaction: (1) competition, (2) bargaining, (3) co-optation, and (4) coalition. [6]

The *competitive* relationship exists where two organizations are competing for the support of a third party. This is illustrated by business firms that compete for material resources, labor inputs, and customers. Government agencies compete for tax dollars; universities compete for students and faculty; and hospitals compete for patients.

Bargaining involves direct negotiations between organizations. Collective bargaining is a prime example of management bargaining directly with the labor union. In a bargaining situation, each party must modify its own goals in response

5 Ibid., p. 27.

6 James D. Thompson and William J. McEwen, "Organizational Goals and Environment: Goal-Setting as an Interaction Process," *American Sociological Review*, February 1958, pp. 23–31.

to the needs of the other party. The business may want to minimize labor costs, whereas the labor union wants to maximize the earnings of employees. To reach agreement, both often modify their goals.

Co-optation involves a more complicated process. "Co-optation has been defined as the process of absorbing new elements into the leadership or policy-determining structure of an organization as a means of averting threats to its stability or existence."[7] For example, the business organization has on its board of directors representatives of banks or other financial institutions. Doctors are frequently members of the board of trustees of hospitals. University administrators have traditionally shared authority with the faculty. Increasingly, students are being included on university committees. Representatives of environmentalist groups are appointed to governmental committees. By giving "outsiders" positions of responsibility, the organization makes them more aware of its problems and hopes to create common understanding. But co-optation also has an important influence on the goals of the organization itself. "Co-optation further limits the opportunity for one organization to choose its goals arbitrarily or unilaterally."[8]

Coalition between organizations requires an even further modification of the goals. "The term coalition refers to a combination of two or more organizations for a common purpose. Coalition appears to be the ultimate or extreme form of environmental conditioning of organizational goals."[9] Coalition is, of course, an important aspect of the political process. Another example occurs when a number of cities and communities develop common transportation facilities or waste disposal systems. Coalition suggests that each organization modify its goals to accommodate those of other parties.

Public and private organizations frequently operate in different environments and have different types of interactions. The private enterprise is more likely to emphasize competitive and bargaining relationships with environmental forces through the market mechanism. The public organization, such as the Department of Health, Education, and Welfare or a local school district, is more likely to engage in co-optation and coalition formation. The public school system must deal with a variety of external forces—legislatures, taxpayers, teachers' professional associations, the PTSA, and the public at large— to obtain support. Co-optation and coalition formation are likely to be most effective in developing and maintaining these relationships. Of course, this distinction between private and public organizations is not absolute. Most organizations use all four forms, but in varying degrees.

Competition, bargaining, co-optation, and coalition are means whereby the organization adapts to forces in its environment. This adapting process fre-

---

7 Ibid., p. 27.

8 Ibid., p. 28.

9 Ibid., p. 28

quently modifies the organization's own goals and also requires adjustments in the means for their accomplishment.

Organizational System Goals

Organizational system goals pertain to the purposes and desired conditions that the organization seeks as a distinct entity. Self-perpetuation, stability of operations, a high rate of return, growth, satisfaction of participants, enhancement of position in field, technological leadership, and innovation are examples of system goals.

Organizations have multiple goals rather than a single goal, and this goal set is determined in response to both external and internal forces. Oganizations, like other open systems, display the characteristic of equifinality—they generally have alternative means for the accomplishment of system objectives. [10] The organization has substantial discretion concerning the goals it attempts to satisfy and also alternatives within its transformation functions as to the means for their accomplishment. However, it must operate within the constraints imposed by environmental forces and the need to maintain the contributions of internal participants.

Nature of Organizational Goals

Wide variations in activities make it difficult to delineate any goal set appropriate for all organizations. In business organizations there is a trend toward more explicitly defining the multiple goals necessary for effective and efficient long-term operations. Peter Drucker was among the first to emphasize the importance of "managing by objectives." He suggested that the enterprise's emphasis on short-term profits alone could lead to adverse long-run consequences. "Objectives are needed in every area where performance and results directly and vitally affect the survival and prosperity of the business." [11] He advocated that the business set objectives in the following eight areas: (1) market standing, (2) innovation, (3) productivity, (4) physical and financial resources, (5) profitability, (6) manager performance and development, (7) worker performance and attitude, and (8) public responsibility.

While this listing of important system goals is appropriate for most business organizations, it is not readily transferable to other organizational types. Gross provides a more generalized model suitable for all organizations as shown in Figure 7.1. This listing recognizes that every organization has multiple goals.

10 Daniel Katz and Robert L. Kahn, *The Social Psychology of Organizations,* 2d ed., John Wiley & Sons, Inc., New York, 1978, p. 30.
11 Peter F. Drucker, *The Practice of Management,* Harper & Brothers, Publishers, New York, 1954, p. 63.

Figure 7.1   Major Categories of Organizational Goals

Satisfaction of interests. Organizations exist to satisfy the interests (or needs, desires, or wants) of various people, both members and outsiders. These interests are multiple, hard to identify, and overlapping. The satisfaction (or dissatisfaction) of these interests may vary by its intensity and by the location and number of people involved. This category of purposes is close to what is often referred to as *welfare, utility, benefit,* or *payoff.*

Output of services or goods. The output of an organization is composed of those products which it makes available for use by clients. These products may consist of services (tangible or nontangible) or goods. The quality and quantity of any product may sometimes be expressed in monetary as well as physical units. From the viewpoint of the organization as a whole, the output of any unit or individual is an intermediate or partial product rather than an end product.

Efficiency or profitability. When available inputs are perceived as scarce, attention is directed toward making efficient use of inputs relative to output. Since there are many ways of calculating input and output and of relating the two, there are many varieties of input-output objectives. Some of them are referred to as "efficiency" or "productivity." "Profitability" is applicable whenever output as well as input may be expressed in monetary terms.

Investment in organizational viability. In a minimal sense viability means the survival of an organization, without which no other purposes are feasible. In a fuller sense it refers to an organization's growth. In either sense viability requires the diversion of inputs from the production of output and their investment in physical, human and organizational assets.

Mobilization of resources. In order to produce services or goods and to invest in viability, an organization must mobilize resources that may be used as inputs. Because of the difficulties of obtaining scarce resources from the environment, "mobilization logic" may differ from "use logic."

Observance of codes. Codes include both the formal and informal rules developed by the organization and its various units and the prescribed behaviors imposed upon the organization by law, morality and professional ethics. These codes may be expressed in terms of what is expected or what is prohibited. In either case, code observance purposes are usually expressed in terms of tolerated margins of deviation.

Rationality. Rationality here refers to action patterns regarded as satisfactory in terms of desirability, feasibility, and consistency. *Technical* rationality involves use of the best methods developed by science and technology. *Administrative* rationality involves the use of the best methods of governing organizations.

Bertram M. Gross, *Organizations and Their Managing.* The Free Press, New York, 1968, pp. 273–274.

Because of obvious difficulties in developing performance criteria to meet these broad goals, it is necessary to translate them into more specific operational goals that can be measured.

This listing also emphasizes that the organizational goal set is not the same as the goals of any one group of participants, such as the board of directors or trustees, top executives, or other employees. Rather, they are the goals of the organization as a collectivity of all of these and other groups that define the primary characteristics and activities of the organization as a system.

In public organizations, the system goals tend to be more varied and complex than in private enterprises. Furthermore, these goals are often constrained by what is politically feasible. [12] There is greater difficulty in specifying goals, in quantifying performance indicators, and in resolving conflicts among objectives.

[12] Hal G. Rainey, Robert W. Backoff, and Charles H. Levine, "Comparing Public and Private Organizations," *Public Administration Review,* March/April 1976, pp. 239–240.

Greater emphasis on the delineation of system goals can be useful for the organization. They provide a sense of direction and purpose that is essential to long-run effectiveness. They help the organization identify the various interest groups and how they place constraints on and contribute to organizational activities. They provide the basis for the entire planning process, both strategic and operational. They can help in motivating participants toward goal accomplishment. They provide the broad standards against which the organization can measure its performance. There is increasing evidence that more explicit attention to the establishment of goals does lead to more effective performance and realization of goals. This is true for individuals as well as for organizations. [13]

The Goal-Setting Process

While the above discussion suggests the nature of organizational goals, it does not provide much insight into the goal-setting process. It was suggested earlier that organizations are learning, adapting systems that have multiple goals. This view is in contrast to that of the organization as a mechanistic, single-goal maximizing system. The goal-setting process is primarily a political process. [14] Goals are formulated as a result of bargaining among the various interest groups. Thus, stockholders require profits, employees want wages and favorable working conditions, managers desire power and prestige, and customers demand quality products. The membership of participating groups and their power change over time; therefore, the goals of the organization are continually shifting to reflect these changes. Because the demands of the various participating groups are frequently in conflict, it is rarely possible to maximize the goals of any one individual or group. Rather, the organization seeks to "satisfy" the goals of all participants in order to maintain their participation.

Goals are also continually being modified because of changing aspiration levels. The business that has achieved its sales quota within a given year will usually adjust its aspirations upward. Lack of success will cause the organization to seek alternative means, or if this is unsuccessful, to adjust the goal downward.

Means-Ends Chain

We have suggested that overall goal statements are usually very general. They are not operational because there are no accepted criteria for determining

---

13 John M. Ivancevich, "Effect of Goal Setting on Performance and Job Satisfaction," *Journal of Applied Psychology,* October 1976, pp. 605–612.

14 Richard M. Cyert and James G. March, op. cit. Their book is a comprehensive extension and elaboration based on a number of writings in the field such as Chester I. Barnard, *The Functions of the Executive,* Harvard University Press, Cambridge, Mass., 1938; Herbert A. Simon, *Administrative Behavior* 3d ed., The Free Press, New York, 1976; and James G. March and Herbert A. Simon, *Organizations,* John Wiley & Sons, Inc., New York, 1958. For an extension of these views see E. Eugene Carter, "The Behavioral Theory of the Firm and Top-Level Corporate Decision," *Administrative Science Quarterly,* December 1971, pp. 413–429.

how particular programs or activities contribute to these goals. It is necessary to translate these broad statements of purpose into operational objectives. [15]

In analyzing goals it is also necessary to decide how they are to be accomplished—the *means* of attainment. In the organization, the relationship between means and ends is hierarchical. Goals established at one level require certain means for their accomplishment. These means then become the subgoals for the next level, and more specific operational objectives are developed as we move down the hierarchy. A fire department has the primary goal of reducing fire losses. The means for attaining this end are prevention of and extinguishing fires. These means then become the goals of the next level in the organization and lead to the creation of two functions—fire prevention and fire fighting. Typical means for accomplishing these goals might be specific programs for location of water hydrants, information to the public, and geographically decentralized fire stations.

The hierarchy of goals has important implications for organization structure. Generally, the division of labor and functional specialization within the organization are based on the means-ends chain. The business organization may have sales, finance, and production departments, each of which has specific subgoals related to its functional area.

Theoretically the rational organization would have perfect integration of the means-ends chain within the hierarchy and through departmental specialization. Typically, however, it is impossible to attain perfect integration. There is usually some disagreement among the organizational units concerning the appropriate means for goal accomplishment. Personal values and biases influence the integration of the means-ends chain.

It is also as true of organizational as of individual behavior that the means-end hierarchy is seldom an integrated, completely connected chain. Often the connection between organization activities and utimate objectives is obscure, or these ultimate objectives are incompletely formulated, or there are internal conflicts and contradictions among the ultimate objectives, or among the means selected to attain them. [16]

Goals at Different Levels

Through the means-ends chain general goals are translated into increasingly specific operational goals. Complex organizations have several administrative levels or subsystems with differing goals and activities.

The *strategic* level relates the activities of the organization to its environmental system. The goals at this level are broad and provide substantial flexibility in the means for their attainment.

15 For further discussion of means and ends see Herbert A. Simon, *Administrative Behavior*, op. cit., pp. 62–66; James G. March and Herbert A. Simon, op. cit., pp. 190–193; Joseph A. Litterer, *The Analysis of Organizations*, John Wiley & Sons, Inc., New York, 1965, pp. 139–142; and R. W. Morell, *Management: Ends and Means*, Chandler Publishing Company, San Francisco, 1969, pp. 5–37.
16 Simon, *Administrative Behavior*, p. 64.

The *coordinative* subsystem translates the broad goals developed at the strategic level into more specific operational goals. The primary purposes of this subsystem are related to the coordination of activities between levels and between functions.

The *operating* subsystem is involved in actual task performance. The goals at this level are usually very specific, short-term, and measurable, such as sales and production quotas.

Interdepartmental Goal Conflict

In addition to greater specification of goals through the means-ends chain on a hierarchical basis, subgoals are established for different functional units within the organization. In a correctional institution there are certain sub-units whose primary responsibility is confinement of inmates, while other subunits have a primary goal of rehabilitation. In a business firm the sales department's goal may be increased sales, the production department's goal may be more efficient production, and the research department's goal may be the development of new products.

Differentiation by function frequently leads to interdepartmental conflict. Maximizing the performance of one functional department may lead to sacrificing the goals of another department. Thus, maximizing the confinement goal in correctional institutions may create conflicts with subunits pursuing the rehabilitation goal. This is another reason why the goal structure of the organization is never perfectly rational. The actual goals of the organization are a result of the power interplay and negotiation among different organizational units and individuals.

Goal Displacement

Ascertaining effectiveness in meeting goals can be a difficult problem. When goals can be precisely stated, as frequently is the case at the operating level, measurement is relatively simple. However, with more general goals, the measurement becomes more difficult. For example, how do we measure effectiveness in meeting the university's goals of creation and dissemination of knowledge, as well as public service? By number of graduates? By analysis of their lifetime earnings? By the volume of research publications? By the won/lost record of the football team?

One of the difficulties that organizations face is overemphasis of specific goals where quantification is possible and underemphasis of more abstract, less easily measured goals.

Most organizations under pressure to be rational are eager to measure their efficiency. Curiously, the very effort—the desire to establish how we are doing and to find ways of improving if we are not doing as well as we ought to do—often has quite undesired effects from the point of view of the organizational goals. Frequent measuring can distort the organizational efforts because, as a rule, some aspects of its output are more measurable than the others. Frequent measuring tends to encourage over-production of highly measurable items and neglect of the less measurable ones. [17]

There are other forces that distort the goal structure of organizations. One of the more important is displacement of goals. Goal displacement stems from the need for the organization to differentiate activities and from the process of downward delegation of authority and responsibility.

In order to accomplish their goals, organizations establish a set of procedures or means. In the course of following these procedures, however, the subordinates or members to whom authority and functions have been delegated often come to regard them as ends in themselves, rather than as means toward the achievement of organization goals. As a result of this process, the actual activities of the organization become centered around the proper functioning of organization procedures, rather than upon the achievement of the initial goals. [18]

Merton says that goal displacement occurs because the bureaucratic organization affects participants' personalities and causes them to seek the security of rigid adherence to rules and regulations for their own sake. "Adherence to the rules, originally conceived as a means, becomes transformed into an end-in-itself; there occurs the familiar process of *displacement of goals* whereby an instrumental value becomes a terminal value." [19] Many control systems may be dysfunctional in getting individuals to meet organizational goals. Lawler suggests that bureaucratic behavior "consists of individuals behaving in ways that are called for by the control system, but that are dysfunctional as far as the generally agreed upon goals of the organization are concerned." [20] In many organizations it is a common observation that "the way to screw up the works is to follow every rule and regulation and to adhere completely to the control system." This was the apparent strategy followed by control tower operators at airports when they engaged in a slowdown.

This problem is apparent in many social welfare agencies. For example, strict adherence to the rule of no welfare payments when there is an employable male in the household may create adverse family and social problems and defeat the overall goals of the agency.

This problem is not easily resolved. If organizational members are bound by rigid role prescriptions as well as rules and regulations to guide their

17 Amitai Etzioni, *Modern Organizations,* Prentice-Hall, Inc., Englewood Cliffs, N.J., 1964, p. 9.
18 David L. Sills, "Preserving Organizational Goals," in Oscar Grusky and George A. Miller (eds.), *The Sociology of Organizations,* The Free Press, New York, 1970, p. 227.
19 Robert K. Merton, *Social Theory and Social Structure,* rev. ed., The Free Press, New York, 1957, p. 199.
20 Edward E. Lawler, III, "Control Systems in Organizations," in Marvin D. Dunnette (ed.), *Handbook of Industrial and Organizational Psychology,* Rand McNally College Publishing Company, Chicago, 1976, p. 1254.

activities, and strong sanctions are used to enforce adherence, goal displacement will occur.[21] This organization might work to develop the means-ends chain more adequately so that individual activities are related to ends. Attempts to translate the intangible, abstract goals into more meaningful, desired states of affairs can be helpful. One such approach, management by objectives, will be discussed in a later section of this chapter.

Individual Participant Goals

We turn now to the third level of analysis: the goals of individual participants and their relationship to organizational goals. Organizations are established to accomplish purposes that cannot be accomplished by individual action. It would be simple to assume that organizational goals and individual participant goals are complementary. This in effect was the assumption of classical economic theory and most traditional management theories. Employees were compensated through monetary and other inducements for their participation in meeting organizational goals, thus "presumably assuring that employees will adhere to the organization's goals except in exceptional, i.e., theoretically pathological, cases."[22] This simple assumption of compatibility failed to recognize many bases for conflict between organizational and individual goals. First, people are much more complex than this theory would suggest. We have many needs and aspirations that are not easily met in purely economic terms. Second, the organization itself has a multiple and complex goal set.

The early human relationists saw the need for greater emphasis on human satisfactions as well as on technical effectiveness. "An industrial organization may be regarded as performing two major functions, that of producing a product and that of creating and distributing satisfactions among the individual members of the organization."[23] Although they saw the need for creating greater human satisfaction, it was viewed as a *means* for obtaining better organizational effectiveness rather than as an *end* in itself. Increased satisfaction would lead to more effective organizational goal accomplishment.

There is a trend toward thinking of the *satisfaction of human participants* within organizations not only as a means for organizational effectiveness but also as an *end in itself.*

21 For a discussion of goal displacement and related issues see: Michel Crozier, *The Bureaucratic Phenomenon,* The University of Chicago Press, 1964, Chicago, pp. 175–208.

22 Peer Soelberg, "Structure of Individual Goals: Implications for Organization Theory," in George Fisk (ed.), *The Psychology of Management Decision,* CWK Gleerup Publishers, Lund, Sweden, 1967, p. 16.

23 F. J. Roethlisberger and William J. Dickson, *Management and the Worker,* Harvard University Press, Cambridge, Mass., 1939, p. 552.

We are not merely interested in the economic success or technological efficiency aspects of a system, but also, and more importantly, in its social efficiency aspects. . . . In general, social efficiency entails personal goal attainment on the part of the members at all levels in an organization, and this includes involvement, satisfaction, participation, and other variables associated with intrinsic motives and psychological rewards. [24]

We raise an even more critical issue when we question whether or not organizational goals and human needs are compatible. Many practices that are developed to increase organizational effectiveness may create human dissatisfactions. A high degree of task specialization may lead to technical efficiency but may also create employee boredom and apathy. A rigid authority structure may seem desirable from the organization's standpoint, but the humans may resist.

However, we should not overemphasize the possible conflicts between organizational goals and human satisfaction.

Within limits, happiness heightens efficiency in organizations and, conversely, without efficient organizations much of our happiness is unthinkable. Without well-run organizations our standard of living, our level of culture, and our democratic life could not be maintained. Thus, to a degree, *organizational rationality and human happiness go hand in hand.* But a point is reached in every organization where happiness and efficiency cease to support each other. Not all work can be well paid or gratifying, and not all regulations and orders can be made acceptable. Here we face a true dilemma. [25]

We are not going to assume either that (1) organizational and individual goals are compatible, or (2) that they are incompatible. To a major extent they are both. Without a minimum degree of compatibility, organizations could not exist. But total agreement is impossible and conflicts do exist.

Reciprocation between Individual and Organization

Frequently, a strong bond develops between the individual and the organization. There is a psychological contract that helps fulfill the goals of each.

This process of fulfilling mutual expectations and satisfying mutual needs in the relationship between a man and his work organization was conceptualized as a process of *reciprocation.* Reciprocation is the process of carrying out a psychological contract between person and company or any other institution where one works. It is a complementary process in which the individual and the organization seem to become a part of each other. The person feels that he is part of the corporation or institution and, concurrently, that he is a symbol personifying the whole organization. [26]

24 Basil S. Georgopoulos, "An Open-System Theory Model for Organizational Research," in Anant R. Negandhi (ed.), *Modern Organizational Theory,* The Kent State University Press, Kent, Ohio, 1973, p. 104.
25 Etzioni, op. cit., p. 2.
26 Harry Levinson, *The Exceptional Executive,* Harvard University Press, Cambridge, Mass, 1968, p. 39.

In modern industrial society there has been a loosening of family, small social group, and other psychological ties—causing the work organization to become increasingly important. This psychological contract is even stronger in other countries. In Japan, the employee and the work organization frequently make lifelong commitments to each other.

Several recent research studies suggest the extent of this reciprocation. Lorsch and Morse found that managers adapted to and found personal satisfaction in organizations with very different structures, interpersonal relations, and environmental forces. The organization that was appropriately designed to meet its task requirements and the demands of its environment provided important psychological rewards for members of the organization and led to a high sense of personal competency.[27] Porter and Lawler found that managers were motivated toward organizational goals when they perceived a high probability of rewards based on performance and when they had an appropriate perception of their organizational role. When managers perceived inducements as rewards for good performance, they performed more effectively. High performers also reported significantly greater fulfillment and satisfaction.[28]

The importance of reciprocation becomes apparent when the psychological contract is broken. When the aerospace industry suffered a severe downturn, organizations discharged many long-term employees, including managers and professionals. These employees had developed a high degree of loyalty and attachment to their organizations, and the results of the layoffs were devastating (both psychologically and economically). We might hypothesize that the stronger the bonds of reciprocation, the more severe the problems of adjustment for the individual when these bonds are severed. Many managers, engineers, scientists, and other professionals had great difficulty in accepting the fact of their dismissal. The importance of reciprocation might also explain the strong and unrelenting demand by most faculty members for maintaining the tenure system.

Internalization of Goals

Internalization occurs when the individual develops a personal commitment to meeting organizational goals. It is one of the most effective means of integration because it removes conflicts between organizational goals and individual motivation. It involves a strong commitment of the individual to the organization.

Commitment embodies three separate but closely related component attitudes: (1) a sense of identification with the organizational mission; (2) a feeling of involvement or

---

27 Jay W. Lorsch and John J. Morse, *Organizations and Their Members: A Contingency Approach,* Harper & Row, Publishers, New York, 1974.

28 Lyman W. Porter and Edward E. Lawler, III, *Managerial Attitudes and Performance,* Richard D. Irwin, Inc., and The Dorsey Press, Homewood, III., 1968.

psychological immersion in the organizational duties; and (3) a feeling of loyalty and affection for the organization as a place to live and work, quite apart from the merits of its mission or its purely instrumental value to the individual. [29]

While this internalization represents the ideal match between organizational goals and individual motivations, it is rarely fully achieved. Few participants make a full commitment toward meeting organizational goals. There may be conflicts between the organizational role and other roles that the individual tries to fulfill. This conflict is apparent for many participants, particularly scientists and other professionals. Traditionally, in professions such as medicine and law, activities were carried out in a nonorganizational context in close interpersonal relationship with clients. Early literature on professionalism focused on the pattern of behavior of these independent professionals and how this differed from that of bureaucrats. This traditional view of independence and autonomy is no longer appropriate for most modern scientists-professionals. They are affiliated with businesses, hospitals, governmental agencies, large law firms, and other complex institutions. "No profession has escaped the advancing tide of bureaucratization." [30]

Numerous studies of scientists-professionals in organizations suggest the problem of role conflict and motivation. [31] These participants place high value on intellectual pursuits, specialized task performance, and autonomy. They have high need for achievement and self-actualization. These values may create many conflicts. The desire for autonomy runs counter to the organization's need for integration. Individuals are more likely to internalize the goals of their professions rather than the goals of the organization. At best, they are likely to make only a "conditional commitment" to organization goals.

The same limited commitment may also be true of other participants, such as the unionized employee. Some situations tend to limit commitment. For example, in professional sports there is the ever-present possibility that the player may be traded or play out an option and move to another team. We have observed numerous situations in which just the rumor of a potential trade had a devastating effect on the commitment of the individual to the team. Because of these possibilities, one of the norms of professional athletes is not to develop too strong an allegiance to a given organization, but to perform to the best of their

29 Bruce Buchanan, "To Walk an Extra Mile: The Whats, Whens, and Whys of Organizational Commitment," *Organizational Dynamics,* Spring 1975, p. 68.

30 Howard M. Vollmer and Donald L. Mills (eds.), *Professionalization,* Prentice-Hall, Inc., Englewood Cliffs, N.J., 1966, p. 264.

31 For example, see William Kornhauser, *Scientists in Industry: Conflict and Accommodation,* University of California Press, Berkeley, Calif., 1962; George A. Miller, "Professionals in Bureaucracy: Alienation among Industrial Scientists and Engineers," *American Sociological Review,* October 1967, pp. 755–768; and Gloria V. Engel, "Professional Autonomy and Bureaucratic Organization," *Administrative Science Quarterly,* March 1970. pp. 12–21.

ability in order to be team players and preserve self-esteem. O. J. Simpson may not have wanted to leave Southern California to play football in Buffalo, but he was expected to put these personal preferences aside and to perform at a maximum level—and he obviously did. It is most likely that the "managerial elites" are the participants who develop the highest degree of internalization of organizational goals. This process is enhanced by bonus systems, profit sharing, and stock options.

The Continuing Dilemma

Many modern behavioral scientists see a continuing conflict between organizational goals and role requirements and individual satisfaction. In a sense, it is unrealistic to expect perfect compatibility and optimal satisfaction of individual and organizational goals. Individuals must give up some of their autonomy and self-expression to participate (and gain the advantages of membership) in the organization. This is as true of participation in the informal group or family as it is in the formal organization. Organization thus reduces personal autonomy in some spheres, but it also enhances opportunities for satisfaction in other areas. It is a trade-off that is never optimal for either the organization or the individual. For example, it could be argued that forced participation in our social security system reduces personal autonomy and individual discretion. However, it also increases independence and autonomy for the retiree.

The Role of Management in Goal Setting and Implementation

Management has a vital role in charting the organization's course. However, it is a mistake to suggest that the goals of management and the goals of the organization are one and the same. Certainly, management is one of the major elements in the coalition, but it is not the only element. Management's power is never absolute.

Monsen's studies of owner-controlled and manager-controlled firms in the same industries suggest that there are important differences in the actual operational goals of these firms. The owner-controlled firms had significantly higher rates of return on investment and lower dividend payouts than did manager-controlled firms within the same industry. It might be suggested that the owner-controlled firm is simply more efficient than the manager-controlled firm. Or (and from our viewpoint more logically) it might be argued that they are responding to different goals. Monsen suggests this difference:

The answer that seems most convincing is that two quite different motivational incentive systems are at work, emanating from the pursuit of different goals. It would seem that our business system is not generally structured to provide the same set of motivations or goals for both owners and managers. As a result, the behavior of our largest firms differs widely depending upon what group controls them. [32]

These findings are consistent with our previous discussion. The professional manager is responding to a different set of influences (including personal motivations) from those of the owner-manager. Because of these variations in actual (rather than publicized) goals, the organizations behave differently.

Management by Objectives (MBO)

Many approaches have been utilized to integrate individual and group goals with overall organizational goals. One of the most comprehensive is "management by objectives" (MBO). MBO attempts to structure this relationship by involving all levels of management in the goal-setting process. In these programs each manager works with subordinates to establish goals and specific action plans for their accomplishment. Odiorne describes this approach as follows:

The system of management by objectives can be described as a process whereby the superior and subordinate managers of an organization jointly identify its common goals, define each individual's major areas of responsibility in terms of the results expected of him and use these measures as guides for operating the unit and assessing the contributions of each of its members. [33]

Over the past two decades many organizations have adopted management by objectives programs. [34] Most of these programs started initially as managerial performance-appraisal procedures. However, many have advanced to a much broader approach encompassing long-range planning, a system of control, and a primary basis of integrating the goals of individual participants with the goals of the organization.

Although management by objectives sounds deceptively simple, in practive organizations adopting this approach have had to spend considerable time in modifying managerial processes in order to make it effective. Figure 7.2 indicates the various stages in the introduction of an MBO program. Stage One is primarily a short-term performance-appraisal approach initiated by the personnel department. Stage Two reflects a more comprehensive approach and affects the entire managerial system of the organization. Stage Three is even longer range (three to

32 R. Joseph Monsen, "Ownership and Management," *Business Horizons,* August 1969, p. 47.

33 George S. Odiorne, *Management by Objectives,* Pitman Publishing Corporation, New York, 1965, pp. 55–56.

34 For a discussion of the operations of a number of these company programs see: Walter S. Wikstrom, *Managing by—and With—Objectives,* Studies in Personnel Policy, no. 212, National Industrial Conference Board, Inc., New York, 1968.

Figure 7.2   Introduction of Management by Objectives by Stages

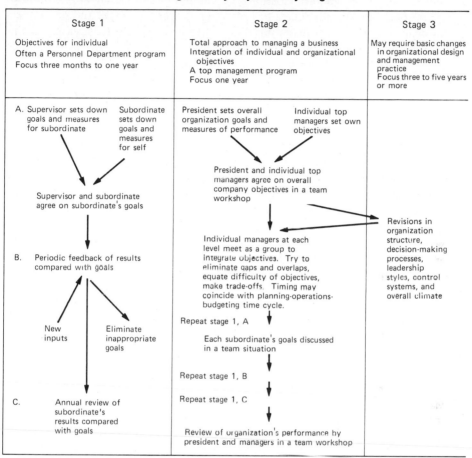

Stage 1	Stage 2	Stage 3
Objectives for individual Often a Personnel Department program Focus three months to one year	Total approach to managing a business Integration of individual and organizational objectives A top management program Focus one year	May require basic changes in organizational design and management practice Focus three to five years or more

Adapted from unpublished manuscript by Robert A. Sutermeister, Graduate School of Business Administration, University of Washington, Seattle, 1973.

five years) and encompasses changes in other subsystems such as the structure. For example, successful MBO programs usually require basic changes in the nature of the management information system. It is obvious that an MBO program cannot be effectively established in a short time period. It usually takes the organization a number of years of learning to develop an effective program. Many of the companies report that learning to operate a successful MBO program is a continuing process. In fact, one of the great advantages of such a program is that it does create a more effective learning-adapting system.

One of the major issues in any MBO program is whether objectives should be established from the top down or from the bottom up. There are advantages in either approach. The bottom-up approach maximizes the participation of lower-level personnel who are closer to the actual operations. However, the top-down approach has the advantage of providing clearer guidelines and parameters for lower-level participants in setting their own objectives. In most cases a compromise is best. "Many companies have discovered that the process cannot be exclusively top-down or bottom-up if it is to be an effective way of managing the business. The communication and planning effort, they find, must go in both directions." [35] However, MBO programs are usually not effective when automatically imposed from the top. Successful programs stress collaboration, cooperative effort, and team building.

Studies of specific MBO programs suggest that such programs do improve communications, increase mutual understanding, improve planning, create more positive attitudes toward the evaluation system, help in utilizing management abilities, and promote innovation. [36] However, there are also problems associated with these programs. Many organizational adjustments are necessary if it is to be successful. It requires long-term effort and is not a short-run panacea. Most programs include only middle- and upper-level managers. It is often difficult to encompass the efforts of many staff groups within such a program. There is a tendency for managers to direct their efforts toward meeting only those objectives on which they are measured. Other, less quantifiable objectives may be short-changed. It is often difficult to set forth clearly definable objectives under conditions of rapid change or environmental turbulence. There are many difficulties in tying performance appraisal into the program. Finally, there may be problems in requiring objective accomplishment under uncertain and adverse conditions. Discussion with executives of companies that have established MBO programs indicates that they worked very well when environmental and market forces were favorable. However, during a business downturn, many managers thought they were held strictly accountable for accomplishment of objectives over which they had limited control. Many programs did not respond adequately to new environmental conditions, and, instead of being a basis for positive motivation, the programs became a source of major conflict.

In spite of these difficulties, management by objectives programs have been used successfully by a number of business organizations to integrate organizational and individual goals. The most successful programs appear to be those that emphasize a total systems approach to MBO and take into consideration its impact on all of the organization's subsystems. MBO seems to be catching on in other types of organizations. For example, within school systems similar types of programs, such as "individual growth contracts," have been advocated for goal setting and measuring the accomplishment of students, teachers, and administrators.

35 Ibid., p. 5.

36 Stephen J. Carroll, Jr., and Henry L. Tosi, "Goal Characteristics and Personality Factors in a Management-by-Objectives Program," *Administrative Science Quarterly*, September 1970, pp. 295–305.

Measuring Organizational Performance

There are many difficulties involved in measuring the performance of organizations. Organizations have a variety of goals and typically use multiple criteria in measuring performance. The business organization may evaluate its performance in terms of profits, return on investment, sales volume, market share, satisfaction of customers, well-being and development of employees, and a host of other measures. The university may measure its performance in terms of output of students, the stature of its alumni, the perceived quality of its faculty, the research output of the institution, and services provided to the community. It is impossible for the complex organization to set forth a single measure of performance for its multiple goals.

Performance measurements involve *effectiveness* (the degree to which goals are accomplished), *efficiency* (the use of resources in attaining goals), and *participant satisfaction* (the motivational climate). In most cases effectiveness and efficiency are related; however, the organization frequently needs to establish different ways of measuring them. Even if the organization is effective in accomplishing goals, it may not be efficient in the utilization of resources. Our nation was effective in reaching its goal of placing a man on the moon by 1970, but many have suggested that this required a very inefficient use of resources. Conversely, an organization could be efficient without being effective. A business might be efficient in the utilization of resources but not effective in reaching its sales goals because of a declining market, severe depression, or other forces. A college basketball coach might achieve near optimal efficiency by getting his or her players to perform beyond their "capacity." However, if the tallest player is 5 feet 11 inches, the team may be very ineffective, as evidenced by a record of 0 wins and 25 losses.

Organizations need to evaluate performance in broad systems terms. [37] The organization should establish measures of performance for all of its transformation processes—not just the financial and technical transactions. Performance in meeting the goals of the environmental suprasystem should be measured more accurately. It is desirable to establish measures of performance in each of the major subsystems—goal setting, effective utilization of technology, creation of an appropriate structure, meeting psychosocial needs, and developing the managerial system.

Measuring organizational performance is a vital concern of the managerial system. The managerial functions of planning and control are directly involved in establishing goals, developing plans for their accomplishment, setting up control processes, and measuring performance. These issues will be discussed more fully in Part 6.

---

37 Richard M. Steers, "Problems in the Measurement of Organizational Effectiveness," *Administrative Science Quarterly,* December 1975, pp. 546–558.

Summary

Goals and values are an integral subsystem of every organization. Social values reflect a system of shared beliefs about desirable goals and norms for human conduct. The organization depends on a minimum level of shared values among internal participants and the external society for its very existence.

Goals can be considered from three primary perspectives: (1) the environmental level—the constraints imposed on the organization by society, (2) the organizational level—the goals of the organization as a system, and (3) the individual level—the goals of organizational participants. Responding to environmental forces leads to continual modification and elaboration in the goal structure of the organization.

Organization system goals pertain to the purposes and desired conditions that the organization seeks as a distinct entity. Continuing existence, growth, profitability, and stability are examples of system goals.

Goals of individual participants are frequently *both* compatible and incompatible with organizational goals. It is necessary to satisfy a certain level of participant needs in order to maintain their contributions. However, it is unrealistic to expect perfect compatibility and optimal satisfaction of individual and organizational goals.

Management has a major role in the setting of operational goals and in providing resources for implementing action programs. Many approaches have been utilized to integrate individual and group goals with overall organizational goals. One of the most comprehensive is "management by objectives" (MBO).

There are many difficulties involved in measuring the performance of organizations in meeting goals. Organizations have a variety of goals and typically use multiple criteria in measuring performance.

Questions and Problems

1 What are goals? Discuss the issue of whether or not organizations have goals.

2 What is meant by organization system goals? What is the distinction between "official" and operational goals? Select a specific organization and report on these differences.

3 How does the environmental suprasystem affect the goals of an organization?

4 Give examples of the interaction between an organization and its environment in terms of (a) competition, (b) bargaining, (c) co-optation, and (d) coalition.

5 What is meant by the means-ends chain? Give examples.

6 Why do organizations frequently have interdepartmental goal conflicts? Select a specific organization and report on these conflicts.

7 What is meant by goal displacement? Give examples.

8 Discuss the issue of the compatibility or conflict between individual and organizational goals. Relate this to your own goals and those of *(a)* the college or university you attend and/or *(b)* an organization in which you have worked.

9 What is meant by management by objectives (MBO)? Using your own experience, or the references and other library resources, report on a specific MBO program.

Rapid change has now left most Americans a little breathless. So complex are effects of changing technology that they have overtaken mankind as problems rather than as opportunities. If men are to utilize technology for the good life, they will have to find a substitute for time, which in the past permitted the human organism, and the community, to adjust to the pace of history.
Charles R. Walker

Technology is the creation of men and is managed by them. Technology and administration are inseparable both in practice and in theory. Therefore the deleterious effects of technology are the responsibility of those who control and administer the complex organizations within which it is embedded.
William G. Scott and David K. Hart

Technology and structure set relatively narrow limits on the boss's freedom to adopt various leadership styles—a production foreman just can't behave like a college dean.
George Strauss

A great many administrators and managers carry in their heads a pattern of the "ideal" organization. That pattern is the classic hierarchy, the family tree; one man at the top, with three below him, each of whom has three below him, and so on with fearful symmetry unto the seventh generation, by which stage there is a row of 729 junior managers and an urgent need for a very large triangular piece of paper.
Antony Jay

Structural relationships are not once and for all prescriptions but are "rules of the game" which are adaptable to changing situations and the changing desires of the participants.
Ogden H. Hall

Technology and Structure

4

The technologies of the organization are based on the knowledge and equipment used in task accomplishment. They affect the types of inputs into the organization and the output from the system. Every modern organization has been influenced by the rapid acceleration of technology in our society. The way an organization adapts to the changing technology has a significant impact on the other organizational subsystems.

The organization structure sets the formal framework for the ways in which tasks are accomplished. Structure is concerned with the differentiation of tasks into operating units and the pattern of established relationships among them. Organizations have both a formal (planned) and an informal structure. The formal structure is depicted by organization charts, position and job descriptions, and procedure manuals. The informal "structure" is determined by informal interactions between participants in the organization and is closely associated with the psychosocial system. Formal and informal relations provide the integrative framework between the technological requirements and the psychosocial and managerial systems.

Chapter 8, "Technology and Organization," is concerned with the impact of the technical systems on the organization—its structural, psychosocial, and managerial systems. Chapter 9, "Organization Structure and Design," considers the forces affecting formal organization, reviews traditional concepts, investigates the elaboration of structure, and considers alternative organizational designs.

Technology and Organization

Eight

The organization is not simply a technical *or* a social system; it requires structuring and integrating human activities around various technologies. The technical system is determined by the task requirements of the organization and is shaped by the specialization of knowledge and skills required, the types of machinery and equipment involved, the information-processing requirements, and the layout of facilities. Any change in the technical system affects other organizational elements. The impact of technology on the organization—its goals, structure, psychosocial system, and managerial system—is the subject of this chapter. The following topics are discussed:

The Concept of Technology
Accelerating Technology
Organizations: Creating and Applying Technology
Classification of Technical Systems
Impact of the Technical System
Social and Behavioral Technologies in Organizations

The Concept of Technology

In the past, science and technology have been viewed as the means for improving human existence—providing more effective human control over the natural, physical, and social environment. More recently, we have come to doubt this view and to wonder whether science and technology really have made a better world. There are conflicting values and attitudes—we recognize the need for continuing technological advancements, but also strive for more effective social control to ensure that these changes are really improvements and do not leave us worse off than before.

Some of the misunderstanding is due to the lack of a precise agreement on the meaning of technology. The terms **technology** and **technological change** have many meanings, ranging from specific to broad connotations. In the narrowest view, these terms are associated with **machine technology,** the mechanization of the means of production of goods and services, the replacement of human effort. This mechanistic view emphasizes such visible manifestations of technology as the supersonic airplane, assembly lines, electronic computers, transportation systems, and the vast complex of facilities and equipment necessary for developing a space shuttle system. This emphasis on physical artifacts is understandable because the machine is the most obvious physical manifestation of technology. From the anthropological approach, the history of technology is often associated with the first use of primitive weapons and tools. The ability to use these instruments was a major distinguishing characteristic of humans from lower animals. However, it is an oversimplification to associate the advancement of technology with the history of tools and machines. Machines are merely the physical artifacts of technology.

Technology as the Application of Knowledge

In the most general sense, technology refers to the application of knowledge for the more effective performance of certain tasks or activities. Technology converts spontaneous and unreflected behavior into behavior that is deliberate and rationalized. Jacques Ellul gives a broad connotation to technology or, as he calls it, technique. "In our technological society, *technique is the totality of methods rationally arrived at and having absolute efficiency* (for a given stage of development) in *every* field of human activity." [1] He suggests that technology has come to dominate every field and is geared to the achievement of efficiency and rationality in all human endeavors. The definition used in this chapter is:

Technology is the organization and application of knowledge for the achievement of practical purposes. It includes physical manifestations such as tools and machines, but also intellectual techniques and processes used in solving problems and obtaining desired outcomes.

A simple example illustrates this concept. The hobbyist purchases a stereo receiver kit to assemble. She receives transistors, resistors, and other physical components. Obviously, these have all been produced using various technologies. She also uses tools—a soldering iron, pliers, screwdrivers—in the assembly process. But this is not enough for most amateurs. In the box containing the components was a detailed set of step-by-step instructions for assembling the receiver. This is the knowledge component of technology—the information required to

[1] Jacques Ellul, *The Technological Society,* trans. by John Wilkinson, © Alfred A. Knopf, Inc., New York, 1964, p. xxv.

accomplish the practical results. If the hobbyist is successful in applying this technology, the stereo works. If not, she will likely take the whole mess to the local radio repair shop, to someone who has more technical knowledge.

In the same sense, computer hardware represents one aspect of technology, but software programs are equally important. The machines on the assembly line represent technology; but so do planning, scheduling, and control procedures. Accounting and budgeting processes, market research surveys, and personnel selection and training procedures all represent parts of technology—the application of knowledge to achieve practical purposes.

By *organizational technology* we mean the techniques used in the transformation of inputs into outputs. In accomplishing this transformation task, for example, the industrial concern utilizes both machine and other specialized technologies. The accountant may employ the computer in performing his task, but he also utilizes a technology based on the knowledge of accounting procedures. Quite clearly, in this case as in many others, there is an interaction between the machine side of technology and specialized technique. When we talk about a change in the technology of the organization and its impact on structure and human relationships, we are not discussing only the impact of such mechanical devices as computers but are also considering changes in the nonmechanical technical system.

Technology as Applicable to All Organizations

Technology is simple to understand in a physical transformation process such as an assembly line, but it is also appropriate for other organizations, such as a hospital or university. The hospital receives human inputs (patients) and utilizes technologies to transform them in some way (physically or mentally). The university receives inputs of students, transforms them through some process of educational technology, and then returns them to the broader society. This view of organizational technology is illustrated in Figure 8.1.

Accelerating Technology

Together, science and technology are providing a new shape to the world. In particular, during the post-World War II period, these forces have brought about a growing discontinuity with the past. "Science and Technology have given our age more of its unique characteristic and coloring than they have any other age. They have done so by altering nearly all the basic components which make up the life of modern man, and altering them in important ways."[2]

The pace of technological change is accelerating. The typical time between a technical discovery and recognition of its commercial usefulness and

2 Charles R. Walker (ed.), *Technology, Industry and Man,* McGraw-Hill Book Company, New York, 1968, p. 9.

Figure 8.1   The Concept of Organizational Technology

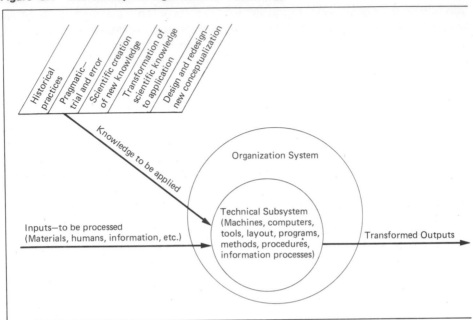

application has decreased from thirty years at the beginning of the century to less than ten years.[3] Scientific and technological changes are more rapidly diffused through the society, as exemplified by the development and utilization of new generations of computers or copiers. Transistor radios and pocket calculators were developed, produced, and distributed worldwide over a short time period. The quartz crystal watch has revolutionized a traditional industry.

Changes stemming from science and technology are not limited to the United States and other industrialized countries. The developing and semi-industrialized countries of the world are gearing their national policies toward increasing industrialism and technical progress. One of the manifestations of this is a convergence in sociocultural systems. For example, there is an emphasis on education. A basic requirement of modern technology is a high level of literacy and specialized training. The effective utilization of technology requires the development of complex organizations that are quite similar, in spite of different cultures, economic systems, and political ideologies.

The Heritage of the Past

We should not overemphasize the accelerating technology of the present and forget the heritage of knowledge from the past. The invention and develop-

3 National Commission on Technology, Automation, and Economic Progress, *Technology and the American Economy*, U.S. Government Printing Office, Washington, D.C., February 1966.

ment of language, the domestication of animals, agriculture, irrigation systems, and processes for preservation of foods are products of past technological developments.[4] The invention of writing by someone or some group "some 5000 years ago set mankind on the road we are still traveling today."[5] Lewis Mumford suggests that the introduction of the mechanical clock during the thirteenth century had a more significant impact on society than any other development. The clock regimented human activities, disassociating them from natural biological and sociological processes. The clock determines when we eat, sleep, go to classes, and work. It provides a basic means for integration of organization endeavors. It is a measuring device for many human activities: productivity (output per work hour), the four-minute mile, the minutes we have available for our computer program, and the fifty-five miles per hour we travel on freeways. As Mumford says:

The gain in mechanical efficiency through coordination and through closer articulation of the day's events cannot be overestimated; while this increase cannot be measured in mere horsepower, one has only to imagine its absence today to foresee the speedy disruption and eventual collapse of our entire society. The modern industrial regime could do without coal and iron and steam easier than it could do without the clock.[6]

We have come to underestimate these vital technological developments from the past because they are so commonplace. But they have had a profound effect on the ways in which our societies and cultures have developed.

Ambivalent Attitudes toward Technology

For much of history we have had positive attitudes toward technology. It was the primary means by which we could minimize human toil, increase productivity, and have a better quality of life. More recently, we have begun to question this assumption and have stressed the negative side of technological "improvements." Many suggest that technology has become an end in itself and that, unabated, it will ultimately drive out humanistic and social considerations. It will dominate and control humankind and reduce us to victims of the machine. Some people have advocated a return to a less sophisticated technological society.

In our view, dismantling of our technological system and returning to the past is not likely, feasible, or desirable. Advancing science and technology will continue to be primary forces for change. Technology can be controlled, but not without some fundamental changes in values and goals. We agree with Mesthene, who suggests that advancing technology should not be viewed as an "unalloyed

---

4 C. D. Darlington, *The Evolution of Man and Society*, Simon and Schuster, New York, 1969.
5 Morris C. Leikind, "The History of Technology: Man's Search for Labor Saving Devices," in Donald P. Lauda and Robert D. Ryan (eds.), *Advancing Technology: Its Impact on Society*, Wm. C. Brown Co. Publishers, Dubuque, Iowa, 1971, p. 9.
6 Lewis Mumford, *Technics and Civilization*, Harcourt, Brace and Company, New York, 1934, pp. 12–18.

blessing" or an "unmitigated curse."[7] In the past we have emphasized the economic advantages of technology. In the future we will develop a better understanding of the environmental, sociological, and psychological consequences of technological change. We agree with Bell, who suggests that the post-industrial society will be based increasingly on the utilization of knowledge.[8] And this knowledge will be used not only to create new science and technology but also to utilize and control it for greater social benefit.

Organizations: Creating and Applying Technology

A phenomenon of modern industrial society is the development of large-scale, complex organizations for the accomplishment of specific purposes. This relatively new development has been pervasive over the past century. Throughout most of human history, social institutions were primarily on an informal face-to-face basis. The industrial revolution, with its demand for concentration of resources and greater scale, fostered larger economic and other organizational units. This condition is not restricted to Western cultures. As other countries pass through the phases of industrialization, they also find it necessary to evolve larger organizational units. It would appear that this trend toward more complex organization is basic in all human society and is moving in a massive wave through many cultures.

It is difficult to determine which comes first—the social structure or the technology. Some would argue that developments in the social structure are a necessary prerequisite to advancing science and technology. Others suggest that developments in technology create the necessity for new social organizations. This is like the chicken and egg controversy, and we are content to consider them as codeterminant forces. It is, however, obvious that individuals and informal groups cannot accomplish certain results in small units. "Large-scale organizations have evolved to achieve goals which are beyond the capacities of the individual or the small group. They make possible the application of many and diverse skills and resources to complex systems of producing goods and services. Large-scale organizations, therefore, are particularly adapted to complicated *technologies,* that is, to those sets of man-machine activities which together produce a desired good or service."[9]

---

7 Emmanuel G. Mesthene, *Technological Changes,* A Mentor Book, The New American Library, Inc., New York, 1970, p. 34.

8 Daniel Bell, *The Coming of Post-Industrial Society,* Basic Books, Inc., Publishers, New York, 1973, pp. 165–265.

9 James D. Thompson and Frederick L. Bates, "Technology, Organization, and Administration," *Administrative Science Quarterly,* December 1957, p. 325.

In the economic sector, corporations are the means for the creation and utilization of industrial technology. They are the vehicle for combining large amounts of capital, extensive mechanization, and comprehensive planning that advanced technology requires. By adapting to and utilizing new technology, the corporation has developed means for growth and diversification and expanding its role in society. This movement toward technological virtuosity has been facilitated by the increasing number of scientists, professionals, and technicians who are aggressively seeking outlets for their creativity.

Other types of organizations are also involved in this process. Large hospitals, with treatment, research, and training functions, are engaged in utilization and creation of technical knowledge. Universities are geared to the two major functions of transmission of knowledge (teaching) and the creation of knowledge (research). The National Aeronautics and Space Administration has engaged in many sophisticated programs that have severely taxed our technical and administrative skills.

A Manifestation of Social Technology

In a broad sense, the development of large-scale organization represents an advancement in social technology. The ability to bring together the material, human, and informational resources necessary to accomplish complex tasks is a major achievement. The development of appropriate structures and information systems, integrated planning and control processes, and programs for more effective selection, training, development, and motivation of human participants is part of this social technology. Organizations of the type that we have today were not possible at the beginning of the twentieth century. The social structure would not have been able to support our modern institutions. [10]

This is readily apparent today. It is impossible to transplant the physical manifestations of technology (plant and equipment) to a developing country without first providing the requisite social technologies of organization and management. If they are not available locally (or at least potentially available through training and development) they have to be imported (in the form of managers, specialists, information, and the like). Frequently, advanced organizational technology conflicts with many of the cultural values and social structures of the developing country.

It is obvious that knowledge about how to organize and manage complex systems is as much a social technology as engineering and design of plant and equipment are a physical technology. Both are manifestations of technology—the rational utilization of knowledge to accomplish human purposes.

[10] Arthur L. Stinchcombe, "Social Structure and Organizations," in James G. March (ed.), *Handbook of Organizations,* Rand McNally & Company, Chicago, 1965, pp. 142–193.

Classification of Technical Systems

Many ways of classifying organizations have been proposed. For example, business firms are frequently classified in terms of industries. The Standard Industrial Classification system divides all manufacturing into twenty major groups with many subgroups. Other organizations are classified on the basis of primacy of functions that they perform: schools, hospitals, prisons, labor unions, and so forth.

While these bases may be appropriate in certain circumstances, there is an increasing tendency to classify organizations in terms of their technical system. "The perspective holds that technology is a better basis for comparing organizations than the several schemes which now exist." [11] Many authors have used technology as a basis for analysis of organizations. James D. Thompson says, "Those organizations with similar technological and environmental problems should exhibit similar behavior; patterns should appear. But if our thesis is fruitful, we should also find that patterned variations in problems posed by technologies and environments result in systematic differences in organizational action." [12]

We agree that a classification of organizations in terms of technology would be a useful starting place for comparative organizational analysis. However, it is difficult to develop a simple classification. For industrial organizations involved in the production of goods, the classification in terms of small batch, mass production, and continuous process provides a general technology continuum. However, it is appropriate primarily for industrial operations. It would be difficult to fit organizations such as department stores, unions, and schools into this classification.

Perrow has proposed a multidimensional model of technology that emphasizes the application of knowledge to the problems the organization faces in performing its transformation functions—the work to be done. [13] Technologies are applied to the task of altering the raw material inputs as in a factory, human inputs as in a hospital or correctional institution, or informational inputs (symbols) as in a bank, advertising agency, or investment firm. He suggests that there are two dimensions of technology based on the problems associated with the processing of these raw material inputs: (1) whether the problems are familiar or exceptional and (2) the degree to which the problems can be solved in known and analyzable ways. Few exceptions and standardized problem-solving procedures describe a routine technology, typically used in many production and service organizations. If there is a large number of exceptions and problem solving is varied and difficult, the technology is described as nonroutine. Research and de-

---

11 Charles Perrow, "A Framework for the Comparative Analysis of Organizations," *American Sociological Review,* April 1967, p. 195.
12 James D. Thompson, *Organizations in Action,* McGraw-Hill Book Company, New York, 1967, pp. 1–2.
13 Perrow, op. cit., pp. 194–208.

velopment laboratories, treatment-oriented psychiatric hospitals, medical research units, and rehabilitation-oriented correctional institutions utilize nonroutine technology.

Classification Based on Complexities and Dynamics

In considering organization technologies, there appear to be two major issues: (1) the degree of complexity of the technology and (2) whether the technology is stable or dynamic. We have used these two dimensions to suggest a continuum ranging from a stable and relatively simple technology, such as basic person-tool, to a dynamic and complex technology (see Figure 8.2). Others have utilized similar classifications. [14]

It is important to recognize that this continuum considers two primary dimensions. One deals with the degree of complexity of the technology required in the transformation process. The second emphasizes the degree of stability in the events, tasks, or decisions that the organization faces. Thus, there are a number of possible combinations along this continuum. At the lower left is the organization that uses very simple and uniform person-tool technology. At the other extreme is the organization that has a dynamic and complex knowledge-based technology, such as an aerospace company, graduate programs in universities, or a research and development laboratory. Obviously, within any complex organization, there may be different departments that are at various positions along this continuum. In a hospital, for example, many housekeeping functions have uniform procedures and stable technology. However, at the other end of the spectrum, the diagnosis and treatment of some patients involves a dynamic and nonuniform technology.

Although the illustration in Figure 8.2 suggests industrial examples, this view of a technological continuum is appropriate for all types of organizations. We will use this model to consider the impact of these various types of technologies on a variety of organizations and the people in them.

Impact of the Technical System

The technical system has received increasing attention in organization theory. In general, technology was neglected by traditional management theorists and human relationists alike. The technological component of the organizational

14 Some of the writers who have adopted similar classifications are Charles Perrow, "A Framework for the Comparative Analysis of Organizations," *American Sociological Review*, April 1967, pp. 194–208; Eugene Litwak, "Models of Bureaucracy Which Permit Conflict," *American Journal of Sociology*, September 1961, pp. 177–184; Raymond G. Hunt, "Technology and Organization," *Academy of Management Journal*, September 1970, pp. 235–252; Beverly P. Lynch, "An Empirical Assessment of Perrow's Technology Construct," *Administrative Science Quarterly*, September 1974, pp. 338–356; Jerald Hage and Michael Aiken, "Routine Technology, Social Structure, and Organization Goals," *Administrative Science Quarterly*, September 1969, pp. 366–376.

Figure 8.2   Classifications of Technologies

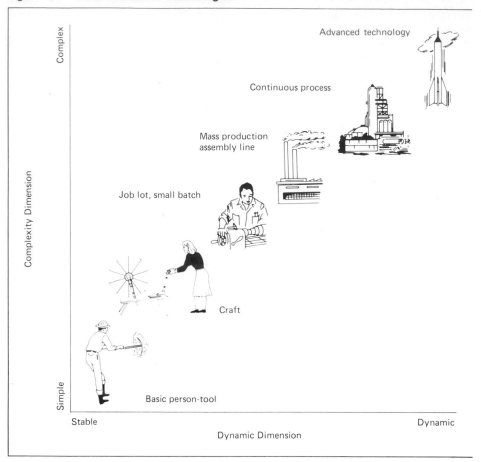

system was often considered a "closed" subsystem, which did not have any dynamic interaction with the other subsystems.

There have been some exceptions to this general neglect of technological factors. Dubin, for example, emphasizes the importance of technology and its impact on the behavioral system.[15] Walker and his associates at Yale University also have made numerous studies of the impact of technology in the work organization.[16] These, however, were exceptions. For the most part, management theorists disregarded the technological factors and attempted to set forth prescriptions that would apply regardless of the technology. However, within the past decade

---

15 Robert Dubin, *The World of Work*, Prentice-Hall, Inc., Englewood Cliffs, N.J., 1958, pp. 62–65.

16 See, for example, Charles R. Walker and Robert H. Guest, *The Man on the Assembly Line*, Harvard University Press, Cambridge, Mass., 1952; and Charles R. Walker, *Modern Technology and Civilization*, McGraw-Hill Book Company, New York, 1962.

the importance of the technological component in the organization has been stressed.

In examining the influence of technology, we must again keep fixed in mind that technology and other system inputs are interdependently related. A useful way to begin our examination of technology, in fact, is to explore three basic ways in which technology influences behavior through its effects on other inputs. First, technology is a determinant of the human inputs required by an organization and, thus indirectly, of the predisposition of employees. Second, technology is a determinant of certain gross features of organizational structure and procedure. Third, technology is an immediate determinant of individual and group job designs and, therefore, indirectly a determinant of social structure and norms. [17]

The technical system is directly related to the environmental suprasystem and to the goals and values of the organization. As a subsystem of the society in which it exists, the organization utilizes the available technical knowledge in its transformation processes. However, new technology is also created by organizations and is made available as an output to society.

The nature of the technical system also has an important impact on the goals and values of the organization. The value of striving for "technical rationality" is apparent in most organizations. The very goals the organization attempts to accomplish are frequently determined by the available technology. We could not adopt the goal of transformation from hydroelectric and fossil fuel generation of electrical energy to nuclear and solar power generation without the available technology. At the operating level in the organization, technology is one of the prime forces in determining the specific goals and the means for their accomplishment.

Impact on Structure

A number of studies have focused specifically on the relationships between technology and organizational structure. Joan Woodward and her associates engaged in extensive research in 100 industrial firms in Great Britain. She divided the firms surveyed into three groups, based on differences in technology. Twenty-four firms had unit or small-batch production, such as job-lot operations; thirty-one were classified as large-batch and mass production, such as assembly lines; and twenty-five were engaged in continuous process production, such as chemical and oil refineries. In addition, twelve firms were classified as combined systems. The transition from unit and small-batch to large-batch and mass production and then to continuous process production was one of increasing technological complexity.

There was a direct correlation between technology and structure. "Among the organizational characteristics showing a direct relationship with

17 Paul R. Lawrence, "Technical Inputs," in John A. Seiler, *Systems Analysis in Organizational Behavior*, Richard D. Irwin, Inc., and The Dorsey Press, Homewood, Ill., 1967, p. 133.

technical advance were the length of the line of command; the span of control of the chief executive; the percentage of total turnover allocated to the payment of wages and salaries, and the ratios of managers to total personnel, of clerical and administrative staff to manual workers, of direct to indirect labour, and of graduate to non-graduate supervision in production departments." [18] The number of vertical levels of management in direct production departments increased with technical advance from unit production to continuous processing. The span of control of the chief executive (the number of people directly responsible to him or her) increased from a medium of four in unit production, to seven in large-batch and mass production, to ten in process production. Management by committee was more common in process industries than in the less complex systems. There was a direct link between a firm's technology and the relative size of its management group. The clerical and administrative personnel, including staff groups, were proportionately larger in the advanced companies.

The study also found a close relationship between successful performance and the organizational structure of companies within each industry. This finding is of key importance; there tended to be an optimal structure for each type of technology. "The fact that organizational characteristics, technology, and success were linked together in this way suggested that not only was the system of production an important variable in the determination of structure, but also that one particular form of organization was the most appropriate to each system of production." [19] A replication of the Woodward study by Zwerman using fifty-six firms in the Minneapolis area generally corroborated her findings. [20]

A series of studies carried out by the Industrial Administration Research Unit of the University of Aston in England provided additional information concerning the impact of the technical system. In a study of forty-six diverse organizations they investigated the relationship between technology and structure. They classified technology into three components. **Operations technology** is the techniques used in the work-flow activities. **Materials technology** refers to the nature of the materials used in the transformation process. **Knowledge technology** refers to the characteristics of the knowledge used in the organization.

The Aston group found that operations technology did not have a major effect on structural relationships except for those structural variables that were centered on the work-flow. They concluded:

Operations technology is shown to affect only those structural variables immediately impinged on by the workflow. Thus the smaller the organization the more completely its structure is pervaded by the immediate effects of this technology; the larger the organization the more these effects are confined to variables such as the proportions employed in

18 Joan Woodward, *Industrial Organization: Theory and Practice*, Oxford University Press, Fair Lawn, N.J., 1965, p. 51. For a discussion of an extension of this research see: Joan Woodward (ed.), *Industrial Organization: Behavior and Control*, Oxford University Press, London, 1970.
19 Ibid., pp. 69–70.
20 William L. Zwerman, *New Perspectives on Organization Theory*, Greenwood Publishing Corporation, Westport, Conn., 1970.

activities that are specifically linked with the workflow, and technology is not related to the wider administrative and hierarchical structure. [21]

More simply stated, the impact of the technical system on structural variables is most apparent in what we have called the "operating subsystem or level." Technology is a prime determinant of the structure on the production line. It is also of major importance in a small organization such as an automobile repair shop. However, the operations technology would have a more limited impact on the structure of the coordinative subsystem. At the strategic level it would have even less importance. These findings would fit in closely with our model as set forth in Figure 5.4. At the coordinative and strategic levels, factors other than operations technology are of major consequence to structure. Environmental influences are important in structuring the strategic level. [22] For example, the nature of the competitive environment would be very important in determining the structural variables within the advertising, market research, and public relations departments of a large industrial organization. The broad administrative structure of the conglomerate or the multinational corporation is influenced more by environmental forces than by technical considerations.

However, we should be reminded that the Aston study considered only "operations technology" and did not include materials and knowledge technology. It is likely that these two components of technology would have an impact on structure at all levels. There have been several additional studies that have attempted to understand the differences in concepts and findings between the Woodward and the Aston studies. It is apparent that at least a part of the disagreement stems from problems associated with the definition and measurement of all the technological and structural variables. [23] These various studies suggest that the relationships between technology and structure are complex.

Impact on Psychosocial System

Traditional management theory gave little consideration to the ways in which technology affected the psychosocial system. The technical system was considered as given and invariable, and the assumption was made that the people would adapt. Fortunately, human beings are adaptable and have responded to rapidly changing technologies. Technological progress in complex organizations

21 David J. Hickson, D. S. Pugh, and Diana C. Pheysey, "Operations Technology and Organization Structure: An Empirical Reappraisal," *Administrative Science Quarterly,* September 1969, p. 378.

22 Jay Galbraith, "Environmental and Technological Determinants of Organizational Design," in Jay W. Lorsch and Paul R. Lawrence (eds.), *Studies in Organization Design,* Richard D. Irwin, Inc., and The Dorsey Press, Homewood, Ill. 1970, pp. 113–39.

23 Lawrence B. Mohr, "Organizational Technology and Organizational Structure," *Administrative Science Quarterly,* December 1971, pp. 444–459; Howard E. Aldrich, "Technology and Organizational Structure: A Reexamination of the Findings of the Aston Group," *Administrative Science Quarterly,* March 1972, pp. 26–43; and John Child and Roger Mansfield, "Technology, Size and Organization Structure," *Sociology,* September 1972, pp. 369–393.

over the past 100 years has required major adjustments on the part of social systems. The techniques of bureaucracy, scientific management, and mass production required fundamental changes. The newer innovations of automation—both in the factory and in the office—are currently having significant impacts; yet we have given little consideration to the relationship between technology and psychosocial systems. Haire states:

Our industrial production layouts are built to utilize the production technique, the machine's characteristics, and the material's qualities to the utmost. The operator is considered the dependent variable. He is expected to (and fortunately does) bend and adjust. It is interesting to speculate on what might happen if we were to build a production line designed to maximize the human resources and motivations of the operators, and then consider the machines as dependent variables which must be built to conform to the requirements of a system designed to maximize the human's potentialities. [24]

Technology affects people in organizations in many ways. It is a key factor in determining the required tasks and the degree of specialization. It often determines the size and composition of the immediate work group and the range of contacts with other workers and supervisors. It frequently prescribes the extent of physical mobility. It affects the various roles and status positions of people in organizations—generally higher technical skills mean more status, pay, and other rewards. It is most influential in setting the specific design of each employee's task—the variety of activities performed, the amount of discretion and autonomy, the types of interactions with others, for example. Technology, particularly in mass-production operations, imposes a time dimension on workers. It requires punctuality in being there to start the process and sets a certain work pace.

Technological changes may create job insecurities and anxieties. Skills developed over a long period may become outmoded, vitally affecting the self-image and motivation of workers. We frequently underestimate or fail to perceive the impact of the technical system on people. With stable operations, the interaction often goes unnoticed. However, a major change in the technology component will often highlight this interdependence. Many of the most important studies showing the relationship between technical systems and people have been conducted during periods of change, when these relationships become more dramatic and observable.

In a study of several industries, Blauner found important differentials in the psychosocial systems with different technologies. For example, alienation and dissatisfaction were greater on the assembly line than in craft and continuous process industries (such as chemicals and oil refining). These latter industries had a higher degree of worker motivation and satisfaction than those on the assembly line. [25]

24 Mason Haire, *Psychology in Management,* 2d ed., McGraw-Hill Book Company, New York, 1964, pp. 6–7.
25 Robert Blauner, *Alienation and Freedom: The Factory Worker and His Industry,* The University of Chicago Press, Chicago, 1964, p. 182.

In a study of 1491 Canadian workers in three different industries—printing, automobile, and oil—Fullan also found that integration and satisfaction were lowest among workers on the mass-production assembly line. [26] In recent contract negotiations between the United Auto Workers and the automobile companies one of the major issues has been the "dehumanizing" nature of the task on the production line. This is further evidence of the impact of technology on the psychosocial system.

Members of the Tavistock Institute in England have engaged in a number of important research studies showing the relationship between technical and psychosocial systems. [27] They have developed a comprehensive sociotechnical systems approach, which seeks to integrate environmental, technical, and social factors. Of key importance in these studies was the finding that changes in a work organization determined only by engineering considerations can disrupt the social system to the extent that the new technology will not work effectively. These studies emphasize another important factor. A given technical system does not automatically lead to one and only one social system. There may be alternatives in designing the social system that lead both to increased productivity and to more personal satisfaction. "Changes that are undertaken from a sociotechnical systems perspective attempt simultaneously to modify *both* the technical and the social aspects of the organization to create work systems that lead both to greater task productivity and to higher personal fulfillment for organization members." [28]

These and many other studies illustrate the complex interrelationship between the technical and the psychosocial systems. Although there appear to be important differences in worker motivation and satisfaction under differing technologies, it has not been easy to determine the contributing factors. Hackman and Oldham have developed a job characteristics model, which helps clarify this relationship. They suggest the five major job dimensions shown in Figure 8.3.

This listing of major job dimensions helps us to put the issue of worker satisfaction in different technologies into a historical perspective. In the traditional craft technologies, jobs ranked high on these five dimensions. However, craft technologies could not meet the increasing demands for products and services in a rapidly growing society. The rise of mass-production technologies at the turn of the century emphasized greatly increased productivity of standardized products. They provided employment opportunities for many foreign immigrants and rural migrants who were moving to industrial centers. These people were basically

26 Michael Fullan, "Industrial Technology and Worker Integration in the Organization," *American Sociological Review,* December 1970, pp. 1028–1039.

27 E. L. Trist and K. W. Bamforth, "Some Social and Psychological Consequences of the Longwall Method of Coal-getting," *Human Relations,* February 1951, pp. 3–38; A. K. Rice, *Productivity and Social Organization: The Ahmedabad Experiment,* Tavistock Publications, London, 1958; E. L. Trist, G. W. Higgins, H. Murray, and A. B. Pollock, *Organizational Choice,* Tavistock Publications, London, 1963; and L. E. Davis and E. L. Trist, "Improving the Quality of Work Life: Sociotechnical Case Studies," in J. O'Toole (ed.), *Work and the Quality of Life,* MIT Press, Cambridge, Mass., 1974.

28 J. Richard Hackman and J. Lloyd Suttle, *Improving Life at Work,* Goodyear Publishing Company, Inc., Santa Monica, Calif., 1977, p. 112.

Figure 8.3   Major Job Dimensions

Skill Variety. The degree to which a job requires a variety of different activities in carrying out the work, which involve a number of different skills and talents of the person.

Task Identity. The degree to which the job requires completion of a "whole" and identifiable piece of work—that is, doing a job from beginning to end with a visible outcome.

Task Significance. The degree to which the job has a substantial impact on the lives or work of other people, whether in the immediate organization or in the external environment.

Autonomy. The degree to which the job provides substantial freedom, independence, and discretion to the individual in scheduling the work and in determining the procedures to be used in carrying it out.

Feedback. The degree to which carrying out the work activities required by the job results in the individual obtaining direct and clear information about the effectiveness of his or her performance.

J. Richard Hackman and Greg R. Oldham, "Motivation through the Design of Work: Test of a Theory," *Organizational Behavior and Human Performance,* August 1976, pp. 250–279.

unskilled and untrained in craft technologies, and it was necessary to design jobs in machine-tending and assembly-line work that utilized the available skills. Specialization, routinization, and tight controls were the answers. However, these jobs ranked low on the dimensions set forth in Figure 8.3 and tended to decrease motivation and satisfaction.

Changing educational levels and increasing aspirations for greater work satisfaction made this approach both less necessary and less acceptable. The new technologies—continuous process, automation, and advanced-knowledge based— require more skill and provide a work climate that is more satisfying. Work in these technologies typically ranks high on the five job dimensions.

As our labor force has become better educated and trained, we no longer need to rely on technologies geared to unskilled workers. Rather, the level of skills available should affect the selection of the appropriate technologies. We would carry this one step further and suggest that the issue of human satisfaction may also be an increasing determinant of the type of technology employed. We may be entering an age in which people no longer are forced to adjust to technology, but rather technology will be adapted to people. This may be the most important characteristic of future industrial revolutions. Improved productivity through technological progress and greater participant satisfaction are not necessarily contradictory goals. Considering both factors as dynamic variables will lead to increased organizational effectiveness, efficiency, and participant satisfaction.

Impact on Managerial System

In many ways, the impact of technology on the managerial system has been even more dramatic than on the other organizational subsystems. We marvel at the obvious technological advancements required to send people to the moon and return them safely. However, the managerial skills required to plan for and integrate all the diverse activities for successful mission accomplishment are equally important.[29] The improvements in management techniques in the United States have perhaps done more to revolutionize society than have scientific-engineering changes.

One of the major consequences of changing technology has been the increasing specialization of knowledge. The managerial system in most organizations includes many participants with specialized skills and training. Many highly trained specialists are in staff positions, and their number is growing: operations researchers, personnel staffs, engineers in research and development, communications experts, and industrial psychologists and sociologists. The modern managerial system is not comprised of a single individual who has overriding knowledge and power; it is composed of a complex team of trained specialists who are contributing their skills to the organization's performance. They are typically the "catalysts" who help the organization utilize and adapt to new technological developments.

Technology has had a primary impact not only on staff and functional personnel but also on middle and lower line managers. The role of first-line supervisors has changed significantly; they are required to integrate activities across a broader spectrum. They are often the mediators between the requirements of the technical system and those of the psychosocial system. Supervisory requirements in terms of both technical and human relations skills are significantly increased as a result of the changing technology.

With accelerating technology, there has been a shift of emphasis for the managerial system. Under traditional management concepts, primary consideration was given to the differentiation or segmentation of activities into subsystems for task performance. Increasingly, with growing differentiation in complex organizations, problems of integration have intensified. *Integration* is the process of achieving coordination of effort among various subsystems in accomplishing the organization's goals.

Many research studies have considered the impact of changing technology on managerial systems. One of the more comprehensive studies was conducted by Burns and Stalker in their investigation of English and Scottish firms. They examined a number of firms with a stable technology and environment, which were attempting to move into the electronics field with its rapidly changing technology. "We hoped to be able to observe how management systems changed in accordance with changes in the technical and commercial tasks of the firm, especially the substantial changes in the rate of technical advance which new interests in electronics development and application would mean."[30] It was their

---

29 See Leonard R. Sayles and Margaret K. Chandler, *Managing Large Systems,* Harper & Row, Publishers, Incorporated, New York, 1971; and James E. Webb, *Space Age Management,* McGraw-Hill Book Company, New York, 1969.

30 Tom Burns and G. M. Stalker, *The Management of Innovation,* Tavistock Publications, London, 1961, p. 4.

hypothesis, substantiated by the research findings, that a different managerial system was appropriate for concerns involved in a stable technology and environment as compared with those adapting to rapidly changing technology. Managerial systems that were adapted to a stable technology were termed **mechanistic.** Such a system was characterized as having a rigidly prescribed organization structure. There were well-defined tasks, and the methods, duties, and powers attached to each functional role were determined precisely. The interactions within the management system tended to be vertical between superior and subordinate—a strong command hierarchy. "Management, often visualized as the complex hierarchy familiar in organization charts, operates a simple control system, with information flowing up through a succession of filters, and decisions and instructions flowing downwards through a succession of amplifiers." [31]

By contrast, **organic** managerial systems are best adapted to conditions of rapidly changing technology and environment. They are suitable to unstable conditions when problems and requirements for action arise that cannot be broken down and distributed among specialized roles within a clearly defined hierarchy. The organic system is characterized by a relatively flexible structure. Continual adjustment and redefinition of individual tasks through interaction with others, a network rather than hierarchical control, emphasis on lateral rather than vertical communications, and a wide dispersal of power and influence based on technical expertise and knowledge rather than on hierarchical position are characteristic of the organic system.

Burns and Stalker also emphasize the difficulties involved in making the transformation from the mechanistic to the organic system by the firms that were trying to move into the electronics industry. The unstructured and highly dynamic nature of the organic system often created anxiety and insecurity on the part of the managers who had been used to working in the structured, mechanistic system.

Burns and Stalker do not attempt to set up an idealized managerial system that would be appropriate for all types of technical and environmental situations. Just the opposite; they strongly emphasize that the most appropriate managerial system is dependent on different kinds of technology and environmental circumstances.

The type of technology can have an important effect on managerial decision making. Organizations with stable, routine technologies tend to adopt computational decision-making approaches, whereas those with a dynamic, diffuse technology require more innovative, judgmental decision-making processes. Organizations with a stable technology emphasize performance goals, whereas organizations with a dynamic technology stress problem solving. [32]

---

31 Ibid., p. 5.
32 Raymond G. Hunt, "Technology and Organization," *Academy of Management Journal,* September 1970, pp. 235–252.

Social and Behavioral Technologies in Organizations

Technology has been defined as the application of knowledge for the achievement of practical purposes. Much of the previous discussion has been concerned with the technology utilized directly in production processes. In addition, organizations utilize a wide variety of social and behavioral technologies in the design of the structure, in planning and controlling operations, in selecting, training, and motivating employees, and in decision-making processes. Many of these techniques are incorporated into our existing knowledge about how to organize and manage large, complex sociotechnical systems. Bell calls this knowledge the "new intellectual technology." He says:

The major intellectual and sociological problems of the post-industrial society are those of "organized complexity"—the management of large-scale systems, with large numbers of interacting variables, which have to be coordinated to achieve specific goals. [33]

The organization of a large corporation, professional association, hospital, or accounting firm represents a *social* technology just as an assembly line or computer-controlled tool is a *machine* technology.

In management, new social technologies are introduced through research, serendipity, and practice. Budgetary control processes, personnel selection, training and development programs, organization charts and position descriptions, and long-range planning have been with us for some time. But there is an emergence of other technologies such as management-by-objectives programs, human asset accounting, management assessment centers, planning-programming-budgeting systems, job design-job enrichment techniques, and a variety of organization change strategies. The management sciences have also contributed many new technologies, such as systems analysis, operations research, and computerized information systems.

Organizations are utilizing new behavioral technologies to directly influence individuals and groups in organizations. Approaches such as sensitivity training, transactional analysis, and behavior modification are examples.

It is impossible to cover all of the newer social technologies in this unit. However, we can illustrate their importance by briefly considering one application—job design-job enrichment.

Job Design– Job Enrichment

Substantial research, experimentation, and actual application of behavioral science concepts have focused on job design and the relationship between

---

33 Bell, op. cit., p. 29.

technology, task, productivity, and worker satisfaction. It is based on certain value premises:

Many managers and behavioral scientists have come to recognize that the missing element of motivation to work may lie in the character of the work itself. For the mature individual, work may be a means of personal growth; it may satisfy his need for achievement, creativity and self-fulfillment. Work, then, becomes more than a means for economic survival, and it is apparent that in this age of affluence with its more sophisticated population, people won't work long or well at a job that offers no challenge or meaning. [34]

We use the term *job design* to include a broad spectrum of approaches, including job enlargement, job enrichment, job restructuring, work reform, autonomous work groups, sociotechnical systems analysis, flexitime, job rotation, and job sharing. Generally speaking, these approaches also include an increased element of worker participation in the job design processes.

More specifically, "job design means specification of the contents, methods, and relationships of jobs in order to satisfy technological and organizational requirements as well as the social and personal requirements of the jobholder." [35] Under this concept, the goal of job design is to enhance productivity/performance *and* to improve the quality of an employee's working life and job satisfaction.

Modern job design concepts consider all aspects of jobs as variables. More specifically, the production technologies and the structural relationships may be modified and redesigned to fit the *needs of the workers.* Rather than increased specialization of tasks, job redesign may advocate job enlargement by increasing the scope of the task or job enrichment by giving the employee greater discretion for planning and control functions. Rather than the worker performing highly specialized work in an assembly line process, job redesign may call for the creation of autonomous work units that are responsible for a complete assembly operation and have substantial leeway in assigning and scheduling tasks among group members. In effect, job design approaches attempt to improve all those job characteristics listed in Figure 8.3.

There have been many different approaches to job design, and this new social technology is being used throughout the world. There seem to be various approaches used, based on differing sociocultural factors. What works in one country may not be appropriate in another setting. [36] Nevertheless, there is a common theme: "How do we design jobs and reform work to increase productivity *and* satisfaction?" This is a common problem for all industrialized countries.

Some of the more comprehensive projects have been undertaken in Sweden and other Scandinavian countries. The development of the new Volvo automobile assembly line at Kalmar, based on autonomous work groups, has received the most publicity. However, there have been more than 500 other experimental

34 Harold M. F. Rush, *Job Design for Motivation,* The Conference Board, Inc., New York, 1971, p. ii.
35 Louis E. Davis, "The Design of Jobs," *Industrial Relations,* October 1966, p. 21.
36 Nancy Foy and Herman Gadon, "Worker Participation: Contrasts in Three Countries," *Harvard Business Review,* May–June 1976, pp. 71–83.

work reform projects carried out by several hundred Swedish companies over the past several years.[37]

    Job design and all of its complementary approaches represents a relatively new social technology, and it is apparent that there are many problems. Although there have been many reported successes on experimental projects in job design, these approaches are slow to spread, even within the same organization.[38]

    It is obvious that this is a social technology with much broader ramifications than just the individual's job productivity and satisfaction. Comprehensive programs may not only require modifications in technologies, structure, and superior-subordinate relationships but in all other aspects of the organizational climate as well. Several such programs have had difficulties because of the failure to recognize and deal with these broader consequences.[39]

    Job design is still in its infancy and we do not understand all of the complex interrelationships. It is a soft social technology that is strongly influenced by values and attitudes. The goal of job and work redesign—to increase both organizational performance and employee satisfaction—is well worth striving for. It is more humanly appropriate than any other orientation and will become an increasingly important consideration for the future.

Summary

    Technology has two aspects—the physical manifestations such as machinery and equipment and the accumulated knowledge concerning the means to accomplish tasks. By organizational technology we mean the complex of techniques utilized in the transformation of the inputs of the system into outputs.

    Science and technology have become a pervasive force in modern society, influencing all of our activities and providing a new shape to the world. In modern industrial society large-scale complex organizations have become the primary means for utilizing technology. In a broad sense, the development of large organizations represents an advancement in social technology. The ability to bring together the material, human, and informational resources necessary to accomplish complex tasks is a major achievement.

    The classification of organizations by type of technology is a useful starting place for comparative analysis. In considering organization technologies, there are two major issues: (1) the degree of complexity and (2) whether the technology is stable or dynamic. We have used these two dimensions to suggest a continuum ranging from a simple and stable technology to a highly complex and dynamic technology.

37 David Jenkins (ed.), *Job Reform in Sweden,* Swedish Employers' Confederation, Stockholm, Sweden, 1975, p. 3.

38 Richard E. Walton, "The Diffusion of New Work Structures: Explaining Why Success Didn't Take," *Organizational Dynamics,* Winter 1975, pp. 3–22.

39 "Stonewalling Plant Democracy," *Business Week,* March 28, 1977, pp. 78–82.

The technical system is directly related to the environmental suprasystem and to the goals and values of the organization. It has an important impact on the structure, social relationships, and managerial system. For a routine technology the stable-mechanistic structure is appropriate. However, with a changing and complex technology, the adaptive-organic form is most effective.

Organizations utilize an increasing variety of social and behavioral technologies that are directed toward improving effectiveness, efficiency, and participant satisfaction. Job design–job enrichment represents an important example of this technology.

An important aspect of the design of organizations is the development of an appropriate fit between the technology and the other subsystems. Throughout this chapter, we have emphasized that different technologies require different adaptations—there is no one best design.

Questions and Problems

1 Compare and contrast machine and knowledge technology.

2 How has technology shaped our sociocultural environment? How is advancing technology related to the growth of complex organizations?

3 Discuss the relationship between technology and organization structure. What are the basic structural differences between the firm with a routine, fixed technology and one with a dynamic, diffused technology?

4 Evaluate the impact of technology on the psychosocial system of organizations.

5 Consider your own work experience. How did the technology affect your job and your relationships with others in the organization?

6 How have managerial systems been affected by changing technology?

7 Discuss the distinctions between mechanistic and organic managerial systems.

8 Based on your own organizational experiences, develop a list of the various social and behavioral technologies that you have observed.

9 Visit a convenient organization (fast food service, supermarket, bank, service station) and observe how the technical system interrelates with the other subsystems.

Organization Structure and Design

Nine

Structural relationships are fundamental considerations of organization theorists and practicing managers. The environmental suprasystem is an important determinant of structure, particularly at the strategic level. The technical system has an effect on the type of structure appropriate for task performance. In turn, the structure sets a framework for the psychosocial system and is inexorably interwoven with the managerial system. The primary emphasis, in this chapter, is on formal rather than on informal relationships. We are concerned with developing the concept of structure, investigating the variables affecting it, considering new developments in organization design, and examining the dynamics of structure in relationship to other organizational subsystems. The following topics are discussed:

Definition of Structure
Traditional Concepts of Organization Structure
Structure: the Linkage Between Environment and Other Subsystems
Differentiation of Organizational Activities
Integration of Organizational Activities
Evolution of Structural Designs
Program Management and the Matrix Form
An Example of Organization Structure
Dynamics of Organization Structure

Definition of Structure

The concept of organization structure is somewhat abstract and illusive. However, it is real and affects everyone in the organization. The student comes in contact with the structure of the university when selecting a major and studying under the direction of a particular academic unit. When you walk into an unfamiliar bank, the information clerk helps you find the "loan department" or the "new accounts department," depending on your needs. New employees in their first assignment are told, "You will be working under Smith in the Market Research Department." One of the more difficult things for the new employee to learn is the name and function of the various departments, the superior-subordinate relationships, and "who does what."

Very simply, **structure** may be considered as *the established pattern of relationships among the components or parts of the organization.* However, the structure of a social system is not visible in the same way as a biological or mechanical system. It cannot be seen but is inferred from the actual operations and behavior of the organization.

The distinction between structure and **process** in systems helps in understanding this concept. In the biological system the structure of the organism may be studied separately from its processes. For example, the study of anatomy is basically the study of the structure of the organism. In contrast, physiology is concerned with the study of the functions of living organisms. In the study of a social system such as an organization, it is difficult to make this clear-cut distinction.

We agree that the structure of the organization cannot be looked at as completely separate from its functions; however, these are two separate phenomena. Taken together, the concepts of structure and process can be viewed as the static and dynamic features of the organization. In some systems the static aspects (the structure) are the most important for investigation; in others the dynamic aspects (the processes) are more important.

In the complex organization, structure is set forth initially by the design of the major components or subsystems and then by the establishment of patterns of relationship among these subsystems. It is this internal differentiation and patterning of relationships with some degree of permanency that is referred to as structure. The formal structure is frequently defined in terms of:

1 The pattern of formal relationships and duties—the organization chart plus job descriptions or position guides.
2 The way in which the various activities or tasks are assigned to different departments and/or people in the organization (differentiation).
3 The way in which these separate activities or tasks are coordinated (integration).
4 The power, status, and hierarchical relationships within the organization (authority system).
5 The planned and formalized policies, procedures, and controls that guide the activities and relationships of people in the organization (administrative system).

Formal and Informal Organization

Formal organization is the planned structure and represents the deliberate attempt to establish patterned relationships among components that will meet the objectives effectively. The formal structure is typically the result of explicit decision making and is prescriptive in nature—a "blueprint" of the way activities should be related. Typically it is represented by a printed chart and is set forth in organization manuals, position descriptions, and other formalized documents. Although the formal structure does not comprise the total organizational system, it is of major importance. It sets a general framework and delineates certain prescribed functions and responsiblities and the relationships among them.

Anyone who has participated in an organization recognizes that many interactions occur that are not prescribed by the formal structure. The *informal organization* refers to those aspects of the system that are not planned explicitly but arise spontaneously out of the activities and interactions of participants.

Informal relationships are vital for the effective functioning of the organization. Frequently groups develop spontaneous means for dealing with important activities that contribute to overall performance. When the formal organization is slow in responding to external and internal forces, informal relationships develop to deal with these new problems. Thus, the organization may be adaptive and serve to perform innovative functions that are not being adequately met by the formal structure. On the other hand, there are occasions in which informal relationships may operate to the detriment of goals—when work groups slow down or sabotage production, for example.

Traditional management theorists concentrated on the formal organization structure. The human relationists, in contrast, were concerned primarily with interpersonal relationships. This diversity of interest led to the view that there is an actual separation between the formal and informal structures. However, they really are intermeshed.

It is impossible to understand the nature of a formal organization without investigating the networks of informal relations and the unofficial norms as well as the formal hierarchy of authority and the official body of rules, since the formally instituted and the informally emerging patterns are inextricably intertwined. The distinction between the formal and the informal aspects of organizational life is only an analytical one and should not be reified; there is only one actual organization. [1]

In this chapter we will discuss the formal structure and will consider the informal patterns and relationships in Part 5. We should keep continually in mind, however, that this cleavage is artificial. In the actual organization the informal and formal structures are so intertwined as to defy separation.

1 Peter M. Blau and W. Richard Scott, *Formal Organizations: A Comparative Analysis,* Chandler Publishing Company, San Francisco, 1962, p. 6.

Authority and Organization Structure

There is a direct interrelationship between organization structure and the pattern of authority. In fact, many traditionalists made the underlying assumption that authority relationships were synonymous with the organization structure. Inasmuch as structure is concerned with the establishment of positions and the relationships between positions, it does provide the framework for authority relationships. However, authority pattern is just one part of the total structure.

Authority refers to a relationship between the participants in the organization and is not an attribute of one individual. The authority structure provides the basis for assigning tasks to the various elements in the organization and for developing a control mechanism to ensure that these tasks are performed according to plan. It provides for the establishment of formalized influence transactions among the members of the organization.

The concept of authority is closely related to the idea of the legitimate exercise of the power of a position and depends on the willingness of subordinates to comply with certain directives of superiors. Obviously, the structure and the positioning of participants in a hierarchical arrangement facilitate the exercise of authority.

Responsibility and Organization Structure

Structure is directly related to the assignment of responsibility and accountability to various organizational units. Delegation is fundamental in the assignment of both authority and responsibility. For example, the personnel department is typically assigned the authority for recruitment, selection, and training of employees, and it has the responsibility for carrying out these assigned activities.

Control systems are based on the delegation of responsibility. Most organizations develop some means to determine the effectiveness and efficiency of the performance of these assigned functions and create control processes to ensure that these responsibilities are carried out. In simple structures there can be clearly defined authority and responsibility assigned to specific departments, and they can be held exclusively accountable for results. In more complex organizations, where substantial integration and coordination are required between departments, both authority and responsibility may be shared by several units.

Organization Charts

A typical way of depicting the structure is through printed organization charts that specify the formal authority and communication networks of the organization. Figure 9.1 presents a simplified chart for a manufacturing company.

Figure 9.1 Simplified Organization Chart for a Manufacturing Company

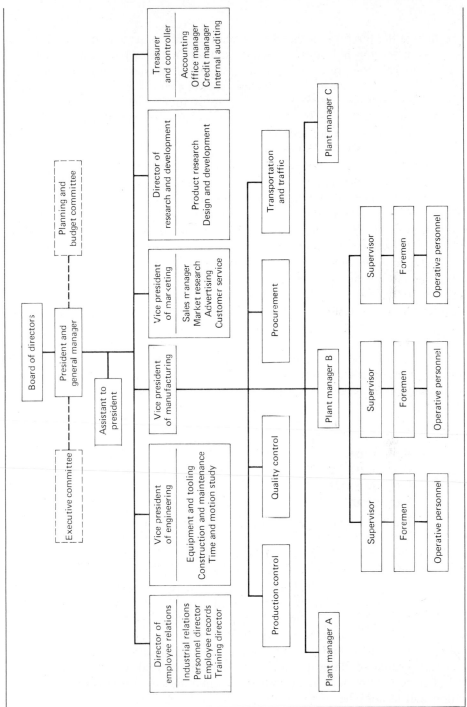

The title of the position on the chart broadly identifies its activities, and its distance from the top indicates its relative status. The lines between positions are used to indicate the prescribed formal interactions. Most organization charts are hierarchical and emphasize relationships between superiors and direct subordinates. They are frequently supplemented by position descriptions and organizational manuals that attempt to define the tasks of the various positions and the interactions between them more specifically.

The organization chart is usually a simplified, abstract model of the structure. It is not an exact representation of reality and therefore has limitations. It shows only a few of the relationships, even in the formal organization, and none of those in the informal organization. It does not, for example, indicate the degree of authority that a superior has over a subordinate. Does the superior have the right to hire and replace the occupant of a subordinate position? More important, it does not indicate the interactions between equals or the lateral relationships between people in different parts of the organization. "It usually errs by not reflecting the nuances of relationships within the organization; it usually deals poorly with informal control and informal authority, usually underestimates the significance of personality variables in molding the actual system, and usually exaggerates the isomorphism between the authority system and the communication system."[2]

In spite of these limitations, the organization chart provides a useful starting point for the investigation of structure. Its inaccuracy generally lies in its simplicity and in its lack of consideration of many other important aspects of the structure.

Traditional Concepts of Organization Structure

Traditional management theorists were primarily concerned with the design of efficient organizations. They emphasized such concepts as objectivity, impersonality, and structural form. The organization structure was designed for the most efficient allocation and coordination of activities. The positions in the structure, not the people, had the authority and responsibility for getting tasks accomplished. The structure was emphasized as the most important and enduring characteristic of the organization. Many of the traditional concepts were based on experiences with stable organizations such as the military, church, and established public bureaucracies. Industrial organizations were concerned with developing a structure geared to stable production. They emphasized a rigid structure with well-defined relationships and clearly established lines of authority and communication. Let us consider some "principles" of organization.

2 Richard M. Cyert and James G. March, *A Behavioral Theory of the Firm,* Prentice-Hall, Inc., Englewood Cliffs, N.J., 1963, p. 289.

Organizational Specialization and Division of Labor

A basic concept of traditional management theory is to divide work into specialized tasks and to organize them into distinct departments. Departmentalization with a natural division of labor is emphasized. It is desirable to determine the necessary activities for the accomplishment of overall organizational objectives and then to divide these activities on a logical basis into departments that perform the specialized functions. The organization structure is the primary means for achieving the technical and economic advantages of specialization and division of labor.

The Scalar Principle

The scalar principle states that authority and responsibility should flow in a direct line vertically from the highest level of the organization to the lowest level. It establishes the hierarchical structure of the organization. It refers to the vertical division of authority and responsibility and the assignment of various duties along the scalar chain. Primary emphasis is on the superior-subordinate relationships. Most organization charts indicate that this principle is still used in designing the structure. The scalar principle is complementary to the concept of unity of command, in which each subordinate has only one superior.

Authority, Responsibility, and Accountability

In the classical view, the legitimatization of authority at a central source ensures that the superior has the *right* to command someone else and that the subordinate person has the *duty* to obey the command. Authority is the right to invoke compliance by subordinates on the basis of formal position and control over rewards and sanctions. It is impersonal and goes with the position rather than the individual. Furthermore, authority and responsibility should be directly linked; that is, if a subordinate is responsible for carrying out an activity, he should also be given the necessary authority. Accountability is associated with the flow of authority and responsibility and is the obligation of the subordinate to carry out his responsibility and to exercise authority in terms of the established policies. This view of authority, responsibility, and accountability provides the framework for much of traditional management theory. It is the basis for legitimatizing organizational hierarchy and control systems and for establishing many other concepts such as span of control and line-staff relationships. Authority is the means for integrating the activities of participants toward objectives and provides the basis for centralized direction and control.

Span of Control

The span of control, or span of supervision, relates to the number of subordinates that a superior can supervise effectively. It is closely related to the hierarchical structure and to departmentalization. Implicit in the span of control concept is the necessity for the coordination of the activities of the subordinates by the superior. It emphasizes superior-subordinate relationships that allow for the systematic integration of activities. Traditional theory advocates a narrow span to enable the executive to provide adequate integration of all the activities of subordinates. It does not recognize the possibility of other means for coordination.

Line and Staff

As organizations grew more complex, it was necessary to integrate personnel with specialized knowledge and functions into the managerial system. This required modifications in the concepts of the scalar structure, unity of command, authority, and responsibility. In many ways, the line and staff concept can be viewed as a necessary compromise in terms of the other classical principles. The line organization is vested with the primary source of authority and performs the major functions of the organization; the staff supports and advises the line. The staff is an aid to the executive, an extension of her personality. Through the use of specialized staffs, reporting directly to the executive, it is possible to use their knowledge without sacrificing the executive's coordinating function. This view maintains the integrity of the line organization as central in the scalar chain and as the source of authority.

Many modern management writers are critical of the application of these traditional principles. However, they do have a place if they are applied with discrimination. They are useful at a certain stage in the development of an organization. They provide a basis for the initial formalizing of relationships as an organization grows from a small, informal operation. They are also appropriate where the organization is dealing with programmed and routine activities and has a stable environment and technology.

However, we would agree with the critics that absolute adherence to these principles is unrealistic. While they may serve as useful guidelines, organizations in a dynamic environment will generally need to have more fluid relationships. These principles were quite useful at the time of their formulation, during the early part of the twentieth century; however, with accelerating technology and new organizational requirements, they need to be modified.

These traditional concepts viewed the organization's structure as a rigid, closed system. They did not recognize the impact of environmental forces, nor did they fully consider the interactions between structure and the other subsystems in the organization.

Structure:
The Linkage Between
Environment and
Other Subsystems

It is useful to think of structure as the **linkage** or network between the organization's environment and the internal subsystems—the technology utilized in the transformation processes, the relationships among people performing various tasks, and the managerial system of planning and control. We use the term linkage because each of these systems is an important determinant of various structural characteristics of the organization. In turn, the structure is a binding element for the integration of these systems.

The fact that an organization is an open system and must receive support from its environment has an important impact on its internal structure. Organizations establish departments to deal with inputs from and outputs to specific sectors of its environment. "Organizations facing heterogeneous task environments seek to identify homogeneous segments and establish structural units to deal with each." [3] In business enterprises many departments interact directly with specific sectors of the environment. Purchasing is concerned with materials inputs; personnel departments recruit and select employees; market research obtains information from the outside. On the output side, sales departments maintain relationships with distributors, advertising departments attempt to influence customers, and public relations departments disseminate information that will enhance the reputation and impact of the corporation. The university's structure is similarly affected by environmental relationships. Separate units may be established to attract and select students, negotiate with legislatures, interact with alumni and donors of resources, attract research funds from the government, place graduates, and engage in many other activities relating to specific environmental forces.

We can generalize by suggesting that the more heterogeneous, dynamic, and uncertain the environment, the more complex and differentiated the internal structuring of the organization. We see many examples of this. With increased pressure from governmental agencies, many organizations respond by establishing lobbying units. Pressure from environmentalists and consumers has resulted in new internal departments. Increasing stress on equal employment opportunities for minorities and women led to new departments to deal with these issues. Obviously, movement into new environments through product diversification or geographic dispersion (e.g., multinational organizations) resulted in restructuring.

The technology that the organization utilizes also has an impact on internal structure. Technology most directly affects those structural characteristics closely related to the transformation process. For example, the technical system is the prime determinant of the structure of the production line, the machine shop, the operating room in the hospital, the oil refining process, and the food process-

3 James D. Thompson, *Organizations in Action*, McGraw-Hill Book Company, New York, 1967, p. 70.

ing plant. At these operating levels, the technology is a major determinant of the specialization and differentiation of activities, the means of integration, the authority relationships, the procedures and rules, and the degree of formalization.

The psychosocial system both affects and is strongly influenced by the structure.[4] For example, people with different educational and work experiences will often respond differently to various structural arrangements. The professional or technical specialist may seek autonomy and freedom from tight structure. This is true, for example, of doctors in hospitals, professors, design engineers, and many other professionals. However, production workers may be conditioned to accept a high degree of control over their activities. Even here, however, the situation may be changing. The desire for more meaningful work and greater participation has led to job redesign, autonomous work groups, and other approaches that affect structure.

Taken together, environmental influences, technological requirements, and psychosocial factors are key determinants of structure. But the cause-and-effect relationships are not easily determined, nor is there substantial agreement about which of these forces is the most important. They are all interactive and interdependent.

The Role of Management in Organizational Design: Strategic Choice

From the foregoing we might assume that, given the environment, technology, and people, the appropriate organization structure would be predetermined. This is certainly not the case. One of management's key functions is to design the organization in response to perceptions of these various contextual and internal factors. Management makes strategic choices that are fundamental in the determination of organization design. "Strategic choice extends to the context within which the organization is operating, to the standards of performance against which the pressure of economic constraints has to be evaluated, and to the design of the organization's structure itself."[5]

In reality, it is not the objective environment to which managerial decision makers respond, but the environment *as they perceive it.* Furthermore, managers often have an important say as to which environment will be relevant—they select an "organizational domain." For example, the corporation decides which markets it will enter in terms of products and/or geographical areas. Managers also make strategic choices concerning the goals of the organization, the nature of the technology, and the internal climate. Although the environment and internal

---

4 For a review of the research concerning the relationships between structural features and attitudes and behavior of people see L. L. Cummings and Cris J. Berger, "Organization Structure: How Does It Influence Attitudes and Performance," *Organizational Dynamics*, Autumn 1976, pp. 34–49.

5 John Child, "Organizational Structure, Environment and Performance: The Role of Strategic Choice," *Sociology*, January 1972, p. 1.

subsystems may place constraints on how managers design the structure of organizations, the importance of managerial decision making should not be underestimated. "Depending on perceptions of both environmental and internal properties, managers have considerable leeway in making strategic choices to meet various contingencies."[6] Figure 9.2 illustrates these determinants and the strategic choice process.

Differentiation of Organizational Activities

Complex organizations are characterized by a high degree of task specialization. Even the simplest enterprise, with just a few employees, has some division of labor among participants. In larger organizations this differentiation is carried much further. For example, a large university can have more specialization in course offerings and faculty personnel than the small liberal arts college that must concentrate on more general, less specialized subject matter. The total task of the organization is differentiated so that particular departments and units are responsible for the performance of specialized activities. "*Differentiation* is defined as the state of segmentation of the organizational system into subsystems,

Figure 9.2   Organization Structure and Strategic Choice

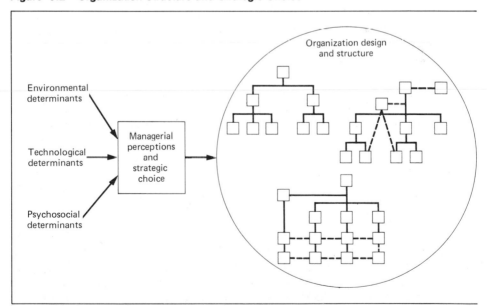

---

6 Carl R. Anderson and Frank T. Paine, "Managerial Perceptions and Strategic Behavior," *Academy of Management Journal*, December 1975, p. 811.

each of which tends to develop particular attributes in relation to the requirements posed by its relevant external environment."[7]

In the organization, this differentiation occurs in two directions: the vertical specialization of activities, represented by the organizational hierarchy, and the horizontal differentiation of activities, called departmentalization. Figure 9.1 illustrates these two bases of separation of activities. The vertical differentiation is represented by the hierarchy moving from the president to the vice-presidents, plant managers, and supervisors, and finally to the operative level. The vertical differentiation establishes the managerial structure, whereas the horizontal differentiation defines the basic departmentalization. Taken together, they set the formal structure of the organization.[8]

Vertical Differentiation: Hierarchy

The vertical division of labor establishes the hierarchy and the number of levels in the organization. Although organizations differ in the degree of their vertical divisions of labor and the extent to which it is made explicit and formalized, they all exhibit this characteristic. In the more formal organizations, such as the military, the vertical specialization is established by specific definitions of roles for the various positions, and there are significant status differences between levels. There is, for example, a basic separation between officers and enlisted personnel. Within the officer ranks, there is a distinct difference of role, status, and position in the hierarchy from second lieutenant to five-star general. Other organizations may not have such a clear-cut hierarchical differentiation in role and function. In the university there is a hierarchy from instructor to assistant professor to associate professor to full professor in the professional ranks. However, the beginning instructor may perform a teaching and research role quite similar to that of the full professor.

In the formal organization this hierarchy sets the basic communications and authority structure, the so-called "chain of command." In the business organization there are typically vertical differentiations of positions ranging from hourly employees to first-line supervisors, middle managers, and top executives. These levels are fairly well defined, with major differences in functions and status for the various positions.

There are substantial rewards for moving upward in the hierarchy. Position in the vertical dimension frequently determines the authority and influence, privilege, status, and rewards enjoyed by the incumbent. This vertical differentia-

7 Paul R. Lawrence and Jay W. Lorsch, "Differentiation and Integration in Complex Organizations," *Administrative Science Quarterly,* June 1967, pp. 3–4.

8 Peter M. Blau, "A Formal Theory of Differentiation in Organizations," *American Sociological Review,* April 1970, pp. 201–218.

tion of activities also has the effect of creating the organizational pyramid. Inasmuch as each superior has more than one subordinate, the organization tends to broaden out (see Figure 9.1).

Horizontal Differentiation: Departmentalization

Organizations typically have some basis for horizontal differentiation of activities. Even in a small retail store operation one partner often performs certain functions, such as purchasing and inventory control, with the other in charge of advertising and sales promotion. In a small organization this differentiation may be informal and may arise out of the natural interests and skills of the individuals involved. In a more complex organization, this horizontal specialization of activities is a necessity because of the need to perform particular functions effectively and efficiently.

The three primary bases of departmentalization are (1) function, (2) product, and (3) location. Departmentalization by *function* is shown in Figure 9.1, wherein the activities of the organization are divided into the primary functions to be performed—manufacturing, marketing, engineering, research and development, employee relations, and finance. This arrangement has the advantage of specialization and the concentration of similar activities within a departmental unit. It is the most prevalent form of departmentalization and is seen not only in business enterprises but in hospitals, governmental agencies, and many other kinds of organizations. The major problem associated with this form is the coordination of the specialized activities.

Product departmentalization has become increasingly important, especially for large, complex organizations. For example, companies such as General Electric, General Motors, and DuPont have major product divisions with substantial autonomy. This form has been used increasingly, with the trend toward heterogeneous diversification.

A third primary basis of departmentalization is *location.* All the organizational activities performed in a particular geographic area are brought together and integrated into a single unit. This has been the pattern adopted by chain stores in establishing regional offices. The geographic basis of departmentalization also has become an important form for multinational business corporations such as IBM, Nestlé Corporation, and Unilever.

In addition to these primary bases of departmentalization, there are several others. Some organizations may departmentalize on a basis of *customers,* with separate units for retail and wholesale or for government and commercial sales. In many manufacturing organizations, departmentalization may relate to the *processes* or *equipment* utilized.

In the large organization, there is no one basis of departmentalization that is carried out uniformly throughout the entire enterprise. For example, at one level in the organization there may be the product divisions. At the next level, there may be functional specialization, and at the third level, departmentalization based on geographic location or customer.

Role of
Staff
Specialists

A traditional basis of differentiation of managerial activities has been in terms of line and staff functions. The line has direct command authority over the activities of the organization and is concerned with the primary functions. In contrast, the staff performs an advisory role and is concerned with supportive or adjutant activities. The development of the line-staff concept was necessary to provide some means of integrating the activities of numerous highly trained specialists who contribute important knowledge and skills.

The role of staff has changed substantially with greater managerial specialization and complexities of many organizations. Staff specialists have come to play much more important roles. With the expansion of this role the clear delineation between line and staff activities is no longer possible. The view of line as only having command authority and staff as only having an advisory role does not always hold true. The staff expert, because of knowledge and technical competence in a particular area of specialization, is frequently viewed as a source of authority and influence in the organization. This is particularly true where the staff has functional authority. Functional authority resides within a specialized staff that exercises control over other operational units. Quite frequently, for example, the industrial relations department has functional authority over many personnel practices in all departments throughout the organization. Functional authority represents a substantial variation from the traditional emphasis on the line structure and unity of command.

Etzioni suggests that in certain types of organizations, such as research laboratories, hospitals, and universities, the roles of staff and line are reversed.

In full-fledged professional organizations the staff-professional line-administrator correlation, insofar as such distinctions apply at all, is reversed. Although administrative authority is suitable for the major goal activities in private business, in professional organizations administrators are in charge of secondary activities; they administer *means* to the major activity carried out by professionals. In other words, to the extent that there is a staff-line relationship at all, professionals should hold the major authority and administrators the secondary staff authority. [9]

Although many organizations, particularly business and the military, attempt to differentiate between the line and staff activities, it is our view that this distinction is becoming increasingly difficult to justify. Newer organizational forms, specifically developed to ensure the integration of activities, both on a

---

9 Amitai Etzioni, *Modern Organizations,* © 1964, p. 81. Reprinted by permission of Prentice-Hall, Inc., Englewood Cliffs, N.J.

vertical and horizontal basis, may be replacing the traditional line-staff form. While organizations with a uniform technology and operating in a stable environment may still find the differentiation of activities in terms of line and staff meaningful, organizations with dynamic technology and changing environment are finding this concept obsolete.

We have looked at some of the ways in which organizations differentiate activities. It appears that in all forms of complex organizations there has been a continual *trend toward the differentiation of activities into specialized subsystems.* Part of this has been a consequence of increased size, but even more significant has been the increasing need for more specialization within organizations.

Integration of Organizational Activities

The second overall consideration in the design of organization structures is that of coordination of activities. "*Integration* is defined as the process of achieving unity of effort among the various subsystems in the accomplishment of the organization's task." [10] The requirements of the environment and the technical system often determine the degree of coordination required. In some organizations, it is possible to separate activities in such a way as to minimize these requirements. This is typically true of chain store operations where each individual store unit has substantial autonomy and the major coordinative activities occur within these separate units. In other organizations, particularly those departmentalized functionally, integration is more important (see Figure 9.1).

It is important to recognize the interaction between the need to specialize activities and the requirements for integration. The more differentiation of activities and specialization of labor, the more difficult the problems of coordination.

Both horizontal and vertical differentiation present organizations with control, communication, and coordination problems. Subunits along either axis are nuclei that are differentiated from adjacent units and the total organization according to horizontal or vertical factors. The greater the differentiation, the greater the potentiality for difficulties in control, coordination, and communications. [11]

Bases of Coordination

Organizations typically establish several different mechanisms for achieving coordination. Litterer suggests three general methods: directive, volun-

[10] Lawrence and Lorsch, op. cit. p. 4.

[11] Richard H. Hall, *Organizations: Structure and Process,* Prentice-Hall, Inc., Englewood Cliffs, N.J. 1972, p. 146.

tary, and facilitated.[12] In one form of directive coordination, **hierarchical** coordination, the various activities are linked together by placing them under a central authority. In Figure 9.1, the major functions are coordinated by the president. In the simple organization, this form of coordination might be sufficient. However, in complex organizations such as General Electric or the National Aeronautics and Space Administration, with many levels and numerous specialized departments, hierarchical coordination becomes more difficult. Although the typical pyramidal chart indicates that there is one central position that is a focal point for coordination of all the activities, this is impossible for the larger organization. It would be difficult for a top-level executive to cope with all the coordinating problems. There are also major problems of communication up and down the hierarchy that make it impossible for the individual at the top to have the information required for the coordination of activities at lower levels. This is particularly true when there are many layers in the organization. Thus, coordination through the hierarchical structure must be supplemented by other means.

The **administrative** system provides a second mechanism for directive coordination of activities. "A great deal of coordinative effort in organization is concerned with a horizontal flow of work of a routine nature. *Administrative systems* are formal procedures designed to carry out much of this routine coordinative work automatically."[13] Many work procedures, such as memos with routing slips, help coordinate efforts of different operating units. To the extent that these procedures can be programmed or routinized, it is not necessary to establish specific structural means for coordination. For nonroutine and nonprogrammable events, specific units such as committees may be required to provide integration.

A second type of coordination is through **voluntary means.** Much of the coordination may depend on the willingness and ability of individuals or groups to voluntarily find means to integrate their activities with other organizational participants. Achieving voluntary coordination is one of the most important yet difficult problems of the manager. Voluntary coordination requires that the individual have sufficient knowledge of organizational goals, adequate information concerning the specific problem of coordination, and the motivation to do something on his or her own.

The problems of integration for the organization with a stable environment, a constant technology, and routine activities are substantially different from those of the organization facing rapidly changing environmental and technological forces. The stable organization can rely on the hierarchical structure and established procedures to ensure coordination. The organization facing change must develop different mechanisms to facilitate integration.

---

12 Joseph A. Litterer, *The Analysis of Organizations*, 2d ed., John Wiley & Sons, Inc., New York, 1973, pp. 455–473.

13 Ibid., p. 466.

Development of
Means to
Facilitate
Integration

Problems of integrating diverse activities in complex organizations have stimulated the development of many means of coordination. One approach to integrating activities is the committee. Committees typically are made up of members from a number of different departments or functional areas and are concerned with problems requiring coordination. Many business organizations have established executive committees at the top level to provide integration. The use of committees for purposes of coordination is a well-established approach in other institutions such as universities and hospitals.

Lawrence and Lorsch studied six organizations operating in the chemical processing industry to determine how they achieved integration. These organizations used a technology that required highly differentiated and specialized activities but also a major degree of integration among them.[14] The study was concerned with how organizations achieve both substantial differentiation and tight integration when these forces seem paradoxical. They found that successful companies used task forces, teams, and project offices to achieve coordination. There was a tendency to formalize coordinative activities that had developed informally and voluntarily. For example, specific individuals were assigned the role of integrator.

In the most successful organizations, the influence of the integrators stemmed from their professional competence rather than from their formal position. They were successful as integrators because of their specialized knowledge and because they represented a central source of information in the operation. These results suggest that it is possible for the complex organization to achieve both differentiation of activities and effective integration but that new organizational arrangements are required to do so.

Others have recommended new structural forms to help with the problems of integration. Likert says, "Increases in functionalization, in turn, make effective coordination both more necessary and even more difficult."[15] He suggests that one mechanism for achieving integration is having people serve as "linking pins" between the various units in the organization (see Figure 9.3). Horizontally, there are certain organizational participants who are members of two separate groups and serve as coordinating agents between them. On the vertical basis, individuals serve as linking pins between their own level and those above and below. Thus, through this system of linking pins, the "voluntary coordination"

---

14 Lawrence and Lorsch, op. cit., pp. 1–47. For a detailed look at the relationship between differentiation and integration in a number of other organizations, see Paul R. Lawrence and Jay W. Lorsch, *Organization and Environment*, Division of Research, Graduate School of Business Administration, Harvard University, Boston, 1967.

15 Rensis Likert, *The Human Organization*, McGraw-Hill Book Company, New York, 1967, p. 156.

Figure 9.3 Linking-Pin Patterns

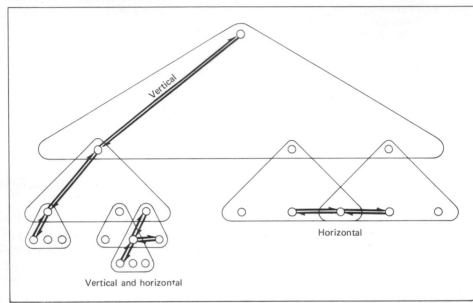

necessary to make the dynamic system operate effectively is achieved. This constitutes a multiple, overlapping group structure in the organization.

To perform the intended coordination well a fundamental requirement must be met. The
entire organization must consist of a multiple, overlapping group structure with *every*
work group using group decision-making processes skillfully. This requirement applies to
the functional, product, and service departments. An organization meeting this requirement will have an effective interaction-influence system through which the relevant communications flow readily, the required influence is exerted laterally, upward, and downward, and the motivational forces needed for coordination are created. [16]

Horizontal and Diagonal Relationships

Most organization charts are drawn to emphasize the vertical hierarchy
and superior-subordinate relationships. Very few indicate horizontal interactions,
those integrative activities that flow between departments, units, or individuals at
approximately the same level.

Horizontal relationships are those whose functions are not primarily the passing down of
orders or the passing up of information and whose nature and characteristics are not
primarily determined by the fact that one actor is superior to the other in the organiza-

16 Ibid., p. 167.

tion's hierarchy. The function of horizontal relationships is to facilitate the solution of problems arising from division of labor, and their nature and characteristics are determined by the participants having different organizational subgoals but interdependent activities that need to intermesh. [17]

As organizations have become more complex, it has been impossible to provide the necessary coordination through the vertical hierarchy. For example, in the modern hospital, a great many horizontal interactions are required. Patient treatment may involve a number of departments and specialized units, many of which are highly technical and impossible for one person to coordinate. "The modern organization depends on lateral relationships precisely because there are so many specialized points of view and so many required contacts that no single manager could handle the communication flow alone." [18]

In the industrial organization, the need for establishing effective horizontal relationships is also important. For example, the required interaction between product research and manufacturing, between sales and inventory control, and between advertising and finance is evident. Increasingly, new organizational units such as operations research groups and data processing centers have been established. They can succeed only if they are able to establish effective horizontal relationships with numerous other units in the organization.

Developing Communication Networks

Traditionally, information has moved up and down the hierarchy. However, increasing differentiation and the growing need for integration required the development of more sophisticated communication networks in organizations.

As organizational structure becomes more diversified and, in particular, as personal specialization increases, the volume of communication increases because of the necessity of co-ordinating the diverse occupational specialists. The major direction of this increased flow of information is horizontal, especially cross-departmental communications at the same status level. . . . As organizations become more diversified, and more specialized (personal specialization, not task specialization) and more differentiated, they have to rely less on a system of programmed interactions to achieve the necessary linkages between parts of the organization and more on a system of reciprocal information flows to achieve co-ordination. We have also suggested that such organizations would more likely rely on socialization rather than use of sanctions as a key mechanism of social control. [19]

Much of this information flow is horizontal and reciprocal between departments, such as the routing of memoranda and the exchange of minutes of

17 Henry A. Landsberger, "The Horizontal Dimension in Bureaucracy," *Administrative Science Quarterly,* December 1961, p. 300.
18 Leonard R. Sayles and George Strauss, *Human Behavior in Organizations,* Prentice-Hall, Inc., Englewood Cliffs, N.J., 1966, p. 424.
19 Jerald Hage, Michael Aiken, and Cora Bagley Marrett, "Organization Structure and Communications," *American Sociological Review,* October 1971, pp. 869–870.

important meetings. Computerized information systems have provided means for more elaborate communication networks. Many organizations have created weekly or monthly newsletters designed to spread the word around concerning major problems, new policies and procedures, and other informational items. By developing more effective communication networks, these organizations hope to create more willing and effective coordination of diverse activities.

Evolution of Structural Designs

One characteristic of large-scale organizations in every field of endeavor has been the increased elaboration and complexity of structure. This is true for business enterprises as well as hospitals, universities, and local, state, and federal governmental (including military) organizations. Although size may be a contributing factor to this elaboration, other forces are also significant.

Impact of Sociocultural Environment

There is a relationship between the sociocultural environment and organization structure. For example, Stinchcombe suggests that firms founded during the nineteenth century have a different structure than do companies founded during the twentieth century.[20] For example, the urban construction industry, with specialized craft workers, craft-specialized subcontractors, and trade unions, was founded in the earlier period and has basically retained this traditional form. Railroads have different organizational designs than do automotive companies, which in turn are different from the newer aerospace and computer companies. The specific structural form depends on the social, cultural, and environmental forces prevailing at the time the organization is established. Even though modifications are made over time, organizations seem to retain a strong flavor of their original form.

There is substantial evidence to verify this thesis. For example, the organization structure for NASA is significantly different from that of older governmental agencies. It has substantially more differentiation and specialization of activities and also has developed different means for achieving integration, such as program orientation. NASA's organization is very dependent on forces in the sociocultural environment. It would have been impossible to adopt the current structure without having highly trained technical specialists available in large numbers from our universities.

20 Arthur L. Stinchcombe, "Social Structure and Organizations," in James G. March (ed.), *Handbook of Organizations,* Rand McNally & Company, Chicago, 1965, pp. 142–143.

Structural Evolution in Industrial Organizations

For large-scale industrial organizations, certain patterns are evident in the structural changes that have occurred over time. Chandler states that as firms developed new strategies in response to the changing social and economic environment, basic changes in structure have been required. [21] In an intensive study of four large corporations, E. I. du Pont de Nemours & Co., General Motors Corporation, Standard Oil Company of New Jersey, and Sears, Roebuck and Company, supported by a survey of seventy other large industrial firms, he found certain evolutionary patterns of structure. Changing population, income, technology, and other forces in the environment have led to the expansion of these firms into new fields. This strategy of diversification and expansion has required major modifications in structure. "A new strategy required a new or at least refashioned structure if the enlarged enterprise was to operate efficiently. . . . Unless new structures are developed to meet new administrative needs which result from an expansion of a firm's activities into new areas, functions, or product lines, the technological, financial, and personnel economies of growth and size cannot be realized." [22]

The pattern of development of large industrial enterprises led to the adoption of a multidivisional structure in which the central corporate office plans and coordinates the activities of a number of operating divisions and makes allocations of personnel, facilities, funds, and other resources. The actual operations of the organization are decentralized to the operating divisions, which have a substantial degree of autonomy. This structural form has been the typical pattern adopted in the past several decades. This evolution is illustrated later in the chapter with a discussion of the Boeing Company.

The development of large-scale conglomerates in recent years has resulted in further structural modifications. Organizations such as International Telephone and Telegraph (ITT), Gulf and Western Industries, Litton Industries, and Textron have grown by encompassing within their structures a number of previously unrelated businesses in different industries (diversification through acquisition). They have accumulated vast financial resources and have spread their risks through expansion into many diverse fields.

The structural forms of these conglomerates are usually quite different from the older diversified organizations such as General Motors and Du Pont. Their strategies of diversification emphasize growth through acquisition and merger rather than through internal expansion. [23] Typically, they have much

---

21 Alfred D. Chandler, Jr., *Strategy and Structure*, The M.I.T. Press, Cambridge, Mass., © 1962.

22 Ibid., pp. 15–16.

23 Robert A. Pitts, "Strategies and Structures for Diversification," *Academy of Management Journal*, June 1977, pp. 197–208.

smaller corporate headquarters staffs and do not attempt to tightly control the operating units or to coordinate activities among them. [24]

Conglomerates have several organizational characteristics which make them a unique corporate form: diversity, comparatively simple integrative devices, pooled interdependence, major subunits which are both self-contained and autonomous to a considerable degree, and interunit coordinative requirements that center mainly around corporate-divisional relationships. [25]

The conglomerates have carried differentiation of activities to an extreme. However, they have generally adopted a loose structure that does not require substantial coordination between the different operating units. Integration is achieved primarily through corporate-divisional interactions with minimum division-to-division integration. The basic strategy is to achieve integration over broad financial and other policies at the strategic level but with very limited attempts to achieve integration between the coordinative and operating subsystems of the different divisions.

Growth of Administrative Structure

There has been substantial research to determine the primary causal factors determining organization structure. We have suggested earlier that the nature of the technical subsystem has a primary impact on structure at the operating level, whereas environmental influences are more important in determining the structure at the strategic level. Two other important factors influencing structure are *size* of the organization and *complexity* of operations.

The research findings relating structure to organizational size are not conclusive. Some have concluded that size is one of the major determinants of the structure of organizations. [26] Others have argued that size is not a critical factor in determining structural form. [27] Almost all researchers do agree that larger organizations have more complex and elaborate structures. However, there may be other intervening variables, such as technology and complexity, that are also characteristics of large organizations. For example, NASA has a very complex structure,

24 Norman A. Berg, "What's Different about Conglomerate Management?" *Harvard Business Review,* November–December 1969, pp. 112–120.

25 Stephen A. Allen, III, "Corporate-Divisional Relationships in Highly Diversified Firms," in Jay W. Lorsch and Paul R. Lawrence (eds.), *Studies in Organization Design,* Richard D. Irwin, Inc., and the Dorsey Press, Homewood, Ill., 1970, p. 22.

26 Peter M. Blau and Richard A. Schoenherr, *The Structure of Organizations,* Basic Books, Inc., Publishers, New York, 1971, pp. 56–62; and D. S. Pugh, D. J. Hickson, C. R. Hinings, and C. Turner, "The Context of Organization Structures," *Administrative Science Quarterly,* March 1969, pp. 91–114.

27 Richard H. Hall, J. Eugene Haas, and Norman J. Johnson, "Organizational Size, Complexity, and Formalization," *American Sociological Review,* December 1967, pp. 903–912.

but this may be due more to the nature of the technology and environmental forces than to size alone. [28]

The research on complexity appears to be more conclusive. There is substantial evidence suggesting that the more differentiated and diverse the activities of the organization and the more integration required, the more complex the structure. "There is a strong tendency for organizations to become more complex as their own activities and the environment around them becomes more complex." [29]

There is a general view that as organizations increase in size, the number of administrative personnel increases more than proportionately. However, research findings suggest that, if anything, the ratio of administrative personnel to operative personnel decreases. However, there is a relationship between the number of administrative personnel and the complexity of operations. As an organization increases in specialization and complexity, the scope of the managerial coordination problems increases. Therefore, it seems logical that the number of people engaged in administrative tasks would also increase.

Program Management and the Matrix Form

The program management approach is geared to changing managerial requirements in the research, development, procurement, and utilization of large-scale military, space, and civilian projects. With the advent of newer, more complex programs, the military services as well as other government agencies and private companies have had to adapt their organizational structures away from traditional functional arrangements. The pressures of accelerating technology and short lead times have made it necessary to establish some formalized managerial agency to provide overall integration of the many diverse functional activities.

Various terms have been used to designate these integrated management functions such as *systems management, program management, product management,* and *project management.* Although there are some differences among these terms and their meanings, they have a thread of commonality—the integrated management of a specific program on a systems basis. "The project manager acts as a focal point for the concentration of attention on the major problems of the project. This concentration forces the channeling of major program considerations through an individual who has the proper perspective to integrate relative matters

28 John R. Kimberly, "Organizational Size and the Structuralist Perspective: A Review, Critique, and Proposal," *Administrative Science Quarterly,* December 1976, pp. 571–597.

29 Hall, *Organizations: Structure and Process,* op. cit., p. 163.

of cost, time, technology, and total product compatibility." [30] This approach has been used in many major military systems and space programs. [31] For example, the National Aeronautics and Space Administration uses this approach in its more complicated projects, such as the space shuttle program. This approach is being used throughout industry as well.

Functions of Program Manager

Program managers are responsible for organizing and controlling all activities involved in achieving the ultimate objective. They are usually superimposed on the functional organization, creating new and complex relationships. This structural approach requires organizational modifications, emphasizes the integrative aspects, and requires the development of effective horizontal and diagonal information-decision networks.

There are various organizational approaches to program management. In the "staff" form the program manager is an adviser to the chief executive or general manager, with little individual authority. The functional managers retain the primary authority. At the other end of the spectrum, the program manager is granted complete authority over all the activities necessary to carry out the program. This is the approach used in many major military or space projects.

The matrix form is a compromise between these two extremes (see Figure 9.4). The functional managers, such as manufacturing, engineering, and marketing, are responsible to the general manager for their special activities. The project manager reports directly to the general manager on a line basis and may have personnel assigned to his or her project from the various functional departments. Under the matrix form there are two primary flows of authority—the vertical flow of authority from the various functional managers and the horizontal flow of project authority.

Authority Relationships

The essence of program management is that it is interfunctional and is often in conflict with the normal organization structure. Thus, when the program

---

30 David I. Cleland, "Why Project Management?" *Business Horizons,* Winter 1964, p. 83.

31 For a discussion of the evolution of the program management concept, see Fremont E. Kast and James E. Rosenzweig, "Organization and Management of Space Programs," in Frederick I. Ordway, III (ed.), *Advances in Space Science and Technology,* Academic Press, Inc., New York, 1965, pp. 273–364; and Richard A. Johnson, Fremont E. Kast, and James E. Rosenzweig, *The Theory and Management of Systems,* 3d ed., McGraw-Hill Book Company, 1973, chap. 13, "Program Management," pp. 388–425.

Figure 9.4 Functional Organization with Project Manager in a Line Capacity

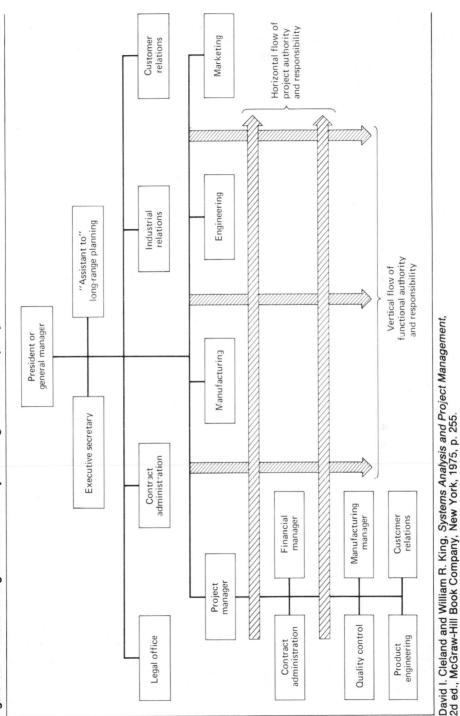

David I. Cleland and William R. King, *Systems Analysis and Project Management*, 2d ed., McGraw-Hill Book Company, New York, 1975, p. 255.

management approach is used, there is a natural conflict system.[32] Instead of an organization operating under the traditional view with a well-defined hierarchical structure, a unity of command, and clear-cut authority and responsibility relationships, the system is much more dynamic and less structured.

The program manager cannot operate effectively by relying solely on the formal authority of the position. Success is more likely to depend on the ability to influence other organizational members. Because the program manager is a focal point in the operation, he or she does have informational and communications inputs that provide a strong basis of influence.[33]

The program manager's authority and influence flow in different directions from hierarchical authority. They flow horizontally across superior-subordinate relationships existing within the functional organization. Throughout the program, personnel at various levels and in many functions must contribute their efforts. For each new program, lateral information-decision networks must be established that differ significantly from the existing networks based on the established structure. The organization should be sufficiently flexible to allow for evolving relationships and networks as program requirements change.

Other Characteristics

Program managers' tasks are finite. They take projects from the beginning and work them through to completion. Once a project is completed, the program management group can be reassigned to new activities. Thus, by its very nature the function is temporary. The organizational structure is dynamic, and people must be prepared to accept change. The emphasis on flexibility rather than permanency of relationships strongly affects the psychosocial and managerial systems.

The program manager and the staff usually serve in an important boundary-spanning capacity. Many activities, particularly in military and space programs, require interorganizational coordination. The program manager is the central point of the information-decision system regarding program activities and is the natural focal point for interorganizational coordination.

Frequently the introduction of the program approach creates additional organizational units and more management positions as well. In several companies that adopted program management, Middleton found a significant increase in the number of departments, the number of vice presidents and directors, and the number of second-level supervisors.[34]

---

32 Arthur G. Butler, Jr., "Project Management: A Study in Organizational Conflict," *Academy of Management Journal,* March 1973, pp. 84–101.

33 Hans T. Thamhain and Gary R. Gemmill, "Influence Styles of Project Managers: Some Project Performance Correlates," *Academy of Management Journal,* June 1974, pp. 216–224.

34 C. J. Middleton, "How to Set up a Project Organization," *Harvard Business Review,* March–April 1967, pp. 81–82.

The Matrix Structural Form

Program management utilizes the matrix form. Many other new organizational designs also take on characteristics of a matrix structure.[35] Essentially, the matrix form is a structural design geared to two primary organizational needs: (1) the need to specialize activities into functional departments that develop technical expertise and provide a permanent home base for employees and (2) the need to have units that integrate the activities of these specialized departments on a program, project, product, or systems basis. This form is a compromise between the traditional functional organization and the autonomous project organization. There are permanently established functional departments that maintain a stable base for specialized activities. Integrative units that have the prime role for coordination of activities are superimposed over this functional structure. The matrix form results in dual authority and responsibility. The functional manager has authority over the technical area and the integrating manager has authority over programs, projects, tasks, or product lines.

The matrix form has been used in a variety of companies. In a major reorganization, Dow Corning Company changed from a conventional divisionalized organization to a matrix form. The matrix structure was separated into *cost centers,* which were the functional activities (marketing, manufacturing, technical service and development, research, and supportive activities) and into *profit centers,* which were the product lines (rubber, resins and chemicals, consumer, medical, and semiconductors). Under this arrangement, a business board was established for each of the company's ten businesses. The managers of the businesses have the direct responsibility for profits, but they rely on the resources allocated from the functional managers. Under this arrangement the majority of the company's professional and managerial personnel work in a dual authority relationship. They report to the business manager *and* to their functional manager. Dow Corning has extended this matrix to reflect the different geographic regions in which the company operates. In reporting on the success of this multidimensional form, William Goggin, board chairman and chief executive officer, suggests that this structural form is not appropriate for all organizations but fits those that meet all or most of the following conditions:

Developing, manufacturing, and marketing many diverse but interrelated technological products and materials.

Having market interests that span virtually every major industry.

Becoming multinational with a rapidly expanding *global* business.

---

35 Jay Galbraith, *Designing Complex Organizations,* Addison-Wesley Publishing Company, Reading, Mass., 1973, pp. 103–106.

Working in a business environment of rapid and drastic change, together with strong competition. [36]

A company operating with a limited product line, mainly in the United States, serving a single industry, and having a relatively stable environment and technology would not find this form appropriate.

A somewhat different use of the matrix form was developed by the microwave cooking division of Litton Industries, Inc. This organization retained the functional departments (engineering, materials, manufacturing, quality control, and marketing) but developed task teams to operate as overlays to this functional structure. Many of the key activities are managed by these task force teams, such as new product development, new marketing programs, cost reduction activities, private-brand business, and new ventures. This approach required major changes in managerial approaches from the more traditional functional organization and altered the individual authority over well-defined activities. "Under the team concept, most decisions require the participation of several people, sometimes formally, sometimes informally. Unilateral decision making is virtually nonexistent. Even decisions delegated solely to a single department are fairly rare. To the manager accustomed to clear-cut lines of authority, this team decision making can be quite frustrating." [37] Litton sees this team approach as an effective means for coping with the problems of a high-growth organization and as providing creativity, flexibility, and adaptability through the task teams, while retaining the stability of the functional organization.

Hospitals have developed matrix type structures. Departments (nursing, social work, dietary, physical therapy, and medical staff specialists) provide for functional specialization; laterally organized units, such as patient care teams, integrate these activities. [38] Universities have functionally organized academic departments, but also have developed specialized interdisciplinary institutes, teaching and research centers, and other units that coordinate academic specialties around programmatic endeavors.

There are many variations of the matrix form in industry and government, but a key common characteristic is that "each matrix involves a set of systems managers sharing or contending for resources controlled by a set of functional managers. [39] This approach differs significantly from traditional concepts and requires new attitudes and behavior.

36 William C. Goggin, "How the Multidimensional Structure Works at Dow Corning," *Harvard Business Review,* January–February 1974, p. 64.

37 William W. George, "Task Teams for Rapid Growth," *Harvard Business Review,* March–April 1977, p. 79.

38 Duncan Neuhauser, "The Hospital as a Matrix Organization," *Hospital Administration,* Fall 1972, pp. 8–25.

39 Leonard R. Sayles, "Matrix Management: The Structure with a Future," *Organizational Dynamics,* Autumn 1976, p. 7.

The matrix is a far cry from the organizations most managers have read about and idealized. Clean lines of authority; unambiguous resource allocation to each problem or goal; clear boundaries separating jobs, divisions, organizations, and loyalties are all part of that simpler life that we need to forsake in a dynamic world of overlapping and contradictory interests and goals. [40]

The matrix organization requires managers at all levels—top, functional, and integrative—and their subordinates to develop new approaches, leadership styles, and ways of operating. "It calls for different kinds of managerial behavior than are typical in conventional line organizations." [41] It is a more complex and difficult form and requires human flexibility in order to provide organizational flexibility.

An Example of Organization Structure

Because of the great diversity among industrial organizations, it would be impossible to set forth a single structure to represent American industry. For purposes of illustration we are showing the structure represented by organization charts for a large company in the aerospace and transportation equipment industry, the Boeing Company.

This company is one of the largest industrial corporations in the United States, ranking among the upper fifty. [42] In 1977 the company had sales of over $4 billion, more than $2 billion in assets, and over 66,000 employees. It is one of the major firms in the aerospace industry and has been the contractor for many of the nation's major defense and space programs, such as the B-52 airplanes, the Minuteman missile system, the Saturn booster program, the Lunar Rover, and the space shuttle program. It is the world's largest producer of commercial aircraft, including the 707, 727, 737, and 747 series. Over 3200 of these jet transports have been sold throughout the world.

Over the past several decades the organization structure of Boeing has become increasingly complex through continual differentiation and elaboration. This resulted from the expansion of the company into a number of new fields and program efforts and from the increasingly complex technology, which requires greater specialization. One of the basic trends has been the vertical elaboration of the structure through the establishment of separate product-line companies, which are composed of several product divisions. Figure 9.5 shows the corporate headquarters structure and the major companies and divisions.

40 Ibid., p. 17.

41 Paul R. Lawrence, Harvey F. Kolodny, and Stanley M. Davis, "The Human Side of the Matrix," *Organizational Dynamics,* Summer 1977, p. 43.

42 "The Fortune Directory of the 500 Largest U.S. Industrial Corporations," *Fortune,* May 8, 1978, p. 240.

Figure 9.5 The Boeing Company—Corporate Organization

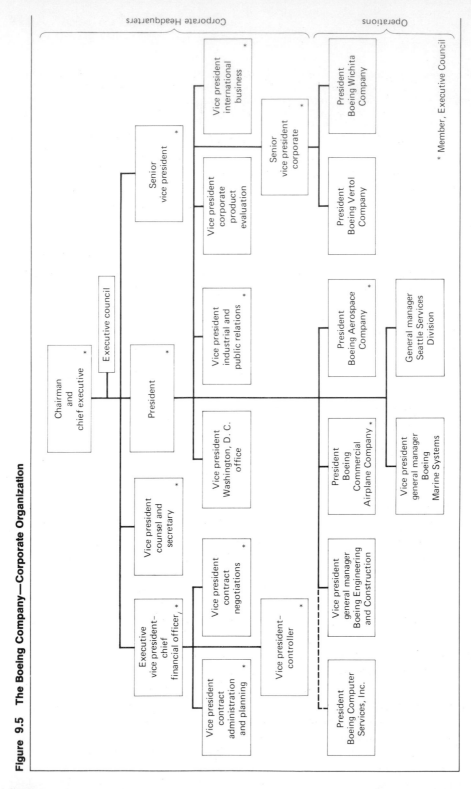

The corporate headquarters, through the executive council, establishes major policies and plans and coordinates the activities of the operating companies and divisions. The actual operations of the company are decentralized. The headquarters staff is composed of a number of functional vice-presidents who establish broad policies and carry on many activities that are important to the corporation as a whole.

The organization structure for the Boeing Commercial Airplane Company is shown in Figure 9.6. This is the largest company in the corporation and is engaged in the production of commercial aircraft and support systems. The 707-727-737 division and the 747 division are responsible for the ongoing production of current aircraft. The commercial products division is engaged in development work on the 7X7 and 7N7, the next generation of advanced-technology airliners. Customer support includes such activities as design and planning of airports and cargo handling systems, providing spare parts to customers, and training of flight and maintenance personnel.

These charts indicate the vertical levels in the organization. They do not, however, show all of the program activities in the total corporation. Each of the other subsidiary companies and divisions is involved in many different programs, such as urban rapid transit systems, military and commercial hydrofoils, nuclear

Figure 9.6   The Boeing Commercial Airplane Company

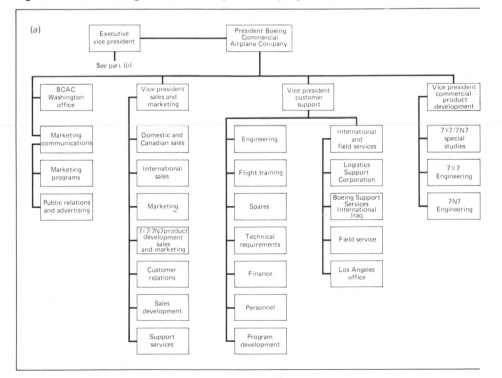

Figure 9.6   The Boeing Commercial Airplane Company (Continued)

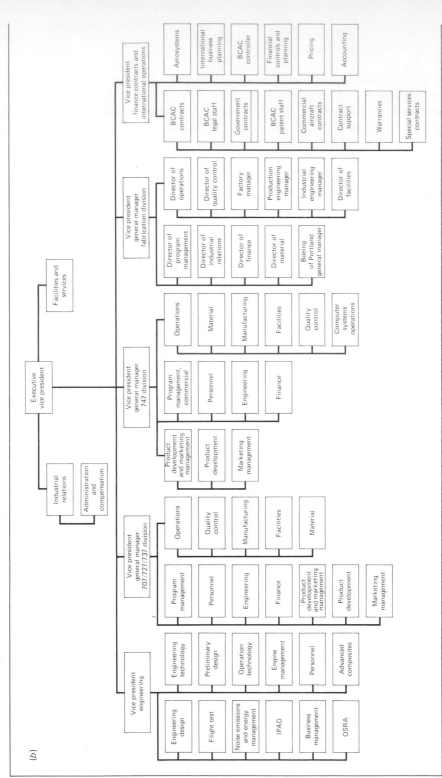

(b)

and solar power projects, and water purification and desalination. A major operating unit, the Boeing Aerospace Company, has a large number of military and space programs. Boeing Computer Services, Inc. is one of the nation's largest suppliers of computer and consulting services.

These charts present a general picture of the structure. In reality, the structure is continually evolving and changing to meet new program requirements, changing technologies, and environmental influences. There have been scores of major changes in structure over the past twenty years and hundreds of changes throughout lower levels in the organization.

This multicompany structure with program efforts in the operating companies provides for both maintenance and adaptability in the organization. The corporate headquarters operates at the strategic level. The companies and divisions are primarily concerned with specific programs. They have broad autonomy in their operations and for the development of new program efforts. When the company undertakes a new program, it is possible to make the changes at the operating company and division levels without upsetting the entire structure. This approach provides the adaptability that is vital in a dynamic industry.

Dynamics of Organization Structure

As a result of various forces, many organizations undergo relatively frequent structural changes. A look at the organization of a modern metropolitan hospital will show that dramatic changes have occurred over the past two decades. Most school systems are currently undergoing structural changes in order to meet changing requirements. In business organizations, the changes are equally dramatic. Daniel reported that in a three-year period at least two-thirds of the nation's top 100 industrial companies reported major organizational realignments.[43] He estimated that on the average, the larger industrial corporations have at least one major restructuring every two years. Many industrial organizations are accepting the necessity for changing their structure as a fact of life and are establishing permanent departments charged with the responsibility for organizational analysis and planning.

The movement toward dynamic, flexible structures and away from the rigid bureaucratic form seems to be a trend in modern organizations. Figure 9.7 summarizes the characteristics of adaptive-organic and stable-mechanistic systems. Instead of providing for permanent, structured positions, as characteristic of the stable-mechanistic system, the adaptive-organic system has less structuring, more frequent change of positions and roles, and more dynamic interplay among the various functions. The organic system requires more time and effort toward

---

43 D. Ronald Daniel, "Reorganizing for Results," *Harvard Business Review,* November–December 1966, p. 96.

integration of diverse activities. The stable-mechanistic form provides for coordination through the hierarchical structure. In the adaptive-organic form, mechanisms for horizontal and diagonal integration are established.

Obviously, the organic form, requiring a dynamic, changing structure, will not be feasible for all organizations. Many organizations can perform most effectively with a more mechanistic structure. These two organizational forms represent polar points on a continuum. In many organizations it will be necessary to operate certain sections such as research and development by utilizing the organic system, and other sections (production operations) with a more mechanistic system. This subject will be discussed in more detail in Part 7, "Comparative Analysis and Contingency Views."

Figure 9.7 Organizational Characteristics of Stable-Mechanistic and Adaptive-Organic Structures

Organizational Characteristic	Types of Structure	
	Stable-Mechanistic	Adaptive-Organic
Openness to environmental influences	Relatively closed. Attempts to select and minimize environmental influences and reduce uncertainty	Relatively open. Designed to adapt to environmental influences and cope with uncertainty
Formalization of activities	More formality based on structure	Less formality based on structure
Differentiation and specialization of activities	Specific, mutually exclusive functions and departments	General, sometimes overlapping activities
Coordination	Primarily through the hierarchy and well-defined administrative procedures	Multiple means and interpersonal interaction
Authority structure	Concentrated, hierarchic	Dispersed, multiple
Source of authority	Position	Knowledge and/or expertise
Responsibility	Attached to specific positions and/or roles	Shared by many participants
Tasks, roles, and functions	Clearly defined and specified in organization charts, position descriptions, and so on	Loosely defined and determined by circumstances, mutual expectations, and so on
Interaction-influence patterns	Superior → subordinate, hierarchical	Superior ⇌ subordinate, horizontal and diagonal
Procedures and rules	Many and specific, usually written and formal	Few and general, often unwritten and informal
Stratification (in terms of power, status, compensation, and so on)	More difference between levels	Less difference between levels
Decision making	Centralized, concentrated toward the top	Decentralized, shared throughout the organization
Permanency of structural form	Tends to be relatively fixed	Continually adapting to new situations

Summary

Structure may be considered as the established pattern of relationships between the components or parts of the organization. Unlike mechanical or biological systems, the structure of the social organization is not visible; it is inferred from operations.

Organizations have both formal and informal structure. The formal structure is the result of explicit decision making concerning organizational patterns and is typically expressed in charts, manuals, and position descriptions.

Traditional management theorists were vitally concerned with the design of efficient organization structures. Many principles were based on experiences with stable organizations such as the military, church, and established public bureaucracies.

Complex organizations are characterized by a high degree of task specialization or division of labor. This differentiation occurs in two directions—the vertical, represented by the hierarchy; and the horizontal, represented by departmentalization. Increased differentiation has magnified the problems associated with integration. Organizations facing a changing environment and accelerating technology have found it necessary to adopt new means for ensuring integration, such as committees, task forces, coordinating teams, and program managers.

Program management and the matrix form have been used effectively to provide the necessary integration of activities on a systems basis. These organizational designs are significantly different from more traditional structural forms.

Most modern organizations undergo frequent changes in structure. Instead of providing for permanent, highly structured relations, as characteristic of the stable-mechanistic system, the adaptive-organic organization has less structuring, more frequent change of positions and roles, and a more dynamic interplay between the various functions. Obviously, however, the organic form is not feasible for all organizations. Many organizations, operating in a stable environment and with a uniform technology, can perform more effectively by utilizing a mechanistic structure.

Questions and Problems

1 What is the structure of an organization? How does this differ from the structure of a physical or biological system?

2 What are advantages and disadvantages of using charts to illustrate organization structure?

3 What is the distinction between the formal and informal organization?

4 Evaluate the contributions of the traditional management theorists to the concept of structure.

5 Why have large organizations increasingly differentiated their activities?

6 Why is integration becoming more important in complex organizations? Discuss alternative means for achieving integration.

7 How is it possible for an organization to achieve both greater differentiation and more effective integration?

8 Investigate a specific organization to determine how it has developed both vertical and horizontal differentiation. Evaluate the means by which this organization achieves integration.

9 Why have horizontal and diagonal relationships become so important in the modern organization?

10 What is program management, and why has it evolved? How does the "authority" of the program manager differ from traditional line authority?

11 Investigate an organization that uses the matrix form. What are the advantages and disadvantages associated with this structural design?

12 Develop a list of organizations that closely reflect characteristics of the stable-mechanistic form.

13 Develop a list of organizations that closely reflect characteristics of the adaptive-organic form.

If you dig very deeply into any problem you will get to "people."
J. Watson Wilson

Every man is in certain respects like all other men, like some other man, like no other man.
Clyde Kluckhohn and Henry A. Murray

We are not only gregarious animals, liking to be in sight of our fellows, but we have an innate propensity to get ourselves noticed, and noticed favorably, by our kind. No more fiendish punishment could be devised, were such a thing physically possible, than that one should be turned loose in a society and remain absolutely unnoticed by all the members thereof.
William James

If we give employees nothing else to create, we cannot complain if they create trouble.
David Willings

I believe the greatest assets of a business are its human assets, and the improvement of their value is a matter of both material advantage and moral obligation.
Clarence Francis

Physical resources unused—lie inert. Coal left alone for a million years is still coal. Human resources left unutilized deteriorate.
Rupert Vance

The Psychosocial System

5

Individuals in social relationships constitute the psychosocial system in organizations. The general "climate" is affected by many variables, some integral, others peripheral. Societal culture sets an overall framework; industry mores and practices have an impact; and many variables are peculiar to specific organizations. Technology and structure affect organizational climate, as do employee attitudes and morale. Within this context, human resources development and utilization is a primary managerial responsibility.

In Chapter 10 we consider behavior and motivation, recognizing that the basic unit for analysis in organizations is the individual. Understanding what motivates behavior toward individual and organizational performance is a fundamental requirement for managerial success.

Status and role systems are considered in Chapter 11. Here we are concerned with how individuals relate to one another in systematic ways within organizations. Each status position has a related role—an expected behavior pattern for any incumbent.

In Chapter 12, we turn to the consideration of group dynamics. Understanding individual behavior is complex enough. However, the organizational context becomes even more complex when the dynamics of interpersonal relations in groups is considered. Small groups mediate between organizations and individuals.

Given the complexity of the psychosocial system in organizations, management is nevertheless charged with coordinating activity toward objective accomplishment. In Chapter 13 influence systems and leadership, important for achieving such coordination, are discussed. Power and authority underlie influence systems and affect the appropriateness and/or effectiveness of various leadership styles.

Individual Behavior and Motivation

Organizations are comprised of individuals; they are the fundamental units of analysis in organization theory. The behavioral sciences—anthropology, psychology, and sociology—provide much of the foundation for our understanding of individual behavior in organizations. Various psychological processes—perception, cognition, and motivation—provide the means through which people develop as personalities. The "whole person" concept reflects the integration of inherent and acquired characteristics. People act and react in environmental settings—cultural and organizational. Individual behavior patterns are the result of many complex factors and represent an integral and important part of the psychosocial system. In this chapter individual behavior and motivation will be discussed in terms of the following topics:

Behavior Patterns
Personality
Individual Similarities
Individual Differences
Theories of Motivation
Expectations and Performance
Hierarchy of Needs
Motivation-Hygiene Concept
Achievement Motivation
Two Views of People
Implications for Managerial Practice

Behavior Patterns

Behavior is a manner of acting; it refers to a person's conduct. Behavioral patterns are modes of conduct used by an individual in carrying out activities. Three relatively distinct divisions in the study of human systems are apparent: the study of *anatomy* provides a view of the organization of the body; the study of *physiology* provides information with regard to the physical processes involved; and the study of *behavior* refers to the overt action patterns of individuals.[1] The desire to behave in a certain way cannot be fulfilled if anatomical and physiological capabilities are not present. Similarly, the anatomical and physiological capacity for a particular activity does not ensure its occurrence. For example, the barriers to improved performance in activities such as athletics are often considered more psychological than physical. Given the determination to push for a "record," the body can respond more nearly to its ultimate capacity. When Roger Bannister became the first human being to run a mile in less than four minutes, his behavior was the result of the combination of anatomical, physiological, and psychological development.

Inherent or Acquired?

Are behavior patterns inherited or learned? Obviously, this question cannot be answered with a yes or no. There is a gradation of relative impact of inheritance or learning, depending on the particular facet of behavior being considered. Anatomy and physiology are relatively more inherited than psychological aspects. We inherit a range of capabilities, but the specific level of performance within that range is acquired through learning.

The developmental range, which always does have limits, is inherited, but the point within that range is acquired. That is why the strict statement that something is *either* inherited *or* acquired becomes meaningless. Human speech is a striking and familiar example. The specifically human capacity for true speech is completely determined by genetic control of development. The particular language spoken . . . is acquired; it is learned.[2]

Life experiences play an important role in modifying the psychological system and shaping behavior patterns. The general relationships involved can be expressed in the equation:

Behavior = f (personality, environment)

But environment and personality are both complex phenomena that must be related to a specific person in order to understand and/or predict behavior.

Personality

Personality theory has occupied a special role in the development of general psychology. It is concerned with the whole person in a total environment

---

1 George Gaylord Simpson and Anne Rowe, "The Evolution of Behavior," in Bernard Berelson (ed.), *The Behavioral Sciences Today,* Basic Books, Inc., Publishers, New York, 1963, p. 90.
2 Ibid., p. 95.

and it is of particular importance for organization theory and management practice. The personality of a human being is a complex combination of physical and mental attributes, values, attitudes, beliefs, tastes, ambitions, interests, habits, and other characteristics that comprise a unique *self.*

In analyzing or comparing personalities, we usually look at general dimensions such as depth, richness, or integration. Some people have deep beliefs or relationships based on intense experiences. Other people's beliefs are more shallow. Some people have wide interests and complex values based on a variety of experiences. Other people's interests are more narrow. Some people "have it all together"; the various facets of their personalities are woven together in a consistent pattern. Others are more fragmented; they are "at loose ends."

From the point of view of personal growth and development, a deep, rich, integrated personality would seem to be optimal. However, these dimensions vary by degrees and many combinations are possible. It is important for managers to recognize differences in order to understand and predict individual behavior in organizational settings.

It is important to distinguish "being a person" from "having personality." For example, we often talk in terms of the presence or absence of personality: "She has no personality" or "He is not very handsome, but he has a lot of personality." These usages imply that personality is equivalent to social skill or adroitness. Other common usage stresses a particular aspect, such as aggressiveness or joviality.

We are interested in personality and behavior as one way to integrate many complex elements into a total system for an individual. Physical, physiological, and psychological functions are fundamental. Both self-perception and the perception of others are important considerations. In short, personality represents a total, complex individual system; it is a key element in the social system; theories of personality are important inputs for organization theory. Understanding and predicting individual behavior requires diagnosis of personality and environment.[3]

Individual Similarities

Anatomically and physiologically, human beings are quite similar. People with more or less than five fingers or toes (on one hand or foot) are rare. To be sure, structural differences are apparent between Caucasian, Oriental, and Negro races. However, even these apparent differences are slight in comparison to the basic similarities involved. Regardless of the superficial physical appearances, physiological processes are similar for all Homo sapiens. More individual differences are evident in psychological processes. The "generation gap" is much more apparent for overt behavior patterns than for physiological differences.

3 Chris Argyris, "Personality and Organization Theory Revisited," *Administrative Science Quarterly,* June 1973, pp. 141–167.

On the other hand, the process of behavior is similar for all individuals. That is, while behavior patterns may vary significantly, the process by which they occur is fundamental to all individuals. Three interrelated assumptions can be made about human behavior.[4]

1 Behavior is caused.
2 Behavior is motivated.
3 Behavior is goal-directed.

These three elements are linked together in the basic model of behavior in Figure 10.1. This model can be applied to all people, of all ages, in all cultures, and at all times.

If these three assumptions are valid, then behavior cannot be spontaneous and aimless. There must be a goal, whether explicit or implicit. Behavior toward goals is generated in reaction to a stimulus—all behavior is caused. Basic to this process is a gap between the current condition and a desired condition with behavior evoked to attempt to close the gap. The process may be relatively unconscious (breathing) or conscious and deliberate (writing a report). A stimulus is filtered through a system of wants or needs, which may take many forms. A lack of water causes thirst and results in behavior such as obtaining a drink of water. Feedback from the goal to the stimulus indicates the sequential nature of this process. If the goal is achieved, the current behavior is terminated, and the individual's attention turns to some other activity. If the goal is not achieved, the individual may partake of a second glass of water and so on until a particular need is satisfied.

This basic model of the behavior process is the same for all individuals.

Figure 10.1   A Basic Model of Behavior

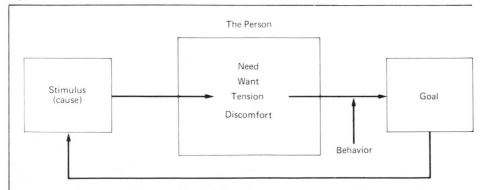

Harold J. Leavitt, *Managerial Psychology,* 4th ed., The University of Chicago Press, Chicago, 1978, p. 8.

4 Harold J. Leavitt, *Managerial Psychology,* 4th ed., The University of Chicago Press, 1978, p. 10.

However, it is easy to see that actual behavior can vary significantly. Differential perception could alter the stimulus phase, for example. Needs or wants vary by individuals, and such differences can be culturally determined or learned. Variations in perception, cognition, and motivation, for example, can lead to different behavior patterns from the same or similar stimuli.

Individual Differences

Many factors lead toward individual differences in behavior. Figure 10.2 shows some of the influences on individual behavior in a work situation. These potential influences filter through personal attitudes via perception, cognition, and motivation. The effect of various events on behavior depends on how they are perceived by the individual. Similarly, if behavior results after a period that allows thinking or problem solving, personal attitudes play an important part in fashioning the specific response. Value systems are affected significantly by total past experience and current personal situations.

A similar model could be developed for other situations in which the individual is involved—family, educational, or recreational, for example.

Perception

Perception is basic to understanding behavior because it is the means by which stimuli affect an organism or individual. A stimulus that is not perceived

Figure 10.2 Some Influences on Behavior in a Work Situation

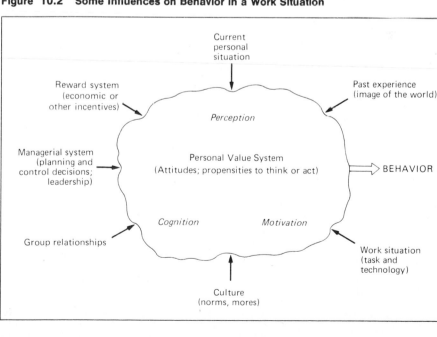

has no effect on behavior. Another key is that people behave on the basis of "what is perceived" rather than "what is." A direct line to "truth" is often assumed, but each person really has only one point of view, based on individualistic perceptions of the real world. Some considerations can be verified in order that several or many individuals can agree on a consistent set of facts. However, in most real-life situations many conditions are not verifiable and are heavily value laden. Even when facts are established, their meaning or significance may vary considerably for different individuals.

Figure 10.3 is a model of the way perceptions are formed and hence influence individual behavior. Numerous external forces such as the stress of the situation, group pressure, and reward systems are involved. Past experience has a direct influence on interpretation of stimuli. Several basic processes (mechanisms) of perception formation can be identified—selectivity, closure, and interpretation.

Figure 10.3   Perception Formation and Its Effect on Behavior

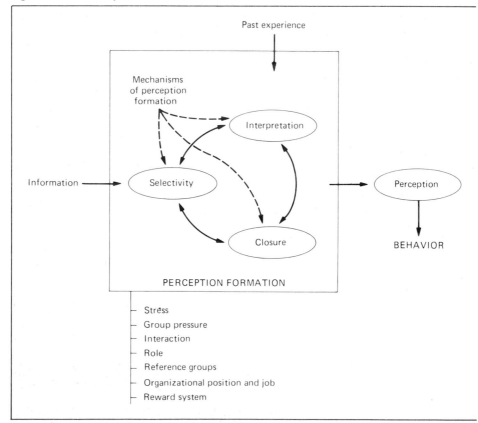

Adapted from Joseph A. Litterer, *The Analysis of Organizations,* 2d ed., John Wiley & Sons, Inc., New York, 1973, p. 103.

The concept of **selective *perception*** is important because voluminous information is received and processed. Individuals select information that is supportive and satisfying.[5] They tend to ignore information that might be disturbing. For example, after purchasing a new automobile, buyers typically will pay more attention to ads for the brand purchased and tend to ignore ads for other models. In this way, they are more likely to be satisfied with their decision.

The same stimulus can be interpreted differently by several individuals. ***Interpretation*** depends on past experience and the value system of each particular person. An attitudinal set or propensity to think or act in a certain way provides a framework for interpreting various stimuli. Not only does the individual perceive selectively, she interprets the situation in ways that will be supportive.

The process of ***closure*** in perception formation relates to the tendency of individuals to have a complete picture of any given situation. Thus a person may perceive more than the information seems to indicate. She adds to the information input whatever seems appropriate in order to close the system and make it meaningful and supportive.

While there is a tendency to perceive supportive information and ignore disturbing information, it is obvious that threatening, bad, or frightening information does "come through." We cannot ignore the real world indefinitely, assuming that we are within the "normal" range in terms of sanity.

Cognition

The term ***cognition*** can be used in two ways. Individuals have ***cognitive systems*** that represent what they know about themselves and the world. These systems are developed through ***cognitive processes,*** which include perceiving, imagining, thinking, reasoning, and decision making. The more we understand about an individual's cognitive system, the better we are able to predict his behavior. "If we understand how man comes by the ideas about things and people which make up his world image, if we understand the principles which govern the growth and development and interaction of these ideas, we will have taken the first step toward understanding man's behavior in this world of his own making."[6]

Cognition implies a conscious or deliberate process toward acquiring knowledge. The term *rational* is often used in conjunction with cognitive processes in order to differentiate irrational acts. Yet rationality should be viewed in the context of the individual involved. "However bizarre the behavior of men, tribes, or nations may appear to an outsider, to the men, to the tribes, to the nations their behavior makes sense in terms of their own world views."[7]

---

5 Ibid., pp. 27–29.

6 David Krech, Richard S. Crutchfield, and Egerton L. Ballachey, *Individual in Society*, McGraw-Hill Book Company, New York, 1962, p. 17.

7 Ibid.

Motivation

A *motive* is what prompts a person to act in a certain way or at least develop a propensity for specific behavior. This urge to action can be touched off by an external stimulus, or it can be internally generated in individual physiological and thought processes. Differences in motivation are undoubtedly the most important consideration in understanding and predicting individual differences and behavior.

Unfortunately, motivation is not a simple concept. "One of the most difficult tasks for psychologists is to describe the urge behind behavior. The motivation of any organism, even the simplest one, is at present only partly understood." [8] It involves needs, wants, tensions, discomfort, expectations. Underlying behavior there is a push or pull toward action. This implies that there is some imbalance or dissatisfaction in the individual's relationship to her environment. She identifies goals and feels a need to engage in some behavior that will lead toward achieving those goals.

It is apparent that needs vary with the individual and hence lead to differential behavior patterns. To confound the matter even further, an individual's needs vary over time. His value system evolves continually, and an integral part of that evolution is the motivational process. As some needs are satisfied, they become less important in the scheme of things. Others develop through experience. Thus, understanding individual motivation requires continual updating in order to reflect the most current mix of goals. An identical stimulus used at two different times may evoke entirely different responses because the value system has been changed.

Theories of Motivation

Performance = *f(ability, motivation)* and experience tells us that individual performance varies considerably, even when people with similar capabilities are working in essentially the same situation. [9] Why? What causes behavior to be energized, directed, and sustained? This question has been of major concern to behavioral scientists and managers. A number of theories have been developed and researched. Evidence has been gathered to support each of the major conceptual models and a cursory, piecemeal review might suggest that the theories and their implications for managerial practice are mutually exclusive. However, there are common threads and a potential for integrating the body of knowledge and setting forth prescriptions for enlightened managerial behavior. In the remainder

8 James Deese, *Principles of Psychology,* Allyn and Bacon, Inc., Boston, 1964, p. 54.

9 John P. Campbell and Robert D. Pritchard, "Motivation Theory in Industrial and Organizational Psychology," in Marvin D. Dunnette (ed.), *Handbook of Industrial and Organizational Psychology,* Rand-McNally College Publishing Company, Chicago, 1976, p. 64.

of this chapter we will explore some of the major theories, identify some common threads, and relate them to managerial practice.

A major distinction in the study of what causes behavior is that of cognitive versus noncognitive explanations. Most work in motivation assumes that it is important to understand internal states and processes of individuals—needs, wants, desires, values, and expectations. The key idea is that it is important to understand what people feel and how they think in order to predict how they will behave in a given situation. An alternative view, represented by the work of B. F. Skinner, emphasizes a **noncognitive** approach that makes no attempt to understand internal conditions and processes. [10] In effect, the individual is a black box wherein feeling and thought processes are unknown and unknowable. Behavior occurs and is directed and sustained via the conditioning effects of reinforcement. Behavior is shaped (directed, amplified, and sustained) because of the consequences that follow it. If behavior is ignored or punished, it tends to decrease or cease, and if it is positively reinforced (rewarded), it tends to increase or persist. To understand and predict behavior, it is sufficient to focus on past overt actions and their consequences as provided by the individual's external environment. There is no need to be concerned about the internal conditions or processes of individuals.

Cognitive theories, on the other hand, focus on internal aspects. This view of motivation has been approached via two dimensions that are relatively distinct but not mutually exclusive—*what* motivates people (content) and *how* behavior is produced (process). [11] **Content** theories focus on the specific variables that influence behavior, such as internal needs or external conditions. What specific needs motivate individuals in work situations? What specific rewards are most powerful in sustaining superior performance? **Process** theories also attempt to identify major variables that explain behavior, but the focus is on the dynamics of how the variables are interrelated in explaining the direction, degree, and persistence of effort. The major variables in process models are incentive, drive, reinforcement, and expectancy.

Expectations and Performance

The common themes in expectancy theories are (1) conscious decisions by individuals (in a work situation or total life space) to behave in certain ways, (2) individual values with regard to choosing desired outcomes, (3) individual expectations concerning the amount of effort required to achieve a specific outcome, and (4) individual expectations concerning the probability of being re-

---

10 B. F. Skinner, *Beyond Freedom and Dignity*, Alfred A. Knopf, Inc., New York, 1971.

11 John P. Campbell, et al., *Managerial Behavior, Performance, and Effectiveness*, McGraw-Hill Book Company, New York, 1970, pp. 340–384.

Figure 10.4 The Process of Motivation: Factors Affecting Individual Effort, Performance, and Satisfaction

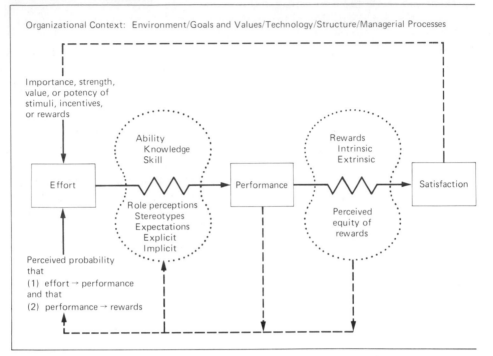

warded for achieving a desired outcome. These concepts have been modeled and tested by many researchers. [12] A number of alternatives have been explored and modifications have been suggested. A composite model, incorporating additional variables (beyond the basic expectations framework) is shown in Figure 10-4. The key elements in this model are effort, performance, and satisfaction. People are motivated to expend effort if they believe that there is a reasonable probability that their effort will accomplish a desired outcome and that the outcome will be followed by intrinsic and/or extrinsic rewards that lead to satisfaction. A positive experience will affect the value system of the individual and the propensity to engage in similar efforts in the future.

As shown in the model, the relationship between effort and performance is affected by an individual's abilities and role perceptions (implicit and explicit expectations of what one is supposed to do). If a person lacks the necessary skill or knowledge to accomplish a task, extraordinary effort will obviously not lead to

---

[12] V. H. Vroom, *Work and Motivation,* John Wiley & Sons, Inc., New York, 1964; Lyman Porter and Edward E. Lawler, III, *Managerial Attitudes and Performance,* Richard D. Irwin, Inc., and the Dorsey Press, Homewood, Ill., 1968; and Terence R. Mitchell, "Expectancy Models of Job Satisfaction, Occupational Preferences and Effort: A Theoretical, Methodological, and Empirical Appraisal," *Psychological Bulletin,* December 1974, pp. 1053–1077.

better performance. If effort is misdirected, improved performance may not be organizationally relevant and hence not rewarded. For example, a basketball player might (1) concentrate on shooting rather than overall team play, (2) win the high scoring honors, and (3) be on the losing team. This suggests the need for continual attention to role expectations so that preconceived notions can be verified and/or modified in order to focus behavior in desired directions. Well-designed management by objectives (MBO) programs can facilitate this process by identifying key results areas and prioritizing the objectives (and action plans) that are most appropriate for a given time frame.

Intrinsic rewards include challenging and/or enjoyable work, responsibility, and self-esteem. Extrinsic rewards include pay, praise, and the esteem of others. The absolute amount of a reward has a direct effect on satisfaction, but it is also affected by perceived equity in the reward system.[13] Individual behavior is affected by a person's perception of the performance-rewards relationship of others. We may compare ourselves with a specific person or with a general class of persons in similar roles. Apparent inequity (others getting the same reward for less output or more reward for the same output) is a source of tension. Tension-reducing behavior could include asking for more rewards (pay or other benefits) or reducing output (quality or quantity) in order to restore the situation to one of perceived equity. In the mid-1970s professional athletics provided a good example of such behavior. Many established "stars" played out their options in order to renegotiate their contracts and/or change teams. They were responding to relatively long-term, no-cut contracts for a few "superstars," particularly individuals who had not proven themselves over the long run. For example, in February 1977 Slick Watts of the Seattle Supersonics, who had led the league the previous year in steals and assists, stated:

I know most people think I'm taking good money, and I am. (Reportedly $70,000 plus bonuses, with increases to $80,000 and $90,000 for the next two years.) But, I bring people into the Coliseum. I'm popular in the community—that isn't just for me, that helps the Sonics. Sam is getting compensated, Russ is getting compensated, Tommy is getting very well compensated, Fred is getting compensated. . . . Me and Norwood get the same salary and he's been in this league a long time and he's on his last legs.

There's a lot of guys in this league making over a hundred grand a year and they don't even get off the bench.[14]

While six-figure equity hassles make the headlines, the equal pay for equal work problem is widespread. Multimillion-dollar retroactive settlements have been made by a number of organizations that apparently were systematically paying women less than men for essentially the same type of work (and performance). Inequities of a few cents per hour or a few dollars per week are enough to create tension, affect satisfaction, and modify subsequent effort.

13 J. Stacy Adams, "Toward an Understanding of Inequity," *Journal of Abnormal and Social Psychology,* November 1963, pp. 422–436.
14 *Seattle Post Intelligencer,* Feb. 20, 1977, p. D-7.

This overall conceptual model is helpful in visualizing the complexity involved in understanding and predicting human behavior in organizations. The basic concept of expectancy theory, that people can process available information (some factual and some perceptual) consciously and then behave so that they will maximize the return on their investment of effort, is intuitively appealing. Testing the entire model empirically is very difficult and probably requires continued research on its various subparts. The model allows consideration of various content theories (*what* motivates behavior) by recognizing the concept of strength or potency of stimuli or incentives. This includes needs or drives (physiological and/or psychological) that occur when there is a gap between a current condition and a desired condition. Effort (conscious or unconscious) is expended to close the gap and achieve satisfaction.

Hierarchy of Needs

The need-hierarchy concept was developed by Abraham Maslow as an alternative to viewing motivation in terms of a series of relatively separate and distinct drives. His concept stressed a hierarchy (Figure 10.5) with certain "higher" needs becoming activated to the extent that certain "lower" needs be-

Figure 10.5 Hierarchy of Needs

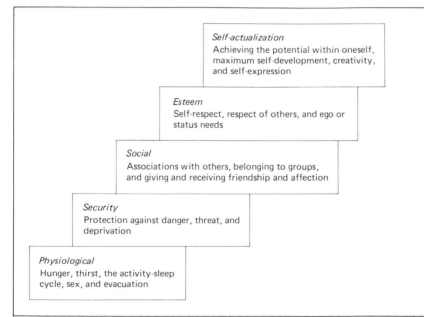

Self-actualization
Achieving the potential within oneself, maximum self-development, creativity, and self-expression

Esteem
Self-respect, respect of others, and ego or status needs

Social
Associations with others, belonging to groups, and giving and receiving friendship and affection

Security
Protection against danger, threat, and deprivation

Physiological
Hunger, thirst, the activity-sleep cycle, sex, and evacuation

come satisfied. [15] These five basic needs are related to each other and arranged in a hierarchy of prepotency. This means that the most prepotent goal will monopolize consciousness and will tend to evoke behavior in response to it.

While these levels in the need hierarchy can be separated for analysis and understanding, they are probably all active in actual behavior patterns. The lower-level needs are never completely satisfied—they recur periodically—and if their satisfaction is deprived for any period of time, they become extremely potent as motivators. On the other hand, a completely satisfied need is not an effective motivator of behavior. Esteem and self-actualization needs are rarely satisfied; we seek indefinitely for more satisfaction of them once they become important to us. Yet they are usually not significant until physiological, security, and social needs are reasonably well satisfied. [16]

On the other hand, a need does not have to be 100 percent satisfied before the next level becomes potent. A more realistic description of the hierarchy would be in terms of decreasing percentages of satisfaction as prepotency increases. The average person is satisfied 85 percent in physiological needs, 70 percent in security needs, 50 percent in social needs, 40 percent in self-esteem needs, and 10 percent in self-actualization needs. [17] Moreover, the relative mix of needs changes during an individual's psychological development. Physiological and security needs are dominant early in life, with social, esteem, and self-actualization needs becoming relatively more important as a person matures. These general tendencies and averages are a good first approximation in understanding human motivation and in predicting behavior. However, there are significant individual differences that must be recognized in any organizational situation.

Motivation-Hygiene Concept

Herzberg and his associates have engaged in extensive research concerning the attitudes of people toward their work. The research was designed to test the concept that people have two sets of needs: (1) their need as animals to avoid physical pain and deprivation and (2) their need as human beings to grow psychologically. The original study involved interviews with 200 engineers and accountants, representing a cross section of Pittsburgh industry. They were asked about events they had experienced at work that had resulted either in (1) a marked improvement or (2) a significant reduction in job satisfaction. [18]

The results of this study and similar ones with other subjects seem to

---

15 A. H. Maslow, "A Theory of Human Motivation," *Psychological Review*, July 1943, pp. 370–396.

16 Douglas M. McGregor, *The Human Side of Enterprise*, McGraw-Hill Book Company, New York, 1960.

17 Maslow, op. cit., pp. 388–389.

18 Frederick Herzberg, *Work and the Nature of Man*, The World Publishing Company, Cleveland, 1966, p. 72.

point to two rather distinct sets of factors—one relating primarily to job satisfaction and the other relating primarily to job dissatisfaction.

Five factors stand out as strong determiners of job satisfaction—*achievement, recognition, work itself, responsibility,* and *advancement*—the last three being of greater importance for lasting change of attitudes. These five factors appeared very infrequently when the respondents described events that paralleled job dissatisfaction feelings. . . .

When the factors involved in the job dissatisfaction events were coded, an entirely different set of factors evolved. These factors were similar to the satisfiers in their unidimensional effect. This time, however, they served only to bring about job dissatisfaction and were rarely involved in events that led to positive job attitudes. Also, unlike the "satisfiers," the "dissatisfiers" consistently produced short-term changes in job attitudes. The major dissatisfiers were *company policy and administration, supervision, salary, interpersonal relations,* and *working conditions.*[19]

The environmental variables were labeled *hygiene* factors, indicating an analogy to the concept of preventive maintenance. The satisfier factors were labeled *motivators,* implying their effectiveness in evoking individual behavior toward superior performance.

Relationship to Need Hierarchy

How does all this fit with the need-hierarchy concept described previously? The dissatisfiers or hygiene factors can be related to physiological and security needs. In modern industry the environmental nature of most jobs has been basically "satisfactory" with regard to these lower-level needs. That is, working conditions (safety, lighting, ventilation) and salaries have generally been acceptable. Thus in Maslow's terms these satisfied needs are not effective motivators. On the other hand, if these conditions are not "reasonably" satisfactory, workers can become disenchanted and not even approach "normal" performance. However, it is unlikely that concentration on improving these facets of the job environment will lead to extraordinary performance—individual effort "above and beyond the call of duty."

Assuming reasonably good environmental conditions are present, how can superior performance be generated? Concentration on motivators involves recognition of higher-level needs such as esteem and self-actualization. Psychological growth comes from working at a task that is inherently interesting, achieving goals, and receiving recognition for such achievement. The system must provide opportunity for individuals to assume responsibility and to be innovative or creative in their work.

One popular myth is that hygiene factors or physiological and security needs are enough to motivate "workers," while motivators such as esteem or self-

---

19 Ibid., pp. 72–74.

Figure 10.6   Relationship of Motivation to Individual Performance

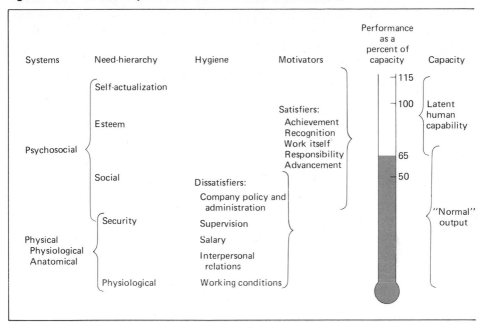

actualization needs should be considered when dealing with "managers." This dichotomy is unfortunate because it perpetuates a chasm between subsystems of organizations that really should be integrated for effective and efficient perform-ance. All are managers; all are workers. There is really no way to draw a meaning-ful line of demarcation. The research findings indicate that the hygiene-motivator concept applies to people in all walks of life and at all levels in both private and public organizations. [20] "Contrary to prevailing belief, the studies show the basic needs of the blue-collar worker or the assembly-line worker are no different from those of the white-collar worker. The primary sources of job satisfaction for both groups are achievement and recognition." [21]

The relationship of motivation to individual performance is summarized in Figure 10.6. Performance is calibrated as a percentage of individual capacity. If related to physical productivity, it could be readily measurable. However, if it refers to artistic or creative output, evaluation would be much more difficult. In either case, we might consider that "normal" output averages somewhat less than 100 percent of capacity. For the sake of illustration, let us assume (rather gener-ously) that individuals normally produce at about 65 percent of capacity over the long run. For short periods of time, performance at 115 percent (maybe even

20 John Newstrom, et al., "Motivating the Public Employee: Fact Versus Fiction," *Public Personnel Management,* January–February 1976, pp. 67–72.

21 Frederick Herzberg, "Motivation, Morale, & Money," *Psychology Today,* March 1968, p. 66.

more) is not uncommon. Sustained effort at such levels is not likely. What factors are involved in moving from 65 to 85 percent performance over the long run? How can we get the subpar (50-percenters) individuals up to "normal" performance?

To the left of the thermometer are indicated various factors that affect performance. Ignoring technology, two basic systems are involved: (1) physical systems, which include physiological and anatomical functions, and (2) psychosocial systems, the individual in organizational endeavor. Relating these systems to the need hierarchy, we find that physiological needs are directly related to physical systems. Security needs likewise relate to physical systems, but they also relate to psychosocial systems. Of particular importance in the psychosocial system are social, esteem, and self-actualization needs.

As indicated, the hygiene and motivator factors can be related to the need hierarchy. The two systems overlap somewhat; dissatisfiers include social, security, and physiological needs, while satisfiers reflect self-actualization, esteem, and social needs. In relating these to individual performance, we see that both satisfiers and dissatisfiers are involved in motivating the individual to "normal" performance. However, the dissatisfiers are relatively more important at this long-run average level of output. In tapping latent human capability and moving beyond the normal range of output, the satisfiers become relatively more important.

Achievement Motivation

The need for achievement, while not set forth explicitly in Maslow's need hierarchy, underlies esteem and self-actualization. Similarly, Herzberg's motivators emphasize the recognition of achievement as critical for long-run job satisfaction.

Like any other physical or psychological attribute, the degree of achievement motivation varies by individual. Some individuals rate very high, others very low; groups, organizations, or societies could be rated according to the degree of achievement motivation evident in the total system. McClelland emphasizes the achievement motive in the propensity for economic growth in various countries.[22] In Western culture, the Protestant ethic and Social Darwinism undoubtedly have fostered high achievement motivation. The free enterprise system has provided an environment within which such an approach could survive and grow. However, the same phenomenon is evident in other economic systems. Economic growth, corporate profits, and individual remuneration are seen as indicators of achievement and are not always sought in themselves. They merely provide an indication to the individual, organization, or society that performance has been good, recognized as such, and rewarded accordingly.

---

22 David C. McClelland, *The Achieving Society,* D. Van Nostrand Company, Inc., Princeton, N.J., 1961.

McClelland found that businesspeople, particularly entrepreneur-managers, have relatively more achievement motivation than other identifiable groups in society. He suggests that achievers:

1 Like situations in which they take personal responsibility for finding solutions to problems
2 Have a tendency to set moderate achievement goals and to take "calculated risks"
3 Want concrete feedback about how well they are doing [23]

Individuals with high achievement motivation are inclined to take moderate risks rather than gamble on situations with high potential payoff *and* high potential failure. This seems to make sense intuitively. The achiever will be interested in a consistent string of successes and not want to spoil her record with a complete flop.

Two Views of People

Assumptions about basic human nature range from *good, industrious, responsible,* and *smart* to *evil, lazy, irresponsible,* and *dumb.* Such summary statements reflect polar oppositions which, admittedly, are unrealistic. Human beings are neither completely good nor completely evil. [24] There are obvious spectra for behavior in terms of cooperation-competition, love-hate, friendship-enmity, or harmony-discord. Given a particular issue, an individual's behavior will reflect a position on one or more of these continua. However, the basic assumption one makes can have a significant impact on organization and management. Relationships are structured in certain ways; compensation systems are designed; communication patterns are established; authority-responsibility relationships are identified; planning and control processes are established; and many other pertinent organizational considerations are affected by management's assumptions about the nature of people. McGregor set forth two alternative views of people, which he termed "Theory X" and "Theory Y." [25]

---

23 David C. McClelland, "Business Drive and National Achievement," *Harvard Business Review,* July–August 1962, pp. 99–112.

24 Henry P. Knowles and Borje O. Saxberg, "Human Relations and the Nature of Man," *Harvard Business Review,* March–April 1967, p. 178. (Knowles and Saxberg cite Occidental philosophers in developing the polar views. For a parallel discussion of Oriental views see Chan K. Hahn and Warren C. Waterhouse, "Confucian Theories of Man and Organization," *Academy of Management Journal,* September 1972, pp. 355–363.)

25 McGregor, op. cit.

Theory X

The average human being has an inherent dislike of work and will avoid it if possible.

Because of this human characteristic of dislike of work, most people must be coerced, controlled, directed, or threatened with punishment to get them to put forth adequate effort toward the achievement of organizational objectives.

The average human being prefers to be directed, wishes to avoid responsibility, has relatively little ambition, and wants security above all.

Theory Y

The expenditure of physical and mental effort in work is as natural as play or rest.

External control and the threat of punishment are not the only means of inducing effort toward organizational objectives. People will exercise self-direction and self-control in the service of objectives to which they are committed.

Commitment to objectives is a function of the rewards associated with their achievement.

The average human being learns, under proper conditions, not only to accept but to seek responsibility.

The capacity to exercise a high degree of imagination, ingenuity, and creativity in the solution of organizational problems is widely, not narrowly, distributed in the population.

Under the conditions of modern industrial life, the intellectual potentialities of the average human being are only partially utilized.

These theories can be related to the need hierarchy in the sense that the traditional view of direction and control, Theory X, relies on the assumption that lower-level needs are dominant in motivating people to perform organizational tasks. Theory Y, on the other hand, assumes that people will exercise self-correction and self-control in working toward objectives to which they are committed.

Based on extensive research in contemporary organizations, Likert has concluded that a managerial system paralleling Theory Y makes significantly better use of human resources and enhances both effectiveness and efficiency of organizational endeavor. Over the years, he has evolved several models of management systems, which he designates by number, one through four. System Four incorporates the basic assumptions and approaches of Theory Y and seems to lead to significant improvement in organizational performance.[26] The conclusions may not be completely generalizable, but they apply to many industries, companies, and subunits within organizations.[27] Moving toward such a managerial system is often a slow process that requires reeducation and reorientation of all organizational participants. However, there does seem to be a trend in this direction.

Implications for Managerial Practice

A primary managerial concern is tapping latent human capability in organizational endeavors. How do we get people to perform at a higher than

26 Rensis Likert, *The Human Organization,* McGraw-Hill Book Company, New York, 1967.

27 David G. Bowers, *Systems of Organizations,* The University of Michigan Press, Ann Arbor, 1976.

"normal" percent of their mental and physical capacities and also maintain satisfaction?

General Approach

An overriding concern is the manager's view of basic human nature. A positive view (good, industrious, responsible, and smart) leads to emphasis on esteem and self-actualization needs, intrinsic rewards, and enriched jobs. A pessimistic view (evil, lazy, irresponsible, and dumb) leads to emphasis on physiological and security needs, extrinsic rewards, and working conditions.

A subtle, but extremely important, aspect is the phenomenon of self-fulfilling prophecies. If it is assumed that people are irresponsible and lazy, interested only in pay and security along with easy, routine tasks, and if our planning and control processes are focused on limiting or circumscribing human behavior, performance is not likely to go beyond what is required. Strict controls, emphasis on external pressure rather than internal desire, and highly programmed activities do not allow much room for growth and development of individual capabilities. Optimistic assumptions can also lead to self-fulfilling prophecies by allowing for and encouraging individual development, growth, and self-actualization. Given the opportunity, people rise to the occasion, are motivated to perform well, and tend to increase their capabilities over time. Thus, unless there is overwhelming evidence to the contrary, it seems advisable for managers to at least start with a reasonably optimistic view of human nature as they apply motivation theory in practice. In Miles' terms, the manager's orientation should be toward human resources and their development rather than merely human relations and their maintenance in terms of morale and satisfaction. [28]

Whether we believe the thinking, feeling, reasoning view of drive or expectancy theory, or whether we believe the nonthinking, external, operant conditioning view of behavior, positive reinforcement plays a major role. [29] Positively reinforced behavior is likely to continue and increase, whether it is viewed as an automatic process or whether it is filtered through the conscious process of increased satisfaction and a decision to exert effort in a future period.

As we indicated in Figure 10.4, the content (what) and process (how) views of motivation can be integrated. It seems obvious that there are a variety of reasons for behavior to be energized, directed, and sustained. Managers should recognize this variety and not focus on a single need such as security or achievement. Indeed, one could be highly motivated to achieve security. The central role of expectations in the motivation process is an important consideration for managerial practice. It seems intuitively obvious that people will work hard if they believe that their effort will lead to good performance and that good performance, in turn, will result in appropriate rewards.

---

[28] Raymond E. Miles, *Theories of Management: Implications for Organizational Behavior and Development,* McGraw-Hill Book Company, New York, 1975, p. 35.

[29] Terence R. Mitchell, "Applied Principles in Motivation Theory," in Peter Warr (ed.), *Personal Goals and Work Design,* John Wiley & Sons, Ltd., London, 1976, pp. 163–171.

Even if we were sure what causes behavior and how effort is energized, directed, and sustained in general, we still have the question of individual differences. People have differential need strengths: some people thrive on teamwork, while others prefer to work alone; some people like a lot of feedback, while others want very little; some people want challenging, varied tasks, while others want more routine, programmed activities. Moreover, individuals change from day to day, thus confounding the managerial problem of motivating people in specific situations. All of this complexity argues for a contingency approach that is flexible, multifaceted, and based on astute diagnosis of the situation. There is no one best way for motivating all people in all situations. Individual differences must be taken into account. For example, it is important to ascertain what is considered rewarding for an individual in order to increase the probability that the effort-performance-reward-satisfaction process will be most meaningful. Indeed, some organizations report success in allowing employees to help design pay systems and/or choose their own rewards. [30] Keeping in mind the need to differentiate managerial practice according to the situation and individual differences, there are some guidelines that may be helpful.

Specific Methods

A primary focus of attention should be the work itself. If the job is inherently interesting, the problem of motivation is much less severe. If doing a task is rewarding and satisfying, we don't have to rely as heavily on rewarding outcomes (performance). Job design and enrichment efforts typically result in reduced absenteeism and turnover as well as increased performance and morale. Key elements of enriched jobs are meaningfulness of work (skill variety, task significance, and task identity), autonomy-responsibility, and knowledge of results (feedback). [31] Not all jobs can be enriched significantly. Some people will not be as motivated by the work itself as others. However, from a managerial perspective it seems obvious that jobs should be designed to be as enriched as possible, recognizing the possible constraints of technology and economics.

Another important consideration for managers is the use of an explicit management by objectives program. If handled correctly, this approach to managing allows us to use elements of the motivation process, as well as several causal factors. Explicit goal setting creates a gap that energizes and directs effort. Participation strengthens commitment. Agreement on key results and action plans clarifies role perceptions and develops mutual expectations. Explicit performance objectives allow us to compare expected versus actual results and to reward good performance. Achievement, accomplishment, recognition, esteem, and self-actual-

30 Edward E. Lawler, "Workers Can Set Their Own Wages—Responsibly," *Psychology Today,* February 1977, pp. 109–112.

31 J. Richard Hackman, et al., "A New Strategy for Job Enrichment," *California Management Review,* Summer 1975, pp. 57–71.

ization are all potential motivators whose use is facilitated via a formalized MBO program.

The complexity involved in motivating people and tapping latent human capabilities is evident in Figures 10.4 and 10.6. Because of the many factors that potentially are involved, it is important for managers to consider many variables simultaneously. We might emphasize higher order needs such as esteem and self-actualization, but we cannot ignore physiological, security, and social needs. Similarly, we can emphasize motivators such as the work itself, accomplishment, and recognition, but we cannot ignore hygiene factors such as pay, supervision, and working conditions. Challenging, realistic goals that are accepted can be highly motivating, but it is important that expectations are clear and understandable. The interaction of effort and ability should be recognized in appraising performance. Both intrinsic and extrinsic rewards are important for satisfaction, but they have differential impact—some individuals will be turned on by increased responsibility while others would rather have more pay. And perceived equity affects the impact of rewards as much as absolute amounts.

Systematic application of these approaches to motivation do lead to improvement. Organizations such Emery Air Freight Corporation say it works—citing improved customer service, profits, and employee satisfaction. In short, Emery believes that it has found a way "to link such theoretical ideas as work measurement, management by objective, job enrichment, productivity and profit improvement, and participative management into a practical program that pays off." [32]

Summary

Individual behavior and motivation are fundamental parts of the psychosocial system of organizations. Personality theory is an important subdiscipline in general psychology, which emphasizes the whole person in his or her environment and current interpersonal relationships.

Individuals are similar in that all behavior is (1) caused, (2) motivated, and (3) goal-oriented. The particular goals vary for individuals, as do the causes underlying motivation. However, the behavioral process outlined by these three ingredients remains the same for all people, in all places, and at all times.

Individual variations in behavior occur primarily because of differences in perception, cognition, and motivation. These processes facilitate the evolution of a system of personal values and knowledge, which is important in mediating between stimulus and response.

Motivation theory is concerned with what (content) and how (process) behavior is energized, directed, and sustained. Noncognitive theories stress operant conditioning via positive reinforcement. Cognitive theories stress needs, drives, and expectations, with emphasis on conscious consideration of the utility of effort

[32] "New Tool: Reinforcement for Good Work," *Business Week*, Dec. 18, 1971, p. 77.

in achieving desired outcomes. However, the seemingly direct relationship of effort → performance → satisfaction is affected by many variables, such as abilities, role perceptions, and reward systems.

The need-hierarchy concept or model includes levels of prepotent needs such as physiological, security, social, esteem, and self-actualization. Many writers have suggested concentration on higher-level need satisfaction in order for people to realize their full potential. McGregor stresses Theory Y (as contrasted to Theory X). Likert has evolved System Four with the same goal in mind. Herzberg stresses motivating factors such as achievement, recognition, responsibility, and the task itself, rather than the hygiene functions such as working conditions, salary, and administrative climate. McClelland describes the achievement motive as related to esteem and self-actualization needs and stresses its importance for many individuals in society, particularly entrepreneur-managers.

In spite of the complexity of motivation theory, there are enough common threads so that practical guidelines can be set forth. General approaches should be flexible enough to take individual differences into account.

Questions
and
Problems

1 What basic disciplines contribute to the understanding of psychosocial systems? How?

2 Relate anatomy, physiology, and psychology to behavior.

3 Are behavior patterns inherited or acquired?

4 Using the basic model in Figure 10.1, trace several examples of behavior—eating, kissing, obtaining a master's degree, or running for president. Why is this model applicable to all people, of all ages, in all cultures, at all times?

5 Summarize the impact of perception, cognition, and motivation on individual differences in behavior.

6 Explain the following relationships:

$$\text{Behavior} = f(\text{personality, environment})$$
$$\text{Performance} = f(\text{ability, motivation})$$
$$\text{Productivity} = f(\text{technology, ability, motivation})$$

7 Using the model in Figure 10.4, give at least two theories for (a) *what* motivates behavior and (b) *how* the process works. Give examples of how advice to practicing managers might be the same regardless of which cause-effect theory is assumed to be correct.

8 Trace your own psychological development in terms of the hierarchy of needs in Figure 10.5. How does the mix of needs affect behavior?

9 What is the motivation-hygiene concept? How is it related to the need-hierarchy concept?

10 What impact does achievement motivation have on individual behavior? On societal behavior?

11 Describe two polar views of people. What is your assumption concerning the basic nature of human beings? Why?

12 What should be the role of the work environment in providing opportunity for self-actualization?

Status
and
Role
Systems

Understanding individual behavior through concepts such as personality and motivation is a necessary but not sufficient condition for coordinating human endeavor in organizations. Managing requires considerable knowledge concerning the organizational environment—the structure and processes that influence individual behavior in many direct and indirect ways. Status and role systems represent two important concepts in this regard. An individual's socially defined status and individually perceived role have a significant effect on how he or she acts and is reacted to. Discussion of these aspects of the organizational psychosocial system will be focused around the following topics:

Status and Role Defined
Status Systems
Classless Society?
Occupational Prestige
Status Symbols
Role Systems
Role Episode
Role Conflict
Bureaucratic Role Behavior

Status
and
Role
Defined

Status refers to the ranking or stratification of people in a social system. It involves degrees of prestige and, unfortunately, implications of good-bad or superiority-inferiority. While "all people are created equal," some are more equal than others. Status hierarchies seem to be an inevitable phenomenon in social systems. An ordering, stratification, or ranking develops among individuals in any group. Status depends on the consensus of group members. Pfiffner and Sherwood describe status as "the comparative esteem which members of the various social systems accord to the positions in them."[1]

It is useful to distinguish social status and organizational status, although the two certainly interact. Social status refers to ranking in a community or society, and an individual's relative position is often based on a number of factors—age, strength, size, wisdom, family relationships, occupation, and personality, for example. The composite impact of ranking on various factors results in an individual's general status within a social system such as the community, state, or country.

Organizational status may also rely on the composite of several characteristics but is usually more narrowly defined than societal status. It typically refers to a specific hierarchical position within a particular organization. Barnard defines such status as follows:

By "status" of an individual in an organization we mean . . . that condition of the individual that is defined by a statement of . . . rights, privileges, immunities, duties, and obligations in the organization and, obversely, by a statement of the restrictions, limitations, and prohibitions governing . . . behavior, both determining the expectations of others In reference thereto. Status becomes systematic in an organization when appropriate recognition of assigned status becomes the duty and the practice of all participating, and when the conditions of the status of all individuals are published by means of differentiating designation, titles, appellations, insignia, or overt patterns of behavior.[2]

This definition of status implies its integral relationship to behavior; certain things can be done, and others cannot be done.

The concept of *role* relates to the activities of an individual in a particular position. It describes the behavior he or she is expected to exhibit when occupying a given position in the societal or organizational system. The relationship of role to individual behavior is apparent. For example, "a role is commonly defined as a set of behaviors which is expected of everyone in a particular position, regardless of who he is. These behaviors are of course socially ordained; and the role therefore sets a kind of limit on the types of personality expression possible in any given situation."[3]

The integration of concepts such as status and role, which are social, and *personality,* which is individual, is important for understanding and predicting individual behavior in organizations. The interaction of these basic ingredients can result in a multiplicity of behavior patterns. Although these concepts are inseparable in real situations, it will be helpful to consider them in detail separately and then to integrate them within the psychosocial system.

1 John M. Pfiffner and Frank P. Sherwood, *Administrative Organization,* Prentice-Hall, Inc., Englewood Cliffs, N.J., 1960, p. 274.

2 Chester I. Barnard, "The Functions of Status Systems," in Robert K. Merton et al. (eds.), *Reader in Bureaucracy,* The Free Press of Glencoe, New York, 1952, p. 242.

3 Pfiffner and Sherwood, op. cit., p. 39.

Status
Systems

Status is derived from a multiplicity of characteristics. However, five basic factors—birth, personal qualities, achievements, possessions, and authority—underlie most societal status systems.[4] The relative importance of these basic factors depends on the particular culture and the point in history one is examining.

Kinds of
Status

Several dichotomies have been identified that facilitate understanding the concept of status. In this section we will discuss the following pairs: ascribed-achieved, functional-scalar, positional-personal, and active-latent.

Ascribed status is that into which a person is born. The individual's family has a certain position in society, and, at least initially, all members of that family are ascribed with that status. The caste system in India and other cultures is an example of such a system. Regardless of personal attributes, an individual is often locked into a particular status from birth. While some mobility has developed, caste status systems are still relatively rigid and upward movement is nominal at best.

More important for the study of organization and management is *achieved* status. Here, education and/or skill provide the means for achieving a specific position in the social system, particularly the work environment. The story of the "self-made person" is common in Western society, particularly the United States. The individual who was "born on the wrong side of the tracks" can achieve high status primarily through occupational prestige. Several routes are open, including politics, education, and entrepreneurial success.

In the United States, education has been the most expedient means of improving status. Thus, many first-generation immigrant families, finding themselves in a low status position in society, have stressed education for their offspring. Most modern large-scale organizations provide opportunity for achieving increased status as one moves up the hierarchical ladder. Here again, however, although an individual might achieve the Presidency after starting on the assembly line with an eighth-grade education, it is very unlikely. A college education is becoming minimal; moreover, the probability of success and increased status improves considerably if the individual has a master's degree.

In organizations the distinction between *scalar* and *functional* status is important.[5] Scalar relates to a position in the vertical hierarchy; functional relates to the particular task or function that an individual performs. In an aerospace

---

4 Talcott Parsons, *Essays in Sociological Theory: Pure and Applied,* The Free Press of Glencoe, New York, 1949, pp. 171–172. Parsons also mentions a sixth category of status—that which is achieved by illegitimate means.

5 Barnard, op. cit., pp. 242–243.

firm, for example, design engineering typically has more functional status than manufacturing or accounting. However, the controller or manufacturing manager has much more scalar status than many design engineers. While scalar status is often quite explicit and set forth formally in the organization charts, functional status is more implicit and dependent on the value system and perception of a particular evaluator. Accountants may perceive their own functional status as much higher than that accorded them by design engineers, and vice versa.

In universities, as in many organizations, a certain general status attaches to particular functions, even though theoretically (according to the structural model) they are all equal. There is a "pecking order" of academic disciplines, which implies relative superiority or inferiority rather than merely difference in function. Mathematicians may accord electrical engineers and political scientists less status than other mathematicians. Such status differentials depend on individual perception, and there is no official, formal published list of functional status. However, it does exist and has an impact on organizational behavior. Scalar status, on the other hand, is explicit and published in chart form. The relative status of the various positions in the system can be readily ascertained, and the privileges and limitations of each position are relatively well known.

Another useful dichotomy in understanding status systems relates to **personal** and **positional** status. A certain amount of status is attached to a particular position in the social system without regard to its occupant. Thus, the position of lawyer or teacher may connote more status than clerk or hobo. On the other hand, Cliff Hangar may be a lousy lawyer and Pete Moss may be an excellent clerk. In these instances, status is attached to the personal performance of an individual in a particular position. Other characteristics, such as attractiveness and gregariousness, affect personal status, which may vary significantly for a given individual in several different groups. In organizations it is helpful if personal and positional status are congruent. If other members hold a person in low esteem but the individual has a relatively high position organizationally, the atmosphere may not be conducive to effective and efficient operation.

The concepts of **active** and **latent** status are also important. Because an individual occupies many positions (plays many roles) in various organizations in society, status attaches to the person in many ways. There are both ascribed and achieved status, both functional and scalar status, and both positional and personal status—separately and together. However, all these factors do not necessarily operate at once. At work, status attaches to a particular position the individual occupies in an organization. Status as a Little League coach or amateur bowler does not have as much impact. Status in these realms would be latent, for the most part, during working hours. Active status would vary, depending on organizational setting and timing—family, work, lodge, church, or other. Latent status may be relevant to active status in varying degrees. For example, an individual's status as a lawyer may affect her status in a community action organization more than her status as a ping-pong player. The concepts of active and latent status can be used to refine the notion of multiplicity of variables in assessing composite status for individuals in social systems.

Equality versus Status

If equalitarianism is one of the cornerstones of our cultural heritage, it would seem that status systems are basically dysfunctional. They certainly emphasize inequality based on various key characteristics. However, status systems are natural and inevitable. In social groups cooperative action requires some division of work, both horizontally (by function) and vertically (scalar concepts). The animal kingdom provides many examples of status systems that require the identification of a leader (or leaders) and followers. Superior-subordinate relationships are evident. There are leaders and followers in elephant herds, lion prides, and chimpanzee bands. Similarly, in human groups, functional specialization and superior-subordinate relationships develop quite naturally. Thus, status serves as a means of organizing endeavor by providing a system within which individuals can relate to one another. It facilitates communication and the implementation of systems of authority and responsibility.[6]

On the other hand, status systems create many problems. Overemphasis on status for its own sake, without recognizing its role in facilitating coordinated group effort, can be detrimental. Individuals can spend great amounts of time, effort, and money in trying to achieve status within a social system. Status differentials can be useful in motivating some people toward superior performance, but others may "break down" in an atmosphere of continual striving. In most large-scale organizations, the hierarchy is pyramidal and narrows quite rapidly toward the top. Thus, many are called, but only a few are chosen. If scalar status is overemphasized, those who do not make it may cease to function at par. Disappointments may be overwhelming and extremely dysfunctional to future organizational endeavor. Yet regardless of the disadvantages, social status systems are inevitable. "Social status in America is somewhat like man's alimentary canal; he may not like the way it works and he may want to forget that certain parts of it are part of him, but he knows it is necessary for his very existence. So a status system, often an object of our disapproval, is present and necessary in our complex social world."[7]

Classless Society?

Many studies of social class have revolved around a classification scheme somewhat as follows: upper upper, lower upper, upper middle, lower

---

6 Robert K. Merton, *Social Theory and Social Structure,* The Free Press of Glencoe, New York, 1957, p. 370.

7 W. Lloyd Warner, Marchia Meeker, and Kenneth Eells, *Social Classes in America,* Science Research Associates, Inc., Chicago, 1949. p. 10.

middle, upper lower, lower lower. By and large, on the basis of income, the four middle categories represent an increasing portion of society. Other status characteristics reflect this as well—education, for example. Class is a psychosocial phenomenon, reflected in attitudes and propensities for decision making. "Those in this country who speak of the 'middle class' as our largest cohesive social group apparently have in mind this conception: they refer to those millions of Americans who share, in general, common values, attitudes, and aspirations."[8]

The increasing proportion of our population in the economic middle class has resulted in increasing use of the term "classless society." In 1959 Packard described this trend by stating that "The rank-and-file citizens of the nation have generally accepted this view of progress toward equality because it fits with what we would like to believe about ourselves. It coincides with the American Creed and the American Dream, and is deeply imbedded in our folklore."[9] In 1977 McGuire concluded that "A strong disposition toward equality . . . has always been a part of the American dream. But people, and especially executives in business and government, should recognize that the attainment of a more equal society requires tradeoffs, and that to make equity a preeminent objective in our society involves the surrender of other important values, among which are freedom, efficiency, and meritocracy."[10]

The focus of efforts in the 1960s and 1970s has been toward decreasing the impact of factors such as race or sex in automatically determining status. The goal has been equal opportunity so that ascribed status does not overwhelm the chance to achieve status via personal accomplishments. We have made some progress toward this goal, but there is still considerable room for improvement.

There are evident disagreements with regard to both the merit and the reality of a classless society. Has it become more homogeneous or more heterogeneous and stratified? Some of the more obvious indicators have disappeared. It is difficult to distinguish a vice-president from a clerk in many organizations on the basis of appearance. The extremes are still quite visible—the opulent can be distinguished from the indigent. However, it is difficult to distinguish the various strata in the vast middle class. On the other hand, while status differentials may be more subtle, they are nevertheless real.[11] Much effort—advertising, for example—goes into distinguishing gradations of status based on material things and activities engaged in.

Mobility

Recognizing the inevitability of stratification and the class system, the concept of social mobility has been stressed in the United States. While other

---

8 Charles H. Page, "Social Class in American Sociology," in Reinhard Bendix and Seymour Martin Lipset (eds.), *Class, Status and Power,* The Free Press of Glencoe, New York, 1953, p. 48.

9 Vance Packard, *The Status Seekers,* David McKay Company, Inc., New York, 1959, pp. 4–5.

10 Joseph W. McGuire, "The 'New' Equalitarianism and Managerial Practice," *California Management Review,* Spring 1977, p. 29.

11 Reeve Vanneman and Fred C. Pampel, "The American Perception of Class and Status," *American Sociological Review,* June 1977, pp. 422–437.

cultures have been characterized as rigid (caste systems, for example), we have emphasized opportunities for upward mobility. The importance of education and entrepreneurial prowess has been stressed.

Of course, this emphasis has led to an environment that almost requires striving for improvement—a reflection of the Protestant ethic and achievement motivation. While opportunities for upward social mobility do exist, there are formidable barriers. Those without entrepreneurial prowess or the capacity to take advantage of educational opportunities find it extremely difficult to better their position. Many current efforts spotlight the tremendous difficulty for the minority groups in lower-income brackets (or the hard-core unemployed) to break out of their position in society. The riots in the ghettos of many large cities reflected the frustration encountered as people tried without much success to better their position within the framework of our society.

Similar problems arise at all levels, but they are not quite so evident. Thus, social mobility has both advantages and disadvantages. It provides opportunity for improved status within our class system, but it also results in an atmosphere where failure can lead to frustration. There are no easy answers. Status systems seem inevitable and useful in structuring organized endeavor, but we must be aware of the dysfunctional aspects and strive for optimal balance.

Occupational Prestige

In modern societies, the hierarchy of occupational prestige is one of the most basic systems of stratification. Extensive empirical studies have shown striking similarities in a variety of nations—socialist and capitalist, developed and developing. "It appears that occupational-prestige hierarchies are similar from country to country and from subgroup to subgroup within a country. This stability reflects the fundamental but gross similarities among the occupational systems of modern nations. Furthermore, knowledge about occupations and relatively strong consensus on the relative positions of occupations are widely diffused throughout the populations involved." [12]

Occupational prestige is important in the social system because it affects the power and influence of occupants of certain positions, as well as the amount of resources that society places at their disposal. In this section we will look at occupational prestige in both the United States and Russia.

United States

Between 1947 and 1963 "scientific occupations were increasing in prestige, culturally oriented occupations were falling, and artisans were enjoying a

---

12 Robert W. Hodge, Paul M. Siegel, and Peter H. Rossi, "Occupational Prestige in the United States, 1925–63," *The American Journal of Sociology*, November 1964, pp. 286–287.

mild upward trend. Nevertheless, the overriding conclusion must be that the structure of occupational prestige is remarkably stable through time as well as space." [13]

Scientific occupations received a tremendous boost in prestige in the post-*Sputnik 1* era. The national goal of putting a man on the moon and returning him safely to earth focused considerable attention on scientific endeavor. The international competition involved has generated repercussions throughout society—government, business, and education. The results of these developments are indicated in the upward movements in prestige of nuclear physicists, scientists, and government scientists. Meanwhile, the physician has remained close to the top of the prestige ladder, second only to Supreme Court justices. Lawyers have moved up significantly from eighteenth to eleventh in the rankings. At the same time, diplomats slipped from fourth to eleventh.

In the wake of Watergate and other similar episodes, confidence in institutions and officials (both public and private) appeared to be decreasing. While relative rankings may still be rather stable, the pedestals of most occupations in the upper half of the hierarchy have been tarnished. This has led to a decrease in the absolute amount of prestige accorded to key roles by the general populace.

Many individual changes of varying degrees can be cited. However, the general stability in the system is evident. Shoeshiners, streetsweepers, garbage collectors, and sharecroppers remain at the bottom of the ladder. The traditional professions rank relatively high. In general, income is probably correlated with the prestige hierarchy. However, there are obvious examples that distort the picture. Business executives, either managers or members of corporate boards of directors, probably enjoy significantly larger incomes than many in occupations ranked above them. Salespeople or nightclub entertainers are often extremely well-paid and yet do not rank very high in occupational prestige as seen by society in general.

Even though occupational prestige is fundamental in social status systems, it is not overriding. It relates primarily to achieved, functional status. In organizations, scalar status may take precedence. The corporate president enjoys a measure of status and prestige over that of the company physician or lawyer. Personal attributes also play an important part, and there is tremendous variation within categories. Some Supreme Court justices acquire more status and prestige than others. The same is true for nuclear physicists, state governors, senators, plumbers, or bartenders. Nevertheless, without detailed knowledge of individual prestige, status is accorded to occupations based on our general impressions of their relative position in the prestige hierarchy. The same ordering holds true in other cultures as well. [14]

13 Ibid., p. 286.

14 Donald J. Treiman, *Occupational Prestige in Comparative Perspective*, Academic Press, New York, 1977.

Union of
Soviet Socialist
Republics

The triumph of the proletariat is supposed to yield a classless society. Russian communism was designed to produce a pure equalitarian social system. Stalin often emphasized that the Soviet population was divided into two major classes: the working class and the peasantry, plus a third group, the intelligentsia. Within Soviet society, the members of all three groups were defined as "equal in rights." In the 1930s, Stalin asserted that the amount of social distance and the political and economic contradictions between the groups were diminishing and, indeed, were being obliterated.[15]

While these goals might be achieved in a very simple society, they appear to be unachievable in complex, technological societies. Indeed, the Soviet Union has recognized the need to differentiate on the basis of many characteristics in order to maintain a viable system. Incentive systems have been developed, and differential rewards have been accorded based on relative contributions to various societal endeavors. The result has been an elaborately and precisely stratified status system, which includes the intelligentsia, divided into several subunits; the working class, also markedly differentiated; and the peasantry, relatively homogeneous but also divided into two distinguishable groups. The whole system can be ranked as follows:

Category	Rank
Ruling elite	1
Superior intelligentsia	2
General intelligentsia	3
Working class aristocracy	4
White-collar workers	5.5
Well-to-do peasants	5.5
Average workers	7
Average peasants	8.5
Disadvantaged workers	8.5
Forced-labor workers	10

This ranking hardly suggests a classless society. The ruling elite refers to the official Communist Party members. On balance, however, the ranking of categories correlates closely with the general occupational categories in the United States. The professional occupations in the United States parallel the relative status of the intelligentsia in Russia. Farm workers and unskilled labor rank very low in both societies. Just as in the United States, many factors are involved in determining an individual's overall status in society. However, the main determi-

15 Alex Inkeles, "Social Stratification in the Soviet Union," in Bendix and Lipset (eds.), *Class, Status and Power*, p. 609.

nants are occupation and income, plus education and technical expertise, which allow one to exert power and authority in certain phases of societal life.

Our own observations and discussions in Russia in 1975 tend to confirm the status rankings shown above. The pay system is formalized for the entire society and parallels, in general, the status hierarchy. Fringe benefits such as housing, vacations, and opportunities to purchase durable goods are also related to occupational status. We spoke to one computer programmer, a recent cybernetics institute graduate, who complained a bit that his salary was lower than that of a lathe operator. But the lathe operator, to whom we also talked, had fifteen years of experience and was really part of the working class aristocracy.

These similarities in occupational prestige in two major world cultures are illustrative of the pervasiveness of status systems throughout the world and over time. Of particular interest in this regard are the various symbols used to identify position in a status hierarchy.

Status Symbols

Numerous symbols can be used to designate status. The most obvious, of course, are those related to physical appearance. The queen wears a crown; the Indian chief has his headdress; the judge has his robe; and the nun has her habit. The military services probably have the most elaborate system of uniform differentials to identify gradations in status. Their visibility leaves no doubt with regard to superior-subordinate relationships and facilitates command and control.

Another prevalent system of status symbols is that of titles. In the military, titles accompany the visible symbols. In other phases of society, however, there are no physical appurtenances. For example, individuals might be indistinguishable in their "Sunday" suits. However, status differentials would be apparent if they were addressed as president, governor, mayor, mister, or ms. Titles often reflect both functional and scalar status. For example, in an aerospace company, there might be as many as six vice-presidents. Therefore, in order to pinpoint his job more accurately, an individual might use the term Vice-president, Research and Development, on his door and/or stationery. In the aerospace environment, it is likely that this title would carry slightly more prestige than Vice-president, Finance, or Vice-president, Manufacturing. The relative status of functional titles would vary according to the industry and the specific company.

In educational institutions it is often difficult to decipher the titular system. The chairperson of a department may use that title only if she assumes it has sufficient prestige. On the other hand, she may sign her letters as "Professor and Chairperson" if the former title seems more prestigious. In a medical school, the term Professor may not "carry much weight" because it ranks eighth on the occupational-prestige hierarchy, whereas physicians rank second.

One of our colleagues was introduced to King Olaf of Norway during a visit to the University of Washington, Seattle, Washington. When asked if he were awed by the experience, he replied, "No, I once shook hands with the Governor of Texas." This illustrates individual perception of the relative ranking of titles.

Many other examples of status symbols could be cited, most of which relate in some way to quantity or quality of material goods, which in turn depend on the amount of money an individual has. Houses, automobiles, furs, jewelry, and extensive travel, for example, can be used to measure relative status of individuals or families in society. It is common to explain purchasing habits in terms of the search for status. This is obviously the case for many individuals who wittingly or unwittingly are caught up in status seeking. On the other hand, there are many who consciously shy away from this approach. For example, the parking concessionaire at one of Seattle's best restaurants suggests that the status seekers drive the Cadillacs and Continentals, while the members of the upper-upper class drive old station wagons.

Status symbols in society in general have received considerable atten-

Figure 11.1   The Paraphernalia That Go with Rank

tion. Even more attention, however, has been devoted to the "signs of office" within large-scale organizations, both public and private.

Signs of Office

Figure 11.1 illustrates the various paraphernalia that go with rank in the corporate environment. Many companies have an elaborate scheme established for differentiating by various levels within the corporate hierarchy. As individuals move from job to job, their status is quite evident by the various physical appurtenances related to their offices. Desks, tables, carpeting, air conditioning, view—all play a role in identifying the status of employees in large-scale organizations.

While some organizations have attempted to establish a "classless society" by maintaining uniform signs of office throughout the system, this approach

Figure 11.1   (Continued)

is rare. [16] As in our general culture, a status system seems natural and inevitable. The signs of office accompany a ranking rather than establish it. Most observers stress the functional nature of the system of differentiated physical appurtenances. They provide an incentive for organizational participants who strive for higher levels and the rewards attendant thereto.

Role Systems

The twin concepts of status and role are fundamental to the description and analysis of social structure. [17] Status relates to positions in a social system occupied by designated individuals; role relates to the expected behavior patterns attributed to that position. "Status and role, in these terms, are concepts serving to connect the culturally defined expectations with the patterned behavior and relationships which comprise social structure." [18]

The term **role** is used to designate the composite of culture patterns associated with a particular status position. It includes attitudes, values, and behavior ascribed by the society to any and all persons occupying a specific position. It includes the legitimate expectations of incumbents with respect to the behavior of other persons toward them. "Insofar as it represents overt behavior, a role is the dynamic aspect of status: what the individual has to do in order to validate his occupation of the status." [19] The term *sergeant* has definite status implications because of its position in the military hierarchy. The behavior expected of sergeants is also reasonably well defined. Some aspects of the role are described in detail in a position description; others are part of the folklore handed down via face-to-face contacts, novels, movies, or other media. A typical stereotype is the seasoned, battle-hardened sergeant who has great difficulty in relating to the new, inexperienced second lieutenant.

Human organizations can be defined as role systems. "In defining human organizations as open systems of roles, we emphasized two cardinal facts: the *contrived nature* of human organizations, and the unique properties of a *structure consisting of acts or events* rather than unchanging physical components." [20] Organizations are much more than aggregates of people, machines, material, time, and space. Predicting organizational behavior requires emphasis on actions and

---

16 The office building of the School of Business Administration (University of Washington) was designed so that all offices and furnishings would be identical, except for several corner ones, which were assigned to senior professors. However, certain locations (differential views) quickly became preferable. Rugs, upholstered chairs, paintings, and other "signs of office" were also added by occupants. Thus a status system developed informally even though the basic space and furnishings were identical.

17 Ralph Linton, *The Study of Man,* Appleton-Century-Crofts, Inc., New York, 1936.

18 Merton, op. cit., p. 368.

19 Ralph Linton, "Concepts of Role and Status," in Theodore E. Newcomb and Eugene L. Hartley (eds.), *Readings in Social Psychology,* Holt, Rinehart and Winston, Inc., New York, 1947, p. 368.

20 Daniel Katz and Robert L. Kahn, *The Social Psychology of Organizations,* 2d ed., John Wiley & Sons, Inc., New York, 1978, p. 187.

events. What happens in organizations? How does it happen? These questions are more important than the question, What is it?

Certain activities are ascribed to particular positions in organizations. A complete set of activities for a particular position is its role. Formal documents such as position descriptions spell out the activities of a particular position or office, including how it relates to other similar positions in the organization. In many cases roles are not set forth explicitly, and yet they seem to be understood by organizational members. Whether formally or informally established, status and role systems are integral parts of any organization—from two-person groups to society as a whole.

Multiple Roles

However, role systems are not clear-cut; there are several complications that make it difficult to define particular roles and often lead to role conflict. The concept of multiple roles is one such phenomenon. Individuals play many roles simultaneously. Usually, however, only one role is active at a particular time, while others are in relative degrees of latency. Multiple roles relate to multiple positions that an individual holds, often in various institutional settings home, church, service organization, fraternal order, or work environment. Within each organization of which he is a member, he occupies a particular position and performs certain activities associated with that role. An individual's existence obviously varies in complexity according to the number of roles played in the organizations of which he is a part. Varying degrees of consistency in role playing may also affect the complexity of the situation.

Role Sets

For any particular position or status there is a variable number of orientations. Some roles are more complex than others.

A particular social status involves, not a single associated role, but an array of associated roles. This is a basic characteristic of social structure. This fact of structure can be registered by a distinctive term, *role-set,* by which I mean that *complement of role relationships which persons have by virtue of occupying a particular social status.* As one example: . . . the status of public school teachers has its distinctive role-set, relating the teacher to . . . pupils, to colleagues, the school principal and superintendent, the Board of Education, and, on frequent occasions, to local patriotic organizations, to professional organizations of teachers, parent-teacher associations, and the like.[21]

It is important to understand the difference between the concept of multiple roles and that of role set. The former refers to different roles in different organizational settings. Role sets, on the other hand, relate to the various orienta-

---

21 Merton, op. cit., p. 369.

tions that a specific position in a particular organization may require. The ultimate in complexity for individual behavior can be seen in the case of someone involved in many different institutional roles, all of which have complex role sets. At the other extreme (the pastoral life of the shepherd, perhaps) is the individual who is involved in very few organizations and whose roles—those he or she does play—are extremely simple and have very narrow role sets.

Role Perception

Accuracy in role perception has a definite impact on effectiveness and efficiency in organizations. Individuals have certain abilities and are motivated in varying degrees to perform designated tasks. However, if a task is incorrectly perceived, the result may be quite ineffective from the organizational point of view. On the other hand, an activity or role associated with a particular position could be perceived quite accurately and yet inefficient performance could result because of deficiencies in ability and/or motivation. These various elements are present in any organizational situation and must be considered together. The numerous factors affecting role perception can be considered in terms of the concept of role episode.

Role Episode [22]

Figure 11.2 illustrates the basic elements of role playing and the numerous confounding variables that influence this process and that illustrate the complexity of the organizational role-taking process. The concept of a role episode is an oversimplification. It implies a beginning, an event or process, and an end. The core part of Figure 11.2 suggests a total sequence: role expectations (I) lead to role sending (II), which leads to a received role (III) with the episode culminating in a behavioral response to the role as received (IV). In reality, it is difficult to establish beginning and ending points for role episodes. The process actually is never-ending, and there are many simultaneous processes going on at any given moment. Moreover, the model does not illustrate the conflict that is inevitable in the process. It is also an oversimplification to treat the role episode in a vacuum. Its context involves "confounding variables," which have an important impact on the process itself.

Baseball managers are expected to behave in certain ways in carrying out the activities of their offices. They get much advice from owners, fans, sportswriters, coaches, and players about how they should behave in certain situations. They filter this advice via selective perception and use the residue, along with their own ideas of the way the job should be done, to develop behavior patterns that

---

[22] This section follows the discussion of "The Role Episode" by Katz and Kahn, op. cit., pp. 185–221.

Figure 11.2   A Theoretical Model of the Role Episode and Factors Affecting the Organizational Role-Taking Process

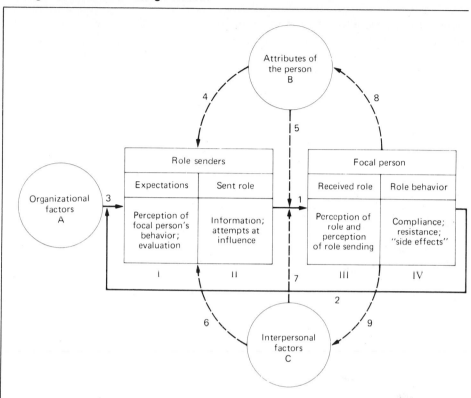

Adapted from Daniel Katz and Robert L. Kahn, *The Social Psychology of Organizations,* 2d ed., John Wiley & Sons, Inc., New York, 1978, pp. 196ff.

guide their actions. Their actual role behavior is the result of their own propensity to act in certain ways as modified by the influence of those persons in their role set.

This same process or role episode can be detailed for any position—president, department head, nurse, file clerk, or janitor.

Confounding Variables

The role episode takes place in the context of confounding variables such as the attributes of the person, as well as organizational and interpersonal influences. These three major confounding variables are indicated as circles in Figure 11.2. They represent the context of typical organizations regardless of the specific individuals occupying positions in them.

Organizational factors (*A*) have a direct causal relationship with role expectations. There are various prescriptions and proscriptions associated with particular positions in organizations. These make up the role expectations usually held by members of a role set and are determined, in part, by the broader organizational context, which includes technology, formal structure, job descriptions, policies and procedures, and reward systems. Many of these are spelled out formally in organizations, regardless of the personalities involved. Certainly, individuals adapt the system somewhat to their own idiosyncratic behavior patterns. However, many properties of organizations can be treated as independent of the particular persons occupying the various positions and "playing" the attendant roles.

Similar to organization factors, there are enduring personality traits (B) that describe the propensity of an individual to behave in certain ways. She has an overall value system and is motivated according to a particular hierarchy of needs or utilities. Role senders often modify their expectations with regard to particular positions based on their knowledge of the personalities involved. The enduring organizational factors are often adjusted in order to compensate slightly for idiosyncratic behavior on the part of a particular role taker.

The most obvious impact of personal attributes is in mediating between the sent role and the received role. Individual selective perception is at work; individuals are much more likely to receive information and be influenced by "sendings" that reinforce their own expectations with regard to a given role. Role senders may perceive considerable distortion between their expectations and the direction of their influence and the resultant behavior of the focal person. Meanwhile, the individual may sincerely believe she is acting as "directed."

Interpersonal factors (C) operate parallel to personal attributes in affecting the role episode process. The way in which the sent role is received will depend in great measure on the interpersonal relationships between the focal person and the role senders. For example, influence varies directly with the degree of confidence an individual has in those who would seek to influence him. If he has no confidence or if an antagonistic atmosphere has developed, effective influence may be quite limited. On the other hand, if the sender or senders are respected and a congenial atmosphere prevails, the resultant behavior is quite likely to be influenced significantly by role senders.

Role Conflict

As complex as the process illustrated in Figure 11.2 is, it does not reflect adequately the concept of role conflict. Some is implied in the selective perception or outright rejection of sent role by the focal person. However, many other types of role conflict can be identified. Conflict in this sense does not mean overt antagonism or violence. Rather, it involves the simultaneous occurrence of two or more role sendings for which the compliance with one precludes compliance with the others.

The supervisor typically has been cited as a prime example of role conflict. On the one hand, management's expectations and related "sendings" stress his or her role in the managerial system and the need for decisiveness in planning and controlling operations. On the other hand, a first-line supervisor often has close ties with the people in the work group—former peers in many cases. Their expectations and sendings may not coincide exactly with those coming from the top down. Similarly, the supervisor has many inputs from other supervisors and his or her own perception of the role to be played. All these work together to provide a complex environment for individual behavior. Let us look at several specific types of role conflict.

Types of Conflict

Four major types of role conflict can be identified: (1) person-role, (2) interrole, (3) intersender, and (4) intrasender. As indicated previously, the concept of **person-role** conflict is implied in Figure 11.2, where personal attributes mediate between the sent role and the one that is received by the focal person. Conflict occurs when the requirements of the role violate the needs, values, or capacities of the focal person. For example, Catholic priests have resigned in order to marry or because they could not espouse the doctrine prescribed by the church on other issues. Or a sheriff may have great difficulty in carrying out the eviction of an aged widow. This type of role conflict relates to the internal cognitive and motivational aspects of behavior. The other primary sources originate externally and provide part of the complex context for individual behavior in organizations.

Interrole conflict relates to the phenomenon of multiple goals for individuals simultaneously acting in several or many organizations. A person may find himself faced with sent expectations for a role in one organization which conflict with those for another role. An employee who is also an officer in the union could experience considerable role conflict. Similarly, an individual's family role may conflict with what is expected of her on the job. The focal person must somehow develop order out of chaos, rank the various demands on her behavior, and develop a system of trade-offs that allows her to decide that "on balance" she should behave in a certain way at a particular time.

Intersender conflict results when various members of the role set have different expectations for a particular role person and hence transmit conflicting sendings. In this case, there are pressures on an individual from many directions as the various senders attempt to influence his behavior. Any office providing service (maintenance perhaps) to many other organizational units experiences such conflict. Everyone presents their projects under the guise of highest priority. Obviously, this is impossible, and some system must be invoked. The matrix organization that has resulted from the imposition of project management on top of traditional functional structure has resulted in intersender role conflict. The project manager expects certain behavior from the manufacturing manager. However, the vice-president of manufacturing has certain expectations with regard to the behavior of anyone in manufacturing, regardless of the particular program on which they function. In universities, department chairpersons are appointed by deans and are expected to function as an extension of the administrative hierarchy from the board of regents through the president, dean, and to the faculty. On the other hand, the chairperson is primarily a faculty member and often seeks to maintain collegial relationships with former peers, who have definite expectations with regard to the role of the chairperson. Intersender role conflict creates a complex environment for the focal person.

Intrasender conflict develops when one sender transmits conflicting instructions or expects behavior that is impossible in the light of earlier directives. A typical example is the supervisor's expectation that the incumbent in a particular position should improve efficiency, while the supervisor explicitly denies the subordinate the authority to fire people or even cut costs in other, less dramatic ways. Intrasender conflict can occur with the transmission of messages that have conflicting parts. It is more common, however, for the conflict to arise from messages sent at different time periods.

Conflict by Organizational Level

Role conflict is evident in all organizations. The degree of conflict can vary significantly and can be related to the levels set forth in Figure 5.5. The more complex the job, the more likely the role conflict. For example, task specialization provides the means for developing a narrowly oriented job description with explicit instructions for anyone who occupies a given position. Therefore, in the operating subsystem, it is possible to forestall role conflict by developing explicit, detailed instructions for a particular task. At other levels—coordinative and strategic—there is much more opportunity for inter- and intrasender conflict to occur. The manager in the coordinative subsystem is typically a mediator and compromiser and hence receives much conflicting information designed to influence the decisions he makes and the role he plays. At the strategic level, the manager is operating at the boundary of her organization and hence is subject to much inter-role conflict. As a member of the chamber of commerce, she is interested in pollution control. As president of a pulp and paper company, she is acutely aware of the cost of pollution control to her own company. This obviously leads to role conflict.

Person-role conflict can occur at any level. However, as one goes upward from operating through coordinative to strategic levels, the manager's job becomes increasingly complex, and the opportunity for person-role conflict increases. In other words, at higher levels there are many more opportunities for expectations for the particular position to be at odds with the individual's own value system with regard to how he or she should behave.

One other type of role conflict should be mentioned—that of overload. In many organizations, the expectations of various senders with regard to a particular position may not necessarily conflict. However, there may be so many of them that it is impossible for one individual to fulfill the requirements.[23] In a sense, this creates a conflict between the expectations for the role and an individual's capacity to perform. Unless the focal person can establish a priority system or ignore some demands, he may "fall apart at the seams" or become ineffective in all his actions. Overload role conflict may be temporary if the various pressures are eventually reduced. On the other hand, they may persist for an indefinite length of time and hence require more than ad hoc adjustments on the part of the focal person. Methods of counteracting the physiological and psychological impacts of stress and anxiety have been receiving increasing attention.[24]

Coupled with the question of overload as a source of role conflict is the general aura surrounding the executive role. What behavior patterns must be exhibited in order to move ahead in today's organizations? Much of the folklore that has developed lauds the aggressive competitiveness of entrepreneurs and laments the unaggressive cooperativeness exhibited in most large-scale, complex organizations. In many organizations, these two general strains of folklore lead to role conflict. "The ambitious, zestful young manager who is eager to make a mark may at first find pyramid-climbing an exasperating experience. For one thing, he will find himself working in a conflicting value system. He must appear a hot competitor, in keeping with the folklore, yet at the same time—and more important—he must prove himself a hot cooperator."[25]

Bureaucratic Role Behavior

"Prior to the 1950's it was part of American folklore that the way to succeed in American business was to follow in the footsteps of great individualists like Henry Ford or John D. Rockefeller. These men were known for their forcefulness and imagination and they were seldom accused of being tactful or cautious."[26] This statement reflects the Protestant ethic and Social Darwinism as described in the discussion of the evolving managerial ideologies in Chapter 2. The general societal value system emphasized imagination and independence as dominant in business success or life in general. The concept of bureaucracy has

---

23 The role of the President of the United States has been described as "impossible" because of the multitude of agencies reporting to the President. The response over several decades was an increase in the White House staff so that the "office," rather than the President, responded to many of the day-to-day pressures. One of President Carter's high-priority objectives was reorganization, including reducing the size of the White House staff, delegating more to cabinet secretaries, and encouraging more direct interaction between himself and key administrators. The presidents of many of today's conglomerates face similar problems. As the number and diversity of subsidiaries increase, role overload becomes a real concern.

24 Herbert Benson, M.D. (with Miriam Z. Klipper), *The Relaxation Response*, Avon Books, New York, 1976.

25 Vance Packard, *Pyramid Climbers*, McGraw-Hill Book Company, New York, 1962, p. 21.

26 Lyman W. Porter and Edward Lawler, III, *Managerial Attitudes and Performance*, Richard D. Irwin, Inc., Homewood, Ill., 1968, p. 99.

been a countertrend. It deemphasizes the human element, particularly capriciousness, and stresses the formal structure of positions and established procedures.

One of the major questions in organization theory in the latter half of the twentieth century has been the role conflict generated by these two opposing concepts. Many "viewers with alarm" have written of the demise of individualism and the triumph of conformism and mediocrity in society in general and business and government organizations in particular. [27] Two of the most widely read works are *The Lonely Crowd*, by Riesman, and *The Organization Man*, by Whyte. The latter introduces the concept of the social ethic that is exemplified by the bureaucratic worker who sacrifices individualism for extreme organizational loyalty. [28] This theme is evident in a number of descriptions (from both inside and outside) of behavior in the Watergate coverup and other similar activities. [29]

Much discussion of organizational life has centered around the two concepts of "inner-directed" and "other-directed" behavior, as set forth by Riesman. In terms of the model of role sending and role taking, inner-directedness emphasizes the internal value system of the focal person and gives greatest weight to his or her own perceptions and expectations with regard to a particular role. It emphasizes creative individualism in identifying and carrying out a particular organizational role. [30]

Other-directedness stresses the dominance of the expectations of others and role playing based on the external influence of other role senders. The extremes of this approach imply conformity and subservient behavior. The focal person keeps foremost in mind the expectations of others while performing his or her tasks. This person must "look good" in the eyes of superiors in order to get ahead. Cooperativeness is critical.

Because executives are prone to promote subordinates with characteristics and value systems similar to their own, this type of behavior seems appropriate and useful to ensure progress. People are likely to emphasize the traits in others that they themselves possess. However, this does not necessarily support a case for other-directedness. Many executives may perceive themselves as individualistic and inner-directed and hence look for similar traits in subordinates.

Large-scale, complex organizations do require cooperative effort. Individualistic (particularly idiosyncratic) behavior patterns may be dysfunctional at low and middle levels. Bureaucratic role behavior seems apparent in organizations and society. It has become popular to decry this phenomenon as a triumph of conformity and go-along-with-the-crowd behavior. The "bureaucratic person" is

27 See, for example, Alan Harrington, *Life in the Crystal Palace,* Alfred A. Knopf, Inc., New York, 1959; C. Wright Mills, *White Collar,* Oxford University Press, Fair Lawn, N.J., 1956; and Robert Heller, *The Great Executive Dream,* Delacorte Press, New York, 1972.

28 William H. Whyte, Jr., *The Organization Man,* Simon and Schuster, Inc., New York, 1956.

29 See for example: John Dean, *Blind Ambition,* Simon and Schuster, Inc., New York, 1976; Jeb Magruder, *An American Life,* Pocket Books, Inc., New York, 1975; Dan Rather, *Palace Guard,* Warner Books, Inc., New York, 1974; and Carl Bernstein and Bob Woodward, *All the President's Men,* Warner Books, Inc., New York, 1976.

30 Robert Townsend, *Up the Organization,* Alfred A. Knopf, Inc., New York, 1970.

supposedly noncontroversial, programmable, and incompetent. [31] The conclusions drawn from the writings of the "viewers with alarm" might well be that the "adaptable, socially attuned individual is going to succeed in business, while the creative, independent individual is in for trouble." [32] However, research has not substantiated such implications. In fact, the research that has been done seems to refute them.

Research on Career Progress

Porter and Lawler summarize their own research and the results of several other studies by stating, "All of these findings point to the conclusion that organizations not only tolerate but even *reward* inner-directed thinking and behavior." [33] Several kinds of research were involved, including tracing the promotions of lower and middle managers in large-scale organizations and measuring attitudes of managers toward the traits that could be identified as relating to either inner- or other-directedness. One study indicated that inner-directedness was tolerated more in large organizations than in small ones. Managers with more inner-directed role perceptions, and presumably behavior, were rated highly both by themselves *and* by their superiors. [34]

Inner-directed behavior was rated higher by top-level managers than by those at lower levels. Presumably, those who have evidenced forceful, individualistic creativity have "fought" their way to the top. Such executives are more likely to prize the traits that they perceive as the keys to success in their own careers.

Other empirical research indicates that:

There is a small but consistent tendency for men who work in bureaucratic organizations to be more intellectually flexible, more open to new experience, and more self-directed in their values than are men who work in nonbureaucratic organizations. This may in part result from bureaucracies' drawing on a more educated work force. In larger part, though, it appears to be a consequence of occupational conditions attendant on bureaucratization—notably, far greater job protections, somewhat higher income, and substantively more complex work. [35]

These findings seem to indicate that the "viewers with alarm" such as Riesman and Whyte were somewhat premature in their conclusions. Their writings were unsupported by empirical research and were probably based on small samples of unsystematic observations. The current scene in most organizations

---

31 "In a hierarchy, every employee tends to rise to his level of incompetence." Lawrence J. Peter and Raymond Hull, *The Peter Principle: Why Things Always Go 'Wrong* Bantam Books, Inc., New York, 1969, p. 7.
32 Porter and Lawler, op. cit., p. 100.
33 Ibid., p. 117.
34 Ibid.
35 Melvin L. Kohn, "Bureaucratic Man: A Portrait and an Interpretation," *American Sociological Review*, June 1971, p. 461.

certainly includes diverse examples of dress and hair styles that are as surprising as they are refreshing. Activism on many dimensions is also apparent. Values—individual and organizational—do change. [36]

It is also true that modern, large-scale organizations probably do not tolerate extremely deviant behavior, particularly at lower levels. Such individuals probably are not hired, but if so, they do not last very long. At the top levels, we have an entirely different atmosphere. Howard Hughes or J. Paul Getty, our society's two most famous billionaires, could extoll the virtues of individualism and, indeed, could "get away with" eccentric behavior. Entrepreneurs in organizations of many sizes can do likewise as long as they are owner-managers.

The most appropriate behavior pattern for progress toward the top of modern, large-scale organizations seems to be forceful, creative individualism, which is *not too far out of line*. Indeed, considerable training is designed to develop originality in problem solving—that is, to encourage behavior that is uncommon, but relevant within a defined organizational context.

Appropriate Managerial Behavior

A number of factors affect the general character of status and role systems in organizations. A formal, unchanging hierarchy, with clearly prescribed roles, is often evident in stable-mechanistic organizations such as military units or factories with routine production processes. On the other hand, an informal, changing hierarchy, with loosely defined roles, is more typical for adaptive-organic organizations such as project teams or consulting groups. On a specific project, status is more often personal and situational, rather than positional, and the importance of various roles typically changes during different phases of the project life cycle.

The managerial philosophy of top executives also has a significant impact on status and role systems. Regardless of the task or technology, management can place different degrees of emphasis on titles, location and size of offices, written job descriptions, protocol, and rules for behavior. The important point is matching situations and approaches. Status and role systems are inevitable and functional. However, rigidity can be detrimental to organizational effectiveness, efficiency, and participant satisfaction.

Summary

Status and role systems are basic to the psychosocial system of organizations. They provide frameworks within which perception, cognition, and motivation operate to influence individual behavior. Status refers to the prestige ranking

---

36 George E. Berkley, *The Administrative Revolution: Notes on the Passing of Organization Man*, Prentice-Hall, Inc., Englewood Cliffs, N.J., 1971.

of an individual in groups—small, informal groups; large, formal organizations; and society as a whole. With each status position is a related role or behavior pattern expected of the incumbent.

Several kinds of status can be identified: (1) ascribed or achieved, (2) functional or scalar, (3) positional or personal, and (4) active or latent. Occupational prestige is one of the most obvious and persistent systems of status. Moreover, the relative position of various occupations is quite similar for many cultures throughout the world.

Roles refer to ongoing behavior or the action related to a particular position in the organizational structure. Multiple roles are evident for individuals who are members of several or many groups. Each particular position has a role set—the organizational interfaces that call for specific behavior patterns.

The *role episode* concept provides a useful framework for understanding the impact of roles on individual behavior. Role senders transmit expectations to the focal person, who is a role taker. The sent role is received by the focal person, who behaves according to his own propensities as modified by the influence of the role senders.

Person-role conflict occurs when an individual's value system is incongruent with the expectations she perceives for her behavior. *Interrole* conflict occurs when the expectations for one or more of the multiple roles precludes the performance of another. *Intersender* conflict occurs when inconsistent expectations are transmitted from several sources of pressure. The focal person cannot carry out both behavior patterns simultaneously. *Intrasender* conflict occurs when two incompatible sets of expectations are transmitted from one influence source.

A major source of current concern is the overall role conflict that is evident. While much of the popular literature seems to suggest that other-directedness and conformity prevail and are undermining the very foundations of American society, empirical research seems to indicate that inner-directedness and individualism are still widespread and rewarded in most organizations.

Questions and Problems

1 Define and compare status and role.

2 Compare and contrast societal and organizational status.

3 Briefly describe the several kinds of status. Illustrate each kind with an example from your own experience.

4 "Status systems are inevitable and inherently useful." Do you agree? Why or why not?

5 What are the functional and dysfunctional aspects of social mobility?

6 Why have occupational prestige rankings been so stable? How do United States rankings compare with those in other cultures?

7 Make a list of various status symbols or "signs of office" that are apparent in your social, school, or work environment.

8 Compare and contrast multiple roles and role sets. How can these concepts be applied in your own situation?

9 Illustrate the concept of role episode (see Figure 11.2) with examples such as a bank vice-president, a traveling salesperson, and a new employee with M.B.A. degree in hand.

10 Define the four major types of role conflict. Relate them to the examples in question 9.

11 Does empirical research support or refute the contentions of "viewers with alarm" that individualism and entrepreneurship are waning and that other-directedness is the best characteristic for success in organizations? What is your view of the "appropriate" behavior pattern for success in organizations? For success in general?

Group Dynamics

Twelve

The human group is a pervasive phenomenon in modern society. As individuals, we are members of families, neighborhood gangs, school cliques, athletic teams, fraternal orders, committees, and work groups. Small groups play an important role in establishing the psychosocial system of large organizations. Without social groups, concepts such as status and role would be meaningless. Social needs such as belonging and esteem are powerful motivators that emanate from group relationships. Dynamic forces operate in small groups to facilitate the integration of individual activity toward collective achievement. Our discussion of group dynamics will be structured around the following topics:

Group Defined
Groups and Organizations
Small Groups
Performance of Work Groups
Committees
Communication
Group Conflict
Organization Improvement via Group Dynamics

Group Defined

A group is an assemblage, cluster, or aggregation of persons considered to be related in some way or united by common ties or interests—family, recreation, or occupation, for example. In psychology and sociology the emphasis is on interrelationships among members; the connotation of aggregation is not stressed. For example, Schein describes a psychological group as "any number of people who (1) interact with one another, (2) are psychologically aware of one another, and (3) perceive themselves to be a group." [1] The criteria of mutual awareness and interaction suggest that a casual crowd, a planeload of travelers, or a nationwide organization are not psychological groups.

In order to emphasize the significant difference between an aggregation and a group, the concept of "small" groups has been used extensively. It is this connotation that we will emphasize in this chapter.

By this term is meant an aggregate of people, from two up to an unspecified but not too large number, who associate together in face-to-face relationships over an extended period of time, who differentiate themselves in some regard from others around them, who are mutually aware of their membership in the group, and whose personal relations are taken as an end in itself. It is impossible to specify a strict upper limit on the size of the informal group, except for the limitation imposed by the requirement that all the members be able to engage in direct personal relations at one time—which means, roughly, an upper limit of around fifteen to twenty. If the aggregate gets much larger than that, it begins to lose some of the quality of a small group or, indeed, begins to break up into small subgroups. [2]

This definition covers families, neighborhood gangs, athletic teams, school cliques, committees, subparts of departments in large organizations, and many other similar groups.

Interaction and Dynamics

The definition of a group, particularly a small group, stresses face-to-face relationships and interaction among individuals. Interaction can be broadly construed as any type of communication—written or oral as well as gestures or facial expressions. "Usually interaction is direct communication—mainly talking and listening, often writing and reading—but it can also include gestures, glances, nods, or shakes of the head, pats on the back, frowns, caresses, or slaps, or any other way in which meaning can be transmitted from one person to another and back again." [3] Without these kinds of interactions a group would be quite static in nature. It would be a collection of individuals. The term **dynamic** in "group dynamics" implies the kinds of interactions indicated above. It also implies continuously *changing* and *adjusting* relationships among group members. This aspect of group behavior is a key ingredient in the overall psychosocial system of organizations.

1 Edgar H. Schein, *Organizational Psychology*, 2d ed., Prentice-Hall, Inc., Englewood Cliffs, N.J., 1970, p. 81.

2 Bernard Berelson and Gary A. Steiner, *Human Behavior*, Harcourt, Brace & World, Inc., New York, 1964, p. 325.

3 Ibid., p. 326.

Groups
and
Organizations

The small group performs a mediating function by linking the individual and the organization. Each individual is a member of various formal and informal small groups within a given organization. Everyone is formally assigned to a work group, which may develop informal subgroups in the process of carrying out the assigned task. Each individual may serve on several or many permanent or temporary committees. While he or she may contribute individually—as a salesperson or researcher—the small group is a typical mechanism through which individuals contribute to organizational endeavor.

An *organized group* is a particular variety of social group. "It is based on the repetition of interaction among members, and the resulting relationships have some degree of permanence. The organized group is a continuous group. It can disperse, reassemble with the same membership, and repeat the relationships established between pairs of positions."[4] The important aspect of this statement is the concept of repetitive relationships. Moreover, there is reference to pairs of "positions" rather than people. This implies the structural nature of organized groups.

An organization structure is an abstract entity comprised of several positions rather than people. Formal organizations are defined by diagrams relating positions or documents describing the duties and responsibilities of various roles. As an organized group persists and develops a unique character, it becomes formalized and structured. Technology often dictates organizational arrangements, as well as the type and degree of interaction in work groups. A noisy assembly line often precludes communication between workers; scientific research may call for isolated individual effort or a team approach; and a planning committee involves considerable group effort by design.

An organization can be thought of as the merger of two concepts: (1) the group as a set of persons and (2) the structure as a set of positions. Obviously, groups change with the addition or subtraction of members. The structure, however, does not change with changes in personnel. The positions remain the same until formal adjustments are made in the set of positions involved. An organization, since it is a combination of these two phenomena, does adjust with changes in personnel. However, the amount of such change varies by organization. Stable-mechanistic organizations may be relatively institutionalized and immune to changes in personnel. Adaptive-organic organizations may be less rigidly defined and show a tendency to adjust continually to the personalities occupying the various positions.

Various kinds of relationships are evident between groups and organiza-

---

4 Theodore Caplow, *Principles of Organization*, Harcourt, Brace & World, Inc., New York, 1964. p. 12.

tions. In some cases the organization may be coterminous with a small group—less than twenty members interacting daily on a face-to-face basis, for example. In most cases, however, the group of persons comprising an organization will be divided into many subunits. Depending on the overall size, the subdivision process may progress through many vertical levels and/or across horizontal departmentation. Many informal, unauthorized subgroups develop spontaneously because of a felt need of the individuals involved.

Peer groups are probably the most common of such relationships. However, informal groups can and do span vertical levels in many organizations. The "tie that binds" may be external in origin, such as ethnic background or common recreational pursuits. It may be related to the organization—a car pool, for example. Or such groups may be based on the development of an interest in a particular idea or project within the scope of the formal endeavor.

While groups of all sizes are important in understanding organizational behavior, the small group is of particular interest because of its integral role in mediating the relationship between the individual and the organization. Much of the research and writing on group dynamics has emphasized small groups in general and small work groups in particular.

Small Groups

Small-group theory has developed as a separate area of study in the behavioral sciences. In this section we will concentrate on a general framework as background for a specific type of small group—the work group. Shull describes the importance of small-group theory in organization and management as follows:

The theoretical relevance of this body of knowledge is evident from a number of standpoints, since the small group: (1) is an ubiquitous and inevitable element of complex social systems; (2) plays an important part in the development and elaboration of personality; (3) is a major factor in processes of socialization and control; (4) bears many resemblances—as a social system—to large-scale social systems; and (5) can be mobilized as a powerful motivational force. [5]

Conceptual Schemes

Homans suggests three concepts for understanding individual behavior in social groups: *activity, interaction,* and *sentiment.* [6] This framework makes explicit some commonsense notions about social groups. The more the people share activities, the more likely they are to interact with one another. The reciprocal is also true; interaction in one sphere of activity often leads to shared activity in

[5] Fremont A. Shull, Jr. (with André L. Delbecq), *Selected Readings in Management* (second series), Richard D. Irwin, Inc., Homewood, Ill., 1962, p. 313.

[6] George C. Homans, *The Human Group,* Harcourt, Brace & World, Inc., New York, 1950, p. 43.

unrelated spheres. Individuals with shared sentiments are more likely to interact with one another and to engage in joint activities. And as activities are shared and interactions increase over a period of time, the degree of shared sentiments is also likely to increase. In other words, individuals in social groups, particularly small groups, are likely to evolve similar value systems. This is particularly true concerning the basic activity of the specific group. However, continued interactions of an intimate, face-to-face nature may result in shared sentiments over a wide range of subjects beyond the legitimate interests of the group itself.

Using a technique called **sociometry,** researchers have analyzed small groups in order to establish patterns of interactions among members. The results of such analysis provide a picture of the way the participants relate to each other when engaged in various activities, both formal tasks and informal activities such as eating lunch or riding to work. A typical set of relationships developed via sociometric analysis is shown in Figure 12.1

The informal leader is A. Other individuals are grouped around the leader in various degrees of "inness." K and L are completely "out of it." G, H, I, and J have fringe status with respect to the primary group. Such status may be temporary, in that an individual may be in the process of working into or out of

6 George C. Homans, *The Human Group,* Harcourt, Brace & World, Inc., New York, 1950, p. 43.

Figure 12.1   The Orbit of Small-Group Relationships

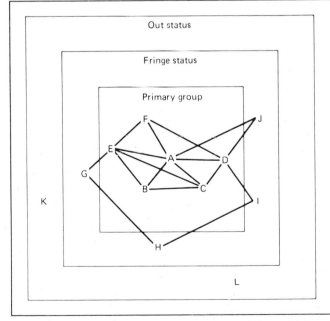

William G. Scott, *Organization Theory,* Richard D. Irwin, Inc., Homewood, Ill., 1967, p. 93

the primary group. Or such status may be relatively permanent in the case where a "fringy" shares only a limited number of the interests of the small group. Out status may be of no consequence to an individual with little or no interest in belonging to the primary group. If the person has a strong desire to join, however, recognition of the excluded condition could have significant impact on his or her personality and behavior. If several individuals recognize such a condition, they may band together and form a primary group whose main tie is the degree of isolation from some other primary group.

Group Development

Two dimensions—personal relations and task functions—are central to the process of group development shown in Figure 12.2. As people progress from a "bunch" to a group, personal relations evolve from apprehensive, tentative interactions and dependence on leaders or formal instructions through confusion and conflict (either overt or covert) to cohesiveness and ultimate interdependence. Obviously, some groups (e.g., athletic teams or work groups) never reach stage four—optimal use of human resources—even when tasks are accomplished reasonably well. Progress on task functions often parallels the development of personal relations, although there is no necessary one-to-one correlation. The first stage involves understanding the task, group goals, and alternative means of achieving them. "Getting organized" means resolving issues (real or potential conflicts) such as leadership, authority-responsibility relationships, and methods of doing and coordinating the work. In stage three the group begins to share information and feelings and build on each other's ideas as it "comes together" to get the job done. The mark of a mature group is its capacity to solve specific problems or to complete tasks, while at the same time improving its ability to do so. This calls for simultaneous attention to task accomplishment and group development.

Figure 12.2   Four Stages of Group Development

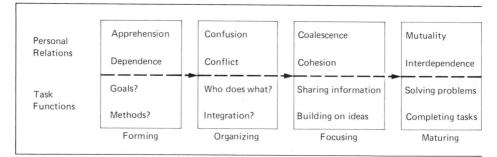

Adapted from John E. Jones, "A Model of Group Development," in John E. Jones and J. William Pfeiffer (eds.), *The 1973 Annual Handbook for Group Facilitators,* University Associates, Inc., La Jolla, Calif. 1973, p. 129.

Other Characteristics

Relatively permanent, primary, spontaneous, informal small groups have a high degree of *naturalness*. Spontaneity leads to the presence of this characteristic. Contrived groups may develop it over a period of time if the natural or informal interactions coincide with the formally designated ones.

Members of small groups typically have the ability to *empathize* to a high degree with other group members. Constant interaction over a relatively long period of time provides the opportunity to gain insight into the value system of other members of the group. This allows the "putting yourself in another's shoes" frame of reference, which is important for empathizing.

Small, informal groups often give evidence of considerable *pressure to conform* to established standards. Constant face-to-face interaction makes most individual behavior an "open book." Thus maintenance of a position in any primary group typically requires behavior patterns that are acceptable, in large measure, to the group.

While many small groups do not guide the behavior of members explicitly, *unity of purpose* is a necessity. Group objectives must be internalized by individual members. Similarly, a *cohesive* relationship is to be expected in small, informal groups.

Social distance is at a *minimum* in small, informal groups. One can deal "at arm's length" with other members of large social groups or organizations. This approach is also possible in dealing with "positions" in bureaucratic institutions. In small, informal groups, however, such formality is impossible; members must interact with other unique and relatively well-defined personalities.

Performance of Work Groups

Many variables affect individual performance in any activity, particularly work. Physical working conditions are important, as are individually oriented elements such as safety or monetary rewards. Many of the factors that motivate individuals to perform are social in nature—prestige or recognition, for example, "Our brief analysis of the role of motivation in productivity reiterates and confirms what the greater bulk of research on motivation in industry has borne out: Motivation is not wholly—nor even primarily—an individual variable. Certainly its force and direction are functions of the social situation in which it arises and is exercised." [7]

Another influence on performance is competition between one individual and another or many others. Allport cites several research studies that compare an individual's normal solitary performance with his or her performance when other people are present. The results indicate that group situations produce

---

7 Hubert Bonner, *Group Dynamics: Principles and Applications,* The Ronald Press Company, New York, 1959, pp. 289–290.

a greater output of energy and achievement.[8] These are generalizations, of course. In some cases individuals do worse in competitive situations—quantitatively and/or qualitatively.

The dynamics of work-group performance is concerned particularly with face-to-face or cooperative groups. While some attention is devoted to the sum of individual output in group situations, more attention has been devoted to the output of the group as a collective entity. In many cases output can be summed for the various individuals because their efforts are independent. In many other cases, however, productivity is dependent on the efficiency of the complete system of interdependent parts. Total performance is only as good as the weakest link.

The dynamic complexity of work-group performance came to light originally as the result of the now legendary experiments at Western Electric's Hawthorne Works in Chicago. The studies, summarized in Chapter 4, were conducted during the late 1920s and early 1930s and focused on sources of employee satisfaction or dissatisfaction at work. The impact of experimental conditions fostered changes in the relationships among operators and between operators and supervisors. It became apparent that group processes were important in facilitating or inhibiting change.[9]

Thus, social interrelationships and many other aspects of group dynamics moved from tangential interest into the spotlight of organization theorists and management practitioners. A great deal of attention has been focused on the problem of work groups restricting output, that is, "pegging" production at some level below the actual capacity of the group and hence suboptimal from the standpoint of the overall organization. There are a number of causes of this tendency; two of the most important are cohesiveness and goal congruence.

Cohesiveness and Commitment to Organizational Goals

The joint or compound impact of cohesiveness and commitment to organizational goals in group effectiveness and efficiency is illustrated in Figure 12.3. The degree of cohesiveness in a group is a complex phenomenon that results from combining the net attraction (or repulsion) for each member. Many forces are at work on each individual, which either attract or repel him. Some members may "go through the motions" as far as group activities are concerned. They may interact perfunctorily and only when absolutely necessary. It is unlikely that such a situation would result in shared sentiments. Hence the group would not be very cohesive.

---

[8] Gordon W. Allport, "Historical Background of Modern Social Psychology," in Gardner Lindzey (ed.), *Handbook of Social Psychology*, Addison-Wesley Publishing Company, Inc., Reading, Mass., 1954, p. 46.

[9] Fritz J. Roethlisberger and William J. Dickson, *Management and the Worker*, Harvard University Press, Cambridge, Mass., 1939.

Obviously, in any group there is a gradation of attraction for individual members. Some will identify more strongly with group values than others. Similarly, the composite of individual attitudes will vary widely. Some groups will be extremely cohesive and integrated; others will be uncohesive and diffuse. Figure 12.3 shows only two distinct categories. However, the left axis indicates a continuum of cohesiveness with a dichotomy identified as uncoordinated versus coordinated behavior. The second dimension, "commitment to organizational goals," is related to direction of effort. This concept, much like cohesiveness, can be viewed as a complex phenomenon that is a composite of individual propensities to internalize organizational goals. Again, there are degrees for each individual and for the group composite.

The joint impact of these two phenomena can be illustrated via the simplified dichotomy in Figure 12.3. The degree of cohesiveness in a work group can lead toward uncoordinated or coordinated behavior. If the group, through its individual members, accepts and internalizes the objectives of the organization, behavior will very likely be functional from the overall system point of view. However, subgroup goals may vary as much as 180 degrees from those of the organization—a subtle slowdown, or strike, or even deliberate sabotage. If the individuals in a subgroup are not committed to organizational goals *and* are not well integrated, the results are unpredictable but probably dysfunctional.

The optimal condition is described as "coordinated behavior in functional directions." In this case the group is cohesive and motivated in directions that are in line with organizational goals. This is the condition that organization theory seeks to understand. The evolving body of knowledge is of utmost interest to managers as they strive to develop work groups with characteristics that lead

Figure 12.3 The Joint Impact of Cohesiveness and Commitment to Organizational Goals on Group Effectiveness and Efficiency

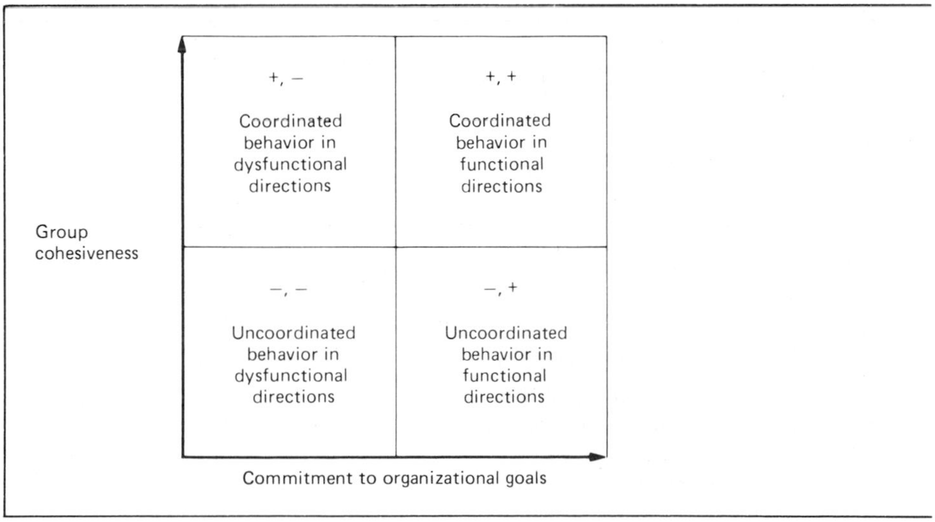

toward organizational effectiveness and efficiency, as well as participant satisfaction.

Productivity

Since the industrial revolution, there has been a relentless trend toward mechanization, automation, and specialization of worker effort. A major thrust of scientific management was the division of tasks into elemental parts that could be mastered by workers with specialized skills. As long as people are involved, individual, small-group, and organizational motivation becomes important for performance. The psychosocial system provides the overall climate within which work groups operate. Specialized mass-production systems often preclude the use of "groups" on the job. Individuals are relatively isolated because of the physical separation of the jobs on an assembly line and/or because the noise level in many operations precludes much communication among workers. However, small groups do develop during lunch breaks or before and after work. Such groups, while not interacting during the actual work period, can, nevertheless, have a significant impact on the productivity of the system.

Considerable attention has been focused in recent years on reversing the trend toward specialization. Job enrichment has been stressed as a means of providing greater worker satisfaction from the task itself. In many cases this approach has involved letting work groups decide on the breakdown of tasks and the assignment of jobs to individuals. Often some system of rotation is developed in order to enlarge the scope of each individual's skill.

Trist and Bamforth describe the impact of increased mechanization in English coal mining. [10] Traditionally the work was organized in such a way that small teams of two to four men performed the entire operation of mining coal. Over a period of time these small face-to-face working groups became extremely cohesive and well-integrated. The introduction of the new, more mechanized longwall method completely disrupted the established system. It specialized the operation, with a separate phase being carried out on each of three shifts during a twenty-four-hour period. Groups of ten or twenty "specialists" worked on each shift.

The abolition of small face-to-face work groups in the mechanization and reorganization led to serious problems of absenteeism, turnover, and sickness among miners, including psychosomatic disorders. Productivity dropped off considerably under the physically improved, mechanized longwall method. The aftermath of these developments has been a gradual, spontaneous, and informal drift back toward the previous system. Trist and Bamforth suggest that these various readjustments focused on restoring small face-to-face work groups with responsible autonomy, greater work-group cohesiveness, and greater satisfaction. They conclude that "it is difficult to see how these problems can be solved effectively

---

10 E. L. Trist and K. W. Bamforth, "Some Social and Psychological Consequences of the Longwall Method of Coal-getting," *Human Relations*, February 1951, pp. 3–38.

without restoring responsible autonomy to primary groups throughout the system and insuring that each of these groups has the satisfying sub-whole as its work task, and some scope of flexibility in work pace." [11]

Similar developments have been evident in Scandinavia, and there have been many successful examples (in terms of productivity and satisfaction) of job redesign with emphasis on more autonomous small work groups. [12] An important ingredient is the basic assumption that employees want to and can make constructive input. The focus is on participation in the day-to-day decisions of small work groups rather than on policy or administrative matters that are being addressed formally through more systematic approaches such as industrial democracy. [13] Job design emphasizing work group dynamics has been successful in the United States and other countries. [14] So far it appears to be easier to "start from scratch", (e.g., in a new plant) than to change existing technology and organization structure. [15] Concern for the individual as well as for primary work groups is an integral part of an overall trend toward human resources development, power equalization, and constitutionalism. [16]

Likert cites a number of researches, both in this country and abroad, with regard to the effect of work-group dynamics on performance. He concludes:

As the importance of group influence has been recognized and as more precise measurements have been obtained, there is increasing evidence which points to the power of group influences upon the functioning of organizations. In those situations where the management has recognized the power of group motivational forces and has used the kind of leadership required to develop and focus these motivational forces on achieving the organization's objectives, the performance of the organization tends to be appreciably above the average achieved by other methods of leadership and management. Membership of groups which have common goals to which they are strongly committed, high peer-group loyalty, favorable attitudes between superiors and subordinates, and a high level of skill in interaction clearly can achieve far more than the same people acting as a mere assemblage. [17]

This statement stresses the potential for group work performance and the role of management in creating an appropriate environment. The role of leadership will be discussed in more detail in the following chapter. We must also recognize that the potential envisioned may or may not be achieved, depending on whether the group goals and those of the overall organization are "in tune."

11 Ibid., p. 38.
12 David Jenkins (ed.), *Job Reform in Sweden,* Swedish Employers' Confederation, Stockholm, 1975.
13 Robert Ball, "The Hard Hats in Europe's Boardrooms," *Fortune,* June 1976, pp. 180 ff.
14 Max Ways, "The American Kind of Worker Participation," *Fortune,* October 1976, pp. 168 ff.
15 Richard E. Walton, "How to Counter Alienation in the Plant," *Harvard Business Review,* November–December 1972, pp. 70–81.
16 David W. Ewing, "What Business Thinks About Employee Rights," *Harvard Business Review,* September–October 1977, pp. 81–94.
17 Rensis Likert, *New Patterns of Management,* McGraw-Hill Book Company, New York, 1961, p. 36.

Committees

Committees have probably had as much "bad press" as any phenom-enon in modern Western civilization. They are described as both ineffective and inefficient. Typical quips are "A camel is a horse designed by a committee" and "The purpose of a committee is to: (1) reduce tranquility, (2) increase dissatisfac-tion, (3) divide responsibility, and (4) stave off action." We all seem hypersensitive to the seemingly endless committee meetings that are a part of organizational activity. Committees function at all levels in organizations from the board of directors to the shop grievance committee.

Why are committees so ubiquitous? Part of the reason lies in our basic nature as social animals. We seek cooperative relationships in all phases of our lives. We typically enjoy face-to-face relationships in groups of all types, including committees.

The dynamic, self-made, entrepreneur type of individual may espouse an abhorrence for committees and say that an individual can and must have the authority and responsibility for decision making—that committees only cloud the issue and make the system both less effective and less efficient. Obviously, there are situations in which an individual approach is both necessary and appropriate. However, there are many other situations in which it is inappropriate if not impos-sible.

A democratic society is based on collective wisdom for planning and controlling activities. We shy away from totalitarian approaches and the fiats of dictators. We use twelve-person juries to decide many legal questions, and a nine-person Supreme Court provides the ultimate interpretation for many complex societal issues. We assume that the collective wisdom of the elected congressional officials is superior in important ways to a "one-person show." At times the pro-cess seems tedious and inefficient because of the seemingly endless fact finding of subcommittees and the long time spans between the introduction of proposed measures and their enactment.

Similar processes are evident in all large-scale organizations—business, government, and others. For many business problems one person simply does not have all the required knowledge and/or skill. Therefore, he or she must call on others for support. Extended committee deliberation is typical among doctors, all of whom may be specialists in different subparts of the medical field, as they attempt to diagnose and prescribe treatments for specific cases.

Often the committee approach is useful in planning the implementation of changes in organization structure and/or processes. Involving several people in the decision-making phase may seem inefficient; however, if the support of these persons is critical in order to ensure wholehearted cooperation of employees dur-ing the implementation phase, such time may be an investment that pays off many times over in the long run.

**Making
Meetings
More
Effective**

In modern organizations committees are seen as not only necessary but functional. The key question is how to make them more effective. By making sure that only relevant people are involved in a particular issue, we can avoid wasting the time of committee members. By involving members in building meeting agendas, we can encourage participation on topics of interest to the group. By paying attention to the process by which the committee functions, as well as to the task it is engaged in, we can improve performance and increase participant satisfaction. For example, it may be useful to encourage the normally quiet members in order to ensure wider participation.

The frustration level of committees can often be reduced by having written information items distributed rather than read and by separating issues into (1) action items and (2) exploratory discussions. In this way the group has a better sense of what it is trying to accomplish during a particular meeting.

The pervasiveness of committee approaches to decision making in all organizations in society fits our contention that many activities are carried out on a group basis. Hence, understanding group dynamics in any setting is important for understanding committee processes. Committees are only one specific example of the countless small groups in society. For committees or task-performing groups, several aspects of group dynamics (communications and conflict) are important enough to warrant specific detailed treatment.

Communication

The core of group dynamics is interaction among members. Interaction, in the broad sense, is any means of communication between people. Thus, communication plays an important role in group dynamics.

Most of the research on communication in small groups has emphasized informal relationships that seem to develop spontaneously. However, certain kinds of communication patterns can be established formally—when a chairperson is appointed to an ad hoc committee or when the physical arrangements of a particular room dictate relationships. Even in these kinds of situations communication patterns can evolve that support or transcend and subvert the supposedly established pattern. The analysis of communication processes in groups often reveals a communication "center" that was not planned.

While countless variations could be identified for small groups, certain basic communication patterns have emerged from numerous research studies. Four typical arrangements of five-member groups are illustrated in Figure 12.4. The numbers refer to how many times that particular individual was recognized as a leader. The data indicate that a leader seems to emerge at the position of highest

Figure 12.4   Basic Communication Networks in Task-Oriented Small Groups. The numbers refer to the frequency of occurrence of recognized leaders at different positions in the various patterns.

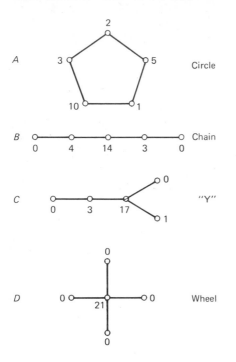

Adapted from Bernard Berelson and Gary A. Steiner, *Human Behavior,* Harcourt, Brace & World, Inc., New York, 1964, p. 356.

centrality—the hub of the wheel, the fork of the Y, and the midpoint of the chain. For the circle, forces other than the communications network obviously become more important in the evolution of the leader in the small group.

These communication patterns could be elaborated in many ways. For example, the ties between any two of the individual group members could be either one-way or two-way communication. Also, in the wheel pattern, communication might flow only outward to peripheral members. Or differential patterns for various pairs within the same basic network may exist. A particular individual may communicate on a two-way basis with one member and on a one-way basis with another. This kind of analysis could superimpose a combination of several patterns—some elements of a wheel and some of a circle, for example—within the primary group identified by sociometric analysis.

The question of one-way versus two-way communication can be related to the discussion of committees. An individual may make a decision and communicate it to group members with the expectation that a particular action will be carried out. However, the probability that what the listener heard coincides with what the speaker or writer said or wrote is quite small. The technical problems of communication are quite severe. Of even more concern are semantic difficulties. Redundancy and feedback (through mutual communication) go a long way to offset the hazards of one-way communication. By sitting down to discuss an issue or plan, people can experience enough interaction to ensure a reasonable amount of understanding.

Mr. B can reply by saying, "This is what I understand you to mean, right?" Ms. A can then nod in agreement or elaborate further if, in her opinion, B has not received the message accurately. This sort of mutual give-and-take can proceed as long as necessary in order to achieve mutual understanding. Obviously, not all issues require such a process. Simple directives might well be issued outward and/or downward from a central source on a one-way channel. However, many other issues should be given more thorough "airing" in order to forestall misunderstandings and long-run dysfunctional consequences.

Two-way communication and "checking for meaning" are typically time-consuming processes, compared to one-way communication. However, research indicates that the accuracy of transmitted messages as well as the confidence of receivers increases when a two-way process is used. There is a need, therefore, to couple a cost/benefit analysis with a sense of the situation. Emphasis on a one-way communication process in order to save time may be shortsighted because the illusion of communication may lead to dysfunctional organizational consequences. We recently noticed a sign in a steno pool that seems apropos:

Why is it that there is never enough time to do it right in the first place, but there is always enough time to do it over again?

Group Conflict

Conflict can have functional as well as dysfunctional effects on persons, groups, and organizations. It has been an important subject in behavioral science and has been studied from many points of view. However, Coser suggests that "the majority of sociologists who dominate contemporary sociology . . . center attention predominately upon problems of adjustment rather than upon conflict; upon social status rather than upon dynamics. Of key problematic importance to them has been the maintenance of existing structures and the ways and means of ensuring their smooth functioning. They have focused upon maladjustments and tensions which interfere with consensus."[18] As an example, he suggests that Parsons' general orientation has led him to view conflict as dysfunctional and disruptive and to disregard its positive functions. Conflict is described as a partly avoidable, partly inevitable and endemic form of sickness in the body social.[19]

---

18 Lewis Coser, *The Functions of Social Conflict,* The Free Press of Glencoe, New York, 1956, p. 20.

19 Ibid., p. 23.

In contrast to these views, there is the notion of conflict not only as inevitable but as an important, positive phenomenon in society. In a decision-making framework, there is always conflict whenever alternatives are apparent. Individuals, groups, and organizations must make choices and "resolve" such conflict. This is a recurring phenomenon with continuing cycles of conflict and resolution.

Coser uses Simmel's basic treatise as a framework for his own analysis and concludes that conflict is a form of socialization. [20]

This means essentially that, to paraphrase the opening pages of Simmel's essay, no group can be entirely harmonious, for it would then be devoid of process and structure. Groups require disharmony as well as harmony, dissociation as well as association; and conflicts within them are by no means altogether disruptive factors. Group formation is the result of both types of processes. The belief that one process tears down what the other builds up, so that what finally remains is the result of subtracting the one from the other, is based on a misconception. On the contrary, both "positive" and "negative" factors build group relations. Conflict as well as cooperation has social functions. Far from being necessarily dysfunctional, a certain degree of conflict is an essential element in group formation and the persistence of group life. [21]

Intragroup Conflict

Intragroup conflict can arise in a variety of ways. [22] In the early stages of group development there is a high probability of disagreements over goals, plans, and member roles. Differences of opinion have to be resolved enough for the group to proceed. Sometimes groups appear to be functioning smoothly, but closer observation reveals a dominant authority figure or a vocal minority, with others "going along for the ride." Such suppressed conflict may have a long-run debilitating effect and/or erupt into open hostility. Recognizing stress, tension, or anxiety in group members is important; coping with it effectively is even more important.

Interpersonal conflict is always present to some extent in groups. Differences in values, beliefs, attitudes, and behavior cause us to like some people better than others. The more positive the relationship, the easier it is to work together. On the other hand, working relationships and teamwork are more difficult and often strained when "personality conflicts" get in the way. Examples of such problems can be seen in professional athletics almost daily; the media seem to focus on interpersonal and intragroup hassles.

Many writers have stressed the difficulty of integrating individual and organizational goals as one of the most critical problems of modern industrial

20 Georg Simmel, *Conflict,* trans. by Kurt H. Wolff, The Free Press of Glencoe, New York, 1955.
21 Coser, op. cit., p. 31.
22 Louis R. Pondy, "Organizational Conflict: Concepts and Models," *Administrative Science Quarterly,* September 1967, p. 298.

civilization.[23] It is an important part of the psychosocial system of organizations. Individuals who are dissatisfied with their situation in a specific small group are not likely to engage wholeheartedly in the group's activities. Thus their levels of interaction will be curtailed and the likelihood that they will develop sentiments "in line" with other organizational members is decreased. Such a condition very likely will lead to conflict among members of the group, decrease cohesiveness, and hence have a significant impact on the group's performance.

However, the constructive and positive role of conflict in fostering creativity and innovation should not be ignored. Some friction should exist between members in the small group as a condition for the generation of fresh ideas. A conflict-free group may be static and operate at considerably less than capacity.

Intergroup Conflict

Conflict within a small group depends to a considerable extent on the external environment in general and intergroup conflict in particular. Manifest conflicts with another small group, or with the large-scale organization of which it is a part, may foster an increased degree of loyalty and cohesiveness (often suppressing intragroup conflict) that would not be the case if its external relationships were conflict-free.

One type of intergroup conflict is competition between subgroups within the organization. Just as conflict is inevitable in social relationships, it is inevitable between subgroups of organizations. The sources of latent conflict are always present and provide seeds for clashes of many types. Such conflicts can develop between groups on the same horizontal level in an organization or between groups on different levels.

Some interdepartmental conflicts seem to gain much publicity—that between the production and distribution phases of manufacturing enterprises, for example. The production group is interested in optimizing its operation and sees the interface in a particular way. The marketing department, on the other hand, may stress salability rather than producibility, and the obvious result is a conflict situation. In a hospital there are conflicts between nurses, doctors, and administrators. In education conflict frequently exists between teachers and administrators or between schools and central staff units. These conflicts can be resolved in a number of ways. One department may dominate the other; there may be a compromise solution that neither really likes; or they may achieve an integration of goals by recognizing their roles in an overall system. This latter approach to conflict resolution would appear to be the most fruitful.[24]

---

23 See, for example, Chris Argyris, *Personality and Organization: The Conflict between the System and the Individual,* Harper & Row, Publishers, Inc., New York, 1957.

24 For a discussion of the consequences of intergroup competition and possible steps toward integration, see Schein, op, cit., pp. 96–103.

However, there is a tendency to personalize intergroup conflict without recognizing that organizational roles are involved. A typical comment goes as follows: "One of the members of research mentioned that he thought of the industrial engineers as just dumb, stupid, and no good. There was no meeting ground on a value which the two groups could bring to a common project." [25] These kinds of attitudes are difficult to overcome until mutual understanding prevails. Such conflict is likely to be dysfunctional to a degree. Until we begin to think of the activities of others as just "different" rather than "inferior" or less useful, we will continue to waste valuable energy in conflict situations.

However, some interdepartmental conflict is inevitable and can be functional in overall organizational endeavor. It can have a positive impact on creativity, innovation, and progress. A conflict-free organization is likely to be static and sterile and without much challenge for group members.

Organization Improvement via Group Dynamics

The term *organization improvement* covers a wide spectrum of formal and informal processes. It includes operational analysis, strategic and comprehensive planning, organization development, and management development. In this section we are concerned with those approaches in which the body of knowledge about group dynamics is used to make organizations more effective and/or efficient, as well as more satisfying for participants. Our coverage will be illustrative rather than exhaustive; it focuses on sensitivity training, team building, and intergroup relations.

The order of presentation is not an indication of importance, nor does it imply where to begin an organization improvement program. Such a decision should be based on thorough diagnosis of specific situations so that change efforts are focused on evident problems.

Sensitivity Training: T Groups

Sensitivity training has several broad objectives: self-insight, better understanding of other persons and awareness of one's impact on them, better understanding of group processes and increased skill in achieving group effectiveness, increased recognition of the characteristics of larger social systems, and greater awareness of the dynamics of change. These objectives are elaborated by the National Training Laboratories as follows:

25 John A. Seiler, "Diagnosing Interdepartmental Conflict, *"Harvard Business Review,* September–October 1963, p. 127.

Self	Interpersonal and Group Relations	Organization
Becoming aware of own feelings and motivations	Establishing meaningful interpersonal relationships	Understanding organizational complexities
Correctly perceiving effects of own behavior on others	Finding a satisfying place in the group	Developing and inventing appropriate new patterns and procedures
Correctly understanding effect of others' behavior on self	Understanding dynamic complexities in group behavior	Helping to diagnose and solve problems between units of the organization
Hearing others and accepting helpful criticism	Developing diagnostic skills to understand group problems and processes	Working as a member and as a leader
Appropriately interacting with others	Acquiring skills of helping the group on task and maintenance problems	

T (for training) groups concentrate on understanding individual behavior as it happens in the group (approximately twelve people) itself. The activities, interactions, and sentiments of the small group are the focal point of attention. Organization improvement is seen as a long-run goal achieved through individuals who have had T-group experience working together in more effective relationships. If such experience is garnered externally to an individual's own organization, he or she may return with new insights, only to be isolated and unable to effect change. This has been a common frustrating experience for many who have been exposed to sensitivity training.

Organizational change is more likely if a T group is drawn from an existing organization, particularly if all members are involved. However, it is difficult to develop enough openness and candor (when all the members are well acquainted) to facilitate T-group training.

By understanding the "driving forces" and "restraining forces" that maintain fixed attitudes, adjustments can be made that foster unfreezing, change, and refreezing of new value systems and behavior patterns. T-group sessions are often uncomfortable for participants because of their unstructured nature. Those with a low tolerance for ambiguity are likely to be frustrated. As the group progresses, however, it begins to recognize and develop its own group dynamics. Most individuals become increasingly comfortable even though conflict and its resolution are an inherent part of this system.

Part of the approach can be described as "confrontation and support." This relates to the feedback that a group provides to individuals with regard to the image projected in general or on specific issues. Such feedback may be painful in some cases, but it is really the only way an individual can gain valuable insights into his or her impact on others. Like most educational experiences, you get out of it what you put into it. If a person will not or cannot project an authentic image and listen actively to feedback from others, the experience is not likely to be of much benefit.

The costs and benefits of such training have been the subject of much debate. Cost effectiveness is not only an economic consideration in this case. Also of concern are the psychological costs and the lasting effects of such training on individuals and organizations. Critics suggest that benefits have not really been demonstrated rigorously and that the cost for participants is high, including nervous breakdowns in some cases.[26] Proponents suggest that mental breakdowns have occurred at the rate of only 4 in 10,000 and that in most of these cases there was a prior history of psychological problems.[27] The T group is stressed as a vehicle for healthy individuals to learn.[28] Some confusion is evident from the standpoint of those with no experience in T groups, however, because the setting for T groups is similar to that for group therapy among mentally disturbed patients.

On the effectiveness question, no real answers are available. Typically, such questions are answered in terms of the responses of trainees after the sessions. In most cases they are positive and stress the tremendous value to the individual. Little has been done to test the lasting value of such training or the degree to which it is damped out when an individual returns to the basic organization.[29]

Will more authentic interpersonal relationships lead to improvements in small-group and overall organizational performance? Is there some optimal level of openness beyond which individuals should not go? Should some façade be maintained in order to achieve optimal effectiveness for the individual, the small group, and the organization as a whole? Much empirical research is needed to answer these questions.

Team Building

Team-building efforts concentrate on existing work groups and solving real problems. Prior T-group experience may facilitate progress in team building, but it is certainly not necessary. Interpersonal issues such as communication skill (listening effectively, for example) may be a focus of attention. However, it is equally likely that more formal tasks, such as role clarification, will be addressed in team-building sessions. Other issues, such as leadership styles, organization structure, mutual expectations, and meeting effectiveness, typically receive attention.

Team-building sessions also involve solving problems related to the spe-

---

26 George S. Odiorne, "The Trouble with Sensitivity Training," *Training Directions,* October 1963.

27 Chris Argyris, "A Comment on George Odiorne's Paper," *Training Directions,* October 1963.

28 Morton A. Lieberman, et al., "Encounter: The Leader Makes the Difference," *Psychology Today,* March 1973, pp. 69–76.

29 For discussions of these questions from the point of view of the practicing manager, see: Robert J. House, "T–Group Training: Good or Bad?" *Business Horizons,* December 1969, pp. 69–77; and William J. Kearney and Desmond D. Martin, "Sensitivity Training: An Established Management Development Tool?" *Academy of Management Journal,* December 1974, pp. 755–760.

cific task of the group. The process includes problem sensing, prioritizing, diagnosing, evaluating alternative solutions, planning action steps, and developing means for follow-up and evaluation.

The effectiveness of team-building efforts depends in large measure on the process of consensus formation and the development of group norms for subsequent behavior. It involves everyone in the problem-solving process and enhances the probability of group cohesiveness and the internalization of group and organizational goals. By taking time to focus on group processes as well as tasks, team building facilitates unfreezing, changing, and refreezing new patterns of behavior.

Intergroup Relations

More sensitive individuals and more cohesive groups may or may not lead to organization improvement. Another dimension that needs attention is intergroup relationships. As indicated previously, conflicts do develop between groups in organizations, and the results can be dysfunctional from an overall point of view. Several means are available to prevent or ameliorate such conflict: (1) avoiding win/lose situations, (2) rotating people among groups in order to facilitate mutual understanding, (3) emphasis on total organizational effectiveness, and (4) increased communication and interaction between groups.[30] Obviously, group dynamics is heavily involved in number (4).

If two groups recognize intergroup problems and are willing to invest time in solving them, several approaches can be beneficial. A simple means of facilitating mutual understanding is to have each group generate a list of positive and negative impressions of the other group—things they like about the other group and things they don't like. It is also helpful to generate a list of predictions of how the other group will respond. The lists then serve as a means to stimulate discussion, understanding, and problem solving.

If a group is interested in how it interacts with a number of other units in an organization, it may be helpful to get input from all of them simultaneously. Therefore, this approach is to get representatives from each unit to sit down with the group seeking help (focal group) and provide feedback concerning how it "comes across." A process similar to the one described above could be used. Representatives could provide feedback concerning what they like and dislike about the focal group's behavior. An important ingredient in either of these approaches is concentration on listening to what others have to say. Questions of clarification are appropriate, but arguing each point as it arises is not likely to be beneficial. After all of the feedback has been generated, it is then appropriate to engage in a problem-solving process that identifies potential new behavior patterns and specific action steps for the future.

30 Schein, op. cit., p. 120.

Grid Organization Improvement

The managerial grid has been used extensively as a framework for organization improvement programs based on group dynamics.[31] Team learning forms a link between individual growth and total organization improvement.

The framework for the program is the managerial grid (see Figure 12.5).

Figure 12.5   The Managerial Grid

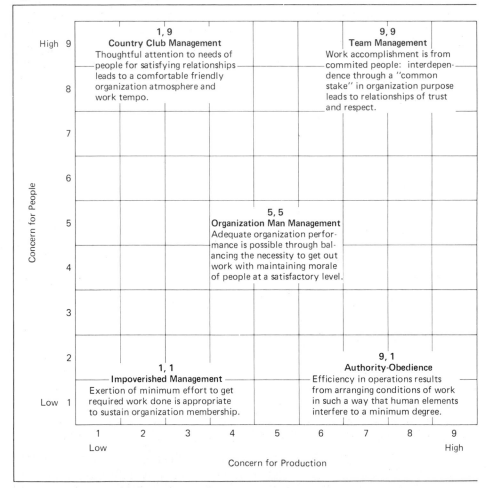

Robert R. Blake and Jane Srygley Mouton, *The New Managerial Grid*, Gulf Publishing Company, Houston, 1978, p. 11.

31 One such program is described in Robert R. Blake and Jane S. Mouton; Louis P. Barnes and Larry E. Greiner, "Breakthrough in Organizational Development," *Harvard Business Review*, November–December 1964, pp. 135–155.

It represents an underlying philosophy of management based on two principal dimensions: (1) the concern for production and (2) the concern for people. Each individual can identify his or her own particular philosophy in terms of degrees on these two basic dimensions. The middle-of-the-road approach is identified along with four extreme positions. The goal is to bring about a "9, 9" managerial philosophy that will influence organization improvement.

The relationship between this approach and the basic concepts of group dynamics is evident. Work is accomplished by team management and the integration of task and human requirements. This can be related directly to the concept of a joint impact of group cohesiveness and internalization of organizational goals. It can also be related to Homans' basic framework of group activities, interactions, and sentiments.

The organization development program involves two parts and six phases.

Part I Management development within an organization

    1 Managerial grid laboratory-seminar training

    2 Team development

Part II Organization development

    3 Horizontal and vertical intergroup linking

    4 Setting organizational improvement goals

    5 Implementing planned change by attaining established goals

    6 Stabilization

"The first two phases involve *management* development so that the other four phases can help managers work toward the 9,9 goals of *organization* development."[32] Teams of small groups are formed using a diagonal slice of the organization chart. Thus different levels are represented, but no one is included with his or her immediate superior. There are approximately fifty hours of intensive problem solving, evaluation of individual and team results, and critiques of team performance. Extensive use is made of simulation of organizational situations in which interpersonal behavior affects the task performance. Teams regularly evaluate their own behavior and problem-solving abilities, and they provide feedback concerning managerial styles. Emphasis is placed on helping the manager understand his or her own attitudes and sentiments and on developing open and effective group interactions.

In phases 3, 4, 5, and 6 these skills and attitudes are extended throughout the organization. Intergroup development concentrates on new approaches to conflict resolution that play down domination and compromise and focus on integration through joint problem-solving efforts that stress total system values. The setting and attainment of overall goals in conjunction with those for various sub-

---

[32] Ibid., p. 137.

systems provide a useful mechanism for integrating activities, interactions, and sentiments.

Considerable attention is devoted to stabilizing the changes that have occurred in managerial philosophies and in the organizational atmosphere. Unless the new approaches become ingrained, much of the program's effort will go for naught as the organization reverts to its original status.

Group dynamics plays an important part in the grid approach because of the central role of small groups in both the training and implementation phases. The small-group setting provides an important facilitating mechanism for unfreezing old individual managerial philosophies, inducing new ones, and stabilizing or refreezing them so that long-lasting change results.

Summary

Group dynamics is a fundamental aspect of psychosocial systems. Human inclination toward sociability is demonstrated by the number of small groups to which we belong.

Group dynamics stresses face-to-face relationships and interaction among individuals. It involves many modes of communication and implies continually changing and adjusting relationships among members. Groups vary in terms of degree of permanence, openness, and formality.

The small group performs a mediating function by linking the individual and the organization. Each individual is a member of formal and informal small groups within larger organizations.

Many conceptual schemes are useful for analyzing small groups as micro systems. One approach stresses activities, interactions, and sentiments. Another approach is sociometry, which focuses on the degree of interaction among participants during various activities. Personal relations and task functions are important dimensions for analyzing group development over time.

Group dynamics has a significant impact on performance. Overall effectiveness and efficiency depend on the coordinated efforts of individuals working together in small groups within a larger organizational system.

Committees have been given much bad publicity as being ineffective and inefficient. They are, nevertheless, a ubiquitous phenomenon. Moreover, research indicates that modern executives view committees in a positive way and stress their usefulness in organizational endeavor.

Communication is the basis of group dynamics, allowing the interactions that are necessary in carrying out the group's activity. Two-way communication, feedback, and "checking for meaning" are means of facilitating mutual understanding.

Conflict has typically been thought of as bad for organizations. It is unlikely, however, that any human group can attain a completely conflict-free situation. Intragroup and intergroup conflict appear to be inevitable. Therefore, its dysfunctional aspects need to be recognized and guarded against, and its functional aspects should be encouraged by managers.

One approach to organization improvement is concentration on individual growth and small-group effectiveness. T groups, team-building sessions, and intergroup problem-solving exercises are typical means of using group dynamics to facilitate management development and organization improvement.

Questions and Problems

1 Compare and contrast a group and an assemblage. What key criteria distinguish a "small" group?

2 What is meant by the term *dynamics* in the phrase "group dynamics"? How is it related to such factors as degree of permanence or openness?

3 In what ways do small groups link individuals and organizations?

4 Describe the interrelationships among activities, interactions, and sentiments in small groups.

5 Illustrate sociometric concepts such as primary group, fringe status, and out status with several examples from your own experience.

6 Reflect on your experience in an actual small group (athletic team, work group, project task force, committee) in terms of the model set forth in Figure 12.2. Illustrate the stages of group development with specific examples of feelings, behavior, and outcomes. How well did the group develop in terms of (a) personal relations and (b) task functions?

7 How do cohesiveness and internalization of organizational goals affect the performance of work groups? Why are positive "readings" on one dimension of Figure 12.3 not sufficient for good performance from the organizational point of view?

8 How can managers use small-group dynamics to improve organizational productivity?

9 What is your view of the role of committees in organizational affairs?

10 How do communication patterns affect the development of leaders in small groups?

11 "Human beings are basically conflictive. They cooperate just enough to get from one conflict situation to the next." Do you agree? Why or why not?

12 Illustrate intergroup conflict with your own experience in an organization.

13 What is organization improvement? What role does group dynamics play in this process?

Influence Systems and Leadership
Thirteen

Management involves coordinating people, machines, material, money, time, and space. The external environment as well as internal factors, such as goals and values, technology, and structure provide a framework for this effort. The psychosocial system pervades the climate affecting the most critical aspect of the managerial task—the integration of individual efforts toward organizational objectives. This aspect of the managerial role is leadership. In this chapter we will discuss ways of influencing the behavior of individuals, groups, and organizations. These various means comprise the influence system which, as part of the psychosocial system, provides a framework within which leadership takes place. We will explore the following topics:

Influence Systems
Power
Authority
Leadership Defined
Traits and Greatness
Effective Leader Behavior
Contingency Views and Flexibility
Facilitating Effective Leadership

Influence Systems

An integral part of the psychosocial system in organizations concerns attempts to influence behavior. Influence is exerted in many directions—up and down the hierarchy and laterally in peer-group relationships. Before discussing various specific ways to influence behavior, we need a more explicit definition. The term *influence* seems to pick up a variety of connotations, depending on the particular field of study and the specific context.

Influence
Defined

Influence denotes any "changes in behavior of a person or group due to anticipation of the responses of others." [1] An influence system involves people taking the roles of influencer and influencee. Behavior changes can be "caused" by ideas or some other inanimate factor. For example, a change in the weather may influence someone to abandon picnic or golf plans. Typically, however, influence systems refer to situations wherein behavioral changes occur as a result of relationships among people. These relationships may involve interaction which is direct or indirect (through the medium of ideas).

The term *influence* is often used in conjunction with other terms such as **power** and/or **authority.** In some cases, they are considered as mutually exclusive concepts, with influence covering those ways of influencing behavior that cannot be termed power or authority. In other cases, they appear to be synonymous or at least overlapping in connotation. Our approach is to consider influence as the all-inclusive concept that covers *any and all* modes by which behavioral change is induced in individuals or groups. [2] Katz and Kahn summarize this position as follows:

Influence includes virtually any interpersonal transaction which has psychological or behavioral effects. Control includes those influence attempts which are successful, that is, which have the effects intended by the influencing agent. Power is the potential for influence characteristically backed by the means to coerce compliance. Finally, authority is legitimate power; it is power which accrues to a person by virtue of his role, his position in an organized social structure. [3]

We shall return to a more detailed discussion of concepts such as power and authority in subsequent sections.

Ways to
Influence
Behavior

A spectrum of ways to influence behavior is indicated in Figure 13.1. Several distinct means are identified—emulation, suggestion, persuasion, and co-ercion—ranging from indirect and invisible approaches to very evident, direct, and forceful methods.

1 Julius Gould and William L. Kolb (eds.), *A Dictionary of the Social Sciences,* The Free Press of Glencoe, New York, 1964, p. 332.

2 Both covert and overt behavior are included. Influence is both an alteration of behavior and a maintenance of behavior as it was, but other than what it would have been without the intervention of the influence. Herbert Goldhammer and Edward A. Shils, "Types of Power and Status," *American Journal of Sociology,* September 1939, p. 171.

3 Daniel Katz and Robert L. Kahn, *The Social Psychology of Organizations,* John Wiley & Sons, Inc., New York, 1966, p. 220.

Figure 13.1   Spectrum of Means for Influencing Behavior

	Influence Spectrum		
Emulation: striving to equal or excel; imitating with effort to equal or surpass; approaching or attaining equality	**Suggestion:** placing or bringing (an idea, proposition, plan, etc.) before a person's mind for consideration or possible action	**Persuasion:** prevailing on a person by advice, urging, reason, or inducements to do something (rather than force)	**Coercion:** forcing constraint; compulsion; physical pressure or compression

Emulation requires no direct contact between individuals; yet it is a powerful influence on behavior. Public figures (famous athletes or elected officials, for example) are usually aware of the degree to which people imitate their behavior. Some professional athletes have refused lucrative contracts to endorse cigarettes because of an image they wish to portray to teenagers. Books (particularly biographies), movies, and television provide tremendous exposure for ideas and life styles. People often pick out certain behavior patterns and strive to equal or surpass them.

Emulation is a much more subtle phenomenon than is indicated by our reference to celebrities. In organizations, participants are aware of the behavioral patterns of coworkers and various executives. Certain individuals become "models," and their behavior patterns are adopted by others who hope to attain similar success. Others "play" certain roles in organizations. Many behavior patterns are perpetuated in organizations primarily on the basis of emulation—with neither formal position descriptions nor direct interaction in the form of persuasion or suggestion needed.

Suggestion involves direct and conscious interaction between individuals or between an individual and a group. It is an explicit attempt to influence behavior by presenting an idea or advocating a particular course of action. Typically, this mode is used when several alternative behavior patterns for individuals or groups are acceptable and the influencer is merely suggesting a preferred pattern.

If this tolerance for different behavior in a particular role were not present, the influencer would use some other mode such as persuasion or even coercion. *Persuasion* implies urging and the use of some inducement in order to evoke the desired response. It involves more pressure than a mere suggestion but falls short of the type of force implied by the term coercion. Applied behavior analysis (a means of behavior modification stemming from Skinnerian operant conditioning) can be viewed as a form of persuasion. Positive reinforcement for desired (from the point of view of the influencer or "shaper") behavior tends to induce the influencee to continue that behavior. Reward systems that may include only recognition and praise have proved successful in modifying individual behavior— reduced absenteeism, for example—in a number of organizational settings.[4]

4 Kenneth Goodall, "Shapers at Work," *Psychology Today*, November 1972, pp. 53 ff. See also B. F. Skinner, *Beyond Freedom and Dignity*, Alfred A. Knopf, Inc., New York, 1971.

Coercion involves forcible constraint, including physical pressure. "We will have to do some arm-twisting" is a typical phrase that figuratively describes a method of persuasion based on physical pressure. Literally, a hammerlock could coerce an individual into a particular bit of behavior ("say uncle," for example). A person wielding a gun, knife, or other similar weapon can forcibly evoke specific behavior from another individual or a group, the typical skyjacking episode.

Many forms of coercion, other than physical force, are evident. In organizations, salaries and/or promotions can be used to constrain or influence behavior. In many cases the threat of dismissal is also a powerful influencer.

Interaction Influence Systems

The concept of an ***influence system*** is critical. The process of influencing behavior is not necessarily attached to an organizational hierarchy. Any interaction between individuals results in a transaction that has psychological and/or behavioral effects. Thus, by definition, influence "happens" in such situations. Taken together, these numerous pairs of relationships in groups or organizations can be termed an ***interaction-influence system.***

Power, the ability to influence behavior, underlies the entire spectrum of means shown in Figure 13.1. The more power an individual has in a given situation, the more effective his or her influence attempts will be. ***Authority,*** as institutionalized power or the right to influence behavior, also underlies the entire spectrum of ways to influence behavior in organizations. Typically, positions high in the hierarchy will have more influence than those at lower levels. However, this is not necessarily the case; it depends on the issues involved and the participants in the interaction-influence system.

The old adage "knowledge is power" is appropriate to this discussion. Quite often the flow of influence is lateral or upward as hierarchical relationships are transcended because an individual has specific knowledge concerning a particular question. A corporate president is likely to be influenced by the advice of tax and/or legal advisors who point out pitfalls in a proposal. If the chief test pilot says the airplane is not ready, the first flight will be postponed even though several hundred dignitaries and high-level corporate officials have gathered for the occasion.

In these examples it is clear that a person in a formal position may be quite dependent on others at the same level or below. This person needs various kinds of support in order to function in the job. This dependence increases the power of others in the organization relative to this person (and increases their ability to influence his or her behavior).

Individuals influence the behavior of others in many ways. Subordinates can influence their superiors if they have technical expertise concerning a particular subject.[5] This form of power is often termed the "authority" of knowledge.[6] The term **functional authority** refers to the degree of dependence on a particular activity or function. Individuals in staff positions theoretically have little formal authority in organizations. However, they influence behavior effectively because of the dependence of other organizational members on them for information concerning procedures or techniques.

Location can have bearing on the ability to influence behavior. An "assistant to," although he or she is low on the status ladder, has considerable power because of his or her close proximity to a high-level executive. With little formal authority, people in such positions find others in the organization dependent on them for information about how the boss is likely to react to various proposals. Also, they are in a position to screen and/or filter messages in both directions—to the boss from other members of the organization and vice versa.

Many organizational relationships involve peer groups. In such cases the interaction-influence system has no relationship to the hierarchy. Thus, power that underlies influence attempts must come from some source other than authority. The potential effectiveness of persuasion and suggestion depends on knowledge, concern for continued social relationships, and other similar factors.

Power

Power is the capability of doing or affecting something.[7] It implies the ability to influence others. In its most general sense, power denotes (1) the ability (exercised or not) to produce a certain occurrence or (2) the influence exerted by a person or group, through whatever means, over the conduct of others in intended ways.[8] This relates to the spectrum of ways to influence behavior as indicated in Figure 13.1 and suggests that power is involved along the entire spectrum as long as there is an ability to produce a certain occurrence.[9]

While power underlies the entire spectrum of ways to influence behavior, its everyday connotation leans toward the persuasive-coercive end of the spectrum. Although power is the *general* ability to produce a certain occurrence, it implies the force, if necessary, to control or command others.

Power is the capacity to affect behavior in predetermined ways. "Only

5 David Mechanic, "Sources of Power of Lower Participants in Complex Organizations," *Administrative Science Quarterly,* December 1962, p. 352.

6 This widely used concept is actually a misnomer because, by definition, authority is institutional rather than personal.

7 Bertrand Russell, *Power,* W. W. Norton & Company, Inc., New York, 1938. Russell contends that power is a fundamental concept in social science in the same sense that energy is fundamental in physics. He defines power as the ability to produce intended effects (p. 35). This is certainly a broad connotation that does not relate to methods used—only the results. For our study of organization and management we are more interested in "intended effects" as they relate to social interaction.

8 Gould and Kolb, op. cit., p. 524.

9 Gerald R. Salancik and Jeffrey Pfeffer, "Who Gets Power—and How They Hold on to It," *Organizational Dynamics,* Winter 1977, pp. 3–21.

groups which have power can threaten to use force and the threat itself is power. Power is the ability to employ force, not its actual employment, the ability to apply sanctions, not the actual application." [10] If coercion or the application of force is ineffective, there is no power. Power exists only when it is effective; it is the capability to influence behavior by limiting the alternatives available in social situations.

Types
of
Power

The power underlying the various means of influencing behavior in an organization has been classified into three categories: physical, material, and symbolic. [11] In some organizations a gun, whip, or actual physical force may be required to influence and control behavior—prisons or custodial mental institutions, for example. In most cases the application of physical force is not necessary. However, the threat of its use underlies coercive power in organizations.

Material rewards or sanctions come primarily in the form of money (or lack of it), which can be used to buy goods and services. Monetary incentive systems, including promotions and layoffs, are examples of utilitarian power that can be used in organizations to influence the behavior of participants.

Symbolic means of influencing behavior are those that are not physical or material. They relate primarily to prestige and esteem or love and acceptance. When organizational participants are encouraged to improve their performance, the appeal is based on what they "ought" to do as "good" employees. The behavior of an individual can be influenced through the medium of a small group. A boss may suggest that other participants in a work group apply pressure on a particular member in order to get him or her to "shape up." The social power— love and acceptance—that peers exercise over one another is an important and integral part of the influence system in groups and organizations.

For a football team, all three types of power underlie the coach's attempt to get a player to improve performance. The coach may appeal to achievement motivation and suggest that the player has not been performing up to capacity and ought out to play much better. Influence attempts may include the focal person's teammates, who are encouraged by the coach to apply a little pressure from the standpoint of the team. The argument is that the team member "should" do better in order that the team might be successful. Without any direction from the coach, the team may use its social power to help influence the behavior of particular members. Ignoring the curfew or not "putting out" on the field may lead to sanctions from teammates—from barbed comments to the silent treatment. If none of these influence attempts is successful, material power can be

---

10 Robert Bierstedt, "An Analysis of Social Power," *American Sociological Review,* December 1950, p. 733.

11 Amitai Etzioni, *Modern Organizations,* Prentice-Hall, Inc., Englewood Cliffs, N.J., 1964, p. 59.

invoked, and the player can be fined for violating regulations or making repeated "bonehead" plays on the field. And coaches have been known to use physical force in attempting to influence the behavior of a player who makes repeated mistakes or does not seem to "get the picture."

In stable-mechanistic organizations the interaction-influence patterns tend to be hierarchical and primarily from superior to subordinate. Power is narrowly held, centralized, and relies heavily on material incentives or sanctions. In adaptive-organic organizations the interaction-influence patterns are more varied, including top-down, bottom-up, horizontal, and diagonal relationships. Power is widely held, decentralized, and relies more on social factors such as esteem and self-actualization.

These comments suggest what is predominant or probable in various types of organizations. Typically, all types of power are used to back up influence attempts in a particular organization, depending on the time and situation. Yet participants come to expect certain kinds of influence attempts as normal. In general, the trend in organizations has been away from reliance on physical and material power bases. Symbolic power tends to be involved in an increasing proportion of influence attempts in organizations.

Power
Equalization

"The general trend of twentieth-century society, particularly in the U.S., is toward a wider distribution of power, a broadening of participation by individuals in controlling their own lives and work." [12] The nature and extent of changes concern managers worldwide. [13] Leavitt describes numerous trends that can be described as power equalization in organizations. [14] We have discussed the trend toward industrial humanism—the primary concern being the individual rather than the work itself or an organization per se. A focal point has been self-actualization and the theory that individuals cannot grow and develop in an atmosphere of overwhelming position power (authority) underlying predominantly downward attempts to influence behavior. There has been a plea for more balance in the distribution of power so that influence can flow in many directions in organizations.

For example, Theory X implies an emphasis on the hierarchy and the use of coercive and/or utilitarian power to back influence attempts in the organization. Theory Y, on the other hand, assumes a balance of power and relatively more use of social power.

---

12 Max Ways, "More Power to Everybody," *Fortune*, May 1970, p. 174.

13 David Oates, "How Far Will Worker Power Go?" *International Management*, February 1977, pp. 10–13.

14 Harold J. Leavitt, "Applied Organizational Change in Industry: Structural, Technological, and Humanistic Approaches," in James G. March (ed.), *Handbook of Organizations*, Rand McNally & Company, Chicago, 1965, pp. 1144–1170.

If power equalization is a recognized objective, several measures can be taken.[15] Decision making can be made more participative, decentralized, and independent. This is particularly true in determining the goals of subgroups and/ or the organization as a whole. But it also applies to the means of implementing strategic decisions. Power equalization can be considered explicitly in assessing cohesiveness and conformity in subgroups. Specific attention can be focused on group pressure, recognizing that decentralized, participative decision making can lead to complex and ambiguous overall situations. Two-way communication and multiple channels can also be helpful in facilitating power equalization in organizations.

The concept of power as both *unilateral* and *bilateral* is quite important. In any social system the power relationships are complex and do not flow on a one-way street. The balance of power between the individual and the organization, as represented by a superior, is decidedly in favor of the organization. It can apply sanctions without regarding too seriously the repercussions that might stem from one individual. However, the group as a whole can wield considerable power, including the ultimate withdrawal of contributions in the form of a strike. This alternative often is extremely unpalatable to the organization, and hence the balance of power swings in favor of the subordinate group—as evidenced by the success of employees in critical fields such as health care or emergency services (police and fire).

Authority

Authority is institutionalized power, an important concept in the study of formal organizations. It is based on legal foundations (legislation, articles of incorporation, partnership agreements, bylaws) that define an organization's mission and empower its members to carry out its activities.

Without formal authority groups typically develop power relationships based on characteristics such as physical prowess, knowledge or wisdom, or some other means of identifying status relationships and positions or roles. Tradition and charisma also help identify power bases within groups. If the organization is a legal entity, relationships are structured and positions are established formally. As we shall see later, the spontaneous system may not necessarily coincide with that which is established legally to achieve the objectives of a formal organization.

Authority
and
Individualism

Natural social groups develop in the form of families, clans, tribes, states, and nations. Within these groups superior-subordinate relationships de-

---

15 Ibid., pp. 1161–1165.

velop in the form of status and role systems. Based on any of a number of characteristics, power structures evolve naturally, and they in turn are perpetuated via tradition. [16]

It is hard to imagine that the human community could proceed in its endeavors without an institutionalized power structure, which we call authority. Anarchy is inconceivable; but so is the other extreme, authoritarianism. As in so many similar conceptual frameworks, we are interested in a workable compromise. We need enough authority to ensure cooperative action and progress toward group goals. However, we also want to encourage individuality, creativity, and innovation.

Authoritarianism results from an obsession with hierarchical relationships to the degree that superiors eschew consultation with subordinates. At the same time, subordinates are disposed toward zealous obedience to hierarchic superiors.

Progress depends on uncommon people and their unwillingness to perpetuate a given system. Often, their struggle is against the societal power structure and the specific authority systems in formal organizations. Benne sums up this perennial struggle as follows:

Authority is a necessity of all stable community life. Today, under the impact of growing collective interdependence men are forced to rethink and reconstruct the operating bases of community authority. The widespread attempt under the historic liberal ideology to deny the principle of authority in human relations has helped to blur the recognition of operating bases of authority necessary to stable and responsible individual and group life, thus paradoxically contributing to the restoration of extreme authoritarianism in human affairs. [17]

Given the inevitability of informal and formal organizations, there is a need for some means to ensure that efforts are directed toward appropriate objectives. "Every organization faces the task of somehow reducing the variability, instability, and unpredictability of individual human acts." [18] Authority, coupled with status and role systems, supplies this necessary element. These key ingredients result in reasonably well-defined roles to be performed by organizational participants so that behavior is not entirely "spontaneous and unrehearsed." In many cases, behavior of organizational members is identical—starting at eight and quitting at five, for example. They may wear certain styles of attire (even uniforms) that distinguish them from other organizations, or they may develop special behavior patterns that are essential to the work of the organization.

16 Anthony Jay, *Corporation Man,* Random House, Inc., New York, 1971.

17 Kenneth D. Benne, *The Conception of Authority,* Bureau of Publications, Teachers College, Columbia University, New York, 1943, p. 27.

18 Daniel Katz and Robert L. Kahn, *The Social Psychology of Organizations,* 2d ed., John Wiley & Sons, Inc., New York, 1978, p. 296.

Types
of
Authority

According to Weber, three basic types of legitimate authority can be identified—rational-legal, traditional, and charismatic. [19] ***Charismatic*** "authority" depends on the magical qualities of individual leaders. No rules or regulations are involved. Charisma is more a concept of power than of authority because it depends on personal characteristics rather than position.

Charismatic authority often evolves into ***traditional*** authority as informal status and role systems become stabilized over time. It is exemplified by the phrase, "it has always been this way." Policies, procedures, and rules are developed by those traditionally "in command." Over a period of time the system evolves to the point where directives are carried out by subordinates without question. Changes or adjustments in the system result when traditional leaders deem it necessary and/or desirable. The traditions in the system may be handed down explicitly in written form or implicitly in a manner similar to the transmission of folklore.

Just as charismatic authority often evolves into traditional authority, so traditional authority can evolve into ***rational-legal*** authority if the system is legitimized formally. Common law has become codified into an elaborate body of official criteria for administering justice in society. Legal authority in organizations is also established by means of specific legislation. Governmental agencies are designated responsibility for a sphere of activity and are accorded commensurate authority in order to carry out their specific tasks. This framework provides the means to structure a hierarchy through which authority is delegated to positions in the system.

Most large-scale business organizations are legal entities called corporations, which derive their authority from the various states. Their charters designate what they can and cannot do, depending on the particular sphere of activity engaged in. Insurance companies have special rules and regulations, as do airlines or drug manufacturers. The authority system in a corporation is based on institutional rights granted to it by the state. This authority is delegated throughout the system on the basis of typical hierarchical patterns. Organizational participants recognize the legitimate authority based on ownership. It may be used by an owner-manager or delegated to a group of "professional" managers, as is the case in many large-scale, complex organizations in society.

While management has the responsibility to achieve organizational goals, an increasing number of external constraints limits traditional authority. Union contracts, regulatory boards or commissions, and new laws circumscribe managerial decision making in matters such as hiring, firing, pricing, safety, and environmental protection.

---

19 Max Weber, *The Theory of Social and Economic Organizations,* trans. by A. M. Henderson and Talcott Parsons, Oxford University Press, Fair Lawn, N.J., 1947, p. 328

But it does not always work as smoothly as it would appear. This approach stresses the flow of authority from the top down and the concept that behavior can be made to conform to the expectations of the influencer. However, there has always been the notion that effective authority depends on the "consent of the governed."

Acceptance Theory of Authority

The institutionalized right to influence behavior may or may not be effective, depending on the consent of organizational participants. Simon suggests that the crux of the authority relationship is that a subordinate "holds in abeyance" his or her own critical faculties for choosing between alternatives and uses the receipt of a command as the basis for choice.[20] This line of reasoning leads to a zone of acceptance from the point of view of the subordinates. They have a certain tolerance level or range within which they will accept directives without analyzing the merits of the behavior as related to the problem at hand. Barnard expressed a similar idea and termed it the zone of indifference.[21]

The concept of "zone of acceptance" is important in understanding effective authority. Unless a directive falls within this range, it will not be effective, and the influence attempt fails. In such cases, repeated attempts to influence behavior can be made with the same means, or a different approach can be used. If it still is not effective, the various sanctions underlying the authority system can be imposed, including dismissal. But if the objective is to coordinate group effort and the result is loss of organizational participants, the overall system has failed. Formal authority is limited by the zone of acceptance.

Individuals typically undergo a socialization process from infancy to adulthood that stresses the acceptance of authority—family, church, school, and work relationships. However, in modern, large-scale organizations a countertrend seems apparent in that the zone of acceptance for participants has narrowed over the years. Employees are likely to exercise their own judgment more often and accept uncritically the directives of others in fewer situations. The educational process has fostered a long-run trend in this direction. As employees at all levels become better educated, they are less likely to defer evaluational and decision-making activities to superiors over wide ranges of activities. More and more people want to know *why* a particular course of action is the desired one. This is occurring in all types of organizations—families, clubs, schools, hospitals, government agencies, and businesses.

---

20 Herbert A. Simon, *Administrative Behavior,* 3d ed., The Free Press, New York, 1976, p. 126.
21 Chester I. Barnard, *The Functions of the Executive,* Harvard University Press, Cambridge, Mass., 1938, p. 167.

Synthesis of
Authority
Concepts

A great deal has been written about the apparent conflict in the nature of authority. [22] Specifically, does authority flow downward in organizations based on an institutionalized right to employ power? Or does authority stem from the bottom up, based on the zone of acceptance that participants maintain with respect to the directives of superiors?

A synthesis is possible if we recognize that the rational-legal authority framework is accepted as legitimate by most participants. And when it is coupled with traditional and charismatic sources of authority, the zone of acceptance is widened significantly. The zone of acceptance should relate to specific influence attempts by particular people. An appeal based on utilitarian aspects may evoke no response; the same appeal based on normative-social or peer-group power may elicit the desired behavior. When positional and personal authority reinforce each other, we have added evidence of the synthesis of the acceptance theory with the right-to-command theory.

Formal authority does give position power, a basis for influencing organizational behavior. However, it is not enough to ensure effective cooperation. When greater reliance must be placed on other means of influencing behavior, leadership becomes a vital factor.

Leadership
Defined

Leadership is (1) a function and (2) a status grouping. Directors, executives, administrators, managers, bosses, and chiefs would typically be included in the category called leadership. Identification of those "in" the group has been important in studying the phenomenon of leadership in the past.

The leadership function involves facilitating the achievement of group goals. In modern organizations leadership functions can be (and often are) performed by several or many participants. However, praise or blame for success or failure is typically focused on the individual—the formal leader. This phenomenon is evident in all organizations, but it is particularly noticeable in the sports world where coaches and managers are either heroes or bums (and fired summarily), in spite of the fact that many variables, including luck, affect team performance. Given our societal propensity to focus on formal leaders, it is important to understand our role expectations.

The leadership function has been defined in many ways—from "that which leaders do" to long, complex paragraphs including several or many elements. Fiedler cites nearly a dozen different definitions with varying connotations and degrees of emphasis on subparts. He concludes that a leader is "the individual

22 Merton J. Mandeville, "The Nature of Authority," *Academy of Management Journal,* August 1960, pp. 107–118.

in the group given the task of directing and coordinating task-relevant group activities or who, in the absence of a designated leader, carries the primary responsibility for performing these functions in the group."[23] Emphasis on coordinating task-oriented group activities seems to indicate that leading is synonymous with managing. Typically, however, management is considered to be a more broadly based function including activities other than leading.

Leadership is part of management, but not all of it. Managers are required to plan and organize, for example, but all we ask of leaders is that they influence others to follow. . . . *Leadership* is the ability to persuade others to seek defined objectives enthusiastically. It is the human factor that binds a group together and motivates it toward goals. . . . It is the ultimate act that brings to success all the potential that is in an organization and its people.[24]

This connotation stresses the role of leadership in eliciting behavioral responses that are more than routine. It suggests the "tapping" of latent human capability in achieving group objectives. And it relates to our concept of an influence system by stressing the role of persuasion.

The differential exertion of influence is one way to define leadership.[25] This approach recognizes that in social groups there are typically bilateral processes of interpersonal influence. Those with a positive balance—a net outflow of influence—would be designated as leaders; those with a minus balance would be followers. Obviously, the process of identifying leaders would have to be repeated for each group because the balance in any one group would shift according to the situation. For example, the physically underdeveloped student may have been forgotten at the senior picnic, where the emphasis was on appearance, physical skill, and strength. On the way home, however, that same student's first-aid training may thrust him or her into the leadership role during the aftermath of an automobile accident.

Differential influence is apparent in informal social relationships and in formal organizations. Typically, designated position holders do have a positive balance in the influence system. However, this may not always be the case. The positional authority of a "leader" may not be enough to persuade subordinates to engage in appropriate activities. Influence attempts fail, and leadership is ineffective.

Tannenbaum and Massarik summarize the relationship between leadership and influence systems by stating that leadership is *"interpersonal influence, exercised in situations and directed, through the communication process, toward the attainment of a specified goal or goals.* Leadership always involves attempts on the

23 Fred E. Fiedler, *A Theory of Leadership Effectiveness*, McGraw-Hill Book Company, New York, 1967, p. 8

24 Keith Davis, *Human Behavior at Work*, 5th ed., McGraw-Hill Book Company, New York, 1977, p. 107.

25 Katz and Kahn, op. cit., p. 528.

part of a *leader* (influencer) to affect (influence) the behavior of a *follower* (influencee) or followers in situation."[26]

We are interested in exactly what makes some people leaders and others followers.

Traits
and
Greatness

For centuries, philosophers have argued the "great person" theory. Was *history made by people* such as Catherine the Great, Napoleon, Lenin, or Churchill? Or, on the other hand, were such *people made by history?* Is there something about the personality of such individuals that enables them to have a significant effect on the course of human events? Or do such people become leaders because they just happen to be in the right place at the right time? Based on most current research, we would answer: some of both. The situation is important in determining the kind of leadership that will be most appropriate. Given the particular environment, there will be one individual whose personality and leadership style fit the situation best. Moreover, he or she happens to be in the right place at the right time.

Debates over the great person theory brought considerable attention to the so-called "trait" approach. It emphasized the personality characteristics, value system, and life style of leaders. The typical approach to such research consisted in identifying characteristics of established leaders. The list of traits could be endless but typically includes such things as size, energy (both nervous and physical), intelligence, sense of direction and purpose, enthusiasm, friendliness, integrity, morality, technical expertise, decisiveness, perceptual skills, knowledge, wisdom, imagination, determination, persistence, endurance, good looks (physical and sartorial splendor), and courage. One obvious problem is that there is little agreement with regard to which traits should be included and which should be excluded. Moreover, there is disagreement with regard to which of those included are the more important.[27]

There have been many attempts to distill out of these long lists of characteristics some key attributes such as intelligence, social maturity and breadth, achievement needs, and genuine respect for people. Their presence does not ensure leadership success, nor does their absence preclude it. However, an individual possessing these basic ingredients may have a higher probability of becoming a

26 Robert Tannenbaum and Fred Massarik, "Leadership: A Frame of Reference," *Management Science,* October 1957, p. 3.

27 For summaries of early research, see Cecil E. Goode, "Significant Research on Leadership," *Personnel,* March 1951, pp. 342–350; and Ralph M. Stogdill, "Personal Factors Associated with Leadership: A Survey of the Literature," *The Journal of Psychology,* January 1948, pp. 35–71. An integrating theory is presented in Warren G. Bennis, "Leadership Theory and Administrative Behavior," *Administrative Science Quarterly,* December 1959, pp. 259–301.

successful leader (regardless of the followers and the situation) than someone without them.

The danger of the trait approach is illustrated by Solomon, who suggests that these qualities are obviously desirable in a leader but that none of them seems to be essential.

The world has seen numerous great leaders who could hardly lay claim to any kind of formal education. History is replete with non-trained, non-academic Fords, Edisons, and Carnegies who couldn't even claim a grammar school education yet managed to become leaders whose influence was felt around the globe. As for appearance of robust health, need we mention more than the delicate Gandhi, or George Washington Carver, the frail, shriveled, insignificant little Negro who was one of America's greatest scientists? And so many more like them? As for high ideals, fine character, etc., where would Hitler, Capone or Attila the Hun rate here? [28]

These may be examples of situations in which a particular personality defect seemed to be called for in the environmental context. A sick society may choose a sick leader. [29]

Effective Leader Behavior

The trait approach refers to what a leader is. Another approach to understanding leadership success concentrates on what the leader does—his or her behavior or style. Terms such as autocratic, democratic, bureaucratic, neurocratic, and laissez-faire have been used to describe the general approach used by leaders in human situations. To research the effectiveness of various styles, it is necessary to hold the situation constant. Thus, any findings have to be interpreted in the light of the environmental situation used in an experiment or observed in real organizations. A study by White and Lippit concentrated on the impact of three leadership styles in task-oriented groups. [30] Three relatively distinct styles are described in Figure 13.2.

In the White-Lippit experiments, the leaders "played" the designated roles over an extended period. With all other aspects of the groups held as constant as possible, the difference in leadership styles allows some conclusions with regard to their impact on individual participants and group behavior.

Although the quantity of work in autocratic groups was slightly more, the quality in democratic groups was consistently better. When the leader left the

28 Ben Solomon, *Leadership of Youth,* Youth Services, New York, 1950, p. 15.

29 J. A. C. Brown *The Social Psychology of Industry,* Penguin Books, Inc., Baltimore, 1954, p. 222.

30 Ralph White and Ronald Lippitt, "Leader Behavior and Member Reaction in Three 'Social Climates,' " in Dorwin Cartwright and Alvin Zander (eds.), *Group Dynamics: Research and Theory,* Harper & Row, Publishers, Inc., New York, 1953, pp. 385–411.

Figure 13.2   Three Leadership Styles

Authoritarian	Democratic	Laissez-Faire
1 All determination of policy by the leader	1 All policies a matter of group discussion and decision, encouraged and assisted by the leader	1 Complete freedom for group or individual decision, with a minimum of leader participation
2 Techniques and activity steps dictated by the authority, one at a time so that future steps were always uncertain to a large degree	2 Activity perspective gained during discussion period. General steps to group goal sketched, and when technical advice was needed, the leader suggested two or more alternative procedures from which choice could be made	2 Various materials supplied by the leader, who made it clear that information would be supplied when requested and took no other part in work discussion
3 The leader usually dictated the particular work task and work companion of each member	3 The members were free to work with whomever they chose, and the division of tasks was left up to the group	3 Complete nonparticipation of the leader
4 The dominator tended to be "personal" in the praise and criticism of the work of each member; remained aloof from active group participation except when demonstrating	4 The leader was "objective" or "fact-minded" in praise and criticism and tried to be a regular group member in spirit without doing too much of the work	4 Infrequent spontaneous comments on member activities unless questioned and no attempt to appraise or regulate the course of events

Ralph White and Ronald Lippitt, *Autocracy and Democracy*, Harper & Row, Publishers, Inc., 1960, pp. 26–27 (our title). By permission of Harper & Row, Publishers.

room, the autocratic groups collapsed completely, whereas the performance in democratic groups decreased only slightly

In general, the findings seem to indicate that a laissez faire approach, or complete permissiveness, was not effective in terms of group performance. Moreover, it did not seem to produce any other benefits, such as improved morale or satisfaction of individual group members. On the contrary, these dimensions were improved, along with performance, in democratic groups. While the quantity of output in autocratic work groups was slightly better than under a democratic approach, there were important negative side effects that cast doubt on the long-run usefulness of such a leadership style. Given the situation as described, it would seem that a democratic-participative approach, on balance, was the most effective and efficient. These findings have been corroborated by other similar experiments and in actual industrial situations.

In stable-mechanistic organizations leadership style based on depersonalized bureaucracy may be appropriate. The system of rules and regulations is designed to cover all exigencies. Hence the role of the leader is one of monitoring routine activity within the guidelines established by the system itself. A bureaucratic style that stresses administrative tidiness, regularity, and accuracy is evident in many of today's large-scale organizations. In adaptive-organic organizations, however, a more flexible style is called for in order to cope with diverse human resources that are engaged in complex activities.

Specific Behaviors

A major focus in leadership research has been to identify specific behaviors that account for leadership effectiveness. In reviewing the research and writing on leadership behavior, Bowers and Seashore concluded that in spite of the variety of terms used, there is a great deal of common conceptual content. They distilled the following four dimensions of effectiveness:

1 *Support.* Behavior that enhances someone else's feeling of personal worth and importance.
2 *Interaction Facilitation.* Behavior that encourages members of the group to develop close, mutually satisfying relationships.
3 *Goal Emphasis.* Behavior that stimulates an enthusiasm for meeting the group's goal or achieving excellent performance.
4 *Work Facilitation.* Behavior that helps achieve goal attainment by such activities as scheduling, coordinating, planning, and by providing resources such as tools, materials, and technical knowledge. [31]

Support and interaction facilitation are obviously "people" concerns. Emphasizing these dimensions recognizes the need to encourage continued support of individuals in organizational endeavor and the need to maintain and improve interpersonal relationships and group processes such as teamwork. Goal emphasis and work facilitation relate to task concerns and to the path-goal theory of leadership. [32] Good leaders are typically seen by subordinates as helpful in both setting goals and in structuring or designing means of achieving them. This approach builds on the concept of achievement motivation; if goals are achieved and performance is rewarded appropriately, there is an increase in satisfaction. Performance leads to satisfaction and increased motivation in the future.

These four dimensions of behavior are an elaboration of several two-factor models that call attention to people versus production, relationship orientation versus task orientation, or group maintenance versus goal achievement. Of primary concern is the question of whether behavior on these dimensions is mutually exclusive. Does emphasis on task preclude emphasis on people or vice versa? In describing leadership behavior in existing organizations, we can find examples

---

31 David G. Bowers and Stanley E. Seashore, "Predicting Organizational Effectiveness with a Four-Factor Theory of Leadership," *Administrative Science Quarterly,* September 1966, p. 247.

32 Robert J. House and Terence R. Mitchell, "Path-Goal Theory of Leadership," *Journal of Contemporary Business,* Autumn 1974, pp. 81–97.

of varying degrees of emphasis on these behaviors. Some managers are relatively task oriented; others focus on relationships. Which is best? We will explore this question in subsequent sections; however, a general guideline is that all four factors in the above model are important and should be emphasized *as much as possible depending on the constraints of the situation.* But it is unrealistic to expect simultaneous attention to all of the dimensions of effective leader behavior. Some tradeoffs are necessary and bound to occur. Goal emphasis may be paramount in initiating a program of management by objectives and results. Interaction facilitation may actually need to be decreased in an organization that seems to spend nearly all of its time in meetings (leaving little time to work on the task). An appropriate balance should be maintained according to the particular situation.

Organizational Context

The external environment of the organization is part of the context within which leadership takes place. Prevailing cultural norms and industry practices provide general guidelines for behavior. Books, periodicals, movies, and television provide explicit role models for leaders in a variety of organizations— business, government, military, church, and educational. These general influences are coupled with specific organizational conditions to provide an overall context for leader behavior.

A basic approach to understanding the internal organizational context is to consider forces in (1) the leader, (2) the followers, and (3) the situation. An example of this approach is provided by Tannenbaum and Schmidt in considering the degree of participation that might be appropriate in decision making: [33]

Leader:

Own value system

Confidence in his or her subordinates

Own leadership inclinations

Feelings of security in an uncertain situation

Follower(s):

Independence-dependence needs

Willingness to assume responsibility for decision making

Tolerance for ambiguity

Degree of interest in participating

Degree of identification with organization goals

Knowledge and experience (or growth potential)

Expectations concerning participation

33 Robert Tannenbaum and Warren H. Schmidt, "How To Choose a Leadership Pattern," *Harvard Business Review*, May–June 1973, pp. 178–179.

Situation:

Values and traditions in the organization

Group effectiveness

Nature of the problem

Pressure of time

Consideration of these factors and forces can also be related to the degree of emphasis on the various behaviors in the four-factor model described previously. For example, the amount of support provided to subordinates might vary with our perception of individual needs in this regard. More emphasis on work facilitation might be provided if subordinate knowledge and experience are minimal. Similarly, interaction facilitation and goal emphasis could be emphasized or not, depending on our own inclinations and our assessment of a group's effectiveness and the specific nature of a given problem.

A number of other variables might be considered in assessing organizational context for leader behavior. However, the aforementioned dimensions and considerations provide evidence of the complexity involved.

Organizational Performance

Organization theory and management practice relate to task-oriented groups. Therefore, productivity is an important measure of managerial performance, which depends in turn on leadership effectiveness. However, attributing organizational outcomes to specific leader behaviors is fraught with danger.

In discussing this issue, Pfeffer suggests three reasons why the observed effects of leaders on organizational outcomes might be small. "First those obtaining leadership positions are selected, and perhaps only certain, limited styles of behavior may be chosen. Second, once in the leadership position, the discretion and behavior of the leader are constrained. And third, leaders can typically affect only a few of the variables that may impact organizational performance." [34] In spite of these inherent problems, there have been numerous attempts to establish a relationship between specific leadership behavior and group performance. At best, the results are mixed. [35]

While the impact of the formal leaders is often constrained by situational factors beyond their control, they can have *some* influence (positive or negative) on performance in almost all cases. Therefore, it is important to understand as much as possible about effective leader behavior, if only in terms of probabilities of success for various styles. Mixed research results concerning the effect of specific behaviors on performance suggests a balanced approach. Multiple long-run

---

34 Jeffrey Pfeffer, "The Ambiguity of Leadership," *Academy of Management Review,* January 1977, p. 106.

35 Ralph Stogdill, *Handbook of Leadership,* The Free Press, New York, 1974, pp. 418–420.

performance criteria (effectiveness, efficiency, and participant satisfaction) suggest emphasis on supporting subordinates, encouraging interaction among group members, setting challenging, realistic goals, and facilitating the work of the organization.

Contingency Views and Flexibility

Our discussion of traits, styles, and behavior inevitably brings us to the conclusion that there is *no one best way to lead; it all depends.* It depends on the leader, the followers, and the situation—the nature of the task, the authority relationships, and the group dynamics. Such factors are part of the organizational context or psychosocial system within which a leader must function. A contingency view in diagnosing situations, coupled with flexibility in behavior, will improve the probability that a leader's influence attempts will be successful.

Figure 13.3 shows a continuum of leadership behavior with the basic variable being the degree of authority used by a manager vis à vis the amount of freedom left for subordinates in making decisions. Different styles can be identified across the continuum from boss-centered leadership to subordinate-centered leadership.

We should not get the implication that some managers always make a decision and announce it and that others always define limits and then ask the

Figure 13.3 Continuum of Leadership Behavior

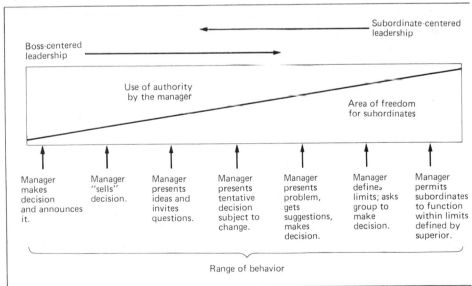

Robert Tannenbaum and Warren H. Schmidt, "How to Choose a Leadership Pattern," *Harvard Business Review,* March–April 1958, p. 96.

group to take a vote. On the contrary, it seems obvious that different styles will be appropriate in different situations. In a military combat situation, subordinates must rely on the decision making of their group leader. The crew of a ship hit by a torpedo would not be inclined to discuss the alternatives and then vote. If the captain announces, "Abandon ship," the order would be carried out immediately. On the other hand, in situations where time permits, it may be useful to include subordinates in the decision-making process. This does not necessarily mean that a vote will be taken and that the majority rules. A manager may be very explicit to the effect that he or she is interested in the various points of view and an exhaustive study of the question. However, the manager may state emphatically, in the beginning, that he or she will make the decision at the end of the discussion. In other cases, the authority to make decisions may be decentralized completely with only broad guidelines established by the manager.

Diagnosing Situations

Vroom has extended this conceptual model and developed prescriptions for leadership behavior based on the answers to a series of questions related to problem attributes.

Problem Attributes [36]	Diagnostic Questions
The importance of the quality of the decision.	Is there a quality requirement such that one solution is likely to be more rational than another?
The extent to which the leader possesses sufficient information/expertise to make a high-quality decision.	Do I have sufficient information to make a high-quality decision?
The extent to which the problem is structured.	Is the problem structured?
The extent to which acceptance or commitment on the part of subordinates is critical to the effective implementation of the decision.	Is acceptance of decision by subordinates critical to effective implementation?
The prior probability that the leader's autocratic decision will receive acceptance by subordinates.	If you were to make the decision by yourself, is it reasonably certain that it would be accepted by your subordinates?
The extent to which subordinates are motivated to attain the organizational goals as represented in the objectives explicit in the statement of the problem.	Do subordinates share the organizational goals to be obtained in solving this problem?
The extent to which subordinates are likely to be in conflict over preferred solutions.	Is conflict among subordinates likely in preferred solutions?

36 Victor H. Vroom, "A New Look at Managerial Decision Making," *Organizational Dynamics,* (AMA-COM, a division of American Management Associations), Spring 1973, p. 69.

By asking each of these questions in sequence, one can classify problems into types. Each type can be identified with an appropriate leadership style or behavior ranging from completely autocratic toward delegation. Participative approaches range from one-on-one consultation to consultation in a group meeting and finally to complete delegation. This type of analysis leads to a matching of leadership behavior with specific problematic situations.

In current management literature it is easy to identify a preference for a participative leadership style. Such an approach may or may not be possible; moreover, it may not even be appropriate. Based on research involving a number of practicing managers responding to case situations, Vroom and Yetton observed that managers typically use a variety of styles, depending on the situation. However, they concluded that most managers would be more effective if they were *both* more autocratic and more participative.[37] They found that managers tended to shy away from an autocratic approach, even when it was most appropriate according to the model, and they tended to be less participative than called for by the model in other situations. This suggests that to be more effective, managers need increased flexibility. A leader must be a good diagnostician and match the situation with an appropriate style—sometimes relatively autocratic and sometimes quite participative.

On balance, it is important for leaders to recognize the complexity of human motivation, group dynamics, and organizational contexts. The best leaders seem to have a tolerance for ambiguity and a conceptual ability to cope with multidimensional situations. They emphasize support and interaction facilitation as well as goal emphasis and work facilitation; and they are both autocratic and participative, depending on the situation.

Facilitating Effective Leadership

Several issues can be identified in the phrase "facilitating effective leadership." First, we need to remember that leadership is the part of management relying most heavily on interpersonal relationships and focused on tapping latent human capability. Leadership functions are important in group activities and not necessarily the responsibility of one person. However, formal leadership roles are crucial in organizations, and it is this person-role that is our concern in this section. We are interested in how leadership can be instrumental in improving organizations—resulting in increased effectiveness, efficiency, and participant satisfaction. The focal point can be self-assessment and development of an organizational program of facilitating better leadership in general.

---

37 Victor H. Vroom and Philip W. Yetton, *Leadership and Decision-Making,* University of Pittsburgh Press, Pittsburgh, Pa., 1973.

An initial concern is our assumption with regard to whether leaders are born or made. If we believe that values, attitudes, knowledge, skills, and behaviors are relatively fixed in early adulthood, then our strategy should emphasize selection of and matching people with appropriate situations. On the other hand, if we believe that values and attitudes can change and that knowledge, skill, and behavior can be improved, our emphasis will be on experience, coaching, and training. Even if our emphasis is on the latter approach, selection and matching are still important in improving the probability of success.

Assuming we have selected people with reasonable potential, what can we do to increase the probability that the potential will be realized? An important aspect is exposure to good leader attitudes and behavior in early organizational experience. Being treated as an important resource is likely to have an impact on an individual's values and lead him or her to develop and grow. Early opportunities to practice leadership skills are also important. Experience as a follower for thirty years is not the best preparation for leadership responsibility. Rotation through a number of jobs and relationships in an organization also helps prepare people for leadership roles. It allows one to experience a variety of superior-subordinate relationships and to assess personal effectiveness in different situations. Explicit coaching can also be helpful in the development process. Formal training programs can be useful in increasing knowledge, developing skills, and changing attitudes. The assessment center approach has been particularly effective in this process because it has a dual impact of helping to identify potential leaders and to provide feedback concerning strengths and weaknesses that can guide future training and development endeavors. [38]

To facilitate the development of flexibility, several approaches might be appropriate. For example, managers should be encouraged to consider the leader (themselves), the followers, and the situation. The first step is self-assessment; this requires feedback from a variety of sources—diagnostic instruments, superiors, peers, and subordinates. If the feedback shows a gap between current behavior and desired behavior, there are two options: (1) maintain it or (2) change it. Leadership style should be relatively natural and comfortable. New behavior can be learned if it is practiced. However, if a desired style is used ineptly or insincerely, the results might be disastrous. Once a general personal style is determined, one should ascertain where that style is most appropriate and where it would need modification in order to be more effective. This includes assessment of potential followers in terms of their abilities, attitudes, and expectations. It is also important to perceive situations accurately in order that an appropriate leadership style might be used—relatively autocratic or relatively participative, for example.

If we believe that growth and development are likely to be minimal and that flexibility in an individual is difficult to achieve, we can then emphasize matching leaders and situations. We can use assessment techniques to determine

---

38 William C. Byham, "The Assessment Center as an Aid in Management Development," *Training and Development Journal*, December 1971, pp. 10–22.

whether an individual is task-oriented or relationship-oriented, and we can diagnose situations in terms of position power, task structure and leader-member relations.[39] Individuals could be reassigned to fit the proper niche, and/or changes could be made in the organization; that is, the situation could be changed to fit a given leader's style. An important part of leadership training is to help managers understand organizational situations wherein their style is likely to be appropriate or inappropriate.

If we believe that leaders can adjust behavior according to the situations, we need at least minimal guidelines so that situations and behavior are matched. The Vroom-Yetton model (p. 330) for assessing the appropriate degree of participation in decision making is an example of this approach. For optimum success, it is important that the leader and the followers are aware of the diagnostic framework so that mutual expectations are synchronized and there are few surprises. This latter point is key. By and large, followers can adjust to variety of leadership styles. Their major complaint concerns inconsistencies and surprises—an autocratic approach when people expected to participate or an invitation to participate when it is deemed unnecessary and burdensome.

The matching approach, coupled with training, provides the means by which to develop leadership talent while using available skills more effectively. Concerted attention in both directions will result in long-run benefits for the system as a whole.

Summary

Influence is an all-inclusive concept that covers any means by which behavioral change is induced in individuals or groups. An influence system involves a spectrum of ways to affect behavior—emulation, suggestion, persuasion, and coercion. The concept of interaction-influence systems stresses the multidirectional nature of influence processes—laterally and diagonally as well as up and down the organizational hierarchy.

Power and/or authority underlie the entire spectrum of ways to influence behavior. Power is the *ability* to induce psychological or behavioral change. Power equalization in organizations is an evident trend toward offsetting coercive and material position power with social power as a basis for influence attempts.

Authority is a special subclass of power; it is an institutionalized *right* to induce psychological or behavioral change. The effectiveness of authority depends on the "consent of the governed." The "zone of acceptance" for employees in most organizations appears to be narrowing as people become better educated and more inclined to think for themselves.

Influence systems provide the broad setting within which leadership occurs. Leadership has two basic connotations: (1) status and (2) active performance

---

[39] Fred E. Fiedler, Martin M. Chemers, and Linda Mahar, *Improving Leadership Effectiveness: The Leader Match Concept,* John Wiley & Sons, Inc., New York, 1976.

of a function. Leadership, as part of management, emphasizes interpersonal relations and the tapping of latent human capabilities. The leadership system involves three basic elements—the leader, the followers, and the situation.

Research indicates that four factors appear to be common in effective leader behavior: support, interaction facilitation, goal emphasis, and work facilitation.

A contingency view and flexibility are important in appropriately matching leader behavior and organizational situations. Improving leadership effectiveness in organizations can be approached in several ways: (1) careful selection of people with a high probability of success, (2) development of managers via experience, coaching, and training, and (3) matching available leaders with situations in which they are most likely to be successful.

Questions and Problems

1 Define influence. Illustrate the four means of influencing behavior shown in Figure 13.1.

2 What is an interaction-influence system? Give examples of influence flowing horizontally, diagonally, and upward in organizations.

3 Compare and contrast power and authority. How do these concepts relate to influence systems?

4 Illustrate the use of *(a)* physical, *(b)* material and *(c)* symbolic power in influencing organizational behavior. Which approach is best? Why?

5 Explain the concept of power equalization. What trends have been apparent? What do you foresee for the future?

6 Compare and contrast anarchy and authoritarianism. How much is "enough" authority to *ensure* cooperative action and progress toward group goals?

7 Explain rational-legal, traditional, and charismatic authority. Compare personal and positional authority.

8 Discuss the zone of acceptance. What affects its scope? In general, will it widen or narrow in the future?

9 Define leadership and relate it to influence systems and management.

10 Identify several leaders in organizations of which you are a member. Check them against the sample list of traits (at least the summary items) in the chapter. How do they compare? Do your findings tend to support or refute trait theory?

11 Compare and contrast autocratic, democratic, and laissez faire leadership styles. Should a leader pick a style and stay with it regardless? Why or why not?

12 Illustrate the four-factor model of effective leader behavior with specific examples (either good or bad) from your experience in organizations.

13 How do variables such as the task, authority relationships, and group dynamics affect the appropriateness of various leadership styles?

14 Outline some steps you will take in developing yourself to be a more effective leader.

*Under any social order from now to Utopia,
management is indispensable and all-enduring. . . . The
question is not: "Will there be a management elite?" but
"What sort of elite will it be?"*
Sidney Webb

*The end products of managers' work are decisions
and actions.*
Peter Drucker

*How do people manage to manage? The answer
seems evident: by knowledge and experience. To be a
manager is not the same thing as to be a leader, although
leadership is a quality too often underrated in modern
management. There are indeed many aspects of the
manager's job that depend on character—on determination,
on drive, on flair. But the tasks of management are
undeniably intellectual tasks . . . policy-making, decision-
taking, and control.*
Stafford Beer

*If we could first know where we are and whither we
are tending, we could then better judge what to do and how to
do it.*
Abraham Lincoln

*Ultimately all policies are made . . . on the basis of
judgments. There is no other way, and there never will be.
The question is whether those judgments have to be made in
the fog of inadequate and inaccurate data, unclear and
undefined issues, and a welter of conflicting personal opinions,
or whether they can be made on the basis of adequate,
reliable information, relevant experience, and clearly drawn
issues. In the end, analysis is but an aid to judgment. . . .
Judgment is supreme.*
Alain C. Enthoven

*Keeping the wheels turning in a direction already
set is a relatively simple task, compared to that of directing
the introduction of a continuing flow of changes and
innovations, and preventing the organization from flying apart
under the pressure.*
H. Edward Wrapp

The
Managerial
System

The managerial system is primarily concerned with decision making for planning and controlling organizational endeavor. Up to this point we have considered in detail the organizational constraints that constitute the complex internal and external context of managerial decision making.

The central theme for Part 6 is set forth in Chapter 14, "Managerial Information-Decision Systems." One approach to the study of organizations is to concentrate on decision-making processes. Similarly, the managerial task can be approached through the study of decision making, particularly if it is broadly construed and includes implementation and a continuous flow of various types of decisions.

Concepts such as open and closed systems plus a programmability continuum provide useful frameworks for discussing managerial decision making. Chapter 15 is concerned with computational decision making, which assumes certainty in relatively closed systems. The concept of rationality is considered in detail, as are quantification and symbolic model building.

Chapter 16 is concerned with judgmental decision making in relatively open systems with uncertain conditions. Emphasis in this chapter is on the behavioral aspects of managerial decision making. It focuses on the human being as a decision maker and on the complexities that arise because of the impact of the beliefs and values that each individual brings to the decision-making process. Attention is devoted to group decision making and the impact of groups on individual decision makers.

Another way of viewing the managerial system would be to think of (1) mobilizing to accomplish a task or achieve an objective, (2) doing the job, and (3) checking the results. The mobilizing process is analogous to organizing and includes all the effort involved in getting ready to do something. The doing or executing function involves planning some action and implementing it. The checking activity is analogous to the control function, which is concerned with maintaining a dynamic equilibrium. This frame of reference provides a means of separating planning (Chapter 17) and controlling (Chapter 18) activities from other organizational considerations.

Managerial Information– Decision Systems

Fourteen

Thinking, problem solving, and decision making are fundamental to human behavior. Managerial decision making receives considerable attention from researchers and practitioners. It is a useful way of viewing what managers actually do in the process of coordinating organizational endeavor. Information is a vital ingredient for decision making. Information-decision systems pertain to both individual and organizational decision making and the attendant information flow relevant to the process. In this chapter we will explore managerial information-decision systems in terms of the following topics:

The Managerial Task
Pervasiveness of Decision Making
Possible Foci of Attention
The Decision-Making Process
Information and Decision Making
Management Information-Decision Systems
Future Promise and Problems

The Managerial Task

Everyone is a manager, if only of his or her personal affairs. Our primary concern, however, is management in organizational settings—the coordination of group effort toward an established purpose. This coordination is effected primarily (1) through people, (2) via techniques, (3) in an organization, and (4) toward objectives. The managerial system is the means of linking other primary subsystems of organizations.

Prescribing Managerial Behavior

The essence of the managerial task is shown in Figure 14.1, where managers are shown as the focal point of a number of interactive processes. The external arrows indicate a logical flow of attention and activities if one were to start an organization from scratch. However, it is more likely that a manager is part of an ongoing operation and that the various functions depicted are carried out in varying sequences. A key aspect of the manager's role is to maintain a dynamic equilibrium among these various elements and keep organizational endeavor "on target" with regard to its overall mission.

The model shown in Figure 14.1 is essentially prescriptive, indicating what managers should do to be effective. From the top management point of view, it is essential to maintain a total system view coupled with a situational perspec-

Figure 14.1   The Managerial Task

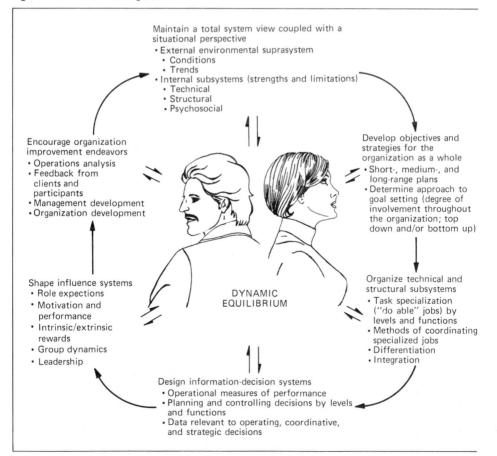

tive. Environmental opportunities and constraints are important considerations in designing or improving overall organizational systems. The same general approach is necessary at lower levels, even though perspectives may be more limited in scope and time horizon. For example, the manager of a department producing components for television sets would need to be aware of economic conditions in general but more concerned about the demand for television sets, specifically those marketed by the company. Production schedules for different models and for engineering design changes would also be of primary concern. These external and internal conditions, along with continuing awareness of the strengths and limitations of the subunit's capabilities, would provide the background for developing objectives and strategies, organizing technical and structural subsystems, and formalizing action plans as well as means of controlling activities and output. Also, regardless of the level in the organization, the manager is concerned with leadership functions—influencing behavior through the effective use of role expectations, motivation principles, group dynamics, and reward systems. Similarly, every manager should encourage organization improvement via a variety of general approaches and specific techniques, depending on the particular situation.

The various functions shown in Figure 14.1 are carried out explicitly or implicitly by all managers. Much of the effort in prescribing better managerial practice has been directed toward making this process more explicit—providing a framework for carrying out the managerial task within a total, integrated system. Management by objectives and results (MBO/R) is an example of such an approach and will be discussed in detail in Chapter 17. The focal point is results rather than activities, even though it is recognized that some managerial attention will be devoted to routine duties, reacting to crises, and putting out fires. MBO/R is an explicit process for maintaining a dynamic equilibrium among a number of activities and focusing them toward relevant goals. The managerial task includes setting long-range goals and short-range objectives; it includes designing sociotechnical systems, information-decision systems, and reward systems; and it includes a variety of organization improvement endeavors. Explicit attention to objectives, action plans, and results comprises a natural, functional means of integrating these essential endeavors.

Describing Managerial Behavior

So far our discussion has been generally prescriptive—what managers should do in order to carry out their task of coordinating human and material resources toward objective accomplishment—and it is reasonably clear that many managers do what is indicated in the model. However, they aren't likely to carry out the steps as clearly nor in the sequences indicated in Figure 14.1. Well, if they don't follow the prescriptions exactly, what do they do? On the basis of his own observations of managers and a review of other related research, Mintzberg suggests that the top manager's job can be described in terms of various roles or organized sets of behaviors that are identified with a position. Formal status and authority give rise to three interpersonal roles, three informational roles, and four decisional roles. [1]

Interpersonal roles: figurehead, leader, liaison

Informational roles: monitor, disseminator, spokesperson

Decisional roles: entrepreneur, disturbance handler, resource allocator, negotiator

These various roles can be illustrated from everyday experience. The pulpmill manager *(figurehead)* greets the high school contemporary problems class to discuss pollution problems. The sales manager *(leader)* exhorts her subordinates to close more sales in order to meet this month's quota and earn individual and group bonuses. The project manager *(liaison)* meets with the chief of engineering design at lunch in order to see if the new specifications will be ready on time. The city manager *monitors* federal and state legislation in order to determine what impact it will have on local funding. He also *disseminates* such information in staff meetings so that it will reach appropriate subordinates. The president of a local savings and loan association *(spokesperson)* testifies before the Senate Banking Committee to lobby for authorization to provide checking and/or other services that have traditionally been reserved to banks. Top managers, regardless of the size of the company, are often involved in *entrepreneurial* endeavors that result in adaptation to changing conditions. For example, if the desired legislation is forthcoming, the savings and loan association president proceeds with full-service banking and a promotional program to call it to the attention of customers. As much as managers try to plan, organize, coordinate, and control activities in a reasonably logical and straightforward manner, much of their time is spent in *handling disturbances,* reacting to crises, and fending off external pressures. When a ten-year-old student who had been expelled sets a fire that destroys half of the building, the principal must react by finding substitute space and coordinating the activities of students, faculty, administrative staff, and parents in implementing a revised plan. The mayor is a *resource allocator* as she attempts to balance the programs proposed by department directors with the anticipated flow of revenues for the coming year. The *negotiating* role is broadly construed to include more than labor-management relations. For example, the executive vice president can be involved in negotiations among several department managers and the director of systems development with regard to the priorities for several computerization projects.

These various roles are carried out to some extent by all managers. However, the amount of time spent may vary with levels or functions. A top manager, for example, is likely to spend relatively more time being a figurehead,

---

1 Henry Mintzberg, "The Manager's Role: Folklore and Fact," *Harvard Business Review,* July–August 1975, pp. 49–61.

spokesperson, or entrepeneur than is a production supervisor. Mintzberg's research indicated that sales managers spent relatively more of their time in interpersonal roles; production managers emphasized decisional roles; and staff managers spent the most time in informational roles.[2] Top managers tend to be involved in many activities (seemingly simultaneously) for relatively short periods of time. It is difficult to separate the various roles and specify that a particular activity is purely interpersonal, or informational, or decisional.

Logical and Intuitive Approaches

Current research on left brain and right brain functioning is relevant to our discussion of prescriptions for and descriptions of managerial behavior.[3] The left hemisphere operates rationally; it takes information bit by bit and processes linearly, as in reading a report. The left brain also controls verbal communication, as well as logical and mathematical reasoning. The right hemisphere, on the other hand, operates intuitively; it dreams and perceives in total images. The right brain controls creativity and artistic capabilities. Our culture, particularly the educational system, tends to overemphasize development of the left hemisphere with less attention to the right.[4] Management education has proceeded along the same lines, emphasizing science, rationality, and logical principles of planning, organizing, coordinating, and controlling activity. Less emphasis has been placed on management as an art, visualizing organizations as total systems, and developing the flexibility appropriate for coping with situational contingencies. In relating his research to the split brain concept, Mintzberg suggests that traditional prescriptions for managerial functions are left-brained, but that, according to his observations, top management is largely an intuitive function. The approaches of the managers he observed seemed to be relational and holistic rather than logical and linear, step-by-step actions.[5]

The following findings support this view:

Managers prefer oral face-to-face communications. Face-to-face communication involves more than linear processing. Gestures, facial expressions, voice tone, and the warp and woof of conversation *all* go into holistic impressions left by oral communication. Top managers particularly seem to gather a large percentage (more than 75%) of their information for decision making in this way.

Managers collect and use soft data. Top managers in particular seldom looked at accounting and other MIS data. They preferred to gather hearsay and general feelings, then form overall impressions.

2 Ibid., p. 59.

3 Wayne Sage, "The Split Brain Lab," *Human Behavior*, June 1976, pp. 25–28.

4 Madeleine Hunter, "Right Brained Kids in Left Brained Schools," *Today's Education*, November–December 1976, pp. 45–48.

5 Henry Mintzberg, "Planning on the Left Side and Managing on the Right," *Harvard Business Review*, July–August 1976, pp. 49–58.

Managers have difficulty disseminating information to their employees. For all the soft data gathering managers go through, they have trouble communicating their models to employees. They have a "dilemma of delegation." What they know in a "right brain" fashion may be inaccessible to the "left brain" or communicative functioning.

Managers don't make decisions by logical analysis. In a study of strategic decision making, only 18 of 83 choices were made by using an explicit strategy. The bulk of the decisions were made intuitively. [6]

How can we integrate our prescriptions for managers with descriptions of their actual behavior? A first approximation is to recognize that top executives often rely on analytical work done by middle and lower-level managers—e.g., engineers, accountants, and market researchers. Also, many managers rely on staff assistants (who often have technical expertise) to analyze complex problems and develop alternative plans for consideration, selection, and implementation. Moreover, the logical-analytical and the intuitive-conceptual approaches are not mutually exclusive; both are important. Their relevance varies with the level in the organization and/or the type of problem involved. Therefore, both left-brain and right-brain skills are necessary in carrying out the managerial task and should be encouraged.

An important step is for managers to recognize how they spend their time. If they decide that more attention should be devoted to strategic issues, action plans, and control processes, then relatively large blocks of time must be set aside and allocated to these important tasks. The necessary time can only be obtained by eliminating some activities and delegating others. [7]

Management and Decision Making

To decide means to pass judgment or to make up one's mind. It implies two or more alternatives under consideration, with the decision maker choosing one of them to end his or her deliberation. Behavior is goal-oriented, and human beings move toward goals by making decisions and implementing them.

An integral element of the managerial task is organizational decision making—choosing an overall strategy, setting specific objectives, designing structures and processes, selecting people, delegating responsibility, evaluating results, and intiating changes. Our understanding of management can be enhanced by viewing it from a decision-making perspective and recognizing that managerial decision making is a sequential process rather than an act, in that problems are seldom resolved once and for all. Subsequent decisions are affected by previous decisions and developments over time. It is a process that includes searching out

6 "What Managers Really Do . . . and Why They Do It," *Training,* October 1976, p. 92.

7 Peter F. Drucker, *The Effective Executive,* Harper & Row, Publishers, New York, 1967; R. Alec Mackenzie, *The Time Trap,* McGraw-Hill Book Company, New York, 1972.

and recognizing problems as well as analyzing them (inventing, developing, and evaluating alternatives) and choosing courses of action to be implemented.

A wide spectrum of decision-making methods are relevant to the managerial system. Within the operating subsystem there is relative certainty; hence, well-defined problems can be solved via straightforward computational techniques. For long-range strategy, the board of directors and top management are faced with considerable uncertainty and novel, ill-structured problems. Computational approaches are less appropriate for decision making at the strategic level except for subparts of some problems. For managers at all levels, subjective judgment plays an important part in many decisions.

Pervasiveness of Decision Making

Decision making is fundamental to organism and organization behavior. It provides the means for control and allows coherence in systems.

The living systems are a special subset of the set of all possible concrete systems, composed of the plants and the animals. They all have the following characteristics (among others):

They are open systems. . . .

They contain a decider, the essential critical subsystem which controls the entire system, causing its subsystems and components to coact, without which there is no system. [8]

From the moment we decide to (1) turn off the alarm, (2) roll over, and (3) go back to sleep, until we reset it (optimistically!) late that night, we are making decisions. Which shoes should I wear? How should I respond to the customer complaint? Where shall we eat lunch? Shall we invest more money in developing a "cloud nine" product idea? And so on throughout the day. We make personal and organizational decisions endlessly.

All managerial activity might be considered decision making. For example, Simon states, "What part does decision making play in managing? I shall find it convenient to take mild liberties with the English language by using 'decision making' as though it were synonymous with 'managing.' " [9] If *all* behavior results from decision making and if managing is a particular kind of behavior, then managing is decision making. Obviously, there are other useful ways to view management—concentration on processes or functions, for example. But decision making is one of the most important tasks of managers. It pervades the perform-

---

8 James G. Miller, "Living Systems: Basic Concepts," *Behavioral Science,* July 1965, pp. 203–204.

9 Herbert A. Simon, *The New Science of Management Decision,* Harper & Row, Publishers, Inc., New York, 1960, p. 1.

ance of all managerial functions. [10] In this context management can be studied in terms of decisions made in planning, organizing, or controlling enterprise activities. In short, decision making is a pervasive activity and provides a useful approach for studying managerial systems.

Conscious or Unconscious

The examples cited above refer to conscious or deliberate choices among alternatives. However, even within this set of examples we have a gradation of consciousness from the relatively automatic shutting off of the alarm to the relatively contemplative approach invoked when deciding on additional investments in new product development.

It seems to us unnecessarily restrictive to require conscious behavior for decision making. It is useful to consider all behavior in the framework of decision making and recognize that there is a gradation of consciousness involved. Such a framework allows the use of terms such as **programmed** and **nonprogrammed decisions.** Relatively automatic (programmed) decisions such as reflex actions appear to be completely unconscious. However, even this type of behavior, according to evolutionists, has been learned over millions of years. For instinctive or impulsive reactions, decisions and behavior are relatively unconscious. Habits are a form of relatively programmed decisions. At some point deliberate consideration was required. Through repetitive processes, however, a choice becomes more and more automatic, given similar stimuli. Organizations develop habits in standard operating procedures and computer programs for coping with repetitive situations. This conserves time and energy that management can devote to nonprogrammable problems. However, habits can stifle innovation—programmed activity can increase to absorb available time.

Within the range of nonprogrammed decision making, there is considerable variation. There is a continuum from one-time decisions such as the Watergate episode or the B-1 bomber controversy to problems that may occur periodically but may call for modified approaches because of changing internal conditions or external environmental factors.

A Basic Unit of Behavior

The question of whether or not unconscious behavior involves decision making has deeper roots in psychological theory. Behaviorists contend that the physiological pattern of the reflex arc explains the stimulus-response relationship.

---

10 This approach is emphasized in the following framework: "*Model-building, model-solving,* and ultimately *model use* are . . . the strongest means by which to consider *decision-making,* which in turn can be viewed as the gateway to the more complex management functions." Martin K. Starr, *Management: A Modern Approach,* Harcourt Brace Jovanovich, Inc., New York, 1971, p. viii.

This school of thought explains behavior in terms of learning new conditioned responses through experience.

Cognitive theorists, on the other hand, support the idea that there is some mediating force between stimulus and response that is much more complex than a simple reflex arc. The "image," or sum total of past experience, is often cited as the mediating force.[11]

The difference between the two positions is illustrated by the following statement:

[The brain] is far more like a map control room than it is like an old-fashioned telephone exchange. The stimuli, which are allowed in, are not connected by just simple one-to-one switches to the outgoing responses. Rather, the incoming impulses are usually worked over and elaborated in the central control room into a tentative, cognitivelike map of the environment. And it is this tentative map, indicating routes and paths and environmental relationships, which finally determines what responses, if any, the animal will finally release.[12]

Miller, Galanter, and Pribram support the cognitive theorists and offer the TOTE (Test-Operate-Test-Exit) unit of behavior (see Figure 14.2) as an alternative to the reflex arc.[13] This unit incorporates the notion of feedback control and suggests that actions are guided constantly by the outcomes of various tests. An organism continually tests the situation for congruity or incongruity. If congruity exists, i.e., if the situation is consonant with some plan or expectation, no further action is called for. However, if the test indicates incongruity, some operation is invoked.

Figure 14.2   The Tote Unit

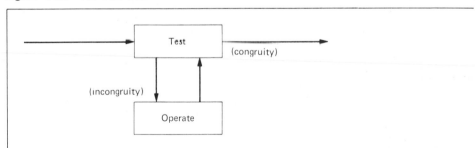

George A. Miller, Eugene Galanter, and Karl H. Pribram, *Plans and the Structure of Behavior,* Holt, Rinehart and Winston, Inc., New York, 1960, p. 26.

11 Kenneth E. Boulding, *The Image,* The University of Michigan Press, Ann Arbor, Mich., 1966.

12 Edward C. Tolman, "Cognitive Maps in Rats and Man," *Psychological Review,* July 1948, pp. 189–208.

13 "It seems obvious to us that a great deal more goes on between the stimulus and the response than can be accounted for by a simple statement about associative strengths. . . . Our theoretical preferences are all on the side of the cognitive theorists. Life is complicated." George A. Miller, Eugene Galanter, and Karl H. Pribram, *Plans and the Structure of Behavior,* Holt, Rinehart and Winston, Inc., New York, 1960, p. 9.

Tests are made repeatedly in order to indicate whether or not the operation should continue.

For example, when parking an automobile parallel to the curb, the driver continually *tests* the situation to ascertain how close he or she has come to achieving the goal. Information concerning distance from the curb and/or other automobiles is processed and checked against the plan. If the current position fits the plan *(congruity),* the driver proceeds to turn off the ignition, set the brake, and get out. If there is *incongruity,* the driver will continue to maneuver *(operate)* the car toward the goal (parking).

The TOTE unit is purposely quite similar to the basic feedback loop in computer programming. Organism behavior is considered analogous to the hierarchical approach used in developing computer programs. Large feedback loops for complete tasks are comprised of many nested subloops, all the way down to the basic instruction step.

In this scheme it appears that decisions are made at all levels, conscious or not. Reflex actions are highly programmed behavior patterns but still involve rapid use of TOTE units to execute the behavior in question. Conscious, deliberate, and cogitative decision processes could also be described under the general model of the TOTE unit. The overall scheme, of which the TOTE unit is the basic unit of analysis, includes the following concepts:

Image. All the accumulated, organized knowledge that a person has about himself and his environment.

Plan. A rough sketch of some course of action (strategy) as well as more detailed operating procedures (tactics).

Execution. Carrying out a plan step by step, completing one part and then moving to the next. It may involve overt action or only the collection and/or transformation of information. [14]

The image provides the environment for planning, which results in strategy, tactics, and execution. Decision making is involved at all levels. This schema is presented for organism behavior, but it could refer to organizations as well. Organizations have images, or "character," which is the sum total of their past experience. They have master plans or strategies, and they operate via tactical, sequential steps. Feedback control is used to check actual results against plans, thus initiating corrective action if needed. We will return to this framework in Chapters 17 and 18, "Managerial Planning" and "Organization Control." The purpose here is to illustrate the pervasiveness of decision making and show how a basic feedback or decision unit can be used to describe all behavior on a continuum of programmability or unconsciousness-consciousness.

[14] Ibid., pp. 16–18.

Possible
Foci of
Attention

The voluminous literature on decision making seems to stem from two basic points of view, descriptive and prescriptive, and to congregate at three levels of interest. The simplified model in Figure 14.3 refers to the decision itself, the decision maker, and the process used. The various disciplines engaged in research on decision making concentrate on whichever focus of attention is most meaningful to them. Management science techniques have emphasized maximization principles in the choice among alternatives. Some psychologists have concentrated on the individual as the decision maker, and others have been concerned with the impact of reference groups on decision making. Considerable attention has been devoted to the decision-making process, both normatively and descriptively. Much has been written on how to make optimal decisions, or at least better decisions than before.[15] A body of knowledge has developed from describing decision processes in real organizations.[16] Such research is concerned primarily with understanding more about how decision makers actually behave, rather than with prescribing better ways to make decisions.[17]

Several dimensions of importance to managerial decision making are shown in Figure 14.4. The context of the decision maker varies from relatively closed to relatively open systems. If the decision maker is continually interacting

Figure 14.3   Levels at Which Decision Making Has Been Studied, With Illustrative Research Questions

	Descriptions of Behavior (What is Happening or What Has Happened)	Prescriptive or Normative Model Building (What Ought to Happen)
The decision	What decisions are made in an organization? How do these decisions "turn out"?	What is an optimal decision? How can decisions be improved?
The decision maker	What are the characteristics of the decision makers in the organization? What factors influence the behavior of decision makers?	How should a rational decision maker behave?
The decision process	How are decisions actually made in the organization?	How should decisions be made in an organization?

Albert H. Rubenstein and Chadwick J. Haberstroh (eds.), *Some Theories of Organization,* rev. ed., Richard D. Irwin, Inc., and the Dorsey Press, Homewood, Ill., 1966, p. 578.

15 Charles H. Kepner and Benjamin B. Tregoe, *The Rational Manager,* McGraw-Hill Book Company, New York, 1965.

16 Graham T. Allison, *Essence of Decision,* Little, Brown and Company, Boston, 1971.

17 Henry Mintzberg, *The Nature of Managerial Work,* Harper & Row, Publishers, Inc., New York, 1973.

Figure 14.4   Several Dimensions of Decision Making

	Contextual Systems	
Closed		Open

	General Processes	
Programmable		Nonprogrammable

	Specific Techniques	
Computational		Judgmental

with the "environment," the system is relatively open. Informational inputs are gathered from diverse sources and become a part of the process. However, if the decision maker does not seek additional information, he or she tends to close the system and routinize the process. Alexis and Wilson describe this phenomenon as follows:

In closed models a few dimensions of the decision environment are selected and admitted into the decision process: action-outcome relations, utility, and so on. The decision maker is assumed to be a logical, methodical maximizer. In contrast, the open decision model parallels an "open system." Like the open system, it is continually influenced by its total environment, and, of course, it also influences the environment. Decisions shape as well as mirror the environment. Contrary to the assumptions of closed decision models, the open model does not assume that the decision maker can recognize all goals and feasible alternatives. A more realistic view of his capabilities is emphasized. He is viewed as a complex mixture of many elements, including his culture, his personality, and his aspirations. [18]

   With human beings in the decision process, the system can vary from relatively open to relatively closed, depending on the individual's propensity and the given situation. In many cases the human element has been eliminated; then the system becomes even more closed. In such cases, computer programs have been developed to handle routine, repetitive decisions.

   The dimension of programmability parallels the open-closed continuum of the contextual system. In those cases in which the contextual complexity is included, the process becomes relatively nonprogrammable. That is, it becomes very difficult to develop a program that eliminates the human element from the decision-making process.

18 Marcus Alexis and Charles Z. Wilson, *Organizational Decision Making,* © 1967, p. 158. Reprinted by permission of Prentice-Hall, Inc., Englewood Cliffs, N.J.

Another dimension relates to specific techniques that may be used. Computational techniques can be programmed to supplant human decision makers when the contextual system is relatively closed. In open systems more judgment is involved, and hence the process cannot be programmed explicitly. In general, these three dimensions parallel each other and provide a meaningful framework for understanding managerial decision making.

In Chapter 15 we will be concerned with computational techniques that can be used by managers in relatively closed systems. In Chapter 16 we will stress the human element—judgmental decision making in open-system contexts. It is recognized that there is no evident demarcation between the open and the closed, the programmable and the nonprogrammable, and the computational and the judgmental dimensions. Rather, there is a gradation along each of these continua. Recognizing the artificial dichotomy, we will discuss the polar positions in the two following chapters.

Regardless of the assumptions concerning the dimensions described above, there is a general model that can facilitate understanding the decision-making process. This general model can be applied computationally or judgmentally, and it can refer to open or closed systems, which may determine its degree of programmability.

The Decision-Making Process

Simon suggests four basic ingredients or phases in the decision-making process.

The first phase of the decision-making process—searching the environment for conditions calling for decision—I shall call *intelligence* activity (borrowing the military meaning of intelligence).

The second phase—inventing, developing, and analyzing possible courses of action—I shall call *design* activity.

The third phase—selecting a particular course of action from those available—I shall call *choice* activity.

The fourth phase, assessing past choices, I shall call *review* activity. [19]

These are elaborations of the general, three-step process outlined by Dewey long ago. [20] The steps in a decision-making process normally are not as discrete as a list would indicate. Much of the decision-making activity goes on simultaneously. That is, evaluation of alternatives can point up another problem to be solved.

19 Herbert A. Simon, *The New Science of Management Decision,* rev. ed., Prentice-Hall, Inc., Englewood Cliffs, N.J., 1977, pp. 40–41.

20 What is the problem? What are the alternatives? Which alternative is best? John Dewey, *How We Think,* D.C. Heath and Company, Boston, 1910, pp. 101–105.

Usually there are a number of problems "in the wind." Thus, the manager is involved simultaneously in intelligence, design, and choice activity. Attempts at designing alternative courses of action may turn up additional problems, setting off new intelligence activities. A continuing problem-solving cycle or decision process might contain a series of subcycles. As the system becomes more complex, it is obvious that refined systems of information flow and tools of analysis must be developed in order to facilitate the decision process.

Figure 14.5 shows a flow chart of the decision-making process. As indicated, there are a number of factors that make up the context for the problem and the decision maker. This could also be termed the state of nature. Some of the factors are external and some are internal to the decision maker. His or her "image" or value system will have an effect on the decision-making process at several stages. Theoretically, the number of alternative solutions could be infinite. However, for all practice purposes only a finite number can be verbalized and isolated.

The next step involves the assessment of the probable future effects of the various alternatives specified. This phase involves a predicting system that may tend toward objectivity or subjectivity, depending on the degree of uncertainty involved. If recorded past experience is available, the probabilities of various outcomes may be ascertained quite readily. With less information, especially for new or unique problems, prediction becomes more speculative and subjective. However, the decision maker does assess the future in some manner—consciously or unconsciously, objectively or subjectively.

Once the effects have been anticipated and an estimate made of the probability of each occurrence, the decision maker then assesses the importance of a particular outcome. If it is inconsequential, it may be discarded from further consideration. If, however, a particular outcome is crucial (even with only a slight chance of occurrence), it may weigh heavily in the decision process. An example is the problem of live virus in vaccine when there might be only a slight (even remote) possibility of actual disease. Yet if the disease is fatal, it becomes a critical factor in the decision process, and steps must be taken to ensure that it does not occur. Space flight, where 95 percent reliability is not good enough, presents a similar example.

After the alternatives have been scrutinized and importance attached to the various outcomes, the decision maker evalutes the relevant information and chooses. Each decision then feeds back into the environment of subsequent decisions.

Obviously, managers do not approach all decisions explicitly via a framework such as shown in Figure 14.5. Many routine or programmed activities are evident in individual and organizational behavior. For nonroutine or nonprogrammed situations, a process such as the one outlined (or something similar) is often followed. Such a diagram is a simplification of the decision-making process; yet it is useful to identify the process explicitly in order to understand it better.

Considerably more detail could be developed for a particular phase of

Figure 14.5 Flow Chart of the Decision-Making Process

Some value framework is invoked when identifying "appropriate" alternatives, attaching importance to the effects anticipated, and balancing the alternatives in the final evaluation. (Refer to items with single asterisk in the figure.) The prediction system is involved in the stages indicated by the double asterisk. Probability of occurrence ranges between 0 and 1—along the continuum of certainty and uncertainty (including risk). Much subjective probability is utilized in the typical decision-making process. A system of information flow is vital to the decision-making process—in the intelligence activity involved in pinpointing problems, in the search activity involved in identifying alternatives, and in the evaluation process leading to a choice.

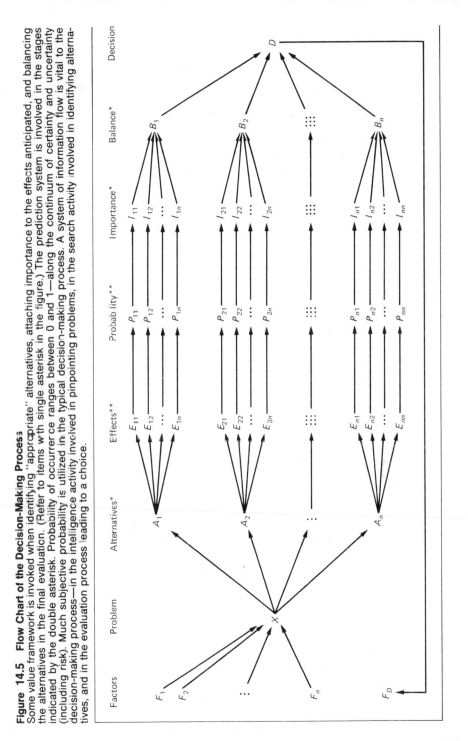

the decision process. For example, in developing alternatives, the complex question of creativity arises. How can innovation be fostered? Descriptive research suggests that most decisions are incremental; that is, they move only a slight way from the approach previously used, particularly if it was successful. In a sense this is satisficing behavior—accepting a workable alternative without being overly concerned that it is "the best."

Information and Decision Making

A system of information flow is vital to the decision-making process. Information is the raw material of intelligence that touches off the recognition that a decision is to be made. Information is essential in evaluating alternative courses of action. A decision maker can be viewed as an information processing system. These two points of view might be termed the micro and macro aspects of information-decision systems.

Communication is intercourse by words, letters, or similar means, and it involves interchange of thoughts or opinions. It also presents the concept of communication systems, for example, telephone, telegraph, or television. Communication implies information; the terms are part of the same family. In the broadest sense information has been defined as "that which is communicated."

Information is often evaluated in terms of its pertinence for decision making. Facts, numbers, and data are processed to provide meaningful information—an increment of knowledge that alters the degree of uncertainty in a particular situation. For example, miscellaneous accounting data provide information when arrayed in balance sheets and income statements. Ratio analysis and graphic displays of pertinent relationships provide even more meaningful information. But if the problem is one of evaluating the effectiveness of a new advertising campaign, traditional accounting data, however elaborately processed, may be meaningless. Thus, what constitutes "information" depends on the problem at hand and the decision maker's frame of reference.

Information can be conveyed in many ways, both formally and informally. Periodic reports with a standard format provide formal feedback on the operating system. The *grapevine* illustrates how informal, interpersonal relationships provide channels of communication. Information is the substance of communications systems. In its various forms—electronic impulses, written or spoken words, informal or formal reports—information is a basic ingredient for decision making.

For many problem-solving tasks, the individual has stored knowledge that he or she brings to bear in the decision-making process. This knowledge or "experience" may be sufficient (at least as the individual sees it) to handle the problem. On the other hand, he or she may seek additional information and hence require service from formal or informal communication systems.

Some psychologists have suggested that mental illness results from information overload. If individuals can remain in equilibrium with their environment, they are healthy. In a sense, they are able to cope with external conditions and maintain a "normal" role in society. If they are unable to process information—both internal and external flows—efficiently, however, a condition of information overload occurs and there is a breakdown in the system. The overload may develop because of the inability to screen out irrelevant data for the individual's decision-making tasks. When a person loses touch with reality, he or she is described as mentally ill.

Information Flow and Organization

Organizations have been faced with dynamic world conditions, rapidly changing technology, changing markets, and other similar phenomena that have required adaptation on their part. Adjustments have been made, but without recognition, in many cases, of the impact of organizational changes on communication systems. Thus, much information that was appropriate under older arrangements has now become obsolete. Furthermore, additional types of information are urgently needed in order to plan and control current operations. "Management often loses sight of the seemingly obvious and simple relationship between organization structure and information needs. Companies very seldom follow up on reorganizations with penetrating reappraisals of their information systems, and managers given new responsibilities and decision-making authority often do not receive all the information they require."[21]

Information geared to managing functions such as engineering, production, and distribution may be irrelevant if a company is reorganized along product lines. Schedule and cost data (among others) per product are essential in order to manage material and energy flow through the total system. Thus, information flow should be adjusted to reflect decision-making needs in the revised organization.

Management Information-Decision Systems

Figure 14.6 shows a skeletal model of an organization with the basic flow of information necessary for the managerial system. Management considers internal and environmental information in the process of establishing objectives (strategic level). Premises with regard to governmental relations, political conditions, the competitive situation, customer needs and desires, internal capabilities, and

---

21 D. Ronald Daniel, "Management Information Crisis," *Harvard Business Review,* September–October 1961, pp. 112–113.

many other factors evolve over a period of time and form a frame of reference for strategic and comprehensive planning. Plans for repetitive and nonrepetitive activities are transmitted to the operating system and to storage in the coordination and control systems for later comparison with operating results (coordinative and operating levels). Detailed orders, instructions, and specifications flow to the operating system.

Feedback is obtained on the output of the system in terms of quality, quantity, cost, and so on. The operating system is monitored in order to maintain process control, and input inspection provides feedback at the earliest stage in the operating system. Information flow is an integral part of the control system because it provides the means of comparing results with plans. Feedback data from various phases of the operating system are collected and analyzed. The analysis involves processing data, developing information, and comparing the results with plans. Decisions are also made within the control system itself because routine adjustments can be preprogrammed in the set of procedures or instructions.

Figure 14.6   Information Flow in an Organization

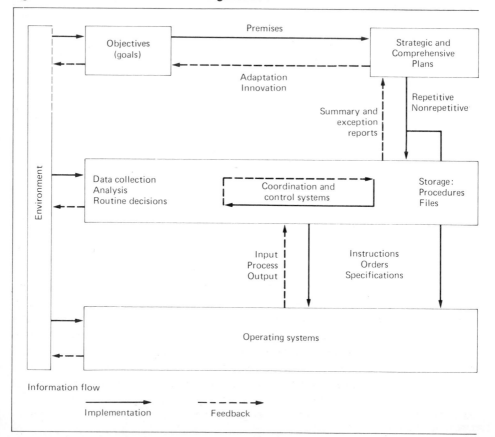

Within the control system there is a flow of information to implement changes to the program based on feedback from the operating system. Thus, procedures are changed and files updated simultaneously with routine decision making and adjustments to the operating system.

Summary and exception reports are generated by the control system and become a part of a higher-level process of review and evaluation that may lead to adaptation or innovation of goals. Subsequent planning activity reflects such feedback, and the entire process is repeated. In time an organization "learns" through the process of planning, implementation, and feedback.[22] Approaches to decision making and the propensity to select certain ends and means change as organizational value systems evolve. This basic or simplified model of information flow can be applied to any organization; it shows the necessary flow of information, regardless of the sophistication of the data processing technology involved.

Although some information exchange with the environment is evident at each level, the boundary is more permeable where top management is concerned. The strategic subsystem is primarily responsible for interacting with the environment and maintaining the organization in a dynamic equilibrium. Nevertheless, some interchange of information occurs between the environment and managers in the operating and coordinative subsystems. Such information is mixed with internal flows to provide the total "picture" for managers at all levels.

The differential nature of the management information-decision system by levels or subsystems is emphasized in Figure 14.7, which shows the relationship of data and information bases. Data processing systems have been developed to facilitate many organizational functions or transactions—payroll, inventory control, accounting (such as accounts payable or accounts receivable), and so on. Such data processing systems provide the raw material for management information-decision systems.

While all data could be considered part of an organizational information base, it is obvious that for any fairly large and complex organization such an approach would be impossible. Therefore, most systems include exception reporting, wherein pertinent information from the various internal data processing activities becomes part of the overall information base when it is brought to the attention of appropriate decision makers. As indicated in Figure 14.7, a considerable amount of such information is used in controlling the operating subsystem of the organization. Some of the internal information is useful for strategic planning. Such information is coupled with that gathered from external sources in order to provide appropriate information for decision making at the top level. Most of the relevant external information flows into the organization through the strategic subsystem.[23] However, some of it comes in via the coordinative and operating

22 Richard M. Cyert and James G. March, *A Behavioral Theory of the Firm*, Prentice-Hall, Inc., Englewood Cliffs, N.J. 1963, p. 123.

23 Judson Gooding, "It's No Easy Trick to Be the Well-Informed Executive," *Fortune*, January, 1973, pp. 85–89.

Figure 14.7   Relationship of Data and Management Information-Decision Systems

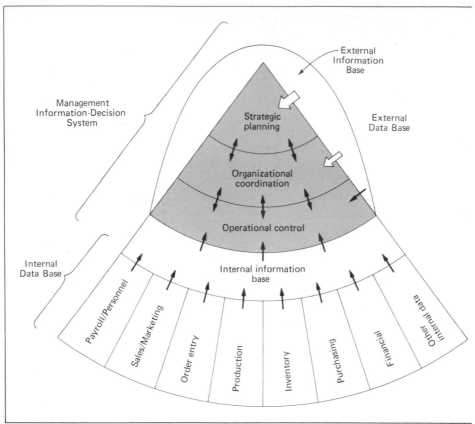

subsystems as well. Information used in the coordinative subsystem comes from both operations and strategic planning activities.

In an age of increasingly sophisticated computerization, it may be possible to include all data from all subsystems in a management information-decision system. But, even if it were possible, it is not clear that it would be an efficient use of resources. The system should be evaluated on the basis of cost/benefit analysis. A balance should be maintained between the cost of the system and the value of the information generated.

Much attention has been focused on computerized management information systems (MIS).[24] However, it is important to recognize that managerial decision making typically requires input of much information—opinions, for ex-

24 "Management Information System: The combination of human and computer-based resources that results in the collection, storage, retrieval, communication, and use of data for the purpose of efficient management of operations and for business planning." Joseph F. Kelly, *Computerized Management Information Systems,* The Macmillan Company, New York, 1970, p. 5.

ample—that cannot be computerized. Thus, overall management information-decision systems should be designed to include explicit attention to nonquantifiable inputs as well as those that result from computerized data processing applications. [25]

Several kinds of information are required for planning: environmental information, competitive information, and internal information. While most companies have some systematic approach to development of internal information for planning purposes, many do not have formal systems at the strategic level for developing information concerning competitors' plans, programs, and past performance. Nor do they deal in a systematic fashion with the social, political, and economic environment of the industry or industries within which they operate. Formal recognition of the decisions that must be made at various points and of the type of information required should point the way toward development of information flows that will be helpful. [26]

The differences between information appropriate for planning purposes and that appropriate for control purposes indicate the importance of carefully designing information-decision systems. Blind adherence to organizational patterns for the flow of information often will hamper the development of an optimal system. Particularly where there have been organizational adjustments and there is a mixture of functional organization and program or product organization, the development of an information-decision system becomes critical.

Designing
Information
Systems

Much of the literature on design emphasizes the development of mechanized systems. Electronic computers have fostered the design of sophisticated systems of information flow, but the analysis involved is applicable to information-decision systems of all kinds—computerized or not. Indeed, designing with reference to existing equipment may result in perpetuating the processing of data irrelevant to management.

Another hazard in designing information systems is that of attempting to develop as much data as possible for use in the system. Voluminous data of many types might be collected and stored in case they are needed at some point in time. It is easy to see that massive amounts of useless data might result. [27]

The best approach is oriented to decision making. It minimizes the development of useless information because only data likely to be meaningful in

25 John Dearden, "MIS Is a Mirage," *Harvard Business Review,* January–February 1972, pp. 90–99.

26 Charles D. Schewe and James L. Wick, "Guide to MIS User Satisfaction," *Journal of Systems Management,* June 1977, pp. 6–10.

27 Henry C. Lucas, Jr., "An Empirical Study of a Framework for Information Systems," *Decision Sciences,* January 1974, pp. 102–113.

decision making at various points are collected. This approach emphasizes the problem involved rather than techniques of analysis. The objective is not optimization of data processing systems; rather, the objective is development of better information-decision systems for management.

Upon installation, the system must be debugged and modified in order to fit the situation. Revised systems do not resemble interchangeable parts. The approach is more like fine watchmaking, where individual parts often must be filed and fitted in order to complement the other parts of the system. This process is vital and requires great skill. Once installed, debugged, and modified, the subsystem under study becomes a part of the total system. The analyst can then look toward other parts of the overall system, possibly those systems that are interconnected with the one most recently under scrutiny. The systems-review function requires periodic checking to ensure that all subsystems maintain their complementary nature and are integrated toward efficient accomplishment of the goals of the system as a whole.

Responsibility for Information Systems Design

Implementation is implicit in the connotation of systems design; otherwise, it would be an empty exercise. Therefore, the interface between managers and information system designers is critical, and mutual understanding should be fostered in order to maximize returns from design efforts. The information-decision system should be tailored to the needs of the organization and adapted continually as circumstances change. Management should play a large and active role in design projects in order to ensure the development of useful systems.

In a general sense, managers engage in systems design work on a day-to-day basis. They plan activities and organize systems to accomplish objectives. However, staff groups have evolved for tasks such as long-range planning, organization studies, and systems design. Special effort should be made to make such activities an extension of the manager's role rather than a separate function.

Four factors interact to determine success in designing and implementing management information systems:

1 Knowledge of decision-making requirements and information needs
2 Interest and ability to implement the system
3 Technical competence in system design
4 Motivation to change the system

Line managers know their own information needs and can specify organizational decision-making requirements. Probability of success in system implementation is enhanced considerably if key managers are interested in the project. On the other hand, technical expertise and motivation for change are more likely to be found in staff groups. The answer would seem to be a team approach, with specialists supporting line managers who would be responsible for the project's success. A manager might work part time on such an effort or full time on a temporary basis if the task requires it.

Many systems do not get beyond the design phase because of unanticipated resistance of people essential to the implementation phase. The following remarks concerning a long-delayed project are typical: "Well, we have good systems. We have them on the drawing board. The hardware and software are okay, but the people are lousing up our system." [28] This condition can be avoided or ameliorated by involving the affected employees in (or at least keeping them aware of) the design process. The most elegant system imaginable will be useless if people are not motivated to implement it.

Future Promise and Problems

The accelerating technological developments in computer-oriented hardware and software systems allow increasing sophistication of information-decision systems. [29] Most discussions of future systems focus on the development of a complete data base pertinent to an organization's activity. Data can be processed to various degrees and be available when needed in decision-making processes. The information thus developed can be utilized in the entire spectrum of programmed-nonprogrammed decision. [30]

Of particular emphasis in some current and more future systems is the concept of fast response. That is, the system provides information to decision makers in a matter of seconds or minutes. The ultimate in this approach involves real-time systems, in which the data base is updated simultaneously with organizational activities and pertinent changes in the environment (airline reservation systems, for example). Decision makers have immediate access to such real-time information via many kinds of input-output devices, including visual consoles. Pertinent statistics or graphic information could be obtained in response to a managerial inquiry.

For data-processing systems in general, the least progress has come in input-output phases. The processing phase has become extremely sophisticated and fast enough to handle most needs. However, problems of source recording and high-speed transmission have not been solved adequately. At Citibank one

28 M. Scott Myers, "The Human Factor in Management Systems," *Journal of Systems Management,* November 1971, p. 13.
29 Robert G. Murdick and Joel E. Ross, "Future Management Information Systems," *Journal of Systems Management,* April and May 1972.
30 Frederic G. Withington, "Five Generations of Computers," *Harvard Business Review,* July–August, 1974, pp. 99–108.

goal was to make the input-output function as analogous as possible to the paper-based routines that people were accustomed to.[31] Voice recognition is another approach that makes use of natural human means of communication.[32] For management information systems an important link will be transmission of pertinent information to the point of decision on a timely basis. For top managers, given Mintzberg's description of their behavior, the means of interaction with the system will have to be as simple as the telephone.

General-purpose, on-line, visually oriented information systems have been used successfully by a variety of organizations. For example, one vice-president reports that "We are now able to put computer power in the hands of our end users—the engineers, operations, and service people."[33] The magnitude of the design task and the costs involved may make such systems out of reach for many organizations. However, technological developments may change this picture in time. Therefore, it is useful for managers in all organizations to be aware of the possibilities of fast-response information-decision systems that utilize a real-time data base.[34]

The
Browsing
Era

Time-sharing computing centers provide engineers, scientists, professors, students, and managers with a new kind of analytical capability—browsing. The decision maker actually evolves a problem-solving technique as he or she goes along; there is no necessity to be a programmer or to know anything about the detailed language of the machine.

The knowledge, versatility, and ingenuity of human problem solvers are coupled with the speed, precision, and storage capacity of computer systems in order to utilize the strengths of both. Trial-and-error learning with self-pacing and reinforcement by the system for correct responses has proven effective in a variety of school situations. Library research and medical diagnosis can also make use of interactive "conversations" with systems that provide fast response concerning (1) stored information or (2) sequential tests of input data against standard criteria. Law-enforcement agencies are making good use of similar systems in both on-line operations and browsing-type investigations. Simulation models of organizations and their environments provide managers with an opportunity to ask "what if" questions in order to test the potential interaction of policy decisions with assumptions about the future (economic conditions, competitor behavior, and the like).

---

31 Robert B. White, "A Prototype for the Automated Office," *Datamation,* April 1977, pp. 83–90.

32 Edward K. Yasaki, Sr., "Voice Recognition Comes of Age," *Datamation,* August 1976, pp. 65–68.

33 "Entry Time Sharing," *Data Processor,* January 1977, pp. 10–12.

34 Richard L. Nolan, "Computer Data Bases: The Future Is Now," *Harvard Business Review,* September–October 1973, pp. 98–114.

The conversational or browsing mode is helpful in getting managers to take advantage of technology that enhances their own inherent capabilities.

While there is a great deal of optimism with regard to the potential for automated information-decision systems, there is also a note of caution in the wind. Pessimistic points of view suggest that it will never work. However, in an era of accelerating technology such as our society has witnessed over the past several decades, this would seem to be a dangerous position. While we may remain skeptical, we should recall our attitude toward Buck Rogers and his space ships of the 1930s.

It is important to assess the total incremental cost of equipment and programming as well as the continuing expense of system development. Such costs should be analyzed in terms of potential benefits from better information and improved managerial decision making. This type of analysis should be made for any information system. We should be concerned with both effectiveness and efficiency. It is important to gear the system to the needs of the decision makers in the organization and to have it work. However, there are also constraints of efficiency that must be recognized. It is not enough that the system be technologically feasible.

It will be important to distinguish types of decisions and design the system accordingly. For example, the browsing concept relies heavily on fast-response systems. However, this does not necessarily require that all information provided by the system has to be on a real-time basis. Some information might be inserted into the data base as events take place. Other information might be fed in daily, weekly, monthly, or annually. A decision maker may want real-time information but be willing to wait several days or weeks for the information to be developed. Figure 14.8 shows a matrix of timeliness of information versus timeli-

Figure 14.8 Timeliness of Response versus Timeliness of Information in Management Information-Decision Systems

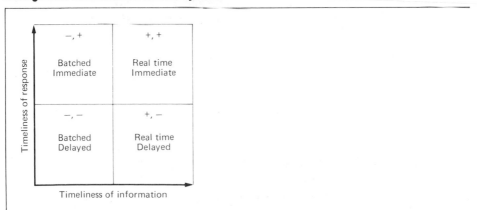

ness of response. Obviously, the most difficult task for an information-decision system is to provide real-time information on a fast-response basis.

Summary

The managerial system is the means of linking subsystems and integrating organizational activities toward relevant goals. The managerial task involves developing strategies, setting objectives, organizing technical and structural subsystems, designing information-decision systems, shaping influence systems, and encouraging improvement endeavors. Managers fill three primary roles—interpersonal, informational, and decisional.

The managerial system functions in organizations by means of information-decision systems. Decision making is a pervasive activity that is fundamental to organism or organization behavior. Types of decisions can be arrayed on a spectrum of programmability, and techniques used range from computational to judgmental.

The decision-making process involves recognition of a problem, identification of alternative courses of action, evaluation of potential outcomes, and a choice. Information is the raw material for the decision-making process; it includes data that are processed meaningfully for a particular decision problem.

An information-decision system is the means by which management carries out its day-to-day functions at all levels—strategic, coordinative, and operating. It involves decision makers (individuals or organization units) and the attendant information flow. In designing information-decision systems, the best approach is a team effort with staff specialists supporting line managers who are primarily responsible for the project.

Accelerating technological developments in computer-oriented hardware and software systems will allow increasing sophistication of information-decision systems in the future. Prognostications focus on a data base for organizations that can be queried at any time by decision makers. The most sophisticated systems couple fast response with a real-time data base.

Questions and Problems

1 Develop a rationale for integrating (or explaining the differences between) prescriptions for the managerial task and descriptions (e.g., Mintzberg's or your own) of actual managerial behavior.

2 Define decision making and discuss three possible foci of attention in studying it.

3 Relate the dimensions of decision making (closed-open context, programmable-nonprogrammable process, and computational-judgmental techniques) to organizational levels (operating, coordinative, and strategic).

4 Do you agree that "managing is decision making"? Why or why not?

5 Relate the TOTE concept of organism behavior to organizations in general.

6 Using the model in Figure 14.6, trace the flow process for several decisions with varying degrees of programmability.

7 Define information and relate it to communication. Relate information flow to organization.

8 Discuss the concept of an information-decision system and its relationship to organization and management. What key concepts are involved?

9 What role should technicians play in the design of information-decision systems? What role should managers play?

10 What has been the impact of electronic computers on information-decision systems? What do you predict for the future?

11 Define the concepts "timeliness of information" and "timeliness of response." Which is more important for managerial decision making?

Computational Decision-Making Techniques

When faced with a difficult problem-solving task, we typically seek ways to simplify the environment. One approach to simplification is that of assuming away some of the complexity of the real world in order to achieve a tidier, more well-defined problem. This process of closing the system to confounding variables is a pervasive behavior pattern. We do it unconsciously by assuming simple, straightforward relationships rather than by considering all the factors involved. On the other hand, we do it consciously when faced with specific problem-solving tasks which, by definition, are complex and require a cogitative approach. The system is deliberately simplified or closed in order to bring to bear applicable analytical techniques. The real test is knowing exactly how much simplification is appropriate without destroying the essence of the problem. In this chapter we will consider computational decision making in relatively closed systems in terms of the following topics:

Problem-Solving Methods
Rationality
Model Building
Quantification
Specific Techniques
Statistical Decision Theory

Problem-Solving Methods

At least six reasonably distinct human methods for problem solving can be identified:

1 Appeal to the supernatural

2 Appeal to worldly authority—the older the better

3 Intuition

4 Common sense

5 Pure logic

6 The scientific method[1]

No chronology is implied by the list because all these approaches are being employed currently in problem-solving situations throughout the world. However, the list does imply a gradation leading toward more careful, searching, and logical approaches. Combinations of several of these are involved in many problem-solving efforts. Intuition can be helpful in the laboratory, as can common sense and logic. Disciplined imagination, a vital ingredient for researchers and decision makers, may depend on both intuition and common sense.

Certain fundamentals are implied by the term *scientific method.* It suggests the use of generally recognized procedures and techniques. Another important ingredient is the attitude of the researcher or decision maker. A relatively formal, systematic, and thorough approach to problem solving suggests objectivity and reasoning rather than emotion. It implies logical solutions to problems, incorporating as little bias as possible. Using the scientific method, either explicitly or implicitly, one reserves judgment until all the pertinent information is available. For many centuries we sought final, definitive answers to problems; more recent approaches have pointed toward a spectrum of possibilities and show a tendency to express knowledge in terms of probability rather than certainty. The scientific method suggests a mind that is constantly challenging, weighing, and explaining—one that is continually diagnosing and asking "Why?"

In organizations, managers are confronted with complex situations at all levels—strategic, coordinative, and operating—and need a contingency view in order to match problems and appropriate methods for solving them. When problems concern only the inanimate economic and technical aspects of the operating system, the application of specific techniques can be relatively straightforward and computational. When the problem deals with the human aspects, the task becomes more difficult and judgmental.[2] And when the analysis includes large-scale, sociotechnical systems, the problem becomes even more complex.

Management science can be defined as the use of the scientific method to answer questions of concern to managers. In this sense it has an extremely broad connotation. However, as indicated in Chapter 4, current common usage suggests a much more restricted sense. It implies a closed, stable-mechanistic system, quantifiable models, and mathematical problem-solving techniques. The term *rationality* is often involved—referring to both the method and the decision maker.

---

1 Stuart Chase, *The Proper Study of Mankind,* Harper & Row, Publishers, Inc., New York, 1956, p. 3.

2 For example, see: James R. Emshoff, *Analysis of Behavioral Systems,* The Macmillan Company, New York, 1971; and John M. Dutton and William H. Starbuck (eds.), *Computer Simulation of Human Behavior,* John Wiley & Sons, Inc., New York, 1971.

Rationality

The management science literature emphasizes recognized procedures and techniques that are relatively formal, systematic, and thorough and used by decision makers who are objective rather than subjective. A rational process is considered to be one "based on reasoning," one that is objective rather than subjective, one that is logical and sensible. However, the use of terms like "sensible" and "reasonable" implies a consensual yardstick. That is, *most of us* would agree with regard to what is a sound or logical approach to problem solving or decision making. Certainly intuition or common sense may suffice in isolated incidents. However, better long-run average results are obtained by the use of more objective methods.

In many problem-solving situations an assumption is made that the objective of the decision maker can be assessed in quantitative terms, most often with money as the common denominator, Rationality in this sense is concerned with the choice that a decision maker makes with reference to clear-cut alternatives. Here again, rationality is measured in terms of a consensual yardstick— what would a "prudent economic person" do under these given circumstances? In this chapter we will utilize, for the time being, the assumptions for rational behavior as developed in classical economics:

1 Complete knowledge of relevant environmental factors
2 Ability to order preferences according to some yardstick of utility (usually money)
3 Ability to choose the alternative that maximizes the decision maker's utility

These assumptions provide the framework for the techniques that are applicable under relatively closed-system conditions. According to Miller and Starr: "The objective of the individual is held to be the maximization of the total utility he can achieve with his limited resources of time, effort, and money. The rationality of the individual is defined in terms of the utilization he makes of his scarce resources to achieve this end of maximum utility."[3] The management science techniques described in this chapter are often prefaced with the adjective "rational," implying both a reasonable, exhaustive, and objective process and an appropriate choice in the light of a well-defined goal. A basic assumption is that of a relatively closed system.

The most commonly used and accepted analytical framework for choice behavior or decision making in organizations is the *closed* decision model. . . . Many of the widely accepted decision models in management science assume a kind of administrative rationality similar to that prescribed for the ideal rational man. These models are structured in

3 David W. Miller and Martin K. Starr, *The Structure of Human Decision,* © 1967, p. 24. Reprinted by permission of Prentice-Hall, Inc., Englewood Cliffs, N.J.

closed frameworks. They are closed because they give little weight to the environment of the decision maker and to the complexity of the act of choice as such. [4]

Individual Rationality

Rather than appraising rationality on the basis of a consensus of what is an appropriate decision-making process or choice, it is important that we look at the problem from the point of view of the decision maker. By not imputing a certain value system that will determine the utility of particular outcomes, the variability of individual value systems is recognized, and hence the system becomes much more open. With such a framework, rational decisions would be those that move decision makers toward their own goal(s). A person's consideration of what is "good" might differ considerably from some other individual's or group's. This view suggests that what is rational for Smith may not be rational for Jones. Philosophers have been concerned about this problem for centuries. The state of this search can be summed up as follows: "Goodness remained a philosophical, theological, and personal matter. Individual truth came to be viewed as a property of cerebral-sensory systems; universal truth was approachable but openly unknowable. And so an operational philosophy of decisions developed, wherein the goodness of a decision would be measured by the extent to which its results satisfied the decision maker's objectives." [5]

Other Dimensions of Rationality

It is also useful to consider individual versus organizational rationality. [6] A decision might be rational from the individual's point of view but not from the standpoint of the organization (as determined by some consensus or some other individual). Organizations involve cooperative effort; hence it is unlikely that each individual can maximize personal objectives at all times. The rationality of organizational behavior should be determined in the light of *group* objectives, not according to "what *I* would do in that situation."

4 Marcus Alexis and Charles Z. Wilson, *Organizational Decision Making,* © 1967, pp. 149–150. Reprinted by permission of Prentice-Hall, Inc., Englewood Cliffs, N.J.

5 Miller and Starr, op. cit., p. 23.

6 Actually, there are a number of ways to view rationality. For example:
> A decision may be called "objectively" rational if *in fact* it is the correct behavior for maximizing given values in a given situation. It is "subjectively" rational if it maximizes attainment relative to the actual knowledge of the subject. It is "consciously" rational to the degree that the adjustment of means to ends is a conscious process. It is "deliberately" rational to the degree that the adjustment of means to ends has been deliberately brought about (by the individual or by the organization). A decision is "organizationally" rational if it is oriented to the organization's goals; it is "personally" rational if it is oriented to the individual's goals.

Herbert Simon, *Administrative Behavior,* 3d ed., The Free Press, New York, 1976, pp. 76–77.

Bounded rationality is the concept that a decision maker does not have complete knowledge of the situation and hence must deal with a limited picture of any given problem. In such a case the person makes a choice that, to the best of his or her knowledge, will help to bring about the objective. An outside agency, with more complete knowledge, may wonder about the rationality of such a decision. The individual may question his or her own sanity at some later time. ("What a crazy thing to do!") In both cases, however, the appraisal is made with the benefit of more complete knowledge concerning the problem in question.

It is also useful to distinguish between a rational choice and a rational process. There may be much more agreement with regard to what is a careful, exhaustive, searching, reasoned approach to problem solving. The scientific method has come to be accepted in all research and problem-solving endeavors as a rational approach. On the other hand, there may be steps in the process that require valuational assumptions. If so, the process may be deemed rational and the choice considered not so rational. In other words, we may evaluate an individual or an organizational decision process in the following manner: "They seemed to go about it in a careful, diligent, and thoughtful manner, but they made a lousy choice."

In the remainder of this chapter we will be concerned with problem-solving techniques that, under the general umbrella of scientific method or management science, make the decision *process* relatively more rational than intuitive, rule-of-thumb, or seat-of-the-pants methods. This assumes that we are discussing relatively closed systems that emphasize economic utility and that decision makers are rational in their *choices* within this framework. In the following chapter we will relax these assumptions and consider decision making in more open systems.

Model Building

Model building and model use provide a framework for managing. "Models are the crux of rational management."[7] They provide a means for simplifying and analyzing complex situations or systems.[8]

A typical step in the management science approach to problem solving is that of constructing a mathematical model to represent the system under study. It involves the quantification of variables. While the development of a mathematical model is an essential step in solving problems under closed-system assumptions, this approach represents only a minute part of the overall endeavor. Indeed, model building is one of our most pervasive activities. In general, models provide a means of abstraction that aids communication. Language itself is a process of abstraction, and mathematics is a particular kind of symbolic language. Model

---

7 Martin K. Starr, *Management: A Modern Approach,* Harcourt Brace Jovanovich, Inc., New York, 1971, p. 26.

8 Ronald J. Ebert and Terence R. Mitchell, *Organizational Decision Processes,* Crane, Russak & Company, Inc., New York, 1975, p. 133.

building is the crux of conceptualization; models are developed to describe, explain, or predict pertinent phenomena in the real world.

Models vary over many dimensions, one of the most important of which is the degree of abstractness involved. A life-size mannikin would be a realistic model of a human being. A photograph would be more abstract, and a page of prose description would be even more abstract. However, in these examples we would be modeling only the physical characteristics of an individual. The mannikin, photograph, or description would not provide much insight with regard to an individual's value system or behavior. A "picture" of this aspect might be obtained via biographical or autobiographical prose.

Similarly, balance sheets and profit and loss statements provide a model of an organization. However, these bare statistics are quite abstract. A better image of the organization is obtained if we have pictures or other descriptive material such as are typically found in annual reports. The more information added to the modeling process, the more difficult the conceptualization. If investors are satisfied with the price/earnings ratio as a model of a particular firm for purposes of deciding whether or not they will invest, the choice may be relatively straightforward. However, many investors are interested in a more detailed analysis which may include less tangible factors such as the astuteness of the management team. The more variables added to the model-building process, the more realistic the picture becomes. However, realism is often nebulous and cumbersome, if not impossible, to deal with. Hence, more simplified, abstract versions of the real world are sought.

The problem of model building can be related to the polar admonitions—"paralysis by analysis" or "extinction by instinct." Continuing to research a problem situation may develop a more and more realistic model of the phenomena in question. In so doing, however, a decision may not result until it is too late. In this case, an elaborate, sophisticated, realistic model would be of little use. In addition to the time dimension, costs are also important. The cost of gathering additional information in order to refine a model may be prohibitive in a particular situation. Thus, the cost of model refinement or enrichment should be balanced against the benefits to be derived therefrom.

At the other end of the spectrum, many decisions are based on oversimplified models of the real world. A decision maker may be very comfortable with his or her particular model of the phenomena involved and make little or no attempt to gain more knowledge of the situation. Bigotry and dogmatism often result from simplified models of the real world. Quite often we find that those with the least knowledge of a particular situation are the most certain about how to solve the problem. Individuals may be quite sure that their straightforward models of the world are realistic and appropriate for problem solving. Closure can develop in two ways. As an unconscious process, and carried to extremes, it can be dysfunctional as far as decision making is concerned. It is much like blinders on a race horse; part of the real world is screened off or shut out. In this way individuals unknowingly have a distorted or partial model of reality.

On the other hand, closure can be deliberate in an attempt to develop models that can be used in analytical work. In this case, simplifying assumptions are made consciously in order to make the analysis amenable to available techniques. If, after solutions are obtained by using simplified models, the restrictions are relaxed and the results interpreted accordingly, there is no particular problem. But if managers or management scientists become enamored with the model and forget the simplifying assumptions made in its development, the results may not be applicable to the real situation. Model building is a useful process but one that must be monitored closely during conception, analysis, and application. Let us turn to model building as a particular phase in applying management science techniques to organizational problem solving.

Management Science Models

Constructing a model is a common technique of abstraction and simplification for studying the characteristics or behavioral aspects of objects or systems under varying conditions. The model itself is usually a representation of objects, events, processes, or systems (a clay mockup of a new automobile design, for example). Manipulation of the model is used to test the impact that proposed changes (in one or more components) will have on the system as a whole. In this way tests can be carried out without disturbing the subject of the model. The various types of models have been classified into three general groups.

1 An *iconic* model pictorially or visually represents certain aspects of a system (as does a photograph or model airplane).
2 An *analogue* model employs one set of properties to represent some other set of properties which the system being studied possesses (e.g., for certain purposes, the flow of water through pipes may be taken as an analogue of the "flow" of electricity in wires).
3 A *symbolic* model uses symbols to designate properties of the system under study (by means of a mathematical equation or set of such equations). [9]

Scale-model airplanes in wind tunnels are iconic models used to simulate actual flight conditions. In operations research, the word "model" usually means a mathematical description of an activity that expresses the relationships among various elements with sufficient accuracy so that it can be used to predict the actual outcome under any expected set of circumstances. Mathematical models are of many types, depending on the real-life situations they are designed to represent. They have both advantages and disadvantages as analytical tools. The model, rather than the system it represents, can be manipulated in a variety of

9 C. West Churchman, Russell L. Ackoff, and E. Leonard Arnoff, *Introduction to Operations Research*, John Wiley & Sons, Inc., New York, 1957, p. 158.

ways until a relatively good solution is found. On the basis of such experimentation, the actual system can be adjusted with a minimum of disruption. Obviously, duplicating reality completely is impossible. Also the process, while beneficial, can be time-consuming and costly.

Model building provides a tool for extending the decision maker's judgment in handling large-scale, complex systems. The use of a model allows creative manipulation in order to test new ideas concerning system components and/or relationships. Any set of equations designed to represent a particular problem area, no matter how narrow, can be thought of as a model. Various assumptions are made about the number of factors that must be included in order to represent the situation accurately. Then numerical values can be assigned to the variables in the problem in order to develop a workable model. Once the system has been described and numerical values have been assigned, the problem can be solved with whatever technique seems appropriate.

Computers
and
Models

Computers have fostered much of the advance in management science over the past several decades. Trivial problems, often used as textbook examples, can be solved quite readily with hand calculations or, at most, the use of a pocket calculator. However, real-life problems in complex industrial settings often are not amenable to such approaches. Numerical solutions to such problems may require thousands of individual steps involving endless hours of clerical work. A computer allows the solution of typical problems in a matter of minutes rather than weeks or months. In fact, real-time problem solving is possible with the system performing computations immediately upon receipt of a query from an input station. The result can be displayed graphically or communicated in any one of several standard media. Moreover, the computer is not subject to fatigue and hence is more likely to provide error-free solutions than the typical statistical clerk. While the programming of solutions to typical problems can be both challenging and time-consuming, the results of such effort can be applied over and over again to similar problems as they arise. The trend toward modular programs, which can be put together in a variety of forms, facilitates the solution of new problems with existing computer programs. [10]

It is dangerous to assume that all management science work involves the use of computers. The problems in question must be analyzed in the light of the most likely techniques and the most efficient processing of data required for solution. As techniques are developed for automating management decisions in areas such as inventory, quality, and production control, the mathematical analysis involved can be integrated into general data processing systems. In such cases the

10 J. W. Pomeroy, "A Guide to Programming Tools and Techniques," *IBM Systems Journal*, vol 11, no. 3, 1972, pp. 234–254.

mathematical analysis required for automatic decisions is imbedded in an overall information-decision system programmed to handle all but the exceptional situations involved in day-to-day operations. Larger-scale mathematical analysis may be required for management decisions in areas such as long-range planning. In this case a computer serves primarily as a calculator in the solution phase rather than as a data processor in the information-decision system.

The Art of Modeling

Problems may fall into classic categories and be solvable by well-defined, specific models. For example, we might have a standard inventory, queuing theory, or linear programming problem and solve it by applying a ready-made technique. Yet such an approach may stifle imagination, impose artificial constraints, and close the system unnaturally.

Dealing with the problem in all its complexity may lead to inaction because managers and/or analysts cannot "get a handle on it." Therefore, it is useful to find ways of simplifying the situation without assuming away the problem. It may be possible to divide the problem into subparts and attack them one at a time. Or it may be possible to develop a model for a simplified version of the problem and then enrich it progressively once a workable model is developed. Real-world problems seldom fall into the classical models of management science. Variations must be developed that involve combinations of several models in order to depict the complete system realistically.

Skill in modeling certainly involves a sensitive and selective perception of management situations. This, in turn, depends on the sort of conceptual structures one has available with which to bring some order out of the perceptual confusion. Models can play the role of giving structure to experience. Yet we seldom encounter a model which is already available in fully satisfactory form for a given management situation, and the need for creative development or modification is almost universally experienced in management science. [11]

A model should be tested against the real world periodically in order to assess its fidelity. Figure 15.1 illustrates the continual looping process, which is fundamental to model building. Actual data and experience provide a starting point for a symbolic model that is referred to the real world in order to determine its fidelity. Test data from the real world are used to evaluate the symbolic model, and adjustments can be made on the basis of such evaluation. The cycle goes on until a satisfactory representation of the real world is obtained.

Figure 15.1 shows a three-step process. However, the amount of testing and refinement will vary with the situation. An acceptable model may result rather quickly, or many tests and refinements may be required to capture the essence of the system. This general modeling process can be applied to many

---

11 William T. Morris, "On the Art of Modeling," *Management Science*, August 1967, p. B–708.

Figure 15.1   The Modeling Process

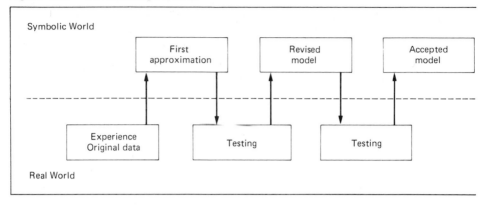

problems—work flow, organizational relationships, PERT-type networks, or linear programming, for example. [12]

Quantification

Models can be broadly characterized as qualitative or quantitative. Typically, there is a transition in the model-building process from qualitative to quantitative concepts. The initial approach in most complex situations is to develop a mental picture of the system. By writing out our description of the system, we attain a simplified (and less realistic) version, but one that can be communicated. However, there are many difficulties in the communication process because of the semantic problems with spoken or written language.

In many cases, real systems are not amenable to modeling. The relationships involved may be too complex to be stated formally in graphic or symbolic terms. Moreover, the pertinent variables may not be well defined, and even if they are, the relationships between them are not clear-cut. Many of the problems faced by managers in today's organizations are of this type. Nonprogrammable decisions arise at all organizational levels but predominate in the environment of middle (coordinative) and top (strategic) management.

On the other hand, there are many problems that can be modeled quantitatively. The symbolic language of mathematics provides a means of relating variables precisely to define the system in detail. When this is possible, powerful techniques of analysis become available. Some suggest that *real* scientific decision making emerges at the point where quantification becomes possible.

Our view is that the scientific method—and hence scientific decision making—can be employed without necessarily quantifying the relationships of the system. Yet the connotation that scientific is related to quantification seems over-

---

12 For a discussion of model suitability based on five major criteria (realism, flexibility, capability, ease of use, and cost) see: William E. Souder, "A Scoring Methodology for Assessing the Suitability of Management Science Models," *Management Science*, June 1972, pp. B526–B543.

whelming. Although we do not accept this view, we are cognizant of the power of quantitative techniques in managerial decision making. Many advantages accrue when quantification of models becomes possible. Mathematics is a compact and efficient language, that minimizes communication problems such as semantics. Translating models into mathematical symbols forces the decision maker to identify pertinent variables and their relationships explicitly. A system of equations can be manipulated in order to test a model's ability to predict. In large, complex systems this testing process may involve many refinements and voluminous calculations. Mathematical models lend themselves to computerization, a step that facilitates the model-building process.

Quantification forces the use of a common denominator as a criterion for optimizing. Frequently, the common denominator is money, because an organization is concerned with solving problems that are related to cost or profit. While monetary terms do have broad usefulness and understanding, there are problems. Although money may have an exact meaning numerically—$100 in Seattle equals $100 in Miami—the value of particular amounts may vary considerably among decision makers. For example, it is not obvious that $10 is worth twice as much as $5 to a particular decision maker. The actual value would relate to an individual's particular situation at a specific time.

One means to achieve a "more common" denominator is the concept of **utiles.** This approach is an attempt to measure precisely the value of potential outcomes to decision makers. The objective is to provide a system whereby preferences can be ordered cardinally on a scale of utiles. That is, 7 utiles is 1 better than 6 utiles, or 10 utiles is twice as good as 5 utiles. This is an attempt to integrate value systems and to achieve quantification of system variables.

Probability must be considered in the quantification of models. Some systems are deterministic in that the parameters are completely defined and the outcomes related to particular courses of action are certain. In real situations, however, there are many probabilistic aspects that must be reduced to quantitative terms. Outcomes might be described as quite likely or remote. In order to incorporate such concepts into quantitative models, it is necessary to attach more precise descriptions to such phenomena. For example, "quite likely" might equal .85 and "remote" might equal .01.

Figure 15.2 shows the relationship between certainty, uncertainty, and risk. Certainty lies at one end of the spectrum and really should be separated, at least conceptually, from the continuum. Similarly, complete uncertainty might be viewed as a separate condition at the opposite end of the spectrum. In theory there may be a continuum between these two points. However, it seems more realistic to consider two separate states with a continuum in between. Certainty involves complete knowledge, and quantitative models that describe such systems are deterministic and can be solved in straightforward fashion. At the other end of the spectrum is uncertainty or a complete lack of knowledge. In such a state of affairs any identifiable potential outcomes would have to be considered equally likely. The continuum between certainty and complete uncertainty is called risk. In situ-

Figure 15.2 Certainty-Uncertainty "Continuum"

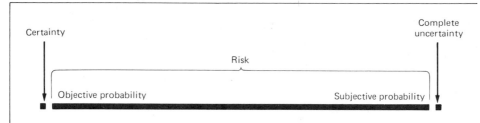

ations of this sort, outcomes are not predictable precisely. However, risk implies some knowledge that can be used to predict the likelihood of anticipated outcomes. Toward the certainty end of the spectrum are objective probabilities that have been obtained through past experience, large samples, or repeated experiments. Such information provides a clue to the likelihood of various possible results. Toward the other end of the spectrum are subjective probabilities that are based on less concrete information and limited experience with the problem under analysis. The decision maker may have a small sample to refer to or may rely on intuition based on similar experience. In any case, subjective estimates of the probability of future outcomes are used. This information must be translated into numerical terms in order that it can become a part of a quantitative model.

Computational Approaches

Two basic computational approaches are algorithmic and heuristic. **Algorithmic** techniques are step-by-step procedures that lead to a solution in a well-defined, closed system. Such "cookbook" approaches are often sufficient. The manager or a technician needs merely to follow the prescribed steps and a solution automatically results. **Heuristic** approaches, on the other hand, involve sophisticated trial-and-error and do not lead invariably to the same results. Heuristic problem-solving techniques rely on relatively more human judgment at various junctures in the decision-making process and hence are useful in relatively open systems. A heuristic approach may be effective but not efficient; a satisfactory solution may be found by a very roundabout path. On the other hand, it may be an efficient method but with no assurance of optimality.

Algorithms set forth a definite procedure that will lead to a solution. However, in many cases the number of steps involved may be prohibitive. For example, an algorithm could be developed to consider every possible combination for a safe. Eventually the correct combination would be identified. However, the number of combination locks in use through the world attests to the fact that an algorithmic approach for this problem is not feasible. A heuristic approach would start by eliminating some "obviously" inappropriate approaches and would concentrate on several that appear to be likely. This sophisticated trial-and-error might not achieve a solution but would cut down the magnitude of the problem-solving task significantly.

Other terms used in describing management science tools are analytical, numerical, and simulation. *Analytical* techniques obtain a unique answer through a process of formal mathematical deduction. Break-even points, economic lot size, and correlation coefficients are examples of unique answers obtained through analytical approaches. *Numerical* analysis involves successive approximations to obtain a solution. In such situations there is also a unique answer, but the method of obtaining it is not as direct as in a case of analytical approaches. *Simulation* processes are used when a system under study is too complex to be conveniently represented by a complete mathematical statement. Or the primary interest may be evaluating the impact of policy decisions on overall system performance. "What if" questions can be asked to test the effect of changes.

"In general, analytical methods are used to solve problems involving relatively simple systems. Numerical solutions can be used in more complex cases, and simulation is usually employed when relationships between variables are too complex for the effective use of either analytical or numerical methods."[13] In order to understand these relationships more clearly, let us turn to some specific examples.

Specific Techniques

The list of specific techniques that might be used in closed-system problem solving is lengthy. Examples might be ratio analysis, break-even analysis, inventory models, mathematical programming, queuing theory, game theory, budgetary control, equipment replacement analysis, payoff matrices, decision trees, network analysis, and simulation. In some cases these categories refer to related mathematical techniques. In others the classification is based on particular types of problems found in the real world. However, it should not be assumed that problems faced by managers fall neatly into such categories. Most decisions require bringing several or many techniques to bear in a particular situation.

Moreover, within these categories there are wide variations in the techniques themselves. For example, linear programming and systems analysis derive their names from generalized models that relate to a broad class of problems. However, the simplified version or general models probably do not apply in specific instances. Managers and/or technicians should tailor the approach to the particular problem at hand; this involves the art of modeling.

Some of the techniques have proved worthwhile in management decision making over a period of years. Some have not been applied fruitfully in real situations as yet. Still others fall in between these extremes, having had limited application in practical situations. It is important for managers to ascertain the

---

13 W.W. Thompson, Jr., *Operations Research Techniques,* Charles E. Merrill Books, Inc., Columbus, Ohio, 1967, p. 6.

usefulness of specific techniques in planning and implementing programs of action. This means enough understanding to evaluate their applicability in particular situations.

In this chapter we will look at one family of techniques as a means of *illustrating* the role of computational methods in decision making under assumptions of relatively closed systems. Statistical decision theory provides a way of looking at a broad spectrum of managerial problems, including strategic issues. The models help us define the problem, clarify the factors and relationships involved, and understand the essential elements. We will make no attempt to be exhaustive in coverage, nor will we go into great detail with regard to the specific techniques. However, a general grasp of the method aids in conceptualizing a variety of managerial problems. The discipline of model building can be helpful by forcing us to think through the system explicitly.

Statistical Decision Theory

The term *statistics* covers a wide range of techniques that are useful for managerial decision making. Descriptive statistics are often important inputs in the decision-making process. Sampling and statistical inference also provide meaningful information in many cases. The term *statistical decision theory* has taken on a particular connotation and relates primarily to the process of evaluating potential outcomes for alternative courses of action in a given situation. The concepts and techniques of statistical decision theory can be related to the general model or flow chart of the decision-making process (Figure 14.5). When the system can be closed enough to allow quantification of all pertinent considerations, statistical decision theory can be utilized. In this section we will consider briefly two concepts—payoff matrices and decision trees—and will outline the fundamentals that are important from the standpoint of managerial decision making.

Payoff Matrices

One way to approach the subject of statistical decision theory is to look at examples of payoff matrices and identify the key concepts involved. Figure 15.3 illustrates the general model. Across the top of the matrix are identifiable and relatively discrete states of nature—N_1, N_2, or N_3. This indicates that the environment of the decision maker includes three mutually exclusive conditions that might prevail at some time in the future. The decision maker may have no idea of the likelihood of each state or may have in mind fairly definite probabilities for each of them.

It is assumed that a decision maker has a definite objective in mind, such as profit maximization or cost minimization. In order to achieve the goal, the

Figure 15.3   General Payoff Matrix Model

	States of nature		
	N_1	N_2	N_3
S_1	P_{11}	P_{12}	P_{13}
S_2	P_{21}	P_{22}	P_{23}
S_3	P_{31}	P_{32}	P_{33}

(Strategies)

decision maker can outline several distinct strategies, indicated along the left-hand side of the matrix as S_1, S_2, or S_3.

The entries in the cells of the matrix indicate the payoffs that will accrue for each strategy coupled with each future state of nature. For example $P_{1,1}$ represents the payoff that will accrue if strategy 1 is chosen and state of nature 1 occurs. Similarly $P_{3,2}$ is the payoff for S_3 and N_2.

In general, two conditions prevail in the decision maker's environment. In one case she is completely certain about a future state of nature and hence can assess payoffs directly and choose the one that maximizes the movement toward an objective. For example, the decision maker may know for sure that N_2 will prevail in the future. Given N_2, she has only to pick the best payoff from among $P_{1,2}$, $P_{2,2}$, and $P_{3,2}$. In this context decision making appears as easy as "falling off a log." However, choosing a strategy under conditions of certainty typically is not as easy as it might appear from our simplified payoff matrix. For example, the decision maker may have fifteen identifiable alternative strategies, and hence the analysis relative to the best payoff may be quite complex. In such deterministic situations linear programming might be used to identify an optimal course of action.

A more typical environment for decision makers is one of uncertainty. As shown in Figure 15.2, an environment of uncertainty ranges from complete ignorance to a condition of relative confidence concerning the probabilities of the various states of nature. If a manager can assign probabilities to the states of nature and can assign values, typically in monetary terms, to each outcome in the matrix, she can ultimately determine the expected value of each individual strategy. The expected value in each cell is the product of its certain value to the decision maker and the probability of that outcome occurring. Expected value for a strategy is the sum of the expected values across all potential states of nature. These basic concepts can be illustrated and reinforced by a specific example.

Figure 15.4(a) shows a payoff matrix that the owner-captain of a fishing boat might develop in assessing his approach to a new season. One strategy with regard to equipment may be to maintain the ship in substantially the same condi-

Figure 15.4 Payoff Matrix for the Owner-Captain of a Fishing Boat

		States of nature					States of nature		
		Poor (1)	Moderate (2)	Excellent (3)			Poor (1) [0.30]	Moderate (2) [0.50]	Excellent (3) [0.20]
Strategies	Same (1)	0	+2	+4		Same (1)	0	+2	+4
	Refit (2)	−4	+4	+8		Refit (2)	−4	+4	+8
	New (3)	−10	0	+20		New (3)	−10	0	+20
		(a)					(b)		

tion as previously. A second alternative might be to refit it with more modern gear and hence increase its effectiveness and efficiency. A third strategy might be to trade it in and obtain a new ship for the coming season. The states of nature could be expressed in terms of the expected volume of the salmon run. Obviously, this aspect of the problem would vary on a continuum; the indicated states of nature—poor, moderate, and excellent—are oversimplifications of the situation. On the other hand, they may be sufficiently identifiable to facilitate thinking in terms of relative payoffs for different strategies under these conditions.

The payoffs (net benefits) in the matrix have been translated from monetary terms to the more general utile form. In this version +4 is twice as good as +2. We can illustrate decision making under certainty (although this is obviously an artificial assumption in this case) by looking at the columns in the matrix. If the captain knew, for example, that a moderate salmon run was forthcoming, he would decide to refit the ship, because +4 is the best payoff under those conditions. If the captain had no preconceived notions about the probability of the three states of nature, he would assume them to be equally likely. Each certainty payoff could then be multiplied by ⅓ and summed across the rows. In this case, strategy 1 would yield 2; strategy 2 would yield 2 ⅔; and strategy 3 would yield 3 ⅓. Therefore, the captain should obtain a new ship because the expected value for this strategy is greater than for the other two.

On the other hand, if the captain could assign probabilities to the various states of nature—perhaps based on historical trend data or intuitive judgment—the computation of expected values could be refined. Let us assume that the probabilities for poor, moderate, and excellent are .30, .50, and .20, respectively, as shown in Figure 15.4(b). In this case strategy 1 has an expected value (EV) of 1.8; for strategy 2, EV=2.4; and for strategy 3, EV=1.0. Given these assumptions, the appropriate strategy would be that of refitting the ship for the new season.

Of particular importance for managerial decision making is the discipline of identifying the states of nature explicitly and coupling them with alternative strategies. This approach enhances the probability that the problem will be considered in a careful systematic manner.

Decision Trees

Decision trees allow management to assess the consequences of a sequence of decisions with reference to a particular problem. The approach involves linking a number of event "branches" which, when fully arrayed, resemble a tree. The process starts with a primary decision that has at least two alternatives to be evaluated. The probability of each outcome must be ascertained as well as its monetary value.

As an illustration, let us take a slightly modified version of our previous fishing boat example. Assume that the captain has two alternatives at the beginning of a new season—keeping the same boat or trading it in on the purchase of a new one. In the previous example there were three states of nature—a poor, moderate, or excellent salmon run—with probabilities attached to each. In this case we will assume either a good run (.7 probability) or a poor run (.3 probability). Obviously, a new boat involves an increase in the captain's investment. In order to simplify the analysis, however, we concentrate on the net cash flow that will result from the various outcomes. For example, as shown in Figure 15.5, the payout or net cash flow would be $90,000 if a new boat were purchased and a good run were to materialize. However, a new boat and a poor run would result in a loss of $10,000. If the captain were to keep the boat, a good run would result in $80,000 and a poor run would net $20,000.

Both sides of the event fork can be evaluated in terms of expected value. Multiplying the probabilities by the payout and summing them results in an expected value of $60,000 for the new boat and $62,000 for the old boat. This approach allows the decision maker to consider each of the alternatives explicitly in terms of the best estimates of future results. A one-step problem, such as that illustrated in Figure 15.5, is quite similar to the payoff matrix. The real contribution of decision trees comes from the ability to link several decisions (of the type illustrated) together in order to see the impact of a sequence of decisions-events-results over time.

For example, we could expand the present analysis to include a second year and develop a decision tree such as the one illustrated in Figure 15.6. In this case, we can trace the impact of decisions made over a period of two fishing seasons. For example, assuming that a new boat were purchased at the beginning of year 1 and that the results as estimated in Figure 15.5 were to accrue, at the beginning of a subsequent season the captain would again be faced with the problem of whether to buy a new boat or keep the old one. Similarly, the second

Figure 15.5   One-Year Decision Tree for the Owner-Captain of a Fishing Boat
Probabilities are in parentheses.

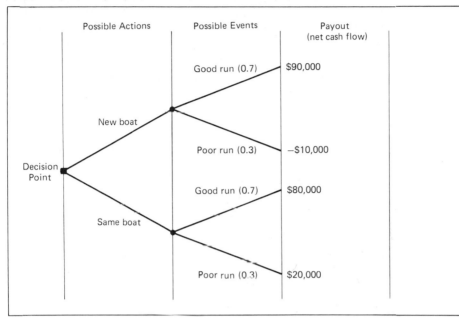

Possible Actions	Possible Events	Payout (net cash flow)

Good run (0.7) — $90,000
New boat
Poor run (0.3) — −$10,000
Decision Point
Good run (0.7) — $80,000
Same boat
Poor run (0.3) — $20,000

season could be described in terms of a good run or a poor run with net cash flows similar to those of the first year.

However, some important differences should be recognized, as illustrated in Figure 15.6. At the beginning of the second year the captain would have had the results of one year's activity and, theoretically, be in a position to adjust the probabilities for the states of nature in the second year. Given some past experience with salmon runs and their cyclical nature, he might be able to adjust the probabilities somewhat. Or even without any extensive past experience with regard to the likelihood of good or bad seasons, the captain may develop some subjective notions on the probability of a good run or a poor run. Regardless of the foundation for appraisal, he will develop some implicit concepts of the future. The decision tree merely makes the thinking process more explicit.

In this case, past experience might indicate that a good run in year 1 makes a poor run in year 2 somewhat more likely. Also past experience might indicate that a poor run is very seldom followed by another poor run. These conditional probabilities are illustrated in Figure 15.6. The payout or net cash flow is the sum of the two years under consideration. The expected value over the entire period can be computed by working backward in the decision tree from right to left. An expected value for each event fork can be calculated and related to each action. Taking the highest value for the possible actions, the decision tree

Figure 15.6 Two-Year Decision Tree for the Owner-Captain of a Fishing Boat

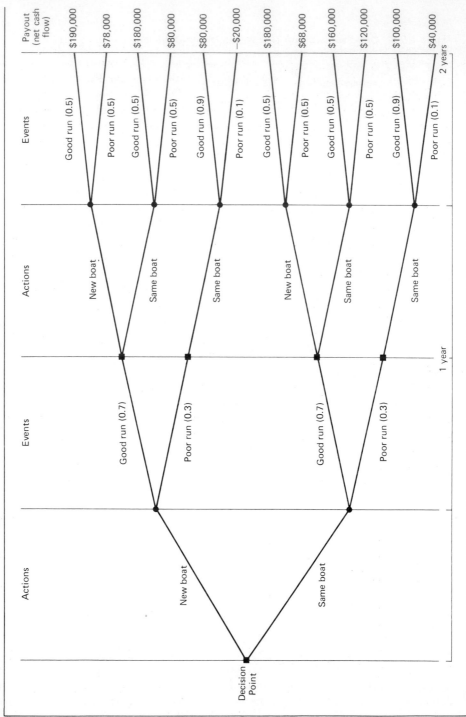

can be simplified and reduced. The same process can then be applied to the reduced tree, and expected values can be obtained for the two principal branches stemming from the original point of decision. We will leave the computations in this case for the student.

The additional decisions in the sequence might result in a changed picture for the overall system. For example, whereas the one-year analysis indicated that the captain should keep the old boat, analysis over a two- or three-year period might indicate that a new boat should be purchased as soon as possible. In this regard, decision trees provide an important tool for short- and medium-range planning. Decision trees for much longer periods become much more cumbersome because of their size and also because estimates for more than two or three years in the future must of necessity be quite speculative. [14]

Opening the System

The use of payoff matrices and decision trees requires simplifying assumptions. To reduce complex problems to a few numbers in a matrix or connected by forked lines may be less than realistic in many cases. However, these approaches do facilitate explicit consideration of the key aspects of many problems.

Theoretically, the states of nature and the various strategies available to a decision maker are infinite. However, for all practical purposes a few reasonably distinct states of nature can be identified, and the strategies often can be reduced to workable proportions, perhaps two to five. The more strategies and states of nature included in the analysis, the more open the system becomes.

Another key assumption in the use of payoff matrices is that of quantification and the development of some system of values for the payoff to a decision maker. The system is often artificially closed by forcing the quantification of outcomes. Figure 15.7 shows an approach that is much less constraining—the use of qualitative payoffs. We are not concerned with the value of any particular outcome; rather, we are interested in their relative values. For example, looking at the future from a decision maker's point of view, if strategy 1 were followed and N_2 were to occur, the outcome would be excellent (e). However, if N_1 were to occur, the outcome would be poor (p). Similarly, if strategy 2 were chosen and N_2 were to occur, the outcome would be fair (f) from the decision maker's point of view.

The use of qualitative payoffs allows the decision maker to consider a wide variety of everyday personal situations wherein specific numerical values

---

14 We have barely scratched the surface with regard to decision trees as a management tool. For additional information see Edward A. McCreary, "How to Grow a Decision Tree," *Think*, March–April 1967, pp. 13–18; John F. Magee, "Decision Trees for Decision Making," *Harvard Business Review*, July–August 1964, pp. 126–138; John S. Hammond, III, "Better Decisions with Preference Theory," *Harvard Business Review*, November–December 1967, pp. 123–141.

Figure 15.7   Qualitative Payoff Matrix
p = poor; f = fair; g = good; e = excellent.

		States of nature	
	N_1	N_2	N_3
S_1	p	e	f
S_2	g	f	g
S_3	p	g	p

(Strategies)

could not be readily ascertained.[15] It may well be that most of the benefits from this type of analysis can be obtained without the constraint of quantification. The concept of states of nature forces the decision maker to anticipate the future environment consciously. Similarly, she must analyze the situation in detail and identify explicit alternative strategies, then systematically relate these strategies to the states of nature and determine the impact or payoff. The decision maker will have some objective or subjective opinion concerning the probability of the various states of nature and hence can, in a rough fashion, determine the expected value of various strategies. For example, she might determine that the expected value of strategy 3 is somewhere between good and poor, probably less than fair. Thus, most of the benefit from the concept of payoff matrices can be obtained even though quantification is impossible or not easily obtained.

Another basic assumption in the case of both payoff matrices and decision trees is that expected values are appropriate for deciding the merits of various strategies. Using expected values assumes that a decision maker is willing to "play" the averages over the long run. In real situations, however, this may be an oversimplification. Individuals vary considerably with regard to their attitude toward risk. In the use of payoff matrices, for example, a pessimistic decision maker may pick the strategy that has the "least-worst" outcome; a large potential gain via some other strategy may be discounted heavily. On the other hand, the optimist selects a strategy that may result in the greatest gain and seemingly ignores the potential substantial losses from unfavorable outcomes. In these cases, the expected values, or long-run averages, do not seem to play an important part in the decision maker's analysis. Our inherent attitude toward risk colors our perception and evaluation of the situation.

Regardless of an individual's inherent attitude toward risk, a particular situation may dictate a strategy other than might seem appropriate according to expected values. In an atmosphere in which management is having difficulty

---

15 Robert Bell and John Coplans, *Decisions, Decisions*, W. W. Norton & Company, Inc., New York, 1976.

Figure 15.8   Potential Results from Developing a Patentable Product

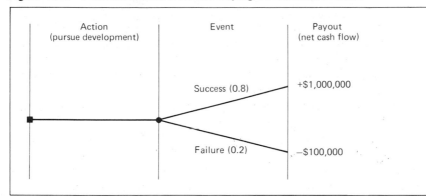

"meeting the payroll," a choice may be dictated on the basis of other than expected values. For example, Figure 15.8 shows a situation in which management
is faced with the choice of whether or not to develop a patentable product. To do
so would require an investment of $100,000. Consumer acceptance is about 80
percent sure once it is developed. However, there is the possibility that consumers
will not accept it or that an innovation will come along almost simultaneously and
make the product obsolete. The payoff for success would be $1,000,000. The
expected value for this example would be

.8 ($1,000,000) − .2 ($100,000) = $780,000

However, if there is even a remote chance of losing $100,000 and such loss would
bankrupt the company, management would be very reluctant to take the risk. A
more solvent firm could afford to gamble. "Them that has, gets."

    We see such behavior in much of life. The player with the largest bank-
roll typically has an advantage in a crap game. Strategy seems to vary with the
size of the pile of chips in front of a poker player. Attitudes toward risk vary
among individuals, and they vary over time for a given individual. [16]

    An interesting phenomenon that seems evident from research concern-
ing individual preference curves is the predominance of conservatism. [17] It appears
that the typical organizational decision maker is overly concerned about the potential negative results of a decision. The entire atmosphere seems to stress the
dangers of losing money. If an individual's career is at stake, he or she may forego
a 50 percent chance for tremendous gain through innovation and accept a 90
percent chance for a small incremental improvement through a relatively routine
approach to a particular problem. Realistically, management should assess decision makers on the basis of the entire decision process rather than on the results

16 Hammond, op. cit.
17 Ralph O. Swalm, "Utility Theory: Insights into Risk Taking," *Harvard Business Review*, November–December 1966, pp. 123–138.

only. "In most situations results are only a surrogate measure of the decision process. . . . If people restrict their evaluation of a decision to its outcomes, they may be rewarding the lucky and punishing the unlucky, falsely encouraging the wrong forms of behavior." [18] Tools such as decision trees make this process visible and allow review of the entire process rather than an ex post evaluation of the results. Organizations can provide a framework for decision making by stating explicitly the attitude that top management considers desirable in assessing risky ventures.

Including preference curves or attitudes toward risk in the decision-making process tends to open up the system considerably. Assuming that all decision makers are "averages" players and hence tuned in to expected values is an oversimplification of the real world. Attitudes vary among individuals, and an individual's attitudes vary over time. All these considerations must be taken into account in applying computational techniques such as payoff matrices and decision trees.

If the system is opened to include nonmonetary aspects, decision making becomes even more complex. For example, the captain in our fishing boat illustration may buy a new vessel even though a two- or three-year analysis shows the net cash flow from the old one to be significantly better. The choice is perfectly rational to the captain because he would "feel better" with a new boat. It may involve safety or prestige; in any case, other factors seem to outweigh the monetary considerations. Other similar examples are evident. Bank presidents may *want* a "showcase" electronic computer facility. Doctors and/or hospital administrators may *want* the latest equipment or processes even though higher "expected values" cannot be demonstrated explicitly. "Potential" lives saved is an extremely forceful argument in some situations.

Summary

The term *computational* suggests a closed system, quantifiable models, and mathematical problem-solving techniques. Management science comes under the general heading of scientific method, which is a relatively formal, systematic, and thorough approach to problem solving and implies objectivity and reasoning rather than emotion.

Management science techniques are typically described as rational approaches to problem solving. The term can apply to both the decision-making process and the choice made. Rational processes are systematic, logical, and reasoned. Choices are clearly rational if they are appropriate in terms of well-defined individual or organizational objectives. However, ill-defined objectives and differing personal values often make it difficult to reach a consensus on what is "appropriate"—or rational.

18 Douglas R. Emery and Francis D. Tuggle, "On the Evaluation of Decisions," *MSU Business Topics*, Spring 1976, p. 47.

Mathematical models are a fundamental part of the management science approach to problem solving. Relatively closed systems can be represented by well-defined relationships that can be quantified and expressed as systems of equations. The development of appropriate mathematical models is an art. Real-world problems do not fall in clear-cut categories, and hence the basic models must be enriched to include the unique aspects of any particular problem.

Many examples of computational approaches to managerial decision making could be cited. In this chapter we have used two techniques as illustrations. Statistical decision theory is represented by the basic concept of a payoff matrix. This approach can be extended for several periods of analysis by means of decision trees. The basic framework is the same, however, because it involves assessing the interaction of alternative strategies and a probabilistic environment. The value system of the decision maker, particularly his or her attitude toward risk, affects the analysis considerably.

If the analysis admits nonmonetary considerations, individual attitudes become an even more integral part of the decision-making process. Quantitative models, often in monetary terms, provide a basic framework or point of departure, but the system is opened significantly when behavioral aspects are included. Such considerations tend to open the system and make it much more complex from the standpoint of the managerial decision maker.

Questions and Problems

1 Define management science. How does it relate to decision making?

2 Discuss the use of the term *rational* in describing (1) the process followed and (2) the choice made by a decision maker.

3 "Model building is one of our most pervasive activities." Do you agree? Why or why not? Is model building functional or dysfunctional for individual decision makers? Why?

4 Describe the modeling process in management science. What has been the role of electronic computers in this endeavor?

5 "Real scientific decision making emerges at the point where quantification becomes possible." Do you agree? Why or why not?

6 Relate the certainty-uncertainty continuum to the quantification of models.

7 Outline the assumptions necessary to "close the system" and allow the use of computational decision making in:

    a Statistical decision theory

    b Break-even analysis

  c Linear programming
  d Ratio analysis
  e Queuing theory
  f Network analysis

Discuss the use of these techniques by managers in relatively open systems.

8 Calculate the expected value for the two-year decision tree shown in Figure 15.6. If the results of one-, two-, and three-year analyses all pointed to keeping the old boat, is there any chance that the captain might purchase a new one anyway? Why or why not?

Behavioral
Aspects of
Decision
Making

Sixteen

Managerial decision making covers a range of situations much broader than can be programmed under closed-system concepts. Judgmental approaches must be used in making the majority of decisions in organizations. Problem solving in the strategic and coordinative subsystems involves mediation and compromise. Social, political, and philosophical considerations become factors in judgmental decision making. Behavioral aspects—beliefs and values of individuals and groups, for example—become increasingly important as we concentrate on the decision maker rather than on the process or technique used. A broad open-system framework, applicable to managerial decision making in general, facilitates identification of situations wherein more definite, explicit, quantifiable techniques can be applied. We will discuss the behavioral aspects of decision making via the following topics.

> Complexity
> Open-System Decision Model
> Individual Decision Making
> Facts and Values
> Beliefs
> Ethical Considerations
> Groups and Decision Making
> The Interface of Computational and Judgmental Approaches

Complexity

Management science techniques have concentrated on mechanistic and deterministic applications. Probabilistic aspects have been included in many problem-solving models, but the emphasis has been on relatively objective probability distributions. These constraints dictate that only simple, well-defined systems are amenable to typical computational approaches. For more complex nonprogrammable problems, the human element plays a more prominent role in the process. Realistic situations often call for sequential decision making wherein a manager's interpretation is necessary at each of several stages. Also, many of the critical factors involved in complex sociotechnical systems are nonquantifiable variables that nevertheless must be included in the managerial decision-making process.

We are concerned with complexity as it relates to the managerial system at all levels. Both the internal organizational climate and the external environment affect managerial decision makers. Increased size, accelerating technology, better educated employees, specialization, both blue- and white-collar unionism, conflicts between organizational and professional allegiance, and other similar factors add up to an exceedingly complex internal climate. Coincidentally, the external environment of organizations is becoming more and more complex— intra- and interindustry relationships, political considerations, legal and governmental aspects, plus the more evident relationships with stockholders, suppliers, and customers. The felt need for social responsibility is also important. All are inputs to managerial decision making in modern organizations. The scope of these considerations makes it evident that many decisions must be made in relatively open systems. It is impossible to mold all the factors that management must consider into an explicit, well-defined model that can be quantified and solved. The scope and complexity of typical problem-solving situations call for a framework of open-system considerations.

The complexities of the real world indicate that traditional concepts of rationality and explicit, computational problem-solving techniques often do not apply. Therefore, a more general model is necessary to provide the framework for managerial decision making and to facilitate understanding of the process as it occurs in typical real-life situations. The open-system decision model provides such a framework.

Open-System Decision Model

The open-system model of decision making is an attempt to describe a more realistic process for individual and organizational decision making. It focuses on human involvement in the various steps of the process and allows for the impact of numerous environmental forces. This view opens the system by eliminating the assumptions of classical rationality. That is, we do not assume that the decision maker has complete knowledge and is a logical, systematic maximizer in economic-technical terms. Concentration on the human element leads to concepts such as learning and adaptation. Continual feedback during the decision process causes adjustments in both ends and means. The system is dynamic rather than static; thus, explicit computational techniques must give way to more judgmental approaches.

An open-system decision model is shown in Figure 16.1. It involves a sequence of decisions that may result from the perception of a problem. As indi-

Figure 16.1   An Open-System Decision Model
Period 1: The individual starts out with an idealized goal structure and defines one or more action goals as a first approximation to the "ideal goal" in the structure. The action goals may be considered as representative of the decision maker's *aspiration level. Period 2:* The individual engages in search activity and defines a limited number of outcomes and alternatives but does not attempt to establish the relations rigorously. Analysis proceeds from loosely defined rules of approximation. The alternatives discovered establish a starting point for further search toward a solution. *Period 3:* Search among the limited alternatives is undertaken to find a satisfactory solution, as contrasted with an optimal one. "Satisfactory" is defined in terms of the aspiration level or action goals.

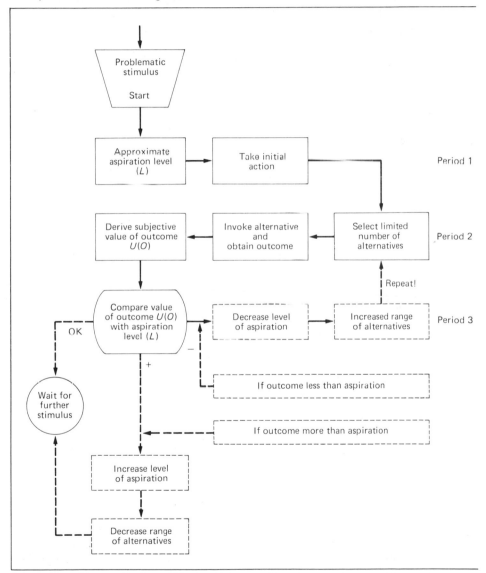

Adapted from Marcus Alexis and Charles Z. Wilson, *Organizational Decision Making,* Prentice-Hall, Inc., Englewood Cliffs, N.J., 1967, p. 160.

cated in the figure, period 1 is devoted primarily to identifying objectives. However, it is recognized that no explicit, clear-cut, "idealized" goal structure is typically available. Therefore, the decision maker has an approximate level of aspiration toward which causal action is taken.

A decision maker typically identifies a limited number of seemingly feasible alternatives rather than an exhaustive list. [1] Usually he or she will select those most readily apparent and relatively close to a current solution or approach to the problem. The alternatives are evaluated in many ways—on a continuum from hunch through "guesstimation" to scientific method. Out of this evaluation comes a choice and its implementation.

The decision maker then considers the outcome and its relationship to the original aspirational level. The possible results are readily apparent; the value of the outcome could meet the aspiration level exactly, or it could be higher or lower. If the outcome is close and there is substantial congruity in the system, the decision maker will probably wait for further problematic stimuli to trigger another decision-making process. If the value of the outcome exceeds the aspiration level, the decision maker is apt to increase the level of aspiration in similar situations and also decrease the range of alternative identification. That is, the decision maker may be quite satisfied with the approach to the problem and not be inclined to "rock the boat" by searching for alternative solutions. He or she will be satisfied to solve the same or similar problems with the approach that has "proved" successful in the past. As in the case of congruency, if the outcome is more than the aspiration level, the decision maker will most likely move to the stage of waiting for further stimuli concerning similar or different problems.

On the other hand, if the outcome turns out to be less than the aspiration level, a different chain of events typically is touched off. The decision maker may decrease the level of aspiration. This may not occur immediately, but it becomes more likely as the number of "failures" increases. Regardless of the ensuing aspiration level, the decision maker must again assess the alternatives available. If there were several that seemed reasonably close in "appropriateness," the decision maker may repeat stage two by selecting one of the other original alternatives to be evaluated. He or she may move from a relatively routine approach toward adaptation and ultimately to innovation.

It should be emphasized that this model of the decision-making process is more descriptive than normative. It depicts what *typical* decision makers *usually* do following a problematic stimulus. It obviously does not hold for every decision maker in every situation. One could think of examples where failures might lead to an increased aspiration level. For example, failure to make the high school

---

1 In this sense the system is relatively open or closed, depending on the decision maker. Although he or she may close the system by considering few alternatives, the *potential* range of alternatives is quite open. Computational techniques consider all the alternatives as identified in the model. However, the model itself usually represents a relatively closed system as compared with reality. The critical aspect of the open-system decision model is emphasis on the human element and the potential scope of continual interaction between the decision maker and the environment.

debating team may cause an individual to raise his or her sights and eventually become a successful debater in college. However, such examples are relatively rare and can be treated as exceptions.

Satisficing Behavior

The general model emphasizes finding satisfactory rather than optimal solutions. In this framework optimality is a utopian concept because of the lack of complete knowledge and a tendency for the decision maker to test alternative solutions that are readily apparent. He or she does not attempt an exhaustive search and evaluation program. However, this does not mean that decision makers cannot approach optimality. On the contrary, studies indicate that even in complex, unstructured situations strategic choices are preceded by reasonably structured decision-making processes (the open-system model) that lead *toward* the best solution. Although there is no clear-cut, cookbook technique that adequately describes managerial decision making in ambiguous situations, patterns are evident in stimuli (crises, problems, and opportunities), solutions (given, ready-made, custom-made, and modified), and processes used (recognition, diagnosis, search, design, and implementation).[2]

Empirical research involving the observation and description of decision-making processes in organizations can be related to the open-system model. In four case studies, for example, researchers found little evidence of explicit objectives.[3] Rather, the very nature of the organization as a coalition of subsystems suggests the presence of multiple objectives. At times the goals are hierarchical in nature and complementary. At other times, conflict among goals is apparent.

The research indicated little conscious comparison of specific alternatives. It seemed that rules of thumb resulted in "reasonably good" solutions to problems. However, there was no way to identify optimality and hence establish a yardstick of goodness. The cases studied involved two crises and two situations that allowed a more cogitative or planning approach. In neither did it appear that an exhaustive list of alternatives was organized and/or evaluated. An alternative was accepted if it satisfied general constraints and enjoyed the support of key managers.

Organizational Search

Organizational search appears to be a more complex process than envisioned in closed-system models of decision making. The classical theory indicates

2 Henry Mintzberg, Duru Raisinghani, and André Théorêt, "The Structure of 'Unstructured' Decision Processes," *Administrative Science Quarterly,* June 1976, pp. 246–275.

3 Richard M. Cyert and James G. March, *A Behavioral Theory of the Firm,* Prentice-Hall, Inc., Englewood Cliffs, N.J., 1963, pp. 44–82.

that there is a search for alternatives followed by evaluation and choice. The empirical research suggests that the search may continue beyond the point of choice as a means of rationalizing the decisions during the implementation phase. Organizations may engage in elaborate processes to justify a decision that has already been made.

If an individual or an organization has an abundance of resources, inefficiencies may be lightly regarded. Effectiveness then becomes of primary concern; a satisfactory solution will be one that works. If resources are limited, then efficiency becomes relatively more important and solutions must be both effective and efficient. In fact, there may be tradeoffs; less effective solutions may be accepted if substantial savings are made in the use of resources. This, of course, involves the continual adjustment of objectives.

Another facet of the classical theory of decision making suggests that the search for alternatives is a one-way street. That is, the individual or organization seeks to identify alternatives and then to evaluate them. Empirical research indicates that the process is somewhat more complex. "Many of the events in these studies suggest a mating theory of search. Not only are organizations looking for alternatives, alternatives are also looking for organizations."[4] Whether a relatively routine decision or a more adaptive or innovative decision, it seems that alternatives are suggested to decision makers by outside agencies such as salespeople, staff specialists, or other similar organizational units. The presentation of alternatives, therefore, may be a problematic stimulus that touches off the managerial decision-making process.

In the cases studied, computation with regard to the anticipated consequences of alternatives were carried out in rough fashion and tended to be quite simple in nature. Only a few calculations were made and elaborate techniques were rarely employed. Two important steps were checking for feasibility and improvement—was money available, and was the proposed solution better than the existing situation? These questions were often difficult to answer, but much less difficult than trying to determine the expected net return on all alternative investments.

The multiplicity of objectives made evaluation of anticipated outcomes quite difficult. Individuals and organizations face a different mix of results for various alternatives. There is no single dimension on which to measure all relevant considerations. Ascertaining the best solution "on balance" is a difficult task. It involves establishing tradeoffs for cost, speed, accuracy, safety, quality, and many other factors that may be pertinent according to the specific problem. However, this balancing act *is performed* by operating managers in organizational settings.

Selective Perception

The situation is even more complex because of the role played by selective perception or even bias. Individuals may unconsciously anticipate outcomes

---

4 Ibid., p. 80.

that are favorable. They may attach a higher than realistic probability to a certain outcome if it is particularly desirable. This type of conscious or unconscious bias may have an important effect on the choice of alternatives.

In each of the cases studied there is some suggestion of unconscious or semiconscious adjustment of perceptions to hope. . . . In addition, there is some evidence of more conscious manipulation of expectations. The classic statement came from a staff member involved in one of the decisions . . . "In the final analysis, if anybody brings up an item of cost that we haven't thought of, we can balance it by making another source of savings tangible."[5]

Where human beings are involved in decision-making processes in dynamic organizations, they are confronted with complex environmental forces. The model shown in Figure 16.1 provides the framework for decision making in relatively open, complex systems. It is a descriptive model developed from observations of decision makers in actual problem-solving situations, and it provides a flexible framework that can be used for all individual and organizational decision making.

Individual Decision Making

An individual's image or value system results from total past experience and is as unique as fingerprints. However, values are extremely difficult to "get a handle on." They cannot be seen or felt. They result in a propensity to decide or act in a specific way, given a particular problem. Value systems must be hypothesized by working backward from overt actions or expressions made by individuals in response to various stimuli.

The individual is the focal point of the open-system model of decision making, and there is a continuum of openness, depending on the individual's frame of mind with regard to a particular question. In many instances people maintain a relatively closed mind on an issue because it is easier than investigating unfamiliar or unpalatable points of view.

Even when considering ill-structured policy issues and using an open-system model such as depicted in Figure 16.1, decision makers may use an approach that results in a relatively closed decision process. If they do not push beyond well-entrenched beliefs, conclusions may follow relatively automatically, given a problematic stimulus. The more decision makers are disposed toward seeking new alternatives and additional information, the more open the decision-making process. The process can be described as relatively open or closed, and decision makers can be described as relatively open-minded or closed-minded.[6]

5 Ibid., p. 81.
6 Milton Rokeach, *The Open and Closed Mind,* Basic Books, Inc., Publishers, New York, 1960, pp. 392–393.

Apparently a particular degree of open-mindedness does not hold true across all issues. Individuals may be closed-minded with regard to religious issues but relatively open-minded on political questions. Similarly, a person might be relatively closed-minded with regard to financial matters and yet quite open-minded with regard to human rights. Moreover, research findings indicate that we can have open-minded conservatives and closed-minded liberals, contrary to popular misconceptions.

Rokeach cites key criteria for open-mindedness, or the ability to form new belief systems, as follows:

1 The ability to remember or to keep in mind all the new parts to be integrated
2 A willingness to "play along" or to entertain new systems
3 Past experience, which determines whether a particular system is, psychologically speaking, new or not new [7]

The implications of related research findings stress the importance of personality rather than intelligence in cognitive functioning, and the ability to synthesize seems much more important for creativity than the ability to analyze. Cognitive and affective (emotional) functioning are not mutually exclusive, they are different facets of a person's total behavior.

The relationship of personal values and organizational strategy seems quite evident. [8] While managers may feel that they are objective in decision making with regard to setting goals and devising strategy, they should recognize that values stem from total past experience and are very subtle yet ever-present factors. Identifying values through introspection will be helpful if an executive wants to understand his or her decisions. Moreover, such an appraisal should be a continuing endeavor because the value profile may change over time. Economic considerations may be paramount at one stage in an individual's career but give way to other values at some later stage. Identifying one's own values is not easy, and it is even more difficult to empathize with someone else.

Facts
and
Values

Values—personal views of what is preferable or what ought to be—affect decision making directly. Value judgments come into play at many stages of the open-system model. Given different backgrounds and perspectives, one man-

---

7 Ibid., p. 398.

8 For a discussion of how individual value profiles (relative strengths of economic, theoretical, political, religious, aesthetic, and social orientations) affect organizational strategy and major policies, see William T. Guth and Renato Tagiuri, "Personal Values and Corporate Strategies," *Harvard Business Review,* September–October 1965, pp. 123–132.

ager may recognize a problem in a particular situation, while another may not. The identification of relevant and appropriate alternatives may depend on individual value systems. An alternative suggested by one individual may be entirely unpalatable to another. Individual hopes or biases have an important effect on the assessment of the probabilities of outcomes related to various alternatives.

Values are involved in determining the importance of various outcomes (see Figure 14.5). Decision makers may agree on the specific probability, but the "importance" of any particular outcome will vary with the perspectives of the decision maker. The general model indicates that a choice is made by balancing the importance of outcomes. "Balancing" is generally laden with value judgments, but the process is very difficult to identify.

While the open-system model of decision making is saturated with value judgments, there are factual considerations as well. In any problem-solving situation, the factual elements are those that can be verified by testing. For example, if the director of athletics is faced with the decision of whether or not to fire the football coach, there are some factual and many value considerations. It is a fact that the team won two and lost nine games during the season. It is a fact that the coach's contract has two more years to run at $30,000 per year. It is a fact that at least some alumni are unhappy, as evidenced by the letters received. On the other hand, there may be a wide difference of opinion regarding the merits of a 2 and 9 record. Similarly, there may be divergent opinions with regard to the importance of the $60,000 necessary to pay off the coach's contract. There may also be differences of opinion with regard to the coach's ability as a tactician, manager, recruiter, or other qualities perceived to be necessary in a good coach. None of these latter considerations can be verified; they are value judgments.

Many values that decision makers hold will be implicit. They will rarely, if ever, consciously introspect enough to identify their own value systems and their impact on the decision-making process. In some cases, however, where decisions are particularly important and visible, decision makers may consciously consider the values that they hold to be important. They may assess explicitly the impact of various alternatives on their value systems and make decisions accordingly. Value systems develop bit by bit over the life cycle of individuals and hence are intricately interwoven with instinctual and habitual behavior as well as more cogitative decision-making activity.

The development of value systems that are in part learned from other individuals or groups distinguishes humans from other animals. We transmit such knowledge across generations. "*Homo sapiens* is physiologically capable, unlike other species, of a wide variety of mutually exclusive responses to given stimuli. This capacity for choice is the essential physio-psychological basis for the development of what we identify as 'values,' namely standards of the desirable which men apply in making choices." [9]

---

[9] Philip E. Jacob et al., *Values and Their Function in Decision-Making*, Supplement no. 9 to *The American Behavioral Scientist*, May 1962, p. 13.

Beliefs

"Beliefs reflect an individual's view of the interrelationship of events either past, present, or future." [10] They are convictions (or at least acceptance) that certain things are true or real. For example, a person's preference for white wine may be based partly on the belief that red wine causes headaches. Product choices reflect beliefs about relationships such as toothpaste-cavities, shampoo-attractiveness, motor oil-engine life, or computer systems-administrative efficiency.

Beliefs (what is true) and values (what is good) are related concepts, but there is an important difference. Because they have some factual basis (often assumed rather than proved), beliefs can be confirmed or disconfirmed. An ad campaign or TV show based on past success patterns may fizzle and lead to some rethinking about cause-effect relationships.

Our sources of beliefs include: [11]

1 *Induction:* The development of a belief based on accumulated observations of past experience; e.g., over time one might find that Tide produces a whiter wash.
2 *Construction:* The adoption of a theory about relationships that may or may not be based on factual observations; e.g., hearsay evidence may lead one to believe that women won't work for a woman boss.
3 *Analogy:* Beliefs formed by generalizing from similar objects, situations, or events; e.g., a person with a volatile red-haired cousin may believe that all red-haired people are volatile.
4 *Authority:* Situations in which the information source has enough authority to maintain the belief; e.g., we believe that the earth goes around the sun because we have confidence in the astronomers who tell us so.

An individual's system of beliefs is accumulated over time and adjusted continually, according to experience and reflective observation. Beliefs and values are integral factors in the decision-making process.

Ethical Considerations

Decision making is affected by ethical considerations—explicit or implicit moral standards that guide behavior. Codes of ethics are prescriptions for what a person's values should be, rather than descriptions of what they actually are. In Chapter 6 we discussed some of the dilemmas for individuals in organizational contexts and for organizations in societal contexts. Here we are concerned with developing some guidelines for making decisions that have ethical overtones and conflicting values.

10 Ronald J. Ebert and Terence R. Mitchell, *Organizational Decision Processes*, Crane, Russak & Company, Inc., New York, 1975, p. 51.
11 Ibid., p. 53.

Many classical philosophers concentrated on developing a moral law or framework that pinpointed a single supreme "good" by which evaluations could be made. Over the years philosophers have attacked the monolithic systems—in some cases advocating an alternative supreme "good" but in many cases offering no substitute system.

The monolithic approach is an example of closed-mindedness in the sense that one yardstick provides the answer in all problematic situations. Given the complexity of modern society, this approach does not seem to offer much to organizational decision makers. Yet the other end of the spectrum does not offer much either. This is the extreme case of situational ethics wherein no framework is available for evaluating the impact of alternative courses of action. Some moderate or middle ground would seem to be appropriate. Leys sets forth this concept as follows:

The "value framework" that I shall articulate consists of a set of standards, tests, or criteria which are always relevant but none of which is always controlling. I believe that, in the making of a decision, it is possible to consider these values in a somewhat orderly fashion. I believe that administrators who learn how to review these criteria in an orderly manner are the ones that have acquired the art of "asking the right questions," and that by practicing this art they improve the quality of their judgment. [12]

It is useful to identify some framework of values explicitly (see Figure 16.2). They may not all apply in a given situation, and the weight of any particular value may change with the situation; but the system should not be infinite because such an approach would not be particularly helpful to decision makers in practical situations. They should have a framework of contingencies to use on a day-to-day basis when they have decisions to make that allow a reflective approach. [13]

When decision makers are confronted with difficult choices, they can "talk to themselves" in terms of various standards or principles. They may have to compromise particular norms or values in a given situation (loyalty to a superior or an organization), but they can be reasonably comfortable if they recognize that certain other values are enhanced by so doing (integrity and self-respect). They must cope with pressures from individuals and/or groups from inside and outside the organization. Formally and informally, various values are "pushed" at decision makers, who either discard them or integrate them into their own value systems. This is the "balancing act" performed in any judgmental decision process. On balance, what is most important? What tips the scale in this particular situation?

Decision makers in the real world cannot afford the luxury of deciding

---

12 Wayne A. R. Leys, "The Value Framework of Decision-making," in Sidney M. Mailick and Edward H. Van Ness (eds.), *Concepts and Issues in Administrative Behavior,* © 1962, p. 81. Reprinted by permission of Prentice-Hall, Inc., Englewood Cliffs, N.J.
13 Theodore V. Purcell, S.J., "Do Courses in Business Ethics Pay Off?" *California Management Review,* Summer 1977, pp. 50–58.

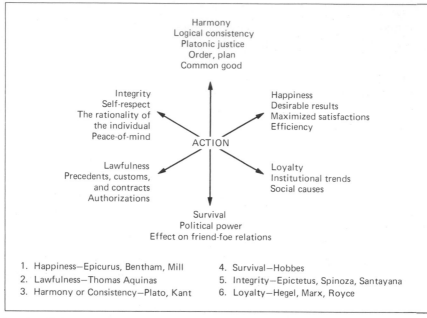

Harmony
Logical consistency
Platonic justice
Order, plan
Common good

Integrity
Self-respect
The rationality of
the individual
Peace-of-mind

Happiness
Desirable results
Maximized satisfactions
Efficiency

ACTION

Lawfulness
Precedents, customs,
and contracts
Authorizations

Loyalty
Institutional trends
Social causes

Survival
Political power
Effect on friend-foe relations

1. Happiness—Epicurus, Bentham, Mill
2. Lawfulness—Thomas Aquinas
3. Harmony or Consistency—Plato, Kant

4. Survival—Hobbes
5. Integrity—Epictetus, Spinoza, Santayana
6. Loyalty—Hegel, Marx, Royce

Figure 16.2   The Relationship of Values to Decision Making
Adapted from Wayne A. R. Leys, "The Value Framework of Decision-making," in Sidney M. Mailick and Edward H. Van Ness (eds.), *Concepts and Issues in Administrative Behavior*, Prentice-Hall, Inc., Englewood Cliffs, N.J., 1962, pp. 87–88.

policy questions in general. This leads to all-encompassing values or standards that do not really apply in specific situations. The decision maker is better advised to develop a sense of the situation and deal with each problem on its own merits. "The philosopher or value-theorist . . . should not try to make the official's decisions. Only the man at the scene of action has access to the factual components of the decision." [14]

It is important to stress the general approach rather than the specific norms or ethical standards identified in a simplified model. Within our culture some consensus may be developed for a model such as the one presented in Figure 16.2. However, even this may be too much to ask. In addition, it is obvious that such a system would not apply across cultural boundaries. The weights given to various objectives or standards of conduct vary considerably. Therefore, a model such as this would have to be developed for each culture in order that managerial decision makers would have a useful value framework for making difficult choices. [15]

14 Leys, op. cit., p. 93.

15 Walter Guzzardi, Jr., "An Unscandalized View of Those 'Bribes' Abroad," *Fortune*, July 1976, pp. 118ff.

Groups and Decision Making

We are interested in the role of groups in the open-system decision model for two reasons. First, there is organizational decision making, in which groups themselves are the agents of choice. Second, in organizational settings there is the impact that groups have on individual choice behavior. Two basic questions: How do groups make decisions, and how do groups affect individual decision making?

To understand group processes, it is important to identify their value systems in order to anticipate their propensity to behave in certain ways. [16] Obviously, if a group is made up of individuals with very similar value systems, prediction of group decisions is relatively easy. On the other hand, if a group is comprised of diverse members, prediction may be much more difficult. Moreover, the degree of cohesiveness may vary with respect to different issues.

There is a spectrum of cohesiveness with regard to individual and group goals. If identical, progress toward group aims is likely. At the other end of the spectrum, minimal agreement between individual and group goals may be evident. Such groups would be relatively unstable and not very well "organized." In some cases group values are quite explicit and endure for long periods of time while organizational membership experiences continuing turnover and change. Those who internalize the group goals remain and become part of a cohesive unit. Those who cannot adjust to the group values will become less active and may eventually drop from the fold. Many religious and other similar volunteer organizations could be described in such terms.

Groups as Decision Makers

A comparison of individuals and groups as decision makers can be useful. A number of issues might be considered—effectiveness, efficiency, open- or closed-mindedness, risk, and rationality.

For example, is a group more effective than an individual decision maker? Often we hear the adage that the best way not to get a decision is to appoint a committee to study the issue. If effectiveness is related only to whether or not a decision is made expeditiously, a committee may be less effective. On the other hand, the evidence on this matter is not clear-cut. Individuals often procrastinate when faced with complex decisions.

A number of specific methods are used by groups to make decisions: (1) *lack of response,* i.e., to a proposed solution by one or a few members; (2) *authority*

16 Patrick E. Connor and Boris W. Becker, "Values and the Organization: Suggestions for Research," *Academy of Management Journal,* September 1975, pp. 550–561.

rule, the leader "announcing" the decision; (3) *minority rule,* a few people with assumed expertise and/or loud voices; (4) *majority rule,* let's take a vote; (5) *consensus,* the most acceptable (not necessarily optimal) solution for all members; and (6) *unanimity,* a possible, but not probable, condition in complex situations. Research has shown that on complex problem-solving tasks to which there is a single correct answer, groups using a consensus mode have been more effective than individuals (except in rare cases), averaging techniques, or other group methods cited above. [17] The strength of the consensus approach is that differences of opinion are used creatively; they are assumed to be natural and are expected. Different points of view are sought out, heard, and encouraged. "Disagreements can help the group's decision because with a wide range of information and opinions, there is a greater chance that the group will hit upon more adequate solutions." [18]

Formal status systems can inhibit social interaction and thereby reduce group effectiveness if all resources are not utilized. This is particularly true if the status system is inversely related to expertise. [19] Obviously, the most effective approach would be to match degree of expertise with degree of participation and influence. This is a very difficult objective to achieve because problems are different, group membership changes, and degree of expertise may be impossible to ascertain, at least a priori.

The effectiveness of a group in decision making relates to the particular values that seem most desirable—speed, accuracy, or creativity, for example. And participation may be important from the standpoint of implementing a decision. In many problematic situations, no decision may be the best solution, at least for the time being. Thus, referring the decision to a group wherein conflicting value systems become evident and no action is taken may be the best approach after all.

With regard to efficiency, it seems obvious that more work-hours are spent in group decision making than if an individual were to tackle the problem alone. Yet, an individual could spend more time in analyzing a problem because of the need for gathering diverse information input. From this point of view, concentrated group attention to the problem may be more efficient in terms of work-hours. The efficiency of specialization can also be brought to bear on the problem. While more time might be spent via the group approach, the cost may be less than if a higher-priced executive were to do it alone. Also, efficiency should be viewed from the broader perspective of both deciding and implementing. In this context the group approach may be more efficient in the long run.

A group tends to open the system more than an individual. An individual, on a particular issue, might range on a spectrum from closed-mindedness to open-mindedness. If a group is involved, it seems likely that a more open total

17 Jay Hall, "Decisions, Decisions, Decisions," *Psychology Today,* November 1971, pp. 51–54ff.
18 Ibid., p. 86.
19 Charles R. Holloman and Hal W. Hendrick, "Effects of Status and Individual Ability on Group Problem Solving," *Decision Sciences,* October 1972, pp. 55–63.

value system would prevail. This is not automatic, however. A group may be extremely cohesive, and individual members may have internalized group goals to the extent that they think as one mind. Groups with divergent member opinions are probably more typical. The decision process in such cases involves information inputs from several or many points of view, and hence the value system would tend to be more open. A possible result from such a group is a decision not to decide. The most hopeless situation would be that of a group composed of closed-minded individuals with diverse value systems. On the other hand, a group of open-minded individuals with diverse value systems might prove to be an effective and efficient problem-solving agent.

Groups are usually considered to be conservative decision makers. The committee, for example, is often accused of recommending solutions that represent "the lowest common denominator." This implies status quo, or at best, moving incrementally not very far from some current practice. In organizational settings groups may be satisfied with relatively small certain improvements in operations rather than risk a loss in an attempt to obtain a bonanza.

There is some evidence to indicate that groups in such situations are more risky.[20] In part, this can be explained by the concept of spreading risk. If one individual is solely responsible for a risky venture, he or she may balk. If a group is involved in making the decision, responsibility is effectively diffused and no one individual feels "under the gun." Therefore groups may, in fact, engage in more risky decision-making behavior than individuals. Other research indicates both risky and cautious shifts, depending on the issue involved. Prevailing cultural values, as expressed in group processes, can influence individuals to shift in whichever direction seems "appropriate."[21] Of course, in all these instances we are considering tendencies. Some individuals will be much more risky than most groups. Some groups, because of the composite of individual value systems, may be much more conservative than most individuals.

Group Rationality

How do groups compare with individuals in terms of rationality and decision making? It is important to remember two views of rationality: (1) the choice and (2) the process. To achieve a logical, methodical, exhaustive, systematic decision process, an organized group effort may be the answer. Weber's normative bureaucratic model was designed in part to offset the capriciousness of individual decision makers. His concept was that explicit, well-defined organizational procedures would tend to eliminate, or at least alleviate, the problems stemming from rule-of-thumb methods used by individual decision makers. He

20 Yeshayahu Rim, "Social Attitudes and Risk Taking," *Human Relations,* August 1965, pp. 259–265.

21 James A. F. Stoner, "Risky and Cautious Shifts in Group Decisions: The Influence of Widely Held Values," *Journal of Experimental Social Psychology,* October 1968, pp. 442–459.

was concerned with the individual bias that often resulted in decisions that were "out of line" with organizational objectives.

Groups may use more rational decision-making processes than individuals when the procedure is formalized and the steps are followed to the letter. This explicit, visible approach tends to make the process more systematic. Again, these are tendencies; some individuals may follow extremely rational approaches to decision making, while some groups may be quite capricious.

In terms of the choice itself, there is no clear way to differentiate between groups and individuals. In both cases decisions are intendedly rational. That is, an alternative is chosen that will move the individual or group toward a goal (expressed or implied). The rationality of choice may appear quite different to someone other than the decision-making agent. If rationality is to be measured in terms of a consensus, then maybe a group approach will result in a greater readiness, on the part of all concerned, to term the decision rational. Having participated in the process, most group members will probably engage in less "second guessing" and accept the chosen alternative as the best under the circumstances.

A group may facilitate the development of more information with regard to a problematic situation and hence move the decision closer to "ideal" rationality, where one of the requirements is complete knowledge. However, the inclusion of diverse information inputs often widens the scope of the problem environment, introduces confounding variables, and, in general, makes the situation more complex. As a result, the evaluation of alternatives, particularly predicting the probability and importance of outcomes, becomes much more difficult.

Group Creativity

The most typical method for group decision making is a face-to-face meeting, where the problem is identified and discussed, solutions are proposed and evaluated, and a choice is made by voting. Because group decision making is so pervasive and because there is so much dissatisfaction with the typical unstructured approach, a number of alternatives have been proposed.

When creativity is an important goal, **brainstorming** methods have been designed to offset the tendency for groups to be hypercritical of new ideas. [22] For example, **synectics** has been developed as an elaborate technique to emphasize "two basic and interrelated approaches: first, procedures that lead to imaginative speculation; second, disciplined ways of behaving so that speculation is not cut down but valued and encouraged." [23]

Other methods have been developed to replace or enhance the typical face-to-face, interacting group approach. The **delphi technique** can be used with physically dispersed participants. The process involves soliciting ideas or opinions

22 Alex F. Osborn, *Applied Imagination,* 3d ed., Charles Scribner's Sons, New York, 1963.
23 George M. Prince, *The Practice of Creativity,* Collier Books, New York, 1972, p. 9.

(via a questionnaire) on a particular problem or issue, collating and summarizing them, and feeding the results back to the participants. Several iterations are typically used to focus the problem solving and move toward consensus. The decision maker (an individual or small group) then uses the results to help make a decision and/or plan appropriate action steps.

The ***nominal group technique*** involves a structured process for integrating individual thinking and group interaction in order to capitalize on the benefits of both. A typical approach includes: (1) silent generation of ideas in writing; (2) recorded round-robin feedback from each member for presentation of ideas to the group, wherein ideas are summarized in a terse phrase and written on a black-board or flip-chart; (3) discussion of recorded ideas to evaluate information; and (4) silent individual voting on priorities. [24]

In research on the creative or information-generation phase of solving a problem that was perceived as difficult, controversial, and emotionally involving, it was found that "nominal and delphi processes generate almost half again as many ideas as interacting groups, and that nominal groups generate slightly more ideas than delphi groups. . . . Groups in the nominal process perceived a significantly higher level of satisfaction than did groups in the interacting and delphi processes. . . . There was no significant difference in perceived group satisfaction between interacting and delphi." [25] These results cannot be generalized to all group decision making. Decision quality and acceptance are key considerations, but efficiency (in terms of time and cost) is also important. For example, the delphi technique obviously takes significantly more chronological time (weeks or months) than may be available for making a decision. However, the nominal group process could be used advantageously in many situations in which interacting groups are used because "that is the way we've always done it."

Groups and Individual Decision Makers

It is apparent that social forces influence individual attitudes and behavior. Decisions about individual goals or actions are affected significantly by "group pressure" in a setting of shared norms regarding such goals or actions.

Asch tested the degree to which subjects move toward group responses to unambiguous visual stimuli, once they perceive themselves to be quite divergent. The essence of the study was to determine the effect of felt pressure on the bona fide subject to conform to the phony responses of the other "subjects." Asch describes the results as follows:

Of course individuals differed in response. At one extreme, about one quarter of the subjects were completely independent and never agreed with the erroneous judgments of

---

24 Andrew H. Van de Ven, *Group Decision Making and Effectiveness,* Kent State University Press, Kent, Ohio, 1974, p. 2.
25 Ibid., p. 63.

the majority. At the other extreme, some individuals went with the majority nearly all of the time. The performances of individuals in this experiment tend to be highly consistent. Those who strike out on the path of independence do not, as a rule, succumb to the majority even over an extended series of trials, while those who choose the path of compliance are unable to free themselves as the ordeal is prolonged. [26]

When the subject was supported to some degree, either deliberately by one of the phony subjects or by a second bona fide subject, the probability of retaining independence was increased significantly. Apparently, the feeling of isolation was overwhelming in many cases, and even the slightest indication of support was used as substantiation of independent judgment.

In spite of these results, subjects, when interviewed, almost without exception maintained that independence was preferable to conformity. Independence may be a normative theory, while conformity may be more descriptive of the real world. The tendency to conformity varies with the individual, and for a given individual, it varies according to particular situations. When experienced or knowledgeable about a particular issue, we may retain our independent judgment. On other issues we may feel less well informed and hence be willing to adjust our thinking according to the majority of peers, subordinates, or superiors. There may be some fine lines between traits such as independence and closed-mindedness. A bigot is not likely to adjust his or her thinking merely because the majority holds a different view. Open-minded independence would be the "golden mean," but such a balance may be hard to achieve.

The reluctance of individuals to voice counterarguments in cohesive groups is a pervasive phenomenon. Janis suggests that "The more amiability and esprit de corps there is among the members of a policy-making ingroup, the greater the danger that independent critical thinking will be replaced by groupthink." [27] The term *groupthink* is used purposely to connote the detrimental aspects of group pressure as described by George Orwell in *1984*. [28] After studying a massive amount of material on policy decision-making processes (formal and informal) concerning major issues such as Pearl Harbor, Vietnam, and the Bay of Pigs, Janis concluded that the groups that committed the fiascos were victims of groupthink.

Several key people in strategic groups under Presidents Kennedy, Johnson, and Nixon later reported that they failed to express their doubts about the alternatives chosen because of the seeming unanimity in the group, only to find later that at least one other person had the same doubts. If either had expressed his opinion and been supported by the other, there is a strong possibility that the group would at least have reconsidered the issue.

Positive steps can offset the groupthink phenomenon; effective groups typically have some or all of the following characteristics or features:

26 Solomon Asch, "Opinions and Social Pressure," in Harold J. Leavitt and Lewis R. Pondy (eds.), *Readings in Managerial Psychology*, The University of Chicago Press, Chicago, 1964, p. 308.
27 Irving L. Janis, "Groupthink," *Psychology Today*, November 1971, p. 44.
28 George Orwell, *1984*, Harcourt, Brace and Company, Inc., New York, 1949.

1 The leader encourages each member to be a critical evaluator.
2 The leader (and key members) should be impartial in the early stages of deliberations.
3 The same problem is assigned to outside groups, who input results.
4 At intervals, before a consensus is reached, each member tests proposals on subordinates and reports the results.
5 Outside experts are invited in and encouraged to challenge views of key group members. [29]
6 At every meeting someone is assigned the role of devil's advocate.
7 There is explicit empathy with rival (nation or organization) to anticipate consequences of actions.
8 Subgroups are used to get more involvement, then differences are addressed in the total group.
9 After consensus is reached, a follow-up meeting should be held (time permitting) in order to allow second thoughts and residual doubts to be aired. [30]

This process can be overdone if diverse points of view are never resolved and inaction results. The leader must maintain an equilibrium in the group's interactive process that encourages critical thinking and involvement but does not preclude consensus when a decision must be made. [31]

Cognitive Dissonance

A tendency toward uniformity results from an individual's internal cognitive processes. The individual recognizes differences in his or her perception of a situation from the perceptions of others or from the group as a whole. The mental state resulting from this situation has been termed ***cognitive dissonance.*** [32] The theory says that two cognitions are dissonant if, considering those two alone, the adverse of one element would follow from the other. The theory further holds that dissonance, being psychologically uncomfortable, will motivate the person to try to reduce dissonance and achieve consonance.

With regard to group pressures on individual decision makers, cognitive dissonance could result if group action were contrary to individual values, beliefs, and perceptions. The individual may play a role in an organization and hence have a need to decide issues in a way that will be organizationally rational. At the

---

29 The importance of truly "outside" and *independent* (maybe even hostile) evaluators cannot be overemphasized. Daniel S. Greenberg, "Don't Ask the Barber Whether You Need a Haircut," *Saturday Review,* Nov. 25, 1972, pp. 58–59.

30 Janis, op cit., p. 76.

31 Norman R. F. Maier, "Assets and Liabilities in Group Problem Solving: The Need for an Integrative Function," *Psychological Review,* July 1967, pp. 239–249.

32 Leon Festinger, *A Theory of Cognitive Dissonance,* Harper & Row, Publishers, Incorporated, New York, 1957.

same time, his or her own private value system may not be able to accept the alternatives implemented (person-role conflict). Because this is an uncomfortable mental state, the individual typically will engage in cognitive behavior that will reduce dissonance and result in a more comfortable state of mind. An individual copes with dissonance and/or strives for cognitive consonance in many ways.

1 He can *blame himself;* i.e., come to believe his own judgment is faulty and that the group is correct.

2 He can *blame the group;* i.e., the group judgment is faulty and his is correct.

3 He can try to *reconcile discrepant judgments* and look for reasons that "explain away" the differences.

4 He can *accept the fact of individual differences,* particularly when the issues involved are subjective and/or personal.

5 He can *avoid evidence of discrepancy* and maintain independence through "isolation" from the group.

6 He can decide that he has been *deceived* (in an experiment or some actual situation) and that no "real" discrepancy exists. [33]

Overt pressure to conform does not create as much dissonance as self-determined discrepancies because the individual can "rationalize" conforming behavior in terms of being forced into it. More dissonance and more change result from felt pressures that are internalized and not easily attributable to an outside agency. A subtle form of dissonance results when a person behaves differently from what he believes is right. The cognitive dissonance resulting from this situation may be resolved via one of the modes described above or by merely concluding that the issue is "not worth it."

Not all group pressure should be viewed as pressure toward conformity or uniformity. Some groups exist to ensure divergent points of view. Discussion groups or legislative bodies may set up elaborate mechanisms so that they can agree to disagree. There is explicit recognition of the need for different opinions and an open-minded approach to decision making.

Because individuals typically belong to many groups simultaneously, the group pressure they feel on various issues may result in their being relatively open-minded. For example, they could (1) come from a small farming community; (2) have a parent who is a relatively conservative merchant; (3) be exposed to liberal teachers; (4) work for a large national company; (5) belong to a rather puritan religious sect; (6) be a registered Democrat; (7) have a Republican spouse; (8) be an Elk and/or a Shriner; (9) coach a gymnastics team; and (10) be active in union affairs. Of course, such pressures (some explicit, many implied) make the individual's environment exceedingly dynamic and complex.

33 David Krech, Richard S. Crutchfield, and Egerton L. Ballachey, *Individual in Society,* McGraw-Hill Book Company, New York, 1962, pp. 516 and 517.

The Interface of Computational and Judgmental Approaches

Managerial decision making—at operating, coordinative, and strategic levels—takes place in systems that can be considered along a continuum from relatively closed to relatively open, from stable-mechanistic to adaptive-organic. Within this framework it is obvious that problems fit anywhere along the spectrum. In some cases all the assumptions required for closed-system, programmed approaches may be appropriate. Factors can be quantified, and sophisticated computational techniques can be applied.

In other cases these assumptions simply do not hold at all. The important thing is to recognize the particular situation for what it is, be it a relatively closed or relatively open system. Quantification and mathematical techniques have been most useful for computational problem solving when few variables have to be considered and value issues are restricted. As managers face decisions that encompass more territory, involve numerous variables, and include nonquantifiable aspects, judgment plays a more important role. Wise decision makers recognize when different approaches will be appropriate. A problem may be made up of numerous subproblems, all of which can be solved with computational techniques. The overall problem, however, requires integrating the "solutions" from subproblems into a total system. Often the larger system will be relatively open because it includes more environmental inputs and relies on the judgment of managerial decision makers. In this latter case the individual or group value system comes into play, adding more openness and complexity.

Unfortunately, the attention devoted to computational problem-solving techniques has far outstripped that devoted to judgmental considerations. The literature of management science or operations research abounds with techniques for decision making. The inordinate amount of time devoted to clear-cut, quantifiable problems is unfortunate from the standpoint that such situations represent such a small proportion of managerial decision making (primarily economic-technical considerations at the operating level). The number of decisions that can be so construed is much less than the number that cannot be approached in that manner. And the importance of such decision problems is much less than that of the more complex, comprehensive policy issues that management faces continually in the coordinative and strategic subsystems.

It seems evident that much of the literature is technique-oriented, dealing with sophisticated refinements of various management science tools. Management scientists have been accused of "talking to themselves" in terms of techniques, with less than desirable orientation to real-world problems.[34] More

34 Donald F. Heany, "Is TIMS Talking to Itself?" *Management Science*, December 1965, pp. B-146–155; and Harry Stern, "Is Information Systems Talking to Itself?" *Interfaces*, August 1972, pp. 54–57.

emphasis on problems rather than techniques has been urged by many writers. For example, Drucker suggests that, "Insight, understanding, ranking of priorities, and a 'feel' for the complexity of an area are as important as precise, elegant mathematical models—and, in fact, are usually infinitely more useful and indeed even more 'scientific.' "[35]

Why has more not been done concerning nonprogrammable problem solving in open systems? The best answer probably relates to the complexity of open systems and the "messy" decisions that are often required. It is not that nothing has been done. On the contrary, much scientific knowledge is available from the behavioral and social sciences that relates to decision making in complex situations, and the scientific method as an approach to problem solving has been stressed in many disciplines and practical settings. The difficult part is putting the general approach together with the untidy aspects of open-system problems in the context of managerial decision making. Much more work needs to be done in this regard.[36]

Algorithmic (cookbook) approaches proceed according to an explicit, programmed set of computations. Heuristic (sophisticated trial-and-error) approaches, on the other hand, rely more heavily on the wisdom and judgment of the human decision maker at all stages in the decision-making process. Lindblom describes the applicability of these approaches to policy decisions as follows:

For complex problems, the first of these two approaches [root or algorithmic or computational] is of course impossible. Although such an approach can be described, it cannot be practiced except for relatively simple problems and even then only in a somewhat modified form. It assumes intellectual capacities and sources of information that men simply do not possess, and it is even more absurd as an approach to policy when the time and money that can be allocated to a policy problem is limited, as is always the case. Of particular importance to public administrators is the fact that public agencies are in effect usually instructed not to practice the first method. That is to say, their prescribed functions and constraints—the politically, or legally possible—restrict their attention to relatively few values and relatively few alternative policies among the countless alternatives that might be imagined. It is the second method [branch or heuristic or judgmental] that is practiced.[37]

Lindblom states that the second method *describes* how most administrators approach complex questions. The first method is not workable for complex policy questions and hence merely *prescribes* how decisions "ought" to be made.

We do not suggest perpetuating existing managerial behavior by teach-

35 Peter F. Drucker, "The Performance Gap in Management Science: Reasons and Remedies," *Organizational Dynamics,* Autumn 1973, p. 29.

36 P. G. Moore, "Technique vs. Judgment in Decision Making," *Organizational Dynamics,* Autumn 1973, pp. 68–80.

37 Charles E. Lindblom, "The Science of 'Muddling Through,' " in Leavitt and Pondy, op. cit., pp. 62–63. (The words algorithmic, heuristic, computational, and judgmental have been added by the authors.)

ing what is done in current organizations. Obviously, many approaches could be improved. On the other hand, it is dangerous to pretend that methods dependent on simplifying assumptions will be applicable in the real world. Naturally, some reasonable middle-ground approach is needed so that normative or prescriptive models are enriched with realism garnered from practical experience. This appears to be a perfectly sound objective, but achieving it is extremely difficult. [38]

The first steps may be the development of mutual understanding on the part of practicing managers and management scientists. Managerial decision making is an art, not a science. Like all arts, however, it is dependent on a body of knowledge stemming from scientific disciplines. There must be mutual respect for the endeavors of both groups. Managers should understand the value systems of management science. Similarly, management scientists should understand the value systems of managers and the complexity of organizational problem-solving situations. Then, and only then, will the applicability of various techniques be appraised realistically.

Shakun suggests that mutual understanding can be enhanced via situational normativism, a process that "involves a search by manager and management scientist for a synthesized situational frame of understanding (involving analytic and heuristic knowledge) within which solutions to the . . . problem can be found." [39] Joint diagnosis requires interaction that leads to mutual understanding. This forms the basis for increased probability of implementing innovative changes because emphasis on situational diagnosis (rather than techniques of analysis) should lead to realism in model building. An ultimate objective is to make the situational-normativism approach an integral part of the organization's problem-solving process.

The complexity of open systems should be recognized, but complexity does not mean chaos. The heuristic approaches often used by competent decision makers can lead to descriptive models that incorporate untidy factors and uncontrollable environmental aspects. Management scientists can be most helpful in testing traditional assumptions, asking questions that help define problems, formulating alternative solutions (rather than *the* solution) to which managerial values, as well as current, specific knowledge and experience can be applied, and focusing on understanding (insight concerning what a decision is all about) rather than techniques. [40] Managerial decision making in open systems can be improved significantly, in many cases, by making the process more explicit. Management can become much more effective if managers consciously think through a process that may have been subconscious before.

38 James E. Rosenzweig, "Managers and Management Scientists (Two Cultures)," *Business Horizons,* Fall 1967, pp. 79–86.

39 Melvin F. Shakun, "Management Science and Management: Implementing Management Science via Situational Normativism," *Management Science,* April 1972, p. B-367.

40 Drucker, op. cit., p. 28.

Summary

Judgmental decision making in relatively open systems recognizes the complexity of the internal organizational climate and the external environment of decision makers. Particularly at strategic and coordinative levels, it is impossible to mold all the factors management must consider into explicit, well-defined models that can be quantified and solved via computational techniques.

The individual is an integral part of the decision-making process and makes any situation relatively open or closed according to his or her mental set (open-minded or closed-minded concerning problem definition, alternative generation, and search for relevant information).

Value systems or "images" result from an individual's total past experience. Value judgments come into play at many stages of the open-system model of decision making, and the personal beliefs and values of managers have a definite impact on their strategic and tactical decisions. Ethical pluralism recognizes that decisions typically cannot be referred to *one* clear-cut standard.

Groups are important in behavioral aspects of decision making for two reasons: (1) they are agents of choice and (2) they have an impact on individual decision makers. Groups have advantages such as more knowledge and information, more alternative solutions, and increased likelihood of a decision being understood and implemented. Potential disadvantages include social pressure (actual or implied) on individuals, domination by one or a few members, and conflict that forestalls action.

Most individual and organizational decision making takes place in relatively open systems. Computational techniques can be applied to many managerial decisions in which economic-technical and other considerations can be quantified. However, coordinative and strategic problems are usually too complex for such approaches and the judgment of the decision maker becomes relatively more important. Within the overall management system it is essential to recognize the context of problems and maintain a contingency view in determining the appropriateness of various approaches, either singly or in combination.

Questions and Problems

1 What trends are evident in the increasing complexity of the internal climate and external environment of organizations? What impact do these trends have on managerial decision making?

2 Using the open-system decision model (Figure 16.1), trace several individual and/or organizational decisions through the steps identified. Does it seem to fit actual behavior? Why or why not?

3 How does the individual's value system or particular approach in a given situation affect the openness of the environmental system for decision making?

4 Distinguish factual and value considerations in decision making. Which are more important? Why?

5 Identify several beliefs that have affected your decision making. Describe an example of a particular personal belief being modified because of concrete experience.

6 How do individual value systems affect organizational strategy? Give examples.

7 What role does ethical pluralism play in managerial decision making? Should we seek an all-encompassing value as a frame of reference for all decisions? Why or why not?

8 Compare and contrast group and individual decision making with respect to: (*a*) effectiveness, (*b*) efficiency, (*c*) open- or closed-mindedness, (*d*) risk, and (*e*) rationality.

9 Discuss the impact of groups on individual decision making, particularly (*a*) pressure to conform and (*b*) cognitive dissonance.

10 "The attention devoted to computational problem-solving techniques has far outstripped that devoted to judgmental considerations." Do you agree? Why or why not?

11 How should open-system, heuristic, judgmental approaches to managerial decision making be integrated with closed-system, algorithmic, computational techniques? What are the prospects?

Managerial Planning

Seventeen

The planning function is an integral part of the managerial information-decision system. It involves setting organizational objectives and designing the means for achieving them. Planning provides a framework for integrated decision making throughout the organization. At the strategic level, long-range, comprehensive plans are developed to achieve overall missions. Short-range plans are used at the operating level and implemented via detailed tactics. In between, at the coordinative level, management is involved in translating strategy into tactics, developing policies and procedures, and coordinating the planning activity. Planning is a key managerial function that provides the means by which individuals and organizations cope with a complex, dynamic, ever-changing environment. Our discussion of planning will involve the following topics:

Planning Defined
The Role of Planning
Setting Goals
Planning Process
Planning Dimensions
Who Does the Planning?
Management by Objectives and Results

Planning Defined

A plan is any detailed method, formulated beforehand, for doing or making something. Planning is the process of deciding in advance what is to be done and how. It involves determining overall missions, identifying key results areas, and setting specific objectives as well as developing policies, programs, and procedures for achieving them. Planning provides a framework for integrating complex systems of interrelated future decisions. *Comprehensive planning is an integrative activity that seeks to maximize the total effectiveness of an organization as a system in accordance with its objectives.*

Planning has an implication of futurity, and it implies that there is some skill involved in designing plans for objective accomplishment. *In short, a plan is a predetermined course of action.* Essentially, a plan has three characteristics. First, it must involve the future. Second, it must involve action. Third, there is an element of personal or organizational identification or causation; that is, the future course of action will be taken by the planner or some other designated person(s) within the organization. Futurity, action, and personal or organizational causation are necessary elements in every plan. [1]

Decision Making and Planning

Decision making and planning are closely related. A decision is basically a resolution of alternative choices. A decision is not a plan, in that it need not involve either action or the future. On the other hand, a decision involving merely the acceptance of an idea can influence future individual or organizational behavior. Decisions, of course, are necessary at every stage of the planning process and therefore inextricably linked to planning.

Planning is something we do in advance of taking action; that is, it is *anticipatory decision making.* It is a process of deciding what to do and how to do it before action is required.

Planning is required when the future state that we desire involves a set of independent decisions; that is, a *system of decisions.* . . . The principal complexity in planning derives from the interrelatedness of the decisions rather than from the decisions themselves. [2]

Managerial decision making is the means of integrating related functions such as goal setting, strategy formulation, planning, and control. Overall organization strategy is the result of decisions about *what* to do (goals) and *how* to do it (tactics). Plans result from decisions and provide *feedforward* information to guide subsequent behavior. Control decisions (to adjust tactics and/or goals) rely on *feedback* information that allows comparison of expected and actual results. Although we will discuss these functions separately for purposes of emphasis, it is important to remember their fundamental interrelatedness. Defining a mission or purpose is a starting point for strategy formulation; strategic and tactical plans include more detailed goals, such as short-range objectives; and all anticipatory planning decisions provide a framework for followup and control decisions.

1 Preston P. LeBreton and Dale A. Henning, *Planning Theory,* Prentice-Hall, Inc., Englewood Cliffs, N.J., 1961, p. 7.
2 Russell L. Ackoff, *A Concept of Corporate Planning,* Wiley-Interscience, New York, 1970, pp. 2–4.

Forecasting

The futurity implication of planning suggests that forecasting is an important part of the process. Anticipation of the states of nature and/or the results of alternative courses of action is a crucial phase of the decision-making process. Individually and organizationally we act on the basis of estimates of the future. Therefore, forecasting is a fundamental part of planning; it is the foundation on which rather elaborate frameworks are often established. As the time element is extended, forecasting becomes increasingly hazardous and more subjective but remains an essential ingredient in the planning process. As the foundation for long-range planning, forecasting is an attempt to make the future environment less uncertain. Conscious effort toward anticipating the technological, economic, political, and social climate for the organization helps the manager avoid pitfalls that might possibly be disastrous. Constant surveillance does not necessarily ensure success; the organization must have the capacity to take advantage of recognized opportunities. However, forecasting and long-range planning should reduce the environmental uncertainty for the organization and provide the framework for managerial decisions that make the best of situations as they arise.

Uncertainty is the complement of knowledge. It is the gap between what is known and what needs to be known to make correct decisions. Dealing sensibly with uncertainty is not a byway on the road to responsible business and governmental decisions. It is central to it. The subject is complex, elusive, and omnipresent. [3]

The Role of Planning

Most organizations operate in an environment of change. They must be prepared to accept change as the inevitable consequence of operating in a dynamic world. The general political, economic, social, and ethical philosophies in our country have promoted an atmosphere of freedom of change for the enterprise. In fact, continued success generally has demanded adaptation and innovation. This is in direct contradiction to many societies—both past and contemporary—in which cultural values and/or political, religious, and other institutions placed major impediments in the path of economic and social progress.

Rapidly advancing technology has also emphasized the need for planning. Companies not abreast of current technology are in trouble over the short run. Moreover, companies unaware of the technical changes likely to occur over the next five to twenty years will be in a disadvantageous position.

On the other hand, the organization faced with a changing environment has often found many obstacles that make planning for optimum adaptation difficult. Even technological advances, which themselves are purveyors of change, can create degrees of inflexibility. For example, automation, while requiring major

---

3 Ruth P. Mack, *Planning on Uncertainty,* Wiley-Interscience, New York, 1971, p. 1.

changes for its establishment, results in some inherent inflexibilities and increased resistance to change. In a typical multiproduct business, for instance, automated operations are predicated on expected variations in volume, product mix, quality, and demand. Since automation establishes a relatively inflexible overall system, it is vitally important that the right decision be made at the outset. Thus, it is evident that effective long-term business planning is of critical importance.

With a stable environment and small, uncomplicated operations, the planning function can be carried out relatively easily with a short-range viewpoint. With a more dynamic environment and large, complex units operating in the face of many forces that restrict flexibility, the planning function becomes critical and must be thought of on a total systems basis. Since the consequence of any decision has such a broad and drastic impact, management, through its planning function, must seek the best possible course of action and yet be ready to change if experience and new information suggest it.[4]

Examples

Let us look at several examples in order to better understand the role of planning. ***Diversification planning*** has become a "way of life" for many so-called "conglomerate" companies. In a dynamic economy, product-line determination is one of the major planning areas because the successful company must adapt continually to changing product-mission requirements. Examples of this need are seen in a variety of industries—automobile companies in expanding their product lines, or aircraft companies in determining whether or not to move into the fields of propulsion and/or electronics. For some companies the product line may range from atomic submarines to sand and gravel. Extreme diversity puts special strains on the management system; therefore, careful consideration should be given to new lines of endeavor. The opportunities must be attractive enough to outweigh the problems of complexity for managerial planning.

Diversification planning is not confined to business enterprise. Government agencies—federal, state, and local—continually reappraise their services in order to ascertain what changes or additions might be in order. The Peace Corps, for example, might change its program mix in the light of feedback concerning performance in relation to its identified mission.

The critical path method is an example of ***network analysis*** that is used in the construction industry to plan and control complex building projects. By laying out a network or flowchart of required steps, the manager can obtain an explicit visual representation of the relationship between all the tasks involved.[5] For example, in the construction of a house, it is evident that the rough wiring, heating, and plumbing must be accomplished before the project can move into the

---

4 Leonard Sayles, "Technological Innovation and the Planning Process," *Organizational Dynamics,* Summer 1973, pp. 68–80.

5 For detailed consideration of the mechanics of network model building, see Richard A. Johnson, Fremont E. Kast, and James E. Rosenzweig, *The Theory and Management of Systems,* 3d ed., McGraw-Hill Book Company, New York, 1973, pp. 244–267.

plastering stage. Obviously, for simple projects, the manager, assuming a reasonable amount of experience, could keep a model tucked away in his or her mind and probably operate quite successfully. On the other hand, if the manager were in charge of a skyscraper or freeway interchange project instead of building a house, the mental model probably would not suffice. For large-scale, complex projects an explicit network is extremely useful, if not absolutely necessary.

In a university the function of *resource allocation* is dependent on planning. Forecasts of total student demand must take into account the number of people in relevant age groups and their propensity to seek a university education. The demand for specific degree programs such as engineering, biology, psychology, or law is affected by the job market and personal interests. Long-range planning is reflected in capital construction decisions for new classrooms, research laboratories, and offices. Short-range planning is reflected in subunit operating budgets for one- or two-year periods.

The role of planning in *coordinating complex interorganizational systems* is exemplified in regional health care. Long-range, comprehensive plans provide a means for matching supply and demand. Considerable voluntary cooperation is necessary among federal, state, and local government agencies plus private organizations and cooperative groups. A master plan for a region identifies gaps and overlaps in health care services. Of particular importance is preventing the duplication of costly, advanced-technology facilities such as cobalt treatment, X-ray scanning, or intensive care units.

Setting Goals

Basically, goals are plans expressed as results to be achieved. In this broad sense, goals include purposes, missions, objectives, targets, quotas, deadlines, and the like. Goals represent not only the end point of planning but the end toward which the other managerial activities, such as organizing and controlling, are aimed. Goals are established for subfunctions such as production or marketing, and subgoals are established as planning moves up and down through the various levels in the organization.

In order to be operational, objectives such as "to make a profit" or "to provide a service" or "to be efficient" should be translated into more specific terms. In other words, an operational objective might be to earn 5 percent on sales or 15 percent on net worth. Service objectives would be related to a specific clientele, such as city playground users, and somehow measured both in terms of number of clients served and degree of user satisfaction achieved.

When goals can be quantified, they can be translated into explicit plans, such as budgets or sales quotas. This provides a relatively clear-cut framework around which activities can be organized and performance measured.

Multiple Goals

Individuals and organizations rarely focus on a single purpose. Multiple goals are common and hence cloud the issue of setting objectives. Profitability is usually required for survival of a business enterprise. However, market share objectives may take precedence at some particular time, or community consciousness may forestall the closing of an unprofitable branch plant. Organizations have objectives with regard to both ends and means. Both quality and quantity of output may suffer in the short run as the organization builds its future capabilities. As the football coach often says, "Just wait 'til next year."

An additional consideration is the time horizon for goal achievement. Is the organization to be measured in terms of short-run or long-run performance? Satisfying stockholders by means of higher dividends in the short run may conflict with long-run viability of the organization, which might require reinvestment of profits in human and physical resources.

Recognizing the Human Element

In stressing the need for clear-cut objectives in order to guide organizational behavior, quantification is probably warranted. Developing explicit quantitative goals enhances clarity and makes objectives operational. On the other hand, management should be cognizant of the multiplicity of organizational performance criteria and be willing to adjust the appraisal of goal achievement in the light of the complexity involved. Recognition that organizations are people systems should also temper management's approach to setting goals and planning activities. According to Gross:

The first elements in both structure and performance, let it be noted, are human; people and the satisfaction of people's interest. All other elements and their many decisions—both financial and technological—are ways of thinking about people and their behavior. An organization's plans for the future are always plans made by people for people—for their future behavior and for their future relations with resources and other people. Financial and technological planners may easily lose sight of these human elements. Another virtue of general-systems analysis, therefore, is that it helps to bring together the "soft" information of human relations people with the "hard" data of accountants and engineers. [6]

Plans should reflect a realistic marriage of environmental opportunity with organizational capability—both physical and human resources. The human element includes inclination or interest as well as capacity. Employees may be quite capable of carrying out a plan developed by top management, and yet

6 Bertram M. Gross, "What Are Your Organization's Objectives?" *Human Relations,* August 1965, p. 199.

performance may fall far short of expectations. Athletic teams often exemplify this phenomenon—"the coach wasn't able to get the best out of the material," or a team is described as "operating at 110 percent of capacity."

The Virtue of Vagueness

Amid the clamor for clarity in organizational goals, it might be wise to consider the possible virtues of vagueness. Clear-cut goals and mechanistic programs for achieving them may discount the human element and lead to a sterile environment that stifles individual initiative and results in underutilization of human resources. Ultrapurposeful action proceeding according to blueprint and schedule may be unpalatable to organizational participants.

In an environment of multiple goals it is impossible to focus on more than a few at any one time. When concentrating on one particular objective, others in the system must of necessity be relatively vague. The same is true for different periods of time. Short-range goals may be rather explicit, while medium- and long-range goals are more vague. It is impossible and unrealistic to identify long-range goals in clear-cut terms. These two concepts are analogous to the task of focusing the lens of a camera. In order to obtain a clear picture of a particular subject, other background or peripheral objects must be slightly fuzzy. It is impossible to obtain a sharp focus across the entire spectrum of a wide angle or over great distances.

If goals are stated in general terms, there is room for organizational participants to fill in details according to their own perception and to modify the pattern to their own liking. Ultraprecision can destroy flexibility and make it more difficult for individuals and organizations to adapt to changing conditions. Vagueness makes it possible to work toward goals by many different means. The concept of equifinality—achieving the same end via different means—is an important consideration in viable systems. Vagueness may also foster serendipity—the achievement of a particular worthwhile goal by accident. Such results may be an unexpected by-product of organizational activity. The probability of such a happening is increased when objectives are relatively vague and there is room for initiative with regard to the means used to achieve them.

Unclear objectives facilitate compromise on the part of participants with diverse value systems. As long as people can read into organizational statements their own interpretation of the ends to be achieved, compromise is feasible. Thus, tacit agreement is often reached with regard to both ends and means in organizational settings. For example, consider the difficulty of achieving unanimous approval and wholehearted commitment toward a set of objectives for a university or college. Agreement on a definitive set of objectives (ends) coupled with a detailed set of policies, procedures, and requirements (means) would not be very likely. If the organization were to go even further and spell out the content and pedagogical approach for each course, the probability of acceptance would approach zero. By maintaining some degree of vagueness with regard to ends and by not detailing the means, agreement and commitment on the part of organizational members is much more likely.

Within the coordinative subsystem, mediation and compromise are essential ingredients in integrating efforts toward short- and long-range goals. The element of vagueness is important in any compromise situation, and its virtues should be recognized. However, it is hard to advocate this approach explicitly. The best approach may be to continue to strive for clarity as a means to make goal setting operational but to recognize that inability to do so may not be necessarily catastrophic and in fact may be beneficial to the organization. This is another example of the necessity for management to maintain a contingency view and flexibility in a complex and dynamic environment. In the following sections we will develop some guidelines for adapting the planning process to specific situations.

Planning Process

An overall model of the planning process is shown in Figure 17.1. Premises underlie the planning process and include objective data concerning the organization and its environment as well as subjective views about environmental problems and opportunities and the organization's strengths and weaknesses. Premises are permeated with the values and beliefs of managers. Also included are societal expectations that are either implicit in the culture or explicit in laws and regulations concerning appropriate organization behavior. Premises culminate in a fundamental organization purpose that, in the last analysis, determines the relevance of strategy—comprehensive, long-range guidelines for decision making.

The key decisions are setting goals, planning action to achieve them, implementing plans, and controlling organizational endeavor (reviewing and evaluating the degree of accomplishment and the appropriateness of plans and actions). Strategy is translated into action via processes that become successively more specific as we move down the organizational hierarchy toward the point of implementation. Tactical plans and procedures are developed to focus on short-range targets.

Strategy Formulation

A key managerial task is the development and continual refinement of an overall strategy. A contingency view of strategy formulation can be set forth in terms of four major components:[7] (1) environmental opportunity—what the organization *might do;* (2) competence and resources—what the organization realis-

7 Kenneth R. Andrews, *The Concept of Corporate Strategy,* Dow Jones-Irwin, Inc., Homewood, Ill., 1971, pp. 37–38.

Figure 17.1 The Structure of Planning

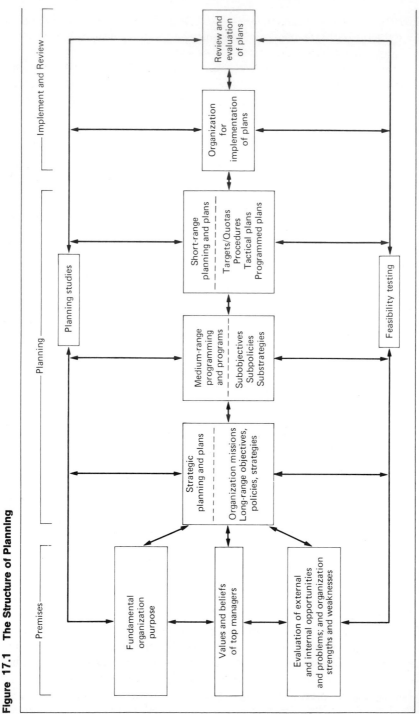

Adapted from George A. Steiner, "Comprehensive Managerial Planning," in Joseph W. McGuire (ed.), *Contemporary Management*, Prentice-Hall, Inc., Englewood Cliffs, N.J., 1974, p. 329.

tically *can do;* (3) managerial interests and desires—what the organization *wants to do;* and (4) responsibility to society—what the organization *should do.* Consideration of each and all of the components should lead to a viable strategic plan— one that has a reasonable probability of success. This approach reflects systems concepts and a contingency view because it recognizes the interrelationships among the various components. An organization may not be able to capitalize on an environmental opportunity (e.g., market demand) if in fact it does not have the competence or resources to do so. Similarly, an organization is unlikely to succeed if its strategic plan is based on managerial interests, without reference to competence, opportunity, or societal responsibilities. Integrating these four components of strategy formulation is a delicate and complex task. Being aware of them is an important first step; reconciling their implications and combining them into a viable strategy is considerably more difficult.

Obviously, some managers and some organizations are "successful" without explicit, time-consuming attention to strategy formulation. Their intuitive feelings about what to do and when to do it may fit the situation. They may be lucky. On the other hand, it is more likely that they have gone through some unconscious strategy formulation process that leads to an appropriate response, even though they cannot articulate their rationale. While such success stories are evident, it is our view that the long-run *probability* of success is enhanced with a more careful, explicit approach to thinking through the various factors involved.

Explicit strategy formulation has a proactive flavor that suggests innovation rather than merely reaction and adaptation. It provides the means for an organization to influence its environment and carve out a niche that is suited to its particular strengths and interests. Some managers shy away from explicit strategy formulation because they are apprehensive about the rigidity that may be implied. However, "long-range" and "comprehensive" are not synonymous with "singleness of purpose" or "rigidity." Organization strategy can be firm and resilient without being brittle or cast in concrete. Strategy formulation is a continuous process of refinement based on past trends, current conditions, and estimates of the future. A visible strategy serves to focus organizational effort, to facilitate commitment on the part of the participants (and perhaps motivate them), and to increase the probability of self-control in subunits and individuals.

Contingency Views of Planning

In our discussion of goal setting we noted the emphasis of most researchers and writers on the need for clear, specific goals as the first step in the planning process. We also noted, however, that there is some virtue in vagueness, particularly in situations in which the complexity and/or long-run time perspective cause considerable uncertainty from the point of view of the decision maker. McCaskey takes this notion a step further by describing two types of planning, each of which

Figure 17.2   Contrast between Planning with Goals and Directional Planning

Planning with Goals	Directional Planning
Characteristics	
Teleological, directed toward external goals	Directional, moving from internal preferences
Goals are specific and measurable	Domain is sometimes hard to define
Rational, analytic	Intuitive, use unquantifiable elements
Focused, narrowed perception of task	Broad perception of task
Lower requirements to process novel information	Greater need to process novel information
More efficient use of energy	Possible redundancy, false leads
Separate planning and acting phases	Planning and acting not separate phases
Contingent Upon	
People who prefer well-defined tasks	People who prefer variety, change, and complexity
Tasks and industries that are quantifiable and relatively stable	Tasks and industries not amenable to quantification and which are rapidly changing
Mechanistic organization forms, "closed" systems	Organic organization forms, "open" systems
"Tightening up the ship" phase of a project	"Unfreezing" phase of a project

Michael B. McCaskey, "A Contingency Approach to Planning: Planning with Goals and Planning without Goals," *Academy of Management Journal*, June 1974, p. 290.

is appropriate in particular situations. [8] The characteristics of such situations are summarized in Figure 17.2. Planning with goals is appropriate in many situations described in the left-hand column. However, the right-hand column describes a significant number of situations that also should be considered. Directional planning, or "planning from thrust" does not mean planning without goals. The goals are merely less clear or more vague than is typical in stable-mechanistic organizations. In adaptive-organic situations it may be enough to have a sense of the domain of relevant activities and an intuitive feeling for appropriate direction. One "goal" in such an approach is to be ready to take advantage of opportunities that may present themselves at any point in time. Short-range plans can then be contingent on current conditions in a particular situation. A contingency view is important in order that the planning process is appropriately matched with the situation. To impose a process that calls for specific measurable goals on a situation that is dynamic and uncertain may lead to oversimplification, a false sense of security, undue rigidity, inability to adopt to internal and external changes, and frustration. On the other hand, failure to develop a conscious strategy with specific and measurable goals when it is possible is also inappropriate—just rolling along with the tide.

   8 Michael B. McCaskey, "A Contingency Approach to Planning: Planning with Goals and Planning without Goals," *Academy of Management Journal*, June 1974, pp. 281–291.

Significant Variables and Specific Strategies

Much of the material on strategy formulation and planning is descriptive, relating the experiences of practicing managers, with most attention focused on a process that can be applied in a variety of situations. Extending the contingency view a step further requires the consideration of significant variables that are important in determining the specific strategy for a particular organization. There are a large number of variables involved, even if strategy formulation is restricted to a particular type of organization such as a business, hospital, community college, or government agency. Figure 17.3 shows some external and internal variables that conceivably could influence the content of a business strategy.

Another refinement in the contingency approach is to consider various stages in the life cycle of a product or service. Typical phases are development, rapid growth, competitive turbulence, maturity, and decline. The relevance of the various factors in Figure 17.3 will vary, depending on the particular phase in the life cycle. For example, "In the introductory stages of the life cycle, the major determinants of business strategy are the newness of the product, the rate of technological change in product design, the needs of the buyer, and the frequency with which the product is purchased. . . . In the decline stage of the life cycle, the major determinants of business strategy are buyer loyalty, the degree of product differentiation, the price elasticity of demand, the company's share of the market, product quality, and marginal plant size."[9]

A comprehensive set of guidelines for determining a specific business strategy is not possible here. Moreover, sets of variables similar to those in Figure 17.3 would be necessary for each type of organization considered. However, we can illustrate the contingency approach by analyzing a particular product-market situation—light aircraft. The first step is recognizing that the product is in the maturity phase of the life cycle, in which "the major determinants of business strategy are the nature of buyer needs, the degree of product differentiation, the rate of technological change in process design, the degree of market segmentation, the ratio of distribution costs to manufacturing value added, and the frequency with which the product is purchased."[10] Based on prior research, case studies, and experience, we would select those variables that have been particularly relevant to the success of light aircraft manufacturers such as Piper or Cessna, ascertain the degree to which they are present in the current situation, and determine the key elements of an appropriate strategy. For example, assume we find that:

1 Product differentiation is high.

2 Customer needs are primarily noneconomic.

---

9 Charles W. Hofer, "Toward a Contingency Theory of Business Strategy," *Academy of Management Journal*, December 1975, p. 799.

10 Ibid., p.799.

Figure 17.3 Some Strategically Significant Environmental and Organizational Variables

Broader Environmental Variables	Industry Structure Variables	Organizational Characteristics and Resources
Economic conditions: GNP trend Interest rates Money supply Energy availability	Type of product Degree of product differentiation Number of equal products Price/cost structure Economies of scale Degree of automation Degree of integration Experience curves Marginal plant size Optimal plant size Rate of product technological change Rate of process technological change Transportation and distribution costs Barriers to entry Critical mass for entry	Market share Degree of customer concentration Quality of products Value added Length of the production cycle Newness of plant and equipment Labor intensity Relative wage rate Marketing intensity Discretionary cash flow/gross capital investment
Demographic trends: Growth rate of population Age distribution of population Regional shifts in population		
Sociocultural trends: Life style changes Consumer activism Career expectations		
Political-legal factors: Antitrust regulations Environmental protection laws		

Supplier Variables	Competitor Variables	Market and Consumer Behavior Variables
Degree of supplier concentration Major changes in availability of raw materials Major changes in conditions of trade	Degree of seller concentration Aggressiveness of competition Degree of specialization in the industry Degree of capacity utilization	Stage of the life cycle Market size Seasonality Cyclicality Market segmentation Buyer concentration Buyer needs Buyer loyalty Elasticity of demand Purchase frequency

Charles W. Hofer, "Toward a Contingency Theory of Business Strategy," *Academy of Management Journal*, December 1975, p. 798.

3 Market segmentation is moderate to high.

4 Product complexity is high.

5 Purchase frequency is low.

6 There are barriers to entering the industry because of technological factors and/or existing channels of distribution.

This combination of conditions would then lead us to a specific strategy that includes elements such as:

1 Focusing our research and development funds first on modifying and upgrading our existing product line, second on developing new products, and last on process innovations

2 Allocating substantial funds to the maintenance and enhancement of our distinctive competences, especially those in the marketing area

3 Developing a strong service capability in our distribution systems

4 Seeking to expand the geographic scope of our operations if possible [11]

A contingency approach to prescribing the various elements of a business strategy is the foundation for comprehensive and long-range planning. Even though prescriptions are not complete (and may never be), understanding and using the process explicitly can be useful to practicing managers. The discipline of consciously thinking through the many factors involved, determining their degree of relevance in a given situation, and hypothesizing the most appropriate course of action will increase the probability that the strategy "fits" the situation. Then all that remains is to implement that strategy via carefully designed programs and tactical plans.

Implementing Strategies and Plans

Considerable attention has been devoted to the strategy formulation and planning process. Less attention has been focused on implementation. The former is an intellectual or thinking activity; the latter is more action oriented.

Planning is one of the two major functions of management and is associated with the "deciding" aspects of the manager's job. The other function—execution—involves implementing decisions. Thus, "deciding" and "doing" are inseparable parts of the manager's job; indeed, developing and operating a comprehensive planning system involves these two parts; deciding what to do—and then doing it. It is much easier to design a planning system than it is to implement it. Most of the literature that has evolved in the past 15 years neglects the planning for the implementation phase of strategic planning. [12]

Implementation involves mobilizing resources, structuring their relationships, integrating diverse activities, and controlling activities in light of policies, plans, and procedures. Accomplishing goals in human systems requires effective personal leadership. Mediocre strategies may be successful because of drive, verve, and brilliant leadership that elicits commitment and effort. It is also possible that a sound strategy can be subverted because leadership is lacking and organizational participants merely "go through the motions." The obvious goal is to couple sound strategy and skillful implementation via effective leadership.

---

11 Ibid., p. 805.

12 David I. Cleland, "Planning Processes and Criteria," in Joseph W. McGuire (ed.), *Contemporary Management,* Prentice-Hall, Inc., Englewood Cliffs, New Jersey, 1974, p. 351.

Planning Dimensions

Understanding the planning function may be enhanced by looking at the process from several points of view, which might be called planning dimensions— repetitiveness, time span, scope, subsystem or level, and flexibility. It will become apparent from the discussion that there are often patterns of relationships among these various dimensions. For example, long-range, comprehensive plans are the primary concern of top management and frequently deal with complex, multidimensional problems. The resulting strategic plans are usually quite flexible and capable of adapting to changing circumstances. In contrast, short-term, operational plans are more limited in scope, tend to be the responsibility of lower management, and usually are more fixed.

Repetitiveness

Essentially, plans for nonrepetitive problems *(single-use plans)* set forth a course of action to fit a specific situation and may be obsolete when the goal is reached. This is in contrast to standing plans, which are designed to have continuing usefulness. There is a hierarchy of single-use plans ranging from (1) major programs, (2) projects, and (3) special tasks to (4) detailed plans.

There are many examples of major programs, such as the design, development, and construction of a rapid transit system. Advancing technology requires long-range planning for large-scale programs. The success of a major program depends on the establishment of more detailed single-use plans for special projects within the total system. These single-use plans should all be integrated into an overall planning hierarchy.

Plans for repetitive action are often called **standing plans.** They include policies, methods, and standard operating procedures designed to cover the variety of repetitive situations that organizations frequently face. These plans are of importance to any established organization. Even relatively informal groups such as garden clubs and bowling teams have established plans. For the more formal organization the standing plans are a primary cohesive force connecting its various subsystems. Plans for repetitive action become the habit patterns of the organization, similar to the habit patterns of individuals.

Policies are the broadest of the standing plans and are general guides to organizational behavior. At the strategic level policies generally set broad premises and constraints within which further planning activities take place. A policy is a general plan of action that guides the members of the organization in the conduct of its operation. Every large organization has a wide variety of policies covering its most important functions, which frequently are formalized and written in organization or policy manuals. Even in those situations in which policies are not written, the organization should have policies that are known and understood by participants. Quite often these informal policies are established because of the habitual pattern of decisions that results when the organization is confronted with a series of similar problems.

Methods and procedures are also standing plans. They are usually less general than policies and establish more definite steps for the performance of certain activities in the organization. The basic difference between a policy and standard methods and procedures is a matter of degree, with both providing guidance for integrated decision making.

There are many organizational advantages to the use of plans for repetitive action. Through the use of standing plans and the concept of "management by exception," top management's influence is extended to all organizational levels. Once a policy decision has been reached, the standing plan serves as a guideline for decision making throughout the organization. Another advantage of the standing plan is that it creates a uniformity of operations throughout the organization. Once established, understood, and accepted, it provides similarity of action in meeting certain situations. This is of vital importance to large-scale, complex business or government organizations. Given established policies, clients of the organization are usually assured of relatively consistent decisions, regardless of the location of facilities or the level in the organization.

The use of standing plans is typical of the stable-mechanistic bureaucracy, whether it is government, business, labor, or any other type of large-scale, complex organization. Herein, perhaps, lies one of the problems. Standing plans are useful when they provide for consistent decisions and when they meet the requirement of the situation. They are not useful when the situation changes so abruptly that the plan does not fit the new situation. Attempting to force new and dynamic situations under a particular standing plan often can lead to dysfunctional consequences.

Nevertheless, the wise use of the standing plans is essential to systematic planning. They provide the basic means of interweaving the organizational processes throughout the entire system.

Time
Span

Much emphasis has been placed on long-range planning, which is closely associated with the goal-setting responsibilities of management at the strategic level. Generally, strategic planning deals with decisions regarding the broad technological and competitive aspects of the organization, the allocation of resources (human and material) over an extended period, and the long-run integration of the organization within its environment. Some authors make a distinction between long-range planning and programming, which is defined as derivative, functional, or operational planning.[13] In the ideal sense, the short- and intermediate-range operational plans are based on and integrated into the strategic planning.

It is our view that strategic or long-range plans are not a separate type of plan. Rather, they are an integral part of the total planning process and establish the basic framework on which more detailed programming and operational plan-

---

13 George A. Steiner (ed.), *Managerial Long-range Planning*, McGraw-Hill Book Company, New York, 1963, pp. 10–12.

ning take place. Figure 17.1 illustrates the interdependency of plans for various time periods. Long- and medium-range plans provide a framework for short-range plans, which refer primarily to current operations. Feedback from ongoing activity is a part of the information flow that management uses in making decisions. Forward planning is based on past history, the current situation, and estimates of the future.

The designation "long range" varies by organization. For a firm engaged in mail-order merchandising, long range may be the next catalog (six months hence). For a firm engaged in growing timber as a crop, the outlook may approximate 100 years. On this relative basis, long range might vary from a matter of months to a matter of centuries. Typically, however, organizations engage in planning for five-, ten-, or fifteen-year intervals. As companies move the planning horizon further out on the time scale, specificity typically decreases. Rather than emphasize specific achievements, goals are stated in terms of acceptable ranges. These are usually tied to forecasts of societal conditions that also must be expressed in terms such as the expected range. Forecasts of economic activity, for example, can be fairly definite over the short run—several quarters or a year. However, in estimating gross national product for 1999, a fairly broad range would be used.

Most authors writing about long-range planning emphasize that it involves decision making that commits resources over the long-run future and that planning is necessary in dealing with the uncertainty of the future. Herein lies a major dilemma. On the one hand, there is rapidly advancing technology, changing competitive and market situations, increasingly active governmental, labor, and other interests, and many other forces that make forecasting the future environment extremely difficult. [14] Yet organizations must plan their activities over a long-run period and must commit resources in spite of future uncertainties. Witness the problems of planning and decision making for a program such as the Alaska pipeline, in which private companies and federal agencies were cooperatively joined in its design and construction. Both parties made commitments based on plans that were subject to drastic changes (e.g., the possibility that society, through Congress, would not tolerate any adverse impact on the environment.)

Thus we find the dilemma—the need for long-run commitments of resources and organizational endeavor in the face of an increasingly dynamic environment and future uncertainities. What is the solution to this long-range planning dilemma? More thorough and complete planning at the early stages runs the risk of complete inflexibility in the face of inevitable changes. Extending the planning period runs the risk of even more uncertainty.

Some of the earlier writers on long-range planning exhibited naïveté in expecting that organizations would be able to establish highly specific and carefully laid out plans that would remain viable for an extended period. This was one

---

14 One speaker introduced his remarks with the statement, "Prediction is hazardous, especially when it relates to the future."

of the major reasons for increasing skepticism regarding the appropriateness of long-range planning. Fortunately, current authors are more sophisticated and recognize that long-range planning must provide for organizational flexibility in meeting changes. Warren says, "The major purpose of planning is the development of processes, mechanisms and managerial attitudes which will do two things. First, they will make it possible to make commitment decisions today with a greater awareness of future implications, and second, they will make it possible to make future decisions more rapidly, more economically, and with less disruptions to the ongoing business." [15] His second point emphasizes that long-run planning must provide for future flexibility in decision making.

Most successful companies seem to have (1) organized programs to seek and promote new business opportunities, (2) an orientation to growth fields and markets, (3) a proven competitive ability in present lines of business, (4) courageous and energetic management, and (5) luck. While luck may be a factor in organizational success, it is not reliable. Long-run probabilities are enhanced by continuing efforts in long-range planning. Whether this means one individual cogitating about the future for a few minutes periodically or a large-scale, departmentalized effort in this regard, the task is the same—coping with the environment and hopefully acting in a way that will be not only adaptive but innovative.

Scope

Another useful dimension in thinking about planning is that of scope. We often hear the term "master plan," which connotes the idea of a general or overall plan for the organization. Within this framework, other more detailed plans are developed for subparts of the total endeavor. Branch describes three types of planning—functional, project, and comprehensive:

We have developed considerable skills in *functional planning*—planning a component or aspect of a large endeavor. We can perform intricate series of actions which lead to a predetermined result, be it in connection with a chemical process, structural design of a beam, manufacturing a watch, or accounting for the transactions of a large enterprise. . . .

Like functional planning, *project planning* has been developing since early historical times. Road building today is the culmination of experience dating back to before Roman times, and modern systems of urban water supply incorporate principles known on the island of Crete some three thousand years ago. The extent to which we have carried the art and science of project planning is represented in such feats as the construction of a Boulder Dam, aircraft carrier, large manufacturing plant, orbiting communication satellite, or any one of the multitude of physical undertakings comparable in their level of accomplishment.

Normally, this form of planning incorporates a greater range of elements than functional planning. It deals with more numerous and diverse parts. . . .

Comprehensive planning is the term describing the ultimate in man's endeavor to perform a major achievement, shape his environment, or affect the future. It includes functional

15 E. Kirby Warren, *Long-range Planning: The Executive Viewpoint,* Prentice-Hall, Inc., Englewood Cliffs, N.J., 1966, p. 29.

and project planning, but transcends them in scope, magnitude, and complexity. It includes not only three-dimensional accomplishments in space but social mechanisms such as laws, regulations, policies, and forms of organization—for example, planning for a nation or large region, city or metropolitan area, far-flung business enterprise, or an extensive sphere of governmental activity such as agriculture, the military services, and space travel. What we are concerned with in comprehensive planning is the spectrum of human awareness, knowledge, capacity to consider and act. [16]

The complexity of the environment increases rapidly as the scope of the planning function increases. Comprehensive or master plans must, of necessity, deal with broad societal elements. [17] Corporate planning for a large industrial firm would include socio-political considerations, legal aspects, and other similar variables that might not be necessary or appropriate at the branch plant level. The necessary information might be provided by headquarters and hence dealt with as "given" in managerial planning at that branch. Planning activity at the subsystem level is complex in a different way because of the increasing amount of detail that must be considered.

Subsystem or Level

As decisions are made with regard to goals and plans are developed to achieve them, the scope of the planning process is constrained for lower levels in the organization, or subsystems. The plan may call for integration of functional efforts in order to achieve a particular objective. Therefore, subgoals are established for the various functions, and plans must be drawn for accomplishing them. Within a particular function, there will be a further breakdown of activity that has to be planned in order that it can fit into the overall system. Goals call for master plans, which in turn foster subplans, and so on down to very detailed operating levels, where procedures are spelled out on a step-by-step basis.

Managers at all levels of the organization are engaged in all the basic functions of the management process. As managers move up to the organizational hierarchy from operating toward strategic levels, however, they are likely to spend relatively more of their time planning than implementing. Moreover, at the top level there is also a gradation of the amount of time spent on planning for varying time periods in the future. Top executives not only devote most of their time to planning but must recognize the necessity for long-range planning. Management at the strategic level defines the desired role of the organization in the future, relates the organization to its various environmental systems, and perceives the niche that the organization can fill.

This does not mean that top executives can plan in a vacuum. Rather, they should develop these long-range plans with the full participation of those

16 Melville C. Branch, *Planning: Aspects and Applications,* John Wiley & Sons, Inc., New York, 1966, pp. 10–11.
17 For example, see Alfred J. Kahn, *Theory and Practice of Social Planning,* Russell Sage Foundation, New York, 1969.

organizational members who have information inputs vital to the decision process. Effective planning is not the exclusive domain of a few top managers but requires the integration of inputs from all levels in the organization. Furthermore, there should be an awareness of the motivational impacts of participation, not only in the actual planning process but also in the implementation of plans. With expanded requirements for innovation, creativity, and flexibility within modern organizations and with increased employment of highly educated participants, it is imperative for management to develop effective means of integrating this knowledge into the planning function.

Flexibility

One of the major considerations in planning is the degree of rigidity or flexibility of plans. Assuming future certainty in the face of a turbulent environment leads to rigidities in plans and limits adaptiveness. This is a **Cook's-tour planning approach**[18] and assumes that the future is sufficiently certain so that we can move in an exact straight line from here to there (see Figure 17.4). Cook's-tour planning requires substantial precision and is most appropriate when the planner is facing a relatively certain environment.

In contrast, the **Lewis-and-Clark planning approach** acknowledges that in the future there will be many decision points and alternative courses of action.[19] From the present viewpoint it is impossible to determine their location or timing. In this approach it is not the function of planning to chart a precise course of

Figure 17.4   Two Approaches to Planning

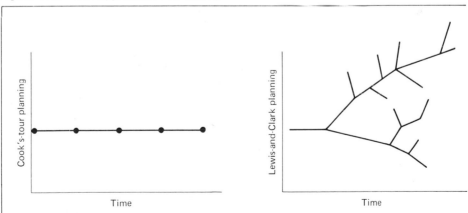

18 Cook's World Travel Service is one of the oldest and largest travel agencies. It was one of the originators of thoroughly planned travel tours with clearly prescribed itineraries and detailed schedules.

19 These two approaches are discussed in detail in James R. Schlesinger, *Organizational Structure and Planning*, The Rand Corporation, Santa Monica, Calif., 1966.

action. Rather, the function of planning is to prepare the organization to cope with the uncertainties of the future, to note the signs in the environment that indicate that a point of decision has been reached, and to develop a means of responding.

The Lewis-and-Clark planning approach is similar to that suggested by Colm for governmental planning:

It is important to recognize that planning means more than merely preparing a plan—it should be understood as a system of decision-making. Government decisions, in part, are always concerned with factors which are outside government control, such as foreign markets, foreign capital, the response of people to government measures, the weather, etc. Estimates can be made concerning these factors, but they are subject to a high degree of error. Consequently, planning is decision-making under conditions of uncertainty which requires a mechanism for adapting the plan to unexpected developments. Under conditions of uncertainty a plan is always tentative and subject to revision in the course of its execution and in the preparation of a subsequent plan. [20]

For the manager it would seem that whenever uncertainties in the internal subsystems and in the environment are substantial, planning should shift toward the Lewis-and-Clark approach. However, there are many organizational pressures to establish long-range plans in a highly specific and exact fashion. This gives the appearance of planning perfection but with the high cost of inflexibility and the likelihood of future events completely destroying the established plans. Organizations can compromise on the rigidity-versus-flexibility dimension by developing relatively fixed short-term operational plans under the general umbrella of more flexible, longer-range, strategic plans.

Who Does the Planning?

In organizations, planning is one of the major functions of line managers. However, with the growing need for investigation, analysis, and evaluation, planning has frequently become a specialized activity. In many cases a specialized staff is set up to aid in the planning function. Those engaged in long-range planning may tend to overemphasize its importance and the role of their subgroup in overall organizational activity.

If planning specialists emphasize generalized approaches or techniques, the organization's particular (maybe even unique) situation may not be recognized. Managers should be directly involved in order to ensure inclusion of their premises with regard to the environment and the organization's special niche in it. No two organizations and no two managers can approach the planning process in

---

20 Gerhard Colm, *Integration of National Planning and Budgeting*, National Planning Association, Washington, D.C., 1968, p. 3.

exactly the same way. Factors are weighted inconsistently, conditions are perceived differently, the importance of outcomes varies in the minds of key people, and there is often disagreement concerning the appropriateness of means of achieving a specific goal. Therefore, the planning process and plans need a heavy emphasis on situational analysis from the point of view of line managers who are "on the scene."

All too frequently, a staff group assumes that its role is planning rather than facilitating the planning activities of line management. Left to its own discretion, this staff proceeds to set goals and develop plans according to its own conception and premises, often developing elaborate research reports to substantiate its positions.

Meanwhile, "back at the ranch," line managers are proceeding to develop their own planning premises, possibly in the executive dining room. Unless there is considerable dialogue and mutual understanding between specialized staff personnel and operating managers, a gap may develop that is dysfunctional for the organization.

The "planning gap" is a divergence in the expectations, premises, objectives, and basic concepts that exists between various units and individuals, within organizations, thus preventing the establishment of an effective, well-defined framework for integrated decision making. The gap we are primarily concerned with in this instance is between operating management and a specialized planning staff. Specialized staff activities must be carried out in relation to the situation as conceived by operating management. Certainly, sophisticated techniques and refined information inputs can lead to adjustments in the manager's perception of the organization and its role in its environment. Staff personnel should ask discerning questions and push for adaptation and innovation. On the other hand, they should be cognizant of all the factors involved and should be in tune with the value system of operating management.

In large-scale organizations with many-leveled departmentation, diverse subobjectives, and organizational and human limits on rationality, it is improbable that the planning gap can be completely eliminated. To do so would be to assume complete knowledge, absolute predictability, perfect communication, and full agreement throughout the organization. These assumptions are too much to ask for. However, the gap can be minimized if specialized staff work is conceived as an extension of the manager's planning function. Continuing dialogue can help to establish a common set of premises to be used throughout the organization.

Management by Objectives and Results

In Chapter 8 we discussed the evolution of MBO/R as a managerial approach, the steps involved in introducing it in an organization, its potential benefits, and some problems that arise because of inadequate preparation and/or faulty implementation. Formal MBO/R programs are typically designed to provide a means for:

Goal setting—identifying and prioritizing missions, key results areas, and objectives

Program planning—designing means for implementing action

Participation—involving organization members on a one-to-one (superior-subordinate) and/or work team basis in the planning process

Development—improving managerial skill in decision making, planning, and controlling

Motivation—tapping latent capability through involvement in setting challenging, realistic objectives

Control—measuring and evaluating results

Performance appraisal—providing feedback to individuals and/or work teams concerning actual versus expected results

Compensation—designing reward systems that emphasize results rather than activities

These ingredients comprise a total system that requires balanced attention if potential benefits are to be realized. In this section, however, we are primarily concerned with MBO/R as an explicit, systematic process for facilitating and integrating managerial decision making, planning, and control. The use of a framework such as MBO/R does not ensure success. There is no guarantee that the "right" objectives will be identified or that "appropriate" action plans will be developed. However, a systematic MBO/R process at least ensures that important issues are considered and discussed. It provides a means for shifting the emphasis from activities toward results and for coordinating objectives and action plans among various individuals and/or subunits.

Roles and missions provide an overall framework for understanding more explicitly the products or services that the organization is designed to provide (see Figure 17.5). Key results areas identify major determinants of organizational success (or failure). Experience indicates that individuals and organizations often devote considerable time and attention to activities that may be trivial when reviewed in the light of the overall mission or purpose. Programmed activity rises to meet available time, leaving little or no time for really significant concerns. Identifying key results areas explicitly is a first step in focusing time, energy, and effort more appropriately. Key results can be related to the basic task (e.g., brewing and marketing beer) or specific problems and opportunities that become apparent in the current time period (e.g., a possible merger or acquisition).

Indicators are measurable factors, related to key results, that facilitate the setting of objectives. They provide another step in explicitness by specifying what will be measured and where effort should be focused. They should include

Figure 17.5   MBO/R Approach to Planning and Controlling Organizational Endeavor

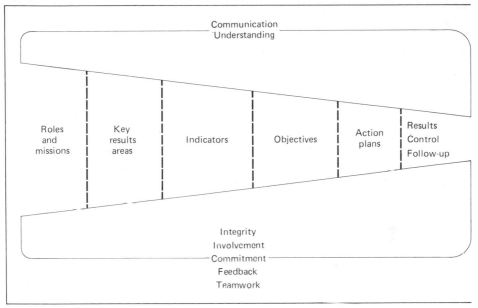

Adapted from George L. Morrisey, *Management by Objectives and Results in the Public Sector,* Addison-Wesley Publishing Company, Reading, Mass., 1976, p. 23.

both "hard" numbers (units of production per work hour, percentage of on-time deliveries) and "soft" data that rely on perceptions of people (employee morale, client satisfaction). Objectives specify results to be achieved and should include target dates and costs (expenditure of money and/or effort). In an overall managerial system, objectives should cover normal work output, improvement in organizational capability, and personal growth and development. Objectives should be challenging and realistic.

Action plans are the means of achieving specific objectives. They involve programming, scheduling, and budgeting as well as explicit designation of who will do what by when. Results are the focal point of the MBO/R system of managerial planning and control. Objectives, by themselves, are meaningless unless there is some way of ensuring their accomplishment. Control involves following up to check actual versus expected results and initiating corrective action when it is called for. Current experience becomes input in the next period when the process is repeated.

As shown in Figure 17.5, communication and understanding are important factors in the overall process. As the various elements are made explicit between superiors and subordinates and/or among team members, communication and understanding are enhanced. Mutual expectations become apparent and coordination of organizational endeavor is facilitated.

Management by objectives and results is a *means* to achieve effectiveness, efficiency, and participant satisfaction rather than an end in itself. Considerable benefit is derived from making the basic functions of the managerial task more explicit. The spotlight is on results—performance in areas that are critical for organizational success.

Depending on how MBO/R is introduced and implemented, it can lead to improvement in a number of key dimensions that underlie improved and sustained performance. Participation of each manager (indeed each employee) in the process of both setting objectives and designing action steps is important for several reasons. Involvement leads to commitment, both publicly and privately. Clear, challenging goals that are accepted by individuals lead to improved performance. Explicit performance objectives make it easier to identify good performance and hence reward it appropriately. Such positive reinforcement increases satisfaction and the probability that desired behavior will be repeated in the future. Explicit objectives also provide an opportunity for specific feedback concerning results. Feedback, responsibility, and meaningful work are central ingredients in enriched jobs. Focusing on key results increases task identity and enhances task significance, two aspects of meaningful work. A properly implemented MBO/R program can enrich jobs while simultaneously emphasizing relevant, challenging, and realistic goals (accepted by participants) that lead to improved performance. [21]

The MBO/R process also allows emphasis on the dimensions of effective leader behavior discussed in Chapter 13: support, interaction facilitation, goal emphasis, and work facilitation. Teamwork can be improved through the process of sharing objectives and action plans among team members, particularly when interdependent activities are involved. The public commitment in a group setting also increases the probability of improved performance. Integrity is a key element in the success or failure of management by objectives and results programs. The process should be approached with genuine respect for the ability of organizational participants to set challenging, realistic objectives that are organizationally relevant. Similarly, each participant must approach the process as a meaningful way to carry out the managerial task. If it is a hollow "exercise," it will not be very effective. Developing the proper overall organizational climate and individual attitudes takes adequate preparation and patience. It cannot be done overnight.

Summary

A plan is a predetermined course of action. Comprehensive plans, established at the strategic level, provide a framework for decision making at lower levels in the organization. Managerial planning is a means of coping with the uncertainty of the future; it facilitates adaptation and innovation.

---

21 Denis Umstot, "MBO + Job Enrichment: How to Have Your Cake and Eat It Too," *Management Review,* February 1977, pp. 21–26.

Strategy formulation and implementation provide overall guidance for organizational endeavor. The general process involves integrating environmental opportunities, organizational competence and resources, managerial interests and desires, and social responsibilities. A contingency approach recognizes important interrelationships among key variables such as market characteristics, technology, and the current phase of a product's (or service's) life cycle.

Some relevant dimensions of planning include repetitiveness, time span, scope, subsystem or level, and flexibility. A number of combinations are possible. Operating level plans are typically repetitive, short range, narrow in scope, and rigid. Strategic level plans (such as a new venture) are more unique, longer range, wider in scope, and more flexible.

Flexibility is an important aspect of planning because some organizational situations—complex and dynamic—are not appropriate for rigid goals, policies, programs, and procedures. The key is maintaining the organization in a state of readiness to respond to contingencies as they arise.

The amount and proportion of time spent on planning typically increases as a manager moves upward in the organizational hierarchy. Specialized staff groups are often established to aid in carrying out the planning function, but line managers must be deeply involved in the planning process.

While planning and control are often separated conceptually for discussion purposes, it is important to recognize that they are inseparable in practice. Management by objectives and results (MBO/R) is an example of an explicit, systematic process for facilitating and integrating managerial decision making, planning, and control.

Questions and Problems

1 Define planning. How does it relate to (a) forecasting and (b) decision making?
2 What factors have increased the importance of planning:
    a In a large business organization
    b In a large community general hospital
    c In a university
    d In a city
    e In the Department of Defense
3 How do multiple goals affect the process of setting objectives? When is vagueness of organizational objectives a virtue?
4 Illustrate a contingency approach to strategy formulation for a new business such as a restaurant, a radio station, or a furniture factory.
5 Discuss the various dimensions of planning and relate them to the plans in an organization with which you are familiar.

6 "The planning process is the means of accomplishing system change." Do you agree? Why or why not?

7 Illustrate Cook's-Tour and/or Lewis-and-Clark planning with personal experiences.

8 What recommendations do you have for minimizing the planning gap?

9 How are planning and control related in the three organizational subsystems or levels—strategic, coordinative, and operating?

10 Using Figure 17.5 as a framework, develop one or more personal objectives (and their related action plans) to cover a period of less than one year.

Organizational Control

Eighteen

Control is the phase of the managerial process concerned with maintaining organizational activity within allowable limits, as measured from expectations. Organizational control is inextricably intertwined with planning. Plans provide the framework against which the control process works. On the other hand, feedback from the control phase often identifies the need for new plans or at least adjustments to existing ones. Typically, individual and organizational behavior involves a continuing sequence of planning-implementing-controlling cycles. The following topics will be considered in our discussion of organizational control:

Control Defined
Elements of Control
Control Process
Closed- and Open-Loop Control
The Time Dimension
Control and Behavior
Designing Control Systems
Examples of Control

Control Defined

The concept of control is quite general and can be used in the organizational context to evaluate overall performance against a five-year strategic plan or specific performance against a production quota of twenty-five units per hour. It relates to both ends (outputs) and means (inputs and transformation processes). Thus, the theory of control is pervasive.

Control theory, like many other broad theories, is more a state of mind than any specific amalgam of mathematical, scientific or technological methods. The term can be defined to include any rational approach used by men to overcome the perversities of either their natural or their technological environment. The broad objective of a control theory is to make a system—any kind of system—operate in a more desirable way: to make it more reliable, more convenient or more economical. [1]

The word *control* has several meanings and, more specifically, several connotations that are meaningful to the discussion in this chapter. For example, it means:

1 To check or verify
2 To regulate
3 To compare with a standard
4 To exercise authority over (direct or command)
5 To curb or restrain

At least three relatively distinct lines of thought are apparent in this definition—(1) curbing or restraining, (2) directing or commanding, and (3) checking or verifying. All are significant for organization theory and management practice. However, we are primarily concerned with the third connotation of control.

Checking or verifying implies some means of measurement and some standard that can serve as a frame of reference in the control process. The planning function typically provides the necessary yardstick—hopefully explicitly but, if not, at least implicitly. Litterer describes the checking or measuring approach to control as "matching" behavior.

We are concerned with control in relation to matching performance with necessary or required conditions to obtain a purpose or objective. The essence here is on directivity and integration of effort, required accomplishment of an end. . . . Control and coordination are closely related. . . .

Control is concerned not only with the events directly related to the accomplishment of major purposes, but also with maintaining the organization in a condition in which it can function adequately to achieve these major purposes. [2]

Homeostasis and Dynamic Equilibrium

The self-regulating or control property of a living process is homeostasis. Provided that the stimulus is not too great, when an organism is disturbed from its "normal" state, it tends to return to it. The organism has built-in control mechanisms which maintain a dynamic equilibrium throughout its life cycle. Many of the self-regulating processes of an organism such as the human being are highly programmed and operate without conscious intervention of the individual. During

1 Richard Bellman, "Control Theory," *Scientific American*, September 1964, p. 186.
2 Joseph A. Litterer, *The Analysis of Organizations*, 2d ed., John Wiley & Sons, Inc., New York, 1973, p. 528.

strenuous exercise, for example, breathing becomes more rapid and the pulse quickens in order to deliver more oxygen via the blood stream to muscles throughout the body. Other self-regulating processes require overt decision-making behavior on the part of the individual. In other words, he or she consciously provides closure in the feedback system that regulates behavior.

For organizations the analogy is not precise; however, the concept of homeostasis is still useful. Organizations have relatively programmed behavior patterns—standard operating procedures—that provide stability over time (maintenance systems). On the other hand, there are processes for making innovative decisions (adaptive systems) that change the organization in response to external and internal stimuli. There is a continuum of programmable control processes, from the relatively mechanistic to those in which conscious and deliberate action is required on the part of human decision makers.

Organisms and organizations are not static; they change and adjust—while exhibiting goal-oriented behavior. The process can best be described as a dynamic equilibrium.

Cybernetics

Cybernetics is another important concept for the control function. The word stems from the Greek *kybernetes,* or helmsman, and thus relates to the connotation "direction of." Cybernetics involves communication and control.[3] It is concerned with information flow in complex systems. Although cybernetics has been applied primarily to mechanistic engineering problems, its model of feedback, control, and regulation has significance for biological and social systems as well. The example of the helmsman illustrates the most important and useful connotation of the control function—maintaining a course toward a goal.

Feedback

Feedback is an essential ingredient in any control process. It provides the information for decisions that adjust the system. As plans are implemented, the system is tracked or monitored in order to ascertain whether or not performance is on target and whether objectives are being met. Feedback is usually obtained with reference to both the ends sought and the means designed to achieve them. In relatively closed systems, feedback leads to automatic adjustments. In relatively open systems, feedback is received by human beings who process it and decide on appropriate action. Many kinds of feedback systems can be designed to facilitate control. The manager may desire a continual flow of information to monitor the system, or assume that "no news is good news" and hence require information on only the exceptional situations. The type and complexity of feedback required also depend on the interrelatedness of organizational subsystems.

---

3 Norbert Wiener, *The Human Use of Human Beings,* rev. ed., Houghton Mifflin Company, Boston, 1954, p. 16.

If the problem of coordination is trivial, control becomes a means of assuring subunit efficiency; if coordination is the overriding concern, control becomes the means for ensuring the collective contribution of organizational subunits. However, and perhaps generally, if neither the separable nor collective aspects of subunit activity can be taken for granted, the control function must be concerned with both and with the conflicts between them. [4]

Organizational control is that phase of the managerial system that monitors performance and provides feedback information that can be used in adjusting both ends and means. Given certain objectives and plans for achieving them, the control function involves measuring actual conditions, comparing them to standards, and initiating feedback that can be used to coordinate organizational activity, focus it in the right direction, and facilitate the achievement of a dynamic equilibrium.

Elements of Control

Four fundamental elements are common to all control systems (see Figure 18.1). They hold true regardless of the degree of sophistication in the system. That is, they are not a function of mechanization or computerization. There is a continuum of refinement in control, from a simple on-off light switch (with a human decision maker involved) to an elaborate heating-cooling system, in which

Figure 18.1   The Basic Elements of a Control System
(1) A measurable and controllable characteristic for which standards are known; (2) a means (sensory device) of measuring the characteristic; (3) a means of comparing actual results to standards and evaluating differences; (4) a means of effecting changes in the system in order to adjust the pertinent characteristic.

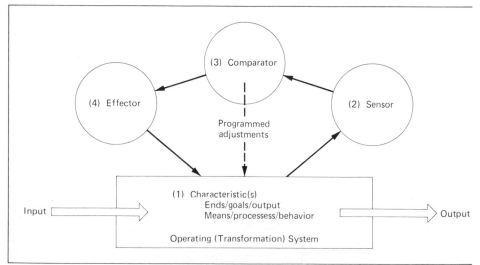

4 John V. Baumler, "Defined Criteria of Performance in Organizational Control," *Administrative Science Quarterly,* September 1971, p. 340.

a computer program might respond not only to changes in the environment but to feedback on rates of change as well. Most sophisticated mechanical or electronic control systems are designed to simulate a human decision maker.

In general, control is maintained by means of decisions that are made as a part of the ongoing process. As for any decision-making process, information flow is the key ingredient. For example, knowing standards implies information about the system. Sensing or measuring also involves information that is used in the comparing phase. Information flow is the essence of the feedback that is necessary to change the system if need be. Internal data processing systems provide information to use in controlling current operations. Summary and exception reports also provide information for management decisions. Internally generated information, coupled with that from the environment, provides the raw material for adaptive and innovative decisions in goal setting and action planning.

Control in Complex Systems

It is important to recognize that control systems typically focus on only one (or at most several) characteristic at a time. A thermostatically controlled home heating system concentrates on temperature and ignores humidity. Automatic street lights are often controlled by time rather than the degree of darkness. In complex social systems it is impossible to control behavior completely. Out of necessity, choosing characteristics to control becomes a sampling process. Considerable managerial skill is required to design a system that provides organizational control effectively and efficiently. Overcontrol may be both expensive (the time and effort involved) and dysfunctional. Picking the appropriate characteristic to monitor is important because individual behavior and organizational performance will be "directed" accordingly. Organizations tend to "get what they measure."

Sophisticated systems have to be designed in order to monitor complex organizations. Performance has many dimensions, such as effectiveness (degree of goal achievement), efficiency (ratios of output to input or benefit to cost), and participant satisfaction (morale or alienation).[5] The key is in recognizing which dimensions are important and controllable. A number of tradeoffs are apparent. Output per day may be increased by tightening supervision and allowing less socialization on the job. However, short-run improvements in efficiency are likely to be accompanied by a decline in morale that may reduce effectiveness and efficiency in future periods.

Managing requires astute selection of performance criteria and appropriate balancing of emphasis among them. Consideration should be given to control of both output (results) and behavior (processes).[6] Control systems are often

[5] Andrew H. Van de Ven, "A Framework for Organizational Assessment," *Academy of Management Review,* January 1976, pp. 64–78.

[6] William G. Ouchi and Mary Ann Maguire, "Organizational Control: Two Functions," *Administrative Science Quarterly,* December 1975, pp. 559–569.

complicated by the fact that key results may be difficult to measure objectively. Therefore, it is often necessary to rely on subjective perceptions of participants and/or clients. It is also important to recognize the continuous process of organizational change (becoming more or less effective, for example) and provide means of feedback and adjustment in improvement efforts.[7]

In some cases, measuring output and monitoring behavior may be complex, costly, and inconclusive—school systems, for example. A degree of control is obtained through the certification process by "ensuring" reasonable competence for teachers and administrators and assuming that competent people, given qualified students and adequate resources, will produce satisfactory results.[8] Certification, licensing, and codes of ethics provide societal controls on the behavior of a variety of professionals in modern organizations.

Control
Process

The fundamental elements in any control system become the control process when linked sequentially in a cycle. Figure 18.2 shows a general model of the control cycle. Objectives are established, programs planned, resources allocated, and work is performed. As actual performance is compared with the plan, feedback is generated to adjust work loads and the allocation of resources. This type of comparison relates primarily to the means used to accomplish objectives. Another comparison is made between actual achievements and the program originally planned. At this stage information is fed back to the program planning phase, as well as forward to a comparison with the original goals. Finally, this comparison leads to a reaffirmation of existing objectives or adjustments for the future. As indicated in the model, this cycle can take place at any level. There is an interface with higher-level control at the step where objectives are determined. Also, there is an interface with lower-level control at the stage where work is performed by the system and possible subsystems. Action plans at one level (region or division) affect objectives and more specific action steps at the next lower level (community or department).

Just as the elements cited previously refer to any control system, the process described herein applies to any control system regardless of the degree of sophistication in the various steps outlined. The *means* employed to sense, compare, and effect may be highly programmed, mechanistic, and computerized, or subjective human beings may be involved in each step of the process. The inclusion of human decision makers in the process tends to make the control system relatively more open.

7 Richard M. Steers, "When Is an Organization Effective?" *Organizational Dynamics*, Autumn 1976, pp. 50–63.

8 Karl E. Weick, "Educational Organizations as Loosely Coupled Systems," *Administrative Science Quarterly*, March 1976, pp. 1–19.

Figure 18.2   The Cycle of Control

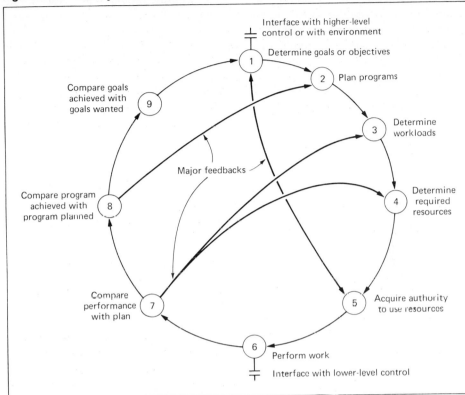

Marvin E. Mundel, *A Conceptual Framework for the Management Sciences,*
McGraw-Hill Book Company, New York, 1967, p. 162.

Closed- and Open-Loop Control

The concept of closed- and open-loop control depends on the presence or absence of automatic feedback. Closed-loop systems involve a sensor, a comparator, and an effector that allow for changes in the system on the basis of the control process, which is operating simultaneously with the performance of the system itself. The classic thermostat example is a closed-loop system because feedback from the environment causes changes in system components to keep the system in balance. The closed loop does not involve information inputs from outside the system. However, the home heating system is closed only in the short run. Human intervention is involved to adjust the thermostat periodically, according to a subjective impression of the environment. Thus, the overall system is open, but we have closed-loop control once the thermostat is set.

Many organizational systems are of this same nature. They can be considered on a continuum from relatively closed to relatively open. In many cases mechanistic systems with closed loops allow the system to perform automatically over a long time. Many computer-based control systems are of this type. However, these systems rely on programs designed by human beings, and the programs can be changed if need be. Thus, in the long run, even highly automated systems are open to human intervention.

The inclusion of human decision makers in control systems as part of the feedback loop moves the systems toward the open end of the spectrum. The individual is subject to many external pressures and sources of information that work their way into the decision-making process. It is true, however, that decision makers can be trained to react on a somewhat programmed basis. Thus habits or standard operating procedures tend to close the system.

The Time Dimension

The time dimension is important to the control function in several ways. Organizations develop ex ante or precontrol by developing standing plans comprised of policies, procedures, and rules or regulations. The development of relatively uniform value systems among organization members provides valuable precontrol. Emphasis is on preventing the system from deviating too far from preconceived norms. Considerable organizational effort goes into maintaining the system within designated limits—preventing undesirable occurrences. Education of the citizenry with regard to traffic laws and the consequences of operating outside the law is an attempt at precontrol of driving behavior.

However, it is apparent that precontrol is often not sufficient to maintain systems within desirable limits. Therefore, considerable effort must also be devoted to postcontrol—ascertaining the results of behavior, evaluating it, and taking action that should correct or adjust behavior in future situations. For example, a flashing red light, siren, and $50 fine are a form of postcontrol designed to induce a particular driver to drive within the posted speed limit. In such a case, the precontrol effort of education and a set of rules did not prove effective. Therefore, postcontrol in the form of punitive action is invoked.

There is considerable disagreement concerning the relative weight that should be placed on pre- and postcontrol. The most extreme position suggests that if enough effort is given to precontrol, there will be no need for postcontrol. That is, if group value systems were internalized completely, all individual and organization actions would fall within desirable limits and the system would be self-regulating. So far, however, this appears to be a utopian concept, and considerable attention continues to be devoted to postcontrol. Many examples of postcontrol in organizations could be cited: reviewing profit performance as related to an established goal, checking the reject or scrap rate quarterly, or checking expense accounts at the end of the month. In each case the difference between actual and expected would be ascertained, and a decision would be made concerning the appropriate corrective action for improved performance in the future.

If feasible, current or real-time control (steering rather than yes-no or postaction) is more satisfactory from the standpoint of maintaining a dynamic equilibrium in organizations.[9] It is often better to adjust behavior as it is happening rather than waiting until the results are in and then initiating corrective action or postcontrol. It is important to identify critical points for controlling operations. For example, the place to detect a flaw in the main landing-gear support is when the part itself is first cast or forged, not after the landing gear has been assembled and attached to the complete airplane.

Real-time control suggests that immediate feedback is important to the process. This is the theory behind teaching machines or programmed learning, in which students are given feedback immediately with regard to the relationship between their response and the correct answer. The same theory has been used in designing incentive systems so that immediate feedback—either reward or punishment—is designed to enhance the probability of an appropriate response on the part of an employee (appropriate from the organization's point of view).

Adjusting minor deviations as they occur is usually easier than correcting wider deviations at some later time. Thus, the notion of current or real-time control is important in maintaining outputs and processes within desired limits as the system continues to function. As measurements are made and comparisons drawn, a system can be adjusted before it deviates too far from present standards. Immediate feedback allows the control process to keep abreast of current operations and helps the system "learn" to operate within the desired limits.

Control and Behavior

A number of behavioral issues should be considered in order to better understand organizational control—for example, congruent values, socialization of participants, and performance appraisal. An overriding concern is the impact of control philosophies and processes on human behavior in organizations.

Congruent Values

The development of reasonably congruent value systems, at least with regard to pertinent organizational issues, is an important means of control. If all key organizational decision makers "think alike," the managerial system is very likely "in control."

9 William H. Newman, *Constructive Control*, Prentice-Hall, Inc., Englewood Cliffs, N.J., 1975, p. 7.

The extreme, of course, is some form of brainwashing, wherein individuals come to think in only one extremely narrow way about pertinent issues. The "organization person" concept, when carried to the extreme, is only a step away from the notion of brainwashing. Certainly there are cases in which conformity is carried too far. We continue to advocate and respect individual initiative. On the other hand, organizations require group effort; the term itself implies cooperation and compromise on the part of the group members as they attempt to achieve some common purpose. Somewhere along the continuum there is a happy medium—perhaps "unity without uniformity."

Tannenbaum suggests that we derive much from organizational membership but often pay heavily for such benefits and that at the heart of this particular exchange lies the control process.

Characterizing an organization in terms of its patterns of control is to describe an essential and universal aspect of organization which every member must face and to which he must adjust. Organization implies control. A social organization has an ordered arrangement of individual human interactions. Control processes help circumscribe idiosyncratic behaviors and keep them conformant with the rational plan of the organization. Organizations require a certain amount of conformity as well as the integration of diverse activities. It is the function of control to bring about conformance to organizational requirements and achievement of the ultimate purposes of the organization. The coordination and order created out of the diverse interests and potentially diffuse behaviors of members is largely a function of control. It is at this point that many of the problems of organizational functioning and of individual adjustment arise. [10]

If managers were so diverse in individual value systems that no agreement on organizational purpose could be achieved, chaos would result. But the other extreme is not very palatable either. If value systems are so consistent that there is absolutely no friction or conflict, we might have a completely static and stale organization. The control function refers to maintaining systems within allowable limits (maintaining a dynamic equilibrium) and suggests that change is acceptable and desirable. However, the system must be stable enough to withstand periodic shocks and still maintain its course toward pertinent goals.

Socialization of Participants

Any individual entering a social system, such as all organizations, is "socialized" to a degree. The new member "learns the value system, the norms, and the required behavior patterns." [11] The amount of overt attention paid to explicit means of socialization depends on the dynamics of the particular organization. Those organizations in relatively stable environments and evidencing little

10 Arnold S. Tannenbaum, *Control in Organizations,* McGraw-Hill Book Company, New York, 1968, p. 3.
11 Edgar H. Schein, "Organizational Socialization and the Profession of Management," in David A. Kolb, Irwin M. Rubin, and James M. McIntyre (eds.), *Organizational Psychology: A Book of Readings,* 2d ed., Prentice-Hall, Inc., Englewood Cliffs, N.J., 1974, p. 3.

growth may develop indirect control without really trying. Individuals may face a long, step-by-step process in moving to positions of real authority and responsibility. In so doing, they gain a value system through long years of experience, almost by osmosis. One of our colleagues spent a summer in a large firm in a rather static industry. Upon his return he said, "I understand now why that industry is so static. It takes forty years for anyone to reach a position in which one can make decisions that have any effect. By that time the person knows only one way to do it." In contrast, Levitt suggests that:

The younger a man is when he reaches the top, or the less dependent his accession is on a generation of selected screening and dedicated commitment to a restricted purpose, the more likely he will see that his company's interests lie in supporting changes coming from outside. He will have escaped the disciplining and narrowing process regarding the external environment that tends to distort his vision. He will be more flexible, more tolerant of diversity, more understanding of the necessity and virtue of . . . change. [12]

In all dynamic industries and organizations there is an influx of people from the outside, and progress may be relatively rapid up through the hierarchy. In this case more overt attention may be paid to developing consistent value systems throughout the organization. Elaborate orientation programs may be put on for new employees. Periodic in-company training programs may be held for supervisors, lower-middle managers, upper-middle managers, and top executives. These development programs are carried on in addition to training for specific skills or functions within the organization. The emphasis is often on general management philosophy and its application in a particular company.

The concept of indirect control has great significance for the relevance of a managerial philosophy such as decentralization of decision making—the delegation of authority and responsibility downward in the organizational hierarchy. If the managerial group, by and large, has a congruent value system with regard to pertinent organizational issues, members of top management can delegate decision making and be reasonably confident that the results will conform to their expectations. That is, the decisions will be made just as if they were doing it themselves. Without this confidence, management is likely to retain centralized control and reserve the right to make decisions or at least review them at the top level.

It is unlikely that many organization members become completely conditioned or developed in today's complex environment. We are part of a pluralistic society and belong to many organizations simultaneously. In general, people become less tractable as they become better educated. This trend alone would seem to indicate difficulty in the future in "developing" employees to narrowly construed organizational value systems.

On the other hand, it is important that general agreement be reached on

---

12 Theodore Levitt, "Why Business Always Loses," *Harvard Business Review*, March–April 1968, pp. 86–87.

important issues such as organizational purposes or objectives and other pertinent areas of concern. A degree of vagueness may be necessary to foster compromise and commitment. The control function must be sophisticated and flexible enough to meet changing conditions. It involves a considerable amount of subjective appraisal. Control decisions require wisdom born of intelligence and experience.

Two Views of Control

Figure 18.3 indicates two alternative views of control—traditional and behavioral. A widespread belief among managers is that the amount of control is fixed. This leads to the assumption that if subordinates have more control over their actions, the boss necessarily has less control as a manager. However, the proper emphasis is on maintaining performance within desired limits, and in this sense the amount of control is variable and increases directly with the amount of concern collectively shown by participants for achieving organizational objectives. Thus, delegation, involvement, motivation, and loyalty may contribute to an increased total amount of control.

A prevalent traditional view is that control is a function of the formal structure and authority (right to command) relationship. An alternative view is that control is a function of interpersonal influence. This suggests that real control takes place via an interaction-influence system that flows in all directions and depends on mutual understanding and acceptance of desired outcomes.

Substantial research evidence suggests that the amount of control and performance are related. Overcontrol can lead to feelings of helplessness, dissatisfaction, and a decrease in productivity. On the other hand, no control can lead to anarchy and an individual sense of uncertainty, anxiety, and frustration.[13] People

Figure 18.3   Two Views of Control

Classical Assumptions (traditional base)	Contemporary Assumptions (behavioral base)
Control is: 1. a fixed amount 2. a *f* (structure and authority) 3. unilateral 4. vertical	Control is: 1. a variable amount 2. a *f* (interpersonal influence) 3. performed via mutual understanding 4. horizontal, vertical, and diagonal

Adapted from J. Timothy McMahon and John M. Ivancevich, "A Study of Control in a Manufacturing Organization: Managers and Nonmanagers," *Administrative Science Quarterly*, 1976, p. 67.)

13 Edward E. Lawler, "Control Systems in Organizations," in Marvin D. Dunnette, (ed.), *Handbook of Industrial and Organizational Psychology*, Rand-McNally College Publishing Company, Chicago, 1976, p. 1265.

do respond positively to clearly defined objectives *and* to feedback concerning their performance. Furthermore, when there is agreement or concordance among organizational members regarding the nature of controls and influence processes, performance is enhanced. [14]

Even though the control system may be reasonably well designed, controls over behavior may be resented, and resistance should be anticipated. Lawler concludes that resistance to control systems is more likely when:

1 The control system measures performance in a new area.
2 The control system replaces a system that people have a high investment in maintaining.
3 The standards are set without participation.
4 The results from the control system are not fed back to the people whose performance is measured.
5 The results from the control system are fed to higher levels in the organization and are used by the reward system.
6 The people who are affected by the system are relatively satisfied with things as they are and they see themselves as committed to the organization.
7 The people who are affected by the system are low in self-esteem and authoritarianism. [15]

Performance Appraisal

Whether done formally or informally, performance appraisal is a phenomenon inherent in organizations. Superiors, subordinates, and peers all form perceptions of each other. Because of its relationship to the reward system, performance appraisal by superiors of subordinates is of primary concern and often formalized, at least in decisions such as hiring, firing, promoting, and reviewing merit for pay increases. Responsibility for performance appraisal gives superiors considerable potential power to control the behavior of subordinates unless there are overriding considerations based on union contracts, automatic step increases, or other built-in means of fairly automatic rewards.

Of crucial importance in formal performance appraisal systems is identification of appropriate criteria. For example, performance on the job should carry more weight than appearance or personality attributes. When results can be measured relatively objectively, appraisal and control are straightforward. When subjective judgments are necessary, the process is facilitated by high levels of trust between superiors and subordinates. Performance appraisal can be functional for the individual and the organization if performance criteria are established jointly,

14 J. Timothy McMahon and John M. Ivancevich, "A Study of Control in a Manufacturing Organization: Managers and Nonmanagers," *Administrative Science Quarterly,* 1976, pp. 66–83.
15 Lawler, *op. cit.,* p. 1274.

appropriate on-the-job behavior is mutually understood, and the review is a continual process focused on growth and development. It can be highly motivating if it taps inherent needs, builds on expectations of appropriate effort leading to desired performance, and includes positive reinforcement via both intrinsic and extrinsic rewards that are equitable in the eyes of all parties concerned.

It is easy to understand, however, how performance appraisal has become dysfunctional in many organizations. Low trust levels, inappropriate criteria, tension-filled appraisal "discussions" long after the fact, and emphasis on shortcomings rather than on accomplishments all work together to create a poor atmosphere, employee dissatisfaction, and decreased organizational efficiency and effectiveness.

Designing Control Systems

While the basic elements of the control process are the same, the specific means of achieving control in organizations should vary according to the situation. Consideration should be given to factors in the environment (such as regulatory agencies) as well as to internal subsystems, such as goals, technology, structure, and human behavior. For stable-mechanistic systems the control process can be relatively fixed, programmed, and hierarchic, with emphasis on impersonal means (such as rules and procedures) and external control of participants. For adaptive-organic systems, the control process should be flexible, dynamic, and reciprocal, with emphasis on interpersonal contacts (such as suggestion and persuasion) and participant self-control.

Most organizations require a variety of control systems to monitor performance—quantity and quality of production, progress on research projects, expenditures versus budgets, ethical behavior, and so on—rather than one unitary, total system. However, it is important that the systems are as integrated as possible, rather than fragmented or piecemeal. Control of overall strategy can rely on relatively subjective appraisal of organizational performance; control of operations can rely on relatively objective criteria and automatic adjustments, based on a comparison of actual and expected results. However, both phases of organizational control should be integrated via coordinative efforts that relate tactics to strategy.

Because organizations "get what they measure," it is crucial to identify those results that are essential for organizational success. There is great temptation to focus on criteria that are easily measured and quantifiable but trivial in determining success. In designing control systems, this temptation must be overcome and attention focused on high-priority objectives, regardless of the degree of difficulty in measuring and evaluating performance. Once this is done, effort should be devoted to making such criteria as measurable as possible.

Managerial Beliefs

In designing control systems it is important to recognize managerial beliefs explicitly. While some aspects of the control function are dictated by task, technology, and structure, there is typically considerable leeway with regard to delegation and reliance on human discretion at various levels. We can relate this issue of beliefs to our previous discussion of Theory X and Theory Y (Chapter 10). If we are basically optimistic concerning our subordinates' ability, integrity, and self-control, we are likely to delegate more, live with loose controls, and rely on people to control their own work activities and behavior. On the other hand, if we are rather pessimistic in these matters, we are likely to delegate less, design tight controls, and rely on policies, procedures, and rules to ensure that work activities and behavior are within prescribed limits.

Overall managerial beliefs are likely to lead to self-fulfilling prophecies. An aura of pessimism and suspicion coupled with tight controls will not encourage growth and development but can foster dependence, hostility, and dissatisfaction. A spirit of optimism and encouragement coupled with participant involvement in setting goals and control processes will likely lead to internalization of organizational control by each individual in his or her own sphere of activity. Of course, there are exceptions that must be taken into account. Some percentage of any work group may require tighter controls than others. However, if this is only five or ten percent, designing the total system with such individuals in mind will stifle the integrity and creativity of the other ninety or ninety-five percent of the work force. Is it better to be optimistic and wrong ten percent of the time or pessimistic and wrong ninety percent of the time? The resulting organizational climate differences can be significant for long-run morale, efficiency, and effectiveness. What if the percentages are reversed? Or seventy-thirty? Or fifty-fifty?

One example of the impact of increased individual discretion in work organizations is the generally positive experience so far with flexitime (the opportunity to work eight hours at any time during some twelve-hour period, such as 6:00 a.m. to 6:00 p.m.). Although this approach is more complex to manage, typical benefits so far include increased service to clientele, less absenteeism and tardiness, increased employee satisfaction, and increased commitment to organizational goals. [16]

Benefit-Cost Analysis

Control can never be complete; variations from expectations are inevitable. It is obvious that organizational resources are consumed in the control func-

---

[16] David Robison, *Alternative Work Patterns,* Work in America Institute, Inc., Scarsdale, New York, 1976.

tion. Therefore, attention should be devoted to benefit-cost analysis of control systems. Figure 18.4 shows the relationship of perfection in control and the cost to attain it. The difference between the cost of control and improvement in system performance is the net economic benefit. A system can be overcontrolled to the extent that the cost of the control subsystem increases faster than improvement in performance. Indeed, such costs theoretically can be greater than the total value realized from the operation itself. As shown in Figure 18.4, there is a range in which net benefit is optimal.

This analysis can be extended beyond economic or financial considerations. Short-run operational control may be attained at the expense of hidden psychological costs. While the system may appear to be in control, pressures may build to an explosion that has severe consequences. Or underlying individual attitudes and group dynamics may have a more subtle impact in the form of specific slowdown tactics or general organizational lethargy. Even if the system appears to be in control, performance is not what it might be if the control system were designed to tap latent human capability and integrate individual and organizational well-being.

Figure 18.4   The Economics of Control

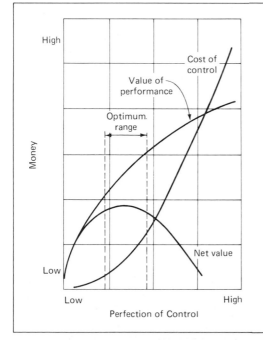

Marvin E. Mundel, *A Conceptual Framework for the Management Sciences,* McGraw-Hill Book Company, New York, 1967, p. 174.

Examples of Control

By considering several examples in detail, we can increase our understanding of the concept of control and illustrate a variety of specific processes that are appropriate in different organizational contexts. In some cases, the foci of control are general, overall characteristics and evaluation depends heavily on subjective appraisal. In other cases, specific criteria can be evaluated via objective measurements. In the examples described, it is difficult to separate planning and control; therefore, the procedures outlined include elements of both.

Social System Control

Increased pressure for social change during the 1960s and 1970s has focused attention on the performance of the total societal system. Previously, the President's economic report made up the bulk of the annual State of the Union message. This no longer suffices. The nation is interested in the President's social report as well. It is becoming increasingly apparent that economic well-being is not a comprehensive measure of societal progress. The "great society" or the "good life" is a much more complex subject. An example of plural concerns is the establishment of the National Center for Productivity and Quality of Working Life.

Many of the objectives of the Declaration of Independence and the Constitution have not been achieved "in general" in society. Some type of feedback reporting will be necessary if we are to monitor progress in all phases of our complex social system. What kind of a system will provide the necessary information? "Economic information itself cannot fully answer these questions. In addition to economic aspects, every situation has political, social, cultural, and biophysical aspects also. Moreover, qualitative information may be fully as important as quantitative information. Overemphasis upon statistics, because they seem more precise, or upon economic data, because they may be more readily available, often yields a narrow, unbalanced view of the state of a nation."[17]

A more meaningful view could be developed through a system of national social accounting that integrates information with regard to concepts developed by economists, political scientists, sociologists, anthropologists, and social psychologists. The task is not an easy one. However, the need is imperative. Managers throughout society, particularly in government positions, need feedback with regard to progress toward identified goals. Also, legislators—federal, state, and local—need some means to appraise the impact of programs that are put into practice. How effective are programs such as Medicare, the Job Corps, or urban

---

[17] Bertram M. Gross, *The State of the Nation: Social Systems Accounting,* Social Science Paperbacks, London, 1966, pp. 1–2.

renewal? What has the Peace Corps really accomplished? Are equal opportunity employment and affirmative action programs achieving stated objectives? Answers to these questions do not come easily in a pluralistic society. However, there may be ways to bring some order out of chaos. [18]

Increased emphasis has been placed on developing more effective performance appraisals of various social programs. Rather than allocate millions or billions of dollars to various programs in the hope that something good will result, more effort is needed to develop effective systems of control and performance appraisal to determine the actual results. In the past a great deal of the emphasis has been on controlling the inputs through budgetary processes and financial accounting. Increasingly, we are attempting to measure the *outputs* of such programs rather than just the inputs. Obviously, this requires more appropriate information concerning actual impact, such as more effective measures of the *results* of the various efforts to reduce automobile emissions and other types of air pollution.

This approach requires a more explicit research orientation to measure the results of any social program. We need to know more about current conditions (such as the state of the nation's health) and how a particular social intervention has led to improvement (or lack thereof). In many areas this may call for field experiments. For example, there has been a controlled field experiment to determine the impact of a guaranteed annual wage to low-income families. Pending legislation before Congress, entitled the Human Resources Development Act, is designed to sponsor pilot experimental projects concerned with enhancing both productivity and the quality of work life. Such experimental field projects, under reasonably controlled conditions, will allow us to measure the *results* of such social interventions more effectively and will provide a great deal more relevant information for future policy decisions.

At the corporate level some tentative steps are being taken toward assessing performance in activities that affect the society around them—"measuring the unmeasurable." Bauer and Fenn provide some guidelines for a social audit process that give managers a more explicit "feel" for the costs and benefits involved. [19] Post and Epstein suggest a method for systematic scanning of the impact of current organizational activities in the context of broad social trends. [20]

Human
Asset
Accounting

The complexity of evaluating the structure or process of complex multi-unit subsystems in society is evident. The task becomes more manageable if a

---

18 For a discussion of these issues, see Michael Springer, "Social Indicators, Reports, and Accounts: Toward the Management of Society," *The Annals of the American Academy of Political and Social Science,* March 1970, pp. 1–13.

19 Raymond A. Bauer and Dan H. Fenn, Jr., *The Corporate Social Audit,* Russell Sage Foundation, New York, 1972.

20 James E. Post and Marc J. Epstein, "Information Systems for Social Reporting," *Academy of Management Review,* January 1977, pp. 81–87.

single unit is involved—a business enterprise or government agency, for example. However, the traditional approaches are still most prevalent—economic-technical variables are used to indicate current status and system performance over time. Financial conditions are monitored via budgets, balance sheets, profit and loss statements, and break-even charts.

Some organizations make periodic attempts to assess human assets by surveying employee morale and/or estimating customer goodwill. Progress is evident in the latter case because many firms formally designate goodwill as an asset and attach a monetary value to it when assessing the financial worth of the firm. In nonbusiness organizations, however, there is no formal way to take into account customer goodwill (or ill will). Typically, we have a "feeling" with regard to how well an organization—a public school system or a general hospital, for example—serves its clientele. In a complex society, unanimity or consensus are probably utopian concepts. However, we may be able to identify major trends with regard to goodwill for a particular organization.

Although business firms and other organizations do attempt to measure employee morale, it is not reflected in the formal accounting statements as an asset or liability. Nevertheless, it certainly affects current performance as well as long-run viability. An organization with a "bad climate" may have difficulty attracting new talent. Therefore, it may gradually decline as a viable organization in spite of significant technological improvements. It is apparent that some organizations do better than others with seemingly the same resources. That is, they have similar technology, and approximately the same number of people. However, the quality of the human resource may vary significantly and hence result in more output per unit of input. Moreover, the latent human capability may be approximately equal, but the inclination to perform may be significantly greater in one organization than in another and hence result in superior performance. Likert suggests a number of conditions that differentiate the human assets in an organization:

1 Level of intelligence and aptitudes
2 Level of training
3 Level of performance goals and motivation to achieve organizational success
4 Quality of leadership
5 Capacity to use differences for purposes of innovation and improvement, rather than allowing differences to develop into bitter, irreconcilable, interpersonal conflict
6 Quality of communication upward, downward, and laterally
7 Quality of decision making
8 Capacity to achieve cooperative teamwork versus competitive striving for personal success at the expense of the organization
9 Quality of the control processes of the organization and the levels of felt responsibility which exist

10 Capacity to achieve effective coordination
11 Capacity to use experience and measurements to guide decisions, improve operations, and introduce innovations[21]

Each of these could vary on a continuum from poor to excellent. An organization that rated excellent across the board would have a significantly different climate from one that rated poor in all categories.

Obtaining feedback on these variables is not always easy. In some cases, measurement is relatively straightforward; in other cases, it is quite difficult. How do we identify quality of communication or capacity to achieve effective coordination? This phase of the organizational control system requires judgmental decision making by experienced executives. The first step is identifying a current structure and performance level to serve as a yardstick for evaluating future conditions. The performance at any given time should be related to past levels of achievement as well as to any absolute standards imposed by the decision maker. This type of evaluation is difficult but absolutely necessary in order to obtain a composite measure of organizational worth. Human assets are receiving increasing attention and undoubtedly will be included in evaluation processes more and more in the future.[22]

The role of human assets in evaluating an organization is illustrated by the importance that security analysts place on company management. They spend many hours evaluating industry data and economic potential. They analyze individual companies within an industry and trace past history and future potential in terms of sales, profits, price earnings ratios, and other similar economic-technical factors. Yet the most important element in most cases is managerial potential. "Knowing the statistics of an industry—prices, production, retailing figures, capital spending—is important, of course, but the main thing is assessing management."[23]

The analyst attempts to assess the energy and astuteness of top management in order to predict whether or not the company will be able to take advantage of opportunities that are likely to present themselves in the future. An energetic, knowledgeable top management group is considered to be a critical determinant of the potential success or failure of the organization. This human asset is not reflected in the financial data published for popular consumption. But this is exactly what the analyst is looking for, because the organization is significantly undervalued if the figures reflect a poor or mediocre situation that is on the verge of blossoming. The likelihood of superior performance in the future is enhanced by excellence in the managerial system.

21 Rensis Likert, *The Human Organization,* McGraw-Hill Book Company, New York, 1967, p. 148.
22 Eric G. Flamholtz, *Human Resource Accounting,* Dickenson Publishing Co., Encino, Cal., 1974; Philip A. Mirvis and Barry A. Macy, "Human Resource Accounting: A Measurement Perspective," *Academy of Management Review,* April 1976, pp. 74–83.
23 "Students of Stocks," *Wall Street Journal,* Jan. 23, 1968, p. 1.

Budgetary
Control

A budget is often described as a plan set forth in financial terms. That is, organizational activity is translated into expected results with dollars as the common denominator. Most writers stress the positive or planning aspects of budgetary control rather than the strictly control phase. Yet the connotation of restriction and constraint is widespread in business and government organizations.

The procedures of budgetary control can be applied to a wide variety of situations. Several basic elements are involved in financial budgeting.

1 *Expressing in dollars the results of plans anticipated in a future period.* These dollar figures are typically set up in the same way as the accounts in a company's accounting system. The budget shows how the accounts should look if present plans are carried out.

2 *Coordinating these estimates into a well-balanced program.* The figures for sales, production, advertising, and other divisions must be matched to be sure that they are mutually consistent; financial feasibility of all plans added together must be assured; and the combined results must be examined in terms of over-all objectives. Some adjustments will probably be necessary to obtain such a balanced program.

3 *Comparing actual results with the program estimates that emerge from step 2.* Any significant differences point to the need for corrective action. In short, the budget becomes a standard for appraising operating results. [24]

Budgetary control, as described above, nearly parallels the management process. It involves planning, coordinating, and controlling.

In many organizations this does, in fact, happen. The budget becomes the primary tool for managing organizational activities. For business enterprises, objectives are typically expressed in terms of dollar sales. Sales forecasts are developed in the light of both external and internal informational inputs, with the results providing a foundation for all organizational activity. An advertising budget is drawn up to fit the sales forecast. The wage and salary budget is designed in view of the number of people required to accomplish the objectives as established. Throughout the organization, future activity is spelled out in dollar terms.

The budgeting process forces management to consider future plans explicitly and attach dollar values to them. By asking organization members at all levels to develop subparts of the budget, a sense of participation and organizational involvement is often achieved. Self-generated plans for budgets often are easier to control than those imposed by others.

Once the various parts of the budget are integrated into a comprehensive financial plan, it becomes a standard against which performance can be measured during the ensuing period. In most cases budgets are flexible enough that adjust-

---

[24] William H. Newman, Charles E. Summer, and E. Kirby Warren, *The Process of Management,* 3d ed. © 1972, pp. 602–603. Reprinted by permission of Prentice-Hall, Inc., Englewood Cliffs, N.J.

ments can be made, if need be, according to the way circumstances develop. It is not necessarily a rigid constraining device.

Budgetary control in many organizations involves dollar allocations whereby a total amount of money is divided and earmarked for certain functions over a period of time. In this sense the budget is a constraining device because activities dependent on available funds must be curtailed if the funds run out. Therefore, the control process is typically one of ascertaining expenditures over time as measured against some planned rate.

A typical problem in organizations of this type is that of running out of funds before the budget period expires. Either funds must be transferred from other endeavors, or activity in this phase of the organization must be curtailed. Another less typical but evident problem is that of coming to the end of a budgetary period with excess funds on hand. At this point there is often a mad scramble to expend the funds in order that the budget officer and/or appropriating agency (legislative body) will not interpret efficient performance as a lack of need and hence cut off the supply of funds in the future. In large, complex organizations, the allocation process is difficult. Matching needs with resources is an important function, and the process should be flexible enough to adjust according to changes in the environment. In most cases, however, changes are rather slow in coming, thus resulting in a continuation of expenditures in relatively obsolete activities and undersupporting new and growing areas of need.

Zero-base budgeting is one approach to the problems of obsolete programs and/or slow response in reallocation of resources.[25] Sunset laws also address these issues.[26] The key concepts are justification of need and demonstrable results from past expenditures. Rather than continuing programs by extrapolating last year's budget, a zero base is assumed and funds are allocated based on the merits of each program in competition with others at that point in time.

The planning-programming-budgeting system (PPBS) developed in the federal government and used by many state and local agencies is also an extension of the traditional budgetary process. This approach requires that programs and missions to be accomplished be clearly identified; then the planning and budgetary processes are developed on a basis of the programs. The overall philosophy and emphasis of this system are on measuring the results or outputs of the various programs, rather than just on the budgetary process of determining and controlling the financial inputs.

Summary

The control function is that phase of the managerial system that maintains organization activity within allowable limits. Planning and controlling are

---

25 Peter A. Phyrr, *Zero-base Budgeting*, Wiley-Interscience, New York, 1973.
26 Legislation creating agencies for specified time periods rather than "in perpetuity." At the end of that time they go out of existence unless reaffirmed.

directly related activities, with plans providing the framework for the control phase of the managerial process. Feedback is critical to control, providing information about past or current performance, which is used to influence future activity or goals.

Four fundamental elements are common to all control systems: (1) a measurable characteristic, (2) a sensor, (3) a comparator, and (4) an effector. Closed-loop control systems involve automatic feedback and adjustment of the system without human intervention. The open-loop system involves a human in the decision making which is part of the control process.

Timing is an important consideration for control theory. Much effort is devoted to precontrol—trying to ensure that operations will remain within allowable limits. However, it seems inevitable that operations get out of control in real life. Thus, considerable attention must also be devoted to postcontrol—adjusting operations after the fact with the intent of keeping the operation in control in the future. Concurrent or real-time control is becoming increasingly prevalent; many operations are adjusted continually and immediately as deviations from expectations occur.

Control of human behavior in organizations is both implicit (congruent value systems and socialization) and explicit (direct attempts to influence people). The total amount of control can vary and be positively related to performance. However, the locus of control—external or internal (self)—is a strong mediating factor in how well control systems function.

Important factors in the design of control systems are managerial beliefs, relevant criteria (key results and high-priority objectives), and functional performance appraisal processes that are continuing rather than sporadic. Complex organizations require a variety of control systems that are as congruent and integrated as possible.

Progress is being made in social system accounting and, in spite of a complex, pluralistic society, more explicit feedback control systems will be forthcoming in the future. At the company or agency level, human asset accounting is being recognized as important feedback concerning organizational well-being.

Questions and Problems

1 Define control. What are its objectives? Illustrate several connotations of control with organizational examples.

2 Relate the following to the concept of control: (a) homeostasis, (b) cybernetics, and (c) feedback.

3 Relate the four basic elements of control to the control cycle.

4 Trace the control process in the following situations: (a) driving to work, (b) coaching a football team, (c) managing an advertising campaign, and (d) administering Medicare.

5 "Even the most detailed and automatic closed-loop systems are open in the ultimate sense." Do you agree? Why or why not?

6 Discuss the relationship between pre-, post-, and current control efforts in organizational control systems.

7 Discuss management "development" (or conditioning) as a means to higher-level organizational control.

8 Relate performance appraisal to the control process. From your own experience, cite good and bad examples, noting personal and organizational effects.

9 What does the phrase "benefit-cost analysis" mean? Give an example of how costs can exceed benefits.

10 What are the prospects for a President's social report in the annual State of the Union message? Why?

11 How do human "assets" affect the value of an organization? What factors are involved? What would you do to increase the value of human assets in your organization?

12 Relate concepts such as inventory control, cost control, and production control to the general models set forth in this chapter.

Knowledge comes from noticing resemblances and recurrences in the events that happen around us.
Wilfred Trotter

We must stop acting as though nature were organized into disciplines in the same way that universities are.
Russell L. Ackoff

What we need are great complexifiers, men who will not only seek to understand what it is they are about, but who will also dare to share that understanding with those for whom they act.
Daniel P. Moynihan

Many seemingly unrelated things follow similar or identical rules of behavior, and . . . knowledge of one therefore provides understanding of another.
Alfred Kuhn

If there is no struggle there is no progress. Those who profess to favor freedom, and yet deprecate agitation . . . want crops without plowing up the ground. They want rain without thunder and lightning. They want the ocean without the awful roar of its many waters.
Frederick Douglass

Comparative Analysis and Contingency Views

7

In the six preceding parts of the book we have developed a framework for studying organizations and management. We have looked at the conceptual foundations and the evolution of theory and have analyzed organizations via a systems approach that focuses on the environmental suprasystem and five sub systems—goals and values, technical, structural, psychosocial, and managerial. This framework provides a basis for considering several other issues.

Comparative analysis and contingency views are particularly important in the development of a body of knowledge that is relevant for management practice. Hypotheses and theories need to be tested across a variety of settings or situations in order to develop concepts that reflect the complexity of organizational phenomena.

In Chapter 19 we look at the pervasiveness and importance of comparative organizational analysis and indicate several foci of attention—internally across functions, levels, or subsystems, as well as externally across institutions and cultures. Various ways of classifying organizations are reviewed and evaluated. The systems model is suggested as a framework for comparative analysis. Systems concepts and contingency views are explored in terms of their relevance and potential contributions to organization theory and management practice.

In Chapters 20, 21, and 22 the systems approach is used to describe and analyze three important institutions in society, the community general hospital, the university, and the city. The systems model is used as a framework to help understand these specific organizations in terms of characteristics or key dimensions common to all organizations.

Comparative Analysis and Contingency Views

Nineteen

Two important issues in the study of organization and management are the universality of concepts and the transferability of skills. Does the body of knowledge—organization theory—apply to any and all organizations? Are managerial skills transferable across institutions and cultures? The answers to these questions obviously depend on the scope and direction of organization theory, as well as the connotation of the term managerial skill. If the manager's skill in situational analysis is emphasized, we can enhance the applicability of current knowledge. But much empirical research remains to be done. Comparative analysis using the systems approach can lead to contingency views that facilitate appropriate organization designs and managerial actions. Current efforts in this direction will be discussed via the following topics:

Comparative Analysis Defined
Types of Organizations
Multivariate Analysis
Cross-Cultural Comparative Analysis
Contingency Views and Organization Theory
Contingency Views and Management Practice

Comparative Analysis Defined

To compare means "to examine in order to observe or discover similarities or differences." We are all continually involved in simplified comparative analysis of organizations. When selecting a college or university to attend, students frequently investigate a number of institutions. They are likely to look at a limited number of dimensions upon which to compare schools: distance from home, tuition costs, academic reputation, where friends are going, and other similar criteria. As consumers, we are continually making comparisons between organizations. Why do we select one automobile repair shop over another? Because it is closer, cheaper, or more reliable? Why do we shop at A & P, Safeway, or an independent grocer? Prospective employees compare a number of organizations for job opportunities. Many will look only at short-term rewards such as the salary and fringe benefits. Other, more sophisticated analysts will scrutinize and compare organizations on many dimensions, including less tangible ones such as long-range career opportunities.

These are rather simple examples of comparative analysis of organizations. They are typically limited to only a few characteristics, usually those most directly pertinent to the observer's role as prospective student, customer, or employee.

For organization theorists and practicing managers, comparative analysis is much more comprehensive—all relevant dimensions should be considered in order to describe, analyze, or plan effectively. The systems approach—consideration of the environmental suprasystem and the major organizational subsystems—provides an appropriate framework for comparative analysis. But several key questions are involved: What organizations should be compared? What characteristics or dimensions should be used in the analysis? How do we obtain information relevant for comparative purposes?

In general, the answer to these questions is "It all depends on the purpose of the analyst." Thus, appropriate analysis includes information (however obtained) on whatever dimensions seem useful in gaining a better understanding of relevant organizations. Comparative analysis can focus on types of organizations or on specific dimensions in terms of their similarities and differences across organizations.

Alternative Approaches

Comparative analysis may be carried out by focusing on one (unidimensional) or several variables (multidimensional). For example, leadership styles might be compared across functions, levels, institutions, or cultures. Such studies provide insight concerning what factors affect a specific variable or dimension.

Typically, however, comparative analysis includes more than one dimension in order to facilitate our understanding of how organizations are similar and different in terms of interrelationships among key variables. The detailed case analysis is a multi-dimensional approach that concentrates on one organization (or subunit) and analyzes as many facets as time and energy will permit. It provides an opportunity to understand a complex social system in great detail. However, the results of such an analysis cannot be generalized. Findings concerning effective organization design or management practice may or may not be applicable to another organization.

In order to identify patterns of relationships that lead to effective performance, it is important to include many organizations. This is the essence of the comparative method—"systematic comparison of a fairly large number of organizations in order to establish relationships between their characteristics."[1] Obviously, the more organizations that are investigated, the more confidence we have in the findings that emerge consistently. Comparative analysis over a variety of institutions and cultures should reveal patterns of relationships. A body of knowledge presented in this way will allow managers to diagnose situations, anticipate possible consequences of their actions, and choose the most appropriate alternative (the one with the highest probability of success). The ultimate body of knowledge will always include a contingency flavor—there are no "absolutes" or guarantees of success. However, better understanding of patterns of relationships should lead to improvement in managerial performance.

It is only after painstaking, exhaustive research in a number of settings that we can be confident of describing relationships with broad applicability. Moreover, normative conclusions or prescriptions for managerial behavior are always tentative, even with such a foundation.

Importance of Comparing

The importance of comparative analysis is underscored by its pervasiveness. Some suggest that "it is formally impossible to study anything without at least implicitly comparing it with something else, or comparing its component parts one with another."[2] Much effort has been devoted to comparative culture, comparative religion, comparative government, and comparative economics. In a sense, comparative analysis gives an indication of maturity in a field. It is a shift toward broader perspectives—away from parochialism and a preoccupation with justifying our own particular system or approach. There has been a tendency throughout history for philosophers to establish universal principles based on narrow experience *and* then to extend the "one best way" (often with considerable missionary zeal) to any and all settings. This conversion process has been evident in culture, religion, politics, and economic systems, as well as in organization theory and management practice.

Comparative analysis says, in effect, "Wait a minute; let's see if our approach is really applicable across the board." It emphasizes empirical research and recognizes an increasing number of relevant phenomena. It is a shift from concentration on a unique organization, country, or culture toward seeking generalizations about patterns of relationships in a variety of settings.[3]

1 Peter M. Blau, "The Comparative Study of Organizations," *Industrial and Labor Relations Review,* April 1965, p. 323.

2 Stanley H. Udy, Jr., "The Comparative Analysis of Organizations," in James G. March (ed.), *Handbook of Organizations,* Rand McNally & Company, Chicago, 1965, p. 679.

3 Dwight Waldo, "Comparative Public Administration," in Preston P. LeBreton (ed.), *Comparative Administrative Theory,* University of Washington Press, Seattle, Wash., 1968, p. 110.

Comparative analysis recognizes that there are many variables and that interactions among them can present a complex situation for the manager. Research continues to show that there is no one best way to achieve organizational goals; the same ends can be gained via a variety of means (equifinality). For example, Perrow sums up his research experience as follows:

I have learned as many others have been learning, that there is no one best way to run any organization and that what works for one firm may not work for another. Thus, any theory which does not have built into its body a mechanism for distinguishing types of organizations and predicting from these types rather than an "other things being equal provision" or a provision for limiting all generalizations to only those organizations that fit those generalizations, is poor theory indeed. . . . I have learned that the name of the game is operationalization. [4]

Comparative studies provide an important stepping-stone in operationalizing organization theory. By identifying the relationships in different settings, there is an opportunity to build a body of knowledge that includes contingent principles or guidelines. Managers are thus provided with relevant information which, coupled with astute diagnosis of specific situations, can lead to appropriate action steps.

Types of Organizations

One of the problems in comparative analysis is "What should be compared to what?" *Classification* means "arrangement according to some systematic division." Alfred Kuhn suggests that:

Things can be classified in numberless ways. Organizations are no exception. Among others, they can be classified as good or bad; profit or nonprofit; public or private; large, medium, or small; producers of commodities or producers of services; centralized or decentralized; primitive or advanced, or as educational, industrial, governmental, religious, philanthropic, or fraternal; and so on and on. No system of classification is "better" in any absolute sense, its usefulness depending on the purpose at hand. [5]

It is important to recognize that there are no right or wrong ways to classify organizations. The goal is better understanding of organizational phenomena—not perfection of classification.

On the basis of popular usage, we might classify organizations by types such as:

4 Charles Perrow, "Some Reflections on Technology and Organizational Analysis," in Anant R. Negandhi (ed.), *Modern Organizational Theory: Contextual, Environmental and Socio-cultural Variables,* Kent State University Press, Kent, Ohio, 1973, p. 51.

5 Alfred Kuhn, *The Study of Society: A Unified Approach,* Richard D. Irwin, Inc. and The Dorsey Press, Homewood, Ill. 1963, p. 431.

Businesses	Political parties
Hospitals	Professional and trade associations
Unions	Military units
Schools	Correctional institutions
Churches	Voluntary and charitable groups
Cooperatives	Local, state, and federal agencies
Social clubs	International agencies

While this classification scheme might be useful for some general purposes, it is not very appropriate for more sophisticated understanding of organizations and their management. It implies that there is substantial uniformity within each organizational type and that there are significant differences between types.

Various approaches have been suggested for the classification of all organizations in our society—typically using one major criterion. Figure 19.1 shows several ways that organizations have been classified using a single dimension, such as means of obtaining compliance, social needs orientation, and primary beneficiary. These intuitively designed classification systems may seem logical, but they have many difficulties as a basis for comparative analysis.

One of the obvious difficulties is overlapping. Many organizations may play multiple roles, but they are slotted into categories based on their primary function. A church or university may meet various social needs, utilize several means of obtaining compliance from their members, and have various beneficiaries of their activities. "A business firm is a profit organization in its normal operations, a service organization in some of its community activities, a pressure organization in its lobbying and some of its institutional advertising, and a cooperative in its nonprofit cafeteria or bowling team."[6]

A more fundamental problem is apparent because of the great diversity of characteristics of organizations within each of these broad types.

Types of organization—in terms of their function in society—will vary as much within each type as between types. Thus, some schools, hospitals, banks, and steel companies may have more in common, because of their routine character, than routine and nonroutine schools, routine and nonroutine hospitals, and so forth. . . . In fact, the variations within one type of organization may be such that some schools are like prisons, some prisons like churches, some churches like factories, some factories like universities, and so on.[7]

This discussion does not mean that it is inappropriate to compare broad organization types such as public and private organizations, corporations and unions, or schools and hospitals. Such comparative analysis can be useful. How-

---

6 Ibid., p. 435.

7 Charles Perrow, "A Framework for the Comparative Analysis of Organizations," *American Sociological Review*, April, 1967, pp. 203–204.

Figure 19.1   Several Ways to Classify Organizations by Types

Means of Obtaining Compliance *

The compliance structure in organizations is determined by the kinds of power (coercive, remunerative, and normative) applied to lower-level participants.

Three Types of Organizations Based on Kinds of Power Used

1 *Coercive organizations* use force (latent or manifest) as the chief means of control over lower-level participants. These participants are generally alienated from the objectives of the organization. Examples include concentration camps, penal institutions, and custodial mental hospitals.
2 *Utilitarian organizations* use remuneration as the basis of control where lower-level participants contribute to the organization with calculative involvement, based on what benefits they can receive. Examples are businesses and most labor unions.
3 *Normative organizations* use moral control as the main source of influence over participants who have a high motivational and moral involvement. Examples include churches, universities, and hospitals, as well as many political and social organizations.

Social Needs Orientation †

Four Types of Organizations Based on Broad Social Needs to Which They Are Oriented

1 *Organizations oriented to economic production* include business firms that are engaged in the production and distribution of goods and services. Their primary function is economic, although there may be other goals which the organization must achieve in order to maintain itself in the environmental system.
2 *Organizations oriented to political goals* are geared to the attainment of valued goals and to the generation and allocation of power in society. This would include most governmental organizations.
3 *Integrative organizations* are concerned with the adjustment of conflicts and the direction of motivation to fulfill certain social expectations. The court system and legal profession is in this group. It also includes hospitals because they provide the mechanism for meeting the social needs for medical care.
4 *Pattern-maintenance organizations* have primary functions that are cultural, educational, or expressive. Examples are churches and schools.

Prime Beneficiary ‡

Four Basic Categories of Organizational Participants
1 The members, or rank-and-file participants
2 The owners or managers of the organization
3 The clients
4 The public at large

Four Types of Organization Based on Prime Beneficiary

1 *Mutual-benefit associations:* the prime beneficiary is the membership; examples are labor unions, trade and professional associations.
2 *Business concerns:* owners are the prime beneficiaries.
3 *Service organizations:* the client group is the prime beneficiary; includes hospitals, universities, religious organizations, and social agencies.
4 *Commonwealth organizations:* The primary beneficiary is the public at large; examples are the military, law enforcement agencies, the post office, and penal institutions.

* Amitai Etzioni, *A Comparative Analysis of Complex Organizations,* rev. ed., The Free Press, New York, 1975, pp. 23–67
† Talcott Parsons, *Structure and Process in Modern Societies,* The Free Press, New York, 1960, pp. 44–47
‡ Copyright © 1962 by Chandler Publishing Company. Reprinted from *Formal Organizations: A Comparative Approach* by Peter M. Blau and W. Richard Scott by permission of Chandler Publishing Company, an Intext publisher.

ever, it is important for the researcher to clearly identify *those characteristics that are used* as the basis for comparison.[8]

We can summarize this discussion of comparative analysis by types of organizations by suggesting several caveats. We should not assume that all organizations within a given type are the same, but should investigate differences as well as similarities. We should not assume differences between common organizational types such as profit and nonprofit, but should look for both similarities and differences. Finally, we should clearly specify the characteristics or attributes we are using for our comparisons.

Intraorganizational Analysis

Comparative studies within organizations relate to similarities and differences across functions or other subunits. For example, we have differentiated the managerial task as it relates to organizational subsystems or levels (see Figure 5.5). The managerial task at the operating, coordinative, and strategic levels is compared according to several dimensions—environmental systems, time perspective, viewpoint (optimizing—satisficing), general problem-solving processes, and decision-making techniques. Comparative analysis is also appropriate and useful across functions such as sales, production, engineering, accounting, and personnel. What are the similarities and differences in organizational settings? Should a manager's approach be altered significantly if he or she moves from one function to another? What are the probable consequences of extending approaches that work in one department to all others?

Numerous studies have focused on intraorganizational analysis. For example, Lawrence and Lorsch investigated differences among sales, production, and research departments in a variety of industries.[9] They compared these functional areas in terms of (1) their emphasis on particular goals, (2) their time orientation, (3) their interpersonal orientations, and (4) their degree of formal structure. Such studies help us better understand which organization designs and managerial practices are appropriate in various internal organizational settings.

Multivariate Analysis

Another approach in comparative analysis is to investigate the important characteristics, dimensions, or attributes that are apparent in all organizations. The key question in this type of analysis is "What characteristics are important for comparative purposes?" A number of researchers have concluded that the nature of the *technology* (routine versus nonroutine) is a key characteristic and

---

8 Hal G. Rainey, Robert W. Backoff, and Charles H. Levine, "Comparing Public and Private Organizations," *Public Administration Review,* March–April 1976, pp. 233–244.

9 Paul R. Lawrence and Jay W. Lorsch, *Organization and Environment,* Division of Research, Graduate School of Business Administration, Harvard University, Boston, 1967.

have suggested that organizations with similar technologies should have similar structural designs. Others have focused on *environment* (certain or uncertain) or *goals* (profit or service) as the key variables. In fact, a wide variety of characteristics have been used in comparative studies of organizations: size, structure, attributes of participants, decision-making processes, leadership styles, and so on.

There is an increasing awareness that no single characteristic is appropriate for meaningful comparative analysis. Currently, researchers are utilizing multivariate analysis to consider a number of major characteristics and their interrelationships.

The systems approach, which has been used as the framework for this book, provides a basis for comparative analysis and suggests the key characteristics for consideration: the environmental suprasystem and the major organizational subsystems. We will use this approach in discussing hospitals, universities, and cities (Chapters 20, 21, and 22). Later in this chapter (Figure 19.2) we will suggest more specific dimensions that can serve as a basis for more comprehensive comparative analysis. However, before looking at this in more detail, we will turn to a discussion of one of the most difficult areas of analysis—comparing organizations and their management across cultures.

Cross-Cultural Comparative Analysis

The universal trend toward more complex organizations suggests the need for cross-cultural comparative analysis. The management literature from societies other than the United States indicates different perspectives of problems and solutions. However, there are also many similarities. For example, in reviewing the rather scarce literature concerning organizations in the People's Republic of China, we note their difficulties in adapting to the need for large-scale organizations. [10] Many of the underlying problems seem to be similar to those facing organizations in the United States and other Western societies—the relationship of the organization to the broader society, the need for specialization of activities, the issues related to hierarchical authority, the effective utilization of technology, and the motivation and satisfaction of human participants.

The open systems approach provides a basic framework for cross-cultural comparative analysis. It recognizes the importance of starting with the broad environmental suprasystem as a basis for understanding organizations and their management. The culture is one of the key determinants. In fact, our organizations are really a reflection of our cultures.

10 Oiva Laaksonen, "The Structure and Management of Chinese Enterprises," *The Finnish Journal of Business Economics,* Vol. 2, 1975, pp. 3–22; Martin King Whyte, "Bureaucracy and Modernization in China: The Maoist Critique," *American Sociological Review,* April 1973, pp. 149–163; and Tai K. Oh, "Theory Y in The People's Republic of China," *California Management Review,* Winter 1976, pp. 77–84.

Organizational systems are cultural answers to the problems encountered by human beings in achieving their collective ends. Although there are objective rational constraints that limit possibilities, there is no one best way in this matter. [11]

We cannot look at organizations and their management apart from the cultural setting. This does not suggest that cultural differences are the prime determinants, but they are necessary considerations. It may be found, for example, that the technologies of mass production create many similarities in the structures and managerial practices in automobile assembly lines in the United States, India, Germany, and Russia. The uniqueness of the cultures may be less significant.

Increasing Interest

There is a growing interest in cross-cultural comparative analysis. Over the past two decades there has been a significant increase in the exchange of organizational and management concepts among practitioners and scholars in different countries. Many of the books that you read for your various courses are found in the Lingnan Institute of Business Administration, Chinese University of Hong Kong library, the Svenska Handelshogskolan in Finland, the Institut Européen d'Administration des Affaires in France, and the main bookstore in Kuala Lampur, Malaysia. Many have been translated into Russian, Chinese, Japanese, and many other languages. (As an example, earlier editions of this book have been translated into Japanese, Spanish, French, Dutch, Portuguese, and Russian.)

These illustrations should not be interpreted to mean that the flow of information is in one direction only—from the United States to the rest of the world. Increasingly, American scholars and practitioners are seeking knowledge and ideas based on research and experience in other cultures. There is growing interest in theory and practice concerning sociotechnical systems design in England, work redesign in Scandinavia, codetermination in Germany, worker councils in Yugoslavia, and managerial decision making in Japan. A worldwide communication network is developing, and the resultant information flow provides a basis for comparing our concepts about organization and management with those from other countries. It also helps us understand how our own culture has influenced our concept development. [12]

There has been less exchange of information with the communist countries, but it is increasing. For example, scholars in the Soviet Union have continually monitored the literature on organization and management theory coming out of the capitalistic countries to determine those concepts and practices that may be appropriate to their system. According to Gvishiani:

11 Michel Crozier, "The Cultural Determinants of Organizational Behavior," in Anant R. Negandhi (ed.), *Environmental Settings in Organizational Functioning,* Comparative Administration Research Institute, Kent State University, Kent, Ohio, 1970, p. 49.

12 For example, see Geert Hofstede and M. Sami Kassem (eds.), *European Contributions to Organization Theory,* Van Gorcum & Company B.V., Assen, The Netherlands. 1976.

Study and critical use of everything positive contained in the concepts of bourgeois theory of organisation and management . . . [is] one of the important tasks facing Soviet scientists. Such a critical analysis presupposes two aspects of investigation: on the one hand, bourgeois concepts must be studied from the viewpoint of their inner logic, consistency and argumentation and, on the other, it is necessary to analyse the different propositions contained in these concepts from the standpoint of Marxism, so as to show where they conform to the objective needs of production, and how they can be used under socialism. [13]

There is evidence of many similarities between current developments in management and organization theory in the United States and the Soviet Union. For example, both countries make extensive use of systems concepts. Milner suggests these applications:

Great attention is given in the Soviet Union to development of the methodology of the systems approach to decision-making in management and organization. . . . Large-scale national programs based on the systems approach are: integrated development of the natural resources of Siberia and the Far East; environmental programs; programs of developing fuel and energy potential; establishment of agricultural and industrial complexes; exploiting the resources of the ocean. [14]

The growth of a more comprehensive worldwide network for the exchange of information concerning organization and management should not lead to the assumption that organization designs and management practices are becoming more uniform. Indeed, one of the major themes of this book is that there is no one set of management principles that is uniformly appropriate, even within a given society. We cannot assume uniformity across cultures, nor should we prescribe it. Our understanding can be enhanced by merging organization and management theory with the developing body of knowledge concerning comparative practices. [15]

Some Confounding Variables

When traveling in other countries, the management scholar or practitioner is often impressed with the similarity of problems faced by organizations in different cultures. It is very easy to discuss the major issues and use familiar terminology. For example, the Ekono Corporation in Helsinki, Finland, uses a project form of organization design for its large-scale forest resource development

---

13 D. Gvishiani, *Organisation and Management: A Sociological Analysis of Western Theories,* Progress Publishers, Moscow, 1972, p. 442. This book provides an interesting analysis of our theories of management and organization from the perspective of a Soviet professor.

14 Boris Milner, "Application of Scientific Methods to Management in the Soviet Union," *Academy of Management Review,* October 1977, p. 556.

15 Anant R. Negandhi, "Comparative Management and Organization Theory: A Marriage Needed," *Academy of Management Journal,* June 1975, pp. 334–344.

and energy utilization programs that is quite similar to the project form used by the Boeing Company in Seattle. Tata Mills Ltd. in Bombay, India, uses similar technology and faces many of the same managerial problems as textile mills in England, the United States, and Japan. The young engineer trained in computer sciences in Russia has learned skills, and may follow a career path, similar to a counterpart in the United States. Thus, one is initially impressed with many similarities concerning organizational and managerial issues in different cultures.

However, these initial impressions are somewhat superficial, and in-depth analysis suggests major differences. In many ways, the *problems* are similar, but the organizational *responses* and specific managerial *actions* may be quite different. The concept of equifinality becomes apparent—there are many alternative ways of reaching a goal. An example may help illustrate this point. Every organization faces the fundamental issue of motivating its participants to achieve organizational objectives, but the types of rewards and punishments may be quite different in various cultures. For example, in Russia the wage levels for employees are strictly determined within a comparatively narrow range. However, the high-performing factory worker is motivated by many side benefits, such as a paid family vacation to the Black Sea, better housing, or preferred status on the waiting list to buy an automobile. Recognition for high performance may be given in ways unfamiliar in our society. In the center of Vladimir, a city about ninety miles from Moscow, there is a large display with pictures of Lenin *and* workers throughout the area who have made the honor role. The local newspapers periodically list an honor roll of individuals "for their success in socialist competition and for their active social work" (lathe operator of the year, pig-keeper of the year, hospital technician of the year, or collective farm manager of the year). It is difficult to imagine this happening in Tulsa or Syracuse, but it is typical of most cities in Russia.

Another example of cultural differences affecting solutions to basic organizational problems can be seen in approaches to the issue of "industrial democracy." [16] There is an underlying trend in most industrial societies toward more worker participation in organizational decision-making processes. However, the *formal means* to create industrial democracy vary widely among different societies. In the United States this concept is associated with the institution of collective bargaining. Participation in decision making is achieved when the union negotiates with management regarding employment relationships. The union is also involved in continual administration of the agreement during the contract period. The same basic approach is used in England, although the stronger class system creates an adversary relationship between management and unions that makes collaborative forms of joint decision making even more difficult.

In many Western European countries, industrial democracy has a significantly different meaning. It involves various programs whereby employees elect

16 "Industrial Democracy in International Perspective," *The Annals of the American Academy of Political and Social Science,* May 1977; and Nancy Foy and Herman Gadon, "Worker Participation: Contrasts in Three Countries," *Harvard Business Review,* May–June 1976, pp. 71–83.

representatives to be directly involved in all the internal decision-making processes of the enterprise.

Industrial democracy in these countries is conceived of as a means of direct employee access to the policy-making and operating levels of individual enterprises, especially the larger ones. The aim is to transform, or to reform, long established patterns of authority and power in industry by granting to employees a degree of influence over all vital affairs of the enterprise which more nearly approximates that of employers, shareholders, and their representatives. [17]

The French use the term "the reform of the enterprise" and the Germans use the concept of codetermination to describe this process. The Codetermination Act of 1976 extended this system to all companies with more than 2000 employees and requires that one-half of the members of the board of supervisors be elected by shareholders and one-half by employees. This board in turn elects a board of managers to manage the organization, subject to its review. This system includes the establishment of works councils at the shop floor level, which are formally independent of the unions. The law grants works councils a broad range of rights of information, consultation, and codetermination in respect to such issues as shop rules, working hours, overtime work, vacation schedules, safety regulations, administration of welfare services, determination of job and piece rates, and the formulation of wage systems. Similar approaches have been adopted in The Netherlands, Austria, Sweden, and the other Scandinavian countries.

The concept of industrial democracy has been extended even further in Yugoslavia under the concept of self-management. This system was initiated in 1950 as an alternative to the highly centralized and bureaucratic communist system of the Soviet Union. Under this decentralized concept, most decision making occurs at the enterprise level, and workers have an important say in all operations.

Yugoslavia's philosophy of industrial relations is based on the assumption that neither the state, as in Soviet-type societies, nor the private owners, as in capitalist societies, shall decide how industry is to be run and how production relations are to be arranged, but instead the workers shall manage their own affairs. Included in "their own affairs" are all decisions concerning the way enterprises are to be managed and production is to be organized. [18]

Under this system the worker-elected council is at the top of the organization and serves as the major policy and decision-making body. It selects the director and the managing board of the enterprise. This self-management system is closely interwoven with the total political and social makeup of the country.

There are many difficulties in making these various programs of industrial democracy operate effectively. However, they illustrate a growing demand

---

17 John P. Windmuller, "Industrial Democracy in International Perspective," *The Annals of the American Academy of Political and Social Science,* May 1977, p. vii.

18 Marius J. Broekmeyer, "Self-Management in Yugoslavia," *The Annals of the American Academy of Political and Social Science,"* May 1977, p. 134.

for greater involvement in decision making and for creating organizational climates more conducive to worker satisfaction. Yet, there are wide differences in the strategies for achieving these goals. The particular approach is strongly influenced by historical relationships and cultural characteristics. For example, the relatively homogeneous Swedish society and the long history of cooperation between labor and management provide a basis for collaborative arrangements that might not be appropriate in other countries, such as England. The Yugoslavian system of self-management has provided one means for a predominantly agrarian country to become a modern semi-industrial society without severe convulsions. This model may not be appropriate for more advanced societies.

The foregoing discussion of *official* national programs to achieve industrial democracy emphasizes the formal, publicized changes and does not consider many informal, grass roots approaches to more worker participation and power equalization. This is particularly true for the United States, where we have greater autonomy for companies, unions, and other organizations and less government control. In the United States a substantial part of the emphasis on employee participation and involvement has occurred within organizations and has not been negotiated officially or legally prescribed. It has been the result of trends toward more knowledge-based jobs, higher educational levels, advancing technologies, and the need for more adaptive-organic organizations.

Emphasis on *official* programs of industrial democracy may tend to underestimate the importance of other types of participation that have a broader and more fundamental base.

The U.S. is in the vanguard of the kind of participation that occurs naturally and organically through the evolution of the economic system. This movement owes nothing to political intervention and little to labor union pressure. [19]

Comparing Japan and the United States

The interest in cross-cultural comparative analysis is reflected in our attempts to understand managerial systems in Japan and to compare them to American practices. Japan is an industrial power and a world leader in the production of automobiles, tankers, steel, electronics products, and many consumer goods. Many United States corporations have established subsidiaries and joint ventures in Japan and, more recently, Japanese firms have created operating subsidiaries in the United States. [20] These experiences provide a unique opportunity to compare Japanese and United States managerial practices.

19 Max Ways; "The American Kind of Worker Participation," *Fortune* October 1976, p. 169.

20 Richard T. Johnson and William G. Ouchi, "Made in America (under Japanese management)," *Harvard Business Review,* September–October 1974, pp. 61–69; and "Japan's Ways Thrive in the U.S.," *Business Week,* Dec. 12, 1977, pp. 156–160.

We should recognize that there is no such thing as a typical Japanese organization or uniformly accepted management practices. Just as in the United States and other countries, there are wide variations. It is simplistic to expect to find one model that is typical for all or most Japanese enterprises. Recognizing these variations, there do appear to be some general characteristics that differentiate Japanese from United States organizations.

In Japanese firms, particularly large enterprises, there is a life-long commitment between the organization and the individual. The *nenko* system of permanent employment provides employees with job security and promotes strong corporate loyalty, high motivation, and group effectiveness. [21] The employee enters the organization upon graduation from school, receives in-company training, and remains as an employee until retirement at age fifty-five. Seniority plays a dominant role in determining pay, status, and position for the individual. Under this system, interfirm mobility is severely limited in exchange for guaranteed job security. It should be emphasized that the *nenko* system does not exist in all organizations nor for all employees. It is used primarily in the larger industrial firms and does not cover temporary, subcontract, and retired workers even in these firms.

Another characteristic of Japanese firms is the greater emphasis on the group rather than on the individual. The concept of *wa,* the spirit of harmony, is a fundamental principle of Japanese thought. [22] This spirit emphasizes a high degree of collaborative rather than competitive behavior among members of the organization. It is reflected in the system of decision making that emphasizes consensus building with proposals moving from lower to higher levels of management. Senior managers are seen as social leaders and facilitators of proposals and decisions made at lower levels, rather than as the primary source of decisions that are then passed down the hierarchy. The *ringi* system is the procedure by which the proposal is informally discussed and then formally circulated among various managers for their inputs, suggestions, and approval.

The central difference between American business and Japanese business lies in decision-making. Japanese decision-making is the gathering of Japanese wisdom. The *ringi* system allows everyone who is likely to be involved in implementation to participate in the making of the decision. This feeling of participation is very important for the spirit of *wa.* [23]

One of the consequences of this approach is the greater amount of time required to reach a consensus decision. This can be frustrating to foreigners trying to negotiate an agreement. However, it has the major advantage of fast and enthusiastic implementation once consensus is reached.

These characteristics have been cited as important factors contributing

---

21 Tai K. Oh, ''Japanese Management-A Critical Review,'' *Academy of Management Review,* January 1976, pp. 14–25.
22 ''Japanese Managers Tell How Their System Works,'' *Fortune,* November 1977, pp. 126–138.
23 Ibid., p. 131. These comments were made by Hajime Sasaki, director and general manager, foodstuffs division, Nissho-Iwai.

to the success of Japanese enterprises. Several American observers have suggested that we have much to learn from the Japanese experience.[24] A number of Japanese firms, such as Sanyo Electric Company, Matsushita Electric Industrial Company, and the Bank of Tokyo have established operations in the United States and have used these concepts with apparent success. However, their executives emphasize that they have adapted their practices to fit the American scene.

Before becoming too enthusiastic, we should recognize that there are some fundamental problems associated with these managerial approaches. The younger Japanese may not hold as strongly to traditional values and consequently may resist the limitations on job entry and mobility, the emphasis on seniority, and the lack of individuality. Many Japanese managers have questioned whether they can retain the concept of lifetime employment. Even though the official unemployment rate is 2 percent, it is estimated that the actual rate is closer to 6 or 7 percent because many permanent employees are not being used productively. Estimates range up to three million for the number of unnecessary employees being carried on corporate payrolls at a cost of $20 billion a year.[25] This represents a substantial fixed cost to the enterprise and, coupled with the heavy fixed debt financing, substantially reduces flexibility in adapting to changing market conditions. Many Japanese executives suggest that it is time for the government to assume the responsibility for unemployment through a greatly expanded social security system, similar to that in the United States.

Overall, there are a number of approaches in the Japanese system that are appropriate for consideration in our organizations.[26] The emphasis on participation, consensus building, and joint problem solving seems appropriate for many organizations. Recognition of the importance of human satisfaction is a vital factor. Yet we would be hesitant to advocate the adoption of specific Japanese approaches in United States organizations because of our cultural emphasis on the individual, competition, and job mobility, rather than on the group, collaboration, and job stability. We have the same doubts about wholesale application of our organization and management concepts to Japan, or any other country.

Contingency Views and Organization Theory

Contingency views are a natural outgrowth of comparative analysis based on systems concepts; they depend on the study of many different organizations.

24 Peter F. Drucker, "What We Can Learn From Japanese Management," *Harvard Business Review*, March–April 1971, pp. 110–122.

25 "Japan's Economy Tomorrow," *Business Week*, Jan. 30, 1978, p. 46.

26 Charles Y. Yang, "Management Styles: American vis-à-vis Japanese," *Columbia Journal of World Business*, Fall 1977, pp. 23–31.

A theory of organizations, whatever its specific nature, and regardless of how subtle the organizational processes it takes into account, has as its central aim to establish the constellations of characteristics that develop in organizations of various kinds. Comparative studies of many organizations are necessary, not alone to test the hypothesis implied by such a theory, but also to provide a basis for initial exploration and refinement of the theory indicating the conditions on which relationships, originally assumed to hold universally, are contingent.[27]

Systems concepts, comparative analysis, and contingency views have contributed significantly to the evolution of organization theory. The field has moved away from closed-system, simplistic views toward recognition of the rich complexities of modern organizations—systems of interdependent psychological, sociological, technical, and economic variables. General systems theory provides the overall model for the study of social organizations, but it involves a relatively high level of abstraction. Contingency views are based on systems concepts but tend to be more concrete and to emphasize more specific characteristics of social organizations as well as patterns of relationships among the subsystems.[28] This trend toward the more explicit understanding of patterns of relationships among organizational variables is essential if theory is to facilitate improved management practice.

The essence of the contingency view is a rejection of universal principles appropriate to all situations. There is no "one best way" to organize and manage. Decentralization is not necessarily better than centralization; bureaucracy is not all bad; explicit objectives are not always good; a democratic-participative leadership style may not fit certain situations; and tight control may be appropriate at times. In short, "it all depends" on a number of interrelated external and internal variables. Prescriptive guidelines should be set forth in statements such as, "If the condition is A, then action X is most likely to be effective. However, if the condition is B, then action Y should be used."

A Conceptual Model

Figure 19.2 is an example of the approach needed to develop a comprehensive conceptual model of contingency views for organization theory and management practice. It is a combination of the systems framework utilized throughout this book plus polar descriptions of organization systems or types: closed/stable/mechanistic and open/adaptive/organic.

In developing this terminology, we were influenced by the dichotomization presented by Burns and Stalker—mechanistic versus organic managerial sys-

---

27 Blau, op. cit., p. 332.

28 For more detail on this subject see Fremont E. Kast and James E. Rosenzweig, *Contingency Views of Organization and Management*, Science Research Associates, Inc., Palo Alto, Calif., 1973.

tems. [29] We were also influenced by the general systems literature and, in particular, the concept of closed and open systems. While these sources provide the fundamental basis for classification into two system types, many others use similar dimensions or characteristics that fit this classification.

A word of caution. Most authors are clear in emphasizing that any polarization is not characteristic of modern organizations. Total organizations simply cannot be described as closed/stable/mechanistic or open/adaptive/organic. They have characteristics that fit somewhere between these extremes. A production line typically is not completely closed/stable/mechanistic, nor is a research laboratory completely open/adaptive/organic. Conceptually we prefer to think of these characteristics on a dimensional basis rather than as polar positions. Moreover, different departments of a single organization may fall on different points of what we view as a continuum. Sales departments tend to be more open and adaptive than production departments. Practically, however, we have great difficulty in presenting these characteristics as dimensions. We can describe the polar positions, but it is much more difficult to look at each of the possible intermediate positions (theoretically infinite) of certain characteristics—for example, between closed and open systems. Further refinements in contingency views are necessary in order to describe and analyze points along the continuum. We have illustrated this approach by identifying several dimensions for each organizational supra- or subsystem. [30]

The analysis of the key subsystems and their important dimensions provides a pattern of relationships for the relatively closed/stable/mechanistic organizational system that is significantly different from that of the relatively open/adaptive/organic organizational system. Concepts about these relationships have not been "proven" via substantial empirical research. In fact, it is doubtful whether or not they can ever be proven conclusively. Organizations and their environments are much too dynamic to allow us to set forth "laws" about relationships. Rather, we can only expect to identify tentative patterns of relationships among the organizational variables.

However, this initial step of identifying patterns of relationships can be of major importance. We can apply this model in the study of many different types of organizations. For example, the research literature suggests that there are significant differences among correctional institutions that could be better understood by using a contingency view. Those institutions that have *confinement* of inmates as a primary goal tend to exhibit characteristics set forth under "closed/stable/mechanistic" in Figure 19.2. Those organizations that emphasize the goal of *rehabilitation* of participants tend to exhibit characteristics set forth under "open/adaptive/organic." The maximum security prison is very closed, highly structured, and exercises tight control (externally imposed) over inmates. The

29 Tom Burns and G. M. Stalker, *The Management of Innovation*, Tavistock Publications, Limited, London, 1961.
30 An expanded version can be seen in Kast and Rosenzweig, op. cit., pp. 315–318.

Figure 19.2 A Conceptual Model of Contingency Views of Organization and Management

Systems and Their Key Dimensions	Characteristics of Organizational Systems	
	Closed/Stable/Mechanistic	Open/Adaptive/Organic
Environmental Suprasystem:		
General nature	Placid	Turbulent
Predictability	Certain, Determinate	Uncertain, Indeterminate
Boundary relationships	Relatively closed. Limited to few participants (sales, purchasing, etc.). Fixed and well defined	Relatively open. Many participants have external relationships. Varied and not clearly defined
Goals and Values:		
Goal structure	Organization as a single-goal maximizer	Organization as a searching, adapting, learning system which continually adjusts its multiple goals and aspirations
Organizational goals in general	Efficient performance, Stability, Maintenance	Effective problem solving, Innovation, Growth
Pervasive values	Efficiency, Predictability, Security, Risk aversion	Effectiveness, Adaptability, Responsiveness, Risk taking
Goal set	Single, Clear-cut	Multiple, determined by necessity to satisfy a variety of constraints
Involvement in goal-setting process	Managerial hierarchy primarily (top down)	Widespread participation (bottom up as well as top down)
Technical System:		
General nature of tasks	Repetitive, Routine	Varied, Nonroutine
Input to transformation process	Homogeneous	Heterogeneous
Output of transformation process	Standardized, Fixed	Nonstandardized, Variable
Methods	Programmed, Algorithmic	Nonprogrammed, Heuristic

Structural System:		
Organizational formalization	High	Low
Procedures and rules	Many and specific. Usually formal and written	Few and general. Usually informal and unwritten
Authority structure	Concentrated, Hierarchic	Dispersed, Network
Psychosocial System:		
Status structure	Clearly delineated by formal hierarchy	More diffuse. Based upon expertise and professional norms
Role definitions	Specific and fixed	General and dynamic. Change with tasks
Motivational factors	Emphasis on extrinsic rewards, security, and lower-level need satisfaction. Theory X view	Emphasis on intrinsic rewards, esteem, and self-actualization. Theory Y view
Leadership style	Autocratic, Task-oriented, Desire for certainty	Democratic, Relationship-oriented, Tolerance for ambiguity
Power system	Power concentration	Power equalization
Managerial System:		
General nature	Hierarchical structure of control, authority, and communications. Combination of independent, static components	A network structure of control, authority, and communications. Co-alignment of interdependent, dynamic components
Decision-making techniques	Autocratic, Programmed, Computational	Participative, Nonprogrammed, Judgmental
Planning process	Repetitive, fixed, and specific	Changing, flexible, and general
Control structure	Hierarchic, specific, short-term. External control of participants	Reciprocal, general, long-term. Self-control of participants
Means of conflict resolution	Resolved by superior (refer to "book")	Resolved by group ("situational ethics")
	Compromise and smoothing	Confrontation
	Keep below the surface	Bring out in open

rehabilitation-oriented correctional institution is more open to society (for example, work-release programs), has a more flexible structure, and tries to develop self-control within each participant.

Even within the military there are differences, depending on the nature of specific activities. The organization for basic military training displays characteristics of the closed/stable/mechanistic system. However, in the design, development, and procurement of advanced weapon systems, the military organization can be described as relatively open/adaptive/organic. New approaches, such as program management and matrix organizations, have emerged to meet changing requirements. Other organizations have gone through similar cycles. For example, our school systems have had to become more open/adaptive/organic in response to social pressures and the individual participant's needs, particularly in the past two decades.

This model may also be useful in looking at the historical evolution of an organization or even an industry. The airline industry provides an illustration of changing organizational characteristics and patterns of relationships between subsystems. In general, airlines have been more open/adaptive/organic organizations than railroads, for example. In their early days they were faced with a turbulent environment—accelerating technology, increasing consumer mobility and affluence, growing acceptance of a new mode of travel, and changing government regulations. During this period they could be characterized by the open/adaptive/organic form. However, as the industry became more stable and operations became more routine, they moved toward a more closed/stable/mechanistic form.

Within the total organization the primary task of the airline—the individual flight—became very routine, programmed, and tightly controlled by specific rules and regulations. Individual tasks became much more specific and routinized. (We can remember earlier days when stewardesses were not simply "programmed" to greet passengers, check coats, demonstrate oxygen masks, and serve drinks and prepared meals; they even had time to fraternize with passengers.) However, at the coordinative level above that of individual flight—the planning, organizing, and controlling of overall flight operations—the airlines must still operate in a more open/adaptive/organic mode. The system must cope with changes in schedules, high rates of employee turnover, and new mixes of personnel for each flight. And even the routine characteristics of the individual flight may change abruptly when the hijacker suddenly says, "Give me $500,000, three parachutes, and let's fly to Tahiti." The operation moves very rapidly to a more open, adaptive system that cannot utilize procedures programmed for routine flights.

We can use this model to investigate even more subtle differences within organizations. For example, the university is typically thought of as an open/adaptive/organic system. However, within the university various subunits, departments, or programs may have different characteristics. The typical university graduate program (particularly doctoral programs) is more likely to exhibit open/adaptive/organic characteristics than the typical undergraduate program. This hypothesis leads to the suggestion that undergraduate and graduate programs should be organized and administered differently—an approach that is not always carried out in practice.

The history department and the campus police represent two rather distinct organization types. In order to understand them, it would be useful to describe them in terms of characteristics or key dimensions within the supra- and subsystems. Until this process of observation and description was completed, it would not be wise to invoke "principles" of organization or management. Situational analysis should precede prescriptions for organization design and management practice.

Much research and conceptualization must be done in order to develop a comprehensive model. Indeed, it is probably an open-ended task. Ideally, empirical research should include multivariate relationships among all of the organizational subsystems or variables. Although this objective is conceptually enticing, it is operationally difficult if not impossible to achieve. The current state of our knowledge about any single variable, such as technology or structure or the psychosocial system, is still very limited. How do we meet this dilemma of needing a more complete understanding of the subsystems and their interrelationships?

Practically, it will be a slow, painstaking process of trying to understand interrelationships and linking variables. After developing a substantial body of knowledge concerning dual relationships, we may be able to introduce additional factors in order to understand multivariate relationships. Lorsch and Morse, for example, studied the relationship of individual motivation to the general organization climate as determined by technology, structure, and environmental influences.[31] Their research was designed specifically to build on earlier work by Lawrence and Lorsch.

There are many other examples of the use of the contingency approach to understand multivariate relationships. For example, in the policy and planning area there is a move toward the development of contingency approaches to managerial strategy formulation and implementation.[32] The strategy-contingency model of power relationships seeks to relate the sources of power within the organization to the environmental uncertainties and strategic problems faced by the key managers.[33] Ultimately, using a multivariate approach, we will be better able to define certain patterns of relationships among organizational variables and/or subsystems, which will facilitate meaningful suggestions for appropriate organization designs and managerial action. This is a major long-run effort on the

31 Jay W. Lorsch and John J. Morse, *Organizations and Their Members: A Contingency Approach,* Harper and Row, Publishers, Incorporated, New York, 1974.

32 Carl R. Anderson and Frank T. Paine, "Managerial Perceptions and Strategic Behavior," *Academy of Management Journal,* December 1975, pp. 811–823; and Charles W. Hofer, "Toward a Contingency Theory of Business Strategy," *Academy of Management Journal,* December 1975, pp. 784–810.

33 Gerald R. Salancik and Jeffrey Pfeffer, "Who Gets Power—And How They Hold on to It: A Strategic-Contingency Model of Power," *Organizational Dynamics,* Winter 1977, pp. 2–21.

part of many researchers, investigating a wide variety of organizations and their subsystems. It involves comparative analysis across functions, levels, institutions, and cultures. While we have really just begun this effort, progress seems to be accelerating and we are adding relevant information to the body of knowledge.

Contingency Views and Management Practice

Traditional management theory emphasized the development of principles that were appropriate and applicable to all organizations and all managerial tasks. These universal principles were quite prescriptive—there was an appropriate way to design and manage organizations. Although the quantitative and behavioral sciences have introduced new concepts to the study of organizations, they, too, have tended toward prescribing the "one best way." The quantitative sciences have emphasized a normative approach and stressed the logical, rational, algorithmic view of management and decision making. Many behavioral scientists have also emphasized a particular approach to management. For example, it is easy to recognize that McGregor considered his Theory X (people are basically lazy and irresponsible) to be less appropriate, in general, than his Theory Y (people are basically industrious and responsible).[34] Similarly, Likert downgraded the highly structured, autocratic System 1 and stressed the functionality and merit of the more democratic, participative System 4 for all organizational situations.[35]

Systems concepts emphasize that organizations are composed of many subsystems, whose interrelationships have to be recognized. Once we accept a systems view, it becomes apparent that it is impossible to prescribe principles that are appropriate to all organizations. There are so many relevant variables that it is impossible for a simplistic model to depict reality. A simple view is appropriate only when the system under consideration is stable, mechanistic, and effectively closed to intervening external variables. Once we begin to consider organizations as open systems with interactive components, we can no longer think in simplistic, unidimensional terms.

If the focus is on *describing* and *understanding* why some organizations have been more successful than others, the resulting body of knowledge should be readily translatable into guidelines for action.[36] Prescriptions with a contingency flavor should be applicable more readily than general principles because managers can relate the theory to their specific situations.

34 Douglas McGregor, *The Human Side of Enterprise*, McGraw-Hill Book Company, New York, 1960.

35 Rensis Likert, *The Human Organization*, McGraw-Hill Book Company, New York, 1967.

36 Ralph H. Kilmann, Louis R. Pondy, and Dennis P. Slevin (eds.), *The Management of Organization Design: Strategies and Implementation*, Elsevier North-Holland, Inc., New York, 1976.

Diagnosis
and
Action

Contingency views have been criticized as being deterministic and conservative. [37] A strict deterministic view suggests that the nature of the environment and the technology dictate the proper organization structure. This in turn requires a particular managerial system in order to maximize performance. Management is an adaptive process of responding to these deterministic forces. Such a view is unrealistic. The organizational environment is not absolute; there are facts that can be verified as well as managerial perceptions of reality. The goals of the organization can include desired changes in the environmental suprasystem. Managers have substantial discretion concerning the task environment they will inhabit (their domain), the goals they will pursue, and the technologies they will use. They can influence the internal climate for participants. They can make strategic choices (both reactive and proactive) in coping with contextual forces—including their own beliefs, values, and attitudes, plus those of other people in the organization.

As we consider contingency views and managerial practice, it is important to recognize that many managers have and will continue to use such an approach implicitly. They have an intuitive "sense of the situation," are flexible diagnosticians, and adjust plans and actions accordingly. Thus, systems concepts and contingency views are not new. However, if this approach to organization theory and management practice can be made more explicit, we can facilitate better management and more effective and efficient organizations. There is nothing as practical as a theory that works.

We can illustrate the application of contingency views by referring to the managerial task shown in Figure 14.1—strategy formulation, organization design, information-decision systems, influence systems and leadership, and organization improvement. A contingency view of strategy formulation recognizes compound interdependencies among factors such as environmental opportunity, competence and resources, managerial interests and desires, and responsibility to society. This approach reflects systems concepts because it recognizes the interrelationships between the various components. A contingency view is used in fitting the strategy and action plans to the situation as diagnosed.

Once the objectives and comprehensive strategies for the organization are defined, the next step is determining key operating and coordinating activities. The basic technical system, as well as structural relationships, should be identified. This typically involves specialization by level and/or function plus coordination of specialized jobs in order to focus activities toward organizational goals. Research

---

37 Leland M. Wooton, "The Mixed Blessings of Contingency Management," *Academy of Management Review,* July 1977, pp. 431–441.

and experience provide guidelines for organization designs that match task, technology, and structure appropriately.

The term "information-decision system" is in itself a contingency view—information is relevant only as it pertains to managerial decision making. Therefore, it is important to begin the design process by identifying the types of decisions made in various parts—functions or levels—of the organization. The system should provide data that are meaningful to the planned tasks and measures of performance. Complex systems may require significantly different approaches in various organizational subsystems or functions (e.g., strategic versus operating or engineering versus marketing).

A key aspect of the managerial task is nurturing the psychosocial system. Contingency views are particularly relevant in discussing applied behavioral science. Assumptions about human nature, balancing extrinsic and intrinsic rewards, and matching leadership styles and situations all give recognition to the importance of diagnosing relationships among variables. For example, in designing a reward system, management should keep the various theories of motivation in mind and apply them where they are appropriate. Piece rates for individuals may be effective in one department, whereas a group bonus might be better in another situation. Non-monetary rewards, such as positive reinforcement through praise and recognition, can be used effectively in many cases.

The task of the manager also includes encouraging organization improvement endeavors—changing the organization to make it more effective and/or efficient as well as more satisfying for its participants. This three-part objective has a contingency flavor because a balance should be maintained in order to ensure long-run viability. Effective solutions to organizational problems should be tempered with cost considerations (cost-benefit analysis) in order to be realistic.

A number of methods or techniques are available for facilitating organization improvement. A contingency view is important in order to match an appropriate planned change effort with the specific problem or opportunity. Diagnosis should come first in order to help the manager to understand the particular situation. If the improvement process is technique-oriented (applying a "canned" approach to any and all situations), there is considerable danger of dysfunctional consequences—for example, wasting substantial amounts of energy on solving the wrong problem.

A Panacea?

Do comparative analysis, systems concepts, and contingency views provide a panacea for solving problems in organizations? The answer is an emphatic *no;* this approach does not provide "ten easy steps" to success in management. Such cookbook approaches, while seemingly applicable and easy to grasp, are usually shortsighted, narrow in perspective, and superficial—in short, unrealistic.

Fundamental ideas, such as systems concepts and contingency views, are more difficult to comprehend. However, they facilitate more thorough understanding of complex situations and increase the likelihood of appropriate actions. This approach requires a considerable amount of conceptual skill on the part of the manager.

Conceptual skill distinguishes really effective managers at all levels and particularly those who progress to the top. It involves the ability to "see the forest for the trees," to discern key interrelationships, and to attach degrees of importance to the various factors bearing on the problem. "The successful manager must be a good diagnostician and must value a spirit of inquiry. . . . There is no one correct managerial strategy that will work at all times." [38] The manager must be flexible in order to cope with a variety of situations. This approach is obviously more difficult than reliance on general principles and rules. It requires a pragmatic approach with heavy emphasis on situational analysis.

The general flavor of the contingency view is somewhere between simplistic, universal principles ("one best way") and complex, vague notions ("it all depends"). It is a mid-range concept that recognizes the complexity involved in managing modern organizations and uses patterns of relationships and/or configurations of subsystems in order to facilitate improved practice. The art of management depends on a reasonable success rate for actions in a probabilistic environment. It is hoped that contingency views, while continually being refined by scientists/researchers/theorists, will also be made more applicable.

Summary

We are all continually involved in informal comparative analysis of organizations. For example, we attempt (by examining or observing) to discover similarities or differences between schools, employers, or taverns. Formal comparative analysis or research can take any one of several directions—intraorganizational analysis across functions, levels, or subsystems and interorganizational analysis across institutions or cultures.

Comparative analysis is a pervasive activity that helps us understand complex affairs (to describe and explain what is happening—including how variables are related, what causes what, and the relative importance of the various forces involved). Comparative analysis is a sign of maturity because it opens the mind to new information from a variety of situations and reduces the tendency to apply the "one best way" in all circumstances.

Classification is a typical step in comparative analysis. Scientific endeavor involves observation and description, which usually lead to categorization in terms of key characteristics. This process has been evident in the development of organization theory. An obvious difficulty with classification schemes is over-

---

38 Edgar H. Schein, *Organizational Psychology*, 2d ed., Prentice-Hall, Inc., Englewood Cliffs, N.J., 1970, pp. 70 and 71.

lapping because of the multiple roles that types of organizations typically play. This is a reflection of the diversity of organizational phenomena.

There is an increasing interest in cross-cultural comparative organizational analysis—investigating similarities and differences in various societies. Organizational systems are cultural answers to the problems people encounter in pursuing collective goals. The problems faced by organizations and managers in different cultures are often similar, but the means of responding to them are frequently quite different.

It is important to develop a framework that facilitates understanding complex organizational phenomena in a variety of settings. The systems approach is helpful in this regard. We can compare organizations in terms of their environmental suprasystem and internal subsystems—goals and values, technology, structure, psychosocial, and managerial. The systems framework aids in the development of organization theory because it focuses attention on meaningful groups of organizational characteristics or relevant dimensions.

The essence of the contingency view is set forth in the chapter and a conceptual model is illustrated. This model provides a framework for research and comparative analysis by focusing on supra- and subsystems and their key dimensions and by describing characteristics for organization types—closed/stable/mechanistic and open/adaptive/organic. The application of these concepts to management practice is discussed and illustrated from a contingency point of view.

Questions and Problems

1 Define comparative analysis and discuss its pervasiveness. Give examples from your own experience.

2 Outline several approaches to comparative analysis. Which approach is most useful?

3 Why is comparative analysis important in developing a body of knowledge such as organization theory?

4 Why is comparative analysis a sign of maturity in organization theory and management practice?

5 Discuss ways of classifying organizations. Which model or framework do you think is the most useful? Why?

6 Using the systems framework in the chapter (and for the book as a whole), sketch out a brief description of a specific organization with which you are familiar.

7 Select a particular foreign country and compare it with the United States in terms of several significant variables relating to managerial behavior.

8 What is the essence of a contingency view of organization and management? Illustrate the concept with several examples.

9 Using the model presented in Figure 19.2, fill in two or three additional dimensions for each of the supra- and subsystems and describe their characteristics for the two polar organization types.

Comparative Organizational Analysis: The Hospital

Twenty

The general hospital is one of the more complex organizational types. Advancing technology, together with changing medical practices, have created new and evolving goals. Hospitals typically employ a large number of professionals—physicians, nurses, and other experts. They have developed distinctive structures, psychosocial systems, and management practices in order to accomplish their goals. Because of the increasing need for coordination of specialized activities, managerial systems in hospitals have become more comprehensive. The hospital is becoming the institutional center for dealing with total community health problems. The boundaries of hospital activities have expanded steadily and will probably continue to do so. The following specific topics are considered in this chapter:

Changing Environment
Goals and Values
Technology
Structure
Psychosocial System
Managerial System

Changing Environment

In order to understand the current environment of the modern hospital, it is necessary to provide a brief historical perspective. Various social institutions have been established to deal with the problem of the sick, disabled, and dependent. At one time, hospitals were more a refuge for the ill and needy than places for medical treatment. They were established on the routes of medieval crusades and pilgrimages and had their roots deep in religious and altruistic hospitality. From these early beginnings, the hospital continued through the nineteenth century to be a haven for the homeless and impoverished. It was the "charitable last resort of the ill pauper." [1]

During the eighteenth and nineteenth centuries in the United States, many voluntary hospitals were established as independent institutions managed by their own boards of governors or trustees. Funds and support for these hospitals came from a rich benefactor or the local community. Physicians stood substantially apart from the hospitals. Their services were often offered free as a charitable endeavor, and the hospitals helped doctors with their training by providing them the opportunity to observe a variety of illnesses. During this period, when medical practice was becoming a profession, the norm was independent practice and close physician-patient relationships, without the necessity for the intervention of the complex organization.

The dramatic developments in medical science and technology in the late nineteenth and early twentieth centuries revolutionized the role and functions of the hospital. No longer was it a place for the ill and poor to go to die; it became the primary institution for treatment. Since the beginning of the twentieth century, the hospital has expanded the boundaries of its activity and has taken on a much greater role in providing medical treatment and service to society in general. However, many of the forces affecting the hospital as an organization stem from its earlier, more restricted role. The technology and structure, as well as psychosocial and managerial systems, are also strongly influenced by the historical pattern of development.

Current Scene

Today there are more than 7100 hospitals in the United States, with approximately 1,500,000 beds. They admit nearly 36,000,000 patients annually and employ over 2,900,000 people, exclusive of physicians. [2] The estimated national expenditure for hospitals is in excess of $44 billion. This excludes the cost of physicians, other services, and drugs.

There are many types of hospitals. Of the 7174 hospitals that existed in this country in 1974, 2698 were operated by federal, state, and local governments; 3576 were voluntary nonprofit hospitals; and 900 were profit or proprietary hospitals. This discussion is primarily concerned with those types classified as voluntary, nonprofit, short-term, and general institutions—representing approximately 3000 hospitals. These have become known as community, voluntary, or general hospitals. They are typically sponsored by voluntary associations or corporations. They are general in the sense that they admit most but not all short-term patients. The general hospital is familiar to most of us. The other types, such as the govern-

---

1 Robert N. Wilson, "The Social Structure of a General Hospital," *The Annals of the American Academy of Political and Social Science*, March 1963, p. 69.

2 These figures are from *Statistical Abstract of the United States, 1976*, U.S. Bureau of Census, 1976, pp. 73–84.

ment hospital, proprietary hospital, state mental hospital, and long-term hospital (such as the tuberculosis hospital), have their own characteristics. Obviously, even within the definition of the general hospital there are wide variations that make this a relatively heterogeneous classification.

Organization of Health Care Services

Historically, the delivery of health care services was highly individualized and emphasized close interpersonal interactions—the doctor-nurse-patient relationship. More recently, it is being transformed into an organizational process.

Delivery of health services to the American people has increasingly become an organizational, as opposed to an individual process. The changing character of health care delivery patterns over the last 10 years reflects this trend. Greater percentages of physicians and related health professionals are employed by organizations; many more consumers are looking to organizations rather than individual practitioners for receipt of health services; and there has been a tremendous growth in hospital emergency room utilization. Furthermore, individual delivery organizations, such as hospitals, clinics, nursing homes, and health departments, are finding themselves enveloped in larger organizational relationships in which they must not only contend with each other, but with a growing number of outside agencies. [3]

Growth of health insurance programs, increased involvement of the federal government, developments in medical technology, professionalization of health service personnel, and changes in social norms and legal requirements have been major forces in reshaping the delivery of health care.

Dynamics of Environment and Organization Design

Rapid changes and problems of adaptation have led to what many have called a "crisis in American health care." The concern is not with the level of knowledge and technology in medicine, but rather with the problems associated with the effective and efficient *delivery* of health care to all our citizens.

The organization of health services has not kept pace with advances in medical science or with changes in society itself. Medical care in the United States is more a collection of bits and pieces (with overlapping duplication, great gaps, high costs, and wasted effort), than an integrated system in which needs and efforts are closely related. [4]

3 Stephen M. Shortell, "Organization Theory and Health Services Delivery," in Stephen M. Shortell and Montague Brown (eds.), *Organizational Research in Hospitals,* an INQUIRY book, Blue Cross Association, Chicago, Ill., 1976, p. 1.
4 Charles E. Odegaard, "Crisis in American Health Care," *Hospital Administration,* Summer 1969, p. 69.

Recent changes have been made in an attempt to respond to these issues. The enactment of Medicare-Medicaid involved the federal government directly in providing health services for segments of our population. The National Health Planning and Resources Development Act of 1974 emphasized the role of health planning and established local and state agencies to integrate health care activities. Various proposals for the creation of some form of national health insurance would have significant implications for the entire health care field. [5]

The federal government has supported the development of Health Maintenance Organizations (HMOs), such as the Kaiser-Permanente Plan in California, the Health Insurance Plan in New York, and the Group Health Cooperative in Washington. These organizations represent a major departure from the traditional fee-for-service approach. "The major characteristics of an HMO are the grouping of facilities, physicians, and other health personnel into a single organizational entity that provides a full range of medical services to a specifically enrolled population for a fixed fee." [6] One advantage of this organizational arrangement is that there is a strong incentive to practice preventive rather than acute medical care.

The development of multi-unit hospital systems under a single corporate type management is a means of achieving more effective planning and utilization of resources. [7] This involves the merger of existing hospitals and the creation of satellite units within a broad geographic area. In some cases this brings together a wide variety of health care units under a single organization and management— hospitals, nursing homes, laboratory facilities, and specialty institutions. It is estimated that the number of hospitals involved in, or considering, some form of cooperative management arrangement is approaching 2500. [8]

The foregoing suggests just a few of the dynamic factors and organizational responses affecting the health delivery system in our society. It is one of our biggest industries; total expenditures on health care are approximately $120 billion annually, about 8 percent of our gross national product. [9] We will look at the internal subsystems of the basic unit in this system, the general hospital.

Goals
and
Values

The general hospital has many diverse objectives. To be sure, the major objective is to satisfy the needs of the patient for care and treatment. But each

5 Richard M. Tomkins, "Evaluating National Health Insurance Legislation: A Summary Review," *Hospital Administration,* Summer 1974, pp. 74–84.

6 Jonathon S. Rakich, Beaufort B. Longest, and Thomas R. O'Donovan, *Managing Health Care Organizations,* W. B. Saunders Company, Philadelphia, 1977, p. 13.

7 Montague Brown, "Multi-Unit Hospital Systems Under Single Management," *Hospital & Health Services Administration,* Spring 1976, pp. 88–95.

8 William H. Money, David P. Gilfillan, and Robert Duncan, "A Comparative Study of Multi-Unit Health Care Organizations," in Shortell and Brown, op. cit., p. 30.

9 Rakich, op. cit., p. 10.

group of participants—patients, medical staff, nurses, administrative staff, trustees, and others—interpret the means for meeting objectives in terms of their own value systems and requirements. Additional objectives, such as medical and nursing education and research, have to be integrated into the organization. "The major hospital embraces multiple goals, chiefly patient care, teaching, and research. It is at once a hotel, a treatment center, a laboratory, a university. Because the institution's work is so specialized, staffed by a variety of professional and technical personnel, there are very important problems of coordination and authority." [10]

The emphasis on patient care and treatment permeates the value system and objectives of the hospital, even though there are constraints of technology, economics, and organizational abilities. [11]

The educational process for most of the professional participants in the hospital emphasizes patient welfare. The standards of conduct prescribed by the specific professional groups reinforce this value—for example, the Hippocratic Oath of physicians, the Florence Nightingale pledge of nurses, and the code of ethics of the American College of Hospital Administrators. Similar codes of other groups operating in hospitals also emphasize patient welfare. This overriding value serves a vital function in unifying the activities of participants in the hospital system and helps explain how it can operate effectively. It causes individual participants to perform their highly professionalized and specialized tasks toward a common end, thus providing voluntary coordination of activities.

The operating goals of hospitals have undergone steady transformation as the boundaries of their activities have expanded. It was suggested that the earlier goal was to provide care for the ill and the poor who did not have the funds to take care of themselves. With advancing technology in the latter part of the nineteenth and early part of the twentieth centuries, there was a major transformation in these goals to give greater emphasis to treatment. Thus, the hospital was changed from a place of last resort for the poor to one where doctors brought their patients for treatment that could not be provided in the home. The hospital became the doctor's workshop, where the physician ordered services *á la carte* for the patients. Gradually the hospital has shifted from being a place where the physician could practice his or her art to include broader objectives. "The hospital began to emerge as a *professional health center,* with institutional responsibility for an identifiable, coordinated program of patient care services, including control of quality, education and research." [12] The objectives and the boundaries of the hospital activities expanded to include emphasis on quality care, on the coordination of the diverse activities of the physician and the hospital staff, and on involvement in educational and research programs. Increasingly, the hospital-practice-oriented

10 Wilson, op. cit., p. 67.

11 Basil S. Georgopoulos and Floyd C. Mann, *The Community General Hospital,* The Macmillan Company, New York, 1962, p. 5.

12 Robert M. Sigmond, "Professional Education for Tomorrow's Hospital Administrators: As Viewed by a Hospital Planner," *Hospital Administration,* Summer 1966, p. 27.

physicians (primarily specialists) became more important as compared with the office-practice-oriented physicians (primarily general practitioners). For these physician specialists, the hospital rather than the private office became the primary institution for their activities.

Thus, the hospital has gradually transformed its objectives, moving from primary concern with individual patient care to the broader problem of total community health service. These changes have influenced the various subsystems of the hospital.

Technology

Throughout the early history of the hospital, crude technical knowledge severely limited its activities. Medicine was not advanced enough to meet the objectives of treatment and cure of patients effectively—the emphasis was on custodial care. The development of medical technology fundamentally changed the achievable goals of the hospital and consequently the organization structure and other subsystems. The development of the germ theory of disease, x-ray, asepsis, pathological examinations, anesthesiology, and surgical techniques all had a profound influence on the hospital. The technological revolution brought fundamental changes in structure and goals. [13]

Because doctors were the primary controllers and users of the new technology, the role of the medical staff in the hospital increased appreciably as a result of these technological changes. The hospital became a place where all patients, not just the poor, came for treatment that could not be provided in the home. The physician and the community at large developed a greater interest in the hospital. It became the primary institution within the community that could accumulate the medical technology—knowledge, skills, and specialized equipment—necessary for patient treatment.

In the modern hospital, the medical staff is the primary source of technology. Physicians have the knowledge for task performance based on intensive training and specialization. Nurses represent a source of knowledge and carry out many of the technical functions in the hospital. There is also an increasing number of specialists who are not part of the medical or nursing staff. The chemist, bacteriologist, physical therapist, recreational director, dietician, social worker, and many other participants are highly trained and are applying their technical knowledge in the hospital setting. The increased number of these specialists has created a more complex organizational situation.

With increased complexities, there has been a growing need for improved techniques of organization and management. In the small, less complicated organization, they were relatively simple. In the modern hospital, more sophisticated approaches for the coordination of activities are necessary.

Not only have the knowledge aspects of technology become more ad-

---

13 Charles Perrow, "Hospitals: Technology, Structure, and Goals," in James G. March (ed.), *Handbook of Organizations,* Rand McNally & Company, Chicago, 1965, p. 948.

vanced and specialized, but the physical aspects of technology—facilities, machinery, and equipment—also are more costly and complex. The modern hospital is faced with the problem of obtaining and financing newly developed diagnostic and treatment equipment. With unsophisticated technology, the black bag was the physician's equipment. Today, doctors require facilities far beyond their own means of acquisition. The hospital has become the central source for the accumulation of the necessary equipment and facilities for patient care and treatment.

Structure

The organization structure of the typical general hospital differs substantially from the design of other large-scale organizations. The hospital establishes a unique relationship between the formal authority of position, as represented by the administrative hierarchy, and the authority of knowledge, as represented by the medical practitioners and other professionals. This creates a somewhat diffused and unusual formal structure. [14] Furthermore, there are variations in structure among hospitals because of differences in their environments and technologies—"the basic assumption being that there is a greater need for internal flexibility when the organization is operating in a highly complex, diverse, unstable, and uncertain environment than when it is not operating in such an environment." [15] Hospitals with a stable and relatively simple environment and technology will be more effective with the stable-mechanistic design, whereas hospitals with a dynamic and complex environment and technology will be more effective with the adaptive-organic design.

However, there are wide variations among the subunits of the hospital. Many routine activities—clerical, maintenance, and some patient care—may best be accomplished with a stable-mechanistic design, whereas unstructured and innovative activities—intensive care units, emergency services, and research activities—may require the adaptive-organic form. Thus, the effective hospital does not follow one basic structural design; it includes a variety of forms, depending on the nature of the environment, task, and technology.

Differentiation of Activities

Extensive differentiation and specialization of activities are evident in the general hospital. "To do its work, the hospital relies on an extensive division of labor among its members, upon a complex organizational structure which encompasses many different departments, staffs, offices, and positions, and upon an elaborate system of coordination of tasks, functions, and social interaction." [16] The

---

14 Ray E. Brown, "Strictures and Structures," in Jonathon S. Rakich (ed.), *Hospital Organization and Management,* The Catholic Hospital Association, St. Louis, Mo., 1972, pp. 21–23.
15 Shortell, op. cit., p. 9.
16 Basil S. Georgopoulos and Floyd C. Mann, "The Hospital as an Organization," *Hospital Administration,* Fall 1962, p. 51.

tasks of the hospital are carried out by a large number of cooperating participants, whose educational backgrounds, training, skills, and functions are diverse and heterogeneous. Much of the treatment task is performed by the doctors, who require the collaboration and assistance of many paramedical professional personnel. The medical staff is specialized because of the complexities of medical technology. The nursing staff includes graduate professional nurses in various supervisory and nonsupervisory positions, practical nurses, and nurse's aides. In addition, there is the hospital administrative staff, which includes a number of supervisory personnel heading departments and services, such as dietetics, admissions, maintenance, pharmacy, medical records, housekeeping, and laundry. There are also medical technicians, who work in the laboratories, x-ray departments, and other units. Apart from these direct participants in the hospital system, there is usually a board of trustees that has overall institutional responsibility for the organization.

Administrative Organization and Medical Staff

A major differentiation of activities occurs because of the distinction between the administrative organization and the medical staff. The functions and the relationships of the medical staff to other segments of the hospital are based on the legal position of the doctor. The hospital as an organization cannot practice medicine; only physicians are legally licensed to practice medicine on patients. The medical staff is largely self-governing and has its primary focus on the therapeutic aspects of patient treatment. The medical staff in most general hospitals is an autonomous structure with a medical director, executive committee, and various functional committees.

Coordination of Activities

A high degree of differentiation and specialization creates critical problems of coordination in the hospital. Two key problems are the dual authority system and the high degree of specialization and professionalization. Coordination by means of the organizational hierarchy is difficult. Hospitals do, however, make extensive use of coordination by administrative rules and procedures. These means of coordination are most effective for the programmable, routine events.

However, because of the diverse problems associated with the care and treatment of patients, it is impossible to rely exclusively on administrative procedures for coordination. Therefore, one of the primary means of integration is voluntary coordination and the willingness of the various participants to work effectively together to deal with unusual and nonroutine events. A basic force ensuring voluntary coordination is the overall value system emphasizing the patient's welfare.

Authority
Structure

A primary characteristic of the bureaucratic model is a single authority pyramid. In the general hospital, there is no one line of authority. "Essentially, authority in the hospital is shared (not equally) by the board of trustees, the doctors, and the administrator—the three centers of power in the organization—and, to some extent, also by the director of nursing. In the hospital, authority does not emanate from a single source and does not flow along a single line of command as it does in most formal organizations." [17]

Each of these three groups—the trustees, the medical staff, and the administrator—has a basis for the exercise of legitimate authority. Hennessey points out the basis of this legitimacy:

1 The legally responsible group in the hospital, charged with legislating policy, is the board of trustees; therefore these . . . must be the policy-makers.

2 The essential activity in the hospital is medical care for the sick, a specialty of physicians; therefore, they should determine the policies of the organization.

3 The person most knowledgeable about all phases of life in the hospital, the only full-time professional with wide perspective . . . the administrator, . . . should decide policy. [18]

Each of these groups has a basis for the exercising of authority; however, they are not clearly delineated and separate. There are many interfaces between these sources of authority, which create conflict. It is difficult to select any one of the three as having central authority. Authority is dispersed and shared rather than adhering to the scalar hierarchy.

One way of looking at this relationship is in terms of the three organizational subsystems. The board of trustees has a strategic role, relating the hospital to its social environment and helping it obtain the necessary resources for its operations. The administrator has a strategic role and a coordinative role of negotiating and integrating the various resources and activities of the participants in the organization. The medical staff has the primary technical role in terms of patient treatment. There is no line of authority between these subsystems. They are three separate sources of authority exercised within the same social organization.

New
Internal
Structures

The problems of coordination of patient care has led to new internal organizational arrangements. The development of emergency and intensive care

---

17 Ibid., p. 59.

18 John W. Hennessey, Jr., "The Administrator and Policy Processes," *Hospital Administration,* Fall 1965, p. 66.

units, patient care teams, and other types of integrated-task activities is increasing in hospitals. Many of these changes are related to the matrix form. "The existence of both hierarchical (vertical) coordination through departmentalization and the formal chain of command and simultaneously lateral (horizontal) coordination across departments (the patient care team) is called a matrix organization." [19] The individual doctor is the project manager, integrating the activities of nurses, dietitians, physical therapists, social workers, and other professionals.

Johnson and Tingey suggest that the professional nurse rather than the physician is the logical person to head the patient care team. They feel that the physician is simply not physically present enough to coordinate the implementation of patient care programs.

The role of the professional nurse in this type of structure is to integrate and coordinate the efforts of a variety of functional team members to accomplish (1) the therapy and treatment prescribed by the physician, (2) the specialized psycho-social needs of the patient, and (3) the physical, nonclinical care of the patient. Matrix authority does not confer upon the nurse the right to command. The nurse's authority is derived from the legitimacy of the assignment, influence with the physician, and expertise. [20]

One of the major advantages of the matrix form is that it overcomes some of the difficulties created by excessive specialization of labor and departmentalization within the hospital. Under this approach, someone is charged with looking after the "total patient person," who is not there just to be medically processed.

Expanding Boundaries

Over a period of ten years the hospital industry has moved from one of predominantly autonomous, independent units to multi-unit hospital systems. [21] This movement has created major problems in the governance of these systems. [22] For example, should one board of trustees direct the activities of all units in the system, or should there be separate and autonomous boards for each unit? Should there be one central medical staff, or should there be separate, decentralized medical staffs in each hospital? In many cases, these systems have created corporate administrative staffs similar to corporate staffs in industrial organizations. The structures of these multi-unit systems are still evolving, and there is no clear-cut

19 Duncan Neuhauser, "The Hospital as a Matrix Organization," *Hospital Administration,* Fall 1972, p. 19.

20 G. Vaughn Johnson and Sherman Tingey, "Matrix Organization: Blueprint of Nursing Care Organization for the 80s," *Hospital & Health Services Administration,* Winter 1976, p. 34.

21 Montague Brown, "Contract Management: Latest Development in the Trend Towards Regionalization of Hospital and Health Services," *Hospital & Health Services Administration,* Winter 1976, pp. 40–59.

22 Lawrence D. Prybil and David B. Starkweather, "Current Perspectives on Hospital Governance," *Hospital & Health Services Administration,* Fall 1976, pp. 67–75.

model of organization design. It is probable that there will continue to be wide variations.

Hospitals have been expanding their domains in many other ways. For example, the hospital emergency room, rather than the private physician, has become the source of primary medical care for many people. In order to meet this need, many hospitals have developed primary care programs to serve patients who are not emergency cases, both in the hospital and in satellite units. "In contrast to the emergency room, where non-urgent demand has been an increasing problem, the primary care programs are designed for routine care and charges are set to be competitive with those of physicians' offices." [23]

Psychosocial System

The hospital makes use of sophisticated technology and has a complex structure. However, one of its fundamental characteristics is the importance of the psychosocial system. "A hospital is basically, fundamentally, and above all, a man-system. It is a complex, human-social system: Its raw material is human; its product is human; its work is mainly done by human hands; and its objective is human—direct service to people, service that is individualized and personalized." [24]

The roles of the various participants—the physicians, the administrators, the nurses, and the paramedical personnel—are rather well defined. This role definition stems from professionalization. The long process of education and training emphasizes certain role precepts, which delineate the individual's actions. However, many role conflicts occur for individual participants when they are cast in two different roles with incongruent demands. For example, the doctor frequently faces a conflict between a professional role as an independent practitioner and an institutional role as a participating member of the hospital. The nursing supervisor may continually be in conflicting roles as a member of the nursing group with an orientation toward professional colleagues and as a member of the administrative hierarchy. Although organizational positions are delineated, shaded areas remain, and there are many possibilities for conflict. In this discussion of psychosocial systems, we will look more specifically at each of the human groups in the hospital organization—the patients, as well as the medical, nursing, and administrative staffs.

The Patient

The patient is obviously one of the key individuals in the hospital—simultaneously the hospital's client and its product. Patients enter the hospital

23 Robin E. MacStravic, "Hospital-Based Ambulatory Care—the Wave of the Future?" *Hospital & Health Services Administration,* Winter 1976, p. 61.
24 Basil S. Georgopoulos, "Hospital Organization and Administration: Prospects and Perspectives," *Hospital Administration,* Summer 1964, pp. 25–26.

reluctantly at best, with a certain amount of suspicion, awe, and fear. Perhaps their one dominant motivation is to be able to walk out of the hospital under their own power as rapidly as possible. Patients' status external to the organization has little bearing on their status in the hospital. "As he strips off his clothing, so he strips off, too, his favored costume of social roles, his favored style, his customary identity in the world."[25]

The role definitions prescribe that patients act in a very passive and responsive way in the hospital. They are there to get well, and they should cooperate with all the professionals in the hospital—the hospital personnel, not the patients, have the technical competence to cure or ameliorate illness. Interestingly enough, there is a growing awareness that there might be therapeutic advantages to having the patient take a more active role in the social structure of the hospital. Greater patient participation is taking place in mental and long-stay hospitals. There are significant barriers to creating a more socially active role for the patient in the general hospital, where the stay is for a relatively short term.[26]

Medical Staff

The medical staff, composed of practicing physicians, has something in common with patients. Private doctors are also "guests" of the hospital, utilizing the facilities provided. They have both a professional *patient-centered* role and an *institutional* role, which they assume as participants in the hospital. Their professional training emphasizes the patient-centered role. The development of the institutional role requires some adaptation. The doctor must make certain adjustments in order to function effectively within the organization. For example, utilization of the hospital's facilities, such as the operating room, has to be scheduled with consideration of the requirements of other physicians. The doctor's motivation in maximizing the care and treatment for individual patients may have to be modified by the organizational requirements for all patients. These two roles for the medical staff often create substantial conflicts. However, physicians are making the necessary adjustments to the institutional role. Training in medical schools, with greater emphasis on internship and clinical practice, supports the institutional role.

The medical staff has a high status position within the hospital organization. Legally, they are the only ones who can prescribe therapeutic care and treatment. We ascribe substantial charisma to physicians. This high societal status carries over into the hospital system. It is further reinforced by the degree of specialization of knowledge and technical competence required for practice.

The group dynamics within the medical staff are very complex. Although many physicians engage in independent practice, they must coordinate their hospital activities with other doctors, nurses, various service departments,

25 Wilson, op. cit., p. 70.
26 Norman Cousins, "The Mysterious Placebo: How Mind Helps Medicine Work," *Saturday Review*, Oct. 1, 1977, pp. 8–16.

and paramedical personnel. This requires the development of effective group relationships. Leadership patterns are determined more by the personal characteristics and charisma of the individual physician than by formal organizational position.

Nursing
Staff

The nursing staff has the difficult but important function of coordination between the "care" functions of the hospital and the "cure" functions of the physician. There is a long tradition that the doctor has direct and immediate authority over the nurse on the medical aspects of the patient's treatment. On the other hand, the nurse is a full-time member of the administrative organization, who reports in the hierarchy through a head nurse, nursing supervisor, and director of nursing to the administrator. To the patient, the nurse is the primary representative of the hospital and is closely associated with his or her care and cure. The doctor may see the patient once a day, but nurses are in continual interaction with patients.

The official position of the nursing staff depicted in the typical organization chart does not really give recognition to the power and influence it has in the hospital organization. The nursing staff plays a vital role in the group dynamics of the hospital. Because of their full-time association with the hospital, their familiarity with established rules and procedures, their ability to develop informal relationships with other participants, and their close association with both patients and doctors, they become a central force of informal influence and leadership throughout the entire organization. The nurse frequently serves as the go-between for the technical subsystem represented by the physician and the coordinative subsystem represented by the administrative staff. In this role the nurse often serves as a negotiator, compromiser, and influencer.

Many forces are changing the status of the professional nurse in the hospital. The education and training of nurses places more emphasis on professional and technical roles. There is an increasing demand for the reduction of time spent on clerical tasks to make more time available for clinical work and direct patient care functions. More specialized nursing roles are developing—in surgery, orthopedics, cardiac units, intensive care, and psychiatric divisions, for example. Nursing is moving away from the concept of "doctor's helpers" toward specialized and technical functions. The registered nurse has increasingly become a specialized professional, less in the shadow of the physician, and the relatively high status differential between doctors and nurses is decreasing. A collegial rather than superior-subordinate relationship is becoming more common.

Various structural designs are being developed to implement this emerging role. As suggested earlier, the matrix form with the nurse coordinating all of the activities necessary for patient care is emerging. This form may also help reduce the clerical overload of nurses and result in significant job enrichment. "The nurse will have a greater opportunity to optimize clinical skills and will have more influence in providing the patient with an effective, tailored, health care program. . . . Better overall health care should result as the nursing staff becomes more motivated and more satisfied with the content and structure of its responsibilities." [27]

Administrative Staff

The administrator has an emerging role in the hospital system. Historically, this function was primarily clerical and housekeeping in nature. Administrators provided the facilities for running the "hotel" side of the hospital, and their status was low as compared to that of the medical staff. However, with the growing complexities, the greater need for coordination of the hospital activities, the development of multi-unit systems, and the increased demands for sophisticated equipment and its effective use, the role of the administrator has expanded.

Carving out the administrator's role has often created substantial conflict with the other power sources in the organization—particularly the medical staff. The medical staff has a desire for a high degree of autonomy based on their professionalization and a strong orientation to individual patient care. In contrast, the hospital administrator is forced to give consideration to optimal utilization of the resources for all patients and for all interest groups. The effective hospital administrator must be prepared to live in a rather ambiguous, uncertain role, one that requires the use of suggestion and persuasion rather than positional authority. The democratic-participative leadership style is generally most effective.

There have been pressures toward professionalization of hospital administration. In some ways, this can be seen as a desire to increase status vis-à-vis the medical practitioners. The move toward professionalization includes specialization of educational requirements through programs at universities, more activities by professional associations, and increasing emphasis on community service objectives. Many factors have increased the relative power and influence of the hospital administrative staff. The increased size and complexity of the organizations, the movement to multi-unit systems, the increasing need to coordinate activities with governmental agencies and other health service institutions, and the demands for reducing costs and creating a more efficient health delivery system have all been factors in increasing the responsibilities of hospital administrators.

Managerial System

The foregoing discussion of the environment, goals, technology, structure, and psychosocial system of the hospital suggests that the managerial system would also be complex. The diversity of the power base and authority structure creates a dispersal of the planning and control decisions in the organization. The

---

27 Johnson and Tingey, op. cit., p. 36.

board of trustees has the legal authority and decides on broad financial matters. Traditionally, it was the focal point for long-range planning and interactions with the community and represented the strategic level in the organizational system. The medical staff, on the other hand, has the technical knowledge and authority concerning patient treatment. The administrator and his or her staff are in charge of the functioning of the hospital and must engage in organizational planning and control. Thus, the managerial system of the hospital is diverse, with all three members of the troika responsible for planning and control decisions in certain spheres of the overall organization.

In addition, various segments establish "hospital procedures," which range all the way from the surgical procedures established by the medical staff to business methods established by the administrator. These hospital procedures provide the basis for control over relatively programmed activities. However, it should be emphasized that many of the functions in the hospital are nonroutine, and it is difficult to establish well-defined controls for such activities. In certain areas control depends primarily on voluntary coordination by the participants themselves.

The planning function in the hospital is carried out in many ways. The medical staff has a vital role in planning related to patient treatment. The administrator is engaged in broader strategic and community planning. He or she is concerned with the financing and procurement of facilities and planning for their effective utilization. Obviously, the administrator must rely on the medical staff for technical inputs regarding plans. However, strategic planning for the hospital system is becoming one of the most important administrative functions.[28] The administrator will also have an expanding role in interhospital planning and coordination and in environmental relationships.

The foregoing discussion of the general hospital suggests that it is a rather special organization, different from other types of institutions. We have considered only one type, the community general hospital. There would be significant differences in the environment, goals, and other subsystems for governmental or other types of hospitals. This discussion of the general hospital, however, has emphasized that it has many management and organizational problems. Over the past two decades few other organizational types have faced such dynamic environments, changing technologies, structural redesigns, and psychosocial adjustments. It is understandable that there would be difficulties in developing managerial systems that can respond effectively to these rapid changes.

Summary

The delivery of health care has been transformed from a highly personalized doctor-patient exchange into an organizational process. The hospital has

28 Douglas C. Mankin and William F. Glueck, "Strategic Planning," *Hospital & Health Services Administration*, Spring 1977, pp. 6–22.

become the central component of the health care system. The general hospital is characterized by a substantial division of labor and application of advanced technology. It embraces many goals and values and has a large number of specialized participants. Although the primary goal is the patient's welfare, there are many additional objectives, such as medical and nursing education, research, and economic viability.

There is a unique relationship between the formal authority of position, as represented by the administrative hierarchy, and the authority of knowledge, as represented by the medical practitioners and other professionals. This creates a diffused and distinctive structure. The administrative organization is headed by the board of trustees, which appoints the hospital administrator as the chief executive. The medical staff is made up of licensed physicians, is basically self-governing, and does not come under the administrative structure.

The hospital has a complex psychosocial system. Although the roles of the various participants—the physicians, the administrative staff, the nurses, and paramedical personnel—are rather well defined, there are substantial conflicts. The psychosocial system is strongly influenced by the norms and values of professionalism, which are internalized by the various participants and focus primarily on patient welfare.

The managerial system is difficult to define. The diversity of the authority structure creates a dispersal of the planning and control functions. The board of trustees has the legal authority and decides on broad financial and other organizational matters. The medical staff has the technical knowledge and decides on matters of patient care and treatment. The administrative staff is in charge of the functioning of the hospital and must engage in managerial planning and organizational control.

Questions and Problems

1 Evaluate the view that advancing technology, together with changing medical practices, has created new and evolving goals for the general hospital.

2 How does the historical development of the hospital affect current structure?

3 How does the overriding value of patient welfare provide a basis for voluntary coordination of activities in the hospital?

4 Does the organization structure of the hospital fit the traditional bureaucratic model? Why or why not?

5 What is the relationship between the medical staff and the administrative staff in the hospital?

6 How is coordination accomplished in the hospital?

7 Discuss the status and roles of the various participants in the psychosocial system of hospitals.

8 In what ways is the managerial system of a hospital different from that in the business organization? In what ways are they similar?

9 What are the administrative and organizational implications of the development of multi-unit hospital systems?

10 Discuss some of the environmental changes that have major influence on hospitals.

Comparative Organizational Analysis: The University

Twenty-one

Institutions of higher education have grown significantly in number and in size. The primary product of colleges and universities is knowledge—its creation and dissemination. With the acceleration of science and technology, they have assumed a greater role in society. The traditional "ivory tower" barriers to interaction with the wider community are being removed. These changes have created some fundamental problems for defining the mission of the university. Furthermore, the university's organizational subsystems are undergoing significant changes. We will discuss these and other aspects of universities in terms of the following framework:

Changing Environment
Goals and Values
Technology
Structure
Psychosocial System
Managerial System

Changing Environment

Today's institutions of higher education are descendants of the university of the medieval period. Medieval universities had a religious beginning and were associated with cathedral schools and monasteries.[1]

Higher education in the American colonies began with Harvard in 1636, and by the time of the Revolution there were nine colleges: "nine home-grown variations on a theme known in the mother country as Oxford and Cambridge."[2]

---

[1] Hastings Rashdall, *The Universities of Europe in the Middle Ages,* ed. by F. M. Powicke and A. B. Emden, Oxford University Press, Fair Lawn, N.J., 1936, 3 vols.
[2] Frederick Rudolph, *The American College and University,* © Alfred A. Knopf, Inc., New York, 1962, p. 3.

These colleges had a religious orientation, strongly affected by the puritan ethic of the times. They were shaped by the aristocratic traditions transmitted from Oxford and Cambridge and cherished the humanistic ideal of classical scholarship, with emphasis on Greek and Latin, logic, rhetoric, ethics, metaphysics, physics, and mathematics. During colonial times, the American colleges began to take a shape of their own, different from their English origins. They moved away from the classical tradition and adopted a curriculum that was more in line with their sociocultural setting.

During the early part of the nineteenth century many new colleges were founded by the various religious denominations, who seemed to be competing to ensure that their views would be perpetuated through institutions of higher learning. There was a democratization of higher education in America, reinforced by the development of a public educational system during the Jacksonian period. "The institutions of the college movement in America intended to be, to the best of their ability and knowledge, democratic institutions for a democratic society."[3] There was a continual conflict between the desire to retain the classical tradition and the overwhelming social necessity for adapting to the requirements of the developing and industrializing nation. The American colleges began to lose their traditional unity of purpose and identity, which had been prescribed within rather narrow limits since their earlier foundations.

Rise of the University

During the second half of the nineteenth century there were major transformations in American higher education—the development of the land-grant colleges and the rise of the true university. In 1862 the Morrill Federal Land Grant Act gave new impetus to the development of colleges emphasizing agricultural and technical subjects. It provided for the support in every state of at least one college, "where the leading objective shall be, without excluding other scientific or classical studies, to teach such branches of learning as are related to agriculture and the mechanical arts." Each state was given public lands equivalent to 30,000 acres for each senator and representative under the apportionment of 1860. This act and its subsequent supporting legislation led to the development of sixty-eight land-grant colleges in a variety of forms.

The development of the land-grant colleges paved the way for a fundamental change from the traditional collegiate pattern. The American university took its form from the German universities, rather than from the English colleges. The German universities placed a strong emphasis on scholarship, creation of knowledge, and training for the learned professions.

The essence of the German university system, which gave it intellectual leadership in the nineteenth century, was the concept that an institution of true higher learning should be,

---

3 Ibid., p. 67.

above all, "the workshop of free scientific research." This emphasis on the disinterested pursuit of truth through original investigation led, on the one hand, to the development of the concept that a true university must maintain freedom of teaching and freedom of learning within certain carefully defined limits. On the other, it led ultimately to a stress on the various services which higher learning could render to the state. [4]

The development of American universities came from a number of directions. Cornell and Johns Hopkins were among the first private institutions to adopt the university pattern. Michigan, Wisconsin, and Minnesota were among the first public institutions to become universities. The earlier colonial colleges such as Harvard, Yale, Princeton, and Columbia superimposed the university system on their collegiate structure. Many variations of the university pattern evolved during the latter part of the nineteenth and early twentieth centuries.

Universities frequently encompassed as part of their institution the collegial pattern in the form of an undergraduate liberal arts college. However, they also included the scientific and technical areas and developed programs in engineering, law, medicine, business administration, and other professional fields. They provided graduate as well as undergraduate education—emphasizing that the university was a primary creator of knowledge with a responsibility for research and investigation into a wide spectrum of subjects.

There developed a new spirit of vocationalism with the incorporation of professional schools within the university. [5] In fact, the universities helped redefine the concept of professions. Traditionally the professions had included only medicine, law, and divinity, but with the growing need for specialized education in many fields, the distinction between vocationalism and professionalism became blurred. Universities recognized the need for professionalized training in a wide variety of fields, such as engineering and other applied sciences, teaching at the elementary and secondary levels, dentistry, business administration, and librarianship. "In assuming responsibility for providing formal professional education, the universities revealed the degree to which American higher education had now broadly entered into the life of the people" [6] The American university system, more than any other in the world, has provided professionally trained people for a wide variety of activities necessary in an advanced industrial society.

Current Scene

Higher education in the United States is characterized by a multiplicity of organizations, functions, and roles. In size, the institutions range all the way from the small liberal arts colleges to the large private and state universities, some

4 John S. Brubacher and Willis Rudy, *Higher Education in Transition: An American History: 1636–1956,* Harper & Row, Publishers, Incorporated, New York, 1958, p. 171.

5 William W. Brickman, "American Higher Education in Historical Perspective," *The Annals of the American Academy of Political and Social Science,* November 1972, pp. 39–41.

6 Rudolph, op. cit., p. 340.

with over 100,000 students. They range in level from the two-year community colleges through universities offering doctoral and post-doctoral work. They range in location from large metropolitan areas to rural settings. The student bodies are also heterogeneous, from beginning undergraduates to doctoral and postdoctoral students—all with differing interests and objectives. There are both privately endowed and state- and community-supported institutions. The role they play in society is complex and is undergoing dynamic change. This great diversity makes it impossible to select one single institution as typical.

Statistics on the current status of higher education in the United States give an indication of this diversity. In 1976 there were 11,215,100 students enrolled in higher education in the United States, of which 8,800,900 were enrolled in public and 2,414,200 in private institutions. [7] The enrollment has increased each year since the early 1950s, rising from 2,102,000 in 1951 to over 11 million in 1976. In 1951, there were 13 college students for each 100 persons eighteen to twenty-four years of age in the population. By 1976, there were 35 college students per 100 persons in the same age group. There were a total of 3026 institutions of higher education, of which 160 were classified as universities, 1738 as four-year colleges, and 1128 as two-year colleges. Universities were classified as those institutions that gave considerable stress to graduate instruction, that confer advanced degrees as well as bachelor's degrees in a variety of liberal arts fields, and that have at least two professional schools that are not exclusively technological.

In 1976 there were over 680,000 faculty, a major increase from the 191,400 in the 1949–1950 academic year. [8] The growing role of the federal government in higher education is seen by the contributions of funds for basic research, facilities, fellowships, student assistants, and other support, which increased from $992 million in 1962 to $7400 million in 1976–1977. The total expenditures on higher education for 1976–1977 were estimated at $49 billion.

Two other trends have had a significant influence on higher education. First, in the post-WW II period public universities have grown more rapidly than private universities, both absolutely and proportionally. Second, there has been an increase in the proportion of graduate to undergraduate students. This is particularly true for the universities, which have taken the role of training at the postbaccalaureate level.

Many of the public and private universities are very complex and have large student enrollments. The university of 30,000 to 50,000 students with a faculty of several thousand and offering a wide range of teaching and research programs is typical. Many of the universities have established branch campuses in various locations throughout their states.

Higher education in the United States has been responsive to changes in its environmental suprasystem. New institutional types and forms have developed

---

7 *The Chronicles of Higher Education*, Feb. 22, 1977, p. 6.

8 *Digest of Education Statistics, 1976 Edition*, National Center for Education Statistics, U.S. Department of Health, Education, and Welfare, Washington, D.C., 1977.

in response to the needs of society. The basic democratic principle holds that every individual, regardless of prior background or status, should have an opportunity for higher education. This, perhaps, has been the one greatest difference between education in the United States and that in Western Europe and England. As a consequence of the basic Jacksonian-democratic view of higher education, the college degree has become one of the primary means for upward mobility in our society. Children of low-income groups have looked to the university as a means of bettering their social positions. [9]

Another distinguishing characteristic is the interest in making higher learning functional and closely related to the needs of society. Again, this is part of the democratizing influence and has led to a multiplicity of educational opportunities. The university system has not fostered an intellectual elite but provides a broad segment of the population with educational opportunities. In return, society has come to expect much of institutions of higher education—they should provide a worthwhile and useful service.

A final consideration relates to the diversity of control. There is no one central source of higher authority over these institutions. Control is decentralized down to a state, local, or private level. There is no single integrating force working toward a master plan for higher education.

Our discussion will concentrate on universities, both private and public, and will not attempt to discuss the other forms of higher education such as colleges, technical institutes, and two-year institutions. However, many of the characteristics of universities will also be true of these other organizations.

Goals and Values

The social role of the university is the creation and dissemination of knowledge. "Higher education has made its province the realm of knowledge. This knowledge may be inherently valuable for its own sake, for the satisfaction it brings to the individual who seeks to escape ignorance and superstition. This knowledge may be useful in solving human problems from health to production, from justice to unemployment. Knowledge for its own sake and for use—knowledge is what higher education would impart." [10] This sets the broad role of the university but does not indicate more specific goals and values. Actually, the role of institutions of higher education has undergone significant changes.

In the colonial colleges the primary function was that of education for the ministry. "The desire of important religious denominations (such as the Angli-

---

9 For a discussion of the relationship between social stratification and higher education, see Christopher Jencks and David Riesman, *The Academic Revolution,* Doubleday & Company, Inc., Garden City, N.Y., 1968, pp. 61–154.

10 John D. Millett, *The Academic Community: An Essay on Organization,* McGraw-Hill Book Company, New York, 1962, p. 34.

can and Calvinist) for a literate, college-trained clergy was probably the most important single factor explaining the founding of the colonial colleges." [11] The dominant views of Christianity set the values, and the majority of the faculty members were members of the clergy. Gradually, however, these institutions and the colleges that followed moved away from their religious orientation toward broader intellectual pursuits. Because of the pragmatic nature of the American society, the colleges did move toward a goal of service. The emerging goals for higher education indicated that knowledge should have application in the professions, government, business, and other social institutions. Education could only be useful if it resulted in change and improvement.

In the latter part of the nineteenth century, universities began to emphasize scholarship, research, and professional training. A primary goal of the institution became the creation of new knowledge through research.

Current Institutional Goals

Three predominant institutional goals for universities are:

1 The dissemination of knowledge to students. This is primarily done through the teaching function.
2 The creation and advancement of knowledge. This is accomplished through the research activities of the faculty and specialized staffs.
3 Service to society. This role is related to the first two goals. It establishes the norm that knowledge creation and dissemination should be useful.

It seems apparent that all three goals of the university are not fully recognized either by the general public or, more important, by major participants in the university system itself. In class discussions concerning the role of the university, students recognize the importance of teaching but frequently have little appreciation for the goal of creation and advancement of knowledge through research. A university does have the function of transmitting the cultural heritage and disseminating current knowledge to the student, but this is a role that is also fulfilled by other institutions in our society. The university has the special function of creating new knowledge through research.

If the university is to accomplish its goals, it must maintain an environment of intellectual freedom, which is necessary for the dissemination of ideas that may not have a popular consensus. There also must be freedom for the pursuit of new knowledge. Historically, universities have always been centers of dissent. Conflict is often evident between different internal groups but also occurs with the external environment. As the university pursues the goals of knowledge creation

11 Brubacher and Rudy, op. cit., p. 6.

and dissemination, conflicts with the established sociocultural norms and values of society are often inevitable.

Technology

We have referred to technology as *knowledge* about the performance of certain tasks or activities. By "organizational technology" we mean the techniques used in the transformation of inputs into outputs in the accomplishment of goals. We will discuss the technology of the university under two headings, academic and administrative.

Academic Technology

Teaching and scholarly research are the primary technical tasks of the system. The academic staff—professors, instructors, and teaching assistants—performs these tasks and is the operating subsystem in the university organization.

The academic staff is specialized in its task performance. The university is departmentalized, and professors within each department have individual expertise. They transmit knowledge to students in specialized disciplines. The second major role, knowledge creation through scholarly and scientific research, is also carried on by the academic staff.

The techniques of teaching have not undergone profound changes. The classroom, with its interpersonal relationships, remains the primary vehicle for the dissemination of knowledge. It is supplemented by the use of textbooks and library resources. There have been modifications in teaching techniques, such as closed-circuit television and teaching machines, but these have not made major inroads into the more traditional methods. While faculties are dedicated to the expansion of knowledge in their disciplines, they have been resistant to experimentation with new teaching techniques. The professor typically adheres to the traditional approach and prefers contact with students in a classroom situation.

Techniques employed in accomplishing the second major goal, that of creation of knowledge through research, have been more subject to change. This is particularly true in the physical sciences, which require research laboratories, cyclotrons, and other equipment, and in such areas as medicine, which must have elaborate research facilities and hospitals. Universities have provided the physical manifestations of technology to enable the staff to perform this role.

At the graduate level, in particular, there is a merging of the technical tasks of knowledge creation and dissemination. Frequently, graduate students are engaged as research assistants in support of the academic staff. The graduate assistant has the dual role of recipient of current knowledge and partner in creating new knowledge.

The diversity of task performance activities in the university suggests the wide differences in technologies in the various disciplines. Each of the academic fields typically has developed techniques that are specialized to its field of endeavor.

Administrative Technology

But a university is more than a professor and a student sitting at opposite ends of a log. Who provides the log? How do we ensure that the student and professor meet at the appropriate time? How are the library resources necessary for an intellectual dialogue accumulated? Who feeds and houses students and takes care of their medical needs? Who provides the parking facilities for the automobiles each of them wants to drive as close as possible to the log? Who records the number of sessions and the professor's evaluation of the student? How is the professor *paid?* These are a few of the functions necessary to support the primary technical tasks of teaching and research. With a university of 30,000 or 40,000 students and an academic staff in excess of 2000, the administrative functions required for servicing the primary technical tasks are complex.

Administrative technology in universities can be classified in four principal areas: [12] (1) *academic administration,* which is the primary concern of the academic staff; (2) *administration of student personnel services,* which includes the selection, admission, and scheduling of students and the recording of their academic achievements; (3) *business administration,* which includes such activities as accounting, auditing, reporting, and budgetary control; receipt, custody, and disbursement of monies; investment of funds; purchasing; management of auxiliary and service activities; operation and maintenance of the institutional plant; selection and promotion of nonacademic personnel; and administration of staff benefits programs; and (4) *public relations,* which includes the relationship with the press, radio, and television stations, alumni, solicitation of funds, and maintenance of contact with possible donors and legislatures. Administrative technology is involved with the latter three areas. Universities are adopting many management concepts from business organizations for these functions. In most modern American universities there has been a significant increase in the number of people on the administrative staff to perform these activities.

Computer technology has already revolutionized the maintenance of student records, the grading process, and many other administrative techniques. It is being applied to library systems in order to aid in information storage and retrieval. [13] Such techniques as systems and procedures analysis and cost-benefit analysis are being used for more efficient utilization of resources. Administrative offices are being established for long-range planning and organizational analysis. These offices use the same type of planning and administrative technologies as in

12 Thomas Edward Blackwell, *College and University Administration,* The Center for Applied Research in Education, Inc., New York, 1966, pp. 14–15.
13 Francis E. Rourke and Glenn E. Brooks, *The Managerial Revolution in Higher Education,* The Johns Hopkins Press, Baltimore, 1966, pp. 20–21.

business and government. Many universities have adopted new planning-programming-budgeting systems (PPBS) to help in the allocation of resources.

There is not a complete separation between academic and administrative technologies. Certainly they are interacting and may be in conflict. The developing administrative techniques have an important effect on the entire academic community. While we share some of the concern over possible conflicts between academe and "the administration," the application of more effective managerial techniques is vital. However, the new directions and techniques in management should be designed to facilitate the primary academic endeavors of teaching and research as well as the internal administrative functions of the university.

Structure

The structure and authority patterns of universities have changed significantly from their medieval form. The early universities appear to have started as scholastic guilds, a combination of teachers and students somewhat similar to trade guilds. In the early Italian universities, the student had substantial authority over administrative and academic affairs. However, this student control broke down, and the church became the primary source of authority. There was continual conflict between the church and the universities' faculties. One of the most significant changes in this relationship occurred in 1231, when Gregory IX recognized the rights of the several faculties of the University of Paris to administer their own activities. This has been called the Magna Charta of the university. The pattern of the University of Paris became the model for the universities in Central Europe and in England. Oxford and Cambridge were organized around faculty authority.

A later development changed this form. The University of Leyden, founded in 1575, had an external board of "curators," who appointed professors and administered the affairs of the university. This pattern was adopted by the University of Edinburgh, founded in 1582, when the charter gave the town council the right to provide for the teaching of all the usual university subjects.[14] Two colonial colleges, Yale and Princeton, were modeled after the University of Edinburgh organization and incorporated the principle of an external board of trustees. This set the precedent for the structure of most American colleges and universities.

Differentiation and Integration

The colonial colleges had a simple structure. They had a strict and prescribed curriculum, small size, and special purpose. With the development of true universities in the latter part of the nineteenth century, the problems of structure became more acute. The university model brought greater complexities due to

14 Blackwell, op. cit., p. 35.

increased specialization and the emphasis on research and knowledge creation. There was also greater diversity of objectives. This process of specialization continued as universities expanded into the various disciplinary fields and added new subject matter.

It became necessary to develop a more complex and elaborate structure. Separate colleges or schools based on academic disciplines were established. These were further divided into departments with even more academic specialization.

The university has undergone the same process and faces the same structural problems as the general hospital—providing for the integration of activities. The primary concern is the integration of the specialized disciplines through new means of coordination. The traditional faculty committee structure and the direct democratic participation in institutional matters are useful devices. However, with increasing size, diversity, and specialization, this system for providing coordination has broken down. It is unrealistic to expect that a full faculty meeting of over 2000 members could provide integration. Consequently, it has been necessary to develop new means for coordinating specialized activities.

The authority structure within the university is not similar to that of the bureaucratic model. There is no way of clearly defining scalar authority from top to bottom of the hierarchy. One university president has likened the university to a collegial partnership between himself and 2000 faculty members. In the university there is a wide dispersal of power. A major source of power is the holders of knowledge and pursuers of research—the academic staff. The authority of knowledge is a fundamental part of the system, and it does not parallel the scalar hierarchy.

Formal Structure

Despite the diffused nature of power, colleges and universities do have a formal structure. It starts with a board of trustees, governors, or regents—an external body at the top of the hierarchy, which is traditional with American universities. The board delegates authority to the president for the administration of the university. Actually, a university president has a dual function. He or she is administrative representative of the board but also the leader of the faculty. An administrative staff consisting of a provost, a number of vice-presidents, the deans of the various colleges or schools, and other administrative personnel all report to the president.

In most universities, the president authorizes the faculty to share the academic duties and responsibilities for the formulation of policies and rules for the government of the institution. The faculty traditionally has primary responsibility over matters of curriculum and a strong voice in the selection and promotion of faculty colleagues. This pattern of shared authority that permeates the university is distinct from that existing in most other complex organizations.

Other Structures

There are other structural aspects of the university that should be considered. Students frequently are in control of many activities. They are formally organized in an overall association of students. Within these associations there are formal structures to carry out specific functions. Students may be organized in fraternities and sororities, dormitory living groups, religious groups, service clubs, professional groups, and a host of other activities. It would be impossible to describe all the structural relationships for student activities in a large university. While the emphasis here has been with the authority of the administration and faculty, the power of the student body should not be underestimated. Any university recognizes that the quality of the students is a prime requisite for first-class status.

Another formal structure existing in most universities is a representative faculty organization such as the university senate or council. There may also be formal college or school councils. These bodies can play a strong academic and administrative role.

This diffused authority structure leads to substantial conflict and uncertainty. "The new university is a conflict-prone organization. Its many purposes push and pull in different directions. Its multiple principles of authority and pluralistic power structure make coordination difficult." [15] However, for the institutions whose basic role is one of creation and dissemination of knowledge, collegial authority appears to be the most appropriate form. It provides for free expression, a high level of commitment of individuals to their disciplinary areas, a strong sense of participation, and an environment conducive to exploring new ideas.

Example of Structure

The organization of the University of Washington serves as an example of structural relationships. This is a large, state-supported university located in a metropolitan area, Seattle. In fall 1976, it had an enrollment of 35,277 students, of which 8717, or nearly 25 percent, were graduate. The growth in student enrollment has been substantial, more than doubling since 1959. This is typical of other large state universities. It had over 2400 regular faculty members and a staff of over 1400 teaching assistants. The nonacademic staff exceeded 9900. Taken together, the students, faculty, and supporting staff represented a university community of nearly 50,000 people. Figure 21.1 shows the administrative organization of the University of Washington. It should be emphasized that this chart shows only part of the structure. It does not show the separate faculty structure, which includes the universitywide faculty senate or councils within the various colleges

---

15 Burton R. Clark, "The New University," *American Behavioral Scientist,* May–June 1968, p. 4.

Figure 21.1 University of Washington Organization Chart (1978)

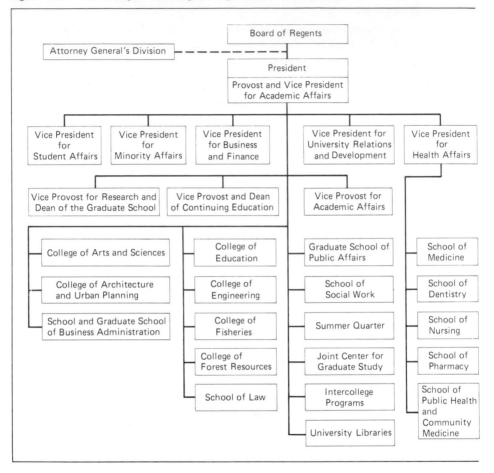

and schools. It does not show the student organizations, such as the Associated Students of the University of Washington, and its board of control. In effect, this organization chart shows just one aspect of the formal structure.

While some of the activities presented on this chart are unique to the University of Washington, the overall concept of the administrative organization is similar to that of other public and private universities. It has a multilevel structure on the academic side moving from the president through the schools and colleges down to the departmental level. In addition, it has an administrative staff to deal with universitywide functions such as business and finance, student affairs, and university relations. These administrative units can be considered as staff activities in support of the primary academic functions.

Psychosocial System

Many diverse participants play roles in the psychosocial system of a university. These participants have different goals and motivations. One of the predominant characteristics is that most of the participants, faculty and students, have a substantial degree of autonomy, and they operate as individuals within the system. Students, for example, have autonomy in the selection of their areas of specialization and interest. Although their classroom participation is on a group basis, their outside preparation is individualized. The same characteristic is also true of the faculty. The professor is primarily responsible for conducting classes and has full control of the evaluational and grading process. Thus, a university community represents a very diffuse and complex psychosocial system, one that is loosely tied together. In the following discussion, we will look at the three predominant participant groups: students, faculty, and the administrative staff.

Students

Students obviously have a vital role in the academic process. They complete the process of knowledge transmission. Their goals and aspirations, values, motivations, and interests have an impact on the academic and social life of every university.

With the evolutionary process from college to university, the basic role and position of students changed dramatically. In the early days the students' lives revolved around the college. The curriculum was prescribed, they lived in residence, and they were isolated from the broader community. They lived in a cloistered environment in which the basis of need satisfaction centered in the college itself.

The movement toward the university system changed this pattern significantly. Students have been placed on their own in a strange environment. They have substantial autonomy in the selection of a curriculum of studies, and the opportunities available to them are varied. Their responsibilities are centered around meeting class obligations, which typically take only twelve to fifteen hours per week. Otherwise, they are substantially on their own. Kerr suggests this new role for the student.

The multiversity is a confusing place for the student. He has problems of establishing his identity and sense of security within it. But it offers him a vast range of choices, enough literally to stagger the mind. In this range of choices he encounters the opportunities and the dilemmas of freedom. The casualty rate is high. The walking wounded are many. *Lernfreiheit*—the freedom of the student to pick and choose, to stay or move on—is triumphant. [16]

Traditionally, colleges and universities accepted the role of *in loco pa-*

16 Clark Kerr, *The Uses of the University,* Harvard University Press, Cambridge, Mass. 1963, p. 42.

rentis, in which the institution adopted a paternalistic attitude toward students. This concept of the university as a second parent to the student is breaking down. The student body is being left to its own devices for the satisfaction of social needs. Obviously, many students respond favorably to this new-found freedom, but for others it creates difficulties of anomie and identification.

Certainly one of the characteristics of university students is their great diversity. A wide variety of programs and curricula exist. Frequently, the value systems that influence students are substantially different between the humanities, physical sciences, and professional schools. There is a substantial age range of students from beginning freshmen to master's and doctoral candidates, as well as those in the professional schools. There is a diversity in their domiciles. In metropolitan universities, many students are commuters, living at home. Others live in university-provided dormitories, others in the sororities and the fraternities, and many live in apartments and other quarters not associated with the university.

Students entering the university come with substantially different goals and expectations of the role they will play in the system. Basically, they are not as committed to the existing norms and values as are the faculty and administration. Many forces have contributed to the feeling of alienation on the part of students— the size of classes, the inability to have close faculty-student contacts, particularly at the undergraduate level, the use of teaching assistants in undergraduate classes, the increased computerization of students' records, and the establishment of bureaucratic procedures in other activities associated with the university. [17] The very transientness of students, typically being in the institution for a few years at most, makes it difficult to find effective means for the assimilation of their interests and influence into the university community.

A significant increase is evident in the number of minority and women students entering institutions of higher education over the past two decades. Minority students grew from 227,000 in 1960 to 1,182,000 in 1975, a jump of 420 percent. This compares with an increase in the number of other students of 155 percent during the same period. Minority students represent nearly 15 percent of total student enrollment, and there is an increasing proportion of minorities in professional and graduate schools.

Women now constitute about half of the first-year enrollment in colleges and universities, but these numbers alone do not indicate the dramatic nature of the shifts. Traditionally, women have received education in a relatively limited range of academic disciplines, such as teacher education, nursing, and liberal arts. Over the past decade they have moved into other fields. The enrollment of women in graduate and professional schools rose by 75 percent between 1970 and 1975 while for men the five-year increase was only 23 percent. [18] Women have been entering medical, dental, and law schools, graduate schools of business and engi-

---

17 William H. Sewell, "Students and the University," *The American Sociologist,* May 1971, pp. 111–117.

18 *The Chronicles of Higher Education,* Feb. 7, 1977, p. 1.

neering, and other traditionally male-dominated academic areas. Between 1970 and 1975 the number of first professional degrees earned by women increased by 184 percent and the number of doctorates received increased by 59 percent.

These increases in the number of women and minorities enrolled in higher education and their entry into new academic areas is a reflection of broader social forces. Higher education is the primary means by which disadvantaged groups have increased their upward mobility and career aspirations. These current trends are in line with the historical pattern in American society.

Faculty

The role of the university faculty in our society has undergone rather dramatic transformation. The traditional concept of the "ivory tower" professor pursuing academic interests in isolation and dealing with the nonpractical has changed. Increasingly, the community looks to the campus for knowledge and expertise in solving real-world problems. This initially occurred in the physical sciences and engineering, as exemplified by the developments in atomic energy. Other academic disciplines have a strong influence on practical affairs—witness the growing role of the economist and other social scientists. Medical schools are among the nation's most important institutions engaged in research on health care problems. This increased reliance on practical knowledge provided by the universities has created a new role for the academician. "Life has changed also for the faculty member. The multiversity is in the main stream of events. To the teacher and the researcher have been added the consultant and the administrator. Teaching is less central than it once was for most faculty members; research has become more important." [19]

The faculty represents a heterogeneous psychosocial system. This diversity stems from the basic differences in the disciplines. Each discipline has established a certain prescribed value system, "ways of thinking" and "methods of research," which sets it apart from other academic specialties.

In the university there is a formal rank structure for the faculty, beginning with the instructor, assistant professor, associate professor, professor, and, in some cases, a distinguished professorial chair. However, this distinction does not affect the role fundamentally. In the United States universities, as differentiated from many European institutions, the instructor and assistant and associate professor perform essentially the same role of teaching and research as the full professor. They have the same degree of autonomy in conducting their classes and research.

Every member of the faculty has a dual role—as an individual and as a member of the community of scholars. As individuals they have various duties to carry out in the performance of their profession. In addition, members of the faculty have certain functions in their collegial role at three levels, the department,

---

[19] Kerr, op. cit., p. 42.

the college or school, and the university. This role is usually performed by service on various academic and administrative committees.

There has been much discussion of the faculty member's role conflict as a teacher (dispenser of knowledge) and as a scholarly researcher (creator of knowledge). Many suggest that this conflict is absolute; the faculty member must choose one of these two roles—to be either a good teacher or a good researcher but, by inference, not both. This popularized dichotomy between "publish or perish" is misleading. Part of the confusion centers on the definition of scholarly research. It might be assumed that scholarly research and a publication record are synonymous, but there may be differences. Many professors engage in research that does not result directly in publication but does contribute to the body of knowledge. Conversely, many publications are not based on scholarly research.

University professors have a dual role of teaching and research, and they cannot adequately fulfill their responsibilities without giving attention to both. This role conflict is not as real as it may appear. It may serve as a rationalization for those who can neither teach nor perform scholarly research effectively. In the university system, both activities are vital to the basic goals of the institution.

There is a growing interest among faculties in many institutions of higher education for developing some form of collective bargaining. Traditionally, each faculty member has negotiated individually with the institution concerning terms of employment. However, there have existed a number of means for joint participation by faculty in university affairs. The tradition of collegiality and sharing of matters of governance between the board of regents, administration, and faculty has created a different role from that of a typical employee in other organizations. However, true collective bargaining as it exists for workers in industry, for many governmental employees, and for certain professionals (e.g., nurses and public school teachers) has not been evident on campuses.

Until recently, collective bargaining by faculty members in public institutions has been severely restricted by state laws. Twenty-four states now allow unionization of faculty members, and there is increasing pressure for many states (and for federal legislation) to extend this right to other faculties.[20] By mid-1977, faculties on 544 campuses had chosen collective-bargaining agents.[21]

Faculties in most universities and colleges have "reluctantly and with skepticism" looked at collective bargaining. There is substantial fear that active collective bargaining will result in an "adversary relationship" between faculty and administration, with a major sacrifice of the concept of collegiality and joint governance of the institution. At the same time, there is a growing concern that the only way for faculty to get a "fair shake" and to maintain their relative position in a period of inflation and limited financial resources is through some form of collective bargaining. In many ways collective bargaining is not compatible with the "professional" norms of the academician. However, the hard realities

20 *The Chronicles of Higher Education,* Mar. 14, 1977, p. 1.
21 *The Chronicles of Higher Education,* May 31, 1977, pp. 10–11.

of life in a large institution where the individual faculty member has a limited individual bargaining position have caused an increasing number of faculty to seek some accommodation between these professional norms and the advantages of collective activity.

Administrative Staff

Members of a university administrative staff—the president, provost, most vice-presidents, deans, and department heads—are also members of the faculty. Most frequently, they have moved from the faculty to an administrative post. Often their assignments as administrators are part time or temporary, and they ultimately return to their faculty positions. Thus, they hold many of the same basic values as the faculty. However, of necessity they are more local in their orientation and are concerned primarily with internal and external institutional matters rather than with their professional disciplines.

The president, deans, and department heads have a dual role in the university system. The president is the chief administrative officer of the university, but he or she is also the presiding member of the faculty, first among equals, and is therefore the educational leader. This duality of function holds for deans and department heads. However, it is increasingly more difficult for academic administrators to fulfill these two roles. The high degree of specialization and the rapid advancements in knowledge make it difficult for administrators to keep up with their disciplines. Furthermore, the complexities of the administrative function take up much of their time and energy. More and more academic administrators are being excluded from the direct, goal-oriented activities of the university—teaching and research.

"Administration or management" does not have the long-established tradition of professionalism that is associated with an academic discipline. The faculty view frequently is that the administration is only there to serve the needs of the professors, who perform the "important" functions of the university. This viewpoint was frequently expressed by one professor as "The dean needs me more than I need him." (However, this was only expressed to colleagues, never to the dean.) This withholding of status and prestige for the academic administrator by faculty colleagues may lead the administrator to orient his or her role to other reference groups—typically other administrators—thus creating additional problems in maintaining an effective "community of scholars."[22] The psychosocial system of academic administrators has many inherent role conflicts and problems

22 "A major effect of these changes has been to erode the informal relationships between administrators and faculty members, relationships which engendered and sustained the trust necessary for an easy exercise of administrative authority, and which muted the potential conflict between administrators and academics in the university of an earlier day. Radical shrinkage of informal contacts has also reduced the actual knowledge that administrators have of faculty and students—and vice versa." Terry F. Lunsford, "Authority and Ideology in the Administered University," *American Behavioral Scientist,* May–June 1968, p. 8.

of identification with particular reference groups. And, all too frequently, the administrative role has more status and prestige as viewed from the external world than from within the university community.

The nonacademic staff represents an important part of the psychosocial system. Architects, engineers, programmers, counselors, budget analysts, and systems designers are examples of professionals who are utilized in various specialized functions. Many others—secretaries, food service workers, mechanics—also make important contributions to university operations.

Managerial System

Planning and control decisions are diffused throughout the entire university system. These functions are shared by many participant groups—students, faculty, administrators, and board of trustees. There is no single managerial system based on a distinct and unified scalar hierarchy. Much of the decision making is in the hands of the individual professor and student. The success of the university system depends on the degree to which the individual internalized objectives mesh with the organization as a whole. We will look briefly at the managerial functions at the department, college or school, and university levels.

Departmental Level

Individual faculty members represent the basic operating units in the university system. To help them to accomplish their tasks, they have traditionally been granted a great deal of autonomy. Because of professional training and discipline specialization, the faculty member is considered the one most appropriate to make decisions concerning the specific conduct of his or her teaching and research. Faculty members determine the course content, texts, instructional methods and procedures, and the means of measuring student performance. However, control is exerted over the faculty member's performance of these tasks. There are formal and informal mechanisms for feedback of information from students about the teacher's performance in the classroom, and professional performance is continually being evaluated by colleagues.

The department is the basic organizational unit in the university. It has the primary function of coordinating the activities of the individual faculty member around a body of knowledge or a discipline. Departments have a substantial role in decision making concerning educational matters. For example, they have a major voice in recruitment of new faculty and in evaluating the performance of their own members. Decisions in these matters are subject to the approval of the dean, president, and board of trustees, but there are strong pressures to confirm departmental decisions unless there are exceptional problems.

The departmental chairperson serves as a coordinator between the department and the college. Because the chairperson is a faculty member, and in most cases will return to a faculty position after tenure as an administrator, his or her value orientation is to departmental colleagues and the discipline area. However, department heads must also be responsive to their relationships with the dean of the school or college.

College or School Level

The college or school is a combination of departments. It provides for a further integration of academic planning and control decisions. Basic decisions are made concerning the broad scope of the curriculum, required courses for majors within the college, and the nature of the various degree programs. In this process, numerous collegewide committees are involved, and the ultimate decisions usually represent a compromise of the viewpoints of the various departmental units. Thus, the decision-making process continues to be one of obtaining consensus rather than one of centralized direction by the dean. However, the dean does have an important role in the use of power to obtain a consensus.

In most universities, the college or school is the primary level at which the budgetary process is initiated. Thus, the dean has substantial influence in the role of fiscal officer. The dean is also a "person in the middle," as a representative of the various departments and faculty members within the college to the higher administration and as the link from the administration to the faculty. One of the most important functions of the dean is to provide the integrative role for the faculty.

The dean reviews the personnel practices of departments. He formulates the budget for his college or school and participates in its administration.

Usually the dean is more than this. He does not issue orders to departments or faculty members, but he stands as a symbol of their collegial responsibility. He is a reminder to all the faculty members of a college or school of their common purpose and common interest. To the extent that he can articulate this common purpose and can win adherents to it, the dean has fulfilled an essential role in the academic process. [23]

The University Level

This level includes the board of trustees, the president, provost, vice-presidents, and other administrative staff. Much of the decision making relating the university to its external environment takes place at this level. It is concerned with financial matters and relationships with legislators, alumni, and many other groups. The president and the administrative staff have two primary decision-making roles. The first is in the overall governance of the university as delegated by the board of trustees. Many activities at this level are concerned with the

23 Millett, op. cit., pp. 92–93.

maintenance of the organization, such as classroom and student facilities, business and financial aspects, and the physical plant. Many of these functions are similar to those in business organizations. The same techniques and approaches for decision making are appropriate. For example, the problems of computerizing and programming the decision-making process in such areas as inventory controls, the payroll, and student records are similar to those faced by business.

The second and more complex decision-making role is that concerned with the president as leader of the faculty. The president reviews and approves the academic offerings of the departments and colleges and establishes broad policy for such activities as faculty selection and promotion. He or she has the help and guidance of a number of groups. For example, there may be a board of deans from the various schools and colleges, which serves as a communications link with the faculty. Many faculty committees report to the president and provide information on academic affairs.

Problems in Decision Making

The discussion on planning and control decisions at the various levels in the university indicates that it is a unique managerial system, significantly different from that found in other organizations. The concept of shared authority and decision making permeates the university. This raises some important questions on how the various groups within the system can effectively participate in the decision-making processes.

As universities have increased in size and complexity and with greater academic specialization, fundamental questions have been raised about how the faculty can exercise its shared decision-making authority.[24] Traditionally, faculty decision making has been based on obtaining a consensus of opinion through democratic processes. Growing size and increased specialization have made the "town meeting" process of decision making ineffective. It is necessary to shift to a more representative form of faculty government. This transformation has not come easily. "College and university faculties must come to terms with this trend by creating and delegating authority to committees and individuals empowered to represent the faculty point of view in the on-going business of a university. If a faculty is to be influential in the affairs of a university it must be able to decide as well as to deliberate. And faculties today are not as well organized for decision and action as they are for deliberation."[25]

Student participation in the university's decision-making processes has become a major issue. If the students' desire for greater participation and involvement in the activities of the university is to become real and effective, some means

---

24 Dennis F. Thompson, "Democracy and the Governing of the University," *The Annals of the American Academy of Political and Social Science,* November 1972, pp. 157–168.
25 Rourke and Brooks, op. cit., p. 129.

must be developed for true representation. Frequently university administrators and faculty are hard-pressed to deal with students because they do not know which groups they represent or their source of legitimization.[26] One of the major problems facing the university is providing for more effective student participation. Some means must be found for legitimizing the power and voice of various student groups. It is evident that students are demanding full rights of university citizenship with academic freedom and provisions for due process. These goals are legitimate (and are similar to those of other groups in our society such as employee unions), and the universities will need to accommodate themselves to these interests.

Summary

There have been major transformations in the functions of institutions of higher education in our society. The advent of the modern university in the latter part of the nineteenth century was a fundamental change from the earlier colleges. The primary goals of the university are the creation and dissemination of knowledge.

The academic staff performs the primary technical tasks of the university—teaching and scholarly research. There is a growing administrative technology associated with the provision of facilities and resources necessary for accomplishing the academic task.

The organization structure of the university cannot be clearly delineated. There have been trends toward greater differentiation of activities because of the high degree of specialization of the various academic disciplines. The process has increased the problems of integration. Coordination is achieved through the "community of scholars" concept with direct participation in institutional matters by the faculty.

There are many participants with various roles in the psychosocial system of the university. These participants have different motivations and goals. Students obviously have a vital role in the academic process; they are the recipients of knowledge. The role of the university faculty has undergone transformation. The traditional concept of the ivory tower professor is no longer a reality. Increasingly, the community looks to the campus for knowledge and expertise in solving practical problems.

Members of the administrative staff have a dual role as administrators and as members of the faculty. This duality frequently creates role conflicts. Increasingly, there appears to be a separation between the administration and the academic faculty in large universities. This process of separation has made the ideal of a "community of scholars" more difficult to achieve.

The functions of planning and control are diffused throughout the entire

26 Joseph R. Gusfield, "Student Protest and University Response," *The Annals of the American Academy of Political and Social Science,* May 1971, pp. 26–38.

university system. They are shared by many participating groups—students, faculty, administrators, and the board of trustees. There is no single managerial system based on a distinct and unified scalar hierarchy. Developing means for effective participation by the students, faculty, and administrators on a collegial basis has become increasingly difficult. This remains one of the most important problems facing the modern university.

Questions and Problems

1 How has the role of institutions of higher education changed in our society? What forces contributed to this transformation?

2 What are the primary goals of universities? Do you see any conflict between these goals?

3 Why is intellectual freedom vital to the university? What are some of the major challenges to this concept?

4 Why is an "administrative technology" of growing importance in higher education?

5 How does the concept of collegial or shared authority differ from bureaucratic authority?

6 Examine the structure of your own college or university. How is it similar or different from that of the University of Washington (see Figure 21.1)? How is integration of activities achieved in your institution?

7 How is the role of the student changing in universities? What means might be developed to provide students with legitimate opportunities for greater participation in internal affairs?

8 How has the role of the faculty been transformed? What are the types of role conflict that the professor faces?

9 What is the role of the administrative staff in the university? What types of conflict face the administrator?

10 What are the major problems in decision making that the university faces? What suggestion do you have for meeting these problems?

Comparative Organizational Analysis: The City

Twenty-two

Cities are pervasive and enduring human organizations. Many centuries ago, extended families of wanderers settled down to grow crops. Since then, numerous forces have combined to foster the development of villages, towns, cities, and metropolitan areas. Almost all of us "belong" to a city—as evidenced by our mailing address. However, our degree of involvement in this organization varies considerably—from inactive resident, to voluntary participant, to paid employee. As human settlements have grown in size and complexity, the problems of coordinating and managing diverse activities have increased dramatically. We will consider the city as an organization in terms of the following framework:

Changing Environment
Goals and Values
Technology
Structure
Psychosocial System
Managerial System

Changing Environment

In simple terms a city is "a place of relatively dense population characterized by frequent and meaningful human interactions."[1] This definition reflects a sociological view and is the one most evident to inhabitants or observers. A city is also a legal entity identified by its incorporated area—an important distinction for purposes of voting, taxation, and eligibility for services. As a political system, a city has all of the complexities of government. From an economic point of view,

---

1 James M. Banovetz, "The Developing City," in James M. Banovetz (ed.), *Managing the Modern City*, International City Management Association, Washington D.C., 1971, p.3.

a city is often a manufacturing and/or trade center with a sphere of influence that may range from local to international scope.

While the formal political and legal boundaries of the city are fixed, the social and economic boundaries are quite variable, as evidenced in metropolitan areas that may include a number of cities and even parts of several counties and/or states. In this discussion we will use the term "city" to cover a municipal government organization and its managers. The issues involved apply to a wide range of entities—villages, towns, and metropolitan areas.

American cities embrace a variety of categories. They are large and small, trade centers and industrial centers, rich and poor. They are as heterogeneous as the people who inhabit them. In assessing the state and fate of American cities, one should distinguish between polymorphic cities like New York or Chicago, and cities like Gary, Detroit, Grand Rapids, or Fall River, that all their lives may lean to one or two industries and might die with their departure. There are American capital cities that never change anything but their governors, cities that are no more than languid milltowns, cities that have more houses than people, cities dominated by the aging, cities with most of their houses on wheels, cities like Los Angeles that spread for miles and are still spreading.[2]

We will focus on medium- to large-sized cities in order to illustrate the wide range of problems and opportunities confronted by the modern city.

Evolution
of the
City

The psychological and sociological foundations of cities have always existed, because people have always banded together for protection and mutual support. They wandered from place to place in small groups, hunting animals and gathering plants for food. About 10,000 years ago the technology of farming was developed, and people began to settle in villages. A source of drinking water was a primary factor in site selection. Other considerations included protection and transportation, which is the reason for the location of today's major cities on rivers or natural ports. Mild climates and the availability of material for clothing and shelter also enhanced the growth of cities in certain locations.

Improved farming skills created surpluses of food and slack resources in the form of nonfarm workers. This led to the development of craft skills and to the bartering of foodstuffs for leather goods, wooden utensils, or metal tools, for example. This approach, within villages, was the forerunner of urban-rural, inter-city, inter-region, and international trade. Expanding trade became a major impetus to the growth of cities throughout the world.

Technological progress supported the growth of cities. Construction skills provided the means to build large structures, protective walls, and other facilities needed to enable a large number of people to live in a concentrated area.

2 Charles A. Abrams, *The City Is the Frontier,* Harper & Row, Publishers, Incorporated, New York, 1965, p. 6.

Improvements in transportation made it feasible both to congregate in urban areas and to interact with outsiders on a continuing basis. Innovations such as the steam engine led to the industrial revolution and the location of factories in existing cities. The need for labor drew additional people and the process of urbanization was accelerated.

The trend has been similar over the world, in spite of protesters such as Thomas Jefferson, who argued that we should "let our workshops remain in Europe" and preserve an agrarian society in the new world. The focal points of Jefferson's concern were overcrowding, pollution, disease, poverty, disorder, and crime. (After 200 years our concerns seem much the same!) Changes and improvements have been made, typically out of sheer necessity rather than foresight and planning.

To master the new intricacies of metropolitan living called for something more than the easy-going ways of colonial times. Yet the municipal authorities, loath to increase taxes, usually shouldered new responsibilities only at the prod of grim necessity. It required the lethal yellow-fever epidemics of the 1790's to induce Philadelphia to set the example of installing a public water system. [3]

Organization has always been important in human settlements. Authority-responsibility relationships were evident in families and tribes. As villages grew in size, it became necessary to have someone coordinate activity when self-control and informal relationships did not suffice. Thus, the custom of elected or appointed officials became the accepted means of organizing and managing municipal affairs. Within regions or nations, local administrators were often appointed and backed up by the power of a ruler to enforce the laws of the land. A small elite was involved in governance; the masses accepted the divine right and/or power of rulers to keep order and make important decisions.

Urbanization

The trend toward urbanization has been persistent and pervasive. It is a complex process that we can merely highlight in order to gain some perspective and begin to understand the modern city.

Both the absolute number and the proportion of people living in cities, as against rural areas, have increased worldwide. The United States serves as a representative example. Over the past 100 years, city population has increased dramatically from 25 to over 70 percent of the total. The primary causes have been immigration from abroad and migration from rural areas. The largest city in Europe in the middle ages was Paris, with a population of 150,000. In the 1970s more than 50 world cities have a population of more than 1,500,000. In the United States alone, there are more than 50 cities with 275,000 or more people.

Within these overall trends there have been shifts of population between

3 Arthur M. Schlesinger, "A Panoramic View: The City in American History," in Paul Kramer and Frederick L. Holborn (eds.), *The City in American Life,* Capricorn Books, New York, 1970, p. 23.

the city and its suburbs. While a few people have chosen to return to rural areas, by far the largest shift has been to contiguous areas immediately adjacent to cities. In early cities the usual pattern was the wealthy in the middle of town with peasants and serfs on the periphery. A later model found the working class close to the center or industrial area because of the need for easy access to their jobs. Wealthy industrialists and merchants lived on the periphery in elite neighborhoods. The move to the suburbs has been primarily a middle-class phenomenon, facilitated by technological advances in transportation systems—automobiles, buses, subways, trains, and ferries. A number of causal factors, such as escape from overcrowding, pollution, inadequate services, and undesirable neighbors, are involved in the move to the suburbs. People have traded commuting time for the benefits they perceive in suburban living.

Some factories (particularly light industry) and offices have moved from the inner city to suburban areas in order to obtain more space and be closer to the local labor force. These trends typically leave the poorer, less educated, and less skilled people in the inner city. In the 1960s and 1970s there have been a number of attempts to revitalize the inner city via urban renewal programs that provide low-income housing, open space, and encouragement for industry to either stay or return, as the case may be. A number of approaches have been used with mixed results—some progress and some failures. [4]

A Rand Corporation study concluded that "broad federal policies have had a greater, though unintended impact on urban development than deliberate urban programs. Overall . . . these policies have contributed to the decline of central-city population and employment." Another interesting conclusion of the study was that "jobs tend to follow people rather than the reverse. Thus, from the local perspective, economic development strategies must be related to efforts to improve the quality of life for city residents." [5]

For many years the plight of the cities went relatively unheeded because state legislatures were dominated by rural interests. However, redistricting has shifted the balance somewhat so that metropolitan areas carry more weight in the voting process. This has facilitated concerted attention to urban problems, particularly school financing and transportation systems.

Governmental Relationships

The city is a legal entity within a complex framework of other governmental units. All governments are limited by the principles set forth in the federal Constitution; all state and local governments are similarly limited by state constitutions and their specific charters. Local governments include counties, townships, incorporated municipalities, and other special districts.

The city is typically the primary governmental unit because it is closest

---

4 Martha Derthick, *New Towns In-Town,* The Urban Institute, Washington D.C., 1972.
5 Mark J. Kasoff, "The Urban Impact of Federal Policies," *Nation's Cities,* November 1977, p. 25.

to the most people. It has the general purpose of protecting and promoting the health, welfare, and safety of its residents. It is in the best position to adapt various programs to local needs and conditions and can respond more quickly to changing problems and opportunities than the state or federal government can.

The environment of the city, from the standpoint of organization and management, includes related local governmental units as well as state and federal systems. Coordination among local governments on programs of service delivery can improve effectiveness and efficiency, but it is often difficult to work out cooperative arrangements for integrating waste disposal systems or consolidating criminal detention facilities. Coordination between major cities and the counties within which they are situated is becoming increasingly important in large-scale public works projects.

Federal programs such as the Urban Renewal Act (1949), the Model Cities Act (1966), and Community Development Block Grants (1974) can be beneficial to cities, but they also carry constraints, responsibilities, and unintended consequences that may be unpalatable to local administrators and citizens. Federal support often calls for local matching money that is difficult to squeeze out of already tight budgets. Sometimes the guidelines change significantly, making contemplated projects and proposals obsolete. [6]

During the 1970s federal revenue-sharing funds provided resources with which the city could implement a number of programs of its own design. [7] This decentralized approach, first funded for 1972–1976 and then extended through 1980, has been well received by local government managers. They have welcomed the flexibility in prioritizing needs according to local situations, in contrast to programmatic, earmarked, and restricted support.

Another aspect of governmental relationships is city compliance with state and federal laws. For example, many projects require an environmental impact statement, and cities are finding it difficult to comply with water quality and clean air standards.

Other
Forces
in the
Environment

The environment of city government includes a wide variety of individuals and interest groups. Businesses, either individually or in associations, are often strong advocates for or against particular projects or programs. The chamber of commerce often has a particular view, as does the central labor council or the local medical society. Neighborhoods have priorities of their own and often request special treatment with regard to police and fire protection or street im-

---

6 "HUD Tightens Block Grant Rules," *The American City & County,* December 1977, p. 13.

7 Richard P. Nathan, et al., *Monitoring Revenue Sharing,* The Brookings Institution, Washington, D.C., 1975.

provements. The concerns of the historical preservation society may result in strong opposition to projects such as urban renewal. "Old, dilapidated, and expendable" may be seen as "unique, restorable, and essential." Environmental protectionists also play a major role in the current environment of city decision makers.

Goals and Values

A composite value system for an organization as complex as a city is impossible. Its values are as diverse as its citizens. They come into play in the expression of special interests of various groups. For example, senior citizens advocate lower property taxes, reduced rates on public transportation, and special recreational centers. Some citizens want more emergency medical services; others place a higher value on additional firefighters or police officers. Still others give first priority to improved traffic flow or better supervised playgrounds.

Periodically these values are expressed in the election of council members, who are charged with developing overall goals and policies for the city. Top management (mayor and/or city manager plus department directors) is also involved in identifying and evaluating alternatives and in making recommendations to the elected council. Thus, the values of key officials become important in determining the ultimate focus and extent of city programs.

During the 1970s the emphasis on growth and quantity was tempered somewhat with recognition of the importance of quality. A number of city goal statements included reference to "the quality of life." Several analyses of American cities were made and published in the media. A number of criteria were considered, and cities were scored on each criterion and ranked according to their overall rating on livability. The criteria used were similar to key results areas in a management by objectives approach. Within each area, specific objectives were identified and programs developed to achieve them. For purposes of illustration, let's consider an actual goal statement for a city of approximately 150,000 population, which we will call Ourtown.

Overall Mission

"To provide a quality city for the citizens of Ourtown" is a simple and uncontroversial goal. However, to make it more meaningful, it was translated into the following subcategories:

1 The basic *physical goal* of the community is to achieve and maintain a safe and healthy environment that will have order, form, and beauty.
2 The basic *social goal* of the community is to ensure the widest range of opportunities for the enrichment of the life of each and every citizen.

3 The basic *economic goal* of the community is to attain an economy capable of sustaining business and employment opportunities and a rising standard of living for each citizen.

4 The basic *management goal* of the community is to provide a form of local government that will be responsive to the needs of the citizens and that will provide services and leadership by the most efficient and democratic means possible.

These goals are directed toward the development of a quality city. They are meaningful but still quite broad and uncontroversial. To make them operational, they were translated into more specific categories representing key results areas.

Key Results Areas

The top management of Ourtown divided the development goals of the city into the following eleven distinctive and functional categories:

1 Education
2 Housing
3 Health
4 Recreation and culture
5 Social services
6 Economic development
7 Utilities
8 Public safety
9 Transportation
10 Intergovernmental relations
11 Environment and design
12 Human resource development

At this level there is more chance for controversy in terms of how the city responsibilities are to be described and which ones (out of a large number of possibilities) are to be included in the primary list. Here again, however, such a list is relatively uncontroversial, even though more specific aims are identified. As specific programs, objectives, and action plans are set forth, there may be disagreement regarding priorities and means of implementation. For example, "improved transportation" can be easily accepted. However, when alternatives such as rapid transit versus more freeways are proposed, there is often heated and prolonged debate. Moreover, achieving a goal of "reduced crime" may require so many resources that it precludes major new programs in the transportation area. Recreation and culture programs compete for the same dollars that could be allocated to social services. Someone has to decide on priorities and allocate resources accordingly.

The overall mission and key results areas may endure over long periods of time. Specific programs or projects designed to meet objectives within the key results areas are more changeable. They are often increased or decreased, even started or stopped, depending on resources available from outside systems—such as general federal revenue sharing or specific (restricted) grants for training, law enforcement assistance, or housing. It is important that the hierarchy of goals be developed explicitly so they will be feasible and supportive rather than contradictory. Once developed and made public, they become the guidelines for planning and controlling organizational endeavors over varying periods of time.

Value judgments are made at all stages of the goal-setting process. It is not a simple process of deciding what is right or wrong, good or bad; it is usually a choice between two very good programs that would benefit some or all of the citizens. However, resource constraints may allow only 20 percent of the proposals to be funded. The values of key administrators come into play in evaluating and ranking the benefit/cost ratios for a new computer, more gardeners for city parks, a new fire truck, equipment for a senior citizens' recreation center, or an alcoholism treatment-rehabilitation program. The value aspects (what is good or desirable) of the above decisions are relatively obvious. In many decisions and actions, however, values and ethical considerations are not clear. Given the amount of attention focused on public officials in the post-Watergate era, it is important for city administrators to consider explicitly the values and ethical standards that will guide decision making. Citizens have increasing expectations for moral conduct on the part of their elected officials and appointed managers.[8]

Technology

The technological system of the city has at least three aspects: (1) the technology of developing and sustaining cities, (2) the equipment, knowledge, and skill involved in delivering services to citizens, and (3) the managerial process involved in planning and controlling city operations. The direct interrelationship of technological advance and urban development is quite evident over the last 100 years.

The thirty years following the Civil War saw a marked acceleration and clear convergence of technology and urbanization. The shape and character of the modern American city were largely cast in that period. With the invention of the elevator and the electric light, with a new capacity to control disease and dispose of waste, with the ability to provide water, gas, and electricity to a wide public, and with the beginnings of new forms of communication such as telephone and telegraphy, life in the American city changed profoundly. . . .

---

8 Frank P. Sherwood, "Professional Ethics," *Public Management,* June 1975, pp. 13–14.

More than any other force the streetcar made possible the metropolitan suburb and ended the dependence of the middle and laboring classes on walking distance between home and place of work. [9]

Technological advancement brought advantages and disadvantages. Skyscrapers and elevators allowed the concentrations of economic activity and people but resulted in overcrowding, noise, and polluted air. Streetcars and automobiles provided opportunities for spreading out but required substantial resources for the many other elements of a transportation system. Increasing demands for citizen services have given impetus to technological improvements in order to provide effective, efficient service with the scarce resources available.

Operative Technology

Many functions, such as police and fire protection, sanitation, and public utilities, had their beginnings in city governments. The technology involved has often been a response to necessity. Primitive open sewers have been replaced with underground systems and elaborate treatment facilities. The garbage dump has been replaced by a process of sorting, reclaiming and recycling, compacting, and planned land filling. The technology of police work has progressed dramatically and now includes sophisticated mechanical and electronic equipment, fast-access information files, and helicopters. Knowledge gained from the physical and behavioral sciences is used in the prevention and detection of crime and the deterrence and apprehension of its perpetrators. Similarly, there has been continual technological progress in fire-fighting equipment. One of the most dramatic technological advancements in recent years is the deployment of emergency medical service via fire department aid cars and highly skilled technicians.

The most visible and tangible technology in the city is the transportation system—streets, freeways, bridges, subways, and traffic controls, plus a variety of public vehicles. It is becoming increasingly difficult to fund new construction, and adequate maintenance of elaborate and aging facilities is also a major concern. [10]

Administrative Technology

The basic process of city government is service delivery and record keeping. The equipment involved in record keeping has evolved from stone tablets to quills and scrolls and then to typewriters and bookkeeping machines. Many medium to large cities today have computerized word-processing systems as well as computers for data processing and information retrieval systems.

The knowledge aspect of technology is evident in modern city administration. The methods of scientific management, industrial engineering, and sys-

---

9 Samuel Bask Warner, Jr., "Streetcar Suburbs: The Consequences," in Kramer and Holborn, op. cit., p. 278.
10 Peter Nye, "The Wearing Out of Urban America," *Nation's Cities,* October 1977, pp. 8–12.

tems analysis have been applied to day-to-day operations. Budgeting techniques are widely used for planning and controlling organizational activities. Formalized methods of long-range planning (LRP), management by objectives and results (MBO/R), and planning-programming-budgeting systems (PPBS) are used by administrators in many cities. [11]

Civil service exams were part of the administrative scene in ancient China. Since that time, public service has been a combination (with relative emphasis shifting from time to time) of merit and spoils systems. Merit systems require that employees be recruited, selected, transferred, and promoted on the basis of their relative ability, knowledge, and skills, without regard for political beliefs or activity. Spoils systems allow elected officials to appoint supporters, friends, and relatives to administrative positions regardless of their technical and/or managerial qualifications. A typical approach at all levels of government today is a combination of (1) middle- and lower-level positions protected by civil service rules and (2) a top level of positions that are exempt from such rules and appointed by elected officials. City managers can use a combination of competitive examinations, interviewing, and assessment center approaches in the selection of their department directors.

Applied behavioral science techniques have been used in many city situations with the aim of solving specific problems and improving the ability of the organization to recognize and solve problems on a continuing basis. The action-research approach of organization development (OD) has received widespread attention. It has been facilitated by the availability of federal grant funds that are earmarked for organization improvement endeavors.

Technology and Productivity

Over the last fifty years employment in the service sector of the economy has grown dramatically, caused both by an increase in the demand for services and a relatively slow increase in output per work-hour in the service sector, including government at all levels. "Most service industries are inherently less subject to technological change than the rest of the economy." [12] In recent years computerization has been a major factor in improving productivity in government services, but opportunities exist for substantial improvements by utilizing other kinds of technology.

During the 1970s the National Science Foundation funded a number of demonstration projects under the heading "technology transfer." The basic aim was to facilitate the transfer of both operative and administrative technology developed in the private sector to municipal government organizations. As an example, Boeing Company employees worked with employees in the city of Ta-

---

[11] George L. Morrisey, *Management By Objectives and Results in the Public Sector,* Addison-Wesley Publishing Company, Reading, Mass., 1976.

[12] Edward F. Renshaw, "Productivity," *The Journal of Urban Analysis,* Vol. 4, No. 2 (1977), p. 302.

coma, Washington, on a variety of projects, including solid waste management, automatic fire hydrants, court scheduling, and telecommunication systems. A number of success stories have been noted in other cities as well. [13] The process is likely to continue in the future if local managers are involved in problem identification and solution, rather than having technology transfer done to them or for them by outside "experts." [14]

Structure

The organization structure of the city always has both political and managerial considerations. A combination of elected officials and appointed administrators makes up the top management of most city governments. Political overtones are heaviest when there are partisan candidates, a full-time council with members coming from specific districts or wards, and a full-time elected mayor, who may appoint top-level officials on the basis of political considerations rather than managerial-technical expertise. The farther the spoils system is extended down through the ranks, the greater the role of politics in organizational life. Although many cities emphasize a nonpartisan approach, political pressures are inevitable, but the pressures are decreased somewhat if council members are elected at large rather than from specific districts.

Municipal reform has been a focus of attention for many years. Emphasis on political rather than managerial approaches to city government has been attacked for its waste, extravagance, graft, and corruption. Of course, such abuses and indictments did not apply to all city governments; some were quite well managed. However, the abuses were evident enough to foster concerted effort toward change. The goals of the reformers were to retain the democratic process *and* develop effective and efficient administration of city affairs. These goals can be elaborated as follows: [15]

1 Administrative arrangements and processes
    a Unification of governmental power, but separation of functions
    b Enhancement of the power of the chief executive through executive integration and provision of stronger managerial tools, such as budgetary and personnel controls
    c Removal of partisan politics from administration through the establishment of merit as the basis for personnel decisions
    d Application of modern managerial techniques, drawn principally from business practices

13 "Aerospace Technology Goes to Town," *Industry Week,* Jan. 8, 1973, pp. 55–58.
14 William V. Donaldson, "Let Cities, Not Technologists, Identify Their Problems, Develop Solutions," *The American City,* April 1973, pp. 38–39.
15 David M. Welborn, "The Environment and Role of the Administrator," in Banovetz (ed.), op. cit., pp. 80–81.

2 Political arrangements and processes
    a Simplification of the task of voters through reducing the number of elected officials and increasing public awareness by improved public reporting and the activities of independent citizen research organizations
    b Enlargement of the capacity of voters to control elected officials through opening the nominating processes and establishment of procedures for initiative, referendum, and recall
    c Insulation of local from partisan politics by holding municipal elections on a nonpartisan basis, electing councils at large rather than from wards, separating the timing of municipal from state and national elections, and home rule

These goals seem appealing, but they could be contradictory. For example, responding in full to expressed citizen desires may preclude fiscal responsibility. However, it is assumed that the electorate wants effective and efficient management of an "appropriate" level of services. Various organizational designs can be used to achieve these purposes; they typically include both legislative and executive functions. Council-mayor and council-manager are two basic approaches that can work, depending on the situation and the specific individuals involved.

Council-Manager Form

The council-manager approach was developed in the early 1900s and has been widely adopted in the United States. By 1978 more than 3000 cities were using this form, including Cincinnati, Phoenix, and Dallas. Many variations can be found, but the basic structure involves a small (perhaps five to nine people) council elected on a nonpartisan, at-large basis. There may be an elected mayor who serves as presiding officer on the council and is an official representative of the city in a variety of capacities. Typically, the mayor and council members serve on a part-time basis. The council appoints a full-time professional manager to be the chief executive officer in the city administration. The city manager has authority and responsibility for the next level of administrators, who are appointed on the basis of experience, technical expertise, and managerial competence. They serve at the pleasure of the city manager, who serves at the pleasure of the council.

Theoretically, the council is concerned with setting policy and the manager is responsible for implementing the programs within established policy guidelines. In practice these clear-cut demarcations become somewhat fuzzy.

Organization Chart for Ourtown

Figure 22.1 shows an example of a city manager form of municipal government. There are nine council members, elected by the citizens. There is an

Figure 22.1   Organization Chart for Ourtown

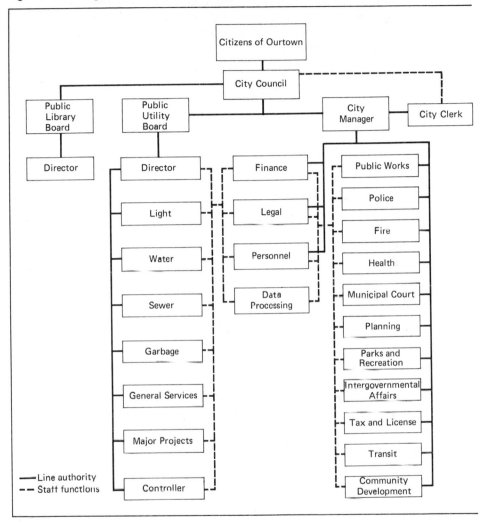

elected mayor, who serves as presiding officer; all elected officials serve on a part-time basis. The council appoints policy-making boards for areas such as libraries and utilities. The city manager has authority and responsibility for all general government functions, as indicated. In this example the director of utilities is responsible to the public utilities board and the council directly, rather than to the city manager. In many cities the director of utilities would report to the city manager. Finance, legal, personnel, and data processing services are provided centrally to all utilities and general government departments. The city clerk provides staff services to the council and is directly responsible to the city manager for other day-to-day functions. The civil service board and the planning commission are not shown on this simplified version of the organizational structure.

The chart of authority-responsibility and reporting relationships does not indicate the true complexity of a city organization. Many programmatic efforts cross departmental lines. Projects are often designed and developed by ad hoc committees or task forces with members from several departments. Economic development and organization improvement are examples of such programmatic efforts.

Psychosocial System

We began our discussion of the city with a definition emphasizing people interacting in meaningful relationships. While it is a physical entity and includes structures and equipment, the essence of the city is people. Therefore, our understanding would not be complete without considering the roles and relationships of the people involved.

Citizens and Clients

The municipal organization exists to serve its clients, the citizens of the city. In bygone days the town meeting provided an opportunity for interested citizens to meet and express themselves directly on community issues. For most cities in the U.S. this approach is simply not feasible. Therefore, other means must be devised for involving people in the issues of the day. The basic process involves electing representatives to make decisions.

Individuals can make their opinions known by telephoning, writing, or personally contacting elected officials or appointed managers. Council meetings are open to citizens, who often do more than observe. Public hearings are standard operating procedure for most important decisions such as major projects, zoning changes, or significant adjustments in service delivery.

Special interest groups—neighborhood associations, ethnic minorities, or municipal workers—make their positions known on important issues that are under consideration by the city administration. Citizen complaints range from a noisy neighbor or a loose dog to more serious matters, such as dangerous traffic patterns or potentially harmful pollution from local plants. Without a systematic means of obtaining input, management can develop an inaccurate perception of collective opinion, because outspoken individuals and/or interest groups may not be truly representative.

Periodic client-citizen surveys provide a means of assessing overall opinion. However, the results are often mixed and may not provide clear-cut guidelines for decision making. In recent years, attempts have been made to include representative citizens in the planning-budgeting process. In some cases, this approach has been mandated by the federal government as a necessary ingredient in proposals for grants. The trend in the 1970s has been toward more and more citizen involvement, and this interactive process is likely to continue.

Top Management

The top management of the city includes elected council members, a mayor, other elected officials, appointed board members (such as civil service, public works, parks, and libraries) and appointed administrators, such as the city manager and directors of the various departments. The roles and relationships among top managers and between them and other employees and citizens vary a great deal according to the circumstances. In very large cities council members may have full-time positions and large individual staffs to facilitate their work. If the mayor is elected separately, there is the potential for considerable conflict unless the legislative and executive functions are spelled out rather clearly.

In the city manager form of government, council members are typically employed only part time, and the legislative policy function is easier to keep separate from the day-to-day administrative functions, which are delegated to the city manager. However, it is never easy to separate these functions completely. Some council members have a propensity to "dabble" in administrative details and do not hesitate to influence department heads directly. Sometimes department directors lobby directly with council members in an attempt to sell programs that may not have been approved at the city manager level.

The city manager is deeply involved in current issues and policy formulation via formal proposals to the council and/or personal lobbying with individual members or subgroups. The city manager is typically in a powerful position because of the vast amount of information that is funneled through that office from within the organization and from outside. The city manager's office is the focal point for relationships with other local governmental units as well as with state and federal agencies. Thus, the city manager can screen or embellish information in order to influence council decisions.

Neither of the extremes—council dominating the manager or the manager dominating the council—are functional in the long run. The city will probably be best served when the manager and council work together in an atmosphere of trust and cooperation, each with a well-defined sphere of responsibility but with ultimate formal responsibility residing with the council.

Today, managers and councils work as a team. They must. The problems and issues are much too complex and difficult for councils to work in the policy areas without a full understanding of the administrative issues. Moreover, the complexity of the issues is such that councils need and expect the advice, information, and assistance the manager can provide in dealing with these issues. Equally important, many administrative issues are much too politically sensitive for the manager to proceed without keeping councils fully informed. [16]

The same prescription is relevant for mayors and councils. However, an elected mayor has a different power base than an appointed manager, and may

16 Arthur A. Mendonsa, "Council-Manager Relations and the Changing Community Environment," *Public Management*, September 1977, p. 7.

feel more directly responsible to the people. The veto process obviously affects the council-mayor relationship when there are significant differences of opinion. The council-mayor approach can work smoothly if the legislative and executive branches develop good relationships, common values, and joint goals, but the potential remains for disagreements and inaction.

The concept of professionalization best characterizes the top management in many cities over the past several decades. While specialized training, such as engineering, has always been essential for areas such as utilities and public works, many administrative positions required no special degree or certification of minimal competence. Increasingly, however, a bachelor's or master's degree in public administration is becoming more the rule than the exception. The International City Management Association and its affiliate, the National Training and Development Service for State and Local Government, have made concerted efforts to involve city managers and other top-level administrators in continuing education. Professional associations in other specialized areas such as finance, data processing, personnel, fire, police, and transit have also been involved in sharing ideas and professionalizing their respective functions. Typically, efforts have been devoted to improve both technical expertise and managerial capability. These efforts appear to be paying off in terms of the general esteem in which city administrators are held by the citizenry.

Employees

The organizational climate of cities has changed significantly during the post-WW II era. Total nonagricultural employment increased about 70 percent from 1950 to 1975. Over the same period, local government employment increased 172 percent (nearly triple), from 3,228,000 to 8,828,000. As a percent of total nonagricultural employment, local government employees increased from 7 percent in 1950 to 11.5 percent in 1975.[17] Thus, the psychosocial system has been affected by the number of people holding municipal jobs. Moreover, the employee mix is changing. The number of state and local government welfare workers nearly doubled from 1965 to 1975, while the number of street and highway workers increased less than four percent.[18]

Another factor is the civil service system, designed to remedy the negative consequences of the spoils or patronage system. Emphasis on demonstrated merit through hiring and promotion examination processes is a primary means of overcoming capricious decision making, cronyism, or favoritism based on irrelevant criteria.[19] However, the system and the employees involved have been maligned because of the rigidity involved and the difficulty in removing "incompe-

---

[17] U.S. Bureau of the Census, *Statistical Abstract of the United States: 1976,* Washington, D.C., 1976, p. 284.

[18] Nye, op. cit., p. 10.

[19] F. Arnold McDermott, "Merit Systems Under Fire," *Public Personnel Management,* July–August 1976, pp. 225–233.

tent" workers. Some see the civil service system as a haven of mediocrity because of the lack of emphasis on financial incentives and the difficulty involved in removing marginal employees. The system obviously has advantages and disadvantages that need to be recognized.

The lack of effectiveness and efficiency in the delivery of city services may be as much a reflection on the complex system as it is on the inadequacy of its employees. Participant satisfaction may be low because of inability to perform up to their own expectations and aspirations, which in turn is caused by the constraints of local, state, and federal regulations, countervailing pressures from outside interests, and traditional operating procedures.

In terms of worker alienation in our society, city employees are not significantly different. Age and education seem to be more important factors than occupation or sector of the economy in determining employee expectations and job satisfaction. In a study comparing public and private employees, it was found that:

Working conditions and compensation ranked high in the estimation of both groups. Self-actualization, a need level normally assumed to emerge only late in one's climb up the need hierarchy, was ranked *most* important by the public employees. This group has clearly adopted some of the characteristics of professional employees, and may not be satisfied until they are treated accordingly. [20]

Most efforts to improve the quality of work life and productivity have come in the private sector, but there are some examples from public agencies. [21] There is an opportunity for local government to set an example; it "can substantially influence the quality of work life in the total society by direct strategies to improve the quality of work life of its own employees." [22]

An important aspect of the psychosocial system in the 1970s has been affirmative action in the hiring, development, and promotion of women and minorities. The city is often a focal point because of the need to set an example for local private organizations. Government at all levels has been relatively more successful in this endeavor than the private sector has been. The backlash from these efforts is the charge of reverse discrimination; some male and nonminority candidates claim they are better qualified according to test scores and other traditional factors. A critical aspect of this process has been the refinement of screening processes to ensure that the criteria used are in fact relevant to the jobs under consideration. Many traditional barriers have been broken down as evidenced by

---

20 John Newstrom, et al., "Motivating the Public Employee: Fact Versus Fiction," *Public Personnel Management,* January–February 1976, pp. 67–72.

21 Raymond A. Katzell, Penney Bienstock, and Paul H. Faerstein, *A Guide to Worker Productivity Experiments in the United States 1971–1975,* New York University Press, New York, 1977.

22 Michael Beer and James W. Driscoll, "Strategies for Change," in J. Richard Hackman and J. Lloyd Suttle (eds.), *Improving Life at Work,* Goodyear Publishing Company, Inc., Santa Monica, Calif., 1977, p. 441.

the increasing number of women and minority employees that can be found in police and fire departments.

Another important dimension of the psychosocial system of the city is collective bargaining. For many years, city employees' notion of holding "public service" jobs seemed to place them "above" collective bargaining and unionization. Such attitudes paralleled those of teachers and nurses. However, as pay and working conditions lagged behind those of workers in the private sector, city employees determined that depending on the good will of the city administration was not enough. Therefore, in recent years city employees have joined unions and engaged in collective bargaining. Their success has been noticed by the "unrepresented" employees, and the trend seems to be accelerating—among office workers as well as skilled craftspeople, transit drivers, firefighters, and police officers. National surveys of public opinion have yielded confusing results, some indicating increasing tolerance of unionization and strikes by public employees, others indicating the opposite.[23] Of course, local opinion would be greatly affected by particular circumstances.

To confound the system even further, strikes are becoming more commonplace. When collective bargaining became acceptable, there seemed to be an understanding that firefighters, police officers, and transit drivers would not strike. It was expected that essential public services would not be interrupted, particularly when loss of property and even life might be at stake. This is no longer a valid assumption. Although it seems that a strike in such areas would be a powerful weapon, recent experience has shown otherwise. Management has weathered strikes by public safety workers and been supported by citizens, who urged not giving in to acts they deemed "intimidation or extortion."[24] In addition, such action has changed the traditional status and role of workers who had been building their image as skilled professionals. The image of the friendly firefighters becomes tarnished as they picket city hall while your house burns down. Police officers also tend to lose prestige after formal strike actions or the informal blue flu. For many medium to large cities, union-management relations is a complex process because there may be fifteen or more separate unions involved.

Managerial System

The chief executive officer of the city (the mayor in some cases or the city manager in the example we have used) is the focal point of the managerial system. Within legislative and policy guidelines, the city manager is responsible for planning and controlling operations.

23 Steve W. Panyan, "Local Surveys as Community Indicators Showing Attitudes toward Unions," *Public Personnel Management,* September–October 1976, pp. 368–372.

24 John L. Taylor, "Fire Fighters Strike," *Public Management,* February 1976, p. 6.

Strategic, Coordinative, and Operating Subsystems

The council, mayor, and/or city manager, with support from department directors, represent the strategic subsystem of the city. They interact with the external environment and are responsible for long-range, comprehensive planning. They define or reaffirm the overall mission of city government, identify key results areas, and develop short-range objectives to be used in allocating resources and establishing budgets.

The operating subsystem of the city is diverse and represents all of the elements of service delivery, including police protection, fire protection, transportation, street repair, utilities (light, water, sewer, and garbage collection), licensing, and judicial processes. A wide variety of unskilled, semiskilled, and highly skilled workers are involved in city operations. File clerks, ditch diggers, detectives, engineers, artists, and lawyers all provide services required to meet the needs of citizens in a modern city.

These efforts are coordinated by middle management, whose responsibility it is to translate plans into action steps and to integrate activities within and across departments. Formal coordination is achieved through the hierarchy, but a great deal of informal integration is accomplished via ad hoc committees that include members from several departments. An urban renewal project, for example, would require the coordination of legal procedures, public relations, public works, utilities, and other functional specialties. A task force with representatives from each of these areas would be responsible for internal integration as well as coordination with interested parties outside the system.

Program Analysis

Managerial responsibility can also be viewed in the context of problem or opportunity sensing and solving. With limited resources, it is important to focus attention on high-priority issues. Each key results area (p. 543) should be scrutinized continually for gaps between expected and actual results or current conditions and desired conditions. Alternative solutions should be generated and evaluated in terms of feasibility and benefit-cost ratios. This type of program analysis is essential before resources can be allocated most appropriately. Figure 22.2 shows illustrative questions within several of the general categories previously identified. Such questions require concerted managerial attention and analysis. Solving them requires creativity, commitment to the implementation of action steps, and diligent followup to monitor progress. These essential steps require no special competence; rather, the main ingredients are sensitivity to the issues, open-minded consideration of new ideas, common sense, and hard work.

Figure 22.2 Illustrative Questions for Program Analysis

Law Enforcement

1 What is the most effective way of distributing limited police forces—by time of day, day of week, and geographical location?

2 What types of police units (foot patrolmen, one- or two-man police cars, special task forces, canine corps units, or others) should be used and in what mix?

3 What types of equipment (considering both current and new technologies) should be used for weaponry, for communications, and for transportation?

4 How can the judicial process be improved to provide more expeditious service, keep potentially dangerous persons from running loose, and at the same time protect the rights of the innocent?

5 How can criminal detention institutions be improved to maximize the probability of rehabilitation, while remaining a deterrent to further crime?

Fire Protection

1 Where should fire stations be located, and how many are needed?

2 How should firefighting units be deployed; and how large should units be?

3 What types of equipment should be used for communications, transportation, and firefighting?
4 Are there fire prevention activities, such as inspection of potential fire hazards or school educational programs, that can be used effectively?

Health and Social Services

1 What mix of treatment programs should do the most to meet the needs of the expected mix of clients?

2 What prevention programs are desirable for the groups that seem most likely to suffer particular ailments?

Housing

1 To what extent can housing code enforcement programs be used to decrease the number of families living in substandard housing? Will such programs have an adverse effect on the overall supply of low-income housing in the community?

2 What is the appropriate mix of code enforcement with other housing programs to make housing in the community adequate?

3 What is the best mix of housing rehabilitation, housing maintenance, and new construction to improve the quantity and quality of housing?

Employment

1 What relative support should be given to training and employment programs which serve different client groups?

2 What should be the mix among outreach programs, training programs, job-finding and matching programs, antidiscrimination programs, and post-employment follow-up programs?

Figure 22.2   Illustrative Questions for Program Analysis (Continued)

<table>
<tr><td align="center">Waste</td></tr>
</table>

1 How should waste be collected and disposed of, given alternative visual, air, water, and pollution standards?
2 What specific equipment and routings should be used?

<table>
<tr><td align="center">Recreation and Leisure</td></tr>
</table>

1 What type, location, and size of recreation facilities should be provided for those desiring them?
2 How should recreation facilities be divided among summer and winter, daytime and night-time, and indoor and outdoor activities?
3 What, and how many, special summer programs should be made available for out-of-school youths?
4 What charges, if any, should be made to users, considering such factors as differential usage and ability to pay?

Harry Hatry, et al., *Program Analysis for State and Local Governments,* The Urban Institute, Washington, D.C., 1976, p. 17.

Designing Structures and Processes: An Example

A typical approach to improving service delivery in complex metropolitan areas is consolidation. This managerial strategy is based on the assumption that spreading technical expertise and administrative overhead across more operations will result in increased effectiveness and efficiency. On the other hand, a single bureaucratic hierarchy with standardized operations may not meet the needs of people in particular circumstances. The benefits of both centralization and decentralization can be realized by differentiating the various functions and designing appropriate structures and processes.

In Los Angeles County the Lakewood Plan has been developed as a midrange strategy between one overall hierarchy for the region and a "crazy quilt" of governments with varying degrees of cooperation, competition, and conflict. It is an open system in a complex environment, structured to meet various community needs and to take advantage of economies of scale in certain functions.

The concept of organizational systems would suggest an alternative and more complex integration process which may involve coordinating bodies such as associations of area governments, special districts for area wide problems such as air and water pollution control, ad hoc and scheduled negotiation among jurisdictions, and a mediating authority such as the court system to resolve disputed issues. As defined in organizational systems, these processes use varying procedures of standardization, planning, and mutual adjustment.[25]

25 Herman L. Boschken, "Organization Logic for Concurrent Government in Metropolitan Areas," *Academy of Management Review,* January 1976. p. 9.

A system of interrelated local governments can consolidate where appropriate (perhaps transportation or sewers) and maintain local control of other functions (perhaps fire protection or education). Within a particular area, such as public safety, some functions may be localized (neighborhood police stations) and others consolidated (criminal information systems). This approach allows the use of both technical expertise and local knowledge in planning and implementing service delivery. Differentiation of types and levels of service requires a relatively complex system of integrating mechanisms. However, it is worth the time and effort if the system preserves representative government, matches service delivery to the needs of a variety of constituents, and increases the probability that accountability will be based on performance.

The external environment and internal conditions of the city are likely to become more complex and turbulent. Systems concepts can be helpful in understanding dynamic interrelationships. Contingency views are necessary in order to design appropriate structures and processes. A variety of approaches can be successful in coordinating organizational endeavor and in cooperative ventures with other local governmental units. In the future, effective management will depend on increasingly astute decision making and dynamic leadership, as well as on committed and motivated employees.

Summary

Cities are complex combinations of people, economic activities, political processes, and legal boundaries. Urbanization is a pervasive phenomenon that reflects the basic human tendency to congregate. The environment of the city is becoming increasingly turbulent and includes other governmental units (local, state, and federal), businesses, and citizens who are often represented by special interest groups.

The general purpose of the city is to protect and promote the health, welfare, and safety of its residents. Within this broad charter many specific functional areas are designed and organized to deliver essential services. A variety of technologies is involved in carrying out day-to-day activities and in the administrative processes necessary for planning and controlling city programs.

The structure and process of city government has been developed to reflect both political and managerial considerations. Technical and administrative expertise are being emphasized in selecting managers at all levels in order to increase effectiveness and efficiency.

The psychosocial system of cities is complex and dynamic. Citizens are becoming actively involved in the functioning of their cities—both formally and informally. Strategic planning and policy formulation is an interactive process that includes elected officials and key managers. City employees are seeking more participation in decision making; they are joining collective bargaining units and strikes are becoming less exceptional. Civil service or merit systems provide a safeguard against capricious personnel decisions but also include rigidities that constrain management's attempts to motivate people by rewarding good performance.

Managing a city requires balanced attention to strategic, operating, and coordinative tasks. The diversity of functions calls for considerable differentiation in approaches to planning and controlling activities. Integration of effort is accomplished via the formal hierarchy, ad hoc interdepartmental committees, and program or project task forces.

Questions and Problems

1 Define a city from several perspectives. What aspects are most important from the point of view of organization and management?

2 Identify the general environmental factors and/or forces that affect the managerial process in United States cities. Identify specific examples of such factors and/or forces that are affecting your city's management.

3 How have the goals of cities changed? Discuss the issue of "quality of life" in formulating city goals.

4 "Technology has made cities both *possible* and *impossible.*" Do you agree? Why or why not?

5 Give specific examples of both operative and administrative technology in the city context. What significant changes have taken place in your city over the past ten years?

6 Why was the council-manager form of city government developed? Does the theory work in practice?

7 Compare the organization structure of your city with the example in Figure 22.1. What are the similarities and differences?

8 Compare and contrast the psychosocial system of a city with that of a business organization.

9 Discuss the leadership role for (a) an elected mayor and (b) an appointed city manager.

10 What approach does your city use in planning and controlling its operations? Are any specific techniques used, such as MBO/R, PPBS, or zero-base budgeting?

Self examination, if it is thorough enough, is nearly always the first step toward change. No one who learns to know himself remains just what he was before.
Thomas Mann

It is an unfinished society that we offer the world—a society that is forever committed to change, to improvement and to growth, that will never stagnate in the certitude of ideology or the finalities of dogma.
John F. Kennedy

Creative organizations or societies are rarely tidy. Some tolerance for inconsistencies, for profusion of purpose and strategies, and for conflict is the price of freedom and vitality.
John Gardner

Future shock is a time phenomenon, a product of the greatly accelerated rate of change in society. It arises from the superimposition of a new culture on an old one. It is culture shock in one's own society.
Alvin Toffler

The world is cluttered up with unfinished business in the form of projects that might have been successful, if only at the tide point someone's patience had turned to active impatience.
Robert Updegraff

We have crossed the threshold from a society that was bound by lack of technical knowledge to one where such knowledge is available in abundance—and becoming ever more so with the passing years. The problem is no longer how to generate new knowledge. Rather, the crucial question is where and how to use it to improve the quality of human life.
Michael Michaelis

Organizational Change and the Future

8

Many organizations have an indefinite life span. Others are more temporal. In any case, organizations must adjust to changing conditions. They must also maintain a system viable enough to accomplish their primary tasks. In short, they need stability and continuity as well as adaptation and innovation.

Organizational change is the topic of Chapter 23. We trace the impetus for change (various external and internal forces) and discuss the typical sources of resistance to change. An important consideration is the development of a process of change that is an integral part of the managerial system. Particular attention is focused on a planned-change process that includes problem sensing, diagnosis, action planning, implementation, and followup. Issues such as coping with differences and managing conflict creatively are also discussed.

Finally, in Chapter 24, we look at management and organization in the future. It is a good probability that uncertainty (turbulent environment, changing value systems, accelerating technology, and other factors) will cause our speculations to be only partially right, at best. In spite of these hazards, we provide our expectations concerning the most significant changes in organizations and in managerial practices.

Organizational Change
Twenty-three

Organizations inevitably change because they are open systems in constant interaction with their environment. Although the impetus for change can be attributed to external and/or internal stimuli, the underlying force is the openness of system boundaries that allows new demands, technologies, skills, and values to affect the system. The concept of organizational change will be discussed in terms of the following topics.

Stability and Continuity as Well as Adaptation and Innovation
Sources of Impetus for Change
Planned Change—Dimensions, Process, and Focus
Resistance to Change
Implementing Planned Change
Dealing with Differences
Approaches to Conflict Resolution

Stability and Continuity as Well as Adaptation and Innovation

Considerable attention has been focused on the need for organizations to adapt to changing conditions. It is popular to emphasize the importance of change without recognizing the need for system maintenance and stability. Any organization must maintain enough stability to function satisfactorily and yet not allow itself to become static, ultraconservative, or oblivious to the need to adapt to changing conditions. A realistic view of organizational change recognizes that both stability and adaptation are essential to survival and growth.

There is, therefore, a clearly recognized need to learn how to construct, how to adapt, how to change organization in a manner better matched to human aspiration. How to organize human effort effectively into complex, specialized structures within a rapidly

563

changing environment, while maintaining the integrity of the system, is a major concern of our time. [1]

In large measure, changes in individuals and organizations are not readily discernible by those who interact with them on a day-to-day basis. For example, an increase of twenty pounds or gray hair around the temples would be much more noticeable to a friend whom you had not seen for ten years than to a member of the household or a working companion.

Similarly, organizations appear more stable to participants than to clients or observers who interact only intermittently with them. A series of small, incremental changes can compound into a significant difference over a long period of time.

Stability and continuity are important attributes to the basic functions of organisms or organizations. An individual's cardiovascular system is essentially the same from birth to death, while increasing in capacity to match body growth. Its overall performance can be modified to meet changed demands—those of a distance runner or swimmer, for example. And short-run increases in capacity can be accommodated to meet the needs of strenuous exercise or a violent struggle for survival. However, the system quickly reverts to normal functioning when the emergency situation no longer exists.

Although organizations are not necessarily destined for a life cycle of birth, growth, maturity, decline, and death, many aspects of such a cycle are apparent. Creation, rapid growth, and bankruptcy are obvious examples. They are traumatic times in the life of an organization when adaptation and innovation are often critical for survival. For organizations that do reach maturity, stability and continuity (maintaining the system) become relatively more important. While changes do occur, the basic functions or operating systems necessary to carry out the transformation process—producing goods or services—remain essentially the same.

Ends and Means

Individuals and organizations undergo changes in both ends and means—the goals they strive for and the methods used. Goals such as survival, profitability, share of the market, service to clients, and growth seem to be quite stable. The means of achieving these goals, however, vary because of factors such as competitive conditions, government regulations, and technological progress. The product range for television manufacturers has widened significantly over the years in order to meet increasingly diverse demands of consumers. Football teams have pursued the same objective through the use of a wide variety of means— single wing, double wing, basic T, split T, pro set, I formation, and wishbone.

---

1 Alexander B. Trowbridge in Wilbur M. McFeely, *Organization Change: Perceptions and Realities,* The Conference Board, Inc., New York, 1972, p. vii.

In rare cases the opposite is true; means stay the same while ends are adjusted. When polio vaccine became a reality, the March of Dimes organization changed its focus of attention to birth defects. The basic means for obtaining and channeling funds remained essentially the same. Other examples of this phenomenon are apparent—Public Interest Research Group and Common Cause, for example. The same investigatory approach is used to increase public awareness and indignation—whether the goal is improved auto safety, better quality meat, congressional reform, more information about campaign contributions, or lower ticket prices for professional sports.

It is also important to recognize that there can be simultaneous adjustments to both ends and means. A goal of racial balance in schools may require new means—redistricting and/or busing (voluntary or mandatory), for example. Acceptance of corporate responsibility for pollution control may require a significantly different production process.

Dynamic Equilibrium

Management is charged with the responsibility for maintaining a dynamic equilibrium by diagnosing situations and designing adjustments that are most appropriate for coping with current conditions. A dynamic equilibrium for an organization would include the following dimensions:

1 Enough stability to facilitate achievement of current goals
2 Enough continuity to ensure orderly change in either ends or means
3 Enough adaptability to react appropriately to external opportunities and demands as well as changing internal conditions
4 Enough innovativeness to allow the organization to be proactive (initiate changes) when conditions warrant

This process is obviously a delicate balancing act, which gets more difficult with the accelerating nature of change, both internally and externally.

Sources of Impetus for Change

The impetus for organizational change comes from many sources. We will discuss this process in terms of the model previously set forth—the environmental suprasystem as well as organizational subsystems (goals and values, technical, structural, psychosocial, and managerial). We are using the systems framework as a means to illustrate the various sources of impetus for change in organizations.

Environment

Organization change is often stimulated by changes in its environment. The *general* environment for any organization in society includes technological, economic, legal, political, demographic, ecological, and cultural factors. Change in these spheres seems to be occurring at an accelerating rate—the pace of change is increasing. Within the general environment, each organization has a more specific set of factors (its *task* environment) that are relevant to its decision-making processes. For example, aerospace technology is likely to be more relevant for an airplane manufacturer than for a food processor. The federal government is a part of the general environment for all organizations, but the Civil Aeronautics Board is a part of the specific environment of every airline. A decision on the general rate structure might affect all airlines, while a decision about who is authorized to fly on specific routes involves only those having expressed an interest in participating.

Competition is obviously a source of impetus for change. Companies adjust their strategies and/or tactics because of new products or services provided by direct competitors, both domestic and foreign. Indirect influences are also felt. Growth in the use of mobile homes has an impact on those engaged in providing permanent housing. Increased expenditures for water skis and sailboats probably detracts from the demand for spectator sports such as baseball.

The strategic subsystem in an organization has a boundary-spanning function; it maintains an interface with its task environment and tries to maintain surveillance of the general environment as well. Organizations typically try to anticipate changes and adjust accordingly. However, some changes occur that are unanticipated and typically result in a flurry of activity to adjust or forestall the impact until the organization is in a better position to react. Economic and technological forecasting and market research are examples of boundary-spanning activities designed to keep the organization in touch with its environment and allow it to adapt and innovate appropriately.

Goals
and
Values

Another impetus for change comes from modifications of the goals of the organization. Changes in values (what is good and desirable) are also important because they lead to changes in goals. Or, if the goals remain constant, changes in values can lead to changes in what is considered "appropriate" behavior. For example, several years ago a large Western brewery was counseled to advertise in *Playboy*. Top management rejected the recommendation because there was a consensus that it was an inappropriate medium. Several years later, after a competitor had begun to advertise in *Playboy* and simultaneously increase its share of the market, management reconsidered its decision and accepted the original recommendation. Thus the goal of market share remained the same and the concept of appropriate advertising strategy was adjusted.

New goals can be imposed from external sources—government regulations concerning product safety features, for example—or they can be developed internally as the organization redefines its overall mission. Organizational strategy is a function of factors such as environmental opportunity, internal competence and resources, managerial interest and desires, and social responsibility.

Technical

The technical system is an obvious source of organizational change. New methods for processing material and/or information have provided dramatic examples. Mechanization, automation, and computerization have had widespread influence in organizations. Such changes have had considerable impact on other subsystems—structural and psychosocial, for example—within organizations. Technical changes include the form and/or function of a product (product design) or service as well as the transformation process used by the organization.

Methods used in analyzing the system (or conducting research) are also considered part of the technical subsystem. Technological forecasting has received increasing attention as organizations attempt to cope with an uncertain and dynamic environment.[2] The Delphi method has been used as a means of systematizing the response of "experts" to questionnaires about future scientific and technological progress.[3] Improvements in analysis and research increase the probability of accelerating changes in the technical subsystem of organizations. On the other hand, the process may be slowed because of problems in translating knowledge and/or technology into action.[4]

Structural

Another source of organizational change is the structural subsystem. Obviously, such changes are related to changes in other subsystems. However, adjustments in structure may be appropriate when all other aspects are relatively stable. Different ways of dividing the work and/or new means of coordination can be designed in order to make an existing organization more effective and efficient. Typical changes might include subdividing an existing department or consolidating three separate units into one department. Such adjustments to the formal ("permanent") organization will have ramifications throughout the total system.

The creation of new structural forms such as conglomerates, multinational corporations, regionwide transportation systems, and multi-unit health care

2 Jerry Richardson, "Tomorrow's Aviation: The Sky Won't Be the Only Limit," *The Futurist,* June 1977, pp. 169–177.

3 See, for example, Harper Q. North and Donald L. Pyke, " 'Probes' of the Technological Future," *Harvard Business Review,* May–June 1969, pp. 68–82; and Alan R. Fusfeld and Richard N. Foster, "The Delphi Technique: Survey and Comment," *Business Horizons,* June 1971, pp. 63–74.

4 Ronald G. Havelock and Kenneth D. Benne, "An Exploratory Study of Knowledge Utilization," in Warren G. Bennis, Kenneth D. Benne, Robert Chin, and Kenneth E. Corey (eds.), *The Planning of Change,* 3d ed., Holt, Rinehart and Winston, Inc., New York, 1976, pp. 151–164.

delivery systems usually leads to many other adjustments. Internal changes such as ad hoc committees, task forces, and program management provide an impetus for change in the organization as a whole. The informal organization—cliques and peer groups, for example—also is a source of change.

Psychosocial

The impetus for change in organizations often comes from the psychosocial system. Success in achieving organizational goals depends to a great extent on human factors. The degree to which latent human capability is tapped can often make the difference in whether or not organizational endeavors are accomplished. Therefore, changes in the morale and motivation of individuals and/or groups can have a significant impact. Group dynamics can enhance organizational performance or detract from it. Management's ability to lead and influence behavior is also a critical factor. Changes in any or all of these variables can lead to discernible changes in organizational performance.

The role of the psychosocial system is crucial in its relationship to implementing change stemming from other sources. If the change requires adaptation on the part of individuals or work groups, such factors must be considered in the overall analysis. If support is required and it is not forthcoming, the impact of a technical change can approach zero (or even be negative). We will discuss resistance to change in more detail in a later section.

Managerial

In planning and controlling activities, the managerial role involves maintaining a dynamic equilibrium between the need for organizational stability and continuity and the need for adaptation and innovation. In most organizations the manager is faced with accelerating change in both the external environmental suprasystem and the other internal organizational subsystems that affect the managerial process.

Accelerating change leads to increasing complexity. In short, the job of managers is not getting any easier. They need a tolerance for ambiguity and a coping style; they are continually involved in diagnosing situations and identifying problems or opportunities. A contingency view is important in making strategic choices—designing changes that respond to specific needs in particular circumstances.

Managers are central figures in organizational change. As decision makers, they are the ultimate change agents, whether they are centrally involved or merely guiding or coordinating activities. Obviously, change can stem from adjustments in managerial behavior per se—leadership style, approaches to planning and controlling, or degree of participation in decision making. Managers may respond to suggestions from others or actively instigate changes when the focus is more technical, structural, or psychosocial. They may use internal and/or external consultants to facilitate organizational changes.[5] Specialists in economic and market research, operations analysis, industrial relations, and organization development are examples of change agents or facilitators. However, it is useful to view the activities of these change agents as an extension of managers, who have ultimate responsibility for organization improvement endeavors.

Planned Change—Dimensions, Process, and Focus

The concept of planned change assumes that the organization in general and the manager in particular can identify gaps between current conditions and desired conditions on a variety of dimensions. This overall activity can be termed "organization improvement." At least three dimensions are relevant to this issue: (1) effectiveness, (2) efficiency, and (3) participant satisfaction. In other words, planned change efforts should be related to the question: "How can this organization be more effective, more efficient, and a more satisfying place to work?"

Short- and long-range considerations should be included in order that appropriate attention may be given to stability and continuity. Expedient changes for the sake of effectiveness (achieving goals) or for the sake of efficiency (better utilization of resources) may have dysfunctional consequences for participant satisfaction and long-run viability of the organization. Whenever the organization can identify differences between where it is and where it would like to be on any dimension, it can engage in a process of planned change—organization improvement.

Dimensions of Planned Change

Figure 23.1 shows three dimensions of planned change with illustrative problem areas, several potential foci of attention, and various improvement strategies. In-depth diagnosis would identify particular problems within these general areas—low morale, inadequate downward communication, inefficient computer programs, lack of quality control, or unwieldy organization structure, for example. Depending on the type of problem identified, an appropriate change effort can be designed. For example, if unclear goals are seen as an organization-wide problem, then an overall program of management by objectives and results would be appropriate. If interdepartmental hassles (production vs. engineering, for example) is the problem, then explicit attention to intergroup conflict resolution would be appropriate.

---

5 "Consultants Move to the Executive Suite," *Business Week,* Nov. 7, 1977, pp. 76–79.

Figure 23.1   Dimensions of Planned Change—Illustrative Problem Areas, Foci of Attention, and Improvement Strategies

Problem Areas	Foci of Attention	Improvement Strategies
Task/technology	Person	Training/education
Authority/responsibility	Role	Job design/enrichment
Motivation	Interpersonal	Management by objectives
Communication	Team/group	and results
Interaction-influence/	Intergroup	Organization behavior
leadership	Organization	modification
Problem solving/		Team building
decision making		Intergroup conflict
Goal setting/planning		resolution
Control		Survey feedback—problem
Culture/climate		sensing and solving
Conflict/cooperation		
Role definition/		
mutual expectations		

The Process of Planned Change

Over and above specific change efforts, there is the question of the organization's overall ability to engage in organization improvement endeavors—to look at itself critically. In this case the focus of attention should be on the *process of planned change* rather than on particular problems. An improved process of planned change should pay dividends because it facilitates continuing review and identification of appropriate problems to be worked on.

Typical steps in a process of planned change are illustrated in Figure 23.2. Problem sensing involves recognizing the need for a change. Awareness may stem from a variety of sources, the most important of which is a formal organizational process of introspection, critique, and followup.

The organization that will remain viable, creative, and relevant must engage in the process of search that the renewal effort involves. Such renewal will not take place by chance. It must be a purposive effort that embodies more than good intention. An organization renewal process takes time, energy, money, and skill. [6]

If the process of planned change is to become an integral part of the organization's "culture," provisions should be made for self-criticism on a relatively routine basis. It should become a natural part of the managerial style.

In order to facilitate a process of planned change, problems should be defined in a way that identifies a gap between a current condition and a desired condition on some relevant dimension. A problem well defined is half solved.

6 Gordon L. Lippitt, *Organization Renewal,* Appleton-Century-Crofts, New York, 1969, p. vii.

Figure 23.2   The Process of Planned Change

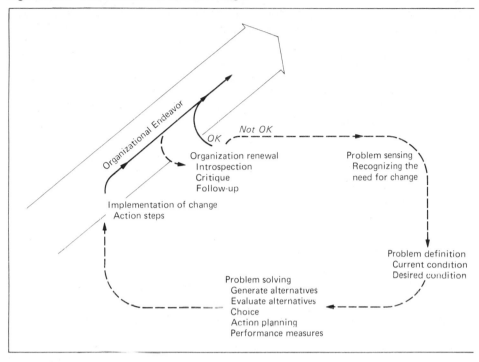

The solution phase involves generating alternatives, evaluating them, and choosing a future course of action. Tentative action steps should be identified and checked for feasibility (requisite skills and/or resources, for example). Performance measures should be established (quantitative and/or qualitative) so that the results of the planned change effort can be evaluated at a later date.

After the change has been implemented, there should be a followup appraisal of actual results compared to the plan. This process may lead to no action if the system is "on target" or to a new cycle of planned change if a problem is sensed. The connotation of "problem" (a gap between a current and a desired condition) is important because any organization has room for improvement, even if things are going along satisfactorily for the most part. If the general process of planned change (as outlined in Figure 23.2) becomes an integral part of the managerial system, many specific types of organization improvement efforts can be included in the solution phase, depending on the particular problems identified.

Operations Analysis

Taken literally, the term ***operations analysis*** could cover a broad spectrum of organization improvement activities. The connotation developed from current usage, however, leans toward symbolic model building, quantification, analytical problem solving, and simulation techniques. Terms such as industrial engineering, work simplification, and operations research are also related. Harrison classifies organization improvement efforts in terms of the depth of emotional involvement and suggests that operations analysis requires the least amount of emotional involvement on the part of organizational participants. [7]

While the human element is often involved in the implementation of results of operation analysis, it can be designed out of the analytical process in order to make quantification and computational solutions possible. An example of operations analysis might be designing a computer program for payroll processing so that it takes twenty-five percent less machine time. The implementation of such a change should have little effect on the people in the system. Defining the optimum number of tellers for various time periods in a branch bank is another example. Implementation of such recommendations might or might not involve significant changes in interpersonal relations of the work group. Recommendations for changes in production processes or the flow of information might or might not require significant changes in social systems. In any case, operations analysis tends to be less personalized than other planned change efforts that focus on individual, group, or organizational behavior.

Individual

Planned change efforts that focus on the individual range from informal orientation for new employees to elaborate management development programs for potential top executives. Whether implicitly or explicitly, most employees are given an overview of organizational activities (mission, scope, and objectives) along with specific instructions regarding their particular job. On-the-job training may include coaching by peers as well as superiors, with the objective of increased technical skill (and maybe interpersonal skill) for the employee. The assumption is that more skillful individuals will somehow lead to overall organization improvement.

Training programs for first-line supervisors, middle managers, and top executives tend to focus on broader organizational issues, interrelationships among functions, and leadership skills. Here again there is an assumption that better leaders will result in organization improvement. In many cases, organizations rely on external training programs (conducted by universities, for example) for development of individual managers. Personal growth is enhanced by exposure to heterogeneous groups of managers from diverse organizations, both public and private.

Groups

Focusing planned change efforts on teams or work groups is another way to improve organizations. This is the approach covered by the term ***organiza-***

---

7 Roger Harrison, "Choosing the Depth of Organizational Intervention," *Journal of Applied Behavioral Science,* April/May/June 1970, pp. 181–202.

tion development (OD), which is typically defined as "a long-range effort to im-prove an organization's problem-solving and renewal processes, particularly through a more effective and collaborative management of organization culture—with special emphasis on the culture of formal work teams—with the assistance of a change agent, or catalyst, and the use of the theory and technology of applied behavioral science, including action research."[8]

In this definition there is an emphasis on improving problem-solving and renewal processes while working on specific issues that are relevant to work groups. A typical feature of organization development activities is inclusion of all participants in the analysis of problems that affect them. The basic steps involved are (1) problem sensing via interviews, questionnaires, or group meetings, (2) pri-oritizing the issues in terms of factors such as importance/urgency/solvability, (3) refinement of problem statements and further diagnosis, (4) generation and evaluation of alternative solutions or tentative courses of action, (5) refinement of action steps in terms of feasibility, (6) implementation, and (7) followup to check actual progress against anticipated results.

Within this general approach, a number of problems that are relevant to group effectiveness might be identified—communication, role ambiguity, leader-ship, and morale, for example. Once a specific issue is identified an appropriate technique (termed "intervention") can be designed to help the members solve their own problem.[9]

If the focus of attention shifts from intragroup to intergroup issues, the same general approach can be followed. However, the methods used to facilitate intergroup problem solving would be tailored for that specific purpose. For exam-ple, people who are in boundary-spanning roles between two groups or depart-ments (engineering and production) may interact in a structured meeting designed to clarify their perceptions of each other and increase mutual understanding. Or one controversial group within an organization may ask for feedback concerning its image as perceived by other units. While improved effectiveness, efficiency, and participant satisfaction cannot be guaranteed as a result of such problem-solving efforts, clarification of perceptions and expectations typically leads to organiza-tional improvement.

Organization

A focus for planned change efforts can be the organization as a whole. OD practitioners typically emphasize that the endeavor includes the total system and is managed from the top.[10] The total organization can be involved by using surveys that solicit responses from all employees. Planned change efforts are then

8 Wendell L. French and Cecil H. Bell, Jr., *Organization Development*, 2d ed., Prentice-Hall, Inc., Englewood Cliffs, N.J., 1978, p. 14.

9 Ibid., pp. 101–176.

10 Richard Beckhard, *Organization Development: Strategies and Models*, Addison-Wesley Publish-ing Co., Boston, Mass., 1969, p. 9; and Chris Argyris, *Management and Organizational Development*, McGraw-Hill Book Co., New York, 1971.

designed according to the needs expressed by the participants. The data are made available to everyone in the system, and periodic followup surveys are taken in order to assess the impact of change efforts over relatively long periods of time. Another approach to organizationwide change efforts involves sequential attention to team building by starting with top management and then branching out by focusing successively on appropriate work groups throughout the system.

Management by objectives and results (MBO/R) can be focused on individuals and/or teams. The ultimate objective, however, is systemwide change and hence organization improvement. The basic elements in a MBO/R program include establishment of objectives by a subordinate, modification in a meeting between superior and subordinate, establishing mutual expectations of appropriate behavior, and subsequent followup to check results. The objectives established can relate to individual and/or work-group performance. The culmination of this systemwide program should result in overall objectives for the organization as a whole.

A planned change effort that focuses on the organization as a whole can, and probably should, involve efforts focused at a variety of target areas—personal growth, team building, intergroup relations, and total organization issues. Depending on the resources available for planned change efforts (managerial skills, consultation skills, money, and time), the various problem areas can be addressed simultaneously or sequentially. The ultimate goal in any case is overall organization improvement.

A Contingency View of Planned Change

A potential problem in organization improvement endeavors is a preconceived notion about what kinds of changes are necessary and desirable. Managers, internal change agents, and consultants sometimes become enamored with particular change strategies or specific techniques. Certain approaches are imposed, regardless of the organizational situation. For example, OD practitioners with humanistic leanings may steer change efforts toward making the system more adaptive-organic. However, this approach may not be appropriate for stable-mechanistic bureaucracies, in which better results might be obtained by concentrating on more realistic changes that recognize inherent constraints. [11]

The key concept is thorough, painstaking diagnosis of the organizational situation and matching problems, appropriate foci of attention, and relevant improvement strategies. For example, ineffectiveness and/or inefficiency in task performance may stem from either human or technological problems. Emphasis on motivation may be a waste of time if in fact an industrial engineering approach

---

11 Virginia E. Schein and Larry E. Greiner, "Can Organization Development Be Fine Tuned to Bureaucracies?" *Organizational Dynamics,* Winter 1977, pp. 48–61; and Cecil H. Bell, Jr. and James E. Rosenzweig, "OD in the City: A Potpourri of Pluses and Minuses," *Southern Public Administration Review,* March 1978, pp. 433–448.

would be more relevant—and vice versa. If the problem is lack of skills on the part of workers, then training is a more appropriate response. Of course, several dimensions can be addressed by considering sociotechnical approaches such as job design or job enrichment when task, technology, individual capability, group dynamics, and motivation are considered simultaneously. Other problems may stem from team ineffectiveness, intergroup conflict, or organizationwide issues. Decisions with regard to specific intervention strategies should be related to the problems as diagnosed by the members of the organization.

Resistance
to
Change

Given the multiple goals of stability and continuity as well as adaptation and innovation while maintaining a dynamic equilibrium in organizations, some resistance to change is not only natural but desirable. However, because of the widespread evidence of change (at an increasing rate), people apparently accept adaptation and innovation. Bennis and Slater suggest that "change has now become a permanent and accelerating factor in American life." [12] Technological changes with obvious benefits and few discernible negative consequences are readily accepted. Changes affecting social relationships take longer to implement.

Resistance to change has sometimes been interpreted as simple inertia in human nature. It is said that people are "in a rut" or "set in their ways." Actually almost everyone is eager for some kind of change in . . . life and situation . . . better health, more money, and more freedom to satisfy . . . desires. Excitement is more attractive than humdrum existence. If people in organizations do not change, it must be because natural drives toward innovation are being stifled or held in check by countervailing forces. [13]

What are the countervailing forces to natural drives for individual and organizational innovation? Obviously, there are a number of specific forces relevant to particular situations. Two major factors are sunk costs (including vested interests) and misunderstandings (of purpose, mechanics, or consequences of change). [14] If the term "sunk costs" is broadly interpreted to include time and energy as well as money, it describes a powerful force in resisting change. Regardless of the merits of a proposal, it is difficult to forget the blood, sweat, and tears that have gone into an existing system. An experienced manager is likely to resist suggestions for changes from internal or external consultants. This concept may explain why curriculum changes come so slowly and why professors use the same texts and lecture notes over long periods of time.

12 Warren G. Bennis and Philip E. Slater, *The Temporary Society,* Harper Colophon Books, New York, 1969, p. 9.

13 This excerpt of "Resistance to Change" by Goodwin Watson is reprinted from *American Behavioral Scientist,* vol. 14, no. 5, pp. 745–766, May–June 1971, by permission of the publisher, Sage Publications, Inc.

14 Steven Kerr and Elaine B. Kerr, "Why Your Employees Resist Perfectly Rational Changes," *Hospital Financial Management,* January 1972, pp. 4–6.

The sunk cost concept may also help explain the different propensities to change for various age groups. Older people obviously have a longer history of sunk costs and hence think they have more to lose than younger people. It also helps to explain why staff people (specialists) are more likely to be change agents in organizations. They have less at stake than line managers, who have invested time and energy in making the existing system work.

Misunderstanding often stems from the illusion of communication. The manager's assumption that subordinates "got the message" is often unfounded. Employees' assumption that management knows how they feel is also often unwarranted. When someone says, "Yes, I understand," that person may (1) really understand, (2) have a fair idea, or (3) not understand at all. The person may not admit he or she does not understand, thinking this would be stupid or would call attention to the manager's inability to communicate clearly. In any event, transferring meaning from one mind to another is a difficult process. We often do not say exactly what we intended to say; others may hear a slightly different message or even a grossly distorted version because they filter the flow of words and delete as well as add to meaning.

How does this affect resistance to change? Whenever individuals do not clearly understand the purpose, mechanics, or potential consequences of a change, they are likely to resist it. If people are involved in the implementation process, it is important for them to understand why the change is being made. When the mechanics of a change are not clearly understood, they cannot be carried out even if the implementer is willing.

Of crucial importance is uncertainty about the consequences of a change. Speculation and rumor about negative consequences are typically part of the change process. Given little explicit information, people will assume the worst. The obvious result is vigorous resistance to proposed changes.

Figure 23.3 illustrates several possible psychological impacts of significant changes on organizational members. Uncertainty concerning consequences often results in high levels of confusion and anxiety. Initial confidence often decreases somewhat, particularly if there is unexpected resistance or if implementation is not as smooth as anticipated. However, as learning and improvement occur, confidence is buoyed and anxiety decreases. This model suggests the importance of thorough communication to all participants of the exact nature, purpose, and potential consequences of a proposed change. It also suggests the need to be realistic concerning improvement efforts and the importance of intermediate checkpoints to ascertain progress and to positively reinforce those involved in the change effort.

Implementing Planned Change

Implementing planned change requires understanding the forces involved in resistance to change and designing appropriate means to overcome

Figure 23.3   Impact of Change on Confidence, Confusion, and Anxiety

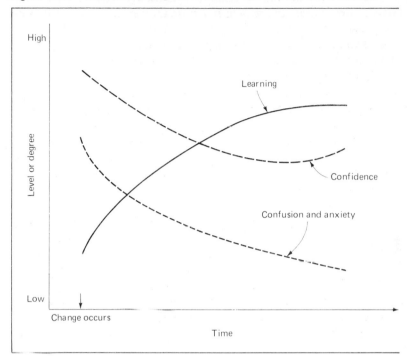

Adapted from William H. Newman, *Constructive Control,* Prentice-Hall, Inc., Englewood Cliffs, N.J., 1975, p. 167.

them. Situational analysis coupled with a contingency view is extremely important. For example, it would be important to understand (1) the historical perspective with regard to past change efforts, (2) the general climate for innovation in the organization, and (3) the specific planned change (purpose, mechanics, and consequences, for example). A thorough situational analysis should provide the opportunity to design a means of implementation that has the highest probability of success. The specific means used in the planned change effort would be contingent on a number of factors, including organizational climate, type of problem, and focus of attention.

Climate
for
Change

The *general* climate for organizational change includes all of the external environment plus internal factors that we have categorized into subsystems—goals and values, technical, structural, psychosocial and managerial. The *specific* climate for planned change depends on a number of factors that are more directly related to the process of adaptation or innovation. A long list of dimensions could be cited, all of which affect the implementability of innovation.[15] However, we will consider only a few of them in order to illustrate the variables involved in the climate for change.

Corwin cites a large number of research studies that point to several conclusions about conditions for success in planned change efforts. For example, it has been postulated that an organization can be changed more easily:

If it is invaded by liberal, creative, and unconventional outsiders with fresh perspectives.

If those outsiders are exposed to creative, competent, and flexible socialization agents.

If it is staffed by young, flexible, supportive, and competent boundary personnel, or "gatekeepers."

If it is structurally complex and decentralized.

If it has outside funds to provide the "organizational" slack necessary to lessen the cost of innovation.

If its members have positions that are sufficiently secure and protected from status risks involved in change.

If it is located in a changing, modern, urbanized setting where it is in close cooperation with a coalition of other cosmopolitan organizations that can supplement its skills and resources.[16]

These tentative conclusions obviously need more research in a variety of settings, as well as careful interpretation, before straightforward guidelines can be developed. However, on balance, the research seems to indicate that "the conditions under which any given strategy is applied, that is, the situation into which an innovation is introduced, seems to be as critical as the strategy itself."[17]

Diagnosis and Action

Figure 23.4 provides a way of looking at problem solving that enhances the probability of implementing recommended action steps. This model is a subpart of the general process of planned change as shown in Figure 23.2. The internal circle emphasizes diagnosis and the external band emphasizes action. There must be an appropriate balance between the two. Overdiagnosis results in "paralysis by analysis"; that is, we never reach the action stage. Underdiagnosis— leaping immediately to action—may result in "extinction by instinct." Of course,

---

15 Gerald Zaltman and Nan Lin, "On the Nature of Innovations," *American Behavioral Scientist,* May–June 1971, pp. 651–673.

16 Ronald G. Corwin, "Strategies for Organizational Intervention: An Empirical Comparison," *American Sociological Review,* August 1972, pp. 441–442.

17 Ibid., p. 452.

Figure 23.4   A Problem-Solving Process—Diagnosis and Action

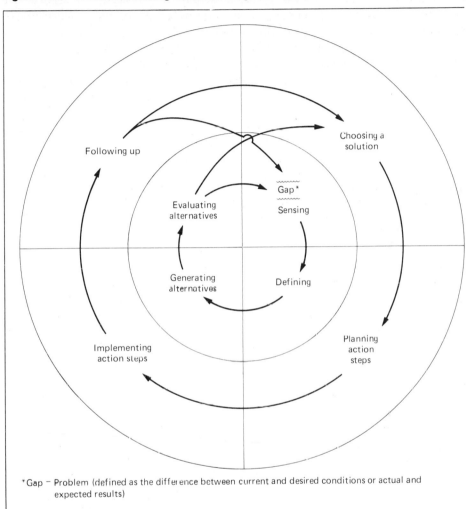

Following up

Choosing a
solution

Evaluating
alternatives

Gap*

Sensing

Generating
alternatives

Defining

Implementing
action steps

Planning
action
steps

*Gap − Problem (defined as the difference between current and desired conditions or actual and
    expected results)

we are concerned here with relatively complex issues that warrant detailed analysis and considered judgment.

The first step is problem sensing, identifying a gap between the perceived
present situation and the desired situation.[18] This may occur in a variety of ways,
such as reviewing expected versus actual operating results, obtaining feedback
from participants, soliciting customer complaints, or receiving a question from the
boss. When several problems are identified, priorities must be established in order

18 Edwin M. Bartee, "A Holistic View of Problem Solving," *Management Science,* December 1973
(Part I), pp. 439–448.

to ensure that effort is focused on the most important issues. The second step involves refining the problem to make sure that relevant organizational members agree on the definition. It also involves dimensions such as:

Who is involved—an individual, a group or groups, the total organization?

Who is causing it—a few people, a specific department or function, top management?

What kind of problem is it—lack of skills, unclear goals, intergroup conflict?

What is the goal for improvement?

How can we evaluate results?

The last question suggests the importance of having an accurate picture of the current condition as well as a clear picture of the desired condition.

The third step in problem diagnosis is the generation of alternative solutions. It is important to note the separation of generation and evaluation. This follows the concept of "brainstorming," in which evaluation is forestalled in order to facilitate the generation of as many alternatives (including "far-out" suggestions) as possible before beginning to evaluate them. The evaluation process includes identifying tentative action steps, anticipating their possible impact, refining them, and, finally, choosing a solution.

The action phase includes planning and implementing specific steps designed to achieve goals or bring activities "back into line." Action steps are followed up at some future time, in order to check the actual situation against the plan. The results of this followup might be reaffirmation of the action plan or reactivation of the problem-solving process if a discrepancy is identified.

Resistance to change is reduced if those involved in implementation of action steps are also involved in the problem-solving process. The inner and outer circles (Figure 23.4) should not be treated as separate functions. That is, problem solvers, analysts, and planners cannot specialize in the activities of the internal circle in relative isolation and then expect others to implement the findings. Continuing interaction between managers and specialists during the problem-solving process should lead to mutual understanding and higher probabilities for success of planned change efforts.

Force Field Analysis

Force field analysis, as illustrated in Figure 23.5 is a general-purpose diagnostic and problem-solving technique. In any situation there are forces that push for change (driving) as well as forces that hinder change (restraining). If the forces offset each other completely, we have equilibrium and status quo. Change can be brought about by increasing the driving forces or by reducing the restraining forces. The latter approach is often more fruitful because to increase driving forces without attention to restraining forces may increase pressure and tension in the system to the point that creative problem solving becomes impossible. This approach facilitates inclusion of a wide variety of factors—technological, structural, and psychosocial (values and feelings, for example). It is particularly important to anticipate antagonism that is likely to be aroused in the implementation of planned change. Accurate assessment will allow creative leadership to cope with hangups at the feeling level.

To illustrate the use of force field analysis, let us pick a common individual and/or organizational problem —lack of time. This is a pervasive problem for harried executives. In order to work on the problem effectively, we need to clarify

Figure 23.5　Force Field Analysis

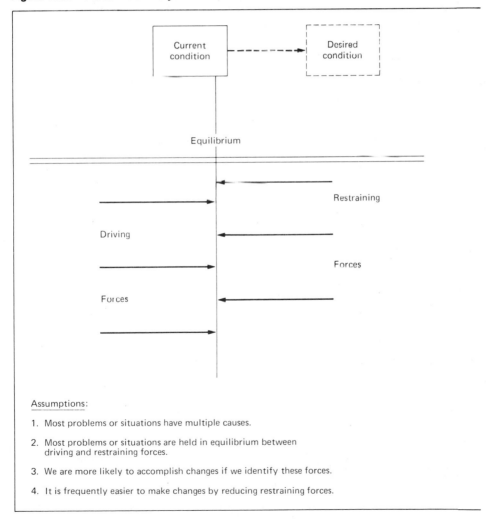

Current condition

Desired condition

Equilibrium

Restraining

Driving

Forces

Forces

Assumptions:

1. Most problems or situations have multiple causes.

2. Most problems or situations are held in equilibrium between driving and restraining forces.

3. We are more likely to accomplish changes if we identify these forces.

4. It is frequently easier to make changes by reducing restraining forces.

it and state it in terms of current and desired conditions. For example, the real issue may be "lack of time to work on important tasks such as developing a comprehensive process for planned change."

Current condition = no time spent on planned change; always react to crisis conditions

Desired condition = large blocks of time for critiquing the organization periodically; a comprehensive and creative process of planned change is an integral part of the managerial system

In order to understand the situation in more detail, we can identify those offsetting forces that keep us in equilibrium—no change from the current condition.

Driving Forces (pushing us toward the desired condition)
1 Knowledge of theory that says it would be "better"
2 Feeling (conviction) that it would be "better"
3 Success stories from current literature (increased productivity, for example)
4 Success stories from acquaintances in similar organizations
5 Consultants (internal or external) "selling" the virtues of a new approach

Restraining forces (keeping us in the current condition)
1 Programmed activity increases to absorb available time.
2 Current deadlines preclude taking time to analyze the problem of lack of time.
3 We seem to be doing satisfactory work—individually and organizationally (we have survived). No sense of urgency.
4 Reluctance of participants to "rock the boat" by analyzing group processes.
5 Assumption that there is no slack in time resources, i.e., time is not currently wasted.

These lists are obviously not exhaustive; the reader can easily add to and/or modify them. However, they do illustrate the approach and lead us to the next step, which is picking one or more of the forces (starting with restraining forces) and generating ideas for increasing or decreasing them. After alternatives have been evaluated, action plans can be designed and implemented.

The analysis can be carried out in as much detail as seems warranted by the problem. For complex issues with probable difficulties in implementation, it may be worthwhile to pursue force field analysis in great depth, with widespread participation. In other cases, it may be sufficient merely to outline the problem in the basic framework and move quickly to the tentative solution phase.

Building
Group
Consensus

The effectiveness of using group norms and consensus decision making to change individual and organizational behavior has been demonstrated in a number of research studies as well as highly publicized programs such as Alcoholics Anonymous and Weight Watchers. Lewin's early studies of the effectiveness of lectures versus group discussion and commitment in changing eating habits have been replicated many times. [19] The key findings were that behavior change is more likely to occur and persist when commitment is on a group, rather than individual, basis. The basic process includes unfreezing existing habits or standard operating procedures, changing to new patterns of behavior, and refreezing in order to ensure lasting effects. The key ingredients involved are changing group norms and making the new norms explicit and visible, as well as encouraging public and explicit commitment to abide by them. As indicated in our discussion of resistance to change, group norms represent a powerful force. Therefore, if those norms can be changed, they will enhance the probability of success of planned change efforts.

Reinforcing
Innovative
Behavior

Another important step in implementing planned change is to concentrate on and enlist the support of influential members of work groups. Energy focused in this direction will often have widespread payoff through the establishment of new norms for behavior. Also, in this same vein, it is important to positively reinforce those who exhibit new behavior in the implementation phase. Positive reinforcement will help perpetuate that behavior and improve the organization's ability to respond to changing conditions by adapting and innovating when appropriate. Promotion and/or monetary rewards (bonus or salary increase) may be used if feasible. For many organizations, however, recognition and praise may be the only means of reinforcement. Fortunately, there is increasing evidence that this rather simple, straightforward approach can be quite successful. [20]

Dealing
with
Differences

One of the questions in organizational change is what to do with the maverick, the person who is "far out." Given the organization's legitimate need

19 Kurt Lewin, "Group Decision and Social Change," in Eleanor E. Maccoby, Theodore M. Newcomb, and Eugene L. Hartley, *Readings in Social Psychology*, Holt, Rinehart and Winston, Inc., New York, 1958, pp. 197–211.

20 "Where Skinner's Theories Work," *Business Week*, Dec. 2, 1972, pp. 64–65; and W. Clay Hamner and Ellen P. Hamner, "Behavior Modification on the Bottom Line," *Organizational Dynamics*, Spring 1976, pp. 3–21.

for stability and continuity, can extreme individualism be accepted? By definition, organization means cooperation and hence the sacrifice of individualism to some extent. But how much? George Bernard Shaw once said, "The reasonable man conforms to the world. The unreasonable man expects the world to conform to him. Therefore, all progress depends on the unreasonable man."

Organizations typically have three general approaches to "differences" in participants: (1) disallow and mold (submerge), (2) accept and tolerate, and (3) understand and value. Over time, organizations in general have moved toward the third approach. Understanding and valuing differences are an important step in keeping the organization tuned to current conditions.

However, it is easy to see a spectrum of all three approaches in modern organizations. Some organizations still maintain rigid codes of dress and hair style, refuse to hire women for executive positions, and avoid employees who are racially and/or ethnically different from current managers. In some organizations for which there are no legal sanctions—particularly small- to medium-sized, closely held corporations that do not sell to the federal government—these conditions might prevail for years to come. However, many organizations will be forced to change because of legal and economic sanctions. Although they may do so reluctantly, they may discover that an initial approach of "accept and tolerate" will gradually change to "understand and value."

Unquestionably, managing participants with widely diverse value systems is more difficult than coordinating a group of people selected in the manager's own image. And we may be surprised to see a process of mutual accommodation as participants recognize the need to submerge individual values and goals to a degree in order to facilitate the accomplishment of organizational objectives.

Approaches to Conflict Resolution

A likely result of increasingly diverse organizational participants is increased interpersonal and intergroup conflict within organizations. Understanding and valuing differences probably rules out unanimity and makes consensus formation much more difficult. The managerial task of coordination will require increasing adroitness. Management will need to become skilled in the creative use of conflicts and tensions that can be potentially beneficial in generating alternative solutions in the problem-solving process. However, conflicts have to be resolved enough to allow the coordination necessary to implement a desired course of action.

Typical approaches to conflict resolution in organizations include (1) withdrawal, (2) smoothing, (3) compromise, (4) confrontation, and (5) forcing. The approaches at either end of the spectrum—withdrawal and forcing—describe a considerable amount of managerial behavior. Henry Ford decided, against the advice of most of his managers, that consumers could have any color car, as long as they wanted black. A cartoon shows a chairperson calling for a vote by stating "All in favor say 'aye'; all opposed say 'I resign.' " Withdrawal may be an appropriate temporary strategy, but it cannot be pursued forever and in all cases. A smoothing approach involves slightly more "working the problem" than withdrawal. However, it still has the connotation of "glossing over" real problems by getting agreement on minor surface issues. Smoothing may be a useful temporary strategy if a more basic approach is followed at a more opportune time.

Compromise and confrontation suggest active attempts to work the problem. Compromise has a slightly negative tone because it assumes that the parties involved have given something up and therefore that neither is completely happy. However, compromise is a fact of life and it will be relevant to organizations as long as there are differences, factions, and power struggles. Political negotiation is an evident part of organizational life. For example, it describes the budgetary process in most large, complex organizations such as a university. The resource allocation process typically involves a series of bids and responses until a final figure that is acceptable to the managers involved is reached. [21]

The aim of creative conflict resolution is integration that allows both parties to achieve their objectives. The basic goal is a win-win approach rather than a win-lose approach. However, the latter is much more common in our competitive society and it does indeed take creative conflict management to find integrative solutions. A confrontation mode might or might not facilitate achieving integrative results. It can mean getting all the cards on the table, good will in empathizing with alternative viewpoints, and actively seeking solutions that satisfy both (or all) protagonists. With increasingly diverse value systems in organizations, this is obviously a difficult assignment.

On the other hand, open confrontation of unresolved issues can be therapeutic, even if the temporary or long-run solution is to decide not to agree. Smoldering, under-the-surface tensions and antagonisms drain off untold amounts of physical and psychic energy. If conflict and confrontation are managed creatively, they can be beneficial in releasing sources to concentrate on the primary organizational task.

Withdrawal and smoothing tend to perpetuate a status quo. Forcing obviously leads to organizational change but may overemphasize expediency while not giving due consideration to medium- and long-run results. Compromise and confrontation provide opportunity for creative conflict resolution leading to substantive change or, at least, therapeutic results that facilitate a healthier organization.

Summary

Organizations must maintain a dynamic equilibrium between stability/continuity and adaptation/innovation. We have used our systems model to iden-

---

21 Gerald R. Salencik and Jeffrey Pfeffer, "Who Gets Power—and How They Hold on to It: A Strategic-Contingency Model of Power," *Organizational Dynamics*, Winter 1977, pp. 3–21.

tify the sources of impetus for change. The environmental suprasystem has an obvious impact on organizations through technological, economic, legal, political, demographic, ecological, and cultural forces. Organizational change also stems from forces within organizational subsystems. The managerial system is in the middle of a patterned swirl of external and internal events and is charged both with managing the change process and making strategic choices.

Planned change efforts (specific changes as well as improved change processes) concentrate on questions of effectiveness, efficiency, and participant satisfaction. The focus of planned change efforts toward organization improvement can be operations analysis, individuals, groups (team building and intergroup relations), and overall organizational issues.

Although people normally seek new and different experiences, resistance to change in organizations stems from countervailing forces such as sunk costs (money, time, and energy), as well as misunderstandings about the purpose, mechanics, and consequences (uncertainty) of planned changes.

The ability to implement planned change requires explicit steps to overcome resistance to change. In general, a problem-solving approach that recognizes the interaction and balance of diagnosis and action is important. A technique such as force field analysis, which allows identification of driving and restraining forces, can be helpful in understanding the problem and ascertaining the most appropriate action steps. Participation, particularly of those to be called on for implementation, is important at all stages in the process of planned change.

The propensity for organizations to change is affected by the way they deal with differences: (1) disallow and mold (submerge), (2) accept and tolerate, and (3) understand and value. Another important factor is the approach generally used in resolving conflict.

Questions and Problems

1 What is meant by the phrase "stability and continuity as well as adaptation and innovation"?

2 Give examples of how disequilibrium in these processes can lead to negative consequences in organizations.

3 For a specific organization with which you are familiar, illustrate how the impetus for change can come from the following sources:

    a External environment

    b Internal subsystems

        (1) Goals and values

        (2) Technical

        (3) Structural

(4) Psychosocial

(5) Managerial

4 Explain the connotation of the word "problem" as used in the process of planned change described in the chapter.

5 Give examples of planned change efforts in the following categories:

a Operations analysis

b Individual

c Group

d Organization

6 For a specific organization with which you are familiar, describe instances of resistance to change based on:

a Sunk costs (vested interests)

b Misunderstanding and/or uncertainty

7 Use the force field analysis technique to diagnose the following problems:

a Current condition = 250 lbs.
Desired condition = 200 lbs.

b Current condition = 2.0 g.p.a.
Desired condition = 3.0 g.p.a.

c Current condition = Downward, one-way communication; much misunderstanding
Desired condition = Upward and downward, two-way communication; mutual understanding

d Any personal or organizational problem that is real for you

8 Give several examples from your own experience of times when your participation in a group commitment has been effective in changing your individual behavior.

9 Do you think organizations are tending toward "understanding and valuing" differences? Give examples.

10 What is the connotation of "confrontation" as used in the chapter? What are its advantages and disadvantages as a means of conflict resolution?

Organization and Management in the Future

Twenty-four

The twentieth century has been a period of growth in size and complexity for organizations in all fields—business, government, military, educational, religious, and medical. We have become an organizational society in which an increasing proportion of all activities occur within the boundaries of these complex social structures. The practice of management has responded to these and other influences. Managerial concepts have adapted to the changing sociocultural environment and internal organizational requirements. In this chapter we set forth a framework for looking at the future of organizations and management and consider some of the primary forces involved. The following topics are discussed:

> The Past is Prologue
> A Rapidly Changing Environment
> Expansion of Organizational Activities
> Response to Technological Change
> Response to Social Change
> Developing a Democratic-Humanistic System
> Dynamic, Flexible Organizations
> Evolving Managerial Systems
> Importance of Research and Experimentation

The Past is Prologue

There are many unforeseeable forces, both in the external environment and in internal operations, which make forecasting the future development of organizations and their management difficult. However, certain factors are paramount in shaping the future, and projection of these factors is not as risky as it might seem there are long-term evolutionary trends. The basic economic and social processes initiated in the nineteenth and twentieth centuries continue to set the stage for the future. Many of the unique characteristics of the environment, structure, and national heritage of American society were set forth in the 1830s by Alexis de Tocqueville, a young French nobleman and an astute observer of the social scene. [1]

Many of the characteristics reported by de Tocqueville over a century ago remain fundamental and profoundly affect our social structure. He emphasized the impact of democracy on American society and its institutions and organizations. He saw the pragmatic nature of the people and their abiding faith in their ability to shape their environment. He discerned the importance attached to knowledge and education. Above all, he emphasized the abiding American faith in the future and the value of change.

On the other hand, we cannot complacently predict the future on the basis of past trends alone. During the 1960s and 1970s strong "counterculture" movements have been evident, rejecting many of the values in our society—the work ethic, the emphasis on economic growth and material betterment, and faith in the virtues of scientific and technological achievements. These counter views suggest that we have been guided over the past several centuries by values associated with an industrializing society, and they foresee a transition to a post-industrial society in which new social values and goals will emerge. One of the most difficult problems facing society will be the integration of traditional values geared to economic growth and technological achievement with the emerging values of greater human dignity, egalitarianism, and social consciousness.

We have become an organizational society, depending increasingly on various forms of complex organizations to accomplish our goals. They cannot be looked at separately from the total social structure; rather, they are a vital, integral part of this structure. Throughout this book we have emphasized that the organization is an open subsystem of the broader sociocultural environment. But the reverse is also true; the nature of our organizations—their goals, values, technologies, structures, and psychosocial systems—has a fundamental effect on the very nature of society. The basic issues of democratic participation, individualism, self-actualization, and a meaningful life are not just broad, theoretical abstractions. They are primary issues involving the day-to-day relationships of individuals and groups in organizations. Organizational life is an integral part of total life.

People can use natural resources to shape their physical and social environment. Their social organizations are the vehicle for further progress. These organizations have played a fundamental role in the social evolution of the past century and will have an even more important role in the future. Managing these organizations not only for economic and productive efficiencies but also to provide for the broader goals of human satisfaction will be one of the most important challenges of the future.

---

1 Alexis de Tocqueville, *Democracy in America,* ed. by Phillips Bradley, Alfred A. Knopf, Inc., New York, 1945. For a discussion of the impact of de Tocqueville's concepts on sociological thinking, see Robert A. Nisbet, *The Sociological Tradition,* Basic Books, Inc., Publishers, New York, 1966.

A Rapidly Changing Environment

One of the more interesting recent developments is the movement toward the scientific study of the future. We have always been interested in predicting what lies ahead. Every society had its prophets. Leonardo da Vinci and Jules Verne made remarkable predictions that have been fulfilled only recently, but these were the predictions of insightful and gifted individuals. More recently there has been an attempt to institutionalize the study of the future. Many governmental commissions and congressional subcommittees, as well as state and local agencies, have been created to predict the future.

With the number and diversity of people and organizations engaged in futurology, it is difficult to reach a consensus on how to study the future, much less any agreement on what the future holds. Figure 24.1 indicates the basic trends

Figure 24.1 Trends of the Future

There Is a Basic, Long-Term, Multifold Trend Toward

1 Increasingly sensate (empirical, this-worldly, secular, humanistic, pragmatic, manipulative, explicitly rational, utilitarian, contractual, epicurean, hedonistic, etc.) culture—recently an almost complete decline of the sacred and a relative erosion of "irrational" taboos, totems, and charismas
2 Bourgeois, bureaucratic, and "meritocratic" elites
3 Accumulation of scientific and technological knowledge
4 Institutionalization of technological change, especially research, development, innovation, and diffusion—recently and increasingly a conscious emphasis on synergisms and serendipities
5 Worldwide industrialization and modernization
6 Increasing capability for mass destruction
7 Increasing affluence and (recently) leisure
8 Population growth—now explosive but tapering off
9 Urbanization and recently suburbanization and "Urban sprawl"—soon the growth of megalopolises
10 Recently and increasingly—macroenvironmental issues (e.g., constraints set by finite size of earth and various local and global reservoirs)
11 Decreasing importance of primary and (recently) secondary and tertiary occupations
12 Increasing literacy and education—recently the "knowledge industry" and increasing numbers and role of intellectuals
13 Future-oriented thinking, discussion, and planning—recently some improvement in methodologies and tools—also some retrogression
14 Innovative and manipulative rationality increasingly applied to social, political, cultural, and economic worlds as well as to shaping and exploiting the material world—increasing problem of ritualistic, incomplete, or pseudo-rationality
15 Increasing universality of the multifold trend
16 Increasing tempo of change in all the above

Herman Kahn, "The 'Emergent United States' . . . Post-Industrial Society," in *The Management of Information and Knowledge,* Committee on Science and Astronautics, U.S. House of Representatives, 1970, p. 26.

suggested by Herman Kahn and his associates at the Hudson Institute. Our own views of the future are in agreement with most of these trends.

In the future the boundaries separating the organization from its environment will become more permeable. Evidence from the recent past suggests that society will be anything but certain and placid. Increasingly, organizations will operate in *turbulent* environments "in which there are dynamic processes arising from the field itself which create significant variances for the component systems."[2] The turbulence will be amplified by the expansion of science and technology, by emphasis on educational achievement, and above all, by the increasing aspirations for people of all nationalities to control, rather than be victims of, their surroundings. "Never in human history have so many people . . . been engaged in attempting to remake the environment, to increase our capacity to use the environment for human purposes, and to remodel the rules and social arrangements that govern man's interaction with his fellows."[3]

Even though the organization of the future may strive for stability and certainty, it will be impossible to achieve. In a turbulent and uncertain environment the organization will have to be adaptive. When the organization cannot achieve and maintain stability because of future uncertainty, it must emphasize dynamic flexibility and responsiveness to change. However, the other side of the issue should be recognized. "In a society in which a wide variety of organizations and organizational forms exist, as in the contemporary United States, social change is also a constant condition."[4] Thus, organizations not only must respond to changes imposed by the environment but they also "output" changes that profoundly affect the society.

As society becomes more "organized," the environment of any individual subsystem is composed of other complex organizations. For example, the business corporation has competitors, suppliers, and customers, as well as interactions with labor unions and public agencies. The problems of integration and interface between organizations will be of critical importance in the future.

Growing Concern for the Environment

We are coming to recognize the importance and limitations of the natural environment itself. We have already discussed ecological issues and the necessity for the organization to consider all the effects of its activities, both good and bad, on the natural environment. According to William Ruckelshaus, first administrator of the national Environmental Protection Agency:

2 F. E. Emery, "The Next Thirty Years: Concepts, Methods and Anticipations," *Human Relations,* August 1967, p. 222.

3 Wilbert E. Moore, "Utility of Utopias," *American Sociological Review,* December 1966, p. 765.

4 Richard H. Hall, *Organizations: Structure and Process,* Prentice-Hall, Inc., Englewood Cliffs, N.J., 1972, p. 326.

We have ridden the abundance of nature into fantastic prosperity, and we have yet to pay full fare for the ride. Only in recent years did we begin to realize that callous treatment of nature's resources not only diminished our own lives, but mortgaged the future of our children. [5]

In the future all organizations, both public and private, will have to be more concerned with the deleterious effects of their activities and outputs. The organization will be held accountable for its environmental impact.

Expansion of the Environment

Until recently, our natural environment has been considered limited to the land masses on earth (and to only a relatively small proportion of these areas). In the future we will see an extension of this environment to the oceans and to outer space. Our first ventures into space open the long-term possibility that we may not be earthbound. Research endeavors suggest that in the future oceans will be developed via farming and mining operations and also serve as undersea habitats for people. Therefore, our environment may not be quite as limited as we have thought heretofore. Also, we should recognize that wherever we go we will take our organizations. There will be organizations and managers on space stations, and there will be organizations and managers in undersea cities.

Expansion of Organizational Activities

Over the past century complex organizations have expanded their activities and boundaries. This process will continue and become even more important in the future. Boundary expansion has resulted from a number of forces. Goal elaboration has caused organizations to increase their scope, and new technologies have caused them to encompass additional activities. Organizations frequently respond to environmental uncertainties by expanding their domain and bringing within internal control those forces creating the uncertainty.

We have indicated how hospitals have expanded their boundaries. In the early days they were typically small units with the primary function of care of indigent patients. Over the past century they have expanded their domain to include all types of care and treatment. The hospital has become a community health service center with a wide variety of medical, psychological, and social functions.

To provide an ever-expanding and complex array of citizen services,

5 William D. Ruckelshaus, "The Beginning of the New American Revolution," *The Annals of the American Academy of Political and Social Science,* July 1971, p. 14.

today's cities have joined with county and federal agencies, as well as with private enterprises and volunteer groups, to plan and act on a region-wide basis.

Similarly, the university has evolved from the small college of a century ago to the multiversity of today. And the modern prison also has expanded its boundaries to include training and rehabilitation activities such as education-release and work-release programs.

In business organizations this process of boundary expansion is quite evident. The development of the corporate form allowed the business to expand its activities beyond that permitted by the resources of the individual owner. The movements in the early part of the twentieth century toward vertical and horizontal integration were an example of boundary expansion by business firms. More recently, the development of large-scale conglomerates with activities in a wide variety of industrial fields has been a primary example of boundary expansion. The managerial system of these conglomerates needs to be substantially more flexible and dynamic than for the more simplified one-product or one-service company.

Multinational Corporations

In the post-World War II period, American business corporations have entered a new, important phase of boundary expansion—international operations. Increasingly, large- and medium-sized corporations are operating in other countries. They are not just investing funds in foreign operations or only establishing sales agencies. Rather, they are engaged in full-scale operations abroad. These multinational corporations have increased greatly in number and size over the past several decades, and this trend will continue.

The move from national to multinational corporation changes the environmental framework within which the organization operates.

The primary distinction between an international and a domestic business lies in their environmental frameworks and in the organizational and behavioral responses that flow from these frameworks. As a company transcends a national setting, its environmental framework changes progressively in countless respects. There arise new ground rules as defined by law, custom, and culture; new values; new contradictions, interactions, and balances among external forces; and new opportunities as well as uncertainties. The wider the company's international scope, the greater the environmental diversities surrounding it. [6]

The multinational corporation has significantly changed the boundaries of its activities and the diversity of its environment. It must operate in new socio-cultural systems and must maintain dynamic flexibility. "The multinational corpo-

---

[6] Endel J. Kolde, *International Business Enterprise*, 2d ed., © 1973, p. 14. Reprinted by permission of Prentice-Hall, Inc., Englewood Cliffs, N.J.

rate firm is an adaptive-learning system."[7] This trend has important ramifications not only for business and economic activities, but for international relationships as well. "Whatever it does, the cosmopolitan corporation should be mindful of the fact that it represents a more successful instance of international cooperation and a closer approach to global thinking than we have thus far encountered among governments. It is the torch-bearer of One World."[8]

A number of questions have been raised about the impact of the multinational corporation on the sovereignty of individual nations—even the United States. "There is an inherent conflict between the multinational firm and nationalism."[9] There is concern that the development of these huge organizations will conflict with the boundaries of the various sovereign nations and that national interests will be sacrificed to the multinational corporate goals. The future may see the development of supranational governmental regulation and control of multinational business enterprises to ensure that they operate within the framework of national sovereignties.

Boundary Expansion in Public Sector

Expansion of the boundaries of organizational activities in the public sector is also inevitable. Many of the problems facing society—urban redevelopment, pollution control, and transportation systems—will require new and different organizational approaches. Traditionally, these problems have been faced on a piecemeal basis with various government agencies each responsible for a single function. It is becoming apparent that these problems cannot be solved fractionally but will have to be approached on a total system basis.

These programs will not be restricted to the public sector. The private sector also will cooperate in dealing with problems such as pollution control and transportation systems. This will alter traditional organizational boundaries and will require the development of new supraorganizational units to solve social problems that can encompass different segments from the public sector (federal, state, and local) *and* the private sector.

The expansion of the boundaries of an organization creates many new and different problems for management. The number of interfaces with environmental units increases, and the organization must be more responsive. Boundary expansion increases internal complexities and creates problems of control. As an organization expands its activities, it cannot continue to use the tight bureaucratic

---

7 Howard V. Perlmutter, "The Multinational Firm and the Future," *The Annals of the American Academy of Political and Social Science,* September 1972, p. 140.

8 Hans B. Thorelli, "The Multi-national Corporation as a Change Agent," in Richard N. Farmer, *International Management,* Dickenson Publishing Company, Inc., Belmont, Calif., 1968, p. 73.

9 John Fayerweather, "The Internationalization of Business," *The Annals of the American Academy of Political and Social Science,* September 1972, p. 5.

form and philosophy but must develop a more dynamic and less structured system.

Interface
between
Organizations

There will be increasing emphasis in the future on problems related to the interface between organizations—interorganizational analysis. Administrative coordinating processes between organizations have been used as substitutes for or complements to marketplace coordination. This has occurred in relationships between the government and the national defense industries and in the National Aeronautics and Space Administration programs. In the future, even more administrative coordination between complex organizations will be necessary.

Most environmental and technical interrelationships also involve organizational interrelationships. To be sure, in the past organizations had relationships with one another. However, most were static or impersonal, defined by rather rigid legal agreements (setting forth mutual responsibilities) or governed by the invisible hand of the marketplace or the more visible hand of the government regulator. Only recently have we come to recognize that most of our contemporary "problem" areas require both the close collaboration of many institutions and rapid, dynamic mutual adaptation. [10]

We do foresee a substantial increase in the interface between government and business. The line between the public sector and private sector in our economy is blurred. Even in the so-called "public sector" the funds may come from federal, state, and local governments but be spent on goods and services produced by the private sector.

There are indications of important developments that will help interorganizational coordination. For example, the program or systems management approach has been used as a means for improving integration within the organization and for better interorganizational coordination. The systems approach will be utilized to deal with many important social and economic problems. Each participating organization will assign personnel to participate with their counterparts from other organizations on a particular program. In the past, this frequently has been accomplished through informal communication and ad hoc committee arrangements. In the future, these approaches will become more formalized.

Organizations will expand the use of "boundary agents," whose primary function will be coordinating activities with the environment. One interesting facet will be an increase in the mobility of various managerial and professional personnel between organizations. As individuals develop greater technical and professional expertise, their services will be in greater demand by other organizations. Professional mobility may be one of the primary forces helping to increase effective interface between organizations.

10 Leonard R. Sayles and Margaret K. Chandler, *Managing Large Systems: Organizations for the Future,* Harper & Row, Publishers, New York, 1971, p. 316.

Response to Technological Change

Technology will continue to be one of the most vital forces affecting organizations and their management in the future. It should be reemphasized that technology is not just mechanical or electronic hardware but relates to the knowledge required for task performance. Not only will the organization of the future be influenced by advancing knowledge, it will be the primary social vehicle creating change.

Technological Forecasting

With a stable technology it is possible for the organization to plan its activities with a high degree of certainty. With a dynamic technology, many uncertainties are introduced into the organizational system. It can no longer take technology as given and then concentrate on other aspects of the situation. Business organizations have come to recognize the importance of environmental and competitive forces and have developed elaborate means for forecasting them. However, with dynamic change it is becoming important to engage in technological forecasting.

For years technology has been the dominant force creating change. . . . Yet only recently have managers in public and private organizations realized the need to forecast technological change and its impact on their activities. Economic forecasts, market forecasts, financial forecasts, even weather forecasts have become standard tools of management. Someday soon, technological forecasting—now in its infancy—must become as accepted and useful as these other analytical devices. [11]

Precise technological forecasting will be impossible in the future as it has been in the past. Too many uncertain forces exist. Who could have predicted the dramatic breakthrough brought by penicillin or the laser or atomic energy? However, this does not mean that the organization should give up on such forecasting. It does not have to be exact in predicting the form of the new developments. Rather, like economic and market forecasts, it can be developed in terms of probabilities and general trends.

In the future, organizations of all types—businesses, hospitals, universities, and governmental agencies—will be actively involved in technological forecasting. They will be aided by improvements in communication systems that provide information from other organizations and the environment. Marshall McLuhan has noted that already the communications revolution has made us into a "global theater." [12] In the past, telegraph, telephone, radio, and television have

11 James Brian Quinn, "Technological Forecasting," *Harvard Business Review,* March–April 1967, p. 89.
12 Marshall McLuhan, *Culture Is Our Business,* McGraw-Hill Book Company, New York, 1970, p. 8.

increased the speed and volume of information flow between people tremendously. In the future, more sophisticated computer-based systems will provide an extensive nervous system that will link together the whole human race. This network of communications is tending to produce a world superculture that is superimposed on the more traditional national and regional cultures of the past.

Technology and Social Engineering

Many of the problems of a modern society, such as education, urban decay, and poverty, can be dealt with either through technology or social engineering. Technology is directed toward solving problems by the utilization of scientific knowledge. The social engineering approach is directed toward inducing social change. For many social problems this approach is more difficult, but offers the greatest long-term benefits.

There is a more basic sense in which social problems are much more difficult than technological problems. A social problem exists because many people behave, individually, in a socially unacceptable way. To solve a social problem one must induce social change—one must persuade many people to behave differently than they have behaved in the past. One must persuade many people to have few babies, or to drive more carefully, or to refrain from disliking Negroes. By contrast, resolution of a technological problem involves many fewer individual decisions. [13]

It is frequently difficult to find solutions to problems by social means— that is, by changing the attitudes, motivations, and behavior of people. The technological approach may offer the best short-run solution. An example of these alternatives may be seen in the various programs for urban redevelopment. One approach would be to try to induce people to return to rural areas (or to refrain from coming to the cities). Currently, this approach is part of the national policy of France, Russia, Japan, and China. The other alternative is to use technical knowledge to redesign the cities, given the high level of urban population concentration. We can see many other situations that have similar alternatives. For example, the development of tranquilizers and other drugs has reduced the number of patients in mental hospitals and has returned them to society. This "technological solution" partially accomplishes the goal without solving the basic underlying psychological and social problems that create mental illness. The technological approach has both advantages and disadvantages:

The Technological Fix accepts . . . intrinsic shortcomings and circumvents them or capitalizes on them for socially useful ends. The Fix is, therefore, eminently practical and, in the short term, relatively effective. One does not wait around trying to change people's minds: if people want more water, one gets them more water rather than requiring them to reduce their use of water; if people insist on driving autos while they are drunk, one provides safer autos that prevent injuries even after a severe accident.

13 Alvin M. Weinberg, "Can Technology Replace Social Engineering?" *The American Behavioral Scientist,* May 1967, p. 7.

But the technological solutions to social problems tend to be incomplete and metastable, to replace one social problem with another.[14]

Technological solutions to social problems provide expedient ways to achieve certain goals. However, in the long run many of the problems facing modern society must be dealt with through basic changes in the value systems and behavior of people. Both these methods will be utilized in the future as they have been in the past. They are not necessarily in conflict, but can be complementary.

Complex organizations of the future will be directly involved in this process of utilizing both technology and social engineering in accomplishing the goals of society. One of the key problems facing organizations is maintaining appropriate internal relationships between the technical and psychosocial systems to ensure both accomplishment of organizational goals and individual satisfaction. Technology should be considered in humanistic terms. It is created by people and should ultimately serve their needs. Taken alone, technology is neither humanistic nor mechanistic. "Modern technology *need not* destroy aesthetic, spiritual and social values, but it will most certainly do so unless the individuals who manage our technology are firmly committed to the preservation of such values."[15] We can determine how advancing knowledge will be used to shape our society.

Response to Social Change

In addition to responding to technological change, in the future organizations will have to adapt to many other forces in the environment. Problems of consumerism, gray power, race relations, poverty, changing family relationships, urban blight, health care, adaptations to leisure, and providing opportunities for greater work satisfaction are just a few examples of broader social issues that will affect organizations. In many ways these social issues are more complex than economic and technological problems. And their solution is more difficult.

The problems are thus infinitely complex and interrelated. No quick, easy, cheap, or final solutions are possible. We must make progress quickly and rapidly, but if we expect to finish the job quickly and get back to our usual concerns, we will certainly be disappointed. The answer is not more education, more money, more jobs, or more and better housing for the disadvantaged, but all of these things and much more. It involves our relations with the rest of the world and our rethinking of whole areas of life. Most of all perhaps, it involves our willingness to pay the price.[16]

These social issues in the general environment will move directly into the

---

14 Ibid., p. 9.

15 John W. Gardner, *Self-renewal: The Individual and the Innovative Society,* Harper & Row, Publishers, Incorporated, New York, 1963, p. 57.

16 Ina Corinne Brown, *Understanding Race Relations,* Prentice-Hall, Inc., Englewood Cliffs, N.J., 1973, p. 240.

task environments of organizations. We have seen this pattern developing over the past several decades. Organizations will need to develop techniques for predicting the social changes of the future and to develop programs in response to such forecasts.

Social Forecasting

"In recent years, researchers have developed the art of forecasting technology (what man can do) but have paid relatively little attention to devising ways to forecast social needs (what man wants)." [17] We have developed sophisticated means for economic forecasting and have increasingly emphasized technological forecasting. In the future, these approaches to forecasting will be broadened to include predictions of other social forces.

Social expectations and changing environment have produced a shift in types of forecasting of most concern to top management. Traditionally, economic forecasting of such environmental factors as gross national product, interest rates, prices, and wage rates has dominated company top level forecasting efforts. Forecasting of noneconomic factors in the environment is becoming more important . . . for managerial decision making. I would not be surprised to see in ten years that forecasting of various social values and social indicators will stand beside such traditional economic forecasts as GNP as major projections important to management in decision making. In mind, of course, are projections of how people feel about such social values as work and leisure, materialism, esthetics, and so on. The social indicators will concern elements of life quality, such as medical care, health, clean air, clean water, and so on. [18]

It is evident that social forecasting is tremendously complex. It is more difficult than either economic or technological forecasting because of the complexities and uncertainties involved in the evolution of value systems.

The fact that social forecasting is difficult does not minimize its importance. A first step is acceptance of the inevitability of social and political change. Historically, organizations, particularly businesses, have accepted and welcomed economic and technological changes but have often resisted social and political change. The prevailing concept has been to emphasize the desirability of social and political stability so that "we can go about our business as usual." But this view is no longer possible. Social, economic, and technological changes are all inevitable (and also interactive) and must be planned for as an ongoing organizational activity. "Only when managers recognize that social and political changes are not transient, and that it is not illegitimate for segments of the public to prod organizations to serve public purposes, will they be able to deal effectively with change." [19]

17 Clark C. Abt, "Forecasting Future Social Needs," *The Futurist*, February 1971, p. 20.
18 George A. Steiner, "Changing Managerial Philosophies," *Business Horizons*, June 1971, p. 8.
19 James E. Post, "The Challenge of Managing under Social Uncertainty," *Business Horizons*, August 1977, p. 52.

Social
Indicators

One of the major problems in social forecasting is the lack of good historical and current information on social conditions. Attempts to develop social indicators and to accumulate these into a national balance sheet of social accounts similar to the national income and product accounts reflect the need for more sophisticated information on social conditions. Although there are obviously many more difficulties than in developing economic indicators, it is apparent that we are moving in this direction. In the future it is likely that individual organizations will be directly tied in with a system of social indicators and accounts that will indicate their social as well as economic effects on society. Organizational performance will be evaluated in terms of social effects as well as economic results.

Developing a
Democratic-
Humanistic
System

Organizations have proved over the past century that they are effective in accomplishing many goals. Witness the tremendous productive capacity of our industrial system. In the future, other key issues will assume importance. Can organizations make use of advancing technology in accomplishing their goals while satisfying human and social needs? In the traditional bureaucratic model, the organization was designed to achieve technical functions with little consideration given to the psychosocial system. A continuation of this approach would be unfortunate for society. "Management must constantly be on guard not to design the human participation in total systems completely in terms of technical functions. This requires that at every level the total man involved must be considered." [20]

A number of writers feel that organizations have failed to provide a humanistic work environment by precluding opportunities for satisfaction and self-actualization. We do not share this pessimistic view. While it may have been true that the traditional organization theory of bureaucracy and scientific management emphasized the technical and structural aspects to the detriment of the psychosocial system, there has been a definite trend toward greater concern for participant satisfaction, quality of work life, and broad social impacts.

Quality of
Work
Life

One of the major problems facing the United States and many other industrialized countries is the quality of work life. The issue is not just one of

---

20 Charles R. DeCarlo, "Changes in Management Environment and Their Effect upon Values," in Charles A. Myers (ed.), *The Impact of Computers on Management*, The M.I.T. Press, Cambridge, Mass., 1967, p. 253.

achieving greater human satisfaction; it is also fundamental to the long-range efficiency, adaptability, and effectiveness of organizations *and* national perform-ance. Organizations and nations that are effective in dealing with these funda-mental issues will be more successful in making the transformation into the post-

Figure 24.2   Improving Life In Organizations

NATIONAL CENTER FOR PRODUCTIVITY
AND QUALITY OF WORKING LIFE
WASHINGTON, D.C.   20036

IMPROVING LIFE IN ORGANIZATIONS

How can work in American society be organized so the individual can enjoy a greater sense of participation, creativity, and dignity? How can we tap more fully the reservoir of ingenuity and intelligence of Americans, the most highly educated people in history, to improve the productivity of the economy? These are among the critical questions we must address to enhance the quality of American life.

As a people, we have made enormous social and economic progress over the past 200 years as a result of our inventiveness, organizing ability, and desire to improve the standard of living, not only for ourselves but also for the next generations. However, as economic life becomes more highly interdependent and complex, there is danger that responsibilities are becoming overspecialized; that organizational goals are being obscured; that the individual's potential for excellence is being overlooked; that we are in risk of losing our dynamism and sense of purpose.

This suggests that we must seek better understanding of how human resources can be used more effectively in large organizations and how present practices can be changed in the light of our knowledge. For our Nation's progress in this last quarter of the twentieth century may hinge as much on social research and invention as advances in earlier decades did on physical science and technology.

Nelson A. Rockefeller
Chairman, Board of Directors
National Center for Productivity
and Quality of Working Life

industrial era. Many countries in Europe and Asia have developed specific national programs of experimentation and research. An overview of these issues from the American perspective is set forth in Figure 24.2.

Quality of work life has many different meanings. To some it means industrial democracy or codetermination with increased employee participation in formal organization decision making. To others, particularly managers and administrators, the term suggests efforts to increase productivity through improvement in the psychosocial rather than the technical and structural systems. Some, particularly unions and work groups, view it as more equitable sharing of the income and benefits and more humane and healthy working conditions. Others see it as breaking down the traditional high degree of specialization typical in many work situations and substituting enlarged and enriched jobs or autonomous work groups that enhance social relationships at the workplace. Finally, others take an even broader view of changing the entire organizational climate by humanizing work, individualizing organizations, and fundamentally changing the structural and managerial systems. Overall, the issue of quality of work life typically addresses questions such as:

How can individuals be helped to develop careers that allow them to realize the full range and extent of their capabilities and interests, while at the same time meeting both the short-term and the long-term manpower needs of the organizations that employ them?

How can jobs be designed so that effective performance is linked with meaningful, interesting, and challenging work?

Under what conditions do various types of rewards (such as pay, promotions, and fringe benefits) and reward systems (such as job-based versus skill-based pay, hourly versus salary payment, and individual versus group incentive plans) prove most effective for encouraging workers to join an organization, come to work regularly, and perform effectively?

What are the dynamics of group and intergroup relations that must be taken into account in any attempt to understand the behavior and improve the quality of work life of group members?

What are the key supervisory strategies that produce the highest quality of work life for people in organizations? What are the structural and other constraints that influence a supervisor's behavior?

How can the desired organizational changes, once identified, actually be brought about? [21]

We think that progress will be made on all these fronts. It is not a question of the luxury of having happier workers; it is a fundamental issue of effectiveness, effi-

---

[21] J. Lloyd Suttle, "Improving Life at Work—Problems and Prospects," in J. Richard Hackman and J. Lloyd Suttle (eds.), *Improving Life at Work*, Goodyear Publishing Company, Inc., Santa Monica, Calif., 1977, pp. 1–2.

ciency, and participant satisfaction that together underlie the survival of our society.

Latent human capability is the most valuable resource of the organization—much more important than physical or financial resources. Increasingly, management will emphasize the importance of human resources and will recognize that maintaining a viable psychosocial system is one of its most vital tasks. Organizations will develop a more adaptive-organic system in place of a stable-mechanistic structure. This is not a revolutionary change; it is a continuation of the trend that has long been evident. Obviously, the battle for a humanistic organization will never be completely won. The manager will have the continuing problem of balancing the technical tasks with the objectives of the psychosocial system. This delicate task of balance and integration will be of major concern to future managers.

Power Equalization in the Future

One of the major forces occurring in organizations in society is the desire on the part of all participants to have greater influence. The rise of labor unions in the 1930s, the growing student demands for participation in university affairs, and the collective activities on the part of public school teachers and nurses are examples of this desire for greater involvement. We see a continuing decline in the gap between organizational elites and lower-level participants. In formal organizations, there appears to be a move toward "power equalization," with all members having greater influence on internal affairs. Organizations of the future wll place less emphasis on a hierarchical structure and will move toward a more equalitarian social system. It is even likely in the not too distant future that a major symbol of stratification, the salute to the superior, will be unceremoniously discarded by the military services.

This movement is exemplified by works councils in most European firms, in which employee representatives are actively involved in decision making. Many of these countries have recently passed codetermination laws that require a certain proportion of the board of directors to be elected by workers.[22] This approach reflects a fundamental redistribution of power within these organizations.

Innovation and Creativity

A popular theme during the 1950s was the growing conformity and lack of initiative on the part of organizational participants. In this view, the organiza-

---

22 Klaus E. Agthe, "Mitbestimmung: Report on a Social Experiment," *Business Horizons,* February 1977, pp. 5–14; and S. Benjamin Prasad, "The Growth of Co-Determination," *Business Horizons,* April 1977, pp. 23–29.

tion had so structured individuals' behavior that performance was typically mediocre and routine—they lacked individuality and initiative. The basic attitude was one of "don't rock the boat," play it safe, and get the organizational rewards without too much effort.

This view was based on the premise that the modern organization required a structuring of human behavior that was more rigid than in earlier, preindustrial society. It romanticized the preorganization social environment to suggest that people had almost complete autonomy. This view seems far from reality. "Man apparently neither wants nor has experienced this postulated state of complete autonomy. People have always demanded structure in their lives. With few exceptions, men depend on human relationships, some fixity of structure, routine, and habit to survive psychologically." [23] While it is true that the organization does structure human behavior, so do the family, the informal group, and all other types of social interaction. The complete state of human autonomy and individualism that has served as the romantic ideal probably never has existed for people since they emerged as social creatures.

In our view, the "problem" of the "organization person" will diminish in the future. While the decade of the fifties may have been one of conformity and passivity, the decade of the seventies appears to be just the opposite. There is greater activism and individual initiative on the part of people in organizations.

A number of forces will continue to reduce pressures to conform. There is a growing sense of professionalism among specialized personnel. They develop loyalties to their professional colleagues and are not as subject to the control and conformity requirements of the organization. Often their loyalty is to a discipline, and they can be innovative and creative within their sphere of competence. Another modifying force is the need for organizations to adapt to dynamic change in the turbulent environment and to stress innovation. The passive organization person was a product of the stable-mechanistic structure. Innovative-creative people will be required and sought in the adaptive-organic systems of the future.

A Mosaic Psychosocial System

In society and in organizations we have generally emphasized the desirability of developing common cultures, values, and even life styles. This has had a homogenizing effect on participants and the psychosocial subsystem in organizations. Current trends allow for more individual and group diversity.

American society up to now has stressed the idea of a "melting pot" and has sought to create through public education a uniform culture. With increased affluence and increased political skill, this ideal can now be called into question. Can we now invent a "mosaic" society, composed of many small subcultures, each of which gives its partici-

---

[23] Leonard R. Sayles, *Individualism and Big Business,* McGraw-Hill Book Company, New York, 1963, p. 179.

pants a sense of community and identity which is so desperately needed in a mass world, and which can at the same time remain at peace with its neighbors and not threaten to pull the society apart?[24]

We see an increasing possibility of allowing more diverse values, views, and life styles among different participants and groups within the confines of organizations. Over the past decade, universities have developed a diversity of programs that do not require all students to conform to a given pattern. Many churches have accommodated themselves to diverse groups in order to keep them within the overall system. Business organizations have shown indications of more tolerance for individual and group variations. The maintenance of a mosaic psychosocial system composed of different subcultures is difficult. Integrating the efforts and interests of people and groups with different values and life styles will tax the skills of managers.

Dynamic, Flexible Organizations

The foregoing discussion of organizations and the factors influencing them in the future can be summarized as follows:

1 Organizations will be operating in a turbulent environment that requires continual change and adjustment.
2 They will have to adapt to an increasing diversity of cultural values in the social environment.
3 Greater emphasis will be placed on technological and social forecasting.
4 Organizations will continue to expand their boundaries and domains. They will increase in size and complexity.
5 Organizations will continue to differentiate their activities, causing increased problems of integration and coordination.
6 Organizations will continue to have major problems in the accumulation and utilization of knowledge. Intellectual activities will be stressed.
7 Concern for the quality of work life will increase. Successful resolution will have a significant impact on human satisfaction *and* productivity.
8 Greater emphasis will be focused on suggestion and persuasion rather than on coercion based on authoritarian power as the means for coordinating the activities of the participants and functions within the organization.

24 Kenneth E. Boulding, "Expecting the Unexpected: The Uncertain Future of Knowledge and Technology," in *Designing Education for the Future,* Colorado Department of Education, Boulder, Colo., 1966, p. 212. For a more complete discussion of these issues, see Martin O. Heisler (ed.), "Ethnic Conflict in the World Today," *The Annals of the American Academy of Political and Social Science,* September 1977.

9 Participants at all levels in organizations will have more influence. Organizations of the future will adopt a power-equalization rather than power-differentiation model.

10 There will be greater diversity in values and life styles among people and groups in organizations. A mosaic psychosocial system will be normal.

11 Problems of interface between organizations will increase. New means for effective interorganizational coordination will be developed.

12 Computerized information-decision systems will have an increasing impact on organizations.

13 The number of professionals and scientists and their influence within organizations will increase. There will also be a decline in the proportion of independent professionals with many more salaried professionals.

14 Goals of complex organizations will diversify. Emphasis will be on satisficing a number of goals rather than maximizing any one.

15 Evaluation of organizational performance will be difficult. Many new administrative techniques will be developed for evaluation of performance in all spheres of activity.

16 Processes of planned change, with widespread involvement of participants, will be institutionalized.

This listing suggests that there will be a movement away from the stable-mechanistic organization toward a more adaptive-organic system. Bennis predicts that bureaucracy, as a formal structure of organization based on logical relationships among functions or tasks, will be replaced within the next twenty-five to fifty years by a new type of organization better suited to the needs of twentieth-century industrialism. "Bureaucracy emerged out of the need for more predictability, order, and precision. It was an organization ideally suited to the values and the demands of the Victorian Empire. And just as bureaucracy emerged as a creative response to a radically new age, so today new organizational shapes and forms are surfacing before our eyes."[25] While we agree that there may be a general movement toward the adaptive-organic form, we cannot agree that the stable-mechanistic organization will disappear. The very essence of the contingency view, as discussed in Chapter 19, suggests that a wide variety of organizational forms will continue to be appropriate, depending on the specific situation. When the environment and technology are relatively routine and certain and when the emphasis is on programmable output and productivity, the stable-mechanistic form may be fitting. However, it is also likely that these conditions will not prevail for as many organizations in the future as in the past.

25 Warren G. Bennis, "Organizations of the Future," *Personnel Administration,* September–October, 1967, p. 6.

Evolving Managerial Systems

With the growth of large-scale organizations and expansion of their activities, management has changed significantly. In medium and large firms there has been a move away from the traditional owner-manager toward the "professional manager." The trend from the stable-mechanistic to adaptive-organic systems has also created fundamental changes for management.

Expanding Management's Role

As more human activities are taking place within larger organizations, the role of management has expanded. There has been a significant increase in the number of managers, professionals, and technical personnel in the labor force. In the future the managerial role will be of even greater importance. "The essential task of modern management is to deal with change. Management is the agency through which most changes enter our society, and it is the agency that then must cope with the environment it has set in turbulent motion." [26]

Management must deal with the dynamics of change and provide coordination for the overall system. We do not agree with some writers who suggest that computerized information-decision systems will take over many managerial functions. While this new technology will help in dealing with the routine, programmable decision-making activities, it will not reduce the more important function of management in dealing with the nonprogrammable, innovative, and creative aspects of organizations.

Will Organizations Become Unmanageable?

The managerial role will not become simpler in the future; it will be even more complex. Some suggest that many of our complex organizations may be approaching unmanageability. [27]

We agree that growing environmental and internal complexities will make organizations unmanageable if traditional stable-mechanistic approaches are used. It is unlikely that these complex systems can be managed effectively "from the top" of the hierarchy. Many of the traditional principles of management reinforced a structured organization well adapted to standardization and

---

[26] Max Ways, "Tomorrow's Management: A More Adventurous Life in a Free-form Corporation," *Fortune*, July 1966, p. 84.

[27] Bertram M. Gross, *Organizations and Their Managing*, The Free Press of Glencoe, New York, 1968, pp. vii–viii.

productivity. However, with a more dynamic environment and the need for flexibility, new managerial systems have developed that emphasize more effective utilization of expert knowledge at all levels, lateral and diagonal communication networks, reliance on group decision-making processes, a project or team approach, and the expansion of the power-equalization concept as a basis for motivation and satisfaction of participants.

Management's Use of Knowledge

Increasingly, management has become a more intellectual activity and involves more effective use of knowledge.

Intellectual processes will be of greater importance to the future manager than to his present-day counterpart; he will spend more time on them. The managerial job will have many more intellectual and educational requirements. It will involve more technical scientific and engineering problems, as well as more complex budgeting and financial decisions. The manager will be functioning in a world where his performance will be evaluated even more than it is today on his intellectual skills in bringing about increases in rate of growth, in quality of services and output. [28]

The increasing importance of managers as knowledge workers will create some rather fundamental problems of obsolescence in the future. When management skills were learned by experience, the longer the service, the better qualified the manager. However, as management has become more dependent on new knowledge of operations and techniques that cannot be learned solely by experience, the likelihood of obsolescence is greater. It is highly unlikely that any formal program of education can be developed that will carry a manager through his or her entire career. The time span for obsolescence of the manager's knowledge will become shorter, just as it has for scientists, professionals, and technicians.

Self-renewal through training and motivation for innovativeness has become a dominant need. Societies, organizations, and individuals grow complacent and stale, and rejuvenation is imperative. The best means for offsetting this paralysis is through emphasis on the individual. "Unless we foster versatile, innovative and self-renewing men and women, all the ingenious social arrangements in the world will not help us." [29] It will be necessary to develop more programs for reeducating managers as they move through their careers. More postexperience programs will be developed for training managers in all types of complex organizations. They will be granted educational leaves to renew their knowledge. The adaptive-organic organization can provide opportunities for participants to change functions, pursue new activities, and meet new challenges.

[28] Reprinted by permission of the publisher from "Implications of Behaviorial Sciences in the Year 2000," by Bernard M. Bass, *Management 2000,* p. 104. © 1968 by the American Foundation for Management Research, New York.
[29] Gardner, op. cit., p. xiv.

Both a Managerial and a Behavioral Scientist

We have suggested that management concepts have been substantially influenced by developments in the management sciences and the behavioral sciences. The manager of the future will have to have substantial knowledge and competence in both areas. In fact, the management role will be one of integrating and coordinating a diversity of techniques and concepts from a number of fields.

Standing squarely between the forces of economic efficiency and technological development and the irresistible psychological and sociological pressures of the human spirit are the representatives of management. The manager must be a technologist and a psychologist, an engineer and a sociologist, . . . analytical and reflective, and a man of action—but . . . deliberate before action. The new manager must indeed be a rare and a *balanced* combination of scientist and humanist! [30]

The manager of the future must deal with both aspects—the technical-economic and the psychosocial—and integrate them to accomplish the goals of both technical efficiency and human satisfaction.

In spite of the growing difficulties of the managerial role, it will offer more opportunities for self-actualization than in the past. Future organizations will be vital in meeting the needs of society, and managers will have increasingly important functions. The managerial role will offer great challenges and rewards for those with a high tolerance for ambiguity plus the skills and propensity to cope with complex issues in dynamic and uncertain situations.

A Flexible Managerial System

The foregoing discussion suggests that managerial life will not become easier. Some of the factors influencing management in the future can be summarized as follows:

1 The managerial role will offer intellectual, emotional, and professional challenge—but there may be high costs. Managers will need a high tolerance for uncertainty, ambiguity, and stress.

2 Management will become more professional in the sense of requiring a more comprehensive body of knowledge, technical expertise, and self-control. Economic and technical skills will continue to be emphasized but augmented by social and political skills.

---

[30] Reprinted by permission of the publisher from "Implications of Behavioral Sciences in the Year 2000," by Forrest H. Kirkpatrick, *Management 2000,* p. 115. ©1968 by the American Foundation for Management Research, New York.

3 Managers will continue to recognize the relevance of a systems and contingency approach. This conceptual framework for analysis will guide strategic choices in organization design and managerial practice.

4 Managers will need greater awareness and concern for social and environmental forces and recognition that the organization's performance will be measured in many new and varied ways.

5 Effective managers will be astute conceptualizers—using environmental and organizational scanning and diagnosis to ensure that decisions and actions fit specific situations.

6 Managers will become relatively more concerned with means (as opposed to ends). They will be more aware of potential unintended consequences (as opposed to anticipated results only).

7 The managerial system will involve greater diversity in terms of sex, ethnicity, and values. Effective managers will recognize, tolerate, and even encourage diversity.

8 Many more managers will be working in less structured situations (such as matrix forms) rather than traditional hierarchical organizations.

9 Managerial recognition that people have the capacity to grow, achieve, and utilize their abilities will become more widespread. A positive view of human nature will be recognized as an important determinant of individual and organizational accomplishment.

10 Managers will continue to exercise power in organizational settings. Although constrained by environmental, technological, structural, and psychosocial forces, managers will have room to maneuver. Organizational performance will depend on the appropriate exercise of discretionary influence.

11 Managers will view the area of people and relationships and the area of task and productivity as mutually supportive rather than mutually exclusive. Emphasizing both areas will lead to increased organization effectiveness and efficiency, as well as participant satisfaction.

12 Managers will be more concerned with developing a climate receptive to change—open communication, trust, and the ability to deal constructively with conflicts. Emphasis on collaboration and teamwork in problem solving, rather than interpersonal and intergroup competition, will increase.

13 Managers will be more adept at combining and integrating several theoretical propositions. For example, management by objectives and results (MBO/R) approaches will be based on theories of effective goal setting, motivation, change, and leadership.

14 Managers will put increasing emphasis on planned change and organization renewal. More attention will be devoted to improving problem-solving processes.

15 Managers will become more directly involved in organizational research. This process will enhance the probability that relevant issues will be investigated and that findings will be implemented in practice.

16 Management education will include more emphasis on developing intuitive thinking processes, creativity, and wisdom in order to balance analytical thinking processes, rationality, and logic.

17 Managers will pay more attention to managing their time—a valuable resource. Prioritization of tasks and astute allocation of scarce time will have increasing impact on performance and satisfaction.

18 Self-renewal via a combination of experience and continuing education will be increasingly important. Career planning will involve questions such as "Who am I?" "What do I want out of life?" "What do I want out of my work life?" Managers will explicitly assess the type of organization climate in which they can be most effective.

19 Managers will be diagnosticians (thinkers) and activists (doers). The art of management will continue to depend on a reasonable success rate for actions in a probabilistic environment.

Importance of Research and Experimentation

We have come far in our understanding of organizations and their management. However, as our knowledge increases, we recognize that there is much more to be known. There also are difficulties in translating new knowledge into practice. Dynamic changes in the nature of organizations and managerial problems will always leave a gap between knowledge and its application, but progress is being made.

There is substantial evidence that we know a great deal about organization design and management practice that is appropriate for relatively stable-mechanistic organizations. There is much less evidence that we have sufficient knowledge and skill to manage the more adaptive-organic organizations. This is understandable, because we have had more experience in dealing with the former and most of our managerial practices are based on this background. Learning to manage the more adaptive-organic form is an evolutionary process, and it is natural for managers to revert to behavior appropriate for mechanistic situations because of its familiarity. For many, the prescriptions seem synonymous with good management. Some managers create subjective certainty by ignoring the confounding aspects of complex, dynamic situations. By assuming that all other things are equal, when in reality they are not, managers develop a false sense of security (Ignorance is bliss!) that can lead to inappropriate strategies and actions.

It is necessary to reconsider much of our traditional knowledge. We see this as a continuing learning process for researchers, theorists, and managers. A systems and contingency approach provides the broad conceptual foundation for improving this process, but obviously the theory is far from complete; there are many gaps in our understanding and in translating concepts into practice.

One of the most important ways to increase our knowledge is through continued research and experimentation on organizations and their management. We need to develop more comprehensive evaluational programs to determine the effectiveness of various organizational innovations. How effective are programs such as management by objectives and results, behavior modification, and job enrichment or techniques such as zero-base budgeting, linear programming, or computerized on-line information systems? We need more sophisticated organizational research to determine the efficacy of these endeavors.

A strong case can be made for the vital importance of assessing the relative effectiveness of different management practices and organization designs by studying what happens when they are introduced into organizations. Failure to do this dooms us to repeating the use of ineffective methods and to the slow development of better approaches to organizational design and theory. [31]

It is vital that managers develop a stronger evaluation research orientation to test the appropriateness of various organizational innovations. [32] In order to advance the field of organization and management theory, it is necessary to merge the energies of the researcher-theorist and the practicing manager. It is not enough to have the academician conduct the research and develop the theories and then have managers attempt the applications. The effort should be interactive and continuous. Theorists should recognize that not all concepts work in practice (at least not without modifications to fit specific situations) and managers should recognize the importance of evaluational research to determine the usefulness of organizational innovations. Working together, they can integrate their perspectives and increase our understanding of organizations *and* improve managerial practices. Sophistication in the study of organizations will come when we have a more complete understanding of organizations as total systems so that we can prescribe more appropriate designs and managerial actions. Ultimately, organization theory should serve as the foundation for more effective management practices.

Questions and Problems

1 How will the turbulent environment affect organizations of the future?
2 Why has there been an expansion of organizational boundaries? Select several organization types and predict the direction of their future boundary expansion.

31 Edward E. Lawler III, "Adaptive Experiments: An Approach to Organizational Behavior Research," *Academy of Management Review,* October 1977, p. 584.
32 Barry M. Staw, "The Experimenting Organization," *Organizational Dynamics,* Summer 1977, pp. 2–41.

3 Why will the problems of interorganizational relationships be of increasing importance in the future? What new means might be used to improve interorganizational coordination?

4 What are the major difficulties in technological forecasting? Given these problems, why should management even attempt such forecasting?

5 Develop a list of various organizations that are engaged in "the scientific study of the future." Investigate the various approaches they have used.

6 Contrast problem solution through technology and problem solution through social engineering. Make a list of social problems that might be dealt with through either technology or social engineering.

7 Why is the issue of quality of work life becoming more important in many societies? Investigate the current developments concerning quality of work life in a specific organization in your community.

8 What is meant by social forecasting? Study the approaches used by several organizations in their social forecasting.

9 What is meant by a humanistic technology? Do you think it is possible in an industrial society?

10 Do you agree or disagree that organizations will move toward greater power equalization? Give examples to support your arguments.

11 What are some of the major difficulties in maintaining a mosaic psychosocial system?

12 Why will the organization of the future be concerned with establishing new measures for evaluation of performance? What types of measures might they use?

13 Use the list of factors influencing management in the future (pp. 609–611) as a basis for considering your own career plans. How will you develop your knowledge and skills to meet these future conditions?

Epilogue

Some men see things as they are and say "Why?";
I dream of things which never were and ask "Why not?"
Robert F. Kennedy

Certitude is not the test for certainty. We have been
cocksure of many things that were not so.
Justice Oliver Wendell Holmes

New times demand new measures and new men;
The world advances, and in time outgrows
The laws that in our fathers' day were best;
And doubtless, after us, some purer scheme
Will be shaped out by wiser men than we,
Made wiser by the steady growth of truth.
James Russell Lowell

We have not succeeded in answering all our
questions. Indeed, we sometimes feel we have not completely
answered any of them. The answers we have found only serve
to raise a whole new set of questions. In some ways we feel
we are as confused as ever. But we think we are confused on
a higher level and about more important things.
Anonymous

Bibliography

Ackerman, Robert W. *The Social Challenge to Business,* Harvard University Press, Cambridge, Mass., 1975.

Ackoff, Russell L. *A Concept of Corporate Planning,* Wiley-Interscience, New York, 1970.

——— "Towards a System of Systems Concepts," *Management Science,* July 1971, pp. 661–671.

Adams, J. Stacy "Toward an Understanding of Inequity," *Journal of Abnormal and Social Psychology,* November 1963, pp. 422–436.

Alexis, Marcus and Charles Z. Wilson *Organizational Decision-Making,* Prentice-Hall, Inc., Englewood Cliffs, N.J., 1967.

Allison, Graham T. *Essence of Decision,* Little, Brown and Company, Boston, 1971.

Anderson, Carl R., and Frank T. Paine Managerial Perceptions and Strategic Behavior," *Academy of Management Journal,* December 1975, pp. 811–823.

Andrews, Kenneth R. *The Concept of Corporate Strategy,* Dow Jones-Irwin, Inc., Homewood, Ill., 1971.

Ansoff, H. Igor *Corporate Strategy,* McGraw-Hill Book Company, New York, 1965.

Anthony, Robert N. *Planning and Control Systems: A Framework for Analysis,* Harvard Graduate School of Business Administration, Boston, 1965.

Aram, John D. *Dilemmas of Administrative Behavior,* Prentice-Hall, Inc., Englewood Cliffs, N.J., 1976.

Argyris, Chris *Integrating the Individual and the Organization,* John Wiley & Sons, Inc., New York, 1964.

——— *The Applicability of Organizational Sociology,* Cambridge University Press, Cambridge, England, 1972.

Banovetz, James M. (ed.) *Managing the Modern City,* International City Management Association, Washington, D.C., 1971.

Barnard, Chester I. *The Functions of the Executive,* Harvard University Press, Cambridge Mass., 1938.

Beckett, John A. *Management Dynamics: The New Synthesis,* McGraw-Hill Book Company, New York, 1971.

617

Beckhard, Richard *Organization Development: Strategies and Models,* Addison-Wesley Publishing Company, Reading, Mass., 1969.

Bell, Cecil H., Jr., and James E. Rosenzweig "OD in the City: A Potpourri of Pluses and Minuses," *Southern Public Administration Review,* March 1978, pp. 433–448.

Bell, Daniel *The Coming of Post-Industrial Society,* Basic Books, Inc., Publishers, New York, 1973.

Bell, Robert, and John Coplans *Decisions, Decisions,* W. W. Norton & Company, Inc., New York, 1976.

Bellman, Richard "Control Theory," *Scientific American,* September 1964, pp. 186–200.

Bendix, Reinhard, and Seymour Martin Lipset (eds.) *Class, Status and Power,* The Free Press of Glencoe, New York, 1953.

Bennis, Warren G. (ed.) *American Bureaucracy,* Aldine Publishing Company, Chicago, 1970.

———, **Kenneth D. Benne, Robert Chin, and Kenneth E. Corey (eds.)** *The Planning of Change,* 3d ed., Holt, Rinehart & Winston, Inc., New York, 1976.

Bent, Alan E., and Ralph A. Rossum (eds.) *Urban Administration: Management, Politics, and Change,* Dunellen Publishing Company, Inc., Port Washington, New York, 1976.

Berelson, Bernard, and Gary A. Steiner *Human Behavior: An Inventory of Scientific Findings,* Harcourt, Brace & World, Inc., New York, 1964.

Berrien, F. Kenneth "A General Systems Approach to Organizations," in Marvin D. Dunnette (ed.), *Handbook of Industrial and Organizational Psychology,* Rand McNally College Publishing Company, Chicago, 1976, pp. 41–62.

Blake, Robert R., and Jane S. Mouton *Corporate Excellence through Grid Organization Development: A Systems Approach,* Gulf Publishing Company, Houston, 1968.

——— **and** ——— *The New Managerial Grid,* Gulf Publishing Company, Houston, 1978.

Blau, Peter M., and Richard A. Schoenherr *The Structure of Organizations,* Basic Books, Inc., New York, 1971.

———, **and W. Richard Scott** *Formal Organizations: A Comparative Analysis,* Chandler Publishing Company, San Francisco, 1962.

Blauner, Robert *Alienation and Freedom,* The University of Chicago Press, Chicago, 1964.

Boulding, Kenneth E. *The Impact of the Social Sciences,* Rutgers University Press, New Brunswick, N.J., 1966.

Bowers, David G. *Systems of Organizations,* The University of Michigan Press, Ann Arbor, 1976.

———, **and Stanley E. Seashore** "Predicting Organizational Effectiveness with a Four-Factor Theory of Leadership," *Administrative Science Quarterly,* September 1966, pp. 238–263.

Brubacher, John S., and Willis Rudy *Higher Education in Transition: An American History: 1636–1956,* Harper & Row, Publishers, Incorporated, New York, 1958.

Bruner, Jerome S., Jacqueline J. Goodnow, and George A. Austin *A Study of Thinking,* John Wiley & Sons, Inc., New York, 1956.

Buckley, Walter (ed.) *Modern Systems Research for the Behavioral Scientist,* Aldine Publishing Co., Chicago, 1968.

Burns, Tom, and G. M. Stalker *The Management of Innovation,* Tavistock Publications, Limited, London, 1961.

Campbell, John P., Marvin D. Dunnette, Edward E. Lawler, III, and Karl E. Weick, Jr. *Managerial Behavior, Performance, and Effectiveness,* McGraw-Hill Book Company, New York, 1970.

Campbell, John P., and Robert D. Pritchard "Motivation Theory in Industrial and Organizational Psychology," in Marvin D. Dunnette (ed.), *Handbook of Industrial and Organizational Psychology,* Rand McNally College Publishing Company, Chicago, 1976, pp. 63–130.

Caplow, Theodore *How to Run any Organization,* The Dryden Press, Hinsdale, Ill., 1976.

Carlisle, Howard M. *Management: Concepts and Situations,* Science Research Associates, Inc., Chicago, 1976.

Carroll, Stephen J., Jr., and Henry L. Tosi, Jr. *Management by Objectives: Applications and Research,* Macmillan Publishing, Inc., New York, 1973.

Cartwright, Dorwin, and Alvin Zander (eds.) *Group Dynamics: Research and Theory,* 3d ed., Harper & Row, Publishers, Incorporated, New York, 1968.

Chandler, Alfred D., Jr. *Strategy and Structure,* The M.I.T. Press, Cambridge, Mass., 1962.

Child, John *Organization: A Guide to Problems and Practice,* Harper & Row, Publishers, Incorporated, New York, 1977.

————— "Organizational Structure, Environment and Performance: The Role of Strategic Choice," *Sociology,* January 1972, pp. 1–20.

Churchman, C. West *The Systems Approach,* Dell Publishing Company, Inc., New York, 1968.

Cleland, David I., and William R. King *Systems Analysis and Project Management,* 2d ed., McGraw-Hill Book Company, New York, 1975.

Cooper, W. W., H. J. Leavitt, and M. W. Shelly, II (eds.) *New Perspectives in Organization Research,* John Wiley & Sons, Inc., New York, 1964.

Corson, John J., and George A. Steiner *Measuring Business's Social Performance: The Corporate Social Audit,* Committee for Economic Development, New York, 1974.

Coser, Lewis A. *The Functions of Social Conflict,* The Free Press of Glencoe, New York, 1956.

Crozier, Michel *The Bureaucratic Phenomenon,* The University of Chicago Press, Chicago, 1964.

—————, **and Jean-Claude Thoenig** "The Regulation of Complex Organized Systems," *Administrative Science Quarterly,* December 1976, pp. 547–570.

Cyert, Richard M., and James G. March *A Behavioral Theory of the Firm,* Prentice-Hall, Inc., Englewood Cliffs, N.J., 1963.

Davis, Keith *Human Behavior at Work,* 5th ed., McGraw-Hill Book Company, New York, 1977.

DeGreene, Kenyon B. *Sociotechnical Systems,* Prentice-Hall, Inc., Englewood Cliffs, N.J., 1973.

Delbecq, Andre L., Andrew H. Van de Ven, and David H. Gustafson *Group Techniques for Program Planning: A Guide to Nominal Group and Delphi Processes,* Scott, Foresman and Company, Glenview, Ill., 1975.

Drucker, Peter F. *Management: Tasks, Responsibilities, Practices,* Harper & Row, Publishers, Incorporated, New York, 1974.

———— *The Practice of Management,* Harper & Row, Publishers, Incorporated, New York, 1954.

Dubin, Robert (ed.) *Handbook of Work, Organization, and Society,* Rand McNally College Publishing Company, Chicago, 1976.

Dunnette, Marvin D. (ed.) *Handbook of Industrial and Organizational Psychology,* Rand McNally College Publishing Company, Chicago, 1976.

Dutton, John M., and William H. Starbuck (eds.) *Computer Simulation of Human Behavior,* John Wiley & Sons, Inc., New York, 1971.

Ebert, Ronald J., and Terence R. Mitchell *Organizational Decision Processes,* Crane, Russak & Company, Inc., New York, 1975.

Edmunds, Stahrl, and John Letey *Environmental Administration,* McGraw-Hill Book Company, New York, 1973.

Ellul, Jacques *The Technological Society,* John Wilkinson (trans.), Alfred A. Knopf, Inc., New York, 1964.

Emery, F. E. (ed.) *Systems Thinking,* Penguin Books Ltd., Harmondsworth, Middlesex, England, 1969.

————, **and E. L. Trist** "The Causal Texture of Organizational Environments," *Human Relations,* February 1965, pp. 21–31.

Etzioni, Amitai *A Comparative Analysis of Complex Organizations,* (rev. ed.), The Free Press of Glencoe, New York, 1975.

———— *Modern Organizations,* Prentice-Hall, Inc., Englewood Cliffs, N.J., 1964.

Feldman, Julian, and Herschel E. Kanter "Organizational Decision Making," in James G. March (ed.), *Handbook of Organizations,* Rand McNally & Company, Chicago, 1965, pp. 614–649.

Festinger, Leon *A Theory of Cognitive Dissonance,* Harper & Row, Publishers, Incorporated, New York, 1957.

Fiedler, Fred E. *A Theory of Leadership Effectiveness,* McGraw-Hill Book Company, New York, 1967.

————, **Martin M. Chemers, and Linda Mahar** *Improving Leadership Effectiveness: The Leader Match Concept,* John Wiley & Sons, Inc., New York, 1976.

Forrester, Jay W. *Industrial Dynamics,* The M.I.T. Press, Cambridge, Mass., and John Wiley & Sons, Inc., New York, 1961.

———— *Urban Dynamics,* The M.I.T. Press, Cambridge, Mass., 1969.

———— *World Dynamics,* Wright-Allen Press, Inc., Cambridge, Mass., 1971.

French, Wendell *The Personnel Management Process: Human Resources Administration,* 4th ed., Houghton Mifflin Co., Boston, 1978.

————, **and Cecil H. Bell, Jr.** *Organization Development,* 2d ed., Prentice-Hall, Inc., Englewood Cliffs, N.J., 1978.

Galbraith, Jay *Designing Complex Organizations,* Addison-Wesley Publishing Company, Reading, Mass., 1973.

Galbraith, John Kenneth *The New Industrial State,* 2d ed., Houghton Mifflin Company, Boston, 1971.

Gardner, John W. *Self-renewal: The Individual and the Innovative Society,* Harper & Row, Publishers, Incorporated, New York, 1963.

Georgopoulos, Basil S., and Floyd C. Mann *The Community General Hospital,* The Macmillan Company, New York, 1962.

Gross, Bertram M. *Organizations and Their Managing,* The Free Press of Glencoe, New York, 1968.

Grusky, Oscar, and George A. Miller (eds.) *The Sociology of Organizations,* The Free Press, New York, 1970.

Gvishiani, D. *Organisation and Management: A Sociological Analysis of Western Theories,* Progress Publishers, Moscow, 1972.

Gyllenhammar, Pehr G. *People At Work,* Addison-Wesley Publishing Company, Reading, Mass., 1977.

Hackman, Richard J., and J. Lloyd Suttle (eds.) *Improving Life at Work,* Goodyear Publishing Company, Inc., Santa Monica, Cal., 1977.

Hage, Jerald, and Michael Aiken *Social Change in Complex Organizations,* Random House, New York, 1970.

Hall, Richard H. *Organizations: Structure and Process,* Prentice-Hall, Inc., Englewood Cliffs, N.J., 1972.

Harrison, Frank E. *The Managerial Decision-Making Process,* Houghton Mifflin Company, Boston, Mass., 1975.

Heller, Frank A. *Managerial Decision-Making: A Study of Leadership Styles and Power-Sharing among Senior Managers,* Tavistock Publications Limited, London, 1971.

Herbst, P. G. *Socio-Technical Design,* Tavistock Publications Limited, London, 1974.

Herzberg, Frederick *The Managerial Choice: To Be Efficient and to Be Human,* Richard D. Irwin, Inc., Homewood, Ill., 1976.

————, Bernard Mausner, and Barbara Snyderman *The Motivation to Work,* John Wiley & Sons, Inc., New York, 1959.

Hickson, D. J., D. S. Pugh, and Diana C. Pheysey, "Operations Technology and Organizational Structures: An Empirical Reappraisal," *Administrative Science Quarterly,* September 1969, pp. 378–397.

Hofer, Charles W. "Toward a Contingency Theory of Business Strategy," *Academy of Management Journal,* December 1975, pp. 784–810.

Hofstede, Geert, and M. Sami Kassem (eds.) *European Contributions to Organization Theory,* Van Gorcum & Company B.V., Assen, The Netherlands, 1976.

Homans, George C. *The Human Group,* Harcourt, Brace & World, Inc., New York, 1950.

Jenkins, David (ed.) *Job Reform in Sweden,* Swedish Employers' Confederation, Stockholm, 1975.

Johnson, Richard A., Fremont E. Kast, and James E. Rosenzweig *The Theory and Management of Systems,* 3d ed., McGraw-Hill Book Company, New York, 1973.

Kahn, Herman, and B. Bruce-Briggs *Things to Come: Thinking about the Seventies and Eighties,* Macmillan Publishing Co., Inc., New York, 1972.

Kast, Fremont E., and James E. Rosenzweig *Experiential Exercises and Cases in Management,* McGraw-Hill Book Company, New York, 1976.

————, **and** ———— ''General Systems Theory: Applications for Organization and Management,'' *Academy of Management Journal,* December 1972, pp. 447–465.

————, **and** ———— ''Hospital Administration and Systems Concepts,'' *Hospital Administration,* Fall 1966, pp. 17–33.

————, **and** ———— **(eds.)** *Science, Technology, and Management,* McGraw-Hill Book Company, New York, 1963.

Katz, Daniel, and Robert L. Kahn *The Social Psychology of Organizations,* 2d ed., John Wiley & Sons, Inc., New York, 1978.

Kerr, Clark *The Uses of the University,* Harvard University Press, Cambridge, Mass., 1963.

Kilmann, Ralph H., Louis R. Pondy, and Dennis P. Slevin (eds.) *The Management of Organization Design: Strategies and Implementation,* Elsevier North-Holland, Inc., New York, 1976.

Knowles, Henry P., and Borje O. Saxberg ''Human Relations and the Nature of Man,'' *Harvard Business Review,* March–April 1967, pp. 22–40ff.

Koontz, Harold (ed.) *Toward a Unified Theory of Management,* McGraw-Hill Book Company, New York, 1964.

Kramer, Paul, and Frederick L. Holborn (eds.) *The City in American Life,* Capricorn Books, New York, 1970.

Kuhn, Thomas S. *The Structure of Scientific Revolutions,* 2d ed., University of Chicago Press, Chicago, 1970.

Lawler, Edward E., III ''Control Systems in Organizations,'' in Marvin D. Dunnette (ed.), *Handbook of Industrial and Organizational Psychology,* Rand McNally College Publishing Company, Chicago, 1976, pp. 1247–1291.

Lawrence, Paul R., and Jay W. Lorsch *Organization and Environment,* Harvard Graduate School of Business Administration, Boston, 1967.

Leavitt, Harold J. ''Applied Organization Change in Industry: Structural, Technical, and Human Approaches,'' in W. W. Cooper, H. J. Leavitt, and M. W. Shelly, II (eds.), *New Perspectives in Organizational Research,* John Wiley & Sons, Inc., New York, 1964, pp. 55–71.

————, **Lawrence T. Pinfield, and Eugene J. Webb (eds.)** *Organizations of the Future: Interaction with the External Environment,* Praeger Publishers, New York, 1974.

LeBreton, Preston P. (ed.) *Comparative Administrative Theory,* University of Washington Press, Seattle, 1968.

Levinson, Harry *The Exceptional Executive: A Psychological Conception,* Harvard University Press, Cambridge, Mass., 1968.

———— *Organizational Diagnosis,* Harvard University Press, Cambridge, Mass., 1972.

Likert, Rensis *The Human Organization,* McGraw-Hill Book Company, New York, 1967.

———— *New Patterns of Management,* McGraw-Hill Book Company, New York, 1961.

Lindblom, Charles E. "The Science of 'Muddling Through,' " in Harold J. Leavitt and Louis R. Pondy (eds.), *Readings in Managerial Psychology,* The University of Chicago Press, Chicago, 1964, pp. 61–78.

Lippitt, Gordon L. *Organizational Renewal,* Appleton-Century-Crofts, Inc., New York, 1969.

Litterer, Joseph A. *The Analysis of Organizations,* 2d ed., John Wiley & Sons, Inc., New York, 1973.

Lorsch, Jay W., and Paul R. Lawrence (eds.) *Studies in Organizational Design,* Richard D. Irwin, Inc., and The Dorsey Press, Homewood, Ill., 1970.

Lorsch, Jay W., and John J. Morse *Organizations and Their Members: A Contingency Approach,* Harper & Row, Publishers, Incorporated, New York, 1974.

Luthans, Fred, and Todd Stewart "A General Contingency Theory of Management," *The Academy of Management Review,* April 1977, pp. 181–195.

Mack, Ruth P. *Planning on Uncertainty,* Wiley-Interscience, New York, 1971.

Maier, Norman R. F. *Problem-solving Discussions and Conferences,* McGraw-Hill Book Company, New York, 1963.

March, James G. (ed.) *Handbook of Organizations,* Rand McNally & Company, Chicago, 1965.

————, **and Herbert A. Simon** *Organizations,* John Wiley & Sons, Inc., New York, 1958.

Maslow, Abraham H. "A Theory of Human Motivation," *Psychological Review,* July 1943, pp. 370–396.

———— *Motivation and Personality,* Harper & Row, Publishers, Incorporated, New York, 1954.

McClelland, David C. *The Achieving Society,* D. Van Nostrand Company, Inc., Princeton, N.J., 1961.

McFeely, Wilbur M. *Organization Change: Perceptions and Realities,* The Conference Board, Inc., New York, 1972.

McGregor, Douglas *The Human Side of Enterprise,* McGraw-Hill Book Company, New York, 1960.

———— *The Professional Manager,* Warren G. Bennis and Caroline McGregor (eds.), McGraw-Hill Book Company, New York, 1967.

McGuire, Joseph W. (ed.) *Contemporary Management,* Prentice-Hall, Inc., Englewood Cliffs, N.J., 1974.

Mesthene, Emmanuel G. *Technological Change: Its Impact on Man and Society,* The New American Library, Inc., New York, 1970.

Miles, Raymond E. *Theories of Management: Implications for Organizational Behavior and Development,* McGraw-Hill Book Company, New York, 1975.

Miller, David W., and Martin K. Starr *Executive Decisions and Operations Research,* 2d ed., Prentice-Hall, Inc., Englewood Cliffs, N.J., 1969.

————, **and** ———— *The Structure of Human Decisions,* Prentice-Hall, Inc., Englewood Cliffs, N.J., 1967.

Miller, E. J., and A. K. Rice *Systems of Organization,* Tavistock Publications, Limited, London, 1967.

Miller, George A., Eugene Galanter, and Karl H. Pribram *Plans and the Structure of Behavior,* Holt, Rinehart and Winston, Inc., New York, 1960.

Miller, James G. "Living Systems: The Group," *Behavioral Science,* July 1971, pp. 302–398.

———— "The Nature of Living Systems," *Behavioral Science,* July 1971, pp. 277–301.

Mintzberg, Henry *The Nature of Managerial Work,* Harper & Row, Publishers, Incorporated, New York, 1973.

Mitchell, Terence R. "Applied Principles in Motivation Theory," in Peter Warr (ed.), *Personal Goals and Work Design,* John Wiley & Sons, Ltd., London, 1976, pp. 163–171.

Morrisey, George L. *Management by Objectives and Results in the Public Sector,* Addison-Wesley Publishing Company, Reading, Mass., 1976.

Mouzelis, Nicos P. *Organization and Bureaucracy,* Aldine Publishing Company, Chicago, 1968.

Mumford, Lewis *The Myth of the Machine,* Harcourt, Brace & World, Inc., New York, 1967.

Negandhi, Anant R. (ed.) *Environmental Settings in Organizational Functioning,* Comparative Administration Research Institute, Kent State University, Kent, Ohio, 1970.

Newman, William H. *Constructive Control,* Prentice-Hall, Inc., Englewood Cliffs, N.J., 1975.

Parsons, Talcott *Structure and Process in Modern Societies,* The Free Press of Glencoe, New York, 1960.

Perrow, Charles "A Framework for the Comparative Analysis of Organizations," *American Sociological Review,* April 1967, pp. 194–208.

———— *Organizational Analysis: A Sociological View,* Wadsworth Publishing Company, Inc., Belmont, Calif., 1970.

Porter, Lyman W., and Edward E. Lawler, III *Managerial Attitudes and Performance,* Richard D. Irwin, Inc., Homewood, Ill., 1968.

————, and ————, and **J. Richard Hackman** *Behavior in Organizations,* McGraw-Hill Book Company, New York, 1975.

Presthus, Robert *The Organizational Society,* Alfred A. Knopf, Inc., New York, 1962.

Prince, George M. *The Practice of Creativity,* Collier Books, New York, 1972.

Pugh, Derek S., D. J. Hickson, and C. R. Hinings "An Empirical Taxonomy of Structure of Work Organizations," *Administrative Science Quarterly,* March 1969, pp. 115–126.

Rakich, Jonathon S., Beaufort B. Longest, and Thomas R. O'Donovan *Managing Health Care Organizations,* W. B. Saunders Company, Philadelphia, 1977.

Rice, A. K. *The Enterprise and Its Environment,* Tavistock Publications, Limited, London, 1963.

Roethlisberger, Fritz J., and William J. Dickson *Management and the Worker,* Harvard University Press, Cambridge, Mass., 1939.

Rosenzweig, James E. "Managers and Management Scientists: Two Cultures," *Business Horizons,* Fall 1967, pp. 79–86.

Rush, Harold M.F. *Behavioral Science: Concepts and Managerial Applications,* The Conference Board, Inc., New York, 1969.

———— *Job Design for Motivation,* The Conference Board, Inc., New York, 1971.

Sayles, Leonard R. *Managerial Behavior,* McGraw-Hill Book Company, New York, 1964.

———— **and Margaret K. Chandler** *Managing Large Systems,* Harper & Row Publishers, Incorporated, New York, 1971.

Schein, Edgar H. *Organizational Psychology,* 2d ed., Prentice-Hall, Inc., Englewood Cliffs, N.J., 1970.

Schoderbek, Peter P. (ed.) *Management Systems,* 2d ed., John Wiley & Sons, Inc., New York, 1971.

Schrieber, Albert N. (ed.) *Corporation Simulation Models,* Graduate School of Business Administration, University of Washington, Seattle, 1970.

Scott, William G., and Terence R. Mitchell *Organization Theory: A Structural and Behavioral Analysis,* 3d ed., Richard D. Irwin, Inc., Homewood, Ill., 1976.

Seiler, John A. *Systems Analysis in Organizational Behavior,* Richard D. Irwin, Inc., and The Dorsey Press, Homewood, Ill., 1967.

Selznick, Philip *Leadership in Administration,* Harper & Row, Publishers, Incorporated, New York, 1957.

Shortell, Stephen M., and Montague Brown (eds.) *Organizational Research in Hospitals,* An Inquiry Book, Blue Cross Association, Chicago, Ill., 1976.

Silverman, David *The Theory of Organizations,* Basic Books, Inc., New York, 1971.

Simon, Herbert A. *Administrative Behavior,* 3d ed., Macmillan Publishing Co., Inc., New York, 1976.

Skinner, B. F. *Beyond Freedom and Dignity,* Alfred A. Knopf, Inc., New York, 1971.

Steiner, George A. *Top Management Planning,* Macmillan Publishing Co., Inc., New York, 1969.

————, **and John B. Miner** *Management Policy and Strategy,* Macmillan Publishing Co., Inc., New York, 1977.

Stogdill, Ralph *Handbook of Leadership,* The Free Press, New York, 1974.

Sutermeister, Robert A. *People and Productivity,* 3d ed., McGraw-Hill Book Company, New York, 1976.

Tannenbaum, Arnold *Control in Organizations,* McGraw-Hill Book Company, New York, 1968.

Tannenbaum, Robert, and Warren H. Schmidt "How to Choose a Leadership Pattern," *Harvard Business Review,* May–June 1973, pp. 162–180.

Thompson, James D. (ed.) *Approaches to Organizational Design,* The University of Pittsburgh Press, Pittsburgh, Pa., 1966.

———— *Organizations in Action,* McGraw-Hill Book Company, New York, 1967.

Toffler, Alvin *Future Shock,* Random House, Inc., New York, 1970.

Udy, Stanley H., Jr. "The Comparative Analysis of Organizations," in James G. March (ed.), *Handbook of Organizations,* Rand McNally & Company, Chicago, 1965, pp. 678–709.

Van De Ven, Andrew H. *Group Decision Making and Effectiveness,* Kent State University Press, Kent, Ohio, 1974.

von Bertalanffy, Ludwig *General System Theory,* George Braziller, New York, 1968.

Vroom, Victor H. *Work and Motivation,* John Wiley & Sons, Inc., New York, 1964.

————, **and Philip W. Yetton** *Leadership and Decision-Making,* University of Pittsburgh, Pittsburgh, Pa., 1973.

Walker, Charles R. (ed.) *Technology, Industry, and Man,* McGraw-Hill Book Company, New York, 1968.

Walton, Clarence (ed.) *The Ethics of Corporate Conduct,* Prentice-Hall, Inc., Englewood Cliffs, N.J., 1977.

Warr, Peter (ed.) *Personal Goals and Work Design,* John Wiley & Sons, Ltd., London, 1976.

Webb, James E. *Space Age Management,* McGraw-Hill Book Company, New York, 1969.

Weber, Max *The Protestant Ethic and the Spirit of Capitalism,* Talcott Parsons (trans.), Charles Scribner's Sons, New York, 1958.

———— *The Theory of Social and Economic Organization,* A. M. Henderson and Talcott Parsons (trans.), The Free Press of Glencoe, New York, 1964.

Weick, Karl E. *The Social Psychology of Organizing,* Addison-Wesley Publishing Company, Reading, Mass., 1969.

Whisler, Thomas L. *Information Technology and Organizational Change,* Wadsworth Publishing Company, Inc., Belmont, Calif., 1970.

Wiener, Norbert *The Human Use of Human Beings,* rev. ed., Houghton Mifflin Company, Boston, 1954.

Wilensky, Harold L. *Organizational Intelligence,* Basic Books, Inc., Publishers, New York, 1967.

Woodward, Joan *Industrial Organization: Theory and Practice,* Oxford University Press, Fair Lawn, N.J., 1965.

Yarmolinsky, Adam *The Military Establishment,* Harper & Row, Publishers, Incorporated, New York, 1971.

Name Index

Subject Index